R. Gupta's®

POPULAR MASTER GUIDE

HSSC Haryana Staff Selection Commission

STAFF NURSE

NURSE / SISTER TUTOR

COMMON ENTRANCE TEST (CET) PHASE-II FOR GROUP 'C' POST

by

RPH Editorial Board

2027 EDITION

RAMESH PUBLISHING HOUSE, NEW DELHI

Published by
O.P. Gupta *for* Ramesh Publishing House

Admin. Office
12-H, New Daryaganj Road, Opp. Officer' Mess,
New Delhi-110002 ✆ 23275224, 23245124

E-mail: info@rameshpublishinghouse.com
For Online Shopping: www.rameshpublishinghouse.com

Showroom
- Balaji Market, Nai Sarak, Delhi-110006 ✆ 23282525 📱 9354373464
- 4457, Nai Sarak, Delhi-110006

Book Code: R-2919

ISBN: 978-93-5477-838-4

Price: ₹ 520

Printed at: Deepak Offset, Delhi

CONTENTS

SCHEME OF EXAMINATION

1. General Awareness, Reasoning, Mathematics, Science, History including Haryana Related History, Current Affairs, Literature, Geography, Civics, Environment, Culture etc.
(Weightage 20%)

2. Computer Terminology, Fundamentals, Word Software, Excel Software, Power Point, Internet, Web Browsing, Communication, Emails, Downloading and Uploading Data on Websites etc.
(Weightage 10%)

3. **Subject Related Syllabus—** **(Weightage 70%)**
    - Anatomy
    - Physiology
    - Nutrition
    - Biochemistry
    - Nursing Foundations
    - Psychology
    - Microbiology
    - Sociology
    - Pharmacology
    - Pathology
    - Genetics
    - Medical Surgical Nursing (Adult including Geriatrics)
    - Community Health Nursing
    - Communication & Education Technology
    - Child Health Nursing
    - Mental Health Nursing
    - Nursing Research and Statistics
    - Midwifery and Obstetrical Nursing
    - Management of Nursing Services & Education.

Previous Years' Paper

Haryana Staff Selection Commission (HSSC)

Staff Nurse Recruitment Exam, 2023

(Exam held on 31-12-2023)

1. ______ are the smallest functional units of the body.
   A. Tissues B. Cells
   C. Fibres D. Cartilages
   E. Not attempted

2. ______ is nonparametric test.
   A. Students t test B. Chi-square test
   C. Z test D. ANOVA
   E. Not attempted

3. Psychoanalysis is propagated by:
   A. William James B. Sigmund Freud
   C. Wilhelm Wundt D. John B. Watson
   E. Not attempted

4. The book 'Ignited Minds' was written by:
   A. A.P.J. Abdul Kalam
   B. Salman Rushdie
   C. Atal Bihari Vajapayee
   D. None of the above
   E. Not attempted

5. ______ is the process of taking corrective action in order to meet objectives.
   A. Decision making B. Implementing
   C. Evaluating D. Problem solving
   E. Not attempted

6. Which of the following lets you to find the text and automatically replace it with something different?
   A. Goto B. Easy text
   C. Copy D. Replace
   E. Not attempted

7. ______ marriage is the form of marriage in which one man marries one woman.
   A. Polygamy B. Group
   C. Polyandry D. Monogamy
   E. Not attempted

8. The Universal Declaration of Human Rights (UDHR) was accepted by the UN through its resolution on:
   A. 24th December 1945
   B. 10th October 1948
   C. 10th December 1948
   D. 10th December 1945
   E. Not attempted

9. The word "rubeola" means:
   A. White spots B. Red spots
   C. Bluish spots D. Black spots
   E. Not attempted

10. ______ is defined as the inflammation of the conjunctiva during first month of life.
    A. Conjunctivitis
    B. Microphthalmia
    C. Anophthalmia
    D. Ophthalmia neonatorum
    E. Not attempted

11. The nervous system consists of a vast number of units called:
    A. Neuroglia B. Protons
    C. Proteins D. Neurones
    E. Not attempted

12. Cooking in water at 100 degree Centigrade is called:
    A. Roasting B. Boiling
    C. Steaming D. None of these
    E. Not attempted

13. Iron requirement during pregnancy is about ______ mg.
    A. 1500 B. 2000
    C. 2500 D. 1000
    E. Not attempted

1. B	2. B	3. B	4. A	5. D	6. D	7. D
8. C	9. B	10. D	11. D	12. B	13. D	

14. Statement: A < B = C, D > C, D ≤ E < F.

Conclusion: I. B < E

II. A < F

A. Only II follows
B. Both I and II follows
C. Neither I nor II follows
D. Only I follows
E. Not attempted

15. A research design in which the researcher relates the present to the future is a:

A. Retrospective research design
B. Ambispective research design
C. Comparative research design
D. Prospective research design
E. Not attempted

16. ______ keyboard is a software device that let you to input data just like a hardware keyboard.

A. Standard B. Ergonomic
C. Compact D. Virtual
E. Not attempted

17. ______ is a set of values recorded on one or more observational units or the factual information collected during research studies.

A. Variable B. Parameters
C. Scales D. Data
E. Not attempted

18. ______ forms the major part of the human brain.

A. Hypothalamus B. Cerebrum
C. Medulla D. Thalamus
E. Not attempted

19. ______ is known as infectious hepatitis or epidemic jaundice.

A. Hepatitis B B. Hepatitis C
C. Hepatitis E D. Hepatitis A
E. Not attempted

20. ______ is the direct visualization of a body system or a part by means of a lighted flexible tube.

A. CT Scan B. MRI
C. Endoscopy D. Chest X-rays
E. Not attempted

21. These are the chemical compounds synthesized by endocrine glands:

A. Gases B. Hormones
C. Nutrient materials D. Antibodies
E. Not attempted

22. ______ is the immunity that is transferred to a recipient in a readymade form.

A. Passive immunity B. Natural active immunity
C. Artificial immunity D. Active immunity
E. Not attempted

23. Fertilizable life span of sperm is:

A. 13-47 hours B. 48-72 hours
C. 73-80 hours D. 6-12 hours
E. Not attempted

24. The error in measuring the current with a tangent galvanometer is minimum when deflection is about:

A. 30° B. 45°
C. 60° D. 0°
E. Not attempted

25. ______ is the issuance of a false statement about another person, which causes that person to suffer harm.

A. Invasion of privacy B. Fraud
C. Battery D. Defamation
E. Not attempted

26. ______ invented a powered loom that used punched wooden cards to automatically weave incredibly detailed patterns including pictures and text.

A. Blaise Pascal B. Joseph Mary Jacquard
C. Napier's Bones D. Gottfried Leibniz
E. Not attempted

27. The word theory comes from the Greek word.

A. theorium B. theoretia
C. theoryia D. theoria
E. Not attempted

28. Which among the following musical instruments is used during Dhamal dance form in Haryana?

A. Damru B. Deru
C. Dholak D. Daf
E. Not attempted

29. Varicella is an acute, highly infectious disease caused by:

A. Influenza virus B. Varicella-Zoster virus
C. Rubella virus D. Polio virus
E. Not attempted

30. Prolonged labour means when the combined duration of first and second stage of labour is more than ______ hours.

A. 17 B. 18
C. 15 D. 16
E. Not attempted

14. B	15. D	16. D	17. D	18. B	19. D	20. C	21. B	22. A
23. B	24. B	25. D	26. B	27. D	28. C	29. B	30. B	

31. ______ is a composite graphical record of key data (maternal and foetal) during labour, entered against time in a single piece of paper.

A. Cervicograph
B. FHR chart
C. Partograph
D. Biometry chart
E. Not attempted

32. ______ rate is defined as "the number of new cases occurring in a defined population during a specified period of time".

A. Incidence
B. Morbidity
C. Mortality
D. Prevalence
E. Not attempted

33. ______ (feeling of life) denotes the perception of active fetal movements by the women.

A. Oslander's sign
B. Goodell's sign
C. Quickening
D. Braxton's-Hicks Contractions
E. Not attempted

34. ______ is the verbal interchange of thought or ideas.

A. Decision making
B. Coordination
C. Conflicts
D. Communication
E. Not attempted

35. Which number will come in the place of question mark?

4832, 5840, 6848, ?

A. 7880
B. 7856
C. 7890
D. 7815
E. Not attempted

36. In spreadsheet, the intersection of rows and columns are called as:

A. cell
B. file
C. folder
D. menus
E. Not attempted

37. ______ study is an example of live experiences of tsunami victims in selected villages of Tamil Nadu.

A. Phenomenological
B. Action
C. Historical
D. Ethnographic
E. Not attempted

38. Second generation ethanol plant was dedicated to the nation at which place in Haryana in 2022?

A. Karnal
B. Panipat
C. Jind
D. Kurukshetra
E. Not attempted

39. Bitot's spots indicate ______ deficiency.

A. Vitamin C
B. Vitamin B
C. Vitamin D
D. Vitamin A
E. Not attempted

40. The total weight gain during the course of a singleton pregnancy for a healthy woman average ______ kg.

A. 11
B. 15
C. 20
D. 6
E. Not attempted

41. ______ cells secrete insulin.

A. Beta
B. Delta
C. Mast
D. Alpha
E. Not attempted

42. ______ is the inflammation of the ureter.

A. Ureteritis
B. Gall bladder
C. Liver
D. Kidneys
E. Not attempted

43. ______ is the organizing process by which we interpret our sensory input.

A. Perception
B. Instincts
C. Motivation
D. Senses
E. Not attempted

44. The Headquarter of United Nations Environment Programme (UNEP) is situated in:

A. Washington
B. Geneva
C. Nairobi
D. New York
E. Not attempted

45. ______ is defined as a person in the population or study group identified as having the particular disease, health disorder or condition under investigation.

A. Agent
B. Cases
C. Host
D. Carrier
E. Not attempted

46. Which among the following is the impact printer?

A. Laser
B. Dot Matrix
C. Thermal
D. Inkjet
E. Not attempted

47. ______ are qualities, properties, or characteristics of person, things or situations that change or vary.

A. Descriptive relationship
B. Constant
C. Variables
D. Cause and effect relationship
E. Not attempted

31. C	32. A	33. C	34. D	35. B	36. A	37. A	38. B	39. D
40. A	41. A	42. A	43. A	44. C	45. B	46. B	47. C	

48. The Constitution of India was enacted on:

A. November 26, 1950 B. November 26, 1949
C. January 26, 1949 D. None of the above
E. Not attempted

49. ______ is unique because it is derived from sunlight and food.

A. Vitamin B B. Vitamin C
C. Vitamin D D. Vitamin A
E. Not attempted

50. ______ refers to the relationship of the long axis of the fetus to the long axis of the centralized uterus or maternal spine.

A. Presentation B. Position
C. Lie D. None of the above
E. Not attempted

51. The term ______ is defined as the amounts of nutrients sufficient for the maintenance of health in nearly all people.

A. Recommended timely allowance
B. Recommended weekly allowance
C. Recommended yearly allowance
D. Recommended daily allowance
E. Not attempted

52. ______ is a crime of violence against another person.

A. Assault B. Fraud
C. Invasion of privacy D. Defamation
E. Not attempted

53. ______ is essentially a cognitive activity.

A. Thinking B. Memory
C. Calculations D. Reasoning
E. Not attempted

54. If $A = \begin{bmatrix} \cos 2\theta & -\sin 2\theta \\ \sin 2\theta & \cos 2\theta \end{bmatrix}$ and $A + A^T = I$, where I is the unit matrix of 2 × 2 and A^T is the transpose of A, then the value of θ is equal to:

A. $\frac{\pi}{3}$ B. π

C. $\frac{3\pi}{2}$ D. $\frac{\pi}{6}$

E. Not attempted

55. Retrospective studies are often called:

A. Case control B. Descriptive
C. Cross-sectional D. Cases
E. Not attempted

56. Which of the following carries out the business dealings by internet?

A. Ecommerce
B. File Transfer Protocol (FTP)
C. News groups
D. Email
E. Not attempted

57. ______ is a formal tentative statement of the expected relationship between two or more variables under the study.

A. Concept definition B. Hypothesis
C. Research questions D. Problem statement
E. Not attempted

58. Haryana Municipal Act was passed in:

A. 1973 B. 1974
C. 1994 D. 1970
E. Not attempted

59. Brucellosis is one of the major ______ zoonoses.

A. Viral B. Fungal
C. Protozoal D. Bacterial
E. Not attempted

60. ______ is the anomaly results from deficient development of the vault of the skull and brain tissue, but the facial portion is normal.

A. Spina bifida
B. Encephalocele
C. Anencephaly
D. Hydrocephalus
E. Not attempted

61. ______ is the structural and functional unit of the kidney.

A. Glomerulus B. Nephron
C. Cortisol D. Neurons
E. Not attempted

62. ______ is the type of correlation when ($r = +1$).

A. Perfect negative correlation.
B. Moderately positive correlation.
C. Moderately negative correlation.
D. Perfect positive correlation.
E. Not attempted

63. ______ is known as serum hepatitis.

A. Hepatitis B
B. Hepatitis C
C. Hepatitis E
D. Hepatitis A
E. Not attempted

48. B	49. C	50. C	51. D	52. A	53. A	54. D	55. A
56. A	57. B	58. A	59. D	60. C	61. B	62. D	63. A

64. A, B, C, D, E, F, and G are seven members of a family. B is the mother of E. C is the son of E. D is the only sister of C and G. E is the father of G. A is the parent of E. K is the parent of G. How is K related of B?

A. Daughter-in-law B. Father
C. Mother D. Daughter
E. Not attempted

65. The smallest unit that can be written to or read from the disk is a:

A. Sector B. Backup
C. Memory D. Track
E. Not attempted

66. ______ is the process in which different people or things work together to attain specific goals or aims.

A. Communication B. Conflict
C. Coordination D. Cooperation
E. Not attempted

67. ______ is the value which has the highest frequency of data.

A. Mode B. Median
C. Range D. Mean
E. Not attempted

68. Chlorobenzene can be converted into ______ by heating in aqueous sodium hydroxide solution at a temperature of 623 K and a pressure of 300 atmospheres.

A. acetone B. phenol
C. aniline D. benzene
E. Not attempted

69. The term enteric fever includes:

A. Flue fever
B. Typhoid fever
C. Dengue haemorrhagic fever
D. Malaria fever
E. Not attempted

70. Average daily fluid intake for adult is about ______ ml.

A. 500-900 B. 1000-1400
C. 1500-2000 D. 100-400
E. Not attempted

71. Riboflavin is also called as:

A. Vitamin B_{12} B. Vitamin B_1
C. Vitamin B_3 D. Vitamin B_2
E. Not attempted

72. ______ is another person or animal where organism is nourished and harboured.

A. Reservoir B. Carrier
C. Vehicle D. Host
E. Not attempted

73. Structuralism is propagated by:

A. William James B. Sigmund Freud
C. Wilhelm Wundt D. John B. Watson
E. Not attempted

74. The classical dance of Tamil Nadu is:

A. Kathak B. Mohiniyattam
C. Kuchipudi D. Bharatnatyam
E. Not attempted

75. ______ is the science that deals with the effects of drugs on living system.

A. Pharmacology B. Pharmacokinetics
C. Pharmacodynamics D. Pharmacy
E. Not attempted

76. A ______ is an equation that performs operations on worksheet data.

A. Formula B. Expression
C. Cell D. Library
E. Not attempted

77. In ______ family the wife goes and lives in the house of the husband after marriage.

A. Matrilocal B. Patrimatrilocal
C. Neolocal D. Patrilocal
E. Not attempted

78. Sirsa is the largest producer of ______ in Haryana.

A. Rice B. Jowar
C. Bajra D. Wheat
E. Not attempted

79. The term disease ______ refers specifically to all current cases (old and new) existing at a given point in time or over a period of time in a given population.

A. Incidence B. Prevalence
C. Detection D. Diagnosing
E. Not attempted

80. A healthy mother while breastfeeding will produce about ______ of breast milk per day.

A. 100-200 ml B. 300-400 ml
C. 500-900 ml D. 10-100 ml
E. Not attempted

64. A	**65.** A	**66.** C	**67.** A	**68.** B	**69.** B	**70.** C	**71.** D	**72.** D
73. C	**74.** D	**75.** A	**76.** A	**77.** D	**78.** D	**79.** B	**80.** C	

81. Heart is in the ______ cavity.
A. Pelvic
B. Thoracic
C. Cranial
D. Abdominal
E. Not attempted

82. Father of immunology is:
A. Robert Koch
B. Edward Jenner
C. Louis Pasteur
D. Antony Van Leeuwenhoek
E. Not attempted

83. ______ are innate and inborn tendencies or psychological dispositions.
A. Perception
B. Instincts
C. Motivation
D. Senses
E. Not attempted

84. The constant term in the expansion of $\left(x^2 - \frac{1}{x^2}\right)^{16}$ is:
A. $^{16}C_7$
B. $^{16}C_9$
C. $^{16}C_{10}$
D. $^{16}C_8$
E. Not attempted

85. The ______ is a system of storage and transport of vaccines at low temperature from the manufacturer to the actual vaccination site.
A. Ice packs
B. Vaccine carriers
C. Cold chain
D. Hot chain
E. Not attempted

86. ______ is an output device that draws pictures on paper based on commands from a computer.
A. Laser
B. Plotter
C. Dot Matrix
D. Inkjet
E. Not attempted

87. ______ is the one in which researcher collects data at the particular point of time.
A. Longitudinal research design
B. Trend studies
C. Panel studies
D. Cross-sectional research design
E. Not attempted

88. The famous Dal Lake is formed by this river:
A. The Jhelum
B. The Ravi
C. The Beas
D. The Chenab
E. Not attempted

89. Chickenpox is transmitted from person to person by ______ infection.
A. Vector
B. Droplet
C. Vehicle
D. Dust
E. Not attempted

90. Hyponatremia is defined as a plasma sodium level less than ______ mEq/L.
A. 140
B. 150
C. 160
D. 135
E. Not attempted

91. The normal life span of RBC is about:
A. 112 days
B. 120 days
C. 122 days
D. 102 days
E. Not attempted

92. ______ is the difference between the highest and the lowest value of the data.
A. Quartile deviation
B. Mean deviation
C. Range
D. Standard deviation
E. Not attempted

93. Measles is also known as:
A. Rubella
B. German measles
C. Mumps
D. Rubeola
E. Not attempted

94. A bag contains 17 tickets numbered from 1 to 17. A ticket is drawn at random, then another ticket is drawn without replacing the first one. The probability that both the tickets may show even numbers is:
A. $\frac{8}{17}$
B. $\frac{7}{16}$
C. $\frac{7}{17}$
D. $\frac{7}{34}$
E. Not attempted

95. ______ drug applied to the skin or mucous membrane at various sites for localized action.
A. Systemic
B. Enteral
C. Parenteral
D. Topical
E. Not attempted

96. Which of the following option lets you to add a border around a selection or change the colour of the paper within a selection?
A. Paragraph
B. Text wrap
C. Columns
D. Borders and shading
E. Not attempted

81. B	**82.** B	**83.** B	**84.** D	**85.** C	**86.** B	**87.** D	**88.** A
89. B	**90.** D	**91.** B	**92.** C	**93.** D	**94.** D	**95.** D	**96.** D

97. ______ is an example of nominal level measurement.

A. Temperature B. Health status
C. Weight D. Gender
E. Not attempted

98. Maharaja Agrasen was associated with which place of Haryana?

A. Pehowa B. Rohtak
C. Agroha D. Sirsa
E. Not attempted

99. ______ is called as slim disease.

A. AIDS B. Chlamydia
C. Gonorrhoea D. Syphilis
E. Not attempted

100. An ______ pregnancy is one in which the fertilized ovum is implanted and develops outside the normal endometrial cavity.

A. interstitial B. ectopic
C. ovarian D. abdominal
E. Not attempted

EXPLANATORY ANSWERS

1. Cells are the smallest structural and functional units of the body because all basic life processes (like respiration, nutrition, excretion, growth, and reproduction) occur within cells. Tissues are made up of groups of similar cells working together, and organs are formed from tissues, so they are larger levels of organization than cells. Hence, "cells" fits exactly as the smallest functional units.

2. The Chi-square test is a nonparametric test because it does not require assumptions about a normal distribution of the population and is commonly used with categorical (frequency) data to test association or goodness of fit. In contrast, Student's t test, Z test, and ANOVA are generally parametric tests that rely on distribution-related assumptions for mean comparisons.

3. Psychoanalysis was propagated by Sigmund Freud, who developed it as a method to understand and treat psychological problems through concepts like the unconscious mind, defense mechanisms, and early childhood experiences. His work laid the foundation of the psychoanalytic school of thought and therapeutic techniques such as free association and dream interpretation.

4. The book "Ignited Minds" was written by A.P.J. Abdul Kalam. The book focuses on inspiring youth and developing a positive, achievement-oriented mindset, emphasizing national development through education, values, and vision. Therefore, the option naming A.P.J. Abdul Kalam matches the book correctly.

5. Problem solving is the process of taking corrective action in order to meet objectives because it involves identifying a gap or obstacle, analyzing its causes, and selecting and applying corrective steps to reach the desired goal. Decision making is choosing among alternatives, implementing is putting a plan into action, and evaluating is judging results, but "taking corrective action to meet objectives" aligns most precisely with problem solving.

6. The "Replace" feature allows the user to search for specific text and automatically substitute it with another text throughout the document. It is commonly used in word processing software to make bulk corrections quickly. Options like Copy or Goto do not perform automatic substitution of text, hence Replace is the correct choice.

7. Monogamy is the form of marriage in which one man marries one woman. It is the most widely accepted form of marriage in many societies and is legally recognized in most countries. Other forms like polygamy involve multiple spouses, so they do not fit the given definition.

8. The Universal Declaration of Human Rights was adopted by the United Nations General Assembly on 10th December 1948. This date is celebrated globally as Human Rights Day. The declaration laid down fundamental rights and freedoms applicable to all human beings.

9. The term "rubeola" refers to measles, which is characterized by red spots or rashes appearing on the skin. The word itself is derived from a Latin term meaning reddish. Hence, "red spots" correctly describes the condition associated with rubeola.

10. *Ophthalmia neonatorum* is defined as inflammation of the conjunctiva occurring within the first month of life in a newborn. It is often caused by infection acquired during birth and requires prompt treatment to prevent complications. Therefore, this option precisely matches the definition given.

11. The nervous system is made up of specialized cells called neurones (or neurons), which are responsible for receiving, processing, and transmitting nerve impulses throughout the body. These cells form the basic functional and structural units of the nervous system. Neuroglia support neurons but do not conduct impulses, hence neurones are the correct units.

12. Cooking in water at 100°C is known as boiling. At this temperature, water reaches its boiling point at normal atmospheric pressure, allowing food to be cooked by direct contact with hot water. Other methods like roasting or steaming involve different conditions and techniques, so boiling fits the definition exactly.

13. During pregnancy, the total iron requirement is approximately 1000 mg. This includes iron needed for the expansion of maternal red blood cell mass, fetal growth, and blood loss during delivery. Hence, 1000 mg is the accepted approximate requirement for a healthy pregnancy.

97. D	**98.** C	**99.** A	**100.** B

14. Given statement: $A < B = C, D > C, D \leq E < F$
First, convert all relations step by step:
From $B = C$, we can replace C with B → so we treat B and C as equal.
From $D > C$, and since $C = B$, it becomes $D > B$.
From $D \leq E$, it means E is either equal to or greater than D → so $E \geq D$.
Now combine these:
Since $D > B$ and $E \geq D$, then E must be greater than B → so $B < E$
→ Conclusion I follows.
Now check Conclusion II:
From the given, $A < B$
We have already proved $B < E$
And given $E < F$
Combine all:
$A < B < E < F$
This clearly shows $A < F$
→ Conclusion II follows.
Therefore, both conclusions logically follow from the given statements.

15. A prospective research design is one in which the researcher studies present conditions and follows subjects into the future to observe outcomes. It is commonly used in longitudinal studies to establish cause-and-effect relationships. Hence, it relates the present to the future, matching the given definition.

16. A virtual keyboard is a software-based input device displayed on the screen that allows users to type using a mouse, touch, or stylus instead of a physical keyboard. It mimics the layout and functions of a hardware keyboard. It is especially useful on touchscreen devices and for accessibility purposes, hence it fits the definition correctly.

17. Data refers to a collection of facts, values, or observations gathered during research. These can be numerical or qualitative and are recorded for analysis. A variable represents a characteristic that can change, but the actual collected information from observations is called data, making it the correct answer.

18. The cerebrum is the largest part of the human brain and occupies the major portion of it. It is responsible for higher functions such as thinking, memory, reasoning, voluntary movements, and sensory perception. Other parts like the hypothalamus, medulla, and thalamus are smaller and perform specific regulatory functions.

19. Hepatitis A is commonly known as infectious hepatitis or epidemic jaundice. It spreads mainly through contaminated food and water and often occurs in outbreaks. It affects the liver and leads to symptoms like jaundice, fatigue, and nausea, which aligns with the given description.

20. Endoscopy is a medical procedure used for direct visualization of internal organs or body systems using a flexible tube with a light and camera. This allows doctors to examine areas like the digestive tract without major surgery. CT scan, MRI, and X-rays provide images but do not involve direct visual inspection with a flexible tube.

21. Endocrine glands produce and secrete chemical substances known as hormones directly into the bloodstream. These hormones act as chemical messengers that regulate various body functions such as growth, metabolism, reproduction, and homeostasis. Therefore, hormones are the correct term for chemical compounds synthesized by endocrine glands.

22. Passive immunity refers to the type of immunity in which ready-made antibodies are transferred to an individual. This can occur naturally, such as antibodies passing from mother to fetus, or artificially through injections. Since the immunity is not produced by the recipient's own body, it is called passive immunity.

23. The fertilizable life span of sperm inside the female reproductive tract is approximately 48 to 72 hours. During this period, sperm remain viable and capable of fertilizing the ovum. This duration allows for a window of fertility around ovulation, making this option correct.

24. In a tangent galvanometer, the current is proportional to the tangent of the deflection angle. The measurement error is minimum when the deflection angle is around 45° because at this angle, small changes in angle produce proportionate changes in tangent value, leading to more accurate readings.

25. Defamation is the act of making a false statement about another person that harms their reputation. It can be in the form of spoken words (slander) or written statements (libel). Since the definition involves issuing a false statement causing harm, defamation is the correct answer.

26. Joseph Marie Jacquard invented the Jacquard loom, a powered loom that used punched cards to control weaving patterns automatically. These punched cards stored instructions, allowing complex designs, including pictures and text, to be woven. This invention was an early step toward programmable machines and influenced later computing concepts.

27. The word "theory" is derived from the Greek word "theoria," which means contemplation, speculation, or viewing. It refers to a system of ideas intended to explain phenomena based on observation and reasoning. Therefore, "theoria" is the correct origin of the term theory.

28. In the Dhamal dance of Haryana, the rhythmic base is provided by traditional folk percussion, and the dholak is the most typical drum used to maintain the beat for group movements. Dhamal is performed with energetic, continuous steps, so a steady, loud, and easily playable drum is required to keep the tempo uniform for all dancers. Among the given options, dholak best matches the commonly used accompanying instrument for this dance form.

29. Varicella, commonly known as chickenpox, is caused by the Varicella-Zoster virus. It is an acute and highly infectious disease characterized by fever and a skin rash. The virus spreads through respiratory droplets or direct contact with lesions, making it highly contagious.

30. Prolonged labour is defined as labour in which the combined duration of the first and second stages exceeds 18 hours. It can lead to complications for both mother and baby if not managed properly. Therefore, 18 hours is the correct threshold used in obstetrics.

31. A partograph is a composite graphical record used during labour to monitor key maternal and fetal parameters against time. It includes cervical dilation, fetal heart rate, uterine contractions, and maternal vital signs on a single chart. This helps in early detection of complications and timely intervention, making it an essential tool in obstetric care.

32. Incidence rate refers to the number of new cases of a disease occurring in a specified population during a defined time period. It measures the risk of developing a disease and is important for understanding the spread of diseases. Prevalence includes both new and existing cases, so it does not fit the definition given.

33. Quickening is the first perception of fetal movements felt by a pregnant woman, usually occurring around 18–20 weeks of gestation. It is an important subjective sign of pregnancy. Other signs like Goodell's sign or Braxton Hicks contractions refer to different physiological changes, not the feeling of fetal movement.

34. Communication is the process of exchanging thoughts, ideas, or information between individuals through verbal or non-verbal means. Since the question specifically mentions verbal interchange of thoughts or ideas, communication fits the definition exactly.

35. Check the pattern step by step:

$$4832 \rightarrow 5840$$
$$5840 \rightarrow 6848$$

Each term increases by 1008:

$$5840 - 4832 = 1008$$
$$6848 - 5840 = 1008$$

So next term:

$$6848 + 1008 = 7856$$

Therefore, 7856 is the correct number in the sequence.

36. In a spreadsheet, the point where a row and a column intersect is called a cell. Each cell is identified by a unique address (like A1, B2) and is used to store data such as numbers, text, or formulas. Hence, "cell" is the correct term for the intersection of rows and columns.

37. A phenomenological study focuses on understanding individuals' lived experiences and perceptions of a particular phenomenon. Studying the real-life experiences of tsunami victims in selected villages fits this approach because it explores personal feelings and experiences, making phenomenological research the correct choice.

38. The second-generation ethanol plant was dedicated to the nation at Panipat in Haryana in 2022. This plant is significant for producing ethanol from agricultural residues like rice straw, contributing to environmental sustainability and reducing stubble burning.

39. Bitot's spots are white, foamy patches on the conjunctiva of the eye and are a classic sign of Vitamin A deficiency. This deficiency affects vision and can lead to night blindness and other eye disorders, so Vitamin A is the correct answer.

40. The average recommended total weight gain during a normal singleton pregnancy for a healthy woman is about 11 kg. This weight gain supports fetal growth, placenta, amniotic fluid, and maternal tissues, ensuring a healthy pregnancy outcome.

41. Beta cells, located in the islets of Langerhans of the pancreas, are responsible for secreting insulin. Insulin helps regulate blood glucose levels by facilitating the uptake of glucose into cells. Other cells like alpha cells secrete glucagon, not insulin, so beta cells are the correct answer.

42. Ureteritis refers to the inflammation of the ureter, which is the tube that carries urine from the kidneys to the bladder. The suffix "-itis" denotes inflammation, and when combined with "ureter," it specifically indicates inflammation of that structure.

43. Perception is the process by which the brain organizes and interprets sensory information to give meaning to what we sense. It involves understanding stimuli from the environment, not just detecting them. Therefore, perception correctly matches the definition of organizing sensory input.

44. The headquarters of the United Nations Environment Programme (UNEP) is located in Nairobi, Kenya. It is the only major UN body headquartered in a developing country and plays a key role in global environmental governance.

45. In epidemiology, a "case" is defined as an individual in the population who has the specific disease, condition, or health disorder being studied. Identifying cases is essential for disease surveillance and research, making this the correct term.

46. An impact printer is a type of printer that works by striking an inked ribbon against paper to produce characters. Dot matrix printers use small pins to hit the ribbon and form characters as a series of dots. Laser, thermal, and inkjet printers do not strike the paper, so they are non-impact printers, making dot matrix the correct answer.

47. Variables are characteristics, qualities, or properties of individuals, objects, or situations that can change or vary. In research, variables are measured, controlled, or manipulated to study relationships. Constants do not change, so they do not fit the definition given.

48. The Constitution of India was enacted (adopted) by the Constituent Assembly on November 26, 1949. It came into force later on January 26, 1950, which is celebrated as Republic Day. Therefore, the enactment date is November 26, 1949.

49. Vitamin D is unique because it can be synthesized in the human body when the skin is exposed to sunlight, and it is also obtained from certain foods. This dual source makes it different from most other vitamins, which are obtained mainly through diet.

50. In obstetrics, the term "lie" refers to the relationship between the long axis of the fetus and the long axis of the uterus or maternal spine. It can be longitudinal, transverse, or oblique. Therefore, "lie" correctly describes the given definition.

51. Recommended Daily Allowance (RDA) refers to the average daily intake level of nutrients considered sufficient to meet the requirements of nearly all healthy individuals in a particular group. It is used as a guideline for maintaining proper nutrition and health, ensuring that people consume adequate amounts of essential nutrients each day.

52. Assault is a crime of violence against another person that involves an intentional act causing fear of imminent harmful or offensive contact. It may or may not involve physical contact, but it creates a reasonable apprehension of injury in the victim. Hence, it is classified as a violent crime.

53. Thinking is essentially a cognitive activity because it involves mental processes such as analyzing, reasoning, problem-solving, and decision-making. It helps individuals process information, form ideas, and arrive at conclusions, making it a core cognitive function.

54. Given, $$A = \begin{bmatrix} \cos 2\theta & -\sin 2\theta \\ \sin 2\theta & \cos 2\theta \end{bmatrix}$$

This is a rotation matrix.

Step 1: Find A^T

$$A^T = \begin{bmatrix} \cos 2\theta & \sin 2\theta \\ -\sin 2\theta & \cos 2\theta \end{bmatrix}$$

Step 2: Add $A + A^T$

$$A + A^T = \begin{bmatrix} \cos 2\theta + \cos 2\theta & -\sin 2\theta + \sin 2\theta \\ \sin 2\theta - \sin 2\theta & \cos 2\theta + \cos 2\theta \end{bmatrix}$$

$$= \begin{bmatrix} 2\cos 2\theta & 0 \\ 0 & 2\cos 2\theta \end{bmatrix}$$

$$= 2 \cos (2\theta)\, I$$

Step 3: Use the given condition

$$A + A^T = I$$

So,

$$2 \cos (2\theta) I = I$$

This gives:

$$2 \cos (2\theta) = 1$$

$$\cos (2\theta) = \frac{1}{2}$$

Step 4: Solve

$$2\theta = \frac{\pi}{3}$$

$$\theta = \frac{\pi}{6}.$$

55. Retrospective studies are commonly referred to as case-control studies because they begin with individuals who already have a particular outcome or disease (cases) and compare them with those who do not (controls), looking back in time to identify possible causes or risk factors. Thus, they study past exposures in relation to present outcomes.

56. Ecommerce refers to the buying and selling of goods and services over the internet. It involves online business transactions, including payments, marketing, and customer interactions. Other options like FTP, email, and newsgroups are communication or data transfer tools, not complete business systems.

57. A hypothesis is a formal, tentative statement that predicts a relationship between two or more variables in a study. It provides a direction for research and can be tested through data collection and analysis. Therefore, it correctly matches the definition given.

58. The Haryana Municipal Act was enacted in 1973 to regulate and govern municipal administration in the state. This Act provided the legal framework for the constitution, powers, duties, and functioning of municipalities in Haryana. It dealt with urban local governance, including sanitation, public health, and civic amenities. The later legislation in 1994 relates to municipal corporations after the 74th Constitutional Amendment, but the original Municipal Act itself was passed in 1973, so this option fits the question exactly.

59. Brucellosis is a bacterial zoonotic disease caused by bacteria of the genus Brucella. It is transmitted from animals to humans, commonly through direct contact or consumption of contaminated animal products, making it a bacterial zoonosis.

60. Anencephaly is a congenital anomaly resulting from the failure of development of the cranial vault and brain tissue, while the facial structures remain relatively normal. It is a severe neural tube defect and is incompatible with life, which fits the given definition precisely.

61. The nephron is the structural and functional unit of the kidney. Each kidney contains millions of nephrons, which are responsible for filtering blood, removing waste products, and forming urine. The glomerulus is only a part of the nephron, not the complete unit, so nephron is the correct answer.

62. When the correlation coefficient $r = +1$, it indicates a perfect positive correlation. This means that as one variable increases, the other variable also increases in exact proportion. There is a complete linear relationship between the two variables without any deviation.

63. Hepatitis B is known as serum hepatitis because it is transmitted through infected blood, body fluids, or contaminated needles. It differs from Hepatitis A, which is transmitted through contaminated food and water, so Hepatitis B fits the given description.

64. Given:

B is mother of E

E is father of G $\rightarrow$ so B is grandmother of G

C is son of E $\rightarrow$ C and G are siblings

D is sister of C and G

A is parent of E $\rightarrow$ A is grandparent of G

K is parent of G $\rightarrow$ K is either mother or father of G

Since E is father of G, the other parent of G must be K $\rightarrow$ so K is the wife of E.

E is the son of B $\rightarrow$ so K is the wife of B's son.

Hence, K is the daughter-in-law of B.

65. A sector is the smallest unit of data that can be read from or written to a disk. Disks are divided into tracks, and each track is further divided into sectors. Data operations are performed at the sector level, making it the correct answer.

66. Coordination is the process by which the activities and efforts of different individuals or groups are organized and harmonized so that they work together effectively to achieve specific goals. It ensures unity of action and proper alignment of tasks, avoiding duplication and conflict. While cooperation refers to voluntary helping behaviour, coordination is a structured and systematic process of integrating efforts toward a common objective, so it fits the definition more precisely.

67. Mode is the value that appears most frequently in a data set. It represents the observation with the highest frequency. Unlike mean or median, which depend on calculations, mode directly identifies the most repeated value in the dataset.

68. Chlorobenzene, when heated with aqueous sodium hydroxide at high temperature (623 K) and high pressure (around 300 atm), undergoes nucleophilic substitution to form phenol. This industrial method is known as the Dow process, making phenol the correct product.

69. Enteric fever is a term that primarily includes typhoid fever and paratyphoid fever, which are caused by Salmonella bacteria. Among the given options, typhoid fever correctly represents enteric fever.

70. The average daily fluid intake for an adult is about 1500–2000 ml. This amount helps maintain proper hydration, supports metabolic processes, and compensates for daily fluid losses through urine, sweat, and respiration.

71. Riboflavin is the chemical name for Vitamin B_2. It is a water-soluble vitamin that plays an important role in energy production, cellular function, and metabolism of fats, drugs, and steroids. It is also essential for maintaining healthy skin, eyes, and nervous system.

72. A host is a person or animal in which an organism (such as a parasite or pathogen) lives, grows, and obtains nourishment. The host provides a suitable environment for the survival and multiplication of the organism. Hence, it exactly fits the definition given.

73. Structuralism was propagated by Wilhelm Wundt, who is considered the father of modern psychology. This school of thought focused on analyzing the structure of the mind by breaking down mental processes into basic elements such as sensations and feelings through introspection.

74. Bharatnatyam is the classical dance form of Tamil Nadu. It is one of the oldest classical dances of India, characterized by fixed upper torso, bent legs, intricate footwork, and expressive gestures. It originated in the temples of Tamil Nadu and is deeply rooted in Indian culture and tradition.

75. Pharmacology is the branch of science that studies the effects of drugs on living systems. It includes how drugs interact with biological systems, their mechanisms of action, therapeutic uses, and side effects. Therefore, it correctly matches the given definition.

76. In a spreadsheet, a formula is an equation used to perform calculations or operations on data present in worksheet cells. It can include numbers, cell references, operators, and functions. Formulas help in automatically computing results such as sums, averages, and other calculations.

77. In a patrilocal family system, the wife moves to live in the husband's house after marriage. This system is common in many traditional societies where the family is centered around the male lineage. Hence, patrilocal correctly describes this arrangement.

78. Sirsa district of Haryana is one of the leading agricultural districts and is widely recognized for its high production of wheat. Due to fertile alluvial soil, extensive irrigation facilities like the Bhakra canal system, and favorable climatic conditions, wheat cultivation is highly productive in this region. Although Sirsa also produces other crops such as cotton, wheat remains the major crop in terms of production, making it the correct answer.

79. Prevalence refers to the total number of cases of a disease (both old and new) present in a population at a given time or over a specified period. It helps in understanding the overall burden of disease in a population, unlike incidence which counts only new cases.

80. A healthy lactating mother typically produces about 500–900 ml of breast milk per day. This amount is sufficient to meet the nutritional needs of an infant during early months and varies depending on factors like nutrition and frequency of feeding.

81. The heart is located in the thoracic cavity, which is the chest region of the body between the neck and abdomen. It lies in the mediastinum between the lungs and is protected by the rib cage. Therefore, the thoracic cavity is the correct anatomical location of the heart.

82. Edward Jenner is known as the father of immunology because he developed the first successful vaccine against smallpox in 1796. His work laid the foundation for the science of immunology and the development of vaccination as a method to prevent infectious diseases.

83. Instincts are innate and inborn tendencies or patterns of behavior present in an individual from birth. They do not require learning or experience and guide basic behaviors such as survival, reproduction, and response to stimuli. Hence, instincts correctly match the given definition.

84. Given expression

$$\left(x^2 - \frac{1}{x^2}\right)^{16}$$

General term of expansion

$$T_{r+1} = \binom{16}{r}(x^2)^{16-r}\left(-\frac{1}{x^2}\right)^r$$

Now simplify powers of x

$$(x^2)^{16-r} = x^{2(16-r)} = x^{32-2r}$$

$$\left(\frac{1}{x^2}\right)^r = x^{-2r}$$

So, $$T_{r+1} = \binom{16}{r}(-1)^r x^{32-2r} \cdot x^{-2r}$$

$$= \binom{16}{r}(-1)^r x^{32-4r}$$

For constant term, power of $x = 0$

$$32 - 4r = 0$$

$$4r = 32$$

$$r = 8$$

Thus, constant term is

$$\binom{16}{8}$$

So, the required answer is ${}^{16}C_8$.

85. The cold chain is a system used for storing and transporting vaccines at recommended low temperatures from the manufacturer to the point of use. It ensures that vaccines remain effective and potent by maintaining a continuous temperature-controlled environment throughout storage and transportation.

86. A plotter is an output device that draws images, diagrams, and graphics on paper based on commands from a computer. It uses pens or other drawing tools to produce high-quality line drawings, often used in engineering and architectural designs.

87. A cross-sectional research design involves collecting data at a single point in time from a population or sample. It provides a snapshot of a situation or phenomenon as it exists at that specific moment, unlike longitudinal studies which observe changes over time.

88. Dal Lake in Jammu and Kashmir is connected to the Jhelum River. It is part of the Jhelum basin and is fed by its tributaries. Hence, Dal Lake is associated with the Jhelum River system.

89. Chickenpox is transmitted through droplet infection, mainly via respiratory secretions when an infected person coughs or sneezes. It can also spread through direct contact with the fluid from skin lesions, but droplet transmission is the primary mode.

90. Hyponatremia is defined as a plasma sodium concentration of less than 135 mEq/L. Sodium is essential for maintaining fluid balance and nerve function, and levels below this threshold indicate a deficiency that can affect normal body functions.

91. The normal life span of a red blood cell (RBC) is about 120 days. RBCs circulate in the bloodstream carrying oxygen from the lungs to body tissues and carbon dioxide back to the lungs. After about 120 days, they are destroyed mainly in the spleen and replaced by new cells formed in the bone marrow.

92. Range is the simplest measure of dispersion and is defined as the difference between the highest (maximum) and lowest (minimum) values in a dataset. It gives a quick idea of the spread of data but does not consider how values are distributed within the range.

93. Measles is also known as rubeola, which is a highly contagious viral disease characterized by fever, cough, and a red rash. It is important to distinguish it from rubella (German measles), which is a different disease.

94. Total tickets = 17 (numbered 1 to 17)

Even numbers = 2, 4, 6, 8, 10, 12, 14, 16 → total = 8

Probability that first ticket is even $= \frac{8}{17}$

After drawing one even ticket, remaining tickets = 16

Remaining even tickets = 7

Probability that second ticket is even $= \frac{7}{16}$

Since drawing is without replacement, multiply probabilities

$$\frac{8}{17} \times \frac{7}{16} = \frac{56}{272} = \frac{7}{34}$$

Hence, required probability $= \frac{7}{34}$.

95. Topical drugs are those applied directly to the skin or mucous membranes for localized action at a specific site. They are used to treat conditions like infections, inflammation, or pain without significant systemic absorption. Hence, topical drugs fit the definition given.

96. The "Borders and shading" option allows users to add borders around selected text or paragraphs and also change the background color (shading) of the selected area. This feature is commonly used in word processing to enhance document appearance.

97. Nominal level measurement involves classification into categories without any order or ranking. Gender is a categorical variable with no inherent order, making it a clear example of nominal scale measurement. Other options like temperature and weight involve numerical values.

98. Maharaja Agrasen is associated with Agroha in Haryana, which is believed to be the ancient capital of his kingdom. Agroha is an important historical and cultural site linked to the Aggarwal community.

99. AIDS is often referred to as the "slim disease" because individuals suffering from it experience severe weight loss and wasting. This condition is caused by the Human Immunodeficiency Virus (HIV), which weakens the immune system.

100. An ectopic pregnancy is a condition in which the fertilized ovum implants outside the normal uterine (endometrial) cavity, most commonly in the fallopian tube. This condition is dangerous and requires prompt medical attention, making "ectopic" the correct term.

Subject Related Knowledge

NURSING

1. Anatomy

1. The smallest functional unit of the human body is

A. Organ B. Cell

C. Tissue mass D. System

2. The anatomical position refers to the body standing

A. With palms backward

B. Supine on table

C. Facing forward

D. Arms above head

3. The plane dividing body into equal right and left halves is

A. Frontal plane

B. Transverse plane

C. Sagittal plane

D. Oblique section

4. The longest bone in the human body is

A. Humerus B. Tibia

C. Femur D. Radius

5. Which part of the brain controls balance and posture?

A. Cerebellum B. Medulla

C. Cerebrum D. Hypothalamus

6. The number of chambers in human heart is

A. Two chambers B. Three cavities

C. Four chambers D. Five sections

7. The functional unit of kidney is

A. Neuron B. Nephron

C. Alveoli D. Tubule

8. The organ responsible for gas exchange is

A. Trachea B. Bronchus

C. Lungs D. Larynx

9. Which structure connects muscles to bones?

A. Ligament B. Tendon

C. Cartilage D. Fascia

10. Match the following:

Column I	Column II
A. Femur	1. Thigh bone
B. Humerus	2. Forearm bone
C. Radius	3. Lower leg bone
D. Tibia	4. Upper arm bone

A. A-1, B-4, C-2, D-3

B. A-4, B-1, C-3, D-2

C. A-1, B-2, C-4, D-3

D. A-3, B-4, C-1, D-2

11. The number of bones in the adult human skeleton is

A. 196 B. 206

C. 216 D. 226

12. The skull consists of ____ bones.

A. Twenty-two B. Twenty-four

C. Twenty D. Twenty-six

13. The vertebral column in an adult has ____ vertebrae.

A. 31 B. 33

C. 35 D. 29

14. The joint present between two vertebrae is

A. Fibrous joint B. Synovial joint

C. Cartilaginous joint D. Ball socket joint

15. Which bone is known as collar bone?

A. Scapula B. Clavicle

C. Sternum D. Rib

16. The scapula is located in the

A. Pelvic region B. Shoulder region

C. Thoracic cavity D. Cranial cavity

17. The patella is present in the

A. Elbow B. Knee

C. Ankle D. Wrist

18. The longest bone of upper limb is

A. Radius B. Ulna

C. Humerus D. Scapula

19. The smallest bone of the body is

A. Incus B. Malleus
C. Stapes D. Cochlea

20. The ribs are attached posteriorly to the

A. Sternum B. Vertebral column
C. Clavicle D. Scapula

21. The sternum is present in the

A. Back region B. Chest region
C. Neck region D. Abdomen

22. The joint that allows maximum movement is

A. Hinge joint
B. Pivot joint
C. Ball and socket joint
D. Gliding joint

23. The joint present in elbow is

A. Pivot joint B. Hinge joint
C. Ball socket D. Saddle joint

24. Cartilage is a type of

A. Epithelial tissue B. Muscular tissue
C. Connective tissue D. Nervous tissue

25. Which of the following bones protects the brain?

A. Rib B. Femur
C. Skull D. Vertebra

26. Match the following:

Column I	Column II
A. Atlas	1. First cervical vertebra
B. Axis	2. Tail bone
C. Sacrum	3. Fused vertebrae
D. Coccyx	4. Second cervical vertebra

A. A-1, B-4, C-3, D-2
B. A-4, B-1, C-2, D-3
C. A-3, B-2, C-4, D-1
D. A-2, B-3, C-1, D-4

27. The number of cervical vertebrae is

A. Five B. Six
C. Seven D. Eight

28. The pelvic girdle is formed by

A. Two bones B. Three bones
C. Four bones D. Five bones

29. Assertion I: Synovial joints allow free movement.
Assertion II: They contain synovial fluid.

A. Both statements are correct
B. I is correct, II is incorrect
C. Both are incorrect
D. I is incorrect, II is correct

30. Assertion I: Red bone marrow produces blood cells.
Assertion II: Yellow bone marrow produces RBCs.

A. Both statements are correct
B. I is correct, II is incorrect
C. Both are incorrect
D. I is incorrect, II is correct

31. The basic functional cell of the nervous system is the

A. Neuroglia cell B. Neuron
C. Epithelial cell D. Muscle fibre

32. The part of neuron that conducts impulses away from the cell body is

A. Dendrite B. Synaptic knob
C. Nissl body D. Axon

33. The gap between two neurons where impulse transmission occurs is called

A. Neuromuscular junction
B. End plate region
C. Synapse
D. Intercalated disc

34. The insulating covering around many axons is

A. Sarcolemma B. Myelin sheath
C. Periosteum D. Synovial capsule

35. The brain part primarily responsible for higher mental functions is

A. Cerebrum B. Cerebellum
C. Medulla oblongata D. Pons

36. The major part of the human brain by volume is

A. Thalamus B. Medulla
C. Cerebrum D. Hypothalamus

37. The structure that connects the two cerebral hemispheres is

A. Pituitary stalk
B. Corpus callosum
C. Optic chiasma
D. Pineal body

38. The brain part that mainly controls breathing and heart rate is

A. Cerebrum B. Cerebellum
C. Medulla oblongata D. Frontal lobe

39. The number of cranial nerves in humans is

A. Ten pairs B. Eleven pairs
C. Twelve pairs D. Thirteen pairs

40. The spinal cord terminates approximately at the level of

A. L5 vertebra B. S1 vertebra
C. L1–L2 vertebrae D. T12 vertebra

41. The protective coverings of brain and spinal cord are called

A. Pleura B. Peritoneum
C. Meninges D. Fascia

42. Match the following:

Column I	Column II
A. Cerebrum	1. Reflex pathway conduction
B. Cerebellum	2. Coordination of movements
C. Medulla oblongata	3. Higher mental functions
D. Spinal cord	4. Vital centres control

A. A-2, B-3, C-4, D-1
B. A-3, B-2, C-4, D-1
C. A-4, B-2, C-3, D-1
D. A-3, B-4, C-2, D-1

43. Assertion I: The central nervous system consists of brain and spinal cord.

Assertion II: Cranial nerves arise from the spinal cord only.

A. Both statements are correct
B. I is correct, II is incorrect
C. Both are incorrect
D. I is incorrect, II is correct

44. The peripheral nervous system consists mainly of

A. Brain lobes
B. Cranial and spinal nerves
C. Meninges only
D. Ventricles of brain

45. The functional and structural unit of nervous tissue is

A. Neuroglia B. Synapse
C. Neuron D. Myelin

46. The heart is located in the

A. Cranial cavity B. Thoracic cavity
C. Abdominal region D. Pelvic cavity

47. The heart has ____ atria.

A. One B. Two
C. Three D. Four

48. The valve present between left atrium and left ventricle is

A. Tricuspid valve B. Pulmonary valve
C. Bicuspid valve D. Aortic valve

49. The largest artery of the body is

A. Pulmonary artery B. Carotid artery
C. Femoral artery D. Aorta

50. The blood vessel that carries oxygenated blood from lungs to heart is

A. Pulmonary artery B. Pulmonary vein
C. Aorta D. Vena cava

51. The right ventricle pumps blood into the

A. Aorta B. Pulmonary artery
C. Vena cava D. Coronary artery

52. The functional unit of circulation is

A. Nephron B. Alveolus
C. Capillary D. Neuron

53. Match the following:

Column I	Column II
A. Right atrium	1. Pumps blood to body
B. Left atrium	2. Receives deoxygenated blood
C. Right ventricle	3. Pumps blood to lungs
D. Left ventricle	4. Receives oxygenated blood

A. A-2, B-4, C-3, D-1
B. A-4, B-2, C-1, D-3
C. A-3, B-1, C-4, D-2
D. A-2, B-3, C-1, D-4

54. Assertion I: Arteries carry blood away from the heart.

Assertion II: All arteries carry oxygenated blood.

A. Both statements are correct
B. I is correct, II is incorrect
C. Both are incorrect
D. I is incorrect, II is correct

55. The wall of the heart is mainly made of

A. Smooth muscle B. Skeletal muscle
C. Connective tissue D. Cardiac muscle

56. The organ responsible for respiration is

A. Heart B. Lungs
C. Liver D. Kidney

57. The trachea divides into two

A. Bronchi B. Bronchioles
C. Alveoli D. Pleura

58. The smallest functional unit of lung is

A. Bronchus B. Bronchiole
C. Alveolus D. Larynx

59. The exchange of gases takes place in the

A. Trachea B. Bronchi
C. Alveoli D. Pleural cavity

60. The covering of lungs is called

A. Peritoneum B. Pleura
C. Pericardium D. Meninges

61. The voice box is known as

A. Pharynx B. Larynx
C. Trachea D. Bronchus

62. The diaphragm separates thoracic cavity from

A. Cranial cavity B. Pelvic cavity
C. Abdominal cavity D. Vertebral cavity

63. Match the following:

Column I	Column II
A. Trachea	1. Site of gas exchange
B. Bronchi	2. Air conducting tube
C. Alveoli	3. Branches of trachea
D. Diaphragm	4. Muscle of respiration

A. A-2, B-3, C-1, D-4 B. A-3, B-2, C-4, D-1
C. A-1, B-4, C-2, D-3 D. A-2, B-1, C-3, D-4

64. Assertion I: Oxygen is transported from lungs to tissues.

Assertion II: Carbon dioxide is transported from tissues to lungs.

A. Both statements are correct
B. I is correct, II is incorrect
C. Both are incorrect
D. I is incorrect, II is correct

65. The right lung has ____ lobes.

A. Two lobes B. Three lobes
C. Four lobes D. One lobe

66. The first part of the digestive tract is

A. Mouth B. Esophagus
C. Stomach D. Duodenum

67. The enzyme present in saliva is

A. Pepsin B. Lipase
C. Amylase D. Trypsin

68. The food pipe is called

A. Trachea B. Esophagus
C. Bronchus D. Ileum

69. The largest gland in the body is

A. Pancreas B. Thyroid
C. Liver D. Salivary gland

70. The bile is produced by

A. Pancreas B. Gall bladder
C. Liver D. Duodenum

71. The main site of digestion is

A. Mouth B. Stomach
C. Small intestine D. Large intestine

72. The enzyme pepsin acts on

A. Fats B. Proteins
C. Carbohydrates D. Vitamins

73. Match the following:

Column I	Column II
A. Stomach	1. Absorption of nutrients
B. Liver	2. Produces bile
C. Pancreas	3. Produces digestive enzymes
D. Small intestine	4. Secretes gastric juice

A. A-4, B-2, C-3, D-1
B. A-2, B-1, C-4, D-3
C. A-1, B-3, C-2, D-4
D. A-3, B-4, C-1, D-2

74. Assertion I: Small intestine is the main site of absorption.

Assertion II: Large intestine absorbs water.

A. Both statements are correct
B. I is correct, II is incorrect
C. Both are incorrect
D. I is incorrect, II is correct

75. The part of stomach that connects to small intestine is

A. Cardiac part B. Fundus
C. Body D. Pylorus

76. The main organ of excretion is

A. Liver B. Kidney
C. Lung D. Skin

77. The functional unit of kidney is

A. Neuron B. Nephron
C. Alveolus D. Glomerulus

78. The urine is transported from kidney to urinary bladder through

A. Urethra B. Nephron
C. Ureter D. Renal artery

79. Match the following:

Column I	Column II
A. Kidney	1. Storage of urine
B. Ureter	2. Conducts urine to outside
C. Urinary bladder	3. Formation of urine
D. Urethra	4. Transport of urine to bladder

A. A-3, B-4, C-1, D-2
B. A-4, B-3, C-2, D-1
C. A-1, B-2, C-3, D-4
D. A-2, B-1, C-4, D-3

80. Assertion I: Kidneys regulate fluid and electrolyte balance.

Assertion II: Kidneys have no role in blood pressure regulation.

A. Both statements are correct
B. I is correct, II is incorrect
C. Both are incorrect
D. I is incorrect, II is correct

81. The male reproductive organ that produces sperm is

A. Prostate gland
B. Testis
C. Epididymis
D. Seminal vesicle

82. The site of fertilization in female is
A. Uterus B. Ovary
C. Fallopian tube D. Cervix

83. The female gamete is called
A. Sperm B. Ovum
C. Zygote D. Embryo

84. The organ where fetus develops is
A. Ovary B. Fallopian tube
C. Uterus D. Vagina

85. The hormone responsible for development of male secondary sexual characters is
A. Estrogen B. Progesterone
C. Testosterone D. Oxytocin

86. The structure that stores sperm temporarily is
A. Vas deferens B. Epididymis
C. Urethra D. Prostate

87. The outermost layer of uterus is
A. Endometrium B. Myometrium
C. Perimetrium D. Cervix

88. The process of release of ovum from ovary is called
A. Fertilization B. Ovulation
C. Implantation D. Menstruation

89. Match the following:

Column I	Column II
A. Testis	1. Female gamete production
B. Ovary	2. Male gamete production
C. Uterus	3. Transport of sperm
D. Vas deferens	4. Development of fetus

A. A-2, B-1, C-4, D-3
B. A-1, B-2, C-3, D-4
C. A-3, B-4, C-1, D-2
D. A-4, B-3, C-2, D-1

90. Assertion I: Fertilization usually occurs in fallopian tube.

Assertion II: Implantation occurs in uterus.

A. Both statements are correct
B. I is correct, II is incorrect
C. Both are incorrect
D. I is incorrect, II is correct

EXPLANATORY ANSWERS

1. **B:** Cells are the basic structural and functional units of life. Every tissue and organ is composed of cells performing specialized roles. Without cells, higher levels of organization cannot exist.

2. **C:** In anatomical position, the body stands erect with face forward, arms at sides and palms facing forward. This standard reference helps in describing body parts consistently.

3. **C:** The sagittal plane divides the body into right and left parts. When equal halves are formed, it is called the median sagittal plane. It is widely used in anatomical descriptions.

4. **C:** The femur is located in the thigh and is the longest and strongest bone. It supports body weight and helps in movement such as walking and running.

5. **A:** The cerebellum coordinates voluntary movements and maintains posture and balance. Damage to it causes loss of coordination and unsteady movements.

6. **C:** The human heart has two atria and two ventricles. This four-chambered structure allows efficient separation of oxygenated and deoxygenated blood.

7. **B:** The nephron is the structural and functional unit of the kidney. It filters blood and forms urine through processes like filtration, reabsorption and secretion.

8. **C:** Gas exchange occurs in alveoli of lungs where oxygen enters blood and carbon dioxide is removed. This process is essential for cellular respiration.

9. **B:** Tendons are fibrous connective tissues attaching muscles to bones. They transmit force generated by muscles to bones, enabling movement.

10. **A:** Femur is thigh bone, humerus is upper arm bone, radius is forearm bone and tibia is lower leg bone. Correct anatomical pairing helps in clinical identification.

11. **B:** Adult human skeleton contains 206 bones. At birth, bones are more in number but fuse during growth. This number is important for clinical and anatomical reference.

12. **A:** The skull is made up of 22 bones including cranial and facial bones. These bones protect the brain and form facial structure. They are mostly fused immovably.

13. **B:** The vertebral column initially has 33 vertebrae. Some fuse to form sacrum and coccyx in adults. It provides support and protects spinal cord.

14. **C:** Intervertebral joints are cartilaginous, allowing slight movement and flexibility. They absorb shock and maintain posture.

15. **B:** The clavicle connects sternum to scapula and is commonly called collar bone. It stabilizes the shoulder and supports arm movements.

16. **B:** Scapula is a flat triangular bone located on posterior thoracic wall. It forms part of shoulder girdle and allows arm movement.

17. **B:** Patella is a sesamoid bone located in front of knee joint. It protects the joint and improves leverage of quadriceps muscle.

18. C: Humerus is the longest bone of upper limb extending from shoulder to elbow. It plays a key role in arm movement.

19. C: Stapes is the smallest bone located in middle ear. It transmits sound vibrations to inner ear structures.

20. B: Ribs are attached posteriorly to vertebrae and anteriorly to sternum. This arrangement forms thoracic cage for protection.

21. B: Sternum lies in the anterior chest and connects ribs. It protects heart and lungs.

22. C: This joint allows movement in all directions. Example is shoulder and hip joints.

23. B: Elbow joint allows movement in one plane like a hinge. It permits flexion and extension.

24. C: Cartilage is a specialized connective tissue providing support and flexibility. It is present in joints and respiratory tract.

25. C: Skull encloses and protects the brain. It also forms structure of face.

26. A: Atlas is first cervical vertebra, axis is second, sacrum is fused vertebrae and coccyx is tail bone. This is important in spinal anatomy.

27. C: There are seven cervical vertebrae in human body. They support head and allow neck movements.

28. A: Pelvic girdle consists of two hip bones. Each is formed by fusion of ilium, ischium and pubis.

29. A: Synovial joints allow free movement due to presence of synovial fluid. The fluid lubricates and reduces friction.

30. B: Red marrow produces RBCs, WBCs and platelets. Yellow marrow mainly stores fat and does not produce blood cells.

31. B: Neurons are specialized cells designed to receive, process, and transmit nerve impulses. Their structure supports rapid communication between different body parts. Other supporting cells (neuroglia) assist but do not conduct impulses as the primary unit.

32. D: The axon carries impulses away from the cell body toward another neuron or effector organ. Dendrites mainly receive impulses toward the cell body. This directionality is essential for organized signal flow in neural pathways.

33. C: A synapse is the functional junction where one neuron communicates with another. Transmission commonly occurs via neurotransmitters across a synaptic cleft. This is the key site for integration and modulation of nervous signals.

34. B: Myelin acts as an insulating layer that speeds up impulse transmission by saltatory conduction. It also protects the axon and improves efficiency of signal travel. Loss of myelin is associated with major neurological dysfunctions.

35. A: The cerebrum controls intelligence, memory, learning, thinking, and voluntary actions. Its cortex is highly developed in humans, enabling complex reasoning. Other brain parts focus more on coordination or vital automatic functions.

36. C: The cerebrum forms the largest portion of brain volume and mass. It contains major sensory, motor, and association areas. This dominance reflects its wide role in controlling body activities and cognition.

37. B: Corpus callosum is a thick band of nerve fibres joining left and right cerebral hemispheres. It allows coordination and transfer of information between hemispheres. This connection supports integrated brain function.

38. C: The medulla contains vital centres regulating respiration, heart rate, and blood pressure. Damage here can be life-threatening because these functions are automatic and continuous. That is why it is called a vital centre region.

39. C: Humans have 12 pairs of cranial nerves emerging mainly from the brain/brainstem. They supply special senses and head-neck regions, with some reaching thorax and abdomen. This number is a standard anatomical fact frequently tested.

40. C: In adults, the spinal cord typically ends around L1–L2 as the conus medullaris. Below this level, nerve roots continue as cauda equina. This is clinically important for safe lumbar puncture levels.

41. C: Meninges are three protective layers covering brain and spinal cord—dura mater, arachnoid mater, and pia mater. They provide mechanical protection and support cerebrospinal fluid circulation. Infections here lead to meningitis.

42. B: Cerebrum is linked with higher functions, cerebellum with coordination, medulla with vital centres, and spinal cord with conduction/reflex pathways. This matching aligns each structure with its primary role. Such mappings are essential in symptom-based clinical MCQs.

43. B: CNS includes brain and spinal cord, so Assertion I is true. Cranial nerves arise from the brain/brainstem, not from the spinal cord only, so Assertion II is false. This distinction separates central components from peripheral outflow pathways.

44. B: The PNS includes nerves that connect CNS to the rest of the body. Cranial nerves serve head/neck and some visceral functions, while spinal nerves supply trunk and limbs. Together they form the major communication network outside CNS.

45. C: Neuron is the structural and functional unit responsible for conducting impulses. It has cell body, dendrites, and axon enabling signal transmission. Neuroglia support neurons but do not replace the neuron's primary impulse-conducting role.

46. B: The heart lies in the mediastinum within the thoracic cavity between the lungs. It is slightly tilted toward the left side. This position allows it to efficiently pump blood to both lungs and body.

47. B: The heart has two atria—right and left—which receive blood. The right atrium receives deoxygenated blood, while the left atrium receives oxygenated blood. These chambers act as receiving chambers.

48. C: The bicuspid (mitral) valve lies between left atrium and left ventricle. It prevents backflow of blood during ventricular contraction. Proper valve function is essential for efficient circulation.

49. D: The aorta is the largest artery, arising from the left ventricle. It distributes oxygenated blood to the entire body through its branches. Its thick wall helps withstand high pressure.

50. B: Pulmonary veins carry oxygenated blood from lungs to the left atrium. This is an exception as veins usually carry deoxygenated blood. It is an important physiological distinction.

51. B: The right ventricle pumps deoxygenated blood to lungs via pulmonary artery. This is another exception as this artery carries deoxygenated blood. Gas exchange occurs in lungs.

52. C: Capillaries are microscopic vessels where exchange of gases, nutrients, and wastes occurs. Their thin walls facilitate diffusion. They connect arteries and veins.

53. A: Right atrium receives deoxygenated blood, left atrium receives oxygenated blood, right ventricle pumps to lungs, and left ventricle pumps to body. This sequence maintains circulation.

54. B: Arteries carry blood away from the heart. However, pulmonary artery carries deoxygenated blood, so not all arteries carry oxygenated blood. This is a common exception.

55. D: The heart wall is made of specialized cardiac muscle that contracts rhythmically. It is involuntary and has unique properties like automaticity. This ensures continuous pumping action.

56. B: Lungs are the primary organs of respiration where oxygen enters blood and carbon dioxide is removed. They contain numerous alveoli for gas exchange. Their large surface area makes diffusion efficient.

57. A: The trachea bifurcates into right and left bronchi. These bronchi further branch into smaller bronchioles inside lungs. This branching ensures proper air distribution.

58. C: Alveoli are tiny air sacs where gas exchange occurs. Their thin walls and rich capillary network allow rapid diffusion of gases. They are considered functional units of lungs.

59. C: Oxygen and carbon dioxide exchange occurs across alveolar walls. This process depends on concentration gradients. Efficient exchange is essential for cellular respiration.

60. B: Pleura is a double-layered membrane covering lungs. It reduces friction during breathing movements. The pleural fluid between layers acts as a lubricant.

61. B: Larynx is called the voice box as it contains vocal cords. It also acts as a passage for air. It plays a role in phonation and protection of airway.

62. C: The diaphragm is a dome-shaped muscle separating thoracic and abdominal cavities. It is the main muscle of respiration. Its contraction increases thoracic volume.

63. A: Trachea conducts air, bronchi are its branches, alveoli are gas exchange sites, and diaphragm aids respiration. Each structure has a specific function in breathing.

64. A: Oxygen moves from lungs to tissues through blood, while carbon dioxide moves in reverse direction. This bidirectional transport maintains gas balance. It is essential for metabolism.

65. B: The right lung has three lobes—upper, middle, and lower. The left lung has two lobes due to space occupied by heart. This asymmetry is a key anatomical fact.

66. A: Digestion begins in the mouth where food is ingested and mechanically broken down. Saliva starts chemical digestion of carbohydrates. It is the entry point of alimentary canal.

67. C: Salivary amylase breaks down starch into simpler sugars. It initiates carbohydrate digestion in the oral cavity. Its activity continues briefly in stomach.

68. B: Esophagus is a muscular tube that transports food from pharynx to stomach. Movement occurs by peristalsis. It does not take part in digestion.

69. C: Liver is the largest gland in the body. It performs many metabolic functions including bile production. It also detoxifies harmful substances.

70. C: Bile is produced by liver and stored in gall bladder. It helps in emulsification of fats. This aids digestion and absorption of lipids.

71. C: Most digestion and absorption occur in the small intestine. It contains enzymes and has large surface area due to villi. This enhances nutrient absorption.

72. B: Pepsin is a proteolytic enzyme secreted in stomach. It breaks proteins into smaller peptides. It works best in acidic medium.

73. A: Stomach secretes gastric juice, liver produces bile, pancreas produces enzymes, and small intestine absorbs nutrients. Each organ has a specific digestive role.

74. A: Small intestine absorbs nutrients while large intestine mainly absorbs water and electrolytes. These processes complete digestion and maintain fluid balance.

75. D: Pylorus is the distal part of stomach that opens into duodenum. It regulates the passage of chyme. It plays an important role in controlled emptying.

76. B: Kidneys are the primary organs responsible for excretion. They filter blood, remove waste products, and regulate water and electrolyte balance. They also help maintain acid-base balance.

77. B: Nephron is the structural and functional unit of kidney. It performs filtration, reabsorption, and secretion to form urine. Each kidney contains millions of nephrons.

78. C: Ureters are tubes that carry urine from kidneys to urinary bladder. They use peristaltic movements to transport urine. They ensure one-way flow of urine.

79. A: Kidney forms urine, ureter transports it to bladder, bladder stores urine, and urethra carries it outside. This sequence ensures proper elimination of waste.

80. B: Kidneys regulate fluid balance and electrolytes. They also regulate blood pressure through renin-angiotensin system. Therefore, second statement is incorrect.

81. B: Testes are the primary male reproductive organs responsible for sperm production. They also secrete testosterone. These functions are essential for reproduction and development of male characteristics.

82. C: Fertilization usually occurs in the ampullary region of fallopian tube. It is the site where sperm meets ovum. The fertilized egg then travels to uterus.

83. B: Ovum is the female gamete produced by ovaries. It combines with sperm during fertilization to form a zygote. It carries half the genetic material.

84. C: The uterus is the organ where embryo implants and develops into fetus. It provides nourishment and protection. It plays a vital role during pregnancy.

85. C: Testosterone is the main male sex hormone. It is responsible for development of secondary sexual characteristics such as beard growth and voice changes. It also supports sperm formation.

86. B: Epididymis is a coiled tube where sperm mature and are stored temporarily. It helps in gaining motility. It is essential for functional sperm.

87. C: The uterus has three layers—endometrium (inner), myometrium (middle), and perimetrium (outer). The perimetrium is the outer protective layer. It covers the uterus.

88. B: Ovulation is the release of mature ovum from ovary. It usually occurs mid-cycle. This is the most fertile period in female reproductive cycle.

89. A: Testis produces sperm, ovary produces ovum, uterus supports fetal development, and vas deferens transports sperm. This reflects normal reproductive physiology.

90. A: Fertilization occurs in fallopian tube and implantation occurs in uterus. These are sequential steps in human reproduction. Both processes are essential for pregnancy.

2. Physiology

1. The basic unit of life is

A. Tissue B. Cell
C. Organ D. System

2. The process by which molecules move from high to low concentration is

A. Active transport B. Diffusion
C. Endocytosis D. Osmosis

3. Movement of water across semipermeable membrane is called

A. Diffusion B. Active transport
C. Osmosis D. Filtration

4. The cell membrane is mainly composed of

A. Proteins only B. Lipids and proteins
C. Carbohydrates only D. Minerals

5. The energy currency of the cell is

A. ADP B. ATP
C. AMP D. NADH

6. The organelle responsible for protein synthesis is

A. Mitochondria B. Ribosome
C. Golgi body D. Lysosome

7. The organelle known as powerhouse of the cell is

A. Ribosome B. Nucleus
C. Mitochondria D. Endoplasmic reticulum

8. The control centre of the cell is

A. Cytoplasm B. Nucleus
C. Mitochondria D. Lysosome

9. Match the following:

Column I	Column II
A. Nucleus	1. Protein synthesis
B. Mitochondria	2. Powerhouse
C. Ribosome	3. Control centre
D. Lysosome	4. Intracellular digestion

A. A-3, B-2, C-1, D-4
B. A-1, B-3, C-4, D-2
C. A-2, B-1, C-3, D-4
D. A-4, B-2, C-3, D-1

10. **Assertion I:** Active transport requires energy.
Assertion II: Diffusion does not require energy.

A. Both statements are correct
B. I is correct, II is incorrect
C. Both are incorrect
D. I is incorrect, II is correct

11. The basic functional unit of nervous system is

A. Neuron B. Axon
C. Dendrite D. Synapse

12. The impulse in a neuron travels from

A. Axon to dendrite B. Cell body to dendrite
C. Dendrite to axon D. Synapse to nucleus

13. The speed of impulse conduction increases due to

A. Synapse B. Myelin sheath
C. Cell body D. Neuroglia

14. The chemical released at synapse is

A. Hormone B. Neurotransmitter
C. Enzyme D. Protein

15. The reflex action is controlled by

A. Brain B. Spinal cord
C. Cerebellum D. Hypothalamus

16. The autonomic nervous system controls

A. Voluntary actions
B. Conscious movements
C. Involuntary activities
D. Sensory perception

17. The sympathetic nervous system prepares body for

A. Rest and digestion B. Relaxation
C. Fight or flight D. Sleep

18. The parasympathetic system mainly causes

A. Increased heart rate B. Dilated pupils
C. Relaxation D. Increased respiration

19. Match the following:

Column I	Column II
A. Sensory neuron	1. Connects neurons
B. Motor neuron	2. Carries impulse to muscle
C. Interneuron	3. Receives stimulus
D. Receptor	4. Carries impulse to CNS

A. A-4, B-2, C-1, D-3 B. A-3, B-4, C-2, D-1
C. A-2, B-1, C-3, D-4 D. A-1, B-3, C-4, D-2

20. **Assertion I:** Neurons cannot regenerate easily.
Assertion II: Neuroglia support neurons.

A. Both statements are correct
B. I is correct, II is incorrect
C. Both are incorrect
D. I is incorrect, II is correct

21. The muscle type present in heart is

A. Skeletal muscle B. Smooth muscle
C. Cardiac muscle D. Voluntary muscle

22. The muscle under voluntary control is

A. Cardiac muscle B. Smooth muscle
C. Skeletal muscle D. Involuntary muscle

23. The functional unit of muscle contraction is

A. Myofibril B. Sarcomere
C. Actin D. Myosin

24. The energy for muscle contraction is provided by

A. ADP B. ATP
C. Creatinine D. Glucose

25. The protein responsible for muscle contraction is

A. Collagen B. Actin and myosin
C. Keratin D. Elastin

26. Smooth muscles are found in

A. Bones B. Heart
C. Intestine D. Skin

27. The contraction of muscle is initiated by

A. Calcium ions B. Sodium ions
C. Potassium ions D. Chloride ions

28. Muscle fatigue is due to accumulation of

A. Oxygen B. Glucose
C. Lactic acid D. ATP

29. Match the following:

Column I	Column II
A. Skeletal muscle	1. Involuntary muscle of organs
B. Cardiac muscle	2. Contractile unit
C. Smooth muscle	3. Voluntary muscle
D. Sarcomere	4. Heart muscle

A. A-3, B-4, C-1, D-2
B. A-1, B-2, C-3, D-4
C. A-2, B-3, C-4, D-1
D. A-4, B-1, C-2, D-3

30. **Assertion I:** Skeletal muscles are striated.
Assertion II: Smooth muscles are non-striated.

A. Both statements are correct
B. I is correct, II is incorrect
C. Both are incorrect
D. I is incorrect, II is correct

31. The normal heart rate in adults is about

A. 60–100 beats/min B. 40–60 beats/min
C. 100–120 beats/min D. 120–140 beats/min

32. The contraction phase of heart is called

A. Diastole B. Systole
C. Relaxation phase D. Filling phase

33. The normal blood pressure is approximately

A. 100/60 mmHg B. 110/70 mmHg
C. 120/80 mmHg D. 140/90 mmHg

34. The pacemaker of the heart is

A. AV node B. Bundle of His
C. SA node D. Purkinje fibres

35. The blood vessel that carries blood away from the heart is

A. Vein B. Artery
C. Capillary D. Venule

36. The oxygen-carrying pigment in blood is

A. Plasma B. Platelets
C. Hemoglobin D. WBC

37. The blood group system is based on

A. RBC size B. Hemoglobin level
C. Antigens on RBC D. Plasma proteins

38. The normal range of hemoglobin in adults is

A. 8–10 g/dL B. 10–12 g/dL
C. 12–16 g/dL D. 16–20 g/dL

39. Match the following:

Column I	Column II
A. Artery	1. Carries oxygen
B. Vein	2. Exchange of substances
C. Capillary	3. Carries blood away from heart
D. Hemoglobin	4. Carries blood to heart

A. A-3, B-4, C-2, D-1 B. A-4, B-3, C-1, D-2
C. A-2, B-1, C-3, D-4 D. A-1, B-2, C-4, D-3

40. **Assertion I:** Platelets help in blood clotting.
Assertion II: RBCs are responsible for immunity.

A. Both statements are correct

B. I is correct, II is incorrect
C. Both are incorrect
D. I is incorrect, II is correct

41. The process of breathing in is called ______.

A. Expiration   B. Ventilation
C. Inspiration   D. Respiration

42. The exchange of gases between alveoli and blood is known as

A. Internal respiration   B. External respiration
C. Cellular respiration   D. Pulmonary ventilation

43. Oxygen is mainly transported in blood by ______.

A. Plasma proteins   B. Hemoglobin
C. Platelets   D. Leukocytes

44. The normal respiratory rate in adults is ______ breaths per minute.

A. 8–10   B. 10–12
C. 12–20   D. 20–30

45. The respiratory centre is located in the ______.

A. Cerebrum   B. Cerebellum
C. Medulla oblongata   D. Hypothalamus

46. The gas exchanged from blood to alveoli is ______.

A. Oxygen   B. Nitrogen
C. Carbon dioxide   D. Hydrogen

47. During inspiration, the diaphragm becomes ______.

A. Relaxed   B. Flattened
C. Elevated   D. Contracted upward

48. The major stimulus for respiration is increased ______ in blood.

A. Oxygen   B. Carbon dioxide
C. Nitrogen   D. pH

49. Match the following:

Column I	Column II
A. Inspiration	1. Gas exchange
B. Expiration	2. Oxygen transport
C. Hemoglobin	3. Breathing out
D. Alveoli	4. Breathing in

A. A-4, B-3, C-2, D-1   B. A-3, B-4, C-1, D-2
C. A-2, B-1, C-4, D-3   D. A-1, B-2, C-3, D-4

50. Assertion I: Oxygen moves from alveoli to blood.
Assertion II: Carbon dioxide moves from blood to alveoli.

A. Both statements are correct
B. I is correct, II is incorrect
C. Both are incorrect
D. I is incorrect, II is correct

51. The enzyme ______ begins digestion of carbohydrates in the mouth.

A. Pepsin   B. Amylase
C. Lipase   D. Trypsin

52. The main site of absorption of nutrients is

A. Stomach   B. Small intestine
C. Large intestine   D. Esophagus

53. The hormone ______ stimulates secretion of gastric juice.

A. Insulin   B. Gastrin
C. Secretin   D. Glucagon

54. The enzyme pepsin acts mainly on

A. Fats   B. Proteins
C. Carbohydrates   D. Minerals

55. The bile helps in digestion of

A. Proteins   B. Fats
C. Carbohydrates   D. Vitamins

56. The pancreatic juice contains enzymes for digestion of

A. Only fats   B. Only proteins
C. All food components   D. Only carbohydrates

57. The movement of food through alimentary canal is called

A. Segmentation   B. Peristalsis
C. Diffusion   D. Filtration

58. The hormone ______ is responsible for secretion of pancreatic juice.

A. Gastrin   B. Secretin
C. Insulin   D. Aldosterone

59. Match the following:

Column I	Column II
A. Amylase	1. Protein digestion
B. Pepsin	2. Fat digestion
C. Lipase	3. Carbohydrate digestion
D. Trypsin	4. Pancreatic enzyme

A. A-3, B-1, C-2, D-4   B. A-1, B-3, C-4, D-2
C. A-2, B-4, C-1, D-3   D. A-4, B-2, C-3, D-1

60. Assertion I: Large intestine absorbs water.
Assertion II: Small intestine is the main site of digestion.

A. Both statements are correct
B. I is correct, II is incorrect
C. Both are incorrect
D. I is incorrect, II is correct

61. The process of formation of urine begins with

A. Reabsorption   B. Filtration
C. Secretion   D. Excretion

62. The filtration of blood occurs in the ______ of nephron.
A. Loop of Henle
B. Glomerulus
C. Collecting duct
D. Distal tubule

63. The reabsorption of useful substances mainly occurs in
A. Proximal convoluted tubule
B. Distal tubule
C. Collecting duct
D. Glomerulus

64. The hormone ADH increases the reabsorption of
A. Sodium B. Glucose
C. Water D. Potassium

65. **Assertion I:** Kidneys help in maintaining acid-base balance.
Assertion II: Kidneys do not regulate electrolyte balance.
A. Both statements are correct
B. I is correct, II is incorrect
C. Both are incorrect
D. I is incorrect, II is correct

66. The hormone ______ regulates blood glucose level.
A. Thyroxine B. Insulin
C. Adrenaline D. Calcitonin

67. The gland known as master gland is
A. Thyroid B. Pituitary
C. Adrenal D. Parathyroid

68. The hormone thyroxine is secreted by
A. Pituitary gland B. Adrenal gland
C. Thyroid gland D. Pancreas

69. Match the following:

Column I	Column II
A. Insulin	1. Increases metabolism
B. Thyroxine	2. Regulates calcium
C. Adrenaline	3. Lowers blood glucose
D. Parathyroid hormone	4. Stress hormone

A. A-3, B-1, C-4, D-2 B. A-1, B-2, C-3, D-4
C. A-2, B-3, C-1, D-4 D. A-4, B-3, C-2, D-1

70. **Assertion I:** Hormones act as chemical messengers.
Assertion II: Hormones are secreted directly into blood.
A. Both statements are correct
B. I is correct, II is incorrect
C. Both are incorrect
D. I is incorrect, II is correct

71. The immunity acquired after vaccination is called
A. Natural immunity
B. Passive immunity
C. Active immunity
D. Artificial passive immunity

72. The cells responsible for immunity are
A. RBC B. Platelets
C. WBC D. Plasma cells

73. The antibodies are produced by ______.
A. T lymphocytes B. B lymphocytes
C. Neutrophils D. Macrophages

74. Match the following:

Column I	Column II
A. Active immunity	1. Foreign substance
B. Passive immunity	2. Protein produced in response
C. Antibody	3. Long lasting immunity
D. Antigen	4. Immediate protection

A. A-3, B-4, C-2, D-1 B. A-4, B-3, C-1, D-2
C. A-2, B-1, C-4, D-3 D. A-1, B-2, C-3, D-4

75. **Assertion I:** Active immunity develops slowly but is long lasting.
Assertion II: Passive immunity provides immediate protection.
A. Both statements are correct
B. I is correct, II is incorrect
C. Both are incorrect
D. I is incorrect, II is correct

EXPLANATORY ANSWERS

1. **B:** Cell is the smallest structural and functional unit capable of performing all life processes. All tissues and organs are composed of cells. Hence, it is considered the basic unit of life.

2. **B:** Diffusion is passive movement of molecules from higher to lower concentration. It does not require energy. It is essential for gas exchange and cellular processes.

3. **C:** Osmosis is the movement of water across a semipermeable membrane from lower solute concentration to higher solute concentration. It helps maintain cell volume and fluid balance.

4. **B:** The cell membrane consists mainly of a phospholipid bilayer with embedded proteins. This structure allows selective permeability. It regulates entry and exit of substances.

5. **B:** ATP stores and provides energy for cellular activities. It is generated mainly in mitochondria. It is required for active processes like transport and synthesis.

6. **B:** Ribosomes are responsible for protein synthesis. They translate genetic information into functional proteins. They can be free or attached to rough ER.

7. **C:** Mitochondria generate ATP through cellular respiration. Due to this role, they are called the powerhouse of the cell. They are essential for energy production.

8. **B:** The nucleus contains genetic material and controls cell activities. It regulates growth, metabolism, and reproduction. It acts as the command center of the cell.

9. **A:** Nucleus controls activities, mitochondria produce energy, ribosomes synthesize proteins, and lysosomes perform digestion. This matching reflects their primary functions.

10. **A:** Active transport requires energy to move substances against concentration gradient. Diffusion is passive and does not require energy. These are fundamental transport mechanisms.

11. **A:** Neuron is the basic unit that conducts nerve impulses. It receives, processes, and transmits signals. Other parts like axon and dendrite are components of neuron.

12. **C:** Impulse travels from dendrites to cell body and then along axon. This direction ensures proper signal transmission. It is essential for coordination.

13. **B:** Myelin sheath increases speed of impulse conduction. It allows saltatory conduction. This makes nerve transmission faster and efficient.

14. **B:** Neurotransmitters are chemicals released at synapse to transmit impulses. Examples include acetylcholine. They play a key role in communication between neurons.

15. **B:** Reflex actions are rapid and involuntary responses controlled by spinal cord. They occur without conscious brain involvement. This ensures quick reaction.

16. **C:** Autonomic nervous system controls involuntary functions like heartbeat, digestion, and respiration. It works without conscious control.

17. **C:** Sympathetic system prepares body for emergency situations. It increases heart rate and blood pressure. It helps body respond to stress.

18. **C:** Parasympathetic system promotes rest and digestion. It decreases heart rate and conserves energy. It maintains normal body functions.

19. **A:** Sensory neurons carry impulses to CNS, motor neurons to muscles, interneurons connect neurons, and receptors receive stimuli. This sequence forms reflex arc.

20. **A:** Neurons have limited regenerative capacity. Neuroglial cells provide support and nourishment. Both are essential for nervous system function.

21. **C:** Cardiac muscle is present only in the heart. It is involuntary and shows rhythmic contraction. It has characteristics of both skeletal and smooth muscle.

22. **C:** Skeletal muscles are under voluntary control. They are attached to bones and help in movement. They have striations and contract rapidly.

23. **B:** Sarcomere is the smallest contractile unit of muscle. It contains actin and myosin filaments. Its shortening leads to muscle contraction.

24. **B:** ATP provides energy required for muscle contraction. It is used during cross-bridge formation and breaking. Without ATP, muscles cannot contract.

25. **B:** Actin and myosin are contractile proteins. Their interaction causes sliding filament mechanism. This results in muscle shortening.

26. **C:** Smooth muscles are found in walls of internal organs like intestine. They are involuntary and help in movement of contents. They do not show striations.

27. **A:** Calcium ions play a key role in muscle contraction. They facilitate interaction between actin and myosin. Their release triggers contraction.

28. **C:** Muscle fatigue occurs due to accumulation of lactic acid during anaerobic respiration. It reduces pH and causes pain and tiredness.

29. **A:** Skeletal muscle is voluntary, cardiac muscle is heart muscle, smooth muscle is involuntary, and sarcomere is contractile unit. This mapping is essential.

30. **A:** Skeletal muscles are striated, whereas smooth muscles lack striations. These structural differences relate to their functions. Both statements are correct.

31. **A:** The normal resting heart rate in adults ranges between 60 and 100 beats per minute. It may vary with age, activity, and health status. It is an important vital sign.

32. **B:** Systole is the phase when the heart contracts and pumps blood out. It is followed by diastole when the heart relaxes. These phases together form the cardiac cycle.

33. **C:** Normal blood pressure is approximately 120/80 mmHg. The first value represents systolic pressure and the second diastolic pressure. It indicates cardiovascular health.

34. **C:** The sinoatrial (SA) node acts as the natural pacemaker. It initiates electrical impulses that regulate heart rhythm. It ensures coordinated contraction of heart.

35. **B:** Arteries carry blood away from the heart to tissues. They have thick elastic walls to withstand high pressure. Most arteries carry oxygenated blood.

36. **C:** Hemoglobin is present in RBCs and carries oxygen. It binds oxygen in lungs and releases it in tissues. It also carries a small amount of carbon dioxide.

37. **C:** Blood groups are determined by presence of specific antigens on RBC surface. The ABO system is based on A and B antigens. This is important for transfusion compatibility.

38. **C:** The normal hemoglobin level in adults is around 12–16 g/dL. It varies with gender and age. Low levels indicate anemia.

39. **A:** Arteries carry blood away from heart, veins bring blood to heart, capillaries allow exchange, and hemoglobin carries oxygen. This mapping reflects circulatory function.

40. **B:** Platelets are involved in clotting and prevent bleeding. RBCs carry oxygen, while WBCs provide immunity. Hence second statement is incorrect.

41. **C:** Inspiration is the process of taking air into the lungs. It occurs when diaphragm contracts and thoracic cavity expands. This allows air to flow into lungs.

42. **B:** External respiration is the exchange of gases between alveoli and blood. Oxygen diffuses into blood while carbon dioxide diffuses into alveoli. This maintains gas balance.

43. B: Hemoglobin carries oxygen by forming oxyhemoglobin. It transports oxygen from lungs to tissues. It plays a key role in respiration.

44. C: Normal respiratory rate in adults ranges from 12 to 20 breaths per minute. It varies with activity and health conditions. It is an important vital sign.

45. C: The respiratory centre is located in medulla. It controls rhythm of breathing automatically. It responds to changes in carbon dioxide levels.

46. C: Carbon dioxide diffuses from blood into alveoli to be exhaled. This helps maintain acid-base balance. Removal of CO_2 is essential for normal function.

47. B: During inspiration, diaphragm contracts and flattens. This increases thoracic volume. As a result, air enters lungs.

48. B: Increased CO_2 levels stimulate respiratory centre. This leads to increased breathing rate. It is the main chemical regulator of respiration.

49. A: Inspiration means breathing in, expiration is breathing out, hemoglobin transports oxygen, and alveoli are sites of gas exchange. Each has a specific function.

50. A: Oxygen moves from alveoli to blood while carbon dioxide moves from blood to alveoli. This exchange occurs by diffusion. Both processes are essential.

51. B: Salivary amylase begins digestion of carbohydrates in the mouth. It converts starch into simpler sugars. This initial digestion continues briefly in stomach.

52. B: Most absorption of nutrients occurs in small intestine. It has villi and microvilli to increase surface area. This ensures efficient absorption.

53. B: Gastrin stimulates secretion of gastric juice. It is released from stomach lining. It plays an important role in digestion of food.

54. B: Pepsin is a proteolytic enzyme that breaks down proteins into peptides. It works in acidic medium of stomach. It is essential for protein digestion.

55. B: Bile emulsifies fats into smaller droplets. This increases surface area for lipase action. It does not contain enzymes but aids digestion.

56. C: Pancreatic juice contains amylase, lipase, and proteases. It digests carbohydrates, fats, and proteins. It plays a major role in digestion.

57. B: Peristalsis is rhythmic contraction of muscles that propels food forward. It occurs throughout alimentary canal. It ensures movement of food.

58. B: Secretin stimulates pancreas to release bicarbonate-rich juice. It neutralizes acidic chyme. It helps maintain optimal pH for enzyme activity.

59. A: Amylase digests carbohydrates, pepsin digests proteins, lipase digests fats, and trypsin is a pancreatic enzyme for proteins. This mapping shows enzyme functions.

60. A: Large intestine absorbs water and electrolytes. Small intestine is main site of digestion and absorption. Both are correct physiological processes.

61. B: Urine formation starts with filtration in the glomerulus. Blood is filtered under pressure and filtrate enters Bowman's capsule. This is the first step in excretion.

62. B: Glomerulus is a network of capillaries where filtration occurs. It allows passage of water and small molecules. Larger molecules like proteins remain in blood.

63. A: Most reabsorption occurs in PCT. Glucose, amino acids, and ions are reabsorbed here. This process conserves useful substances.

64. C: ADH increases water reabsorption in distal tubules and collecting ducts. It helps concentrate urine. It plays a role in maintaining body fluid balance.

65. B: Kidneys maintain acid-base balance by regulating hydrogen and bicarbonate ions. They also regulate electrolytes like sodium and potassium. Hence second statement is incorrect.

66. B: Insulin is secreted by pancreas and lowers blood glucose level. It promotes uptake of glucose into cells. It plays a vital role in metabolism.

67. B: Pituitary gland is called master gland because it controls other endocrine glands. It secretes various stimulating hormones. It regulates body functions.

68. C: Thyroxine is secreted by thyroid gland. It regulates metabolism and growth. It influences many physiological processes.

69. A: Insulin lowers glucose, thyroxine increases metabolism, adrenaline is stress hormone, and parathyroid hormone regulates calcium. This reflects endocrine functions.

70. A: Hormones are chemical messengers transported by blood. They are secreted directly into bloodstream. They regulate body processes.

71. C: Vaccination introduces antigen into the body which stimulates immune system to produce antibodies. This leads tó active immunity. It is long lasting and provides protection against future infections.

72. C: White blood cells play a key role in immune response. They protect the body against infections. Different types like lymphocytes, neutrophils, and macrophages perform specific functions.

73. B: B lymphocytes differentiate into plasma cells which produce antibodies. These antibodies neutralize pathogens. They are essential for humoral immunity.

74. A: Active immunity is long lasting, passive immunity provides immediate protection, antibodies are proteins, and antigens are foreign substances. This reflects basic immunological concepts.

75. A: Active immunity takes time to develop but lasts long. Passive immunity provides immediate but temporary protection. Both are important defense mechanisms.

3. Nutrition and Biochemistry

1. The main source of energy in diet is

A. Proteins B. Carbohydrates
C. Vitamins D. Minerals

2. The energy provided by 1 gram of carbohydrate is ______ kcal.

A. 2 B. 4
C. 7 D. 9

3. The body-building nutrient is

A. Carbohydrate B. Fat
C. Protein D. Vitamin

4. The energy provided by 1 gram of fat is

A. 4 kcal B. 7 kcal
C. 9 kcal D. 2 kcal

5. The essential fatty acids are mainly obtained from

A. Animal fats B. Vegetable oils
C. Water D. Minerals

6. The nutrient required for growth and repair is

A. Carbohydrates B. Proteins
C. Fats D. Vitamins

7. The main storage form of carbohydrate in body is

A. Glucose B. Glycogen
C. Fructose D. Lactose

8. The deficiency of protein leads to

A. Obesity B. Kwashiorkor
C. Diabetes D. Hypertension

9. Match the following:

Column I	Column II
A. Carbohydrates	1. Body building
B. Proteins	2. Energy source
C. Fats	3. Protective food
D. Vitamins	4. Concentrated energy

A. A-2, B-1, C-4, D-3 B. A-1, B-2, C-3, D-4
C. A-3, B-4, C-2, D-1 D. A-4, B-3, C-1, D-2

10. **Assertion I:** Carbohydrates are the primary source of energy.

Assertion II: Proteins are mainly used for energy production.

A. Both statements are correct
B. I is correct, II is incorrect
C. Both are incorrect
D. I is incorrect, II is correct

11. The daily energy requirement of an adult depends on

A. Age B. Activity level
C. Sex D. All of these

12. The protein rich food is

A. Rice B. Wheat
C. Pulses D. Sugar

13. The excess carbohydrates are stored in liver as ______.

A. Fat B. Glycogen
C. Protein D. Starch

14. The nutrient that provides insulation to body is

A. Protein B. Carbohydrate
C. Fat D. Mineral

15. The minimum daily protein requirement is approximately

A. 0.5 g/kg B. 1 g/kg
C. 2 g/kg D. 3 g/kg

16. Vitamin A deficiency leads to

A. Rickets B. Scurvy
C. Night blindness D. Beriberi

17. The vitamin ______ is responsible for blood clotting.

A. Vitamin A B. Vitamin D
C. Vitamin K D. Vitamin C

18. The deficiency of Vitamin D causes

A. Scurvy B. Rickets
C. Pellagra D. Night blindness

19. Vitamin C is also known as

A. Retinol B. Calciferol
C. Ascorbic acid D. Thiamine

20. The vitamin essential for calcium absorption is

A. Vitamin A B. Vitamin D
C. Vitamin E D. Vitamin K

21. Deficiency of Vitamin B1 leads to

A. Pellagra B. Beriberi
C. Scurvy D. Anemia

22. The vitamin ______ is required for vision.

A. Vitamin A B. Vitamin B
C. Vitamin C D. Vitamin D

23. Deficiency of Vitamin C causes

A. Rickets B. Scurvy
C. Osteomalacia D. Beriberi

24. Vitamin E acts mainly as

A. Hormone B. Enzyme
C. Antioxidant D. Coenzyme

25. The vitamin responsible for red blood cell formation is

A. Vitamin B12 B. Vitamin A
C. Vitamin D D. Vitamin K

26. Match the following:

Column I	Column II
A. Vitamin A	1. Blood clotting
B. Vitamin D	2. Vision
C. Vitamin C	3. Bone health
D. Vitamin K	4. Wound healing

A. A-2, B-3, C-4, D-1 B. A-1, B-2, C-3, D-4
C. A-3, B-4, C-1, D-2 D. A-4, B-1, C-2, D-3

27. The vitamin synthesized in skin by sunlight is

A. Vitamin A B. Vitamin D
C. Vitamin C D. Vitamin E

28. Deficiency of niacin causes

A. Scurvy B. Pellagra
C. Rickets D. Beriberi

29. **Assertion I:** Fat soluble vitamins can be stored in body.

Assertion II: Water soluble vitamins are excreted in urine.

A. Both statements are correct
B. I is correct, II is incorrect
C. Both are incorrect
D. I is incorrect, II is correct

30. The vitamin required for collagen synthesis is

A. Vitamin A B. Vitamin B12
C. Vitamin C D. Vitamin D

31. The mineral required for formation of hemoglobin is

A. Calcium B. Iron
C. Phosphorus D. Sodium

32. The deficiency of iron leads to

A. Rickets B. Scurvy
C. Anemia D. Goiter

33. The mineral ______ is essential for bone and teeth formation.

A. Iron B. Calcium
C. Sodium D. Potassium

34. Iodine deficiency leads to

A. Anemia B. Goiter
C. Rickets D. Scurvy

35. The mineral important for nerve impulse transmission is

A. Iron B. Calcium
C. Sodium D. Iodine

36. The mineral required for muscle contraction is

A. Calcium B. Iron
C. Chloride D. Zinc

37. The mineral ______ helps in maintaining fluid balance.

A. Iron B. Calcium
C. Sodium D. Magnesium

38. Zinc plays an important role in

A. Oxygen transport B. Enzyme function
C. Bone formation D. Water balance

39. Match the following:

Column I	Column II
A. Iron	1. Thyroid function
B. Calcium	2. Hemoglobin formation
C. Iodine	3. Fluid balance
D. Sodium	4. Bone formation

A. A-2, B-4, C-1, D-3 B. A-1, B-2, C-3, D-4
C. A-3, B-1, C-4, D-2 D. A-4, B-3, C-2, D-1

40. **Assertion I:** Calcium is essential for bone formation.

Assertion II: Iron is required for oxygen transport.

A. Both statements are correct
B. I is correct, II is incorrect
C. Both are incorrect
D. I is incorrect, II is correct

41. The normal daily water requirement for an adult is approximately ______ liters.

A. 1–1.5 B. 2–3
C. 4–5 D. 5–6

42. The main intracellular cation is

A. Sodium B. Potassium
C. Calcium D. Magnesium

43. The main extracellular cation is

A. Potassium B. Sodium
C. Calcium D. Iron

44. Match the following:

Column I	Column II
A. Sodium	1. Bone formation
B. Potassium	2. Intracellular cation
C. Calcium	3. Extracellular cation
D. Chloride	4. Acid-base balance

A. A-3, B-2, C-1, D-4 B. A-2, B-3, C-4, D-1
C. A-1, B-4, C-3, D-2 D. A-4, B-1, C-2, D-3

45. Assertion I: Electrolytes help maintain fluid balance.
Assertion II: Electrolytes have no role in nerve conduction.

A. Both statements are correct
B. I is correct, II is incorrect
C. Both are incorrect
D. I is incorrect, II is correct

46. A balanced diet contains

A. Only carbohydrates
B. Only proteins
C. All nutrients in proper proportion
D. Only fats

47. The Recommended Dietary Allowance (RDA) is defined as

A. Minimum nutrient intake
B. Maximum nutrient intake
C. Average requirement of nutrient
D. Daily intake sufficient for healthy individuals

48. The energy requirement of a person mainly depends on

A. Climate B. Age, sex and activity
C. Religion D. Food habits only

49. The diet of a pregnant woman should be rich in ______.

A. Carbohydrates only B. Proteins and iron
C. Fats only D. Vitamins only

50. The extra calorie requirement during pregnancy is about

A. 100 kcal B. 200 kcal
C. 300 kcal D. 500 kcal

51. The diet providing all nutrients in adequate amount is called ______.

A. Therapeutic diet B. Balanced diet
C. Liquid diet D. Special diet

52. The protein requirement increases during

A. Old age
B. Childhood
C. Pregnancy and lactation
D. Rest

53. The diet for infants should be rich in

A. Proteins B. Fats
C. Carbohydrates D. All nutrients

54. Match the following:

Column I	Column II
A. Balanced diet	1. Extra food for specific group
B. RDA	2. Deficiency or excess of nutrients
C. Malnutrition	3. Adequate intake for healthy life
D. Supplementary diet	4. Recommended daily intake

A. A-3, B-4, C-2, D-1 B. A-4, B-3, C-1, D-2
C. A-2, B-1, C-4, D-3 D. A-1, B-2, C-3, D-4

55. Assertion I: Balanced diet prevents deficiency diseases.
Assertion II: RDA varies with age and sex.

A. Both statements are correct
B. I is correct, II is incorrect
C. Both are incorrect
D. I is incorrect, II is correct

56. The method of cooking that preserves maximum nutrients is

A. Frying B. Boiling
C. Steaming D. Roasting

57. Cooking food improves

A. Digestibility B. Nutrient loss
C. Spoilage D. Toxicity

58. The method ______ uses dry heat for cooking food.

A. Boiling B. Steaming
C. Roasting D. Poaching

59. Overcooking of vegetables leads to loss of

A. Carbohydrates B. Proteins
C. Vitamins D. Minerals

60. Assertion I: Cooking destroys microorganisms in food.
Assertion II: Cooking always increases vitamin content.

A. Both statements are correct
B. I is correct, II is incorrect
C. Both are incorrect
D. I is incorrect, II is correct

61. The cell membrane is mainly composed of ______ and proteins.

A. Carbohydrates B. Lipids
C. Minerals D. Water

62. The movement of substances from higher to lower concentration is called

A. Active transport B. Diffusion
C. Endocytosis D. Osmosis

63. The enzyme ______ acts as a biological catalyst.

A. Protein B. Enzyme
C. Lipid D. Hormone

64. The specific site where substrate binds to enzyme is called

A. Binding region B. Active site
C. Surface area D. Reaction site

65. Match the following:

Column I	Column II
A. Diffusion	1. Movement of water
B. Osmosis	2. Requires energy
C. Active transport	3. Passive transport
D. Facilitated diffusion	4. Carrier mediated transport

A. A-3, B-1, C-2, D-4 B. A-1, B-2, C-3, D-4
C. A-2, B-3, C-4, D-1 D. A-4, B-3, C-1, D-2

66. The sum of all chemical reactions in the body is called

A. Digestion B. Metabolism
C. Respiration D. Circulation

67. The breakdown of complex substances into simpler ones is called

A. Anabolism B. Catabolism
C. Metabolism D. Digestion

68. The synthesis of complex molecules from simple ones is called

A. Catabolism B. Digestion
C. Anabolism D. Respiration

69. The process of glycolysis occurs in the ______.

A. Nucleus B. Cytoplasm
C. Mitochondria D. Ribosome

70. The end product of aerobic respiration is

A. Lactic acid
B. Carbon dioxide and water
C. Ethanol
D. Pyruvic acid

71. The organelle responsible for energy production is

A. Ribosome B. Nucleus
C. Mitochondria D. Golgi body

72. The energy released from food is stored in the form of ______.

A. ADP B. ATP
C. AMP D. NADH

73. The process of formation of glucose from non-carbohydrates is called

A. Glycolysis
B. Glycogenesis
C. Gluconeogenesis
D. Glycogenolysis

74. Assertion I: Anabolism requires energy.
Assertion II: Catabolism releases energy.

A. Both statements are correct
B. I is correct, II is incorrect
C. Both are incorrect
D. I is incorrect, II is correct

75. The metabolic process that converts glucose into glycogen is called

A. Glycogenolysis B. Glycolysis
C. Glycogenesis D. Gluconeogenesis

EXPLANATORY ANSWERS

1. B: Carbohydrates are the main source of energy in diet. They are easily broken down into glucose. This glucose is used by cells for energy.

2. B: Carbohydrates provide 4 kcal per gram. This is a standard value used in nutrition calculations. It helps determine daily energy intake.

3. C: Proteins are essential for growth and repair of tissues. They form structural components of body. They are called body-building nutrients.

4. C: Fats provide 9 kcal per gram, making them the most concentrated energy source. They also help in insulation and storage of energy.

5. B: Essential fatty acids like linoleic acid are obtained from vegetable oils. They are important for cell structure and metabolism.

6. B: Proteins help in repair and maintenance of body tissues. They are required for enzymes, hormones, and antibodies. They are essential for growth.

7. B: Glycogen is the storage form of glucose in liver and muscles. It can be converted back to glucose when needed. It helps maintain blood sugar levels.

8. B: Kwashiorkor is caused by protein deficiency. It leads to edema, muscle wasting, and growth retardation. It is common in children.

9. A: Carbohydrates provide energy, proteins build body, fats provide concentrated energy, and vitamins protect body. This classification is basic nutrition concept.

10. B: Carbohydrates are primary energy source. Proteins are mainly used for growth and repair, not energy. Hence second statement is incorrect.

11. D: Energy requirement depends on age, sex, and activity level. These factors influence metabolism. Hence all options are correct.

12. C: Pulses are rich in proteins. They are important plant sources of protein. They are widely used in diet.

13. B: Excess carbohydrates are converted into glycogen. It is stored in liver and muscles. It serves as reserve energy.

14. C: Fats provide insulation and protect organs. They also help maintain body temperature. They act as energy reserves.

15. B: The average protein requirement is about 1 gram per kilogram body weight. It may vary with age and condition. It ensures proper growth and repair.

16. C: Vitamin A deficiency affects vision, especially in dim light. It leads to night blindness due to impaired retinal function. It can progress to xerophthalmia.

17. C: Vitamin K is essential for synthesis of clotting factors. Its deficiency leads to bleeding disorders. It plays a key role in coagulation.

18. B: Vitamin D deficiency leads to defective bone mineralization. In children, it causes rickets characterized by soft bones. In adults, it causes osteomalacia.

19. C: Vitamin C is chemically known as ascorbic acid. It is important for collagen synthesis and wound healing. It also acts as antioxidant.

20. B: Vitamin D helps in absorption of calcium and phosphorus from intestine. It is essential for bone formation. Its deficiency affects skeletal system.

21. B: Vitamin B1 (thiamine) deficiency leads to beriberi. It affects nervous and cardiovascular systems. It may present as weakness and edema.

22. A: Vitamin A is essential for vision, especially in low light. It forms part of visual pigments. Its deficiency leads to visual disturbances.

23. B: Vitamin C deficiency causes scurvy. It leads to bleeding gums, poor wound healing, and weakness. It is due to defective collagen formation.

24. C: Vitamin E acts as antioxidant. It protects cells from oxidative damage. It helps maintain cell membrane integrity.

25. A: Vitamin B12 is essential for RBC formation. Its deficiency leads to megaloblastic anemia. It also affects nervous system.

26. A: Vitamin A is for vision, Vitamin D for bones, Vitamin C for healing, and Vitamin K for clotting. This classification is important in clinical nutrition.

27. B: Vitamin D is synthesized in skin under sunlight. UV rays convert precursors into active vitamin. It is unique among vitamins.

28. B: Niacin deficiency leads to pellagra characterized by dermatitis, diarrhea, and dementia. It is commonly seen in malnutrition.

29. A: Fat soluble vitamins (A, D, E, K) are stored in body. Water soluble vitamins (B, C) are not stored and excreted in urine. This affects toxicity and deficiency.

30. C: Vitamin C is required for collagen synthesis. It helps maintain connective tissue. It also aids in wound healing.

31. B: Iron is an essential component of hemoglobin. It helps in transport of oxygen in blood. Deficiency leads to reduced oxygen carrying capacity.

32. C: Iron deficiency results in anemia. It leads to fatigue, weakness, and pallor. It is one of the most common nutritional deficiencies.

33. B: Calcium is required for development and maintenance of bones and teeth. It also plays a role in blood clotting and muscle contraction.

34. B: Iodine deficiency leads to enlargement of thyroid gland known as goiter. It affects thyroid hormone production. It can lead to metabolic disturbances.

35. C: Sodium plays an important role in nerve impulse transmission. It helps in maintaining membrane potential. It is essential for nerve and muscle function.

36. A: Calcium is necessary for muscle contraction. It facilitates interaction of contractile proteins. It is also important for nerve transmission.

37. C: Sodium maintains osmotic balance and fluid distribution in body. It regulates water balance and blood pressure. It is a major extracellular ion.

38. B: Zinc acts as a cofactor for many enzymes. It plays a role in growth, immunity, and healing. Its deficiency affects multiple body functions.

39. A: Iron is for hemoglobin, calcium for bones, iodine for thyroid, and sodium for fluid balance. This classification is important for understanding mineral roles.

40. A: Calcium is necessary for bone formation and strength. Iron is required for oxygen transport through hemoglobin. Both are essential minerals.

41. B: The average daily water requirement for an adult is around 2–3 liters. It varies depending on activity, climate, and health status. Adequate intake is essential for metabolism and temperature regulation.

42. B: Potassium is the main intracellular cation. It helps in maintaining cell function, nerve impulse transmission, and muscle contraction. Its imbalance can affect cardiac function.

43. B: Sodium is the major extracellular cation. It regulates fluid balance and osmotic pressure. It also plays a role in nerve and muscle function.

44. A: Sodium is extracellular cation, potassium is intracellular cation, calcium is for bones, and chloride helps in acid-base balance. This reflects electrolyte functions.

45. B: Electrolytes maintain fluid balance and osmotic pressure. They also play a key role in nerve conduction and muscle activity. Hence second statement is incorrect.

46. C: A balanced diet contains carbohydrates, proteins, fats, vitamins, minerals, and water in proper amounts. It ensures proper growth and health. It prevents deficiency diseases.

47. D: RDA represents the daily nutrient intake level sufficient to meet the needs of most healthy individuals. It varies with age, sex, and physiological state.

48. B: Energy requirement depends on age, sex, and physical activity. Active individuals need more energy. These factors influence metabolic rate.

49. B: During pregnancy, protein is needed for fetal growth and iron for hemoglobin formation. Deficiency can lead to complications. Hence these nutrients are essential.

50. C: During pregnancy, an additional 300 kcal per day is required. This supports fetal growth and maternal health. Requirements increase further in lactation.

51. B: A balanced diet provides all nutrients in adequate amounts. It maintains health and supports normal body functions. It is essential for all age groups.

52. C: Protein requirement increases during pregnancy and lactation. It supports growth of fetus and milk production. It is essential for tissue repair.

53. D: Infants require all nutrients for rapid growth and development. A balanced intake is necessary. Breast milk provides complete nutrition.

54. A: Balanced diet ensures adequate nutrition, RDA gives daily requirement, malnutrition is imbalance of nutrients, and supplementary diet provides extra nutrients.

55. A: Balanced diet prevents deficiency diseases. RDA varies with age, sex, and physiological condition. Both statements are correct.

56. C: Steaming preserves most nutrients as food is not in direct contact with water. It minimizes loss of water-soluble vitamins. It is considered a healthy cooking method.

57. A: Cooking improves digestibility by softening food. It also enhances taste and flavor. It makes food easier to consume and absorb.

58. C: Roasting uses dry heat for cooking. It enhances flavor and texture. It is commonly used for grains and meat.

59. C: Overcooking destroys heat-sensitive vitamins like vitamin C and B-complex. These vitamins are easily lost during prolonged cooking. Proper cooking methods help preserve nutrients.

60. B: Cooking kills harmful microorganisms making food safe. However, excessive cooking reduces vitamin content. Hence second statement is incorrect.

61. B: Cell membrane consists of phospholipid bilayer with embedded proteins. Lipids provide structure and flexibility. It helps in selective permeability.

62. B: Diffusion is passive movement from higher to lower concentration. It does not require energy. It is important for gas exchange.

63. B: Enzymes are biological catalysts that speed up reactions. They are specific to substrates. They are not consumed in reactions.

64. B: Active site is the region where substrate binds. It determines enzyme specificity. It forms enzyme-substrate complex.

65. A: Diffusion is passive, osmosis involves water movement, active transport requires energy, and facilitated diffusion uses carriers. This reflects membrane transport mechanisms.

66. B: Metabolism includes all chemical reactions in body. It includes both synthesis and breakdown processes. It is essential for life.

67. B: Catabolism involves breakdown of complex molecules. It releases energy. It is important for energy production.

68. C: Anabolism involves synthesis of complex molecules. It requires energy input. It is important for growth and repair.

69. B: Glycolysis occurs in cytoplasm. It is the first step of glucose breakdown. It does not require oxygen.

70. B: Aerobic respiration produces CO_2 and water. It releases large amount of energy. It occurs in mitochondria.

71. C: Mitochondria produce energy in form of ATP. They are called powerhouse of cell. They perform cellular respiration.

72. B: ATP stores energy released from food. It is used for cellular activities. It is called energy currency.

73. C: Gluconeogenesis is formation of glucose from non-carbohydrate sources. It occurs in liver. It maintains blood glucose levels.

74. A: Anabolism requires energy while catabolism releases energy. Both processes are essential parts of metabolism.

75. C: Glycogenesis converts glucose into glycogen. It helps in storage of energy. It mainly occurs in liver and muscles.

4. Nursing Foundations

1. The first step of nursing process is
   A. Diagnosis B. Assessment
   C. Planning D. Evaluation

2. The process of collecting patient data is called
   A. Diagnosis B. Assessment
   C. Implementation D. Evaluation

3. The nursing diagnosis is based on ______.
   A. Medical findings B. Patient data
   C. Lab reports only D. Doctor's orders

4. The planning phase includes setting ______.
   A. Diagnosis B. Goals
   C. Treatment D. Assessment

5. The implementation phase involves
   A. Planning care B. Providing care
   C. Evaluating care D. Diagnosing

6. The evaluation step determines
   A. Patient condition B. Achievement of goals
   C. Diagnosis D. Assessment

7. The nursing process is a ______ approach.
   A. Static B. Dynamic
   C. Linear D. Fixed

8. The nursing process consists of ______ steps.
   A. 3 B. 4
   C. 5 D. 6

9. The nursing diagnosis is different from medical diagnosis because it focuses on
   A. Disease B. Patient response
   C. Treatment D. Pathology

10. The data collected during assessment can be
    A. Objective B. Subjective
    C. Both A and B D. Only lab data

11. The step ______ involves setting priorities of care.
    A. Assessment B. Diagnosis
    C. Planning D. Evaluation

12. The evaluation phase answers whether ______ are achieved.
    A. Diagnoses B. Goals
    C. Assessment D. Treatment

13. The nursing process is patient-centered and ______.
    A. Disease oriented B. Goal oriented
    C. Task oriented D. Time oriented

14. The process of identifying patient problems is called
    A. Assessment B. Diagnosis
    C. Planning D. Evaluation

15. The step ______ involves carrying out nursing interventions.
    A. Assessment B. Planning
    C. Implementation D. Evaluation

16. Match the following:

Column I	Column II
A. Assessment	1. Data collection
B. Diagnosis	2. Identify problems
C. Planning	3. Set goals
D. Implementation	4. Provide care

    A. A-1, B-2, C-3, D-4 B. A-2, B-3, C-4, D-1
    C. A-3, B-1, C-2, D-4 D. A-4, B-3, C-1, D-2

17. **Assertion I:** Nursing process is cyclic in nature.
    Assertion II: Evaluation is the final step but process continues.
    A. Both statements are correct
    B. I is correct, II is incorrect
    C. Both are incorrect
    D. I is incorrect, II is correct

18. The assessment includes collecting _____ data from patient.
A. Only objective
B. Only subjective
C. Both subjective and objective
D. Only laboratory

19. The nursing care plan is prepared during ______ phase.
A. Assessment B. Diagnosis
C. Planning D. Evaluation

20. The outcome of nursing care is determined during ______.
A. Implementation B. Planning
C. Evaluation D. Diagnosis

21. The normal body temperature in adults is about
A. 35°C B. 36.5–37.5°C
C. 38°C D. 39°C

22. The normal pulse rate in adults is ______ beats per minute.
A. 40–60 B. 60–100
C. 100–120 D. 120–140

23. The normal respiratory rate in adults is
A. 8–10 B. 10–12
C. 12–20 D. 20–30

24. The instrument used to measure blood pressure is
A. Thermometer B. Stethoscope
C. Sphygmomanometer D. Spirometer

25. The systolic blood pressure represents pressure during ______.
A. Relaxation B. Contraction
C. Rest D. Filling

26. The diastolic pressure occurs during ______ of heart.
A. Contraction B. Relaxation
C. Pumping D. Ejection

27. The most common site for measuring pulse is
A. Carotid artery B. Radial artery
C. Femoral artery D. Brachial artery

28. The normal blood pressure is about
A. 100/60 mmHg B. 110/70 mmHg
C. 120/80 mmHg D. 140/90 mmHg

29. The body temperature is regulated by ______.
A. Brain B. Hypothalamus
C. Spinal cord D. Pituitary

30. The pulse rate increases in ______.
A. Rest B. Exercise
C. Sleep D. Relaxation

31. The fever is defined as body temperature above ______.
A. 36°C B. 37°C
C. 38°C D. 39°C

32. The respiratory rate is counted by observing ______.
A. Pulse B. Chest movement
C. Heart sound D. Blood pressure

33. The unit of blood pressure is
A. mmHg B. cm
C. mL D. mg

34. The normal oxygen saturation is
A. 70–80% B. 80–90%
C. 95–100% D. 60–70%

35. The device used to measure oxygen saturation is
A. Thermometer B. Pulse oximeter
C. Sphygmomanometer D. ECG

36. The body temperature is measured in ______.
A. Celsius B. Meter
C. Liter D. Gram

37. The pulse deficit is the difference between
A. Heart rate and pulse rate
B. BP and pulse
C. Respiration and pulse
D. Temperature and pulse

38. The respiration is controlled by ______.
A. Cerebrum B. Medulla
C. Hypothalamus D. Pituitary

39. Match the following:

Column I	Column II
A. Temperature	1. Chest movement
B. Pulse	2. Arterial pressure
C. Respiration	3. Heat of body
D. Blood pressure	4. Heart beats

A. A-3, B-4, C-1, D-2 B. A-1, B-2, C-3, D-4
C. A-2, B-3, C-4, D-1 D. A-4, B-1, C-2, D-3

40. **Assertion I:** Fever indicates infection in many cases.
Assertion II: Pulse rate decreases during exercise.
A. Both statements are correct
B. I is correct, II is incorrect
C. Both are incorrect
D. I is incorrect, II is correct

41. The process of admitting a patient to hospital is called
A. Discharge B. Admission
C. Referral D. Transfer

42. The purpose of admission procedure is to ______ the patient.
A. Treat B. Assess and orient
C. Diagnose D. Discharge

43. The first step in admission is

A. Treatment B. Assessment
C. Registration D. Diagnosis

44. The belongings of patient should be ______ at admission.

A. Ignored B. Checked and recorded
C. Discarded D. Stored without record

45. The orientation of patient includes explaining ______.

A. Disease B. Ward routines
C. Treatment D. Surgery

46. The discharge planning should begin at the time of

A. Treatment B. Admission
C. Diagnosis D. Surgery

47. The discharge of patient is done when ______.

A. Patient requests B. Doctor orders
C. Nurse decides D. Relative decides

48. The discharge summary includes ______.

A. Diagnosis B. Treatment given
C. Follow-up advice D. All of these

49. **Assertion I:** Proper admission reduces patient anxiety.
Assertion II: Discharge planning is done only at the end.

A. Both statements are correct
B. I is correct, II is incorrect
C. Both are incorrect
D. I is incorrect, II is correct

50. The patient education at discharge includes ______.

A. Diet advice B. Medication instructions
C. Follow-up care D. All of these

51. Communication is defined as exchange of

A. Words B. Information
C. Signals D. Ideas only

52. The basic elements of communication include sender, message and ______.

A. Noise B. Receiver
C. Channel D. Feedback

53. The process of receiving and interpreting message is called

A. Encoding B. Decoding
C. Feedback D. Transmission

54. Non-verbal communication includes

A. Speaking B. Writing
C. Gestures D. Reading

55. The communication that occurs without words is called

A. Verbal B. Non-verbal
C. Written D. Oral

56. The therapeutic communication is used to

A. Entertain B. Build relationship
C. Instruct D. Inform

57. Active listening involves

A. Hearing only B. Paying attention
C. Ignoring D. Talking

58. The barrier of communication includes

A. Noise B. Clarity
C. Feedback D. Understanding

59. The communication ______ helps in clarifying doubts.

A. Feedback B. Encoding
C. Noise D. Channel

60. The eye contact in communication shows

A. Disinterest B. Attention
C. Anger D. Fear

61. The tone of voice is part of ______ communication.

A. Verbal B. Non-verbal
C. Written D. Formal

62. The communication between nurse and patient is called ______.

A. Social communication
B. Therapeutic communication
C. Formal communication
D. Group communication

63. The effective communication requires

A. Clarity B. Simplicity
C. Understanding D. All of these

64. Match the following:

Column I	Column II
A. Sender	1. Response
B. Message	2. Person who sends
C. Receiver	3. Content
D. Feedback	4. Person who receives

A. A-2, B-3, C-4, D-1 B. A-3, B-4, C-1, D-2
C. A-1, B-2, C-3, D-4 D. A-4, B-1, C-2, D-3

65. **Assertion I:** Communication improves patient care.
Assertion II: Communication is not important in nursing.

A. Both statements are correct
B. I is correct, II is incorrect
C. Both are incorrect
D. I is incorrect, II is correct

66. Documentation in nursing means recording of

A. Treatment only B. Patient care
C. Diagnosis only D. Medicines only

67. The purpose of documentation is to ______ patient care.
A. Delay B. Improve
C. Ignore D. Avoid

68. The documentation should be ______ and accurate.
A. Incomplete B. Clear
C. Rough D. Delayed

69. The legal document in nursing is
A. Verbal report
B. Written record
C. Oral communication
D. Telephone message

70. The documentation must be done ______.
A. Before care B. After care
C. During care D. Anytime

71. The abbreviation used in documentation should be
A. Unapproved B. Standard
C. Personal D. Complex

72. The documentation helps in _____ among health team.
A. Confusion B. Communication
C. Delay D. Conflict

73. The entry in record should be made using ______ ink.
A. Red B. Blue or black
C. Green D. Pencil

74. Match the following:

Column I	Column II
A. Accuracy	1. Record all data
B. Timeliness	2. Protect patient information
C. Completeness	3. Correct information
D. Confidentiality	4. Record immediately

A. A-3, B-4, C-1, D-2 B. A-1, B-2, C-3, D-4
C. A-2, B-3, C-4, D-1 D. A-4, B-3, C-2, D-1

75. Assertion I: Documentation is important for legal purposes.
Assertion II: Documentation is not required in patient care.
A. Both statements are correct
B. I is correct, II is incorrect
C. Both are incorrect
D. I is incorrect, II is correct

76. Infection is defined as invasion of body by
A. Chemicals B. Microorganisms
C. Cells D. Tissues

77. The chain of infection includes agent, host and ______.
A. Treatment B. Environment
C. Medication D. Diagnosis

78. The first step in infection control is
A. Sterilization B. Hand hygiene
C. Disinfection D. Isolation

79. The most common method to prevent infection is
A. Mask B. Gloves
C. Hand washing D. Gown

80. The mode of transmission of infection includes ______.
A. Air B. Contact
C. Droplet D. All of these

81. The term ______ refers to absence of microorganisms.
A. Disinfection B. Sterilization
C. Cleanliness D. Isolation

82. The isolation technique is used to
A. Treat patient
B. Prevent spread of infection
C. Diagnose disease
D. Improve immunity

83. The personal protective equipment includes
A. Gloves B. Mask
C. Gown D. All of these

84. The infection acquired in hospital is called
A. Community infection B. Nosocomial infection
C. Chronic infection D. Acute infection

85. The reservoir of infection is
A. Source of microorganisms
B. Host
C. Vector
D. Carrier

86. The portal of entry is
A. Exit route B. Entry route
C. Transmission D. Carrier

87. The use of gloves is to prevent
A. Injury B. Infection
C. Pain D. Bleeding

88. The sterilization method using steam is
A. Dry heat B. Autoclaving
C. Radiation D. Filtration

89. The disinfectant is used to
A. Kill spores B. Kill pathogens
C. Remove dirt D. Clean surface

90. The hand washing should be done for at least ______ seconds.
A. 10 B. 20
C. 30 D. 60

91. The infection control includes proper ______ disposal.
A. Waste B. Water
C. Food D. Air

92. The biomedical waste is segregated using _____.

A. Bags B. Colors
C. Labels D. Boxes

93. The mask is used to prevent ______ transmission.

A. Contact B. Droplet
C. Vector D. Direct

94. The sterilization destroys ______.

A. Bacteria only B. All microorganisms
C. Viruses only D. Fungi only

95. The cleaning is the process of removing ______.

A. Microbes B. Dirt
C. Spores D. Viruses

96. The infection spreads through contaminated _____.

A. Food B. Water
C. Air D. All of these

97. The use of PPE reduces the risk of ______.

A. Infection B. Injury
C. Pain D. Fatigue

98. Match the following:

Column I	Column II
A. Hand washing	1. Kill all microbes
B. Sterilization	2. Reduce microbes
C. Disinfection	3. Prevent spread
D. Isolation	4. Remove transient flora

A. A-4, B-1, C-2, D-3 B. A-1, B-2, C-3, D-4
C. A-2, B-3, C-4, D-1 D. A-3, B-4, C-1, D-2

99. Assertion I: Infection control reduces disease spread.
Assertion II: Hand hygiene is not important in infection control.

A. Both statements are correct
B. I is correct, II is incorrect
C. Both are incorrect
D. I is incorrect, II is correct

100. The standard precautions include ______.

A. Hand hygiene B. PPE use
C. Safe disposal D. All of these

101. Asepsis means

A. Presence of infection
B. Absence of microorganisms
C. Spread of infection
D. Growth of bacteria

102. The type of asepsis used to reduce microorganisms is called

A. Surgical asepsis B. Medical asepsis
C. Isolation D. Disinfection

103. The surgical asepsis is also known as ______ technique.

A. Clean B. Sterile
C. Dirty D. Disinfection

104. The principle of asepsis is to prevent

A. Injury B. Infection
C. Pain D. Bleeding

105. The sterile field should be kept

A. Below waist level B. Above waist level
C. At ground level D. Anywhere

106. The sterile objects should not be touched by

A. Sterile hands B. Clean hands
C. Unsterile hands D. Gloved hands

107. The outer 1 inch of sterile field is considered

A. Sterile B. Contaminated
C. Clean D. Safe

108. The medical asepsis includes

A. Sterilization B. Cleaning
C. Disinfection D. All of these

109. The sterile gloves are used in

A. Clean procedure B. Surgical procedure
C. Routine care D. Basic care

110. The sterile field becomes contaminated if

A. Touched with sterile object
B. Left unattended
C. Kept dry
D. Covered

111. The aseptic technique is essential in ______ procedures.

A. Routine B. Surgical
C. Daily D. Basic

112. The sterile solution should be poured from a height of ______ inches.

A. 1 B. 2
C. 4 D. 6

113. The hand hygiene is part of ______ asepsis

A. Surgical B. Medical
C. Isolation D. Disinfection

114. Match the following:

Column I	Column II
A. Medical asepsis	1. Clean technique
B. Surgical asepsis	2. Kill all microbes
C. Sterilization	3. Reduce microbes
D. Disinfection	4. Sterile technique

A. A-1, B-4, C-2, D-3 B. A-2, B-3, C-1, D-4
C. A-3, B-2, C-4, D-1 D. A-4, B-1, C-3, D-2

115. Assertion I: Aseptic technique prevents infection.

Assertion II: Sterile field can be touched with bare hands.

A. Both statements are correct
B. I is correct, II is incorrect
C. Both are incorrect
D. I is incorrect, II is correct

116. Activities of daily living include

A. Bathing B. Feeding
C. Dressing D. All of these

117. The purpose of bed making is to provide _____ to patient.

A. Comfort B. Treatment
C. Diagnosis D. Exercise

118. The position used to improve breathing is

A. Supine B. Fowler's
C. Lateral D. Prone

119. The oral hygiene helps to prevent _____.

A. Infection B. Pain
C. Bleeding D. Injury

120. The bed bath is given to patients who are _____.

A. Ambulatory B. Immobile
C. Active D. Walking

121. The purpose of back care is to prevent

A. Pain B. Pressure sores
C. Infection D. Bleeding

122. The turning of patient should be done every _____ hours.

A. 1 B. 2
C. 4 D. 6

123. The pressure sore is caused by prolonged _____.

A. Movement B. Pressure
C. Exercise D. Massage

124. The position used for rectal examination is

A. Fowler's B. Sims'
C. Supine D. Prone

125. The purpose of mouth care is to maintain _____.

A. Cleanliness B. Nutrition
C. Hydration D. Comfort

126. The range of motion exercises help to maintain

A. Strength B. Flexibility
C. Mobility D. All of these

127. The use of bedpan is for patients who are _____.

A. Walking B. Immobile
C. Active D. Sitting

128. The personal hygiene includes _____.

A. Bathing B. Grooming
C. Oral care D. All of these

129. Match the following:

Column I	Column II
A. Fowler's position	1. Lying on abdomen
B. Sims' position	2. Lying on back
C. Supine position	3. Side-lying
D. Prone position	4. Sitting position

A. A-4, B-3, C-2, D-1 B. A-3, B-2, C-1, D-4
C. A-2, B-4, C-3, D-1 D. A-1, B-4, C-2, D-3

130. Assertion I: Regular repositioning prevents pressure sores.

Assertion II: Immobile patients do not need skin care.

A. Both statements are correct
B. I is correct, II is incorrect
C. Both are incorrect
D. I is incorrect, II is correct

131. The right patient is one of the _____ of drug administration.

A. Principles B. Rights
C. Rules D. Methods

132. The route of drug administration through mouth is called

A. Intravenous B. Oral
C. Intramuscular D. Subcutaneous

133. The abbreviation IM stands for

A. Intradermal B. Intramuscular
C. Intravenous D. Internal medicine

134. The injection given under the skin is called

A. Intradermal B. Subcutaneous
C. Intramuscular D. Intravenous

135. The fastest route of drug administration is

A. Oral B. Intramuscular
C. Subcutaneous D. Intravenous

136. The drug order should be verified for _____.

A. Dose B. Route
C. Time D. All of these

137. The purpose of checking drug expiry date is to prevent

A. Infection B. Toxicity
C. Ineffectiveness D. Allergy

138. The nurse should wash hands _____ administering drugs.

A. After B. Before
C. During D. Anytime

139. The correct site for IM injection in adults is

A. Deltoid B. Gluteal
C. Vastus lateralis D. All of these

140. The sublingual route means placing drug ______.

A. Under tongue B. On tongue
C. In cheek D. In throat

141. The purpose of drug administration is to ______.

A. Cure disease B. Prevent disease
C. Relieve symptoms D. All of these

142. The nurse must check patient identity using ______.

A. Name B. ID band
C. Bed number D. All of these

143. The medication error can be prevented by following ______.

A. Experience
B. Rights of drug administration
C. Speed
D. Guessing

144. Match the following:

Column I	Column II
A. Oral	1. Under skin
B. Intravenous	2. Into vein
C. Intramuscular	3. Into muscle
D. Subcutaneous	4. By mouth

A. A-4, B-2, C-3, D-1 B. A-2, B-3, C-4, D-1
C. A-3, B-1, C-2, D-4 D. A-1, B-4, C-3, D-2

145. Assertion I: Correct drug administration ensures patient safety.

Assertion II: Drug errors do not affect patient outcome.

A. Both statements are correct
B. I is correct, II is incorrect
C. Both are incorrect
D. I is incorrect, II is correct

146. The care given before surgery is called

A. Postoperative care
B. Preoperative care
C. Intraoperative care
D. Emergency care

147. The purpose of preoperative care is to ______ patient for surgery.

A. Diagnose B. Prepare
C. Treat D. Discharge

148. The consent taken before surgery is called ______ consent.

A. Written B. Verbal
C. Informed D. Legal

149. The patient should be kept NPO before surgery to prevent

A. Pain B. Infection
C. Aspiration D. Bleeding

150. The shaving of surgical site is done to prevent

A. Pain B. Infection
C. Bleeding D. Injury

151. The vital signs should be checked ______ surgery.

A. After B. Before
C. During D. Anytime

152. The postoperative care begins immediately ______ surgery.

A. Before B. After
C. During D. End of day

153. The most important observation after surgery is

A. Pain B. Bleeding
C. Vital signs D. Dressing

154. The complication after surgery includes

A. Infection B. Hemorrhage
C. Shock D. All of these

155. The position after surgery depends on

A. Patient choice B. Type of surgery
C. Nurse decision D. Room condition

156. The deep breathing exercises are advised to prevent

A. Pain B. Infection
C. Atelectasis D. Bleeding

157. The wound dressing should be kept ______.

A. Dry and clean B. Wet
C. Loose D. Open

158. The postoperative patient should be monitored for ______.

A. Vital signs B. Pain
C. Complications D. All of these

159. Match the following:

Column I	Column II
A. Preoperative care	1. After surgery
B. Postoperative care	2. Before surgery
C. NPO	3. Nothing by mouth
D. Consent	4. Patient permission

A. A-2, B-1, C-3, D-4 B. A-1, B-2, C-4, D-3
C. A-3, B-4, C-1, D-2 D. A-4, B-3, C-2, D-1

160. Assertion I: Preoperative care reduces surgical risk.

Assertion II: Postoperative care is not important.

A. Both statements are correct
B. I is correct, II is incorrect
C. Both are incorrect
D. I is incorrect, II is correct

161. Patient safety means prevention of
A. Disease B. Harm
C. Pain D. Infection

162. The most common cause of patient injury in hospital is
A. Burns B. Falls
C. Infection D. Allergy

163. The side rails are used to prevent
A. Infection B. Falls
C. Pain D. Bleeding

164. The identification band is used to ensure ______ patient.
A. Correct B. Safe
C. Proper D. Treated

165. The medication error can be prevented by
A. Experience
B. Carelessness
C. Following protocols
D. Speed

166. The fire safety equipment includes
A. Extinguisher B. Alarm
C. Sprinkler D. All of these

167. The safety during patient transfer includes use of
A. Force B. Proper technique
C. Speed D. Ignoring rules

168. The nurse should assess patient for risk of ______.
A. Infection B. Fall
C. Pain D. Bleeding

169. The electrical equipment should be
A. Broken B. Checked regularly
C. Old D. Uncovered

170. **Assertion I:** Patient safety is essential in nursing care.
Assertion II: Safety measures are not required in hospital.
A. Both statements are correct
B. I is correct, II is incorrect
C. Both are incorrect
D. I is incorrect, II is correct

EXPLANATORY ANSWERS

1. **B:** Nursing process begins with assessment. It involves collecting complete data about patient. It forms the basis for all further steps.
2. **B:** Data collection is done during assessment phase. It includes history, examination, and investigations. It helps in identifying problems.
3. **B:** Nursing diagnosis is based on collected patient data. It focuses on patient's response to illness. It is different from medical diagnosis.
4. **B:** Planning includes setting measurable goals. These goals guide nursing interventions. They should be patient-centered.
5. **B:** Implementation involves performing planned interventions. It is the action phase. It includes direct patient care.
6. **B:** Evaluation checks whether goals are achieved. It helps in modifying care plan. It ensures effectiveness of care.
7. **B:** Nursing process is dynamic and continuous. It changes according to patient condition. It is flexible in nature.
8. **C:** Nursing process has five steps: assessment, diagnosis, planning, implementation, and evaluation. It is systematic approach.
9. **B:** Nursing diagnosis focuses on patient's response. Medical diagnosis focuses on disease. This difference is important.
10. **C:** Assessment includes both subjective (patient statements) and objective (observed data). Both are essential for care.
11. **C:** Planning includes setting priorities and goals. It helps in organizing care. It ensures systematic approach.
12. **B:** Evaluation determines whether goals are achieved. It assesses effectiveness of interventions. It guides further care.
13. **B:** Nursing process is goal-oriented. It aims at improving patient health. It ensures quality care.
14. **B:** Diagnosis identifies patient problems. It is based on assessment data. It guides planning.
15. **C:** Implementation involves performing interventions. It is execution of care plan. It includes all nursing actions.
16. **A:** Assessment collects data, diagnosis identifies problems, planning sets goals, and implementation provides care. This sequence forms nursing process.
17. **A:** Nursing process is cyclic and continuous. Evaluation may lead to reassessment. It ensures continuous improvement.
18. **C:** Assessment includes subjective data like symptoms and objective data like signs. Both are needed for accurate diagnosis.
19. **C:** Nursing care plan is prepared during planning phase. It includes goals and interventions. It guides patient care.
20. **C:** Evaluation determines outcome of care. It checks effectiveness of interventions. It helps in revising care plan.
21. **B:** Normal body temperature ranges between 36.5°C and 37.5°C. It may vary with age, time of day, and activity. It reflects metabolic activity.
22. **B:** Normal adult pulse rate is 60–100 beats per minute. It varies with activity and health status. It is an important vital sign.

23. C: Normal respiratory rate is 12–20 breaths per minute. It reflects respiratory function. It changes in illness.

24. C: Blood pressure is measured using sphygmomanometer. It is used with stethoscope. It measures systolic and diastolic pressure.

25. B: Systolic pressure occurs during contraction of ventricles. It represents maximum pressure. It is the higher value.

26. B: Diastolic pressure occurs during relaxation phase. It represents minimum pressure. It indicates peripheral resistance.

27. B: Radial artery is most commonly used site. It is easily accessible. It provides accurate pulse reading.

28. C: Normal blood pressure is about 120/80 mmHg. It varies with age and health. It is important for circulation.

29. B: Hypothalamus regulates body temperature. It maintains homeostasis. It responds to environmental changes.

30. B: Pulse rate increases during exercise. It supplies more oxygen to tissues. It reflects cardiac activity.

31. C: Fever is defined as temperature above 38°C. It indicates infection or inflammation. It is a protective response.

32. B: Respiratory rate is counted by observing chest rise and fall. It should be measured discreetly. It reflects breathing pattern.

33. A: Blood pressure is measured in millimeters of mercury. It is standard unit. It indicates pressure in arteries.

34. C: Normal oxygen saturation is 95–100%. It reflects oxygenation status. Low values indicate hypoxia.

35. B: Pulse oximeter measures oxygen saturation. It is non-invasive. It is widely used in clinical practice.

36. A: Body temperature is measured in Celsius. It can also be measured in Fahrenheit. It is a vital parameter.

37. A: Pulse deficit is difference between apical pulse and peripheral pulse. It indicates cardiac inefficiency. It is clinically important.

38. B: Medulla controls respiration. It regulates rhythm of breathing. It responds to CO_2 levels.

39. A: Temperature is heat, pulse is heart beats, respiration is chest movement, and BP is arterial pressure. This mapping reflects vital signs.

40. B: Fever often indicates infection. Pulse rate increases during exercise, not decreases. Hence second statement is incorrect.

41. B: Admission is the process of accepting a patient into hospital for care. It includes registration and initial assessment. It ensures proper documentation.

42. B: Admission helps assess patient condition and orient them to hospital environment. It reduces anxiety. It prepares patient for treatment.

43. C: Registration is the first formal step in admission. It records patient details. It ensures identification and legal documentation.

44. B: Patient belongings should be checked and documented. It prevents loss and disputes. It ensures accountability.

45. B: Orientation includes explaining ward rules, routines, and facilities. It helps patient adjust to environment. It promotes cooperation.

46. B: Discharge planning starts at admission. Early planning ensures continuity of care. It helps in better recovery.

47. B: Patient is discharged only on doctor's order. It ensures patient is medically fit. It maintains legal safety.

48. D: Discharge summary includes diagnosis, treatment, and follow-up advice. It ensures continuity of care. It is an important document.

49. B: Proper admission reduces anxiety by providing information. Discharge planning begins early, not only at end. Hence second statement is incorrect.

50. D: Patient education includes diet, medication, and follow-up. It ensures proper recovery. It prevents complications.

51. B: Communication is the process of exchanging information, ideas, and feelings. It is essential for understanding. It forms the basis of interaction.

52. B: Communication involves sender, message, and receiver. Receiver interprets the message. Feedback completes the process.

53. B: Decoding is interpreting the received message. It helps in understanding communication. It depends on knowledge and perception.

54. C: Non-verbal communication includes gestures, posture, and facial expressions. It conveys emotions. It supports verbal communication.

55. B: Non-verbal communication occurs without words. It includes gestures and expressions. It is important in patient care.

56. B: Therapeutic communication helps in building trust. It improves nurse-patient relationship. It enhances care quality.

57. B: Active listening involves giving full attention. It includes understanding and responding. It improves communication.

58. A: Noise interferes with communication. It acts as a barrier. It reduces clarity.

59. A: Feedback helps in confirming understanding. It clarifies doubts. It completes communication cycle.

60. B: Eye contact shows interest and attention. It improves communication. It builds trust.

61. B: Tone of voice reflects emotions. It is part of non-verbal communication. It influences message interpretation.

62. B: Nurse-patient communication is therapeutic. It aims to improve patient well-being. It builds rapport.

63. D: Effective communication requires clarity, simplicity, and understanding. These factors improve message delivery. They prevent misunderstanding.

64. A: Sender sends message, message is content, receiver gets it, and feedback is response. This forms communication process.

65. B: Communication improves patient care. It is essential in nursing practice. Hence second statement is incorrect.

66. B: Documentation includes recording all aspects of patient care. It provides a permanent record. It ensures continuity of care.

67. B: Proper documentation improves patient care. It helps in communication and planning. It ensures quality care.

68. B: Documentation should be clear, accurate, and complete. It should be easy to understand. It prevents errors.

69. B: Written records are legal documents. They can be used in court. They provide evidence of care.

70. B: Documentation is done immediately after care. It ensures accuracy. Delayed recording can lead to errors.

71. B: Only standard abbreviations should be used. It prevents misunderstanding. It ensures clarity.

72. B: Documentation facilitates communication among healthcare team. It ensures coordinated care. It improves patient outcomes.

73. B: Documentation should be done in permanent ink like blue or black. It prevents alteration. It maintains record integrity.

74. A: Accuracy means correct data, timeliness means immediate recording, completeness means full data, and confidentiality protects information.

75. B: Documentation is legally important. It is essential for patient care. Hence second statement is incorrect.

76. B: Infection occurs when microorganisms invade the body. These include bacteria, viruses, fungi, and parasites. They can cause disease.

77. B: Chain of infection includes agent, host, and environment. Breaking any link prevents infection. It is important in control measures.

78. B: Hand hygiene is the most important step. It prevents transmission of microorganisms. It is simple and effective.

79. C: Hand washing removes pathogens from hands. It reduces infection risk. It is the most common preventive method.

80. D: Infection spreads through air, contact, and droplets. Multiple modes exist. Proper precautions are required.

81. B: Sterilization means complete destruction of all microorganisms. It includes spores. It is used for critical items.

82. B: Isolation separates infected patients. It prevents transmission. It protects others.

83. D: PPE includes gloves, masks, and gowns. They protect healthcare workers. They reduce infection risk.

84. B: Hospital-acquired infections are called nosocomial. They occur during hospital stay. They are preventable.

85. A: Reservoir is the source where microorganisms live. It can be human, animal, or environment. It is part of infection chain.

86. B: Portal of entry is the route through which pathogens enter. It includes skin, mucosa, etc. It leads to infection.

87. B: Gloves protect against infection. They prevent direct contact with pathogens. They are part of PPE.

88. B: Autoclaving uses steam under pressure. It destroys all microorganisms including spores. It is widely used method.

89. B: Disinfectants kill pathogenic organisms. They are used on surfaces. They do not kill spores.

90. B: Hand washing should be done for at least 20 seconds. It ensures proper removal of microbes. It is recommended standard.

91. A: Proper waste disposal prevents spread of infection. Biomedical waste must be handled carefully. It reduces contamination.

92. B: Biomedical waste is segregated using color-coded bags. It helps in safe disposal. It prevents mixing of waste.

93. B: Masks prevent droplet transmission. They protect against respiratory infections. They are essential in infection control.

94. B: Sterilization destroys all forms including spores. It ensures complete elimination. It is essential for surgical items.

95. B: Cleaning removes dirt and organic matter. It reduces microbial load. It is first step before disinfection.

96. D: Infection can spread through food, water, and air. Multiple routes exist. Prevention is necessary.

97. A: PPE protects healthcare workers from infection. It acts as barrier. It reduces exposure.

98. A: Hand washing removes transient flora, sterilization kills all microbes, disinfection reduces microbes, and isolation prevents spread.

99. B: Infection control reduces disease spread. Hand hygiene is essential in prevention. Hence second statement is incorrect.

100. D: Standard precautions include hand hygiene, PPE, and safe disposal. These measures prevent infection. They are universally applied.

101. B: Asepsis means absence of disease-causing microorganisms. It helps prevent infection. It is essential in patient care.

102. B: Medical asepsis reduces number of microorganisms. It includes cleaning and disinfection. It is used in routine care.

103. B: Surgical asepsis is also called sterile technique. It ensures complete absence of microorganisms. It is used in invasive procedures.

104. B: Asepsis aims to prevent infection. It protects patient and healthcare workers. It maintains safety.

105. B: Sterile field must be kept above waist. Objects below waist are considered contaminated. This prevents contamination.

106. C: Sterile objects must not be touched by unsterile hands. It leads to contamination. Proper technique is required.

107. B: The outer one inch of sterile field is considered contaminated. It should not be used. This maintains sterility.

108. D: Medical asepsis includes cleaning, disinfection, and reducing microbes. It prevents spread of infection. It is widely used.

109. B: Sterile gloves are used during surgical procedures. They prevent contamination. They maintain sterility.

110. B: A sterile field left unattended is considered contaminated. It must be continuously observed. It ensures safety.

111. B: Aseptic technique is essential in surgical procedures. It prevents entry of microorganisms. It reduces infection risk.

112. C: Sterile solutions are poured from about 4–6 inches. It prevents splashing and contamination. It maintains sterility.

113. B: Hand hygiene is part of medical asepsis. It reduces microorganisms. It is the simplest preventive measure.

114. A: Medical asepsis is clean technique, surgical asepsis is sterile technique, sterilization kills all microbes, and disinfection reduces microbes.

115. B: Aseptic technique prevents infection. Sterile field should not be touched with bare hands. Hence second statement is incorrect.

116. D: ADL includes basic self-care activities like bathing, feeding, and dressing. These are essential for daily living. Nurses assist patients in performing these activities.

117. A: Bed making provides comfort and cleanliness. It helps prevent infection and pressure sores. It is an essential nursing activity.

118. B: Fowler's position improves breathing by expanding lungs. It is commonly used for respiratory distress. It enhances oxygenation.

119. A: Oral hygiene prevents infection and maintains oral health. It reduces bacterial growth. It improves comfort.

120. B: Bed bath is given to immobile patients. It helps maintain hygiene. It prevents complications.

121. B: Back care prevents pressure sores by improving circulation. It reduces prolonged pressure. It maintains skin integrity.

122. B: Patients should be repositioned every 2 hours. It prevents pressure sores. It improves circulation.

123. B: Pressure sores occur due to prolonged pressure on tissues. It reduces blood supply. It leads to tissue damage.

124. B: Sims' position is used for rectal examination. It provides better access. It is comfortable for patient.

125. A: Mouth care maintains oral cleanliness. It prevents infection. It improves comfort.

126. D: Range of motion exercises improve strength, flexibility, and mobility. They prevent stiffness. They are important for immobile patients.

127. B: Bedpan is used for immobile patients. It helps in elimination. It maintains hygiene.

128. D: Personal hygiene includes bathing, grooming, and oral care. It maintains cleanliness. It improves health.

129. A: Fowler's is sitting, Sims' is side-lying, supine is lying on back, and prone is lying on abdomen. These positions are used in care.

130. B: Repositioning prevents pressure sores. Immobile patients require more skin care. Hence second statement is incorrect.

131. B: The rights of drug administration include right patient, drug, dose, route, and time. These ensure safety. They prevent medication errors.

132. B: Oral route is the most common method. Drugs are taken by mouth. It is convenient and safe.

133. B: IM means intramuscular injection. Drug is given into muscle. It allows moderate absorption.

134. B: Subcutaneous injection is given under skin. It is used for insulin and vaccines. Absorption is slower.

135. D: IV route provides fastest action. Drug directly enters bloodstream. It is used in emergencies.

136. D: Drug order must be checked for dose, route, and time. It ensures correct administration. It prevents errors.

137. C: Expired drugs may lose effectiveness. They may not produce desired effect. Some may become harmful.

138. B: Hand washing before drug administration prevents infection. It is essential for safety. It maintains hygiene.

139. D: IM injections can be given in deltoid, gluteal, and vastus lateralis muscles. Site depends on age and drug.

140. A: Sublingual route places drug under tongue. It allows rapid absorption. It bypasses first-pass metabolism.

141. D: Drugs are used to cure, prevent, and relieve symptoms. They play important role in treatment. They improve health.

142. D: Patient identification must be confirmed using name, ID band, and other details. It prevents errors. It ensures correct patient.

143. B: Following rights prevents medication errors. It ensures safety. It is essential practice.

144. A: Oral is by mouth, IV is into vein, IM into muscle, and SC under skin. This classification is basic.

145. B: Correct drug administration ensures safety. Drug errors can harm patient. Hence second statement is incorrect.

146. B: Preoperative care is given before surgery. It prepares patient physically and psychologically. It reduces complications.

147. B: Preoperative care prepares patient for surgery. It includes assessment and instructions. It ensures safety.

148. C: Informed consent is taken after explaining procedure. It is legal requirement. It protects patient rights.

149. C: NPO prevents aspiration during anesthesia. It reduces risk of vomiting. It ensures safety.

150. B: Shaving reduces infection risk. It removes hair from surgical site. It ensures cleanliness.

151. B: Vital signs are checked before surgery. They provide baseline data. They help in monitoring.

152. B: Postoperative care starts after surgery. It focuses on recovery. It prevents complications.

153. C: Monitoring vital signs is most important. It indicates patient condition. It helps detect complications.

154. D: Complications include infection, hemorrhage, and shock. Early detection is important. It improves outcome.

155. B: Position depends on surgery type. It ensures comfort and safety. It aids recovery.

156. C: Deep breathing prevents lung collapse. It improves ventilation. It reduces complications.

157. A: Dressing should be clean and dry. It prevents infection. It promotes healing.

158. D: Patient must be monitored for vital signs, pain, and complications. It ensures proper recovery.

159. A: Preoperative is before surgery, postoperative after surgery, NPO means nothing by mouth, and consent is permission.

160. B: Preoperative care reduces risk. Postoperative care is equally important. Hence second statement is incorrect.

161. B: Patient safety focuses on preventing harm to patients. It includes avoiding errors and injuries. It ensures quality care.

162. B: Falls are the most common cause of injury. They can lead to fractures and complications. Prevention is important.

163. B: Side rails prevent patients from falling from bed. They are used especially in weak or unconscious patients. They ensure safety.

164. A: Identification band ensures correct patient identification. It prevents errors in treatment. It is essential for safety.

165. C: Following protocols reduces medication errors. It ensures safe practice. It improves patient outcomes.

166. D: Fire safety includes extinguisher, alarm, and sprinkler. These help control fire. They ensure safety.

167. B: Proper technique prevents injury during transfer. It protects both patient and nurse. It ensures safe handling.

168. B: Fall risk assessment is important. It helps prevent accidents. It ensures patient safety.

169. B: Equipment should be checked regularly. It prevents accidents. It ensures proper functioning.

170. B: Patient safety is essential in nursing. Safety measures are always required. Hence second statement is incorrect.

5. Psychology

1. Psychology is the study of
A. Body B. Behavior and mind
C. Disease D. Society

2. The father of modern psychology is
A. Freud B. Watson
C. Wundt D. Skinner

3. The first psychological laboratory was established by
A. Freud B. Pavlov
C. Wundt D. Skinner

4. The study of observable behavior is called ______.
A. Psychoanalysis B. Behaviorism
C. Functionalism D. Structuralism

5. The founder of psychoanalysis is
A. Freud B. Watson
C. Wundt D. James

6. The behaviorism school focuses on ____ behavior.
A. Conscious B. Unconscious
C. Observable D. Hidden

7. The functionalism school focuses on _____ of mind.
A. Structure B. Function
C. Behavior D. Emotion

8. The structuralism school studies _____ of mind.
A. Function B. Structure
C. Behavior D. Emotion

9. The humanistic approach focuses on
A. Behavior B. Unconscious
C. Self-actualization D. Reflexes

10. The cognitive psychology studies
A. Reflexes B. Thinking and memory
C. Behavior only D. Emotions

11. Learning is defined as a relatively permanent change in
A. Behavior B. Body
C. Structure D. Health

12. The process of retaining information is called
A. Learning B. Memory
C. Thinking D. Perception

13. The trial and error learning is given by
A. Pavlov B. Skinner
C. Thorndike D. Watson

14. Classical conditioning was proposed by
A. Skinner B. Pavlov
C. Thorndike D. Freud

15. Operant conditioning is given by
A. Pavlov B. Skinner
C. Watson D. Freud

16. The memory that lasts for a few seconds is called
A. Long-term memory B. Short-term memory
C. Sensory memory D. Permanent memory

17. The process of recalling stored information is called
A. Encoding B. Storage
C. Retrieval D. Learning

18. The process of converting information into memory is called
A. Storage B. Retrieval
C. Encoding D. Recall

19. The forgetting curve was given by
A. Freud B. Pavlov
C. Ebbinghaus D. Skinner

20. The repetition of information helps in ______ memory.
A. Weakening B. Strengthening
C. Losing D. Ignoring

21. Motivation is the process that initiates and directs
A. Thoughts B. Behavior
C. Emotions D. Perception

22. The basic physiological needs are described in

A. Freud theory B. Maslow hierarchy
C. Pavlov theory D. Skinner theory

23. The lowest level in Maslow's hierarchy is

A. Esteem needs B. Safety needs
C. Physiological needs D. Self-actualization

24. The desire to achieve success is called ______.

A. Emotion B. Motivation
C. Perception D. Learning

25. The theory of motivation given by Maslow is called ______ theory.

A. Instinct B. Drive
C. Hierarchy of needs D. Reinforcement

26. Emotion is a state of

A. Thinking B. Feeling
C. Acting D. Learning

27. The James-Lange theory states that emotion follows ______.

A. Thinking
B. Behavior
C. Physiological changes
D. Perception

28. The Cannon-Bard theory states that emotion and physiological changes occur

A. Separately B. Simultaneously
C. Sequentially D. Independently

29. The emotion of fear prepares the body for

A. Rest B. Fight or flight
C. Sleep D. Relaxation

30. Match the following:

Column I	Column II
A. Maslow	1. Classical conditioning
B. Pavlov	2. Hierarchy of needs
C. Skinner	3. Operant conditioning
D. Thorndike	4. Trial and error

A. A-2, B-1, C-3, D-4 B. A-1, B-2, C-4, D-3
C. A-3, B-4, C-1, D-2 D. A-4, B-3, C-2, D-1

31. Personality is the sum of individual's

A. Behavior B. Traits
C. Characteristics D. All of these

32. The theory of personality given by Freud is called

A. Behavioral B. Psychoanalytic
C. Humanistic D. Trait

33. According to Freud, the part of personality that operates on pleasure principle is

A. Ego B. Superego
C. Id D. Conscious

34. The part of personality that follows reality principle is

A. Id B. Ego
C. Superego D. Unconscious

35. The superego represents

A. Desire B. Reality
C. Morality D. Behavior

36. The humanistic theory of personality was given by

A. Freud B. Skinner
C. Rogers D. Pavlov

37. The concept of self-actualization was given by

A. Freud B. Maslow
C. Skinner D. Watson

38. The personality traits are relatively ______.

A. Changeable B. Stable
C. Temporary D. Weak

39. The assessment of personality can be done by

A. Interview B. Observation
C. Tests D. All of these

40. **Assertion I:** Personality influences behavior.

Assertion II: Personality is fixed and cannot change.

A. Both statements are correct
B. I is correct, II is incorrect
C. Both are incorrect
D. I is incorrect, II is correct

41. Developmental psychology studies changes in

A. Behavior B. Mind
C. Life span D. All of these

42. The stage of development from birth to 1 year is called

A. Childhood B. Infancy
C. Adolescence D. Adulthood

43. According to Piaget, the stage of sensorimotor development occurs from

A. 0–2 years B. 2–7 years
C. 7–11 years D. 11–15 years

44. The stage of adolescence is characterized by

A. Physical growth B. Emotional changes
C. Identity formation D. All of these

45. The ability to think abstractly develops in ______ stage.

A. Sensorimotor B. Preoperational
C. Concrete operational D. Formal operational

46. Mental health is defined as state of

A. Illness B. Well-being
C. Disease D. Disorder

47. The ability to cope with stress indicates good
A. Intelligence B. Personality
C. Mental health D. Behavior

48. The mental illness affects
A. Body B. Mind
C. Society D. All of these

49. The promotion of mental health includes
A. Counseling B. Stress management
C. Support D. All of these

50. Assertion I: Mental health is important for overall health.
Assertion II: Mental illness affects only physical health.
A. Both statements are correct
B. I is correct, II is incorrect
C. Both are incorrect
D. I is incorrect, II is correct

51. Behavior is defined as any observable ______ of an individual.
A. Thought B. Action
C. Feeling D. Idea

52. Instinct is an ______ pattern of behavior.
A. Learned B. Innate
C. Temporary D. Variable

53. The reflex action is an example of ______ behavior.
A. Learned B. Voluntary
C. Involuntary D. Conscious

54. The behavior is influenced by ______ factors.
A. Biological B. Environmental
C. Social D. All of these

55. Assertion I: Instinctive behavior is inborn.
Assertion II: Behavior is not influenced by environment.
A. Both statements are correct
B. I is correct, II is incorrect
C. Both are incorrect
D. I is incorrect, II is correct

EXPLANATORY ANSWERS

1. B: Psychology studies behavior and mental processes. It includes thoughts, emotions, and actions. It helps understand human behavior.

2. C: Wilhelm Wundt is called father of modern psychology. He established first lab. He introduced scientific study of mind.

3. C: First psychology laboratory was set up in 1879 by Wundt. It marked beginning of scientific psychology. It was in Germany.

4. B: Behaviorism studies observable behavior. It ignores mental processes. It focuses on stimulus-response.

5. A: Sigmund Freud founded psychoanalysis. He studied unconscious mind. He emphasized role of childhood.

6. C: Behaviorism focuses on observable behavior. It can be measured objectively. It excludes internal thoughts.

7. B: Functionalism studies functions of mental processes. It focuses on adaptation. It was developed by William James.

8. B: Structuralism studies structure of mind. It analyzes components of consciousness. It uses introspection.

9. C: Humanistic psychology focuses on personal growth. It emphasizes self-actualization. It highlights human potential.

10. B: Cognitive psychology studies thinking, memory, and perception. It focuses on mental processes. It explains behavior.

11. A: Learning is a change in behavior due to experience. It is relatively permanent. It involves adaptation.

12. B: Memory is the ability to store and recall information. It is essential for learning. It involves encoding, storage, and retrieval.

13. C: Thorndike proposed trial and error learning. He gave the law of effect. Learning occurs through consequences.

14. B: Pavlov developed classical conditioning. It is based on association. It involves stimulus-response learning.

15. B: Skinner proposed operant conditioning. Behavior is influenced by reinforcement. It focuses on consequences.

16. B: Short-term memory holds information for a few seconds. It has limited capacity. It is temporary.

17. C: Retrieval is recalling stored information. It is essential for memory use. It depends on cues.

18. C: Encoding converts information into memory form. It is first step of memory. It involves attention.

19. C: Ebbinghaus studied forgetting curve. It shows rapid forgetting initially. It emphasizes importance of revision.

20. B: Repetition strengthens memory. It improves retention. It helps in long-term storage.

21. B: Motivation initiates and directs behavior. It provides energy and direction to actions. It is essential for goal achievement.

22. B: Maslow proposed hierarchy of needs. It includes physiological, safety, social, esteem, and self-actualization. It explains motivation.

23. C: Physiological needs are basic needs like food and water. They are lowest level in hierarchy. They must be satisfied first.

24. **B:** Motivation drives behavior toward goals. It includes desires and needs. It influences actions.

25. **C:** Maslow's theory is hierarchy of needs. Needs are arranged in levels. Higher needs are fulfilled after lower ones.

26. **B:** Emotion is a state of feeling. It involves psychological and physiological changes. It affects behavior.

27. **C:** James-Lange theory states that emotion follows physiological changes. First body changes occur, then emotion is experienced.

28. **B:** Cannon-Bard theory states that emotion and physiological changes occur at the same time. Both are independent processes.

29. **B:** Fear prepares body for fight or flight response. It increases heart rate and energy. It helps survival.

30. **A:** Maslow proposed hierarchy, Pavlov classical conditioning, Skinner operant conditioning, and Thorndike trial and error learning.

31. **D:** Personality includes behavior, traits, and characteristics. It defines how a person thinks and acts. It is unique to each individual.

32. **B:** Freud proposed psychoanalytic theory. It focuses on unconscious mind. It explains personality development.

33. **C:** Id operates on pleasure principle. It seeks immediate satisfaction. It is present from birth.

34. **B:** Ego works on reality principle. It balances id and superego. It deals with real world.

35. **C:** Superego represents moral values. It develops from social norms. It controls impulses.

36. **C:** Carl Rogers proposed humanistic theory. It focuses on self-concept. It emphasizes personal growth.

37. **B:** Maslow introduced self-actualization. It is highest level of need. It involves achieving potential.

38. **B:** Personality traits are relatively stable over time. They influence behavior. They are consistent.

39. **D:** Personality can be assessed through interview, observation, and tests. These methods provide information. They help in evaluation.

40. **B:** Personality influences behavior. It can change over time. Hence second statement is incorrect.

41. **D:** Developmental psychology studies changes in behavior, mind, and development across life span. It explains growth patterns. It covers all age groups.

42. **B:** Infancy is from birth to one year. It involves rapid physical and mental growth. It is crucial stage.

43. **A:** Sensorimotor stage occurs from birth to 2 years. Child learns through senses and actions. Object permanence develops.

44. **D:** Adolescence involves physical, emotional, and social changes. Identity formation is key feature. It is transitional stage.

45. **D:** Formal operational stage involves abstract thinking. It develops after 11 years. Logical reasoning improves.

46. **B:** Mental health is a state of well-being. It allows a person to cope with stress and work productively. It is essential for overall health.

47. **C:** Ability to cope with stress shows good mental health. It indicates emotional stability. It helps in daily functioning.

48. **D:** Mental illness affects mind, body, and social functioning. It impacts overall health. It requires holistic care.

49. **D:** Mental health promotion includes counseling, stress management, and support. These help maintain balance. They prevent disorders.

50. **B:** Mental health is essential for overall well-being. Mental illness affects both mental and physical health. Hence second statement is incorrect.

51. **B:** Behavior includes observable actions of an individual. It can be measured and studied. It reflects mental processes.

52. **B:** Instinct is inborn behavior. It does not require learning. It is present from birth.

53. **C:** Reflex action is involuntary. It occurs automatically. It is not under conscious control.

54. **D:** Behavior is influenced by biological, environmental, and social factors. These factors interact. They shape personality.

55. **B:** Instinct is inborn behavior. Behavior is influenced by environment. Hence second statement is incorrect.

6. Microbiology

1. Microbiology is the study of

A. Cells B. Microorganisms
C. Tissues D. Organs

2. Microorganisms are organisms that are

A. Large B. Visible
C. Microscopic D. Multicellular

3. Bacteria are

A. Eukaryotic B. Prokaryotic
C. Multicellular D. Complex

4. The study of bacteria is called ______.

A. Virology B. Mycology
C. Bacteriology D. Parasitology

5. Viruses are

A. Living cells B. Non-living outside host
C. Multicellular D. Eukaryotic

6. The study of viruses is called

A. Mycology B. Bacteriology
C. Virology D. Parasitology

7. Fungi are

A. Prokaryotic B. Eukaryotic
C. Non-living D. Viruses

8. The study of fungi is called

A. Mycology B. Virology
C. Bacteriology D. Parasitology

9. Protozoa are

A. Multicellular B. Unicellular
C. Non-living D. Viruses

10. The microorganism without cellular structure is

A. Bacteria B. Virus
C. Fungi D. Protozoa

11. The bacteria reproduce by ______.

A. Budding B. Binary fission
C. Spore formation D. Fragmentation

12. The bacteria can be seen using

A. Telescope B. Microscope
C. Lens D. Naked eye

13. The shape of bacteria can be

A. Cocci B. Bacilli
C. Spirilla D. All of these

14. Match the following:

Column I	Column II
A. Bacteria	1. Unicellular organism
B. Virus	2. Non-cellular
C. Fungi	3. Eukaryotic
D. Protozoa	4. Prokaryotic

A. A-4, B-2, C-3, D-1 B. A-2, B-3, C-4, D-1
C. A-3, B-4, C-1, D-2 D. A-1, B-2, C-3, D-4

15. **Assertion I:** Viruses require host to reproduce.
Assertion II: Bacteria cannot reproduce independently.

A. Both statements are correct
B. I is correct, II is incorrect
C. Both are incorrect
D. I is incorrect, II is correct

16. A pathogen is an organism that causes

A. Health B. Disease
C. Growth D. Immunity

17. The ability of a microorganism to cause disease is called

A. Immunity B. Pathogenicity
C. Virulence D. Resistance

18. The degree of pathogenicity is known as

A. Immunity B. Virulence
C. Infection D. Resistance

19. The toxins produced by bacteria are called

A. Antigens B. Toxins
C. Enzymes D. Hormones

20. The exotoxins are produced by ______ bacteria.
A. Gram-positive B. Gram-negative
C. Both D. None

21. The endotoxins are present in ______ bacteria.
A. Gram-positive B. Gram-negative
C. Both D. None

22. The transmission of pathogens through direct contact is called ______ transmission.
A. Indirect B. Direct
C. Vector D. Airborne

23. The vector-borne disease is transmitted by
A. Water B. Food
C. Insects D. Air

24. The host that harbors pathogen without symptoms is called
A. Patient B. Carrier
C. Vector D. Reservoir

25. The infection acquired from community is called
A. Nosocomial B. Community-acquired
C. Chronic D. Acute

26. The portal of exit is the route through which pathogen ______ the host.
A. Enters B. Leaves
C. Multiplies D. Attacks

27. The reservoir of infection can be
A. Human B. Animal
C. Environment D. All of these

28. The incubation period is the time between ______ and symptoms.
A. Exposure B. Treatment
C. Recovery D. Diagnosis

29. Match the following:

Column I	Column II
A. Pathogenicity	1. Degree of disease
B. Virulence	2. Cause disease
C. Carrier	3. Spread disease
D. Vector	4. Asymptomatic host

A. A-2, B-1, C-4, D-3 B. A-1, B-2, C-3, D-4
C. A-3, B-4, C-1, D-2 D. A-4, B-3, C-2, D-1

30. **Assertion I:** Pathogens can cause disease.
Assertion II: All microorganisms are pathogenic.
A. Both statements are correct
B. I is correct, II is incorrect
C. Both are incorrect
D. I is incorrect, II is correct

31. Immunity is the ability of body to resist
A. Growth B. Disease
C. Injury D. Pain

32. The immunity present at birth is called
A. Acquired B. Passive
C. Innate D. Artificial

33. The immunity developed after infection is called
A. Innate B. Acquired
C. Passive D. Natural

34. The immunity obtained through vaccination is called
A. Natural B. Passive
C. Artificial active D. Innate

35. The immunity obtained from mother to child is called
A. Artificial B. Passive
C. Active D. Acquired

36. The cells responsible for immunity are
A. RBC B. WBC
C. Platelets D. Plasma

37. The antibody is produced by
A. RBC B. Platelets
C. Lymphocytes D. Neutrophils

38. The antigen is a substance that
A. Protects body B. Produces antibodies
C. Causes reaction D. Destroys cells

39. The lymphocytes are of two types
A. T and B cells
B. RBC and WBC
C. Platelets and plasma
D. Neutrophils and eosinophils

40. The T-cells are responsible for ______ immunity.
A. Humoral B. Cellular
C. Passive D. Artificial

41. The B-cells are responsible for ______ immunity.
A. Cellular B. Humoral
C. Passive D. Artificial

42. The vaccine stimulates ______ immunity.
A. Passive B. Active
C. Innate D. Artificial passive

43. The immunity developed naturally after disease is called ______ immunity.
A. Artificial active B. Natural active
C. Artificial passive D. Innate

44. The immunoglobulin is also known as
A. Antigen B. Antibody
C. Toxin D. Enzyme

45. The first line of defense includes
A. Skin B. Mucous membrane
C. Secretions D. All of these

46. The phagocytosis is carried out by
A. RBC B. Neutrophils
C. Platelets D. Plasma

47. The immunity obtained by injection of antibodies is called
A. Active B. Passive
C. Natural D. Innate

48. The memory cells are responsible for
A. Immediate response B. Long-term immunity
C. Weak immunity D. No response

49. Match the following:

Column I	Column II
A. Innate immunity	1. Develops after exposure
B. Acquired immunity	2. Present at birth
C. Passive immunity	3. Antibody transfer
D. Active immunity	4. Antibody production

A. A-2, B-1, C-3, D-4 B. A-1, B-2, C-4, D-3
C. A-3, B-4, C-1, D-2 D. A-4, B-3, C-2, D-1

50. Assertion I: Vaccination provides immunity.
Assertion II: Innate immunity is developed after birth.
A. Both statements are correct
B. I is correct, II is incorrect
C. Both are incorrect
D. I is incorrect, II is correct

51. Sterilization is the process of destroying
A. Bacteria only B. Viruses only
C. All microorganisms D. Fungi only

52. Disinfection is the process of destroying
A. All microbes B. Pathogens
C. Spores D. Viruses only

53. The method of sterilization using steam is
A. Dry heat B. Autoclaving
C. Radiation D. Filtration

54. The autoclave works on the principle of
A. Dry heat B. Moist heat
C. Radiation D. Filtration

55. The temperature used in autoclave is ______ °C.
A. 100 B. 121
C. 150 D. 180

56. The time required for autoclaving is ______ minutes.
A. 10 B. 15
C. 30 D. 60

57. The dry heat sterilization is done by
A. Autoclave B. Hot air oven
C. Filtration D. Radiation

58. The filtration method is used for sterilizing
A. Solids B. Liquids
C. Metals D. Glass

59. The radiation sterilization is used for
A. Liquids B. Disposable items
C. Metals D. Food

60. The chemical disinfectant is used on
A. Living tissue B. Non-living objects
C. Both D. None

61. The antiseptics are used on ______.
A. Skin B. Instruments
C. Metals D. Glass

62. The boiling is a method of
A. Sterilization B. Disinfection
C. Filtration D. Radiation

63. The alcohol is used as
A. Sterilizing agent B. Disinfectant
C. Antiseptic D. Both B and C

64. The phenol is used as
A. Antiseptic B. Disinfectant
C. Sterilizing agent D. Antibiotic

65. The spores are destroyed by
A. Disinfection B. Sterilization
C. Cleaning D. Boiling

66. The UV radiation is used for
A. Surface sterilization B. Deep sterilization
C. Liquids D. Food

67. The chemical used for fumigation is
A. Alcohol B. Formaldehyde
C. Phenol D. Chlorine

68. The chlorine is used for disinfecting
A. Air B. Water
C. Skin D. Instruments

69. Match the following:

Column I	Column II
A. Autoclave	1. Moist heat
B. Hot air oven	2. Dry heat
C. Filtration	3. Liquids
D. Radiation	4. Disposable items

A. A-1, B-2, C-3, D-4 B. A-2, B-1, C-4, D-3
C. A-3, B-4, C-1, D-2 D. A-4, B-3, C-2, D-1

70. **Assertion I:** Sterilization destroys all microorganisms.
Assertion II: Disinfection destroys spores.
A. Both statements are correct
B. I is correct, II is incorrect
C. Both are incorrect
D. I is incorrect, II is correct

71. Infection control aims to prevent
A. Disease B. Infection
C. Injury D. Pain

72. The most effective method of infection control is
A. Mask B. Gloves
C. Hand hygiene D. Isolation

73. The chain of infection includes agent, host and ______.
A. Environment B. Treatment
C. Medication D. Diagnosis

74. The isolation of patient is done to prevent
A. Pain B. Infection spread
C. Injury D. Bleeding

75. The PPE includes
A. Gloves B. Mask
C. Gown D. All of these

76. The infection acquired in hospital is called
A. Community infection B. Nosocomial infection
C. Chronic infection D. Acute infection

77. The biomedical waste is segregated using ______ coding.
A. Color B. Number
C. Letter D. Symbol

78. The hand washing should be done for at least ______ seconds.
A. 10 B. 20
C. 30 D. 60

79. The standard precautions include
A. Hand hygiene B. PPE
C. Safe disposal D. All of these

80. The mask prevents ______ transmission.
A. Contact B. Droplet
C. Vector D. Direct

81. The portal of entry is the route through which pathogen ______ body.
A. Leaves B. Enters
C. Multiplies D. Spreads

82. The vector-borne disease is transmitted by
A. Water B. Air
C. Insects D. Food

83. The infection control includes proper ______ disposal.
A. Food B. Water
C. Waste D. Air

84. Match the following:

Column I	Column II
A. Hand hygiene	1. Prevent spread
B. PPE	2. Reduce microbes
C. Isolation	3. Protect staff
D. Waste disposal	4. Safe disposal

A. A-2, B-3, C-1, D-4 B. A-3, B-1, C-4, D-2
C. A-1, B-2, C-3, D-4 D. A-4, B-3, C-2, D-1

85. **Assertion I:** Infection control reduces spread of disease.
Assertion II: PPE is not required in healthcare.
A. Both statements are correct
B. I is correct, II is incorrect
C. Both are incorrect
D. I is incorrect, II is correct

86. Tuberculosis is caused by
A. Virus B. Bacteria
C. Fungi D. Protozoa

87. Malaria is caused by
A. Virus B. Bacteria
C. Protozoa D. Fungi

88. AIDS is caused by
A. Bacteria B. Virus
C. Fungi D. Protozoa

89. The vector of malaria is
A. Housefly B. Mosquito
C. Tick D. Louse

90. Cholera is transmitted through
A. Air B. Water
C. Food D. Contact

91. The causative agent of typhoid is
A. Virus B. Bacteria
C. Fungi D. Protozoa

92. The disease spread by droplets is
A. Malaria B. Tuberculosis
C. Cholera D. Typhoid

93. The vaccine for tuberculosis is
A. DPT B. BCG
C. OPV D. MMR

94. Hepatitis B affects the
A. Heart B. Liver
C. Kidney D. Lungs

95. The disease transmitted by sexual contact is

A. Malaria
B. AIDS
C. Cholera
D. Typhoid

96. The disease spread by contaminated food is

A. Malaria
B. Tuberculosis
C. Cholera
D. Typhoid

97. The dengue is transmitted by

A. Housefly
B. Mosquito
C. Tick
D. Louse

98. The rabies is transmitted by

A. Insects
B. Animal bite
C. Water
D. Food

99. Match the following:

Column I	Column II
A. Tuberculosis	1. Protozoa
B. Malaria	2. Bacteria
C. Cholera	3. Waterborne
D. AIDS	4. Virus

A. A-2, B-1, C-3, D-4
B. A-1, B-2, C-4, D-3
C. A-3, B-4, C-1, D-2
D. A-4, B-3, C-2, D-1

100. Assertion I: Vaccination prevents diseases.

Assertion II: All diseases are non-communicable.

A. Both statements are correct
B. I is correct, II is incorrect
C. Both are incorrect
D. I is incorrect, II is correct

EXPLANATORY ANSWERS

1. B: Microbiology studies microorganisms. These are tiny organisms not visible to naked eye. It includes bacteria, viruses, fungi, and protozoa.

2. C: Microorganisms are microscopic. They require microscope for observation. They are present everywhere.

3. B: Bacteria are prokaryotic cells. They lack true nucleus. They are simple organisms.

4. C: Bacteriology is study of bacteria. It deals with structure and function. It is important in medicine.

5. B: Viruses are non-living outside host. They need host cells to reproduce. They show both living and non-living features.

6. C: Virology is study of viruses. It includes their structure and replication. It is important in disease study.

7. B: Fungi are eukaryotic organisms. They have true nucleus. They can be unicellular or multicellular.

8. A: Mycology is study of fungi. It includes molds and yeasts. Some fungi cause diseases.

9. B: Protozoa are unicellular organisms. They are eukaryotic. Some are pathogenic.

10. B: Virus lacks cellular structure. It is acellular. It depends on host for replication.

11. B: Bacteria reproduce by binary fission. It is asexual reproduction. It is rapid process.

12. B: Bacteria are seen under microscope. They are too small to see with naked eye. Microscopy is essential.

13. D: Bacteria have different shapes like cocci, bacilli, and spirilla. Shape helps in identification. It is important in classification.

14. A: Bacteria are prokaryotic, viruses are non-cellular, fungi are eukaryotic, and protozoa are unicellular. This classification is basic.

15. B: Viruses require host for reproduction. Bacteria can reproduce independently. Hence second statement is incorrect.

16. B: Pathogens are organisms that cause disease. They invade host and multiply. They lead to infection.

17. B: Pathogenicity is ability to cause disease. It varies among organisms. It determines disease potential.

18. B: Virulence is degree of pathogenicity. It indicates severity of disease. Higher virulence means more severe disease.

19. B: Bacteria produce toxins that damage tissues. They cause symptoms. They play role in disease.

20. A: Exotoxins are mainly produced by Gram-positive bacteria. They are highly potent. They are secreted.

21. B: Endotoxins are part of Gram-negative bacteria cell wall. They are released on cell death. They cause fever.

22. B: Direct transmission occurs through physical contact. It spreads pathogens easily. It includes touch.

23. C: Vector-borne diseases are transmitted by insects. Examples include malaria. Vectors carry pathogens.

24. B: Carrier harbors pathogen without symptoms. It can spread infection. It is important in epidemiology.

25. B: Community-acquired infections occur outside hospital. They are common. They differ from nosocomial infections.

26. B: Portal of exit is route by which pathogen leaves host. It spreads infection. Examples include respiratory tract.

27. D: Reservoir can be human, animal, or environment. It is source of infection. It maintains pathogen.

28. A: Incubation period is time from exposure to symptom onset. It varies by disease. It is important in diagnosis.

29. A: Pathogenicity means ability to cause disease, virulence is degree, carrier is asymptomatic host, and vector spreads disease.

30. B: Pathogens cause disease. Not all microorganisms are harmful. Many are beneficial. Hence second statement is incorrect.

31. B: Immunity is the body's ability to resist infection. It protects against pathogens. It is essential for health.

32. C: Innate immunity is present at birth. It provides immediate defense. It is non-specific.

33. B: Acquired immunity develops after exposure. It is specific. It has memory.

34. C: Vaccination induces artificial active immunity. It stimulates antibody production. It provides long-term protection.

35. B: Maternal antibodies provide passive immunity. It is temporary. It protects newborn.

36. B: White blood cells are responsible for immunity. They fight infection. They include lymphocytes.

37. C: Lymphocytes produce antibodies. B-cells produce antibodies. They are important in immune response.

38. B: Antigen stimulates antibody production. It triggers immune response. It is foreign substance.

39. A: Lymphocytes include T and B cells. T-cells provide cellular immunity. B-cells provide humoral immunity.

40. B: T-cells provide cellular immunity. They destroy infected cells. They are important in defense.

41. B: B-cells produce antibodies. They provide humoral immunity. They act against pathogens.

42. B: Vaccination stimulates active immunity. Body produces its own antibodies. It provides long-term protection.

43. B: Natural active immunity develops after infection. It is long-lasting. It involves memory cells.

44. B: Immunoglobulin is antibody. It binds to antigen. It neutralizes pathogens.

45. D: Skin, mucous membranes, and secretions form first line of defense. They prevent entry of pathogens.

46. B: Neutrophils perform phagocytosis. They engulf pathogens. They are part of innate immunity.

47. B: Passive immunity is obtained by antibody injection. It provides immediate protection. It is temporary.

48. B: Memory cells provide long-term immunity. They respond quickly on re-exposure. They ensure protection.

49. A: Innate is present at birth, acquired develops after exposure, passive is antibody transfer, and active is antibody production.

50. B: Vaccination provides immunity. Innate immunity is present at birth. Hence second statement is incorrect.

51. C: Sterilization destroys all microorganisms including spores. It ensures complete elimination. It is used for surgical instruments.

52. B: Disinfection destroys pathogenic organisms. It does not kill spores. It is used on surfaces.

53. B: Autoclaving uses steam under pressure. It is effective method. It kills all microbes.

54. B: Autoclave works on moist heat principle. Steam penetrates materials. It destroys microorganisms.

55. B: Standard autoclave temperature is 121°C. It ensures sterilization. It is widely used.

56. B: Standard time is 15 minutes. It ensures effectiveness. It depends on load.

57. B: Dry heat sterilization is done in hot air oven. It is used for glassware. It requires high temperature.

58. B: Filtration is used for heat-sensitive liquids. It removes microbes. It does not kill them.

59. B: Radiation sterilizes disposable items. It uses gamma rays. It is used industrially.

60. B: Disinfectants are used on non-living objects. They destroy pathogens. They are not used on skin.

61. A: Antiseptics are used on living tissues. They prevent infection. They are safe for skin.

62. B: Boiling kills many microbes but not spores. It is a disinfection method. It is simple.

63. D: Alcohol acts as disinfectant and antiseptic. It kills bacteria. It is widely used.

64. B: Phenol is used as disinfectant. It kills microbes on surfaces. It is effective.

65. B: Spores are resistant. Only sterilization can destroy them. Disinfection is not sufficient.

66. A: UV radiation is used for surface sterilization. It does not penetrate deeply. It is used in rooms.

67. B: Formaldehyde is used for fumigation. It sterilizes air and surfaces. It is effective.

68. B: Chlorine is used for water disinfection. It kills pathogens. It ensures safe water.

69. A: Autoclave uses moist heat, hot air oven uses dry heat, filtration is for liquids, and radiation for disposables.

70. B: Sterilization kills all microbes. Disinfection does not kill spores. Hence second statement is incorrect.

71. B: Infection control focuses on preventing infection. It reduces transmission. It protects patients and staff.

72. C: Hand hygiene is most effective method. It removes pathogens. It prevents spread.

73. A: Chain of infection includes agent, host, and environment. Breaking chain prevents infection. It is important concept.

74. B: Isolation prevents spread of infection. It separates infected patients. It protects others.

75. D: PPE includes gloves, masks, and gowns. They protect healthcare workers. They reduce exposure.

76. B: Hospital-acquired infections are nosocomial. They occur during hospital stay. They are preventable.

77. A: Biomedical waste is segregated by color coding. It ensures safe disposal. It prevents contamination.

78. B: Hand washing should be at least 20 seconds. It ensures removal of microbes. It is recommended.

79. D: Standard precautions include hand hygiene, PPE, and safe disposal. These reduce infection risk. They are essential.

80. B: Masks prevent droplet transmission. They protect respiratory system. They reduce spread.

81. B: Portal of entry is route of entry. Pathogens enter body through it. It leads to infection.

82. C: Vector-borne diseases are transmitted by insects. They carry pathogens. Examples include malaria.

83. C: Proper waste disposal prevents infection spread. Biomedical waste must be handled carefully. It ensures safety.

84. A: Hand hygiene reduces microbes, PPE protects staff, isolation prevents spread, and waste disposal ensures safety.

85. B: Infection control reduces disease spread. PPE is essential. Hence second statement is incorrect.

86. B: Tuberculosis is caused by Mycobacterium tuberculosis. It affects lungs. It spreads through air.

87. C: Malaria is caused by Plasmodium. It is transmitted by mosquito. It affects blood.

88. B: AIDS is caused by HIV virus. It affects immune system. It reduces immunity.

89. B: Malaria is transmitted by female Anopheles mosquito. It acts as vector. It spreads infection.

90. B: Cholera spreads through contaminated water. It causes diarrhea. It is preventable.

91. B: Typhoid is caused by Salmonella typhi. It spreads through food and water. It causes fever.

92. B: Tuberculosis spreads by droplets. It is airborne disease. It affects lungs.

93. B: BCG vaccine protects against tuberculosis. It is given in childhood. It provides immunity.

94. B: Hepatitis B affects liver. It causes inflammation. It spreads through blood.

95. B: AIDS spreads through sexual contact. It is viral disease. It affects immune system.

96. D: Typhoid spreads through contaminated food. It causes fever. It is preventable.

97. B: Dengue is transmitted by Aedes mosquito. It causes fever. It is vector-borne disease.

98. B: Rabies spreads through animal bites. It affects nervous system. It is fatal if untreated.

99. A: Tuberculosis is bacterial, malaria is protozoal, cholera is waterborne, and AIDS is viral.

100. B: Vaccination prevents diseases. Many diseases are communicable. Hence second statement is incorrect.

7. Sociology

1. Sociology is the study of

A. Society B. Body
C. Mind D. Disease

2. The basic unit of society is

A. Community B. Group
C. Family D. Institution

3. The marriage between one man and one woman is called

A. Polygamy B. Monogamy
C. Polyandry D. Endogamy

4. The marriage between one man and multiple women is

A. Polyandry B. Monogamy
C. Exogamy D. Polygyny

5. The marriage within same group is called

A. Endogamy B. Exogamy
C. Monogamy D. Polygamy

6. The marriage outside the group is called

A. Endogamy B. Polygyny
C. Exogamy D. Polyandry

7. The family consisting of parents and children is called

A. Joint family B. Nuclear family
C. Extended family D. Large family

8. The family consisting of multiple generations is called

A. Nuclear B. Joint
C. Small D. Single

9. The functions of family include

A. Socialization B. Protection
C. Reproduction D. All of these

10. Marriage is a ______ institution.

A. Social B. Economic
C. Political D. Religious

11. A social group is a collection of individuals who

A. Work together B. Share common interests
C. Live alone D. Have no interaction

12. The primary group is characterized by

A. Formal relations
B. Secondary relations
C. Close and personal relations
D. Temporary relations

13. The example of secondary group is

A. Family B. Friends
C. School D. Neighbours

14. The group with direct face-to-face interaction is

A. Secondary group B. Formal group
C. Large group D. Primary group

15. The characteristics of secondary group include

A. Informal relations B. Emotional attachment
C. Personal contact D. Formal relations

16. A social problem is a condition that affects

A. Individuals only B. Society
C. Family only D. Community only

17. Population refers to number of

A. Houses B. Animals
C. People D. Resources

18. Overpopulation leads to

A. Development B. Resource shortage
C. Better living D. Employment

19. The literacy rate is an indicator of

A. Health B. Economy
C. Education D. Culture

20. **Assertion I:** Population growth affects resources.
Assertion II: Overpopulation improves quality of life.

A. Both statements are correct
B. I is correct, II is incorrect
C. Both are incorrect
D. I is incorrect, II is correct

EXPLANATORY ANSWERS

1. **A:** Sociology studies society and social relationships. It explains human interaction. It helps understand social structure.

2. **C:** Family is basic unit of society. It provides care and support. It plays important role in development.

3. **B:** Monogamy is marriage between one man and one woman. It is common form. It promotes stability.

4. **D:** Polygyny is marriage of one man with multiple women. It is type of polygamy. It is less common.

5. **A:** Endogamy is marriage within same group. It maintains cultural identity. It is common in some societies.

6. **C:** Exogamy is marriage outside group. It promotes social interaction. It prevents inbreeding.

7. **B:** Nuclear family includes parents and children. It is small family unit. It is common in modern society.

8. **B:** Joint family includes multiple generations. It provides support. It is common in traditional societies.

9. **D:** Family performs functions like socialization, protection, and reproduction. It supports members. It is essential institution.

10. **A:** Marriage is a social institution. It regulates relationships. It is recognized by society.

11. **B:** Social group consists of individuals sharing common interests and interacting with each other. Interaction is essential. It creates social relationships.

12. **C:** Primary group has close and personal relationships. Members have emotional attachment. Example is family.

13. **C:** School is a secondary group. It has formal relationships. Interaction is goal-oriented.

14. **D:** Primary group involves face-to-face interaction. It includes family and friends. It has strong bonds.

15. **D:** Secondary groups have formal and impersonal relations. They are large in size. They are goal-oriented.

16. **B:** Social problems affect large number of people in society. They require collective action. Examples include poverty and unemployment.

17. **C:** Population refers to total number of people in an area. It is important for planning. It affects resources.

18. **B:** Overpopulation leads to shortage of resources. It increases pressure on environment. It affects quality of life.

19. **C:** Literacy rate reflects level of education. It indicates development. It helps in social progress.

20. **B:** Population growth affects resources and environment. Overpopulation reduces quality of life. Hence second statement is incorrect.

8. Pharmacology/Pathology/Genetics

1. Pharmacology is the study of
A. Diseases B. Drugs
C. Cells D. Tissues

2. Pharmacodynamics deals with
A. Drug absorption B. Drug action on body
C. Drug excretion D. Drug metabolism

3. Pharmacokinetics includes
A. Drug action B. Drug effects
C. ADME D. Drug toxicity

4. The term ADME stands for
A. Absorption, Distribution, Metabolism, Excretion
B. Action, Dose, Metabolism, Effect
C. Absorption, Dose, Movement, Excretion
D. Action, Distribution, Metabolism, Elimination

5. The process of movement of drug from blood to tissues is
A. Absorption B. Distribution
C. Metabolism D. Excretion

6. The organ mainly responsible for drug metabolism is
A. Kidney B. Liver
C. Heart D. Lung

7. The elimination of drug from body is called
A. Absorption B. Distribution
C. Metabolism D. Excretion

8. The effect produced by drug is called
A. Pharmacokinetics B. Pharmacodynamics
C. Pharmacology D. Toxicology

9. The unwanted effect of drug is called
A. Side effect B. Therapeutic effect
C. Action D. Dose

10. The study of harmful effects of drugs is called
A. Pharmacology B. Toxicology
C. Pharmacodynamics D. Pharmacokinetics

11. The dose of drug depends on
A. Age B. Weight
C. Condition D. All of these

12. The route of drug administration affects
A. Absorption B. Distribution
C. Metabolism D. Excretion

13. The drug given through vein is called
A. Oral B. Intramuscular
C. Intravenous D. Subcutaneous

14. The drug that relieves pain is called
A. Antibiotic B. Analgesic
C. Antipyretic D. Sedative

15. The drug that reduces fever is called
A. Analgesic B. Antibiotic
C. Antipyretic D. Sedative

16. The drug that kills bacteria is called
A. Antipyretic B. Antibiotic
C. Analgesic D. Sedative

17. The drug that induces sleep is called
A. Antibiotic B. Analgesic
C. Sedative D. Antipyretic

18. The bioavailability of drug refers to
A. Distribution B. Absorption
C. Excretion D. Effect

19. The half-life of drug is the time taken for ______ of drug to be eliminated.
A. Half B. Full
C. Quarter D. Double

20. The first-pass effect occurs in
A. Kidney B. Liver
C. Heart D. Lung

21. The adverse drug reaction is
A. Desired effect B. Unwanted effect
C. Therapeutic effect D. Normal effect

22. The therapeutic index indicates
A. Safety of drug B. Toxicity of drug
C. Effectiveness D. Dose

23. The loading dose is given to
A. Maintain level B. Achieve rapid effect
C. Reduce toxicity D. Increase excretion

24. The maintenance dose is given to
A. Achieve effect B. Maintain level
C. Reduce effect D. Stop drug

25. The tolerance means
A. Increased response B. Decreased response
C. No response D. Toxic response

26. The drug interaction occurs when
A. One drug acts B. Two drugs act together
C. Drug is absorbed D. Drug is excreted

27. The placebo is a
A. Active drug B. Inactive substance
C. Antibiotic D. Hormone

28. The contraindication means
A. Indication B. Prohibition
C. Recommendation D. Suggestion

29. Match the following:

Column I	Column II
A. Analgesic	1. Reduces fever
B. Antipyretic	2. Kills bacteria
C. Antibiotic	3. Relieves pain
D. Sedative	4. Induces sleep

A. A-3, B-1, C-2, D-4 B. A-1, B-2, C-3, D-4
C. A-2, B-3, C-4, D-1 D. A-4, B-3, C-1, D-2

30. **Assertion I:** Pharmacology studies drugs.
Assertion II: Drugs have no side effects.
A. Both statements are correct
B. I is correct, II is incorrect
C. Both are incorrect
D. I is incorrect, II is correct

31. Chemotherapy is the use of drugs to treat
A. Pain B. Infection
C. Disease D. Fever

32. Antibiotics are used to treat
A. Viral infections B. Bacterial infections
C. Fungal infections D. Parasitic infections

33. The drug resistance occurs when microorganisms
A. Die easily B. Become sensitive
C. Become resistant D. Multiply slowly

34. The broad-spectrum antibiotics act against
A. Specific bacteria B. All bacteria
C. Limited bacteria D. Many types of bacteria

35. The narrow-spectrum antibiotics act against
A. Many bacteria B. Few bacteria
C. All bacteria D. Viruses

36. The drug used for fungal infection is called
A. Antibiotic B. Antiviral
C. Antifungal D. Antipyretic

37. The drug used for viral infection is
A. Antibiotic B. Antiviral
C. Antifungal D. Analgesic

38. The sulfonamides are used as
A. Antifungal B. Antibiotic
C. Antiviral D. Analgesic

39. The penicillin acts by inhibiting
A. Protein synthesis B. DNA synthesis
C. Cell wall synthesis D. RNA synthesis

40. The tetracycline acts by inhibiting
A. Cell wall synthesis B. Protein synthesis
C. DNA synthesis D. RNA synthesis

41. The drug used in tuberculosis is
A. Penicillin B. Streptomycin
C. Insulin D. Aspirin

42. The drug used for malaria is
A. Penicillin B. Chloroquine
C. Aspirin D. Paracetamol

43. The antifungal drug is
A. Amphotericin B B. Penicillin
C. Tetracycline D. Aspirin

44. The antiviral drug is
A. Acyclovir B. Penicillin
C. Streptomycin D. Insulin

45. The combination therapy is used to
A. Reduce effect B. Increase resistance
C. Improve effectiveness D. Stop drug

46. The superinfection occurs due to
A. Overuse of antibiotics
B. Underuse of drugs
C. No treatment
D. Proper treatment

47. The drug toxicity is related to

A. Low dose B. High dose
C. No dose D. Proper dose

48. The chemotherapy drugs should be given as per

A. Patient choice B. Doctor's order
C. Nurse decision D. Relative advice

49. Match the following:

Column I	Column II
A. Antibiotic	1. Fungal infection
B. Antifungal	2. Viral infection
C. Antiviral	3. Bacterial infection
D. Antimalarial	4. Malaria

A. A-3, B-1, C-2, D-4 B. A-1, B-2, C-3, D-4
C. A-2, B-3, C-4, D-1 D. A-4, B-3, C-1, D-2

50. Assertion I: Chemotherapy drugs treat infections.
Assertion II: Antibiotics are effective against viruses.

A. Both statements are correct
B. I is correct, II is incorrect
C. Both are incorrect
D. I is incorrect, II is correct

51. The drug used to reduce gastric acidity is

A. Antacid B. Antibiotic
C. Analgesic D. Antipyretic

52. The proton pump inhibitors act by inhibiting ______ secretion.

A. Enzyme B. Acid
C. Hormone D. Water

53. The H2 blockers reduce secretion of ______ in stomach.

A. Enzyme B. Bile
C. Acid D. Mucus

54. The drug used for constipation is

A. Antacid B. Laxative
C. Antiemetic D. Antibiotic

55. The drug used to control vomiting is

A. Antacid B. Laxative
C. Antiemetic D. Analgesic

56. The drug used in diarrhea is

A. Laxative B. Antidiarrheal
C. Antibiotic D. Antacid

57. The drug metoclopramide is used as ______ agent.

A. Laxative B. Antacid
C. Antiemetic D. Antibiotic

58. The drug omeprazole belongs to ______ group.

A. Antacid B. PPI
C. H2 blocker D. Laxative

59. The antacid works by ______ gastric acid.

A. Increasing B. Neutralizing
C. Producing D. Absorbing

60. The drug used in peptic ulcer is ______ inhibitor.

A. Enzyme B. Pump
C. Protein D. Acid

61. Match the following:

Column I	Column II
A. Antacid	1. Prevent vomiting
B. Laxative	2. Relieve constipation
C. Antiemetic	3. Reduce acidity
D. Antidiarrheal	4. Control diarrhea

A. A-3, B-2, C-1, D-4 B. A-2, B-3, C-4, D-1
C. A-1, B-4, C-2, D-3 D. A-4, B-1, C-3, D-2

62. Match the following:

Column I	Column II
A. Omeprazole	1. Antidiarrheal
B. Ranitidine	2. PPI
C. Metoclopramide	3. Antiemetic
D. Loperamide	4. H2 blocker

A. A-2, B-4, C-3, D-1 B. A-4, B-2, C-1, D-3
C. A-3, B-1, C-4, D-2 D. A-1, B-3, C-2, D-4

63. Assertion I: Antacids neutralize gastric acid.
Assertion II: Antacids increase acid secretion.

A. Both statements are correct
B. I is correct, II is incorrect
C. Both are incorrect
D. I is incorrect, II is correct

64. Assertion I: Laxatives are used in constipation.
Assertion II: Laxatives reduce bowel movement.

A. Both statements are correct
B. I is correct, II is incorrect
C. Both are incorrect
D. I is incorrect, II is correct

65. The drug used to protect gastric mucosa is

A. Sucralfate B. Aspirin
C. Paracetamol D. Antibiotic

66. The drug ______ acts by blocking histamine receptors in stomach.

A. Omeprazole B. Ranitidine
C. Loperamide D. Metoclopramide

67. The drug used in diarrhea reduces ______ motility.

A. Gastric B. Intestinal
C. Cardiac D. Pulmonary

68. The side effect of antacids may include ______.

A. Diarrhea B. Constipation
C. Both D. None

69. The drug ______ is used to stop loose motions.

A. Loperamide B. Omeprazole
C. Ranitidine D. Sucralfate

70. The drug used to increase gastric motility is

A. Loperamide B. Metoclopramide
C. Omeprazole D. Ranitidine

71. The drug used to relieve bronchospasm is

A. Antacid B. Bronchodilator
C. Diuretic D. Laxative

72. Salbutamol is a

A. Antihistamine B. Bronchodilator
C. Antibiotic D. Antipyretic

73. The drug used in allergic rhinitis is

A. Antacid B. Antiemetic
C. Antihistamine D. Antidiarrheal

74. Theophylline belongs to ______ group.

A. Methylxanthine B. Steroid
C. Antibiotic D. Analgesic

75. The corticosteroids used in asthma reduce airway

A. Bleeding B. Spasm only
C. Inflammation D. Acidity

76. The drug ______ is used as expectorant to loosen sputum.

A. Ranitidine B. Salbutamol
C. Guaifenesin D. Furosemide

77. The drug used to suppress cough is called

A. Expectorant B. Antitussive
C. Bronchodilator D. Decongestant

78. The opioid antitussive drug is

A. Codeine B. Salbutamol
C. Guaifenesin D. Cetirizine

79. The drug used to reduce nasal congestion is

A. Antacid B. Decongestant
C. Antitussive D. Laxative

80. In asthma, bronchodilators mainly act by relaxing

A. Cardiac muscle
B. Skeletal muscle
C. Smooth muscle of bronchi
D. Intestinal muscle

81. Match the following:

Column I	Column II
A. Salbutamol	1. Antitussive
B. Cetirizine	2. Expectorant
C. Codeine	3. Antihistamine
D. Guaifenesin	4. Bronchodilator

A. A-4, B-3, C-1, D-2 B. A-3, B-4, C-2, D-1
C. A-1, B-2, C-3, D-4 D. A-2, B-1, C-4, D-3

82. Match the following:

Column I	Column II
A. Decongestant	1. Relieves allergy
B. Bronchodilator	2. Reduces swelling in nose
C. Antihistamine	3. Reduces inflammation
D. Steroid	4. Relieves bronchospasm

A. A-2, B-4, C-1, D-3 B. A-4, B-1, C-3, D-2
C. A-1, B-2, C-4, D-3 D. A-3, B-4, C-2, D-1

83. Assertion I: Antihistamines help in allergic conditions.
Assertion II: Antihistamines increase histamine action.

A. Both statements are correct
B. I is correct, II is incorrect
C. Both are incorrect
D. I is incorrect, II is correct

84. Assertion I: Steroids help in asthma by reducing inflammation.

Assertion II: Steroids are used to increase mucus secretion.

A. Both statements are correct
B. I is correct, II is incorrect
C. Both are incorrect
D. I is incorrect, II is correct

85. The drug used for emergency relief in acute asthma is

A. Cetirizine B. Guaifenesin
C. Codeine D. Salbutamol inhalation

86. The drug used to relieve pain is

A. Sedative B. Analgesic
C. Antidepressant D. Antipsychotic

87. Morphine is a

A. Sedative B. Antipyretic
C. Opioid analgesic D. Antibiotic

88. The drug used to induce sleep is

A. Sedative B. Analgesic
C. Antibiotic D. Antipyretic

89. Diazepam belongs to ______ group.

A. Barbiturate B. Benzodiazepine
C. Opioid D. Antidepressant

90. The drug used for depression is

A. Analgesic B. Antipsychotic
C. Antidepressant D. Sedative

91. The antipsychotic drugs are used in

A. Anxiety B. Depression
C. Schizophrenia D. Pain

92. The drug used in epilepsy is

A. Phenytoin B. Paracetamol
C. Aspirin D. Ranitidine

93. The drug ______ is used as general anesthetic.
A. Diazepam B. Ketamine
C. Paracetamol D. Ibuprofen

94. The local anesthetic blocks ______ conduction.
A. Hormonal B. Nerve
C. Blood D. Enzyme

95. The drug used to treat anxiety is
A. Antipsychotic B. Antidepressant
C. Anxiolytic D. Antibiotic

96. The opioid drugs act on ______ receptors.
A. Alpha B. Beta
C. Dopamine D. Opioid

97. The side effect of opioids includes
A. Diarrhea B. Constipation
C. Hypertension D. Fever

98. The drug used in Parkinson's disease is
A. Levodopa B. Paracetamol
C. Aspirin D. Ranitidine

99. The drug used to reduce fever and pain is
A. Antibiotic B. Antidepressant
C. Analgesic D. Antipyretic

100. The drug ______ acts as antidepressant by increasing serotonin.
A. Diazepam B. Fluoxetine
C. Morphine D. Ketamine

101. Match the following:

Column I	Column II
A. Morphine	1. Antipsychotic
B. Diazepam	2. Analgesic
C. Fluoxetine	3. Antidepressant
D. Haloperidol	4. Anxiolytic

A. A-2, B-4, C-3, D-1 B. A-3, B-1, C-2, D-4
C. A-1, B-3, C-4, D-2 D. A-4, B-2, C-1, D-3

102. Match the following:

Column I	Column II
A. Phenytoin	1. Antiepileptic
B. Levodopa	2. Anesthetic
C. Ketamine	3. Analgesic
D. Paracetamol	4. Anti-Parkinson

A. A-1, B-4, C-2, D-3 B. A-2, B-1, C-3, D-4
C. A-3, B-2, C-4, D-1 D. A-4, B-3, C-1, D-2

103. Assertion I: Opioids relieve severe pain.
Assertion II: Opioids have no side effects.
A. Both statements are correct
B. I is correct, II is incorrect
C. Both are incorrect
D. I is incorrect, II is correct

104. Assertion I: Antidepressants improve mood.
Assertion II: They decrease neurotransmitters.
A. Both statements are correct
B. I is correct, II is incorrect
C. Both are incorrect
D. I is incorrect, II is correct

105. The drug used to control seizures is
A. Analgesic B. Antiepileptic
C. Antidepressant D. Antibiotic

106. The drug ______ is used for sedation and anxiety.
A. Haloperidol B. Diazepam
C. Fluoxetine D. Paracetamol

107. The drug used in psychosis is
A. Analgesic B. Antiepileptic
C. Antipsychotic D. Antibiotic

108. The local anesthetics act by blocking ______ channels.
A. Potassium B. Calcium
C. Sodium D. Chloride

109. The drug ______ is used for mild pain and fever.
A. Morphine B. Ketamine
C. Haloperidol D. Paracetamol

110. The sedation effect is produced by drugs acting on ______ system.
A. Cardiovascular B. Respiratory
C. Nervous D. Digestive

111. The drug used to reduce blood pressure is
A. Antihypertensive B. Analgesic
C. Antibiotic D. Antacid

112. The drug ______ is used as diuretic to remove excess fluid.
A. Atenolol B. Furosemide
C. Digoxin D. Nitroglycerin

113. The drug used to increase cardiac output is
A. Antibiotic B. Diuretic
C. Cardiac glycoside D. Antacid

114. Digoxin is used in
A. Hypertension B. Heart failure
C. Infection D. Pain

115. The drug used to dilate blood vessels is called
A. Vasodilator B. Antibiotic
C. Antacid D. Analgesic

116. Nitroglycerin is used in
A. Hypertension B. Angina
C. Diabetes D. Infection

117. The beta-blockers act by blocking _____ receptors.

A. Alpha B. Beta
C. Dopamine D. Histamine

118. The drug propranolol is a

A. Diuretic B. Vasodilator
C. Beta-blocker D. Antibiotic

119. The ACE inhibitors act by inhibiting ______ enzyme.

A. Renin
B. Angiotensin converting enzyme
C. Insulin
D. Histamine

120. The drug used to prevent clot formation is

A. Anticoagulant B. Antibiotic
C. Analgesic D. Antacid

121. Match the following:

Column I	**Column II**
A. Digoxin	1. Diuretic
B. Furosemide	2. Beta-blocker
C. Propranolol	3. Vasodilator
D. Nitroglycerin	4. Cardiac glycoside

A. A-4, B-1, C-2, D-3 B. A-2, B-3, C-4, D-1
C. A-1, B-4, C-3, D-2 D. A-3, B-2, C-1, D-4

122. Match the following:

Column I	**Column II**
A. Antihypertensive	1. Prevent clot
B. Diuretic	2. Reduce BP
C. Anticoagulant	3. Dilate vessels
D. Vasodilator	4. Remove fluid

A. A-2, B-4, C-1, D-3 B. A-3, B-2, C-4, D-1
C. A-4, B-3, C-2, D-1 D. A-1, B-3, C-2, D-4

123. Assertion I: Diuretics increase urine output.
Assertion II: Diuretics cause fluid retention.

A. Both statements are correct
B. I is correct, II is incorrect
C. Both are incorrect
D. I is incorrect, II is correct

124. Assertion I: Beta-blockers reduce heart rate.
Assertion II: Beta-blockers increase blood pressure.

A. Both statements are correct
B. I is correct, II is incorrect
C. Both are incorrect
D. I is incorrect, II is correct

125. The drug ______ is used to treat hypertension.

A. Paracetamol B. Atenolol
C. Ranitidine D. Loperamide

126. The drug used in angina reduces ______ demand.

A. Oxygen B. Blood
C. Glucose D. Enzyme

127. The anticoagulants act by preventing ______ formation.

A. Urine B. Acid
C. Clot D. Enzyme

128. The diuretics act on ______ to increase urine output.

A. Heart B. Liver
C. Kidney D. Brain

129. The side effect of diuretics may include

A. Dehydration B. Fever
C. Infection D. Pain

130. The drug used to reduce cholesterol is called

A. Antibiotic B. Analgesic
C. Antacid D. Hypolipidemic

131. Hormones are chemical substances produced by

A. Glands B. Organs
C. Cells D. Tissues

132. Insulin is used to treat

A. Hypertension B. Diabetes mellitus
C. Infection D. Pain

133. The hormone ______ regulates blood glucose level.

A. Thyroxine B. Insulin
C. Cortisol D. Estrogen

134. The deficiency of insulin leads to

A. Hypoglycemia B. Diabetes
C. Hypertension D. Obesity

135. The hormone thyroxine is secreted by

A. Pituitary B. Thyroid
C. Adrenal D. Pancreas

136. The drug used in hypothyroidism is

A. Insulin B. Thyroxine
C. Cortisol D. Estrogen

137. The corticosteroids are used for their ______ effect.

A. Antibacterial
B. Anti-inflammatory
C. Analgesic
D. Antipyretic

138. The hormone ______ is involved in stress response.

A. Estrogen B. Insulin
C. Cortisol D. Thyroxine

139. The oral contraceptives contain

A. Insulin B. Estrogen
C. Cortisol D. Thyroxine

140. The hormone ______ is used to treat infertility.

A. Estrogen B. Progesterone
C. Insulin D. Gonadotropin

141. Match the following:

Column I	Column II
A. Insulin	1. Stress hormone
B. Thyroxine	2. Female hormone
C. Cortisol	3. Metabolism
D. Estrogen	4. Blood glucose

A. A-4, B-3, C-1, D-2 B. A-3, B-4, C-2, D-1
C. A-2, B-1, C-4, D-3 D. A-1, B-2, C-3, D-4

142. Match the following:

Column I	Column II
A. Pancreas	1. Cortisol
B. Thyroid	2. Insulin
C. Adrenal	3. Estrogen
D. Ovary	4. Thyroxine

A. A-2, B-4, C-1, D-3 B. A-4, B-3, C-2, D-1
C. A-1, B-2, C-3, D-4 D. A-3, B-1, C-4, D-2

143. Assertion I: Insulin lowers blood glucose level.
Assertion II: Insulin increases glucose production.
A. Both statements are correct
B. I is correct, II is incorrect
C. Both are incorrect
D. I is incorrect, II is correct

144. Assertion I: Corticosteroids reduce inflammation.
Assertion II: They increase immune response.
A. Both statements are correct
B. I is correct, II is incorrect
C. Both are incorrect
D. I is incorrect, II is correct

145. The hormone used to increase calcium level in blood is
A. Calcitonin B. Insulin
C. Thyroxine D. Parathyroid hormone

146. An adverse drug reaction is
A. Desired effect B. Unwanted effect
C. Therapeutic effect D. Intended action

147. The term toxicity refers to
A. Safety B. Harmful effect
C. Benefit D. Normal action

148. The drug allergy is an example of ______ reaction.
A. Predictable B. Toxic
C. Hypersensitivity D. Therapeutic

149. The idiosyncratic reaction is
A. Common reaction B. Dose-related
C. Unusual reaction D. Predictable

150. The adverse drug reactions should be ______ to authority.
A. Ignored B. Reported
C. Stopped D. Avoided

151. Match the following:

Column I	Column II
A. Side effect	1. Dose related harmful effect
B. Toxic effect	2. Expected minor effect
C. Allergy	3. Unusual reaction
D. Idiosyncrasy	4. Immune response

A. A-2, B-1, C-4, D-3 B. A-3, B-2, C-1, D-4
C. A-1, B-3, C-2, D-4 D. A-4, B-2, C-3, D-1

152. Match the following:

Column I	Column II
A. Drug safety	1. Drug monitoring
B. Pharmacovigilance	2. Adverse effect
C. Toxicity	3. Immune reaction
D. Allergy	4. Safe use

A. A-4, B-1, C-2, D-3 B. A-2, B-3, C-4, D-1
C. A-3, B-2, C-1, D-4 D. A-1, B-4, C-3, D-2

153. Assertion I: Pharmacovigilance monitors drug safety.
Assertion II: It ignores adverse reactions.
A. Both statements are correct
B. I is correct, II is incorrect
C. Both are incorrect
D. I is incorrect, II is correct

154. Assertion I: High dose increases toxicity.
Assertion II: Low dose always causes toxicity.
A. Both statements are correct
B. I is correct, II is incorrect
C. Both are incorrect
D. I is incorrect, II is correct

155. The term ______ refers to safe use of drugs.
A. Toxicity B. Pharmacology
C. Drug safety D. Allergy

156. The monitoring of adverse drug reactions is called ______.
A. Pharmacodynamics B. Pharmacovigilance
C. Toxicology D. Pharmacokinetics

157. The allergic reaction involves ______ system.
A. Nervous B. Digestive
C. Cardiovascular D. Immune

158. The nurse should check ______ before administering drug.
A. Price B. Color
C. Expiry date D. Brand

159. The safe administration of drug requires following ______ rights.
A. Five B. Four
C. Three D. Six

160. The most important step in drug safety is

A. Storage B. Prescription
C. Administration D. Correct identification

161. Inflammation is a protective response to

A. Injury B. Disease
C. Infection D. All of these

162. The cardinal signs of inflammation include redness, heat, swelling and ______.

A. Pain B. Fever
C. Vomiting D. Fatigue

163. The redness in inflammation is due to increased ______.

A. Blood flow B. Lymph flow
C. Oxygen D. Enzymes

164. The swelling in inflammation is due to ______ accumulation.

A. Blood B. Fluid
C. Air D. Cells

165. The loss of function in inflammation is called

A. Rubor B. Tumor
C. Dolor D. Functio laesa

166. The cell injury may be reversible or ______.

A. Temporary B. Mild
C. Irreversible D. Partial

167. The most common cause of cell injury is ______.

A. Infection B. Hypoxia
C. Trauma D. Toxins

168. Hypoxia means deficiency of ______.

A. Blood B. Oxygen
C. Nutrients D. Enzymes

169. The necrosis is

A. Normal cell death
B. Programmed death
C. Accidental cell death
D. Reversible injury

170. The apoptosis is a form of ______ cell death.

A. Accidental B. Uncontrolled
C. Programmed D. Necrotic

171. Match the following:

Column I	Column II
A. Redness	1. Increased blood flow
B. Swelling	2. Chemical mediators
C. Pain	3. Fluid accumulation
D. Heat	4. Increased temperature

A. A-1, B-3, C-2, D-4 B. A-2, B-1, C-4, D-3
C. A-3, B-2, C-1, D-4 D. A-4, B-3, C-2, D-1

172. Match the following:

Column I	Column II
A. Necrosis	1. Oxygen deficiency
B. Apoptosis	2. Programmed death
C. Hypoxia	3. Cell injury response
D. Inflammation	4. Uncontrolled death

A. A-4, B-2, C-1, D-3 B. A-2, B-3, C-4, D-1
C. A-1, B-4, C-3, D-2 D. A-3, B-1, C-2, D-4

173. **Assertion I:** Inflammation is a defense mechanism.
Assertion II: Inflammation always causes harm.

A. Both statements are correct
B. I is correct, II is incorrect
C. Both are incorrect
D. I is incorrect, II is correct

174. **Assertion I:** Necrosis is irreversible cell death.
Assertion II: Apoptosis is uncontrolled process.

A. Both statements are correct
B. I is correct, II is incorrect
C. Both are incorrect
D. I is incorrect, II is correct

175. The most severe form of cell injury results in

A. Adaptation B. Reversible injury
C. Recovery D. Necrosis

176. A tumor is an abnormal mass of

A. Tissue B. Blood
C. Cells D. Fluid

177. The benign tumor is

A. Malignant B. Non-cancerous
C. Metastatic D. Invasive

178. The malignant tumor is

A. Localized B. Non-invasive
C. Cancerous D. Harmless

179. The spread of tumor to distant sites is called

A. Metaplasia B. Dysplasia
C. Hyperplasia D. Metastasis

180. The uncontrolled cell division is known as

A. Apoptosis B. Necrosis
C. Differentiation D. Neoplasia

181. The tumor ______ remains localized and does not spread.

A. Malignant B. Benign
C. Secondary D. Metastatic

182. The cancer causing agents are called ______.

A. Mutagens B. Pathogens
C. Carcinogens D. Antigens

183. Match the following:

Column I	Column II
A. Benign tumor	1. Cancer causing agent
B. Malignant tumor	2. Spread of tumor
C. Metastasis	3. Non-cancerous
D. Carcinogen	4. Cancerous

A. A-3, B-4, C-2, D-1 B. A-2, B-1, C-4, D-3
C. A-1, B-3, C-2, D-4 D. A-4, B-2, C-3, D-1

184. Assertion I: Benign tumors do not invade tissues.
Assertion II: Malignant tumors spread to distant sites.
A. Both statements are correct
B. I is correct, II is incorrect
C. Both are incorrect
D. I is incorrect, II is correct

185. The loss of normal control of cell growth leads to
A. Inflammation B. Necrosis
C. Infection D. Tumor formation

186. Anemia is a condition of decreased
A. WBC B. RBC
C. Platelets D. Plasma

187. The most common cause of anemia is
A. Infection B. Iron deficiency
C. Trauma D. Dehydration

188. The hemoglobin carries ______ in blood.
A. Carbon dioxide B. Nitrogen
C. Oxygen D. Hydrogen

189. The deficiency of vitamin B12 leads to ______ anemia.
A. Iron deficiency B. Aplastic
C. Hemolytic D. Megaloblastic

190. The increase in WBC count is called
A. Leukopenia B. Thrombocytopenia
C. Leukocytosis D. Anemia

191. The decrease in platelets is called ______.
A. Leukocytosis B. Anemia
C. Hemophilia D. Thrombocytopenia

192. The disorder of clotting is called
A. Anemia B. Leukemia
C. Hemophilia D. Thrombosis

193. Match the following:

Column I	Column II
A. Anemia	1. Bleeding disorder
B. Leukemia	2. Low platelets
C. Hemophilia	3. Cancer of blood
D. Thrombocytopenia	4. Low hemoglobin

A. A-4, B-3, C-1, D-2 B. A-3, B-4, C-2, D-1
C. A-1, B-2, C-3, D-4 D. A-2, B-1, C-4, D-3

194. Assertion I: Hemoglobin carries oxygen.
Assertion II: RBC do not contain hemoglobin.
A. Both statements are correct
B. I is correct, II is incorrect
C. Both are incorrect
D. I is incorrect, II is correct

195. The increase in RBC count is called
A. Anemia B. Leukemia
C. Thrombocytosis D. Polycythemia

196. Clinical pathology deals with study of
A. Diseases B. Laboratory tests
C. Drugs D. Surgery

197. The complete blood count (CBC) measures ______ components.
A. Blood B. Urine
C. Tissue D. Cells

198. The normal hemoglobin level in adults is about ______ g/dL.
A. 5–8 B. 8–10
C. 12–16 D. 18–22

199. The ESR test is used to detect
A. Infection B. Inflammation
C. Cancer D. Diabetes

200. The urine examination helps to detect ______ disorders.
A. Kidney B. Heart
C. Brain D. Lung

201. The blood sugar test measures ______ level.
A. Protein B. Fat
C. Glucose D. Enzyme

202. The normal fasting blood glucose is about ______ mg/dL.
A. 50–60 B. 70–100
C. 150–200 D. 200–300

203. Match the following:

Column I	Column II
A. Hemoglobin	1. Kidney function
B. ESR	2. Oxygen carrying
C. Blood sugar	3. Inflammation
D. Urine test	4. Glucose level

A. A-2, B-3, C-4, D-1 B. A-3, B-4, C-1, D-2
C. A-1, B-2, C-3, D-4 D. A-4, B-1, C-2, D-3

204. Match the following:

Column I	Column II
A. CBC	1. Kidney function
B. ESR	2. Liver function
C. RFT	3. Blood cells
D. LFT	4. Inflammation

A. A-3, B-4, C-1, D-2 B. A-2, B-3, C-4, D-1
C. A-1, B-2, C-3, D-4 D. A-4, B-1, C-2, D-3

205. **Assertion I:** ESR increases in inflammation.
Assertion II: ESR decreases in infection.
A. Both statements are correct
B. I is correct, II is incorrect
C. Both are incorrect
D. I is incorrect, II is correct

206. **Assertion I:** Blood sugar increases in diabetes.
Assertion II: Blood sugar is unrelated to metabolism.
A. Both statements are correct
B. I is correct, II is incorrect
C. Both are incorrect
D. I is incorrect, II is correct

207. The test used to assess kidney function is
A. LFT B. CBC
C. RFT D. ESR

208. The test used to assess liver function is
A. CBC B. LFT
C. RFT D. ESR

209. The decrease in hemoglobin indicates ______.
A. Leukemia B. Infection
C. Anemia D. Cancer

210. The urine may show glucose in ______ condition.
A. Hypertension B. Diabetes
C. Infection D. Anemia

211. Genetics is the study of
A. Cells B. Heredity
C. Tissues D. Organs

212. The unit of heredity is called
A. Cell B. Chromosome
C. Gene D. DNA

213. The DNA is located in ______ of cell.
A. Cytoplasm B. Nucleus
C. Membrane D. Ribosome

214. The chromosome is composed of ______.
A. Protein B. Lipid
C. DNA D. Enzyme

215. The normal number of chromosomes in human is
A. 23 B. 44
C. 46 D. 48

216. The ______ determines sex of individual.
A. Gene B. Chromosome
C. Hormone D. Cell

217. The XX chromosome represents ______.
A. Male B. Female
C. Both D. None

218. The XY chromosome represents ______.
A. Female B. Male
C. Both D. None

219. Match the following:

Column I	Column II
A. Gene	1. Carries genetic material
B. DNA	2. Hereditary unit
C. Chromosome	3. Contains DNA
D. Nucleus	4. Controls cell

A. A-2, B-1, C-3, D-4 B. A-3, B-2, C-4, D-1
C. A-1, B-3, C-2, D-4 D. A-4, B-1, C-2, D-3

220. Match the following:

Column I	Column II
A. Autosome	1. Expressed always
B. Sex chromosome	2. Requires two copies
C. Dominant gene	3. Determines sex
D. Recessive gene	4. Non-sex chromosome

A. A-4, B-3, C-1, D-2 B. A-3, B-4, C-2, D-1
C. A-2, B-1, C-4, D-3 D. A-1, B-2, C-3, D-4

221. **Assertion I:** Genes are located on chromosomes.
Assertion II: Genes do not control inheritance.
A. Both statements are correct
B. I is correct, II is incorrect
C. Both are incorrect
D. I is incorrect, II is correct

222. **Assertion I:** DNA carries genetic information.
Assertion II: Chromosomes lack DNA.
A. Both statements are correct
B. I is correct, II is incorrect
C. Both are incorrect
D. I is incorrect, II is correct

223. The dominant gene is expressed in ______ condition.
A. Homozygous only B. Heterozygous only
C. Both conditions D. None

224. The recessive gene is expressed in ______ condition.
A. Homozygous B. Heterozygous
C. Both D. None

225. The genetic material is transferred from parents to offspring through ______.
A. Cells B. Chromosomes
C. DNA D. Genes

226. Genetic disorders are caused by abnormalities in
A. Organs B. Cells
C. Genes D. Tissues

227. Down syndrome is caused by

A. Monosomy
B. Trisomy 21
C. Deletion
D. Mutation

228. The Turner syndrome is due to

A. XXY
B. XXX
C. XO
D. XY

229. The Klinefelter syndrome is represented by

A. XO
B. XY
C. XX
D. XXY

230. The sickle cell anemia is caused by mutation in ______.

A. WBC
B. Platelets
C. Plasma
D. Hemoglobin

231. The genetic disorder ______ is characterized by mental retardation and facial features.

A. Turner syndrome
B. Down syndrome
C. Hemophilia
D. Thalassemia

232. Hemophilia is a ______ disorder.

A. Blood clotting
B. Metabolic
C. Infectious
D. Hormonal

233. Match the following:

Column I	Column II
A. Down syndrome	1. XO
B. Turner syndrome	2. Trisomy 21
C. Klinefelter syndrome	3. XXY
D. Sickle cell anemia	4. Hemoglobin defect

A. A-2, B-1, C-3, D-4
B. A-3, B-2, C-1, D-4
C. A-1, B-3, C-2, D-4
D. A-4, B-2, C-3, D-1

234. Assertion I: Genetic disorders can be inherited.

Assertion II: Genetic disorders are always infectious.

A. Both statements are correct
B. I is correct, II is incorrect
C. Both are incorrect
D. I is incorrect, II is correct

235. The mutation refers to change in ______.

A. Cell
B. Tissue
C. Organ
D. Gene

236. Prenatal diagnosis is done to detect abnormalities in

A. Mother
B. Father
C. Fetus
D. Family

237. The test ______ is used to detect chromosomal abnormalities before birth.

A. ECG
B. X-ray
C. Urine test
D. Amniocentesis

238. Match the following:

Column I	Column II
A. Amniocentesis	1. Chromosomal analysis
B. Ultrasound	2. Imaging technique
C. Karyotyping	3. Early genetic test
D. Chorionic villus sampling	4. Amniotic fluid test

A. A-4, B-2, C-1, D-3
B. A-3, B-1, C-2, D-4
C. A-1, B-4, C-3, D-2
D. A-2, B-3, C-4, D-1

239. Assertion I: Prenatal tests help in early detection of disorders.

Assertion II: Prenatal testing has no risk.

A. Both statements are correct
B. I is correct, II is incorrect
C. Both are incorrect
D. I is incorrect, II is correct

240. The karyotyping is used to study ______.

A. Cells
B. Genes
C. Chromosomes
D. Tissues

EXPLANATORY ANSWERS

1. **B:** Pharmacology is study of drugs and their effects. It includes sources, actions, and uses. It is essential in healthcare.

2. **B:** Pharmacodynamics deals with effects of drugs on body. It explains mechanism. It studies response.

3. **C:** Pharmacokinetics includes absorption, distribution, metabolism, and excretion. It describes drug movement. It determines dose.

4. **A:** ADME explains drug journey in body. It affects effectiveness. It is key concept.

5. **B:** Distribution is movement of drug to tissues. It depends on blood flow. It affects action.

6. **B:** Liver is main site of metabolism. It converts drugs to inactive form. It helps elimination.

7. **D:** Excretion removes drug from body. Kidney is main organ. It prevents accumulation.

8. **B:** It studies effects of drug. It explains how drug works. It is action on body.

9. **A:** Side effects are unwanted effects. They occur along with therapeutic effects. They may be harmful.

10. **B:** Toxicology studies harmful effects. It deals with poisoning. It ensures safety.

11. **D:** Dose depends on age, weight, and condition. It ensures proper effect. It avoids toxicity.

12. **A:** Route affects absorption of drug. It determines onset of action. It influences effectiveness.

13. **C:** IV route delivers drug into vein. It acts rapidly. It is used in emergencies.

14. **B:** Analgesics relieve pain. They do not affect consciousness. They improve comfort.

15. **C:** Antipyretics reduce fever. They act on hypothalamus. They restore normal temperature.

16. **B:** Antibiotics kill or inhibit bacteria. They treat infections. They are widely used.

17. **C:** Sedatives induce sleep. They calm patient. They reduce anxiety.

18. **B:** Bioavailability refers to amount of drug absorbed. It reaches circulation. It affects efficacy.

19. **A:** Half-life is time for half drug elimination. It determines dosing interval. It is important concept.

20. **B:** First-pass effect occurs in liver. It reduces drug concentration. It affects oral drugs.

21. **B:** Adverse reaction is unwanted effect. It may be harmful. It needs monitoring.

22. **A:** Therapeutic index indicates safety. Higher value means safer drug. It compares toxic and effective dose.

23. **B:** Loading dose gives immediate effect. It raises drug level quickly. It is initial dose.

24. **B:** Maintenance dose keeps drug level constant. It ensures therapeutic effect. It prevents fluctuation.

25. **B:** Tolerance means reduced response to drug. Higher dose needed. It develops over time.

26. **B:** Drug interaction occurs when two drugs interact. It alters effect. It may be harmful.

27. **B:** Placebo has no active ingredient. It is used for comparison. It has psychological effect.

28. **B:** Contraindication means drug should not be used. It may harm patient. It is important safety measure.

29. **A:** Analgesic relieves pain, antipyretic reduces fever, antibiotic kills bacteria, sedative induces sleep.

30. **B:** Pharmacology studies drugs. Drugs can have side effects. Hence second statement is incorrect.

31. **C:** Chemotherapy refers to use of drugs to treat diseases, especially infections and cancer. It targets causative agents. It helps in recovery.

32. **B:** Antibiotics act against bacteria. They do not affect viruses. They are commonly used.

33. **C:** Resistance occurs when microbes adapt. They survive drug action. It reduces effectiveness.

34. **D:** Broad-spectrum antibiotics act against wide range of bacteria. They are useful in mixed infections. They are commonly used.

35. **B:** Narrow-spectrum antibiotics act against specific bacteria. They reduce side effects. They preserve normal flora.

36. **C:** Antifungal drugs treat fungal infections. They inhibit fungal growth. Example is amphotericin.

37. **B:** Antiviral drugs treat viral infections. They inhibit virus replication. They are specific.

38. **B:** Sulfonamides are antibacterial drugs. They inhibit folic acid synthesis. They treat infections.

39. **C:** Penicillin inhibits bacterial cell wall synthesis. It leads to cell death. It is bactericidal.

40. **B:** Tetracycline inhibits protein synthesis. It stops bacterial growth. It is bacteriostatic.

41. **B:** Streptomycin is used in tuberculosis. It is effective against Mycobacterium. It is combined therapy.

42. **B:** Chloroquine is used in malaria. It kills parasite. It is antimalarial drug.

43. **A:** Amphotericin B is antifungal. It treats severe infections. It is potent drug.

44. **A:** Acyclovir is antiviral. It treats herpes infection. It inhibits viral replication.

45. **C:** Combination therapy increases effectiveness. It reduces resistance. It improves outcome.

46. **A:** Superinfection occurs due to overuse. Normal flora is destroyed. It allows opportunistic infection.

47. **B:** Toxicity occurs at high dose. It can damage organs. Dose should be controlled.

48. **B:** Drugs should be given as per prescription. It ensures safety. It prevents errors.

49. **A:** Antibiotics treat bacteria, antifungals treat fungi, antivirals treat viruses, and antimalarials treat malaria.

50. **B:** Chemotherapy treats infections. Antibiotics do not act on viruses. Hence second statement is incorrect.

51. **A:** Antacids neutralize gastric acid. They provide relief in acidity. They are commonly used.

52. **B:** PPIs inhibit acid secretion. They act on proton pump. They reduce acidity effectively.

53. **C:** H2 blockers reduce acid secretion. They block histamine receptors. They treat ulcers.

54. **B:** Laxatives relieve constipation. They increase bowel movement. They are widely used.

55. **C:** Antiemetics control vomiting. They act on CNS. They prevent nausea.

56. **B:** Antidiarrheal drugs control diarrhea. They reduce motility. They prevent fluid loss.

57. **C:** Metoclopramide prevents vomiting. It increases motility. It acts centrally.

58. **B:** Omeprazole is proton pump inhibitor. It reduces acid secretion. It is used in ulcers.

59. **B:** Antacids neutralize acid. They increase pH. They relieve symptoms.

60. **B:** PPIs inhibit proton pump. It reduces acid production. It is effective therapy.

61. A: Antacid reduces acidity, laxative relieves constipation, antiemetic prevents vomiting, antidiarrheal controls diarrhea.

62. A: Omeprazole is PPI, ranitidine is H2 blocker, metoclopramide antiemetic, loperamide antidiarrheal.

63. B: Antacids neutralize acid. They do not increase acid secretion. Hence second statement is incorrect.

64. B: Laxatives increase bowel movement. They do not reduce it. Hence second statement is incorrect.

65. A: Sucralfate protects mucosa. It forms protective layer. It prevents ulcer damage.

66. B: Ranitidine blocks histamine receptors. It reduces acid secretion. It is H2 blocker.

67. B: Antidiarrheal drugs reduce intestinal motility. They slow movement. They control diarrhea.

68. C: Antacids may cause diarrhea or constipation. It depends on composition. It is common side effect.

69. A: Loperamide controls diarrhea. It reduces motility. It is effective drug.

70. B: Metoclopramide increases gastric motility. It improves emptying. It prevents vomiting.

71. B: Bronchodilators relieve bronchospasm by opening airways. They relax bronchial smooth muscle. They give quick symptom relief in asthma.

72. B: Salbutamol is a beta-2 agonist bronchodilator. It provides rapid relief from wheezing. It is commonly given by inhalation.

73. C: Antihistamines reduce allergy symptoms like sneezing and runny nose. They block histamine receptors. They are useful in allergic rhinitis.

74. A: Theophylline is a methylxanthine bronchodilator. It helps relax bronchial smooth muscle. It also improves diaphragmatic function.

75. C: Corticosteroids reduce airway inflammation in asthma. They decrease edema and mucus. They help prevent exacerbations.

76. C: Guaifenesin loosens sputum by thinning secretions. This makes cough more productive. It helps in chest congestion.

77. B: Antitussives suppress cough reflex. They are used for dry irritating cough. They should be avoided in productive cough if sputum needs clearance.

78. A: Codeine suppresses cough by acting on cough center. It is an opioid antitussive. It can cause drowsiness and constipation.

79. B: Decongestants reduce nasal swelling. They improve nasal airflow. They provide relief in common cold.

80. C: Bronchodilators relax bronchial smooth muscle. This opens the airways. It reduces wheezing and breathlessness.

81. A: Salbutamol is bronchodilator, cetirizine is antihistamine, codeine is antitussive, and guaifenesin is expectorant. This matches their common clinical uses.

82. A: Decongestant reduces nasal swelling, bronchodilator relieves bronchospasm, antihistamine relieves allergy, and steroid reduces inflammation. These are standard respiratory drug roles.

83. B: Antihistamines block histamine receptors and reduce allergic symptoms. They do not increase histamine action. Hence the second statement is incorrect.

84. B: Steroids reduce inflammation and airway hyperreactivity. They do not increase mucus secretion. Hence the second statement is incorrect.

85. D: Acute asthma needs quick bronchodilation. Inhaled salbutamol acts rapidly. It is used as a rescue medication.

86. B: Analgesics relieve pain without causing unconsciousness. They act on central or peripheral pathways. They are widely used in clinical practice.

87. C: Morphine is a strong opioid analgesic. It acts on opioid receptors. It is used in severe pain.

88. A: Sedatives induce sleep and relaxation. They depress CNS activity. They are used in anxiety and insomnia.

89. B: Diazepam is a benzodiazepine. It has sedative and anxiolytic effects. It is commonly used.

90. C: Antidepressants improve mood. They increase neurotransmitter levels. They treat depression.

91. C: Antipsychotics are used in schizophrenia. They control hallucinations and delusions. They act on dopamine receptors.

92. A: Phenytoin is antiepileptic. It stabilizes neuronal membranes. It prevents seizures.

93. B: Ketamine is a general anesthetic. It produces dissociative anesthesia. It is used in surgeries.

94. B: Local anesthetics block nerve conduction. They inhibit sodium channels. They prevent pain sensation.

95. C: Anxiolytics reduce anxiety. They calm CNS. Diazepam is an example.

96. D: Opioids act on opioid receptors. They relieve pain. They can cause dependence.

97. B: Opioids reduce bowel motility. They cause constipation. It is a common side effect.

98. A: Levodopa increases dopamine. It is used in Parkinson's disease. It improves movement.

99. D: Antipyretics reduce fever and pain. They act on hypothalamus. Paracetamol is common.

100. B: Fluoxetine increases serotonin. It is SSRI. It improves mood.

101. A: Morphine is analgesic, diazepam anxiolytic, fluoxetine antidepressant, haloperidol antipsychotic. This matches drug classification.

102. A: Phenytoin is antiepileptic, levodopa anti-Parkinson, ketamine anesthetic, paracetamol analgesic. This reflects their uses.

103. B: Opioids relieve severe pain. They have side effects like respiratory depression. Hence second statement is incorrect.

104. B: Antidepressants increase neurotransmitters like serotonin. They do not decrease them. Hence second statement is incorrect.

105. B: Antiepileptics control seizures. They stabilize neurons. They prevent abnormal firing.

106. B: Diazepam reduces anxiety and induces sedation. It acts on GABA receptors. It is widely used.

107. C: Antipsychotics treat psychosis. They reduce hallucinations. They act on dopamine pathways.

108. C: Local anesthetics block sodium channels. This prevents impulse conduction. It produces anesthesia.

109. D: Paracetamol is used for mild pain and fever. It has fewer side effects. It is widely used.

110. C: Sedatives act on nervous system. They depress CNS activity. They produce calmness.

111. A: Antihypertensives reduce blood pressure. They prevent complications. They are widely used in hypertension.

112. B: Furosemide is a loop diuretic. It increases urine output. It removes excess fluid.

113. C: Cardiac glycosides increase heart contraction. They improve cardiac output. Digoxin is example.

114. B: Digoxin is used in heart failure. It increases contractility. It improves circulation.

115. A: Vasodilators widen blood vessels. They reduce resistance. They lower blood pressure.

116. B: Nitroglycerin relieves angina. It dilates coronary vessels. It improves blood flow.

117. B: Beta-blockers block beta receptors. They reduce heart rate. They lower BP.

118. C: Propranolol is beta-blocker. It reduces heart workload. It is used in hypertension.

119. B: ACE inhibitors block this enzyme. They reduce BP. They prevent vasoconstriction.

120. A: Anticoagulants prevent clot formation. They reduce risk of thrombosis. They are important drugs.

121. A: Digoxin is cardiac glycoside, furosemide diuretic, propranolol beta-blocker, nitroglycerin vasodilator. This matches their use.

122. A: Antihypertensive reduces BP, diuretic removes fluid, anticoagulant prevents clot, vasodilator dilates vessels. These are correct matches.

123. B: Diuretics increase urine output. They do not cause fluid retention. Hence second statement is incorrect.

124. B: Beta-blockers reduce heart rate and BP. They do not increase BP. Hence second statement is incorrect.

125. B: Atenolol is beta-blocker. It lowers BP. It is used in hypertension.

126. A: Antianginal drugs reduce oxygen demand. They improve supply. They relieve chest pain.

127. C: Anticoagulants prevent clot formation. They reduce risk of thrombosis. They maintain blood flow.

128. C: Diuretics act on kidney. They increase urine output. They remove excess fluid.

129. A: Diuretics can cause dehydration. They lead to fluid loss. Monitoring is required.

130. D: Hypolipidemic drugs reduce cholesterol. They prevent atherosclerosis. They improve heart health.

131. A: Hormones are secreted by endocrine glands. They regulate body functions. They act through bloodstream.

132. B: Insulin is used in diabetes. It lowers blood glucose. It is essential hormone.

133. B: Insulin regulates glucose level. It promotes uptake of glucose. It prevents hyperglycemia.

134. B: Insulin deficiency leads to diabetes mellitus. Blood glucose rises. It needs treatment.

135. B: Thyroxine is secreted by thyroid gland. It regulates metabolism. It affects growth.

136. B: Thyroxine is used in hypothyroidism. It replaces deficiency. It normalizes metabolism.

137. B: Corticosteroids reduce inflammation. They suppress immune response. They are widely used.

138. C: Cortisol is stress hormone. It increases glucose. It helps body adapt to stress.

139. B: Oral contraceptives contain estrogen and progesterone. They prevent ovulation. They regulate cycle.

140. D: Gonadotropins stimulate ovulation. They are used in infertility. They act on gonads.

141. A: Insulin controls glucose, thyroxine regulates metabolism, cortisol is stress hormone, estrogen is female hormone. This matches endocrine functions.

142. A: Pancreas secretes insulin, thyroid secretes thyroxine, adrenal secretes cortisol, ovary secretes estrogen. This shows gland-hormone relation.

143. B: Insulin lowers blood glucose. It does not increase glucose production. Hence second statement is incorrect.

144. B: Corticosteroids reduce inflammation and suppress immunity. They do not increase immune response. Hence second statement is incorrect.

145. D: Parathyroid hormone increases calcium in blood. It acts on bone and kidney. It regulates calcium balance.

146. B: Adverse drug reaction is unintended harmful effect. It occurs at normal dose. It requires monitoring.

147. B: Toxicity refers to harmful effects of drugs. It depends on dose. It can damage organs.

148. C: Drug allergy is immune-mediated reaction. It is not dose dependent. It can be severe.

149. C: Idiosyncratic reaction is abnormal response. It is unpredictable. It varies among individuals.

150. B: ADRs must be reported. It improves drug safety. It helps in monitoring.

151. A: Side effect is expected, toxic effect is dose related, allergy is immune response, idiosyncrasy is unusual reaction. This classification is standard.

152. A: Drug safety ensures safe use, pharmacovigilance monitors drugs, toxicity causes harm, allergy is immune reaction. This links concept correctly.

153. B: Pharmacovigilance monitors adverse effects. It does not ignore them. Hence second statement is incorrect.

154. B: High dose increases toxicity. Low dose usually does not. Hence second statement is incorrect.

155. C: Drug safety ensures proper use. It reduces errors. It protects patient.

156. B: Pharmacovigilance monitors ADRs. It improves safety. It is essential in practice.

157. D: Allergy involves immune system. It produces hypersensitivity. It can be dangerous.

158. C: Checking expiry date prevents harm. Expired drugs may be ineffective or toxic. It is essential step.

159. A: Five rights include right patient, drug, dose, route, time. It ensures safety. It prevents errors.

160. D: Correct patient identification prevents errors. It ensures right drug. It is most important.

161. D: Inflammation is response to injury, infection, or tissue damage. It is protective. It helps healing.

162. A: Cardinal signs include redness, heat, swelling, and pain. Pain occurs due to chemical mediators. It indicates tissue damage.

163. A: Redness occurs due to vasodilation. Increased blood flow causes redness. It is early sign.

164. B: Swelling occurs due to fluid accumulation. It results from increased permeability. It leads to edema.

165. D: Loss of function is fifth sign. It results from tissue damage. It affects organ function.

166. C: Cell injury can be reversible or irreversible. Irreversible leads to death. It cannot recover.

167. B: Hypoxia is most common cause. It reduces oxygen supply. It affects cell metabolism.

168. B: Hypoxia means lack of oxygen. It affects cell function. It leads to injury.

169. C: Necrosis is uncontrolled cell death. It occurs due to injury. It causes inflammation.

170. C: Apoptosis is programmed cell death. It is controlled. It does not cause inflammation.

171. A: Redness due to blood flow, swelling due to fluid, pain due to mediators, heat due to temperature. These are classic signs.

172. A: Necrosis is uncontrolled death, apoptosis is programmed, hypoxia is oxygen deficiency, inflammation is response. This explains pathology.

173. B: Inflammation is protective. It does not always harm. It helps healing. Hence second is incorrect.

174. B: Necrosis is irreversible. Apoptosis is controlled process. Hence second is incorrect.

175. D: Severe injury leads to necrosis. Cells die permanently. It causes tissue damage.

176. C: Tumor is abnormal mass of cells. It results from uncontrolled growth. It may be benign or malignant.

177. B: Benign tumors are non-cancerous. They do not spread. They grow slowly.

178. C: Malignant tumors are cancerous. They invade tissues. They can spread.

179. D: Metastasis is spread of tumor. It occurs via blood or lymph. It is feature of malignancy.

180. D: Neoplasia is uncontrolled cell growth. It leads to tumor formation. It is abnormal process.

181. B: Benign tumors remain localized. They do not invade. They are less harmful.

182. C: Carcinogens cause cancer. They induce mutations. Examples include chemicals and radiation.

183. A: Benign is non-cancerous, malignant is cancerous, metastasis is spread, carcinogen causes cancer. This is standard classification.

184. A: Benign tumors do not invade tissues. Malignant tumors spread to distant sites. Both statements are correct.

185. D: Loss of growth control leads to tumor. Cells divide uncontrollably. It is pathological condition.

186. B: Anemia is due to reduced RBC or hemoglobin. It leads to decreased oxygen supply. It causes fatigue.

187. B: Iron deficiency is most common cause. It affects hemoglobin synthesis. It leads to anemia.

188. C: Hemoglobin carries oxygen from lungs. It supplies tissues. It is essential for metabolism.

189. D: Vitamin B12 deficiency causes megaloblastic anemia. It leads to large RBC. It affects DNA synthesis.

190. C: Increased WBC is leukocytosis. It occurs in infection. It indicates immune response.

191. D: Low platelets cause thrombocytopenia. It leads to bleeding. Platelets are essential for clotting.

192. C: Hemophilia is clotting disorder. It is genetic. It causes prolonged bleeding.

193. A: Anemia is low hemoglobin, leukemia is blood cancer, hemophilia is bleeding disorder, thrombocytopenia is low platelets. This classification is standard.

194. B: Hemoglobin carries oxygen. RBC contain hemoglobin. Hence second statement is incorrect.

195. D: Increased RBC is polycythemia. It increases blood viscosity. It affects circulation.

196. B: Clinical pathology focuses on lab investigations. It helps in diagnosis. It includes blood and urine tests.

197. D: CBC measures blood cells like RBC, WBC, and platelets. It gives information about health. It is basic test.

198. C: Normal hemoglobin is 12–16 g/dL. It varies with age and sex. It is important indicator.

199. B: ESR increases in inflammation. It is non-specific test. It helps detect disease.

200. A: Urine examination detects kidney disorders. It shows protein, sugar. It indicates renal function.

201. C: Blood sugar test measures glucose. It is important in diabetes. It shows metabolic status.

202. B: Normal fasting glucose is 70–100 mg/dL. It indicates normal metabolism. It is diagnostic parameter.

203. A: Hemoglobin carries oxygen, ESR shows inflammation, blood sugar measures glucose, urine test shows kidney function. This matches clinical use.

204. A: CBC measures blood cells, ESR shows inflammation, RFT checks kidney, LFT checks liver. These are standard tests.

205. B: ESR increases in inflammation. It does not decrease in infection. Hence second statement is incorrect.

206. B: Blood sugar increases in diabetes. It is part of metabolism. Hence second statement is incorrect.

207. C: Renal function test checks kidney function. It includes urea and creatinine. It assesses renal health.

208. B: Liver function test assesses liver. It measures enzymes. It detects liver disease.

209. C: Low hemoglobin indicates anemia. It reduces oxygen supply. It causes weakness.

210. B: Glucose in urine indicates diabetes. It occurs when blood sugar is high. It is diagnostic sign.

211. B: Genetics studies heredity and variation. It explains transmission of traits. It is important for inheritance.

212. C: Gene is basic unit of heredity. It controls traits. It is located on chromosome.

213. B: DNA is present in nucleus. It contains genetic information. It controls cell activities.

214. C: Chromosomes are made of DNA and proteins. DNA carries genetic code. It is essential for inheritance.

215. C: Humans have 46 chromosomes. They are arranged in 23 pairs. It is normal number.

216. B: Sex is determined by chromosomes. X and Y chromosomes decide gender. It is genetic mechanism.

217. B: XX represents female. Both chromosomes are X. It determines female sex.

218. B: XY represents male. Presence of Y chromosome determines male sex. It is key factor.

219. A: Gene is hereditary unit, DNA carries genetic material, chromosome contains DNA, nucleus controls cell. This explains genetic structure.

220. A: Autosome is non-sex chromosome, sex chromosome determines sex, dominant gene expressed always, recessive needs two copies. This shows inheritance.

221. B: Genes are on chromosomes. They control inheritance. Hence second statement is incorrect.

222. B: DNA carries genetic information. Chromosomes contain DNA. Hence second statement is incorrect.

223. C: Dominant gene expresses in both homozygous and heterozygous conditions. It masks recessive gene. It shows trait.

224. A: Recessive gene expresses only in homozygous condition. It requires two copies. It is masked by dominant.

225. D: Genes transfer traits from parents. They carry genetic information. They determine characteristics.

226. C: Genetic disorders arise from abnormalities in genes or chromosomes. They affect inheritance. They may be inherited or spontaneous.

227. B: Down syndrome is due to extra chromosome 21. It leads to developmental delay. It has characteristic features.

228. C: Turner syndrome has only one X chromosome. It occurs in females. It leads to infertility and short stature.

229. D: Klinefelter syndrome has XXY chromosomes. It occurs in males. It leads to infertility and gynecomastia.

230. D: Sickle cell anemia is due to mutation in hemoglobin gene. It alters RBC shape. It causes anemia.

231. B: Down syndrome causes intellectual disability. It has characteristic facial features. It is chromosomal disorder.

232. A: Hemophilia is clotting disorder. It causes prolonged bleeding. It is inherited condition.

233. A: Down syndrome is trisomy 21, Turner XO, Klinefelter XXY, sickle cell affects hemoglobin. This is standard mapping.

234. B: Genetic disorders can be inherited. They are not infectious. Hence second statement is incorrect.

235. D: Mutation is change in gene. It alters DNA sequence. It can cause disorders.

236. C: Prenatal diagnosis detects abnormalities in fetus. It helps early management. It improves outcomes.

237. D: Amniocentesis examines amniotic fluid. It detects genetic disorders. It is prenatal test.

238. A: Amniocentesis tests fluid, ultrasound is imaging, karyotyping studies chromosomes, CVS is early test. This matches diagnostic methods.

239. B: Prenatal tests detect disorders early. Some tests have risks. Hence second statement is incorrect.

240. C: Karyotyping studies chromosomes. It detects abnormalities. It is genetic test.

9. Medical Surgical Nursing

1. The respiratory system is responsible for
   A. Digestion B. Circulation
   C. Respiration D. Excretion

2. The normal respiratory rate in adults is ______ per minute.
   A. 8–10 B. 12–20
   C. 25–30 D. 30–40

3. The exchange of gases occurs in ______.
   A. Bronchi B. Trachea
   C. Alveoli D. Larynx

4. The disease characterized by inflammation of bronchi is
   A. Asthma B. Bronchitis
   C. Pneumonia D. Tuberculosis

5. The asthma is caused by narrowing of
   A. Alveoli B. Bronchi
   C. Trachea D. Larynx

6. The pneumonia is infection of ______.
   A. Bronchi B. Larynx
   C. Lungs D. Trachea

7. The tuberculosis affects mainly ______.
   A. Heart B. Lungs
   C. Liver D. Kidney

8. The COPD includes chronic bronchitis and ______.
   A. Pneumonia B. Asthma
   C. Emphysema D. Tuberculosis

9. The emphysema is characterized by destruction of ______.
   A. Bronchi B. Alveoli
   C. Trachea D. Larynx

10. The dyspnea means difficulty in ______.
    A. Breathing B. Walking
    C. Talking D. Sleeping

11. The cyanosis is due to decreased ______ in blood.
    A. CO_2 B. Oxygen
    C. Nitrogen D. Hydrogen

12. The hypoxia is deficiency of ______ in tissues.
    A. Blood B. Oxygen
    C. Glucose D. Protein

13. The oxygen therapy is used to treat ______.
    A. Fever B. Hypoxia
    C. Pain D. Infection

14. The device used to deliver oxygen is
    A. Catheter B. Mask
    C. Syringe D. Cannula

15. The oxygen is given through nasal cannula at ______ flow rate.
    A. 1–6 L/min B. 8–10 L/min
    C. 10–15 L/min D. 20–30 L/min

16. The sputum examination is used to detect ______.
    A. Infection B. Pain
    C. Fever D. Injury

17. The ABG analysis measures ______ in blood.
    A. Sugar B. Gases
    C. Protein D. Enzymes

18. The pH of blood is normally ______.
    A. 6.8–7.0 B. 7.35–7.45
    C. 7.5–8.0 D. 8.0–8.5

19. The respiratory acidosis is caused by ______.
    A. Hyperventilation B. Hypoventilation
    C. Fever D. Pain

20. The respiratory alkalosis is caused by ______.
    A. Hypoventilation B. Hyperventilation
    C. Infection D. Pain

21. Match the following:

Column I	Column II
A. Asthma	1. Infection of lungs
B. Pneumonia	2. Chronic airway obstruction
C. Tuberculosis	3. Bacterial infection
D. Emphysema	4. Alveolar destruction

A. A-2, B-1, C-3, D-4 B. A-1, B-2, C-4, D-3
C. A-3, B-4, C-1, D-2 D. A-4, B-3, C-2, D-1

22. Match the following:

Column I	Column II
A. Dyspnea	1. Low oxygen
B. Cyanosis	2. Blue discoloration
C. Hypoxia	3. Difficulty breathing
D. Cough	4. Reflex action

A. A-3, B-2, C-1, D-4 B. A-2, B-3, C-4, D-1
C. A-1, B-4, C-2, D-3 D. A-4, B-1, C-3, D-2

23. Assertion I: Oxygen therapy treats hypoxia.
Assertion II: Oxygen is harmful in all cases.
A. Both statements are correct
B. I is correct, II is incorrect
C. Both are incorrect
D. I is incorrect, II is correct

24. Assertion I: COPD is a chronic disease.
Assertion II: COPD is completely reversible.
A. Both statements are correct
B. I is correct, II is incorrect
C. Both are incorrect
D. I is incorrect, II is correct

25. The respiratory distress is indicated by ______.
A. Normal breathing B. Rapid breathing
C. Slow breathing D. No breathing

26. The tracheostomy is an opening in ______.
A. Lung B. Trachea
C. Bronchi D. Alveoli

27. The incentive spirometer is used to improve ______.
A. Circulation B. Respiration
C. Digestion D. Excretion

28. The chest physiotherapy helps in ______ removal.
A. Blood B. Air
C. Secretion D. Water

29. The pleural effusion is accumulation of fluid in ______.
A. Lung B. Pleural cavity
C. Bronchi D. Trachea

30. The pneumothorax is presence of ______ in pleural space.
A. Fluid B. Air
C. Blood D. Pus

31. The hemoptysis means coughing of ______.
A. Blood B. Sputum
C. Air D. Water

32. The orthopnea is difficulty in breathing when ______.
A. Standing B. Sitting
C. Lying D. Walking

33. The bronchodilators act by relaxing ______.
A. Cardiac muscle B. Smooth muscle
C. Skeletal muscle D. Intestinal muscle

34. The peak flow meter measures ______.
A. Lung capacity B. Blood flow
C. Heart rate D. BP

35. The tuberculosis spreads through ______.
A. Water B. Food
C. Air D. Contact

36. Match the following:

Column I	Column II
A. Pneumothorax	1. Fluid in pleura
B. Pleural effusion	2. Air in pleura
C. Hemoptysis	3. Blood in sputum
D. Dyspnea	4. Difficulty breathing

A. A-2, B-1, C-3, D-4 B. A-1, B-2, C-4, D-3
C. A-3, B-4, C-1, D-2 D. A-4, B-3, C-2, D-1

37. Match the following:

Column I	Column II
A. Nasal cannula	1. Measures lung function
B. Oxygen mask	2. Delivers oxygen
C. Ventilator	3. Mechanical breathing
D. Spirometer	4. Low flow oxygen

A. A-4, B-2, C-3, D-1 B. A-2, B-1, C-4, D-3
C. A-3, B-4, C-1, D-2 D. A-1; B-3, C-2, D-4

38. Assertion I: Pneumonia causes lung infection.
Assertion II: Pneumonia improves oxygenation.
A. Both statements are correct
B. I is correct, II is incorrect
C. Both are incorrect
D. I is incorrect, II is correct

39. Assertion I: Asthma is reversible airway disease.
Assertion II: Asthma causes airway narrowing.
A. Both statements are correct
B. I is correct, II is incorrect
C. Both are incorrect
D. I is incorrect, II is correct

40. The main function of lungs is
A. Digestion B. Respiration
C. Circulation D. Excretion

41. The heart pumps blood through

A. Respiratory system B. Circulatory system
C. Digestive system D. Nervous system

42. The normal pulse rate in adults is ______ per minute.

A. 40–50 B. 60–100
C. 100–120 D. 120–140

43. The blood pressure is measured using

A. Thermometer B. Sphygmomanometer
C. Stethoscope D. ECG

44. The normal blood pressure is around

A. 90/60 mmHg B. 140/90 mmHg
C. 160/100 mmHg D. 120/80 mmHg

45. The hypertension is defined as BP above

A. 90/60 B. 110/70
C. 120/80 D. 140/90

46. The hypotension is defined as low

A. Pulse B. BP
C. Temperature D. Respiration

47. The myocardial infarction is caused by

A. Infection
B. Injury
C. Blockage of coronary artery
D. Hypertension

48. The angina pectoris is due to

A. Increased oxygen
B. Decreased oxygen supply to heart
C. Infection
D. Trauma

49. The ECG is used to assess

A. Lung function B. Brain activity
C. Kidney function D. Heart activity

50. The tachycardia means

A. Slow heart rate B. Irregular rhythm
C. Fast heart rate D. Weak pulse

51. The bradycardia is heart rate less than ______ bpm.

A. 60 B. 80
C. 100 D. 120

52. The atherosclerosis is

A. Infection B. Narrowing of arteries
C. Tumor D. Bleeding

53. The thrombus is a

A. Fluid B. Clot
C. Gas D. Tissue

54. The embolism is caused by

A. Clot traveling B. Infection
C. Injury D. Fever

55. The heart failure is inability of heart to

A. Pump blood B. Produce blood
C. Filter blood D. Store blood

56. The edema is accumulation of ______.

A. Blood B. Air
C. Fluid D. Cells

57. The cyanosis indicates lack of ______.

A. Blood B. Oxygen
C. Glucose D. Enzyme

58. The cardiac output is product of heart rate and ______.

A. BP B. Stroke volume
C. Respiration D. Pulse

59. The drug used in angina is

A. Aspirin B. Digoxin
C. Insulin D. Nitroglycerin

60. The diuretics are used to reduce ______.

A. Pain B. Infection
C. Fluid overload D. Fever

61. Match the following:

Column I	Column II
A. Hypertension	1. Slow heart rate
B. Hypotension	2. High BP
C. Tachycardia	3. Low BP
D. Bradycardia	4. Fast heart rate

A. A-2, B-3, C-4, D-1 B. A-3, B-2, C-1, D-4
C. A-1, B-4, C-3, D-2 D. A-4, B-1, C-2, D-3

62. Match the following:

Column I	Column II
A. ECG	1. Blood pressure
B. Echo	2. Heart imaging
C. Angiography	3. Heart activity
D. BP	4. Vessel study

A. A-3, B-2, C-4, D-1 B. A-2, B-1, C-3, D-4
C. A-1, B-4, C-2, D-3 D. A-4, B-3, C-1, D-2

63. **Assertion I:** Hypertension increases risk of heart disease.

Assertion II: Hypertension is harmless.

A. Both statements are correct
B. I is correct, II is incorrect
C. Both are incorrect
D. I is incorrect, II is correct

64. **Assertion I:** MI occurs due to lack of blood supply.

Assertion II: MI improves heart function.

A. Both statements are correct
B. I is correct, II is incorrect
C. Both are incorrect
D. I is incorrect, II is correct

65. The heart has ______ chambers.
A. 2 B. 3
C. 5 D. 4

66. The right side of heart carries ______ blood.
A. Oxygenated B. Mixed
C. Nutrient rich D. Deoxygenated

67. The left ventricle pumps blood to
A. Lungs B. Brain
C. Body D. Heart

68. The pulmonary artery carries ______ blood.
A. Oxygenated B. Mixed
C. Nutrient rich D. Deoxygenated

69. The coronary arteries supply blood to
A. Brain B. Lungs
C. Kidney D. Heart

70. The cardiac arrest means
A. Slow heart
B. Fast heart
C. Weak heart
D. Sudden stoppage of heart

71. The CPR stands for
A. Cardiac pulse rate
B. Cardiopulmonary resuscitation
C. Cardiac pressure regulation
D. Circulatory process rate

72. The first step in CPR is
A. Breathing B. Chest compression
C. Check pulse D. Check response

73. The normal heart sound is
A. Lub-dub B. Tick-tock
C. Tap-tap D. Beat-beat

74. The murmur indicates
A. Normal flow B. Turbulent flow
C. Slow flow D. No flow

75. The valvular disease affects ______ of heart.
A. Muscle B. Nerves
C. Vessels D. Valves

76. Match the following:

Column I	Column II
A. Angina	1. Chest pain
B. MI	2. Heart attack
C. Atherosclerosis	3. Artery narrowing
D. Embolism	4. Clot movement

A. A-1, B-2, C-3, D-4 B. A-2, B-3, C-4, D-1
C. A-3, B-4, C-1, D-2 D. A-4, B-1, C-2, D-3

77. Match the following:

Column I	Column II
A. Diuretics	1. Reduce BP
B. Beta blockers	2. Reduce fluid
C. ACE inhibitors	3. Dilate vessels
D. Vasodilators	4. Reduce heart rate

A. A-2, B-4, C-1, D-3 B. A-1, B-2, C-3, D-4
C. A-3, B-1, C-4, D-2 D. A-4, B-3, C-2, D-1

78. Assertion I: CPR saves life.
Assertion II: CPR is not needed in cardiac arrest.
A. Both statements are correct
B. I is correct, II is incorrect
C. Both are incorrect
D. I is incorrect, II is correct

79. Assertion I: Atherosclerosis narrows arteries.
Assertion II: It improves blood flow.
A. Both statements are correct
B. I is correct, II is incorrect
C. Both are incorrect
D. I is incorrect, II is correct

80. The main function of heart is
A. Digestion B. Respiration
C. Circulation D. Excretion

81. The digestive system is responsible for
A. Respiration B. Circulation
C. Digestion D. Excretion

82. The process of breaking food into simpler substances is called ______.
A. Absorption B. Digestion
C. Assimilation D. Ingestion

83. The enzyme amylase helps in digestion of ______.
A. Protein B. Fat
C. Carbohydrate D. Vitamin

84. The stomach secretes ______ acid.
A. Sulfuric B. Nitric
C. Acetic D. Hydrochloric

85. The liver produces ____.
A. Insulin B. Bile
C. Enzyme D. Hormone

86. The bile helps in digestion of ______.
A. Protein B. Fat
C. Carbohydrate D. Vitamin

87. The pancreas secretes ______.
A. Bile B. Saliva
C. Digestive enzymes D. Hormones

88. The absorption of nutrients mainly occurs in ______.

A. Stomach B. Large intestine
C. Mouth D. Small intestine

89. The constipation is difficulty in passing ______.

A. Urine B. Stool
C. Gas D. Blood

90. The diarrhea is characterized by frequent _____ stools.

A. Hard B. Formed
C. Watery D. Bloody

91. The appendicitis is inflammation of _____.

A. Liver B. Appendix
C. Stomach D. Intestine

92. The gastritis is inflammation of ______.

A. Intestine B. Liver
C. Pancreas D. Stomach

93. The jaundice is due to increase in ______.

A. Hemoglobin B. Bilirubin
C. Protein D. Glucose

94. The hepatitis is infection of _____.

A. Kidney B. Heart
C. Liver D. Brain

95. The peptic ulcer is caused by ______

A. Virus B. Bacteria
C. Trauma D. All of these

96. The vomiting is forceful expulsion of ______.

A. Air B. Food
C. Blood D. Fluid

97. The dysphagia means difficulty in ______.

A. Breathing B. Swallowing
C. Walking D. Talking

98. The ascites is accumulation of fluid in ______.

A. Chest B. Abdomen
C. Brain D. Heart

99. The cirrhosis is chronic disease of ______.

A. Kidney B. Lung
C. Heart D. Liver

100. The melena is passage of ______ stools.

A. Red B. Green
C. White D. Black

101. Match the following:

Column I	Column II
A. Hepatitis	1. Liver disease
B. Gastritis	2. Stomach inflammation
C. Appendicitis	3. Appendix inflammation
D. Cirrhosis	4. Liver infection

A. A-4, B-2, C-3, D-1 B. A-3, B-4, C-1, D-2
C. A-1, B-3, C-2, D-4 D. A-2, B-1, C-4, D-3

102. Match the following:

Column I	Column II
A. Amylase	1. Fat digestion
B. Lipase	2. Protein digestion
C. Protease	3. Carbohydrate digestion
D. Bile	4. Emulsification

A. A-3, B-1, C-2, D-4 B. A-1, B-3, C-4, D-2
C. A-2, B-4, C-1, D-3 D. A-4, B-2, C-3, D-1

103. Match the following:

Column I	Column II
A. Constipation	1. Yellow skin
B. Diarrhea	2. Hard stool
C. Vomiting	3. Watery stool
D. Jaundice	4. Expulsion of food

A. A-2, B-3, C-4, D-1 B. A-3, B-2, C-1, D-4
C. A-1, B-4, C-3, D-2 D. A-4, B-1, C-2, D-3

104. **Assertion I:** Liver produces bile.
Assertion II: Bile helps in digestion of fats.

A. Both statements are correct
B. I is correct, II is incorrect
C. Both are incorrect
D. I is incorrect, II is correct

105. **Assertion I:** Diarrhea leads to dehydration.
Assertion II: Diarrhea increases fluid balance.

A. Both statements are correct
B. I is correct, II is incorrect
C. Both are incorrect
D. I is incorrect, II is correct

106. **Assertion I:** Jaundice causes yellow discoloration.
Assertion II: Jaundice decreases bilirubin.

A. Both statements are correct
B. I is correct, II is incorrect
C. Both are incorrect
D. I is incorrect, II is correct

107. The enzyme for protein digestion is ______.

A. Amylase B. Lipase
C. Protease D. Bile

108. The large intestine mainly absorbs ______.

A. Protein B. Fat
C. Vitamins D. Water

109. The normal pH of stomach is ______.

A. 1–3 B. 5–7
C. 7–8 D. 8–10

110. The gall bladder stores ______.

A. Enzyme B. Hormone
C. Acid D. Bile

111. The urinary system helps in removal of
A. Oxygen B. Nutrients
C. Waste products D. Hormones

112. The functional unit of kidney is called ______.
A. Neuron B. Nephron
C. Alveoli D. Glomerulus

113. The kidneys are located in ______ region.
A. Thoracic B. Pelvic
C. Cranial D. Abdominal

114. The urine is formed in ______.
A. Ureter B. Bladder
C. Kidney D. Urethra

115. The urine is stored in ______.
A. Kidney B. Ureter
C. Urethra D. Bladder

116. The process of urine formation is called ______.
A. Digestion B. Respiration
C. Filtration D. Circulation

117. The normal urine output in adults is about ______ ml/day.
A. 200–400 B. 500–800
C. 1000–1500 D. 2000–3000

118. The oliguria means urine output less than ______ ml/day.
A. 50 B. 100
C. 200 D. 400

119. The anuria means urine output less than ______ ml/day.
A. 200 B. 100
C. 150 D. 50

120. The polyuria means increased ______.
A. Blood B. Urine output
C. Respiration D. Pulse

121. The dysuria means difficulty in ______.
A. Breathing B. Walking
C. Urination D. Talking

122. The hematuria is presence of ______ in urine.
A. Pus B. Protein
C. Sugar D. Blood

123. The UTI stands for ______.
A. Upper tract infection B. Urinary tract infection
C. Ureter infection D. Urine toxic infection

124. The renal failure is failure of ______.
A. Heart B. Liver
C. Brain D. Kidney

125. The dialysis is used to remove ______.
A. Nutrients B. Oxygen
C. Hormones D. Waste products

126. Match the following:

Column I	Column II
A. Hematuria	1. Low urine
B. Dysuria	2. Painful urination
C. Polyuria	3. Blood in urine
D. Oliguria	4. Increased urine

A. A-3, B-2, C-4, D-1 B. A-2, B-1, C-3, D-4
C. A-1, B-3, C-2, D-4 D. A-4, B-2, C-1, D-3

127. Match the following:

Column I	Column II
A. Kidney	1. Stores urine
B. Ureter	2. Forms urine
C. Bladder	3. Carries urine
D. Urethra	4. Excretes urine

A. A-2, B-3, C-1, D-4 B. A-3, B-1, C-4, D-2
C. A-1, B-4, C-2, D-3 D. A-4, B-2, C-3, D-1

128. **Assertion I:** Kidneys filter blood.
Assertion II: Kidneys produce urine.
A. Both statements are correct
B. I is correct, II is incorrect
C. Both are incorrect
D. I is incorrect, II is correct

129. **Assertion I:** Dialysis replaces kidney function.
Assertion II: Dialysis produces hormones.
A. Both statements are correct
B. I is correct, II is incorrect
C. Both are incorrect
D. I is incorrect, II is correct

130. The stone in kidney is called ______.
A. Tumor B. Infection
C. Ulcer D. Calculus

131. The catheterization is insertion of tube into ______.
A. Kidney B. Ureter
C. Bladder D. Urethra

132. The prostate gland is present in ______.
A. Female B. Male
C. Both D. None

133. The nephritis is inflammation of ______.
A. Liver B. Lung
C. Brain D. Kidney

134. The proteinuria is presence of ______ in urine.
A. Blood B. Sugar
C. Fat D. Protein

135. The glycosuria is presence of ______ in urine.
A. Protein B. Blood
C. Ketones D. Glucose

136. The endocrine system regulates body through

A. Nerves B. Blood
C. Hormones D. Enzymes

137. The pituitary gland is called ______ gland.

A. Thyroid B. Master
C. Adrenal D. Pineal

138. The hormone insulin is secreted by ______.

A. Liver B. Pancreas
C. Kidney D. Heart

139. The insulin helps to regulate ______.

A. Protein B. Fat
C. Blood sugar D. Enzyme

140. The diabetes mellitus is caused by deficiency of ______.

A. Thyroxine B. Insulin
C. Cortisol D. Estrogen

141. The hyperglycemia means increased ______.

A. BP B. Sugar
C. Temperature D. Pulse

142. The hypoglycemia means decreased ______.

A. Protein B. Fat
C. Glucose D. Water

143. The thyroid gland secretes ______.

A. Insulin B. Thyroxine
C. Adrenaline D. Cortisol

144. The hypothyroidism is deficiency of ______.

A. Insulin B. Adrenaline
C. Cortisol D. Thyroxine

145. The hyperthyroidism causes ______ metabolism.

A. Decreased B. Normal
C. Absent D. Increased

146. The adrenal gland secretes ______.

A. Thyroxine B. Insulin
C. Estrogen D. Cortisol

147. The Cushing's syndrome is due to excess ______.

A. Insulin B. Thyroxine
C. Cortisol D. Estrogen

148. The Addison's disease is due to deficiency of ______.

A. Cortisol B. Insulin
C. Thyroxine D. Glucagon

149. The growth hormone is secreted by ______.

A. Thyroid B. Pituitary
C. Adrenal D. Pancreas

150. The gigantism is due to excess ______.

A. Thyroxine B. Insulin
C. Cortisol D. Growth hormone

151. Match the following:

Column I	Column II
A. Insulin	1. Metabolism
B. Thyroxine	2. Stress hormone
C. Cortisol	3. Blood sugar
D. Growth hormone	4. Growth

A. A-3, B-1, C-2, D-4 B. A-2, B-3, C-4, D-1
C. A-1, B-4, C-3, D-2 D. A-4, B-2, C-1, D-3

152. Match the following:

Column I	Column II
A. Diabetes mellitus	1. Low cortisol
B. Hypothyroidism	2. Low thyroxine
C. Cushing's syndrome	3. High cortisol
D. Addison's disease	4. High blood sugar

A. A-4, B-2, C-3, D-1 B. A-2, B-3, C-4, D-1
C. A-1, B-4, C-2, D-3 D. A-3, B-1, C-4, D-2

153. **Assertion I:** Insulin lowers blood glucose.
Assertion II: Insulin increases blood glucose.

A. Both statements are correct
B. I is correct, II is incorrect
C. Both are incorrect
D. I is incorrect, II is correct

154. **Assertion I:** Thyroxine regulates metabolism.
Assertion II: Thyroid has no role in metabolism.

A. Both statements are correct
B. I is correct, II is incorrect
C. Both are incorrect
D. I is incorrect, II is correct

155. The hormone glucagon increases ______.

A. Protein B. Fat
C. Glucose D. Water

156. The diabetes insipidus is due to deficiency of ______.

A. Insulin B. Thyroxine
C. Cortisol D. ADH

157. The goiter is enlargement of ______.

A. Pituitary B. Adrenal
C. Pancreas D. Thyroid

158. The hormone estrogen is secreted by ______.

A. Kidney B. Ovary
C. Liver D. Heart

159. The hormone testosterone is secreted by ______.

A. Ovary B. Thyroid
C. Pituitary D. Testis

160. The endocrine glands are ______ glands.

A. Exocrine B. Mixed
C. Tubular D. Ductless

161. The musculoskeletal system provides
A. Digestion B. Support and movement
C. Circulation D. Respiration

162. The bones are connected by ______.
A. Muscles B. Ligaments
C. Tendons D. Cartilage

163. The joint is formed between ______.
A. Muscles B. Bones
C. Nerves D. Vessels

164. The muscle is responsible for ______.
A. Protection B. Circulation
C. Movement D. Digestion

165. The ligament connects ______.
A. Muscle to bone B. Bone to bone
C. Bone to tendon D. Muscle to muscle

166. The tendon connects ______.
A. Bone to bone B. Muscle to bone
C. Muscle to muscle D. Bone to cartilage

167. The osteoporosis is
A. Joint inflammation B. Bone infection
C. Muscle injury D. Bone weakness

168. The fracture is break in ______.
A. Muscle B. Bone
C. Nerve D. Joint

169. The sprain is injury to ______.
A. Muscle B. Bone
C. Ligament D. Tendon

170. The strain is injury to ______.
A. Ligament B. Bone
C. Joint D. Muscle

171. The arthritis is inflammation of ______.
A. Muscle B. Bone
C. Joint D. Tendon

172. The osteoarthritis mainly affects ______
A. Muscles B. Joints
C. Nerves D. Skin

173. The rheumatoid arthritis is ______ disease.
A. Infectious B. Autoimmune
C. Genetic D. Nutritional

174. The gout is due to deposition of ______.
A. Calcium B. Cholesterol
C. Protein D. Uric acid

175. The dislocation is displacement of ______.
A. Muscle B. Bone
C. Joint D. Tendon

176. Match the following:

Column I	Column II
A. Ligament	1. Movement
B. Tendon	2. Bone to bone
C. Joint	3. Muscle to bone
D. Muscle	4. Junction of bones

A. A-2, B-3, C-4, D-1 B. A-3, B-2, C-1, D-4
C. A-1, B-4, C-2, D-3 D. A-4, B-1, C-3, D-2

177. Match the following:

Column I	Column II
A. Fracture	1. Bone break
B. Sprain	2. Ligament injury
C. Strain	3. Muscle injury
D. Dislocation	4. Joint displacement

A. A-1, B-2, C-3, D-4 B. A-2, B-1, C-4, D-3
C. A-3, B-4, C-1, D-2 D. A-4, B-3, C-2, D-1

178. **Assertion I:** Osteoporosis weakens bones.
Assertion II: Osteoporosis increases bone strength.
A. Both statements are correct
B. I is correct, II is incorrect
C. Both are incorrect
D. I is incorrect, II is correct

179. **Assertion I:** Arthritis causes joint pain.
Assertion II: Arthritis affects muscles only.
A. Both statements are correct
B. I is correct, II is incorrect
C. Both are incorrect
D. I is incorrect, II is correct

180. The main function of skeleton is
A. Digestion B. Respiration
C. Protection D. Support

181. The nervous system controls
A. Digestion B. Respiration
C. Coordination D. Circulation

182. The basic unit of nervous system is ______.
A. Neuron B. Nephron
C. Alveoli D. Osteon

183. The brain is protected by ______.
A. Skin B. Muscle
C. Bone D. Meninges

184. The spinal cord is located in ______.
A. Skull B. Chest
C. Abdomen D. Vertebral column

185. The cerebrum is responsible for ______.
A. Balance B. Respiration
C. Reflexes D. Thinking

186. The cerebellum controls ______.

A. Memory B. Thinking
C. Emotion D. Balance

187. The medulla controls ______.

A. Voluntary action B. Thinking
C. Movement D. Vital functions

188. The reflex action is ______.

A. Slow B. Voluntary
C. Controlled D. Involuntary

189. The meninges are ______ layers.

A. One B. Two
C. Four D. Three

190. The cerebrospinal fluid protects ______.

A. Heart B. Liver
C. Kidney D. Brain

191. The stroke is caused by ______ supply to brain.

A. Increased blood B. Decreased blood
C. Increased oxygen D. Decreased glucose

192. The paralysis is loss of ______.

A. Memory B. Speech
C. Movement D. Sensation

193. The epilepsy is characterized by ______.

A. Pain B. Infection
C. Fracture D. Seizures

194. The meningitis is inflammation of ______.

A. Brain B. Spinal cord
C. Nerves D. Meninges

195. The coma is state of ______.

A. Alertness B. Consciousness
C. Activity D. Unconsciousness

196. The GCS is used to assess ______.

A. Heart function B. Consciousness
C. Respiration D. BP

197. The aphasia is difficulty in ______.

A. Walking B. Talking
C. Breathing D. Sleeping

198. The hemiplegia is paralysis of ______.

A. Whole body B. One limb
C. Both limbs D. One side

199. The Parkinson's disease affects ______.

A. Heart B. Lungs
C. Liver D. Brain

200. The tremors are seen in ______ disease.

A. Diabetes B. Asthma
C. Hypertension D. Parkinson's

201. Match the following:

Column I	Column II
A. Cerebrum	1. Balance
B. Cerebellum	2. Thinking
C. Medulla	3. Protection
D. Meninges	4. Vital functions

A. A-2, B-1, C-4, D-3 B. A-1, B-2, C-3, D-4
C. A-3, B-4, C-1, D-2 D. A-4, B-3, C-2, D-1

202. Match the following:

Column I	Column II
A. Stroke	1. Infection
B. Epilepsy	2. Seizures
C. Meningitis	3. Loss of movement
D. Paralysis	4. Blood supply problem

A. A-4, B-2, C-1, D-3 B. A-2, B-1, C-4, D-3
C. A-1, B-3, C-2, D-4 D. A-3, B-4, C-1, D-2

203. Match the following:

Column I	Column II
A. Aphasia	1. Unconscious
B. Hemiplegia	2. Speech defect
C. Coma	3. Involuntary action
D. Reflex	4. One side paralysis

A. A-2, B-4, C-1, D-3 B. A-3, B-2, C-4, D-1
C. A-1, B-3, C-2, D-4 D. A-4, B-1, C-3, D-2

204. Assertion I: Stroke affects brain.
Assertion II: Stroke improves blood supply.

A. Both statements are correct
B. I is correct, II is incorrect
C. Both are incorrect
D. I is incorrect, II is correct

205. Assertion I: Epilepsy causes seizures.
Assertion II: Epilepsy is infectious disease.

A. Both statements are correct
B. I is correct, II is incorrect
C. Both are incorrect
D. I is incorrect, II is correct

206. Assertion I: Reflex is involuntary action.
Assertion II: Reflex requires conscious effort.

A. Both statements are correct
B. I is correct, II is incorrect
C. Both are incorrect
D. I is incorrect, II is correct

207. The neuron transmits ______.

A. Blood B. Impulses
C. Oxygen D. Nutrients

208. The synapse is junction between ______.

A. Bones B. Muscles
C. Cells D. Neurons

209. The spinal cord controls ______.

A. Thinking B. Reflexes
C. Emotion D. Memory

210. The main function of nervous system is

A. Digestion B. Respiration
C. Circulation D. Control

211. Communicable diseases are those diseases which can be transmitted from one person to another through

A. Air B. Water
C. Contact D. All of these

212. Tuberculosis is a communicable disease that primarily affects which organ of the body?

A. Heart B. Kidney
C. Liver D. Lungs

213. The causative organism of tuberculosis is

A. Virus B. Bacteria
C. Fungus D. Parasite

214. Malaria is transmitted by the bite of which mosquito?

A. Culex B. Aedes
C. Anopheles D. Housefly

215. The dengue fever is transmitted by which vector?

A. Anopheles mosquito B. Culex mosquito
C. Housefly D. Aedes mosquito

216. The human immunodeficiency virus (HIV) primarily affects which system of the body?

A. Respiratory system B. Digestive system
C. Nervous system D. Immune system

217. The vaccine BCG is used to prevent which disease?

A. Hepatitis B. Tuberculosis
C. Measles D. Polio

218. The disease cholera is caused by

A. Virus B. Bacteria
C. Protozoa D. Worms

219. The transmission of cholera mainly occurs through consumption of

A. Air
B. Contaminated food and water
C. Blood
D. Skin contact

220. Measles is a disease caused by

A. Bacteria B. Fungus
C. Parasite D. Virus

221. Which of the following diseases is transmitted through contaminated water?

A. Tuberculosis B. Malaria
C. Dengue D. Cholera

222. The hepatitis B virus is transmitted mainly through

A. Air B. Water
C. Food D. Blood and body fluids

223. The term 'carrier' in communicable disease refers to a person who

A. Shows symptoms
B. Has severe disease
C. Is immune
D. Transmits infection without symptoms

224. Match the following:

Column I	Column II
A. Tuberculosis	1. Water-borne disease
B. Malaria	2. Air-borne disease
C. Dengue	3. Mosquito-borne disease
D. Cholera	4. Protozoal disease

A. A-2, B-4, C-3, D-1 B. A-3, B-2, C-1, D-4
C. A-1, B-3, C-2, D-4 D. A-4, B-1, C-3, D-2

225. Match the following:

Column I	Column II
A. HIV	1. Blood transmission
B. Hepatitis B	2. Viral disease
C. Measles	3. Immune deficiency
D. Tuberculosis	4. Air-borne disease

A. A-3, B-1, C-2, D-4 B. A-2, B-3, C-1, D-4
C. A-1, B-2, C-4, D-3 D. A-4, B-3, C-2, D-1

226. Assertion I: Vaccination helps in prevention of communicable diseases.

Assertion II: Vaccination has no role in immunity.

A. Both statements are correct
B. I is correct, II is incorrect
C. Both are incorrect
D. I is incorrect, II is correct

227. Assertion I: Malaria is transmitted by mosquito bite.

Assertion II: Malaria spreads through air.

A. Both statements are correct
B. I is correct, II is incorrect
C. Both are incorrect
D. I is incorrect, II is correct

228. The isolation of a patient is done to prevent ______ infection of.

A. Treatment B. Spread
C. Cure D. Diagnosis

229. The incubation period refers to the time between

A. Treatment and recovery
B. Diagnosis and death
C. Exposure and symptoms
D. Infection and cure

230. The best method to prevent communicable diseases is

A. Surgery B. Medication
C. Observation D. Immunization

231. A burn is defined as injury to the skin caused by

A. Cold B. Pressure
C. Infection D. Heat

232. Burns are classified based on the depth of tissue damage into how many degrees?

A. One B. Two
C. Three D. Four

233. A first-degree burn affects only the

A. Dermis B. Muscle
C. Bone D. Epidermis

234. A second-degree burn affects both epidermis and

A. Muscle B. Dermis
C. Bone D. Nerve

235. A third-degree burn involves destruction of

A. Epidermis only B. Dermis only
C. Skin layers only D. Full thickness of skin

236. The most important complication of severe burns is

A. Hypertension B. Fever
C. Pain D. Shock

237. The rule of nine is used to estimate

A. Depth of burn
B. Cause of burn
C. Severity of burn
D. Percentage of body surface area burned

238. The immediate first aid for minor burns includes application of

A. Oil B. Ice
C. Ointment D. Cold water

239. Infection in burn patients occurs due to loss of

A. Blood B. Immunity
C. Protein D. Skin barrier

240. The fluid resuscitation in burns is important to prevent

A. Pain B. Infection
C. Fever D. Shock

241. Cancer is defined as uncontrolled growth of

A. Tissues B. Organs
C. Fluids D. Cells

242. The spread of cancer from one part of body to another is called

A. Mutation B. Metaplasia
C. Hyperplasia D. Metastasis

243. The common symptom of cancer includes

A. Pain B. Lump
C. Weight loss D. All of these

244. The carcinogens are substances that

A. Cure cancer B. Prevent cancer
C. Detect cancer D. Cause cancer

245. The biopsy is a procedure used to

A. Treat cancer B. Prevent cancer
C. Diagnose cancer D. Cure cancer

246. Match the following:

Column I	Column II
A. First-degree burn	1. Epidermis only
B. Second-degree burn	2. Dermis involvement
C. Third-degree burn	3. Full thickness
D. Rule of nine	4. Surface area estimation

A. A-1, B-2, C-3, D-4 B. A-2, B-1, C-4, D-3
C. A-3, B-4, C-1, D-2 D. A-4, B-3, C-2, D-1

247. Match the following:

Column I	Column II
A. Carcinogen	1. Drug treatment
B. Biopsy	2. Tissue examination
C. Chemotherapy	3. Cancer causing
D. Radiotherapy	4. Radiation treatment

A. A-3, B-2, C-1, D-4 B. A-2, B-1, C-4, D-3
C. A-1, B-4, C-3, D-2 D. A-4, B-3, C-2, D-1

248. **Assertion I:** Severe burns can cause shock.
Assertion II: Burns increase fluid loss.

A. Both statements are correct
B. I is correct, II is incorrect
C. Both are incorrect
D. I is incorrect, II is correct

249. **Assertion I:** Cancer cells grow uncontrollably.
Assertion II: Cancer cells follow normal regulation.

A. Both statements are correct
B. I is correct, II is incorrect
C. Both are incorrect
D. I is incorrect, II is correct

250. The radiation therapy is used to ______ cancer cells.

A. Increase B. Protect
C. Nourish D. Destroy

251. The chemotherapy involves use of ______.

A. Radiation B. Surgery
C. Drugs D. Hormones

252. The staging of cancer is done to determine

A. Cause B. Diagnosis
C. Prevention D. Extent of disease

253. The most common type of cancer is
A. Bone cancer B. Skin cancer
C. Liver cancer D. Brain cancer

254. The palliative care in cancer focuses on
A. Cure B. Diagnosis
C. Prevention D. Relief of symptoms

255. The grafting in burns is done to
A. Increase pain B. Reduce infection
C. Diagnose burn D. Replace skin

256. Emergency care is provided to patients who have
A. Chronic illness
B. Minor injury
C. Stable condition
D. Life-threatening condition

257. The primary survey in emergency includes assessment of
A. Nutrition
B. Elimination
C. Hygiene
D. Airway, breathing, circulation

258. The first step in emergency management is to assess the ______ of the patient.
A. Temperature B. Airway
C. Pulse D. BP

259. The term 'triage' refers to
A. Treatment B. Diagnosis
C. Prevention D. Prioritization of patients

260. Cardiopulmonary resuscitation (CPR) is performed in case of
A. Fever B. Infection
C. Injury D. Cardiac arrest

261. The ratio of chest compression to ventilation in adult CPR is
A. 15 : 2 B. 30 : 2
C. 10 : 2 D. 20 : 2

262. The shock is defined as inadequate ______ to tissues.
A. Oxygen B. Blood supply
C. Nutrients D. Perfusion

263. The hypovolemic shock is caused by
A. Infection B. Allergy
C. Cardiac failure D. Blood loss

264. The anaphylactic shock is caused by
A. Trauma B. Infection
C. Blood loss D. Severe allergic reaction

265. The septic shock is due to
A. Injury B. Blood loss
C. Dehydration D. Infection

266. The intravenous fluid is given to maintain ______.
A. Temperature B. Respiration
C. BP D. Circulation

267. The oxygen therapy is used to improve ______.
A. BP B. Pulse
C. Digestion D. Oxygenation

268. The defibrillator is used to treat
A. Fracture B. Stroke
C. Hypertension D. Cardiac arrhythmias

269. The ventilator is used to support ______.
A. Heart B. Kidney
C. Liver D. Respiration

270. The Glasgow Coma Scale is used to assess ______.
A. Pulse B. BP
C. Temperature D. Consciousness

271. The ICU stands for ______.
A. Intensive care unit B. Immediate care unit
C. Internal care unit D. Integrated care unit

272. The monitoring in ICU includes ______.
A. BP B. Pulse
C. Respiration D. All of these

273. The suctioning is done to clear ______.
A. Blood B. Fluid
C. Air D. Secretions

274. The intubation is insertion of tube into ______.
A. Esophagus B. Stomach
C. Nose D. Trachea

275. The emergency drug for anaphylaxis is
A. Atropine B. Insulin
C. Morphine D. Adrenaline

276. Match the following:

Column I	Column II
A. CPR	1. Clears airway
B. Defibrillator	2. Artificial breathing
C. Ventilator	3. Restores heart rhythm
D. Suction	4. Resuscitation

A. A-4, B-3, C-2, D-1 B. A-3, B-4, C-1, D-2
C. A-2, B-1, C-4, D-3 D. A-1, B-2, C-3, D-4

277. Match the following:

Column I	Column II
A. Hypovolemic shock	1. Allergy
B. Septic shock	2. Infection
C. Anaphylactic shock	3. Blood loss
D. Cardiogenic shock	4. Heart failure

A. A-3, B-2, C-1, D-4 B. A-2, B-1, C-4, D-3
C. A-1, B-4, C-3, D-2 D. A-4, B-3, C-2, D-1

278. Match the following:

Column I	Column II
A. Airway	1. Oxygenation
B. Breathing	2. Consciousness
C. Circulation	3. Blood flow
D. Disability	4. Open airway

A. A-4, B-1, C-3, D-2 B. A-1, B-3, C-2, D-4
C. A-2, B-4, C-1, D-3 D. A-3, B-2, C-4, D-1

279. Assertion I: Shock reduces tissue perfusion.
Assertion II: Shock improves circulation.
A. Both statements are correct
B. I is correct, II is incorrect
C. Both are incorrect
D. I is incorrect, II is correct

280. Assertion I: CPR is lifesaving.
Assertion II: CPR is not required in cardiac arrest.
A. Both statements are correct
B. I is correct, II is incorrect
C. Both are incorrect
D. I is incorrect, II is correct

281. Assertion I: Oxygen therapy improves oxygenation.
Assertion II: Oxygen therapy reduces oxygen level.
A. Both statements are correct
B. I is correct, II is incorrect
C. Both are incorrect
D. I is incorrect, II is correct

282. The emergency management aims to ______ life.
A. End B. Delay
C. Control D. Save

283. The term 'code blue' refers to
A. Infection B. Trauma
C. Surgery D. Cardiac arrest

284. The pulse oximeter measures ______.
A. BP B. Pulse
C. Temperature D. Oxygen saturation

285. The main goal of ICU care is to provide ______ support.
A. Basic B. Routine
C. Preventive D. Critical

286. The ear is the organ of hearing and
A. Vision B. Balance
C. Taste D. Smell

287. The external ear includes pinna and ______.
A. Cochlea B. Tympanic membrane
C. Auditory canal D. Ossicles

288. The middle ear contains ______.
A. Nerves B. Muscles
C. Fluids D. Ossicles

289. The inner ear contains cochlea and
A. Pinna B. Auditory canal
C. Semicircular canals D. Tympanic membrane

290. The tympanic membrane is also known as
A. Ear canal B. Eardrum
C. Cochlea D. Ossicle

291. The infection of middle ear is called
A. Otitis externa B. Otitis media
C. Otitis interna D. Labyrinthitis

292. The hearing loss is called ______.
A. Aphasia B. Dysphagia
C. Anosmia D. Deafness

293. The Meniere's disease affects
A. External ear B. Middle ear
C. Inner ear D. Nerve

294. Match the following:

Column I	Column II
A. Pinna	1. Hearing
B. Cochlea	2. Balance
C. Semicircular canals	3. Sound collection
D. Tympanic membrane	4. Vibration

A. A-3, B-1, C-2, D-4 B. A-2, B-3, C-1, D-4
C. A-1, B-2, C-3, D-4 D. A-4, B-3, C-2, D-1

295. Assertion I: The ear helps in maintaining balance.
Assertion II: The ear has no role in equilibrium.
A. Both statements are correct
B. I is correct, II is incorrect
C. Both are incorrect
D. I is incorrect, II is correct

296. The eye is the organ of
A. Hearing B. Vision
C. Smell D. Taste

297. The retina contains ______.
A. Blood vessels B. Nerves
C. Photoreceptors D. Muscles

298. The lens helps in ______.
A. Protection B. Nourishment
C. Blood supply D. Focusing

299. The glaucoma is characterized by increased ______ pressure.
A. Blood B. Intracranial
C. Arterial D. Intraocular

300. The cataract is opacity of ______.

A. Cornea B. Retina
C. Iris D. Lens

301. In geriatric nursing, the term "geriatrics" refers to the care and study of

A. Children B. Adults
C. Elderly people D. Newborns

302. In older adults, the most common risk factor for falls is

A. Poor hearing only
B. Muscle weakness and poor balance
C. Excess appetite
D. Increased hemoglobin

303. Occupational health mainly focuses on preventing illness related to

A. Home environment B. Workplace environment
C. School environment D. Community environment

304. The term "polypharmacy" means that a patient is taking

A. Only one medicine
B. Two medicines together
C. Herbal medicines only
D. Many medicines at the same time

305. In elderly patients, the common physiological change in skin is that the skin becomes

A. Thick and oily B. Thicker and darker
C. Thin and fragile D. Thick and moist

306. The nursing measure that best prevents pressure ulcers in a bedridden elderly patient is

A. Providing a high-protein diet only
B. Keeping the patient fasting
C. Restricting fluids strictly
D. Changing position regularly

307. Occupational hazards can include physical, chemical, and

A. Nutritional hazards
B. Financial hazards
C. Environmental hazards
D. Biological hazards

308. Match the following:

Column I	Column II
A. Noise exposure	1. Carpal tunnel risk
B. Dust exposure	2. Hearing loss risk
C. Needle-stick injury	3. Respiratory problem risk
D. Repetitive work	4. Blood-borne infection risk

A. A-2, B-3, C-4, D-1 B. A-3, B-2, C-1, D-4
C. A-4, B-1, C-3, D-2 D. A-1, B-4, C-2, D-3

309. Assertion I: Regular exercise helps older adults maintain mobility and balance.

Assertion II: Regular exercise always increases the risk of falls in older adults.

A. Both statements are correct
B. I is correct, II is incorrect
C. Both are incorrect
D. I is incorrect, II is correct

310. In occupational health, the correct use of personal protective equipment is important because it helps to

A. Increase exposure to hazards
B. Delay treatment
C. Reduce risk of injury and infection
D. Replace vaccination completely

311. The immune system is responsible for protecting the body against which of the following?

A. Injury only
B. Infections
C. Temperature changes
D. Hormonal imbalance

312. The primary function of antibodies is to

A. Produce energy B. Destroy red blood cells
C. Fight antigens D. Carry oxygen

313. The lymphocytes are mainly produced in which organ?

A. Heart B. Liver
C. Brain D. Bone marrow

314. The term immunity refers to the ability of the body to

A. Grow
B. Digest food
C. Maintain temperature
D. Resist disease

315. The natural immunity is also known as ______ immunity.

A. Acquired B. Active
C. Artificial D. Innate

316. The acquired immunity develops after exposure to

A. Food B. Water
C. Pathogens D. Air

317. The vaccine helps in developing which type of immunity?

A. Passive immunity
B. Artificial active immunity
C. Natural passive immunity
D. Natural active immunity

318. The allergy is defined as

A. Normal response
B. Reduced immunity
C. Exaggerated immune response
D. Absence of immunity

319. The anaphylaxis is a type of ______ reaction.

A. Mild B. Chronic
C. Slow D. Severe allergic

320. The antigen is a substance that

A. Produces energy B. Causes immune response
C. Carries oxygen D. Protects body

321. The antibody is produced by which cells?

A. RBC B. Platelets
C. T cells D. B cells

322. The HIV infection mainly affects which cells of immune system?

A. RBC B. Platelets
C. Neutrophils D. T helper cells

323. The autoimmune disease is a condition in which the body

A. Destroys pathogens only
B. Produces more hormones
C. Attacks its own cells
D. Increases immunity

324. Match the following:

Column I	Column II
A. Antigen	1. Immune response trigger
B. Antibody	2. Protection
C. Vaccine	3. Hypersensitivity
D. Allergy	4. Protein defense

A. A-1, B-4, C-2, D-3 B. A-2, B-3, C-1, D-4
C. A-3, B-2, C-4, D-1 D. A-4, B-1, C-3, D-2

325. Match the following:

Column I	Column II
A. Innate immunity	1. Antibody transfer
B. Acquired immunity	2. Natural defense
C. Active immunity	3. Immunological memory
D. Passive immunity	4. Antibody production

A. A-2, B-3, C-4, D-1 B. A-3, B-2, C-1, D-4
C. A-1, B-4, C-2, D-3 D. A-4, B-1, C-3, D-2

326. Assertion I: Vaccination helps in prevention of diseases.

Assertion II: Vaccination weakens the immune system.

A. Both statements are correct
B. I is correct, II is incorrect
C. Both are incorrect
D. I is incorrect, II is correct

327. Assertion I: Autoimmune diseases attack self-cells.

Assertion II: Autoimmune diseases improve immunity.

A. Both statements are correct
B. I is correct, II is incorrect
C. Both are incorrect
D. I is incorrect, II is correct

328. The hypersensitivity reaction is an example of

A. Normal immunity B. Weak immunity
C. Immune deficiency D. Excess immune response

329. The immunodeficiency refers to

A. Increased immunity
B. Normal immunity
C. Lack of immune response
D. Excess immunity

330. The function of lymph nodes is to

A. Pump blood B. Filter lymph
C. Produce bile D. Store oxygen

EXPLANATORY ANSWERS

1. **C:** Respiratory system performs gas exchange. It supplies oxygen and removes CO_2. It is vital for survival.

2. **B:** Normal adult respiratory rate is 12–20/min. It indicates adequate ventilation. It varies with age.

3. **C:** Gas exchange occurs in alveoli. They provide large surface area. Oxygen diffuses into blood.

4. **B:** Bronchitis is inflammation of bronchi. It causes cough and sputum. It affects airflow.

5. **B:** Asthma causes bronchial narrowing. It leads to wheezing. It is reversible.

6. **C:** Pneumonia is infection of lung tissue. It causes inflammation. It impairs oxygenation.

7. **B:** Tuberculosis mainly affects lungs. It spreads via air. It is chronic disease.

8. **C:** COPD includes bronchitis and emphysema. Emphysema destroys alveoli. It reduces gas exchange.

9. **B:** Emphysema damages alveoli. It reduces surface area. It causes breathlessness.

10. **A:** Dyspnea means difficulty breathing. It is common symptom. It indicates respiratory distress.

11. **B:** Cyanosis occurs due to low oxygen. It causes bluish skin. It indicates hypoxia.

12. **B:** Hypoxia is deficiency of oxygen in tissues. It affects organ function. It is serious condition.

13. **B:** Oxygen therapy corrects hypoxia. It improves oxygen supply. It is essential treatment.

14. **B:** Oxygen mask delivers oxygen. It provides higher concentration. It is commonly used.

15. **A:** Nasal cannula provides low flow oxygen. It is comfortable. It is used in mild cases.

16. **A:** Sputum test detects infection. It identifies organisms. It helps diagnosis.

17. **B:** ABG measures oxygen, CO_2, and pH. It evaluates respiratory status. It is important test.

18. **B:** Normal blood pH is 7.35–7.45. It maintains acid-base balance. It is tightly regulated.

19. **B:** Hypoventilation causes CO_2 retention. It leads to acidosis. It affects breathing.

20. **B:** Hyperventilation causes CO_2 loss. It leads to alkalosis. It alters pH.

21. **A:** Asthma causes obstruction, pneumonia infection, TB bacterial, emphysema alveolar damage. This explains diseases.

22. **A:** Dyspnea is breathing difficulty, cyanosis blue color, hypoxia low oxygen, cough reflex. These are symptoms.

23. **B:** Oxygen treats hypoxia. It is not harmful in all cases. Hence second is incorrect.

24. **B:** COPD is chronic and not fully reversible. Hence second statement is incorrect.

25. **B:** Tachypnea indicates distress. It shows increased effort. It is sign of hypoxia.

26. **B:** Tracheostomy is opening in trachea. It helps breathing. It is surgical procedure.

27. **B:** Spirometer improves lung expansion. It prevents complications. It enhances breathing.

28. **C:** Chest physiotherapy removes secretions. It improves ventilation. It prevents infection.

29. **B:** Pleural effusion is fluid accumulation. It compresses lung. It affects breathing.

30. **B:** Pneumothorax is air in pleural space. It collapses lung. It is emergency.

31. **A:** Hemoptysis is coughing blood. It indicates serious disease. It needs evaluation.

32. **C:** Orthopnea occurs in lying position. It is seen in heart failure. Sitting relieves it.

33. **B:** Bronchodilators relax smooth muscle. They open airways. They improve breathing.

34. **A:** Peak flow meter measures airflow. It assesses lung function. It is used in asthma.

35. **C:** TB spreads by air droplets. It is contagious. It requires isolation.

36. **A:** Pneumothorax air, effusion fluid, hemoptysis blood, dyspnea breathing difficulty. These define conditions.

37. **A:** Cannula low flow, mask oxygen, ventilator breathing, spirometer lung function. This matches equipment.

38. **B:** Pneumonia causes infection and reduces oxygenation. Hence second is incorrect.

39. **A:** Asthma is reversible and causes narrowing. Both statements are true.

40. **B:** Lungs perform gas exchange. They supply oxygen. They remove CO_2.

41. **B:** Heart pumps blood through circulatory system. It supplies oxygen and nutrients. It maintains life.

42. **B:** Normal pulse is 60–100 bpm. It reflects heart function. It varies with activity.

43. **B:** BP is measured using sphygmomanometer. It gives systolic and diastolic values. It is essential tool.

44. **D:** Normal BP is 120/80. It maintains perfusion. It is healthy range.

45. **D:** Hypertension is BP above 140/90. It increases risk of disease. It needs management.

46. **B:** Hypotension is low blood pressure. It reduces perfusion. It may cause shock.

47. **C:** MI occurs due to blockage. It stops blood supply. It damages heart muscle.

48. **B:** Angina is chest pain due to low oxygen. It is reversible. It indicates ischemia.

49. **D:** ECG records electrical activity. It detects abnormalities. It is diagnostic tool.

50. **C:** Tachycardia means rapid heart rate. It may be due to stress. It needs evaluation.

51. **A:** Bradycardia is <60 bpm. It is slow rate. It may be normal in athletes.

52. **B:** Atherosclerosis causes plaque formation. It narrows arteries. It reduces blood flow.

53. **B:** Thrombus is clot formed in vessel. It blocks flow. It can cause infarction.

54. **A:** Embolism occurs when clot travels. It blocks distant vessel. It is dangerous.

55. **A:** Heart failure is inability to pump. It causes fluid accumulation. It affects organs.

56. **C:** Edema is fluid accumulation. It occurs in heart failure. It causes swelling.

57. **B:** Cyanosis indicates low oxygen. It causes bluish color. It is serious sign.

58. **B:** Cardiac output = HR × stroke volume. It indicates heart performance. It is important.

59. **D:** Nitroglycerin relieves angina. It dilates vessels. It improves blood flow.

60. **C:** Diuretics remove excess fluid. They reduce edema. They are used in heart failure.

61. **A:** Hypertension high BP, hypotension low BP, tachycardia fast HR, bradycardia slow HR. These are definitions.

62. **A:** ECG heart activity, echo imaging, angiography vessels, BP measures pressure. These tests are used.

63. **B:** Hypertension increases risk. It is not harmless. Hence second is incorrect.

64. **B:** MI damages heart. It does not improve function. Hence second is incorrect.

65. **D:** Heart has four chambers. Two atria and two ventricles. It ensures circulation.

66. **D:** Right heart carries deoxygenated blood. It sends to lungs. It removes CO_2.

67. **C:** Left ventricle pumps blood to body. It supplies oxygen. It is strong chamber.

68. **D:** Pulmonary artery carries deoxygenated blood. It goes to lungs. It is unique.

69. **D:** Coronary arteries supply heart. They provide oxygen. Blockage causes MI.

70. **D:** Cardiac arrest is sudden stop. It is emergency. CPR is needed.

71. **B:** CPR restores circulation. It is lifesaving. It is emergency procedure.

72. **D:** First step is checking responsiveness. It ensures safety. Then CPR starts.

73. **A:** Heart sounds are lub-dub. They represent valve closure. They are normal sounds.

74. **B:** Murmur indicates abnormal flow. It may be due to valve defect. It needs evaluation.

75. **D:** Valvular disease affects valves. It alters flow. It causes murmur.

76. **A:** Angina pain, MI heart attack, atherosclerosis narrowing, embolism clot movement. These are conditions.

77. **A:** Diuretics reduce fluid, beta blockers HR, ACE inhibitors BP, vasodilators dilate vessels. These are actions.

78. **B:** CPR saves life. It is needed in arrest. Hence second is incorrect.

79. **B:** Atherosclerosis narrows arteries. It reduces flow. Hence second is incorrect.

80. **C:** Heart circulates blood. It supplies oxygen. It is essential function.

81. **C:** Digestive system breaks food into simpler forms. It helps absorption. It provides energy.

82. **B:** Digestion converts complex food into simple forms. It allows absorption. It is essential process.

83. **C:** Amylase breaks carbohydrates into sugars. It acts in mouth. It begins digestion.

84. **D:** Stomach secretes HCl. It kills bacteria. It activates enzymes.

85. **B:** Liver produces bile. It helps fat digestion. It is stored in gall bladder.

86. **B:** Bile emulsifies fats. It increases surface area. It aids enzyme action.

87. **C:** Pancreas secretes enzymes. It digests proteins, fats, carbs. It is important organ.

88. **D:** Most absorption occurs here. It has villi. It increases surface area.

89. **B:** Constipation is difficulty passing stool. It is due to low fiber. It causes discomfort.

90. **C:** Diarrhea involves watery stools. It leads to dehydration. It needs management.

91. **B:** Appendicitis is inflammation. It causes pain. It may need surgery.

92. **D:** Gastritis is inflammation of stomach lining. It causes pain. It may be due to infection.

93. **B:** Jaundice occurs due to bilirubin increase. It causes yellow color. It indicates liver disease.

94. **C:** Hepatitis affects liver. It causes inflammation. It may be viral.

95. **D:** Ulcers can be due to bacteria, stress, drugs. Multiple causes exist. It damages lining.

96. **B:** Vomiting expels stomach contents. It is protective reflex. It may cause dehydration.

97. **B:** Dysphagia means difficulty swallowing. It may be neurological. It needs evaluation.

98. **B:** Ascites is fluid in abdomen. It occurs in liver disease. It causes distension.

99. **D:** Cirrhosis is chronic liver damage. It leads to fibrosis. It affects function.

100. **D:** Melena is black stool. It indicates upper GI bleeding. It needs attention.

101. **A:** Hepatitis liver infection, gastritis stomach, appendicitis appendix, cirrhosis liver disease. These are definitions.

102. **A:** Amylase carbs, lipase fats, protease proteins, bile emulsifies. This is digestion process.

103. **A:** Constipation hard stool, diarrhea watery, vomiting expulsion, jaundice yellow skin. These are signs.

104. **A:** Liver produces bile and bile digests fats. Both statements are true.

105. **B:**Diarrhea causes dehydration. It does not increase fluids. Hence second is incorrect.

106. **B:** Jaundice increases bilirubin. It does not decrease. Hence second is incorrect.

107. **C:** Protease digests proteins. It breaks them into amino acids. It is secreted by pancreas.

108. **D:** Large intestine absorbs water. It forms stool. It maintains balance.

109. **A:** Stomach is acidic. Low pH helps digestion. It kills microbes.

110. **D:** Gall bladder stores bile. It releases during digestion. It aids fat digestion.

111. **C:** Urinary system removes metabolic wastes. It maintains fluid balance. It regulates electrolytes.

112. B: Nephron is functional unit of kidney. It filters blood. It forms urine.

113. D: Kidneys are in abdominal region. They lie retroperitoneal. They filter blood.

114. C: Urine is formed in kidneys. It results from filtration. It is excretory process.

115. D: Bladder stores urine. It holds until voiding. It expands as needed.

116. C: Urine formation begins with filtration. Blood is filtered in glomerulus. It forms filtrate.

117. C: Normal urine output is about 1–1.5 L/day. It varies with intake. It indicates kidney function.

118. D: Oliguria is <400 ml/day. It indicates reduced output. It suggests kidney problem.

119. D: Anuria is <50 ml/day. It is severe condition. It indicates renal failure.

120. B: Polyuria is increased urine output. It occurs in diabetes. It causes dehydration.

121. C: Dysuria is painful urination. It occurs in infection. It causes discomfort.

122. D: Hematuria is blood in urine. It indicates pathology. It needs investigation.

123. B: UTI affects urinary tract. It causes pain and burning. It is common.

124. D: Renal failure is kidney failure. It leads to waste accumulation. It needs dialysis.

125. D: Dialysis removes wastes. It substitutes kidney function. It maintains balance.

126. A: Hematuria blood, dysuria painful urination, polyuria increased urine, oliguria low urine. These are conditions.

127. A: Kidney forms urine, ureter carries, bladder stores, urethra excretes. This is flow.

128. A: Kidneys filter blood and produce urine. Both functions are correct.

129. B: Dialysis replaces function. It does not produce hormones. Hence second is incorrect.

130. D: Kidney stones are called calculi. They cause pain. They obstruct flow.

131. D: Catheter is inserted through urethra. It drains urine. It is nursing procedure.

132. B: Prostate is male gland. It surrounds urethra. It affects urination.

133. D: Nephritis is kidney inflammation. It affects function. It may cause proteinuria.

134. D: Proteinuria indicates protein in urine. It shows kidney damage. It needs evaluation.

135. D: Glycosuria is glucose in urine. It occurs in diabetes. It indicates hyperglycemia.

136. C: Endocrine system uses hormones for regulation. They act through blood. They control body functions.

137. B: Pituitary is master gland. It controls other glands. It secretes many hormones.

138. B: Insulin is secreted by pancreas. It regulates glucose. It is essential hormone.

139. C: Insulin lowers blood sugar. It helps glucose uptake. It maintains balance.

140. B: Diabetes mellitus is due to insulin deficiency. It leads to hyperglycemia. It needs treatment.

141. B: Hyperglycemia is high blood sugar. It occurs in diabetes. It causes complications.

142. C: Hypoglycemia is low glucose. It causes dizziness. It needs correction.

143. B: Thyroid secretes thyroxine. It controls metabolism. It affects growth.

144. D: Hypothyroidism is low thyroxine. It slows metabolism. It causes weight gain.

145. D: Hyperthyroidism increases metabolism. It causes weight loss. It increases heart rate.

146. D: Adrenal secretes cortisol. It is stress hormone. It regulates metabolism.

147. C: Cushing's is excess cortisol. It causes obesity. It affects metabolism.

148. A: Addison's is cortisol deficiency. It causes weakness. It is serious condition.

149. B: Growth hormone is from pituitary. It controls growth. It affects height.

150. D: Excess GH causes gigantism. It leads to abnormal growth. It occurs in childhood.

151. A: Insulin sugar, thyroxine metabolism, cortisol stress, GH growth. These are functions.

152. A: Diabetes high sugar, hypothyroid low thyroxine, Cushing high cortisol, Addison low cortisol. These are disorders.

153. B: Insulin lowers glucose. It does not increase. Hence second is incorrect.

154. B: Thyroxine regulates metabolism. Thyroid is essential. Hence second is incorrect.

155. C: Glucagon raises glucose. It acts opposite to insulin. It increases blood sugar.

156. D: Diabetes insipidus is due to ADH deficiency. It causes polyuria. It leads to dehydration.

157. D: Goiter is thyroid enlargement. It occurs in iodine deficiency. It causes swelling.

158. B: Estrogen is female hormone. It controls reproduction. It affects secondary characters.

159. D: Testosterone is male hormone. It controls male traits. It is produced in testes.

160. D: Endocrine glands have no ducts. They release hormones into blood. They act distantly.

161. B: Musculoskeletal system provides structure and movement. Bones support body. Muscles help movement.

162. B: Ligaments connect bone to bone. They stabilize joints. They prevent excessive movement.

163. B: Joints are formed between bones. They allow movement. They provide flexibility.

164. C: Muscles contract to produce movement. They work with bones. They enable actions.

165. B: Ligaments join bones. They maintain stability. They support joints.

166. B: Tendons connect muscles to bones. They transmit force. They enable movement.

167. D: Osteoporosis reduces bone density. It weakens bones. It increases fracture risk.

168. B: Fracture is break in bone. It may be complete or partial. It needs immobilization.

169. C: Sprain is ligament injury. It occurs due to twisting. It causes pain and swelling.

170. D: Strain is muscle injury. It occurs due to overuse. It causes pain.

171. C: Arthritis is joint inflammation. It causes pain and stiffness. It affects mobility.

172. B: Osteoarthritis affects joints. It causes degeneration. It is common in elderly.

173. B: Rheumatoid arthritis is autoimmune. Body attacks joints. It causes inflammation.

174. D: Gout is due to uric acid crystals. It causes severe pain. It affects joints.

175. C: Dislocation is displacement of joint. It causes deformity. It needs reduction.

176. A: Ligament bone-bone, tendon muscle-bone, joint junction, muscle movement. These define structures.

177. A: Fracture bone break, sprain ligament, strain muscle, dislocation joint. These are injuries.

178. B: Osteoporosis weakens bones. It does not increase strength. Hence second is incorrect.

179. B: Arthritis affects joints. It causes pain. It does not affect only muscles.

180. D: Skeleton supports body. It protects organs. It helps movement.

181. C: Nervous system coordinates body activities. It controls responses. It maintains balance.

182. A: Neuron is basic unit. It transmits impulses. It controls functions.

183. D: Brain is protected by meninges. They cover brain. They provide safety.

184. D: Spinal cord lies in vertebral column. It is protected. It conducts impulses.

185. D: Cerebrum controls thinking. It manages memory. It handles voluntary actions.

186. D: Cerebellum controls balance. It coordinates movement. It maintains posture.

187. D: Medulla controls vital functions. It regulates breathing. It controls heart rate.

188. D: Reflex is automatic action. It does not require thinking. It is rapid.

189. D: Meninges have three layers. They protect brain. They include dura, arachnoid, pia.

190. D: CSF protects brain. It cushions it. It maintains pressure.

191. B: Stroke occurs due to reduced blood flow. It damages brain. It causes paralysis.

192. C: Paralysis is loss of movement. It may affect body parts. It is serious.

193. D: Epilepsy causes seizures. It is neurological disorder. It needs treatment.

194. D: Meningitis is inflammation of meninges. It is infection. It causes fever.

195. D: Coma is unconscious state. Patient is unresponsive. It needs care.

196. B: GCS assesses consciousness. It evaluates response. It is clinical tool.

197. B: Aphasia affects speech. It occurs in stroke. It impairs communication.

198. D: Hemiplegia affects one side. It occurs in stroke. It causes disability.

199. D: Parkinson's affects brain. It affects movement. It causes tremors.

200. D: Tremors are symptom of Parkinson's. It is neurodegenerative. It affects movement.

201. A: Cerebrum thinking, cerebellum balance, medulla vital, meninges protection. These are functions.

202. A: Stroke blood supply, epilepsy seizures, meningitis infection, paralysis movement loss. These are disorders.

203. A: Aphasia speech, hemiplegia one side, coma unconscious, reflex involuntary. These are definitions.

204. B: Stroke reduces blood supply. It damages brain. Hence second is incorrect.

205. B: Epilepsy causes seizures. It is not infectious. Hence second is incorrect.

206. B: Reflex is involuntary. It does not need conscious effort. Hence second is incorrect.

207. B: Neurons transmit impulses. They carry signals. They control actions.

208. D: Synapse is junction between neurons. It transmits signals. It is functional unit.

209. B: Spinal cord controls reflexes. It gives quick response. It bypasses brain.

210. D: Nervous system controls body. It coordinates activities. It maintains homeostasis.

211. D: Communicable diseases spread through air, water, and contact. Multiple routes exist. Prevention requires hygiene.

212. D: Tuberculosis mainly affects lungs. It spreads via droplets. It causes chronic infection.

213. B: TB is caused by Mycobacterium tuberculosis. It is bacterial disease. It needs antibiotics.

214. C: Malaria is transmitted by female Anopheles mosquito. It carries parasite. It spreads infection.

215. D: Dengue is spread by Aedes mosquito. It breeds in clean water. It causes fever.

216. D: HIV attacks immune system. It reduces resistance. It leads to AIDS.

217. B: BCG vaccine protects against TB. It is given in childhood. It provides immunity.

218. B: Cholera is caused by Vibrio cholerae. It spreads through contaminated water. It causes diarrhea.

219. B: Cholera spreads through contaminated food. It is water-borne. Hygiene prevents it.

220. D: Measles is viral disease. It spreads by air. It is preventable by vaccine.

221. D: Cholera spreads through water. It causes diarrhea. It is preventable.

222. D: Hepatitis B spreads through blood. It includes transfusion and needles. It is infectious.

223. D: Carrier has no symptoms. It spreads disease. It is important in epidemiology.

224. A: TB airborne, malaria protozoal, dengue mosquito, cholera water-borne. These are transmission types.

225. A: HIV immune deficiency, hepatitis blood, measles viral, TB airborne. These define diseases.

226. B: Vaccination provides immunity. It prevents disease. Hence second is incorrect.

227. B: Malaria spreads by mosquito. It is not airborne. Hence second is incorrect.

228. B: Isolation prevents spread. It protects others. It controls infection.

229. C: Incubation is time between exposure and symptoms. It varies by disease. It helps diagnosis.

230. D: Immunization prevents disease. It builds immunity. It is effective method.

231. D: Burns are injuries caused by heat, chemicals, or radiation. Heat is most common cause. It damages skin.

232. C: Burns are classified into first, second, and third degree. It depends on depth. It guides treatment.

233. D: First-degree burn affects epidermis only. It causes redness. It heals quickly.

234. B: Second-degree burn involves dermis. It causes blisters. It is more severe.

235. D: Third-degree burn destroys entire skin. It may affect deeper tissues. It needs grafting.

236. D: Severe burns cause fluid loss. It leads to shock. It is life-threatening.

237. D: Rule of nine estimates burn area. It helps management. It guides fluid therapy.

238. D: Cold water cools burn. It reduces damage. It is first aid.

239. D: Skin protects body. Burns destroy barrier. It increases infection risk.

240. D: Fluid loss in burns causes shock. Resuscitation prevents it. It maintains circulation.

241. D: Cancer is uncontrolled cell growth. It forms tumor. It invades tissues.

242. D: Metastasis is spread of cancer. It occurs via blood. It worsens prognosis.

243. D: Cancer shows multiple symptoms. Pain, lump, weight loss occur. Early detection is important.

244. D: Carcinogens cause cancer. They damage DNA. Examples include chemicals.

245. C: Biopsy examines tissue. It confirms diagnosis. It is important test.

246. A: First epidermis, second dermis, third full thickness, rule of nine area. This shows classification.

247. A: Carcinogen causes cancer, biopsy diagnosis, chemo drugs, radiotherapy radiation. These are treatments.

248. A: Burns cause fluid loss leading to shock. Both statements are true.

249. B: Cancer cells grow uncontrollably. They are abnormal. Hence second is incorrect.

250. D: Radiation kills cancer cells. It damages DNA. It reduces tumor.

251. C: Chemotherapy uses drugs. It kills cancer cells. It affects rapidly dividing cells.

252. D: Staging shows spread. It guides treatment. It predicts prognosis.

253. B: Skin cancer is common. It is due to UV exposure. It is preventable.

254. D: Palliative care reduces suffering. It improves quality of life. It is supportive care.

255. D: Skin graft replaces damaged skin. It promotes healing. It reduces complications.

256. D: Emergency care is for serious conditions. It needs immediate action. It saves life.

257. D: ABC is primary survey. It ensures survival. It is priority.

258. B: Airway is checked first. It ensures breathing. It prevents obstruction.

259. D: Triage sorts patients. It gives priority. It ensures proper care.

260. D: CPR is done in cardiac arrest. It restores circulation. It saves life.

261. B: CPR ratio is 30 compressions and 2 breaths. It maintains circulation. It is standard.

262. D: Shock is poor perfusion. It leads to organ failure. It is emergency.

263. D: Hypovolemic shock is due to loss of blood. It reduces volume. It causes shock.

264. D: Anaphylactic shock is due to allergy. It causes collapse. It is emergency.

265. D: Septic shock is due to infection. It causes vasodilation. It is severe.

266. D: IV fluids improve circulation. They maintain BP. They prevent shock.

267. D: Oxygen therapy improves oxygen. It supports tissues. It prevents hypoxia.

268. D: Defibrillator restores rhythm. It treats arrhythmia. It is lifesaving.

269. D: Ventilator supports breathing. It is used in ICU. It helps patients.

270. D: GCS measures consciousness. It assesses brain function. It is important.

271. A: ICU is for critical care. It has advanced equipment. It provides monitoring.

272. D: ICU monitors vital signs. It includes BP, pulse, respiration. It ensures stability.

273. D: Suction clears airway. It removes secretions. It improves breathing.

274. D: Intubation inserts tube into trachea. It maintains airway. It supports ventilation.

275. D: Adrenaline treats anaphylaxis. It reverses shock. It is emergency drug.

276. A: CPR resuscitation, defibrillator rhythm, ventilator breathing, suction clears airway. These are uses.

277. A: Hypovolemic blood loss, septic infection, anaphylactic allergy, cardiogenic heart failure. These are types.

278. A: Airway open, breathing oxygenation, circulation blood flow, disability consciousness. These are ABCD.

279. B: Shock reduces perfusion. It does not improve circulation. Hence second is incorrect.

280. B: CPR saves life. It is needed in arrest. Hence second is incorrect.

281. B: Oxygen therapy increases oxygen. It does not reduce. Hence second is incorrect.

282. D: Emergency care saves life. It prevents death. It is priority.

283. D: Code blue means arrest. It requires CPR. It is emergency call.

284. D: Pulse oximeter measures SpO_2. It shows oxygen level. It is important.

285. D: ICU provides critical care. It supports vital functions. It is essential.

286. B: Ear helps in hearing and balance. Inner ear maintains equilibrium. It is essential for coordination.

287. C: External ear includes pinna and auditory canal. It collects sound. It directs to eardrum.

288. D: Middle ear has three ossicles. They transmit sound. They amplify vibrations.

289. C: Inner ear contains semicircular canals. They maintain balance. They detect movement.

290. B: Tympanic membrane is eardrum. It vibrates with sound. It transmits signals.

291. B: Otitis media is middle ear infection. It causes pain. It affects hearing.

292. D: Hearing loss is deafness. It may be partial or complete. It affects communication.

293. C: Meniere's disease affects inner ear. It causes vertigo. It affects balance.

294. A: Pinna collects sound, cochlea hearing, canals balance, tympanic vibration. These are functions.

295. B: Ear helps in balance. It maintains equilibrium. Hence second is incorrect.

296. B: Eye is organ of vision. It detects light. It forms images.

297. C: Retina has rods and cones. They detect light. They convert signals.

298. D: Lens focuses light on retina. It adjusts shape. It ensures clear vision.

299. D: Glaucoma increases eye pressure. It damages optic nerve. It may cause blindness.

300. D: Cataract is opacity of lens. It reduces vision. It needs surgery.

301. C: Geriatrics deals with the health needs of older adults. It includes prevention, treatment, and rehabilitation. Nursing care focuses on safety and independence.

302. B: Age-related muscle loss and balance problems increase fall risk. Falls can cause fractures and disability. Preventive measures include mobility support and safe surroundings.

303. B: Occupational health prevents and controls workplace-related disease. It identifies hazards and promotes safe practices. It protects workers' health and productivity.

304. D: Polypharmacy means multiple medicines used together. It increases risk of adverse drug reactions in elderly. Careful review prevents drug interactions.

305. C: Aging makes skin thin and less elastic. It tears easily and heals slowly. Proper skin care reduces injury and infection.

306. D: Regular repositioning reduces continuous pressure on bony areas. It improves blood flow and prevents tissue breakdown. It is the most effective basic preventive step.

307. D: Occupational hazards include biological risks like infections. They also include physical and chemical hazards. Safety protocols reduce exposure.

308. A: Noise causes hearing loss, dust causes respiratory problems, needle-stick risks blood-borne infections, repetitive work increases carpal tunnel risk. This mapping matches common workplace hazards.

309. B: Exercise improves strength, balance, and mobility. It generally reduces fall risk when done safely. Therefore the second statement is incorrect.

310. C: PPE acts as a protective barrier against hazards. It reduces exposure to harmful agents. It supports overall safety practices.

311. B: Immune system protects body from pathogens. It identifies and destroys harmful organisms. It maintains health.

312. C: Antibodies bind antigens. They neutralize pathogens. They help immune response.

313. D: Bone marrow produces lymphocytes. It is primary lymphoid organ. It supports immunity.

314. D: Immunity is body's defense mechanism. It protects from infections. It ensures survival.

315. D: Innate immunity is present from birth. It provides immediate defense. It is non-specific.

316. C: Acquired immunity develops after exposure. It builds memory. It is specific.

317. B: Vaccines stimulate immune response. They produce antibodies. They provide protection.

318. C: Allergy is hypersensitivity. It reacts strongly to harmless substances. It causes symptoms.

319. D: Anaphylaxis is severe reaction. It is life-threatening. It needs emergency treatment.

320. B: Antigen triggers immunity. It activates lymphocytes. It leads to antibody production.

321. D: B cells produce antibodies. They are part of immune system. They provide humoral immunity.

322. D: HIV attacks T helper cells. It weakens immunity. It leads to AIDS.

323. C: Autoimmune diseases target self tissues. It causes damage. It is abnormal response.

324. A: Antigen triggers, antibody protein, vaccine protection, allergy hypersensitivity. These define terms.

325. A: Innate natural, acquired memory, active antibodies, passive transfer. These types differ.

326. B: Vaccines protect from disease. They strengthen immunity. Hence second is incorrect.

327. B: Autoimmune diseases damage body. They do not improve immunity. Hence second is incorrect.

328. D: Hypersensitivity is overreaction. It causes allergy. It is harmful.

329. C: Immunodeficiency reduces immunity. It increases infection risk. It needs management.

330. B: Lymph nodes filter lymph. They trap pathogens. They support immunity.

10. Community Health Nursing

1. The determinants of health are the factors that influence the health status of

A. Individual and community
B. Hospitals only
C. Doctors only
D. Environment only

2. Which of the following is considered a biological determinant of health?

A. Income level　B. Education
C. Age　D. Housing

3. The environmental determinant of health includes factors such as ______.

A. Nutrition　B. Air and water quality
C. Income　D. Occupation

4. Lifestyle is an important determinant of health because it affects

A. Only income
B. Only environment
C. Only genetics
D. Daily habits and behaviors

5. The social determinant of health includes

A. Age　B. Sex
C. Education　D. Climate

6. Which of the following factors is included under economic determinants of health?

A. Income　B. Air quality
C. Water supply　D. Climate

7. The term "health" according to WHO includes physical, mental, and ______ well-being.

A. Emotional　B. Social
C. Economic　D. Spiritual

8. The cultural practices of a community mainly affect which aspect of health?

A. Biological　B. Environmental
C. Social　D. Economic

9. The genetic factors influence which aspect of health?

A. Behavior　B. Environment
C. Disease susceptibility　D. Occupation

10. Match the following:

Column I	Column II
A. Biological factors	1. Income
B. Environmental factors	2. Age
C. Social factors	3. Education
D. Economic factors	4. Water quality

A. A-2, B-4, C-3, D-1　B. A-3, B-2, C-1, D-4
C. A-1, B-3, C-2, D-4　D. A-4, B-1, C-3, D-2

11. Match the following:

Column I	Column II
A. Lifestyle	1. Heredity
B. Genetics	2. Daily habits
C. Environment	3. Surroundings
D. Health services	4. Medical care

A. A-2, B-1, C-3, D-4　B. A-3, B-2, C-1, D-4
C. A-1, B-4, C-2, D-3　D. A-4, B-3, C-2, D-1

12. **Assertion I:** Lifestyle choices influence health status.
Assertion II: Lifestyle has no impact on disease occurrence.

A. Both statements are correct
B. I is correct, II is incorrect
C. Both are incorrect
D. I is incorrect, II is correct

13. **Assertion I:** Clean environment promotes good health.
Assertion II: Pollution has no effect on health.

A. Both statements are correct
B. I is correct, II is incorrect
C. Both are incorrect
D. I is incorrect, II is correct

14. The availability of healthcare services is considered a ______ determinant of health.

A. Biological　B. Environmental
C. Social　D. Health service

15. The nutrition of an individual mainly affects which component of health?

A. Physical health B. Social health
C. Economic health D. Cultural health

16. Epidemiology is the study of distribution and determinants of diseases in

A. Individuals only B. Communities
C. Hospitals D. Animals

17. The term incidence refers to the number of

A. Existing cases B. New cases
C. Deaths D. Recoveries

18. The prevalence of a disease is defined as the total number of _____ cases at a given time.

A. New B. Old
C. Existing D. Future

19. The agent, host, and environment form which epidemiological model?

A. Web of causation B. Iceberg phenomenon
C. Chain of infection D. Epidemiological triad

20. The incubation period is the time between

A. Exposure and onset of symptoms
B. Diagnosis and treatment
C. Treatment and recovery
D. Infection and cure

21. The epidemic refers to the occurrence of disease in excess of

A. Expected level B. Minimum level
C. Maximum level D. Average level

22. The pandemic is an epidemic that spreads across

A. Village B. District
C. Country D. Continents

23. The endemic disease is constantly present in

A. One person B. Specific area
C. Hospital D. Whole world

24. The mortality rate indicates the number of

A. New cases B. Deaths
C. Recoveries D. Admissions

25. The case fatality rate is defined as the proportion of

A. Cases recovered B. Cases admitted
C. Cases dying D. Cases diagnosed

26. The source of infection refers to

A. Host B. Agent
C. Environment D. Origin of infection

27. The mode of transmission includes direct and _____ transmission.

A. Active B. Passive
C. Indirect D. Artificial

28. The vector is defined as an organism that

A. Causes disease B. Transmits infection
C. Prevents disease D. Diagnoses disease

29. The reservoir of infection is the place where the pathogen

A. Dies B. Multiplies
C. Leaves D. Enters

30. The host is defined as the organism that

A. Produces pathogen B. Destroys pathogen
C. Diagnoses pathogen D. Harbors pathogen

31. Match the following:

Column I	Column II
A. Incidence	1. Illness rate
B. Prevalence	2. Death rate
C. Mortality	3. Existing cases
D. Morbidity	4. New cases

A. A-4, B-3, C-2, D-1 B. A-3, B-4, C-1, D-2
C. A-2, B-1, C-4, D-3 D. A-1, B-2, C-3, D-4

32. Match the following:

Column I	Column II
A. Epidemic	1. Worldwide spread
B. Pandemic	2. Constant presence
C. Endemic	3. Occasional cases
D. Sporadic	4. Sudden increase

A. A-4, B-1, C-2, D-3 B. A-1, B-2, C-3, D-4
C. A-2, B-3, C-1, D-4 D. A-3, B-4, C-2, D-1

33. Match the following:

Column I	Column II
A. Agent	1. Living organism
B. Host	2. Carrier
C. Environment	3. Surroundings
D. Vector	4. Cause of disease

A. A-4, B-1, C-3, D-2 B. A-1, B-4, C-2, D-3
C. A-2, B-3, C-4, D-1 D. A-3, B-2, C-1, D-4

34. Match the following:

Column I	Column II
A. Direct transmission	1. Contact
B. Indirect transmission	2. Mosquito
C. Airborne transmission	3. Droplets
D. Vector-borne transmission	4. Fomites

A. A-1, B-4, C-3, D-2 B. A-2, B-1, C-4, D-3
C. A-3, B-2, C-1, D-4 D. A-4, B-3, C-2, D-1

35. **Assertion I:** Incidence measures new cases of disease.

Assertion II: Prevalence measures total cases of disease.

A. Both statements are correct

B. I is correct, II is incorrect
C. Both are incorrect
D. I is incorrect, II is correct

36. Assertion I: Vector transmits infection.
Assertion II: Vector destroys pathogens.
A. Both statements are correct
B. I is correct, II is incorrect
C. Both are incorrect
D. I is incorrect, II is correct

37. Assertion I: Endemic diseases occur constantly in an area.
Assertion II: Endemic diseases are rare.
A. Both statements are correct
B. I is correct, II is incorrect
C. Both are incorrect
D. I is incorrect, II is correct

38. Assertion I: Pandemic affects large population worldwide.
Assertion II: Pandemic is limited to a small area.
A. Both statements are correct
B. I is correct, II is incorrect
C. Both are incorrect
D. I is incorrect, II is correct

39. The attack rate is a type of
A. Mortality rate B. Incidence rate
C. Prevalence rate D. Recovery rate

40. The secondary attack rate measures spread among
A. General population B. Hospital patients
C. Close contacts D. Health workers

41. The screening test is used for
A. Diagnosis B. Treatment
C. Prevention D. Early detection

42. The sensitivity of a test refers to its ability to
A. Detect negatives B. Detect positives
C. Measure accuracy D. Measure error

43. The specificity of a test refers to its ability to
A. Detect positives B. Detect negatives
C. Measure sensitivity D. Measure risk

44. The surveillance is defined as continuous ______ of disease.
A. Treatment B. Prevention
C. Control D. Monitoring

45. The epidemic curve is used to study
A. Mortality B. Spread of disease
C. Treatment D. Diagnosis

46. The chain of infection includes agent, host, and ____.
A. Vector B. Environment
C. Reservoir D. Transmission

47. The natural history of disease includes pre-pathogenesis and ______ stages..
A. Recovery B. Prevention
C. Pathogenesis D. Diagnosis

48. The primary prevention aims to prevent
A. Complications B. Disability
C. Death D. Disease occurrence

49. The secondary prevention aims to
A. Prevent disease B. Detect early disease
C. Reduce disability D. Provide rehabilitation

50. The tertiary prevention focuses on
A. Prevention B. Diagnosis
C. Cure D. Rehabilitation

51. The herd immunity protects
A. Individuals only B. Community
C. Animals D. Environment

52. The outbreak is defined as sudden occurrence of
A. Few cases B. Many cases
C. Expected cases D. Rare cases

53. The quarantine refers to restriction of
A. Healthy individuals B. Sick individuals
C. Exposed individuals D. Immune individuals

54. The isolation is applied to
A. Healthy persons B. Carriers
C. Exposed persons D. Sick persons

55. The epidemiological study that follows subjects over time is called
A. Cross-sectional study
B. Case-control study
C. Descriptive study
D. Cohort study

56. Communicable diseases are those diseases which can be transmitted from one person to another.
A. True B. False
C. Only in hospitals D. Only in children

57. Which disease is mainly transmitted through droplet infection in the air?
A. Malaria B. Tuberculosis
C. Cholera D. Dengue

58. Malaria is caused by which type of organism?
A. Protozoa B. Virus
C. Fungus D. Bacteria

59. Dengue fever is transmitted by which mosquito?

A. Anopheles mosquito B. Culex mosquito
C. Aedes mosquito D. Sandfly

60. Cholera is mainly transmitted through contaminated food and water.

A. True B. False
C. Only by air D. Only by insects

61. BCG vaccine is given to prevent which disease?

A. Tuberculosis B. Measles
C. Hepatitis B D. Tetanus

62. Which of the following is a viral communicable disease?

A. Cholera B. Typhoid
C. Tuberculosis D. Measles

63. HIV is mainly transmitted through which route?

A. Food B. Water
C. Air D. Blood and body fluids

64. The incubation period is the time interval between exposure to an infection and the appearance of the first symptoms.

A. True
B. False
C. Only for chronic diseases
D. Only for non-communicable diseases

65. Isolation of an infected patient is done to prevent transmission of infection to others.

A. True B. False
C. Only for injuries D. Only for diabetes

66. The female Anopheles mosquito transmits which disease?

A. Dengue B. Malaria
C. Cholera D. Typhoid

67. Measles is mainly spread through which route of transmission?

A. Airborne droplets B. Contaminated water
C. Blood transfusion D. Vector bite

68. Which of the following is a water-borne communicable disease?

A. Influenza B. Dengue
C. Cholera D. Tuberculosis

69. Hepatitis B is most commonly transmitted through blood and body fluids.

A. True B. False
C. Only by food D. Only by air

70. A carrier is a person who harbours the infectious agent and can transmit it without showing symptoms.

A. True B. False
C. Only after vaccination D. Only during fever

71. Match the diseases with the correct mode/type.

Column I	Column II
A. Tuberculosis	1. Water-borne
B. Malaria	2. Viral disease
C. Cholera	3. Air-borne
D. Measles	4. Protozoal disease

A. A-3, B-4, C-1, D-2 B. A-4, B-1, C-3, D-2
C. A-1, B-3, C-2, D-4 D. A-2, B-4, C-1, D-3

72. Match the disease with the common transmission route.

Column I	Column II
A. HIV	1. Mosquito-borne
B. Hepatitis B	2. Water-borne
C. Dengue	3. Blood transmission
D. Cholera	4. Immune deficiency illness

A. A-4, B-3, C-1, D-2 B. A-3, B-4, C-2, D-1
C. A-1, B-2, C-3, D-4 D. A-2, B-1, C-4, D-3

73. Match the infection-control term with its correct meaning.

Column I	Column II
A. Isolation	1. Separation of infected persons
B. Quarantine	2. Restriction of exposed persons
C. Disinfection	3. Destruction of many pathogens (not spores)
D. Sterilization	4. Destruction of all micro-organisms including spores

A. A-1, B-2, C-3, D-4 B. A-2, B-1, C-4, D-3
C. A-3, B-4, C-1, D-2 D. A-4, B-3, C-2, D-1

74. Match the epidemiological term with its correct description.

Column I	Column II
A. Agent	1. Living organism that harbours infection
B. Host	2. Place where pathogen lives and multiplies
C. Vector	3. Cause of disease
D. Reservoir	4. Carrier that transmits infection

A. A-3, B-1, C-4, D-2 B. A-1, B-2, C-3, D-4
C. A-2, B-3, C-1, D-4 D. A-4, B-1, C-2, D-3

75. Assertion I: Vaccination helps in preventing communicable diseases.

Assertion II: Vaccination has no role in immunity.

A. Both statements are correct
B. I is correct, II is incorrect
C. Both are incorrect
D. I is incorrect, II is correct

76. Assertion I: Malaria is transmitted through the bite of an infected mosquito.

Assertion II: Malaria spreads through contaminated drinking water.

A. Both statements are correct
B. I is correct, II is incorrect
C. Both are incorrect
D. I is incorrect, II is correct

77. Assertion I: Cholera is commonly transmitted through contaminated water.

Assertion II: Cholera is mainly an airborne infection.

A. Both statements are correct
B. I is correct, II is incorrect
C. Both are incorrect
D. I is incorrect, II is correct

78. Assertion I: HIV infection weakens the immune system.

Assertion II: HIV infection improves the body's resistance to infections.

A. Both statements are correct
B. I is correct, II is incorrect
C. Both are incorrect
D. I is incorrect, II is correct

79. Immunization is one of the most effective methods to prevent many communicable diseases.

A. True B. False
C. Only for adults D. Only for newborns

80. Sterilization is the process of destroying all forms of microorganisms including spores.

A. True B. False
C. Only for floors D. Only for food

81. Which disease is classically spread through droplet nuclei and close contact in crowded settings?

A. Cholera B. Tuberculosis
C. Malaria D. Dengue

82. Which of the following diseases is caused by bacteria?

A. Measles B. Dengue
C. Cholera D. HIV

83. Hand hygiene is considered a key measure for preventing transmission of infections in the community.

A. True B. False
C. Only in ICUs D. Only during surgery

84. Communicable diseases are also commonly referred to as infectious diseases.

A. True
B. False
C. Only seasonal diseases
D. Only childhood diseases

85. Vector-borne diseases are transmitted by living carriers such as mosquitoes and ticks.

A. True B. False
C. Only by water D. Only by air

86. Disinfection is a process that destroys many pathogenic microorganisms but may not destroy bacterial spores.

A. True B. False
C. Only for food D. Only for blood

87. Primary prevention for communicable diseases includes immunization and health education.

A. True B. False
C. Only isolation D. Only surgery

88. Modes of transmission of infection include direct and indirect transmission routes.

A. True
B. False
C. Only direct transmission
D. Only indirect transmission

89. Proper sanitation and safe drinking water supply help in preventing many communicable diseases.

A. True
B. False
C. Only prevents cancer
D. Only prevents diabetes

90. Which one of the following is the most appropriate community-level step to prevent cholera outbreaks?

A. Early ambulation
B. Vector control only
C. Safe water and sanitation
D. Increase fat intake

91. Non-communicable diseases do not spread from person to person and usually have a long duration.

A. True B. False
C. Only in children D. Only in elderly

92. Which condition among the following is classified as a non-communicable disease?

A. Tuberculosis B. Malaria
C. Diabetes mellitus D. Cholera

93. High intake of salt is strongly associated with which health condition?

A. Diabetes mellitus B. Hypertension
C. Asthma D. Tuberculosis

94. Obesity develops when there is excessive accumulation of ______ in the body.

A. Protein B. Water
C. Minerals D. Fat

95. Which of the following is a characteristic feature of diabetes mellitus?

A. Increased hemoglobin
B. High blood glucose
C. Low blood pressure
D. Decreased pulse rate

96. Smoking significantly increases the risk of developing which disease?
A. Asthma B. Cancer
C. Influenza D. Measles

97. The term "lifestyle diseases" is best associated with which type of factors?
A. Infectious agents
B. Genetic mutations
C. Environmental disasters
D. Unhealthy habits

98. Cardiovascular diseases primarily involve which organ system?
A. Respiratory system
B. Digestive system
C. Cardiovascular system
D. Nervous system

99. Match the following diseases with their correct features.

Column I	Column II
A. Diabetes	1. Excess body fat
B. Hypertension	2. High blood pressure
C. Cancer	3. Uncontrolled cell growth
D. Obesity	4. High blood sugar

A. A-4, B-2, C-3, D-1 B. A-2, B-1, C-4, D-3
C. A-3, B-4, C-1, D-2 D. A-1, B-3, C-2, D-4

100. Match the risk factors with their categories.

Column I	Column II
A. Smoking	1. Protective factor
B. Alcohol intake	2. Risk factor
C. Balanced diet	3. Lifestyle factor
D. Physical exercise	4. Health promotion

A. A-2, B-2, C-1, D-4 B. A-3, B-1, C-2, D-4
C. A-2, B-3, C-1, D-4 D. A-1, B-4, C-2, D-3

101. Assertion I: Non-communicable diseases are usually chronic in nature.
Assertion II: Non-communicable diseases spread rapidly through contact.
A. Both statements are correct
B. I is correct, II is incorrect
C. Both statements are incorrect
D. I is incorrect, II is correct

102. Assertion I: Regular physical activity reduces the risk of many non-communicable diseases.
Assertion II: Sedentary lifestyle increases the risk of disease.
A. Both statements are correct
B. I is correct, II is incorrect
C. Both statements are incorrect
D. I is incorrect, II is correct

103. Prevention of non-communicable diseases mainly depends on adopting a ______ lifestyle.
A. Sedentary B. Unhealthy
C. Balanced D. Irregular

104. Screening programmes for diseases like cancer are mainly intended for ______ detection.
A. Late B. Delayed
C. Wrong D. Early

105. Health education plays a key role in reducing the burden of non-communicable diseases.
A. True B. False
C. Only in hospitals D. Only in urban areas

106. Demography is the study of human population with respect to size, structure, and distribution.
A. True B. False
C. Only size D. Only distribution

107. The crude birth rate refers to the number of live births per ______ population in a year.
A. 100 B. 1,000
C. 10,000 D. 100,000

108. Which indicator measures the number of deaths per 1,000 population per year?
A. Birth rate B. Fertility rate
C. Mortality rate D. Growth rate

109. The population pyramid is used to represent the ______ of a population.
A. Income level B. Age and sex structure
C. Literacy D. Occupation

110. The total fertility rate indicates the average number of children born to a woman during her reproductive period.
A. True B. False
C. Only for males D. Only for children

111. Which of the following best defines population density?
A. Number of births
B. Number of deaths
C. Number of people per area
D. Growth rate

112. Migration refers to the movement of people from one place to another.
A. True B. False
C. Only within country D. Only outside country

113. Which of the following factors directly influences population growth?

A. Climate only B. Birth and death rates
C. Occupation only D. Culture only

114. Match the following demographic indicators with their meanings.

Column I	Column II
A. Birth rate	1. Deaths per 1,000 population
B. Death rate	2. Births per 1,000 population
C. Fertility rate	3. Children per woman
D. Population density	4. People per unit area

A. A-2, B-1, C-3, D-4 B. A-3, B-2, C-4, D-1
C. A-1, B-3, C-2, D-4 D. A-4, B-1, C-3, D-2

115. Match the following terms with their definitions.

Column I	Column II
A. Migration	1. Movement of people
B. Urbanization	2. Increase in population
C. Census	3. Official population count
D. Population growth	4. Increase in city population

A. A-1, B-4, C-3, D-2 B. A-3, B-1, C-2, D-4
C. A-2, B-3, C-4, D-1 D. A-4, B-2, C-1, D-3

116. Assertion I: Population growth depends on birth and death rates.

Assertion II: Population growth is independent of migration.

A. Both statements are correct
B. I is correct, II is incorrect
C. Both statements are incorrect
D. I is incorrect, II is correct

117. Assertion I: Census provides detailed population data.

Assertion II: Census is conducted every year in India.

A. Both statements are correct
B. I is correct, II is incorrect
C. Both statements are incorrect
D. I is incorrect, II is correct

118. The census is an official count of population conducted at regular intervals.

A. True B. False
C. Only for cities D. Only for villages

119. High population growth may lead to increased pressure on resources such as food, water, and housing.

A. True
B. False
C. Only in developed countries
D. Only in rural areas

120. Which of the following is the most important source of demographic data in India?

A. Hospital records B. School records
C. Surveys only D. Census

121. National Health Programs in India are designed to control and prevent major health problems at the community level.

A. True B. False
C. Only for hospitals D. Only for urban areas

122. The National Tuberculosis Elimination Programme (NTEP) aims to eliminate tuberculosis by which target year in India?

A. 2025 B. 2030
C. 2035 D. 2040

123. The Revised National Tuberculosis Control Programme (RNTCP) is now known as ______.

A. NHM B. NTEP
C. UIP D. NRHM

124. The Universal Immunization Programme (UIP) provides vaccines to prevent diseases among which group?

A. Elderly
B. Adults only
C. Children and pregnant women
D. Only workers

125. The National AIDS Control Programme is implemented to control which disease?

A. Tuberculosis B. HIV/AIDS
C. Malaria D. Diabetes

126. The National Vector Borne Disease Control Programme covers diseases like malaria, dengue, and ______.

A. Cancer B. Hypertension
C. Tuberculosis D. Filariasis

127. The Janani Suraksha Yojana is a scheme aimed at promoting ______ deliveries.

A. Home B. Institutional
C. Traditional D. Private

128. The National Health Mission (NHM) focuses mainly on strengthening which level of healthcare?

A. Primary healthcare B. Tertiary care
C. Private sector D. Corporate hospitals

129. Match the following programmes with their objectives.

Column I	Column II
A. NTEP	1. Immunization
B. UIP	2. Tuberculosis control
C. NACP	3. HIV control
D. NVBDCP	4. Vector-borne diseases

A. A-2, B-1, C-3, D-4 B. A-1, B-3, C-4, D-2
C. A-3, B-2, C-1, D-4 D. A-4, B-1, C-2, D-3

130. Match the following schemes with their benefits.

Column I	Column II
A. Janani Suraksha Yojana	1. Health insurance
B. Ayushman Bharat	2. Maternal care
C. ICDS	3. Child nutrition
D. Mid-Day Meal	4. School nutrition

A. A-2, B-1, C-3, D-4 B. A-1, B-2, C-4, D-3
C. A-3, B-4, C-1, D-2 D. A-4, B-3, C-2, D-1

131. Assertion I: National Health Programs help in disease control.

Assertion II: These programs are limited to urban areas only.

A. Both statements are correct
B. I is correct, II is incorrect
C. Both statements are incorrect
D. I is incorrect, II is correct

132. Assertion I: Immunization reduces incidence of infectious diseases.

Assertion II: Immunization increases risk of infections.

A. Both statements are correct
B. I is correct, II is incorrect
C. Both statements are incorrect
D. I is incorrect, II is correct

133. The Ayushman Bharat scheme provides financial protection for ______ care.

A. Primary B. Emergency
C. Hospitalization D. Preventive

134. The Integrated Child Development Services (ICDS) programme mainly focuses on health, nutrition, and ______ development.

A. Economic B. Social
C. Cultural D. Child

135. The Mid-Day Meal Programme is implemented to improve nutritional status of ______ children.

A. College B. School
C. Preschool D. Working

136. The National Programme for Prevention and Control of Cancer, Diabetes, Cardiovascular Diseases and Stroke is abbreviated as ______.

A. NPCB B. NACP
C. NHM D. NPCDCS

137. The purpose of family welfare programmes is to promote ______.

A. High fertility B. Population control
C. Disease spread D. Migration

138. The Accredited Social Health Activist (ASHA) works at which level of healthcare?

A. Hospital level B. District level
C. Community level D. State level

139. The National Programme for Control of Blindness aims to reduce ______ in the population.

A. Deafness B. Blindness
C. Cancer D. Diabetes

140. The main objective of National Health Programs is to improve the overall health status of the population.

A. True B. False
C. Only for rich people D. Only for urban areas

141. Health services are organized activities aimed at promoting, maintaining, and restoring health.

A. True
B. False
C. Only curative services
D. Only preventive services

142. The primary health care system focuses mainly on which type of care?

A. Specialized care
B. Hospital care
C. Community-based care
D. Emergency care

143. The first point of contact between the community and the health system is usually the ______ level of care.

A. Primary B. Secondary
C. Tertiary D. Super-specialty

144. The secondary level of health care includes which of the following facilities?

A. Sub-centres
B. Primary Health Centres
C. Community Health Centres
D. Home care services

145. Tertiary health care provides specialized services such as advanced diagnostic and surgical care.

A. True B. False
C. Only preventive care D. Only basic care

146. The concept of "health for all" emphasizes which approach?

A. Curative approach B. Preventive approach
C. Holistic approach D. Hospital-based approach

147. The Alma-Ata Declaration (1978) is associated with which concept?

A. Hospital management
B. Primary health care
C. Medical education
D. Drug policy

148. The health planning process involves setting objectives, identifying resources, and _____ implementation.

A. Ignoring B. Delaying
C. Evaluating D. Avoiding

149. Match the levels of care with their facilities.

Column I	Column II
A. Primary care	1. Super-specialty hospital
B. Secondary care	2. Sub-centre
C. Tertiary care	3. District hospital
D. Community level	4. PHC

A. A-4, B-3, C-1, D-2 B. A-3, B-1, C-2, D-4
C. A-2, B-4, C-3, D-1 D. A-1, B-2, C-4, D-3

150. Match the components of primary health care with their functions.

Column I	Column II
A. Health education	1. Disease prevention
B. Nutrition	2. Awareness
C. Immunization	3. Balanced diet
D. Safe water	4. Sanitation

A. A-2, B-3, C-1, D-4 B. A-1, B-2, C-3, D-4
C. A-3, B-1, C-4, D-2 D. A-4, B-3, C-2, D-1

151. Assertion I: Primary health care is accessible and affordable.

Assertion II: Primary health care focuses only on treatment.

A. Both statements are correct
B. I is correct, II is incorrect
C. Both statements are incorrect
D. I is incorrect, II is correct

152. Assertion I: Health planning improves utilization of resources.

Assertion II: Health planning is not required for health services.

A. Both statements are correct
B. I is correct, II is incorrect
C. Both statements are incorrect
D. I is incorrect, II is correct

153. The referral system helps in transferring patients from one level of care to another for better management.

A. True B. False
C. Only for emergencies D. Only for rural areas

154. Community participation is an important principle of primary health care.

A. True B. False
C. Only for hospitals D. Only for urban areas

155. The goal of health planning is to provide effective, efficient, and equitable health services to the population.

A. True B. False
C. Only for rich people D. Only for cities

156. The community health nurse plays an important role in promoting and maintaining health at the community level.

A. True B. False
C. Only curative role D. Only hospital work

157. Which of the following is a primary role of a community health nurse?

A. Surgery B. Health education
C. Laboratory work D. Radiology

158. A community health nurse is responsible for identifying health problems and planning care for the community.

A. Only planning B. Only diagnosis
C. Only treatment D. Assessment and planning

159. The nurse provides immunization services to prevent diseases in the community.

A. True B. False
C. Only in hospitals D. Only in emergencies

160. Which activity best represents the role of a nurse in disease prevention?

A. Surgery B. Health teaching
C. Lab diagnosis D. Imaging

161. Match the roles of a nurse with their functions.

Column I	Column II
A. Educator	1. Protects patient rights
B. Care provider	2. Provides nursing care
C. Advocate	3. Organizes services
D. Manager	4. Gives health education

A. A-4, B-2, C-1, D-3 B. A-2, B-3, C-4, D-1
C. A-1, B-4, C-2, D-3 D. A-4, B-2, C-1, D-3

162. The nurse acts as a link between the community and health services.

A. True B. False
C. Only in hospitals D. Only in urban areas

163. Assertion I: Health education is an important responsibility of a nurse.

Assertion II: Nurses have no role in prevention of disease.

A. Both statements are correct
B. I is correct, II is incorrect
C. Both statements are incorrect
D. I is incorrect, II is correct

164. A nurse supervises health workers and ensures proper implementation of health programs in the community.

A. Only clinical role B. Only teaching role
C. Only research role D. Administrative role

165. Home visits by a nurse help in assessing the health status of families and providing care.

A. True
B. False
C. Only for sick patients
D. Only for children

166. Health education aims to change the behavior of individuals and communities towards better health practices.

A. True
B. False
C. Only knowledge improvement
D. Only treatment

167. Which principle of health education emphasizes participation of the community in planning and implementation?

A. Interest
B. Reinforcement
C. Motivation
D. Participation

168. Health education should be based on the needs and interests of the people.

A. True
B. False
C. Only for schools
D. Only for hospitals

169. Match the methods of health education with their examples.

Column I	Column II
A. Lecture	1. Showing a procedure
B. Demonstration	2. Acting a situation
C. Group discussion	3. One-way communication
D. Role play	4. Exchange of ideas

A. A-3, B-1, C-4, D-2
B. A-1, B-3, C-2, D-4
C. A-4, B-2, C-1, D-3
D. A-2, B-4, C-3, D-1

170. Assertion I: Health education helps in prevention of diseases.

Assertion II: Health education has no effect on behavior change.

A. Both statements are correct
B. I is correct, II is incorrect
C. Both statements are incorrect
D. I is incorrect, II is correct

EXPLANATORY ANSWERS

1. **A:** Determinants of health affect both individuals and communities. They influence overall health status. They include multiple factors.
2. **C:** Age is biological factor. It affects disease risk. It influences health outcomes.
3. **B:** Environment includes air and water. Pollution affects health. Clean environment improves health.
4. **D:** Lifestyle includes habits like diet and exercise. It affects health. It influences disease risk.
5. **C:** Education is social determinant. It affects awareness. It influences health behavior.
6. **A:** Income affects living conditions. It determines access to resources. It impacts health.
7. **B:** WHO defines health as physical, mental, and social well-being. It is complete state. It is not just absence of disease.
8. **C:** Cultural practices affect social behavior. They influence health practices. They affect lifestyle.
9. **C:** Genetics influence risk of disease. It determines inheritance. It affects health status.
10. **A:** Biological age, environmental water, social education, economic income. These define determinants.
11. **A:** Lifestyle habits, genetics heredity, environment surroundings, health services care. These factors affect health.
12. **B:** Lifestyle affects health. Poor habits cause disease. Hence second is incorrect.
13. **B:** Clean environment promotes health. Pollution harms health. Hence second is incorrect.
14. **D:** Health services include hospitals. They provide care. They affect health outcomes.
15. **A:** Nutrition affects body function. It maintains strength. It supports health.
16. **B:** Epidemiology studies disease patterns in populations. It helps in prevention. It improves public health.
17. **B:** Incidence measures new cases. It shows risk of disease. It helps in planning.
18. **C:** Prevalence includes all cases. It shows burden of disease. It is important for planning.
19. **D:** It includes agent, host, environment. It explains disease causation. It is basic model.
20. **A:** Incubation period is time between exposure and symptoms. It varies by disease.
21. **A:** Epidemic is increase above expected level. It indicates outbreak. It needs control.
22. **D:** Pandemic spreads globally. It affects large population. It is serious.
23. **B:** Endemic diseases persist in area. They occur regularly. They are constant.
24. **B:** Mortality rate measures deaths. It indicates severity. It helps evaluation.
25. **C:** Case fatality shows proportion dying. It indicates severity. It is useful.

26. **D:** Source is origin. It spreads infection. It may be human or animal.

27. **C:** Transmission may be direct or indirect. Indirect includes vectors. It spreads disease.

28. **B:** Vector carries disease. It spreads pathogens. Example mosquito.

29. **B:** Reservoir is place of growth. Pathogen survives there. It is source.

30. **D:** Host is organism. It supports pathogen. It may get disease.

31. **A:** Incidence new, prevalence existing, mortality death, morbidity illness. These rates differ.

32. **A:** Epidemic sudden, pandemic worldwide, endemic constant, sporadic occasional. These describe patterns.

33. **A:** Agent cause, host organism, environment surroundings, vector carrier. These define triad.

34. **A:** Direct contact, indirect fomites, airborne droplets, vector mosquito. These modes differ.

35. **A:** Incidence new, prevalence total. Both are measures. Both correct.

36. **B:** Vector transmits disease. It does not destroy pathogens. Hence second incorrect.

37. **B:** Endemic is constant. It is not rare. Hence second incorrect.

38. **B:** Pandemic is global. It is not limited. Hence second incorrect.

39. **B:** Attack rate is incidence. It measures risk. It is used in outbreaks.

40. **C:** Secondary attack is among contacts. It shows spread. It is important.

41. **D:** Screening detects early disease. It prevents complications. It improves outcome.

42. **B:** Sensitivity finds true positives. It reduces false negatives. It is important.

43. **B:** Specificity finds true negatives. It reduces false positives. It ensures accuracy.

44. **D:** Surveillance monitors disease. It tracks spread. It helps control.

45. **B:** Epidemic curve shows pattern. It indicates outbreak. It helps control.

46. **B:** Chain includes environment. It helps transmission. It affects disease.

47. **C:** Natural history has stages. It includes pathogenesis. It shows progression.

48. **D:** Primary prevention stops disease. It prevents onset. It is important.

49. **B:** Secondary prevention detects early. It reduces severity. It improves outcome.

50. **D:** Tertiary reduces disability. It provides rehab. It improves quality.

51. **B:** Herd immunity protects population. It reduces spread. It protects vulnerable.

52. **B:** Outbreak is sudden rise. It needs control. It is similar to epidemic.

53. **C:** Quarantine restricts exposed. It prevents spread. It is preventive.

54. **D:** Isolation separates sick. It prevents transmission. It is important.

55. **D:** Cohort follows subjects. It studies incidence. It is longitudinal.

56. **A:** Communicable diseases spread from an infected source to a susceptible person. Transmission can occur via air, water, contact, or vectors. Control focuses on breaking the chain of infection.

57. **B:** Tuberculosis spreads mainly through airborne droplets from coughing or sneezing. Prolonged close contact increases risk. Early detection and treatment reduce transmission.

58. **A:** Malaria is caused by Plasmodium, which is a protozoan parasite. It multiplies in human blood after mosquito transmission. Prevention includes mosquito control and chemoprophylaxis in risk areas.

59. **C:** Dengue is transmitted by Aedes mosquitoes, especially Aedes aegypti. These mosquitoes often bite during daytime. Preventing breeding in clean stagnant water is essential.

60. **A:** Cholera commonly spreads through ingestion of contaminated food or water. Poor sanitation and unsafe water supply increase risk. Community prevention focuses on safe water, sanitation, and hygiene.

61. **A:** BCG vaccine provides protection mainly against severe childhood TB forms. It is part of routine immunization in India. It supports community-level prevention of TB.

62. **D:** Measles is caused by a virus and spreads rapidly through the air. It can lead to complications like pneumonia. Vaccination is the most effective preventive measure.

63. **D:** HIV spreads through infected blood, sexual contact, and from mother to child. It does not spread through casual contact or air. Safe practices and screening reduce risk.

64. **A:** Incubation period is the silent period before symptoms appear. It differs between diseases. Understanding it helps in quarantine and surveillance.

65. **A:** Isolation separates infected persons to prevent transmission. It is different from quarantine, which restricts exposed persons. It is an important public health measure.

66. **B:** Malaria is transmitted by infected female Anopheles mosquitoes. The parasite enters bloodstream and affects RBCs. Prevention includes bed nets and vector control.

67. **A:** Measles spreads mainly through droplets and airborne transmission. It is highly contagious. Immunization reduces outbreaks.

68. **C:** Cholera is typically water-borne and spreads through contaminated water. It causes acute watery diarrhea and dehydration. Safe water is central to prevention.

69. **A:** Hepatitis B spreads through blood and body fluids, including unsafe injections and transfusion. It can also

spread from mother to baby. Vaccination and safe injection practices prevent it.

70. A: A carrier can transmit infection without symptoms. Carriers contribute to hidden spread. Identifying and controlling carriers supports outbreak control.

71. A: TB is air-borne, malaria is protozoal, cholera is water-borne, and measles is viral. This mapping reflects both agent type and major transmission pattern. It helps in choosing preventive strategies.

72. A: HIV leads to immune deficiency, hepatitis B spreads via blood, dengue is mosquito-borne, and cholera is water-borne. Correct identification helps in targeted control measures. It also guides patient counseling.

73. A: Isolation is for infected persons, quarantine is for exposed persons, disinfection reduces pathogens, and sterilization destroys all microbes including spores. These are core infection-control concepts. They are used in both community and hospital settings.

74. A: Agent causes disease, host harbours infection, vector transmits infection, and reservoir is the habitat of pathogen. Understanding these terms helps in breaking the chain of infection. It supports community prevention planning.

75. B: Vaccines stimulate immune response and build protection. They help reduce incidence and outbreaks. The second statement is incorrect because vaccination strengthens immunity.

76. B: Malaria is mosquito-borne and not water-borne. Contaminated water is linked with diseases like cholera and typhoid. Hence, the second statement is incorrect.

77. B: Cholera spreads mainly through water/food contamination. It is not primarily airborne. Therefore, the second statement is incorrect.

78. B: HIV reduces immune function by affecting T helper cells. It increases susceptibility to infections. It does not improve resistance, so the second statement is incorrect.

79. A: Immunization prevents many vaccine-preventable diseases. It protects individuals and strengthens herd immunity. It is a key community health strategy.

80. A: Sterilization removes all microorganisms including spores. It is used for surgical instruments and critical items. It ensures safety in healthcare settings.

81. B: TB spreads in crowded and poorly ventilated settings. Droplet nuclei remain suspended in air. Control includes ventilation and early treatment.

82. C: Cholera is caused by Vibrio cholerae, a bacterium. It causes profuse watery diarrhea. Prompt rehydration is lifesaving.

83. A: Hand hygiene breaks the transmission chain. It reduces spread via contact and fomites. It is one of the simplest and most effective measures.

84. A: Infectious and communicable diseases are often used interchangeably. Both refer to diseases caused by pathogens. Communicable highlights transmission between people.

85. A: Vector-borne diseases spread via carriers like mosquitoes and ticks. Control includes eliminating breeding sites and personal protection. It reduces disease burden.

86. A: Disinfection reduces pathogens on surfaces. It may not kill spores reliably. Sterilization is required when complete elimination is needed.

87. A: Primary prevention prevents disease occurrence. Immunization and health education are key tools. They reduce incidence in the community.

88. A: Transmission can be direct (contact, droplets) or indirect (vectors, fomites). Recognizing routes guides prevention. It helps control outbreaks.

89. A: Sanitation and safe water reduce fecal-oral diseases. They prevent outbreaks like cholera. Community infrastructure plays major role.

90. C: Preventing cholera requires safe water supply and sanitation measures. It reduces contamination and transmission. Community awareness and hygiene support control.

91. A: Non-communicable diseases are not infectious. They develop slowly and persist for long duration. Examples include diabetes and hypertension.

92. C: Diabetes is a metabolic disorder. It is not caused by pathogens. It requires long-term management.

93. B: High salt intake increases blood pressure. It contributes to hypertension. It is a modifiable risk factor.

94. D: Obesity is excess fat accumulation. It increases risk of heart disease and diabetes. It affects overall health.

95. B: Diabetes is characterized by elevated blood sugar levels. It can cause complications if uncontrolled. Monitoring is essential.

96. B: Smoking is a major risk factor for lung cancer and other diseases. It damages tissues. It increases mortality.

97. D: Lifestyle diseases result from habits like poor diet and lack of exercise. They are preventable. Behavior change is important.

98. C: Cardiovascular diseases affect heart and blood vessels. They include hypertension and heart attack. They are leading cause of death.

99. A: Diabetes relates to sugar, hypertension to BP, cancer to cell growth, obesity to fat. These features define each disease.

100. A: Smoking and alcohol are risk factors. Balanced diet is protective. Exercise promotes health.

101. B: NCDs are chronic. They do not spread by contact. Hence second statement is incorrect.

102. A: Exercise reduces risk. Inactivity increases disease risk. Both statements are true.

103. C: Healthy lifestyle prevents NCDs. Balanced diet and exercise are essential. It improves quality of life.

104. D: Screening helps detect disease early. It improves prognosis. It reduces complications.

105. A: Health education increases awareness. It promotes healthy behavior. It reduces disease burden.

106. A: Demography studies population size, distribution, and structure. It helps in planning health services. It is essential for public health.

107. B: Crude birth rate is number of live births per 1,000 population per year. It is a standard measure. It helps assess fertility.

108. C: Mortality rate measures deaths in population. It indicates health status. It helps planning.

109. B: Population pyramid shows age and sex distribution. It indicates growth pattern. It helps policy making.

110. A: Total fertility rate reflects reproductive behavior. It shows average children per woman. It helps in population control planning.

111. C: Population density shows how crowded an area is. It affects resource use. It influences health services.

112. A: Migration is movement of people. It may be internal or external. It affects population distribution.

113. B: Population growth depends on births and deaths. Migration also affects it. These are key factors.

114. A: Birth rate births, death rate deaths, fertility children per woman, density people per area. These are indicators.

115. A: Migration movement, urbanization city growth, census count, growth increase. These are definitions.

116. B: Growth depends on birth, death, and migration. Migration also affects population. Hence second is incorrect.

117. B: Census gives data. It is conducted every 10 years in India. Hence second is incorrect.

118. A: Census collects population data. It is official. It helps planning.

119. A: High population increases pressure. It affects resources. It leads to problems.

120. D: Census is main source. It gives accurate data. It is important for policy.

121. A: National Health Programs target major public health issues. They aim at prevention, control, and elimination. They operate at community level.

122. A: India aims to eliminate TB by 2025. This is ahead of global targets. It requires strong implementation.

123. B: RNTCP was renamed NTEP. It focuses on TB elimination. It uses modern strategies.

124. C: UIP provides vaccines to vulnerable groups. It prevents diseases. It improves child health.

125. B: NACP targets HIV prevention and control. It includes awareness and treatment. It reduces transmission.

126. D: NVBDCP includes malaria, dengue, and filariasis. These are vector-borne diseases. Control involves vector management.

127. B: JSY promotes hospital deliveries. It reduces maternal mortality. It provides incentives.

128. A: NHM strengthens primary care. It improves accessibility. It supports rural health.

129. A: NTEP TB, UIP immunization, NACP HIV, NVBDCP vector diseases. These match objectives.

130. A: JSY maternal care, Ayushman insurance, ICDS nutrition, Mid-Day Meal school nutrition. These programs.

131. B: Programs cover both rural and urban areas. They are not limited. Hence second is incorrect.

132. B: Immunization protects. It reduces infections. Second statement is incorrect.

133. C: Ayushman Bharat covers hospitalization costs. It provides financial protection. It benefits poor families.

134. D: ICDS supports child development. It includes nutrition and education. It improves growth.

135. B: Mid-Day Meal supports school children. It improves nutrition. It encourages attendance.

136. D: NPCDCS focuses on NCDs. It includes cancer and diabetes. It promotes prevention.

137. B: Family welfare reduces population growth. It promotes planning. It improves health.

138. C: ASHA works at village level. She connects community and health system. She promotes awareness.

139. B: Program aims to reduce blindness. It provides treatment. It improves vision care.

140. A: Programs aim to improve health. They reduce disease burden. They enhance quality of life.

141. A: Health services include promotive, preventive, curative, and rehabilitative care. They aim to improve health status. They serve individuals and communities.

142. C: Primary care focuses on community needs. It is accessible and affordable. It is the first level of contact.

143. A: Primary care is the entry point to health system. It provides basic services. It is closest to the community.

144. C: CHCs are secondary-level facilities. They provide specialized services. They act as referral units.

145. A: Tertiary care includes advanced hospitals. It provides specialized services. It deals with complex cases.

146. C: "Health for all" includes physical, mental, and social well-being. It is comprehensive. It emphasizes prevention.

147. B: Alma-Ata Declaration promoted PHC. It emphasized accessibility and equity. It is a milestone.

148. C: Planning includes evaluation. It checks effectiveness. It improves services.

149. A: Primary PHC, secondary district hospital, tertiary super-specialty, community sub-centre. These are levels of case.

150. A: Education awareness, nutrition diet, immunization prevention, water sanitation. These are functions.

151. B: PHC includes prevention and promotion. It is not only treatment. Hence second statement is incorrect.

152. B: Planning improves resource use. It is essential. Hence second statement is incorrect.

153. A: Referral system ensures proper care. It moves patients appropriately. It improves outcomes.

154. A: Community participation is key. It improves acceptance. It strengthens programs.

155. A: Planning aims for efficient services. It ensures equity. It improves health outcomes.

156. A: Community health nurse promotes health. She provides preventive and promotive care. She works in community settings.

157. B: Nurse educates people. It prevents disease. It improves health awareness.

158. D: Nurse assesses community needs. She plans interventions. It improves care delivery.

159. A: Immunization prevents disease. Nurse administers vaccines. It reduces morbidity.

160. B: Teaching promotes healthy behavior. It prevents illness. It is key role.

161. D: Educator teaches, care provider gives care, advocate protects rights, manager organizes services. These are roles.

162. A: Nurse connects community and system. She facilitates services. She promotes care.

163. B: Nurse plays role in prevention. Health education is important. Second statement is incorrect.

164. D: Nurse supervises and manages programs. She ensures implementation. It is administrative function.

165. A: Home visits assess family health. They provide care. They improve outcomes.

166. A: Health education aims at behavior change. It promotes healthy practices. It improves community health.

167. D: Participation involves community involvement. It increases acceptance. It improves effectiveness.

168. A: Education should meet people's needs. It becomes effective. It ensures better results.

169. A: Lecture is one-way, demonstration shows procedure, discussion exchanges ideas, role play acts situation. These are methods.

170. B: Health education changes behavior. It prevents disease. Second statement is incorrect.

11. Communication & Education Technology

1. Communication is the process of exchanging information between individuals.

A. True B. False
C. Only verbal D. Only written

2. The person who sends the message in communication is called the ______.

A. Receiver B. Sender
C. Channel D. Feedback

3. Which element of communication is responsible for converting ideas into a message?

A. Decoding B. Feedback
C. Encoding D. Noise

4. The response given by the receiver to the sender is known as feedback.

A. Channel B. Noise
C. Message D. Feedback

5. Effective communication requires clarity and understanding between sender and receiver.

A. True B. False
C. Only written form D. Only oral form

6. The process of interpreting the message by the receiver is called ______.

A. Encoding B. Transmission
C. Noise D. Decoding

7. Which of the following is a barrier to effective communication?

A. Clarity B. Feedback
C. Noise D. Understanding

8. Match the elements of communication with their functions.

Column I	Column II
A. Sender	1. Medium of communication
B. Message	2. Person who interprets
C. Channel	3. Information transmitted
D. Receiver	4. Person who initiates

A. A-4, B-3, C-1, D-2 B. A-3, B-4, C-2, D-1
C. A-2, B-1, C-4, D-3 D. A-1, B-2, C-3, D-4

9. Assertion I: Feedback helps in improving communication.

Assertion II: Communication is always one-way.

A. Both statements are correct
B. I is correct, II is incorrect
C. Both are incorrect
D. I is incorrect, II is correct

10. The medium through which a message is transmitted is called the ______.

A. Sender B. Receiver
C. Message D. Channel

11. The ability to understand and share the feelings of another person is called ______.

A. Sympathy B. Empathy
C. Attitude D. Behavior

12. Which of the following is an essential element of effective interpersonal relationship?

A. Authority B. Dominance
C. Trust D. Isolation

13. Interpersonal relationship involves interaction between two or more individuals.

A. True B. False
C. Only one person D. Only groups

14. Respect for others is an important component of healthy interpersonal relationships.

A. Communication B. Feedback
C. Listening D. Respect

15. Active listening means paying full ______ to the speaker.

A. Judgment B. Criticism
C. Attention D. Ignorance

16. Good interpersonal relationships help in reducing conflicts and improving cooperation.

A. True B. False
C. Only at home D. Only at workplace

17. Which of the following is a barrier to interpersonal relationships?

A. Trust B. Respect
C. Miscommunication D. Understanding

18. Match the interpersonal skills with their meanings.

Column I	Column II
A. Empathy	1. Paying attention
B. Listening	2. Belief in others
C. Respect	3. Understanding feelings
D. Trust	4. Valuing others

A. A-3, B-1, C-4, D-2 B. A-1, B-3, C-2, D-4
C. A-2, B-4, C-1, D-3 D. A-4, B-2, C-3, D-1

19. **Assertion I:** Interpersonal relationships are important in nursing practice.

Assertion II: Nurses do not need communication skills.

A. Both statements are correct
B. I is correct, II is incorrect
C. Both are incorrect
D. I is incorrect, II is correct

20. A strong interpersonal relationship is built on mutual ______ between individuals.

A. Conflict B. Competition
C. Trust D. Authority

21. Counseling is a process that helps an individual to solve personal ______.

A. Conflicts B. Problems
C. Issues D. Tasks

22. Guidance is a continuous process aimed at helping individuals in making appropriate decisions.

A. True B. False
C. Only for students D. Only for patients

23. Which of the following is an important principle of counseling?

A. Judgment B. Criticism
C. Confidentiality D. Authority

24. The role of a counselor includes providing emotional support and helping individuals cope with problems.

A. Teaching only B. Diagnosing disease
C. Prescribing drugs D. Emotional support

25. **Assertion I:** Counseling helps in improving mental well-being.

Assertion II: Counseling has no role in solving personal problems.

A. Both statements are correct
B. I is correct, II is incorrect
C. Both are incorrect
D. I is incorrect, II is correct

26. Teaching is a process of imparting knowledge, skills, and ______ to learners.

A. Habits B. Values
C. Attitudes D. Beliefs

27. Learning is defined as a relatively permanent change in behavior due to experience.

A. True
B. False
C. Only temporary change
D. Only physical change

28. Which of the following is a principle of effective teaching?

A. Ignoring learners B. One-way communication
C. Active participation D. No feedback

29. Motivation plays an important role in the teaching-learning process by increasing interest in learning.

A. Only external B. Only internal
C. Not required D. Essential

30. Teaching should be learner-centered rather than teacher-centered.

A. True B. False
C. Only for schools D. Only for colleges

31. The use of examples and illustrations helps in better ______ of the subject matter.

A. Teaching B. Understanding
C. Writing D. Memorizing

32. Reinforcement is used to strengthen desired learning behavior.

A. True B. False
C. Only punishment D. Only reward

33. Which method is most suitable for active involvement of learners?

A. Lecture B. Reading
C. Discussion D. Observation

34. Match the teaching principles with their meanings.

Column I	Column II
A. Motivation	1. Encouragement
B. Reinforcement	2. Response to learner
C. Feedback	3. Involvement
D. Participation	4. Strengthening behavior

A. A-1, B-4, C-2, D-3 B. A-2, B-1, C-4, D-3
C. A-3, B-2, C-1, D-4 D. A-4, B-3, C-2, D-1

35. **Assertion I:** Teaching should be based on learner's needs.

Assertion II: Teaching does not require planning.

A. Both statements are correct
B. I is correct, II is incorrect
C. Both are incorrect
D. I is incorrect, II is correct

36. The lecture method is mainly a ______ type of communication.

A. Two-way B. Interactive
C. Informal D. One-way

37. Demonstration is a teaching method in which a procedure is shown to learners.

A. True B. False
C. Only theoretical D. Only written

38. Which teaching method encourages exchange of ideas among learners?

A. Lecture B. Demonstration
C. Group discussion D. Drill

39. Role play is used to develop communication skills by acting out real-life situations.

A. Only observation B. Only reading
C. Only writing D. Simulation of situations

40. **Assertion I:** Different teaching methods should be used according to learning objectives.

Assertion II: One teaching method is suitable for all situations.

A. Both statements are correct
B. I is correct, II is incorrect
C. Both are incorrect
D. I is incorrect, II is correct

41. Evaluation is the process of assessing the achievement of ______ in teaching.

A. Objectives B. Methods
C. Teachers D. Books

42. Evaluation helps in improving the teaching-learning process.

A. True B. False
C. Only for exams D. Only for teachers

43. Which type of evaluation is done during the teaching-learning process?

A. Summative evaluation
B. Final evaluation
C. Formative evaluation
D. Annual evaluation

44. Evaluation also helps in identifying the strengths and weaknesses of learners.

A. Only strengths
B. Only weaknesses
C. Only marks
D. Both strengths and weaknesses

45. **Assertion I:** Evaluation is a continuous process.

Assertion II: Evaluation is done only at the end of teaching.

A. Both statements are correct
B. I is correct, II is incorrect
C. Both are incorrect
D. I is incorrect, II is correct

EXPLANATORY ANSWERS

1. **A:** Communication involves exchange of ideas and information. It can be verbal or non-verbal. It is essential for understanding.

2. **B:** Sender initiates communication. He conveys message. It starts the process.

3. **C:** Encoding converts ideas into message form. It is essential for communication. It ensures clarity.

4. **D:** Feedback is response from receiver. It confirms understanding. It completes communication.

5. **A:** Effective communication requires clarity. It ensures proper understanding. It avoids confusion.

6. **D:** Decoding is interpretation of message. It is done by receiver. It ensures understanding.

7. **C:** Noise interferes with communication. It distorts message. It acts as barrier.

8. **A:** Sender initiates, message is information, channel is medium, receiver interprets. These are elements.

9. **B:** Feedback improves communication. Communication is two-way. Second statement is incorrect.

10. **D:** Channel is medium of communication. It carries message. It connects sender and receiver.

11. **B:** Empathy means understanding feelings of others. It helps in communication. It builds strong relationships.

12. **C:** Trust is essential for relationships. It promotes openness. It strengthens interaction.

13. **A:** Interpersonal relations involve interaction. It includes communication. It is between individuals.

14. **D:** Respect maintains dignity. It builds healthy relations. It improves cooperation.

15. **C:** Active listening requires focus. It ensures understanding. It improves communication.

16. **A:** Good relations reduce conflicts. They improve teamwork. They promote harmony.

17. **C:** Miscommunication creates misunderstanding. It damages relations. It acts as barrier.

18. **A:** Empathy understanding, listening attention, respect valuing, trust belief. These are skills.

19. **B:** Relationships are important. Nurses need communication skills. Second statement is incorrect.

20. **C:** Trust strengthens relationships. It ensures cooperation. It builds understanding.

21. **B:** Counseling helps individuals deal with personal issues. It improves coping ability. It supports decision-making.

22. **A:** Guidance is ongoing process. It helps individuals make choices. It supports development.

23. **C:** Confidentiality builds trust. It protects privacy. It is essential in counseling.

24. **D:** Counselor supports emotionally. It helps coping. It improves mental health.

25. **B:** Counseling improves well-being. It helps solve problems. Second statement is incorrect.

26. **C:** Teaching includes knowledge, skills, and attitudes. It develops personality. It influences behavior.

27. **A:** Learning is permanent change. It occurs through experience. It modifies behavior.

28. **C:** Active involvement improves learning. It increases understanding. It makes teaching effective.

29. **D:** Motivation encourages learning. It increases interest. It improves performance.

30. **A:** Learner-centered approach is effective. It focuses on needs. It improves learning.

31. **B:** Examples clarify concepts. They improve comprehension. They make learning easy.

32. **A:** Reinforcement strengthens behavior. It encourages learning. It improves retention.

33. **C:** Discussion involves participation. It promotes interaction. It enhances understanding.

34. **A:** Motivation encourages, reinforcement strengthens, feedback gives response, participation involves learners. These are principles.

35. **B:** Teaching needs planning. It should meet learner needs. Second statement is incorrect.

36. **D:** Lecture is one-way communication. Teacher delivers content. Learner listens passively.

37. **A:** Demonstration shows procedures. It improves understanding. It is practical method.

38. **C:** Discussion involves exchange of ideas. It promotes interaction. It improves learning.

39. **D:** Role play simulates real situations. It develops skills. It improves communication.

40. **B:** Methods vary by objective. No single method suits all. Second statement is incorrect.

41. **A:** Evaluation measures achievement of objectives. It checks learning outcomes. It guides improvement.

42. **A:** Evaluation improves teaching. It identifies gaps. It enhances learning.

43. **C:** Formative evaluation is ongoing. It monitors progress. It helps improvement.

44. **D:** Evaluation identifies strengths and weaknesses. It guides learning. It improves performance.

45. **B:** Evaluation is continuous. It is not limited to end. Second statement is incorrect.

12. Child Health Nursing

1. Growth refers to an increase in the size and weight of the body.
   A. True B. False
   C. Only mental change D. Only emotional change

2. Development refers to qualitative changes in the child's
   A. Weight B. Height
   C. Abilities D. Age

3. Which of the following is a principle of growth and development?
   A. Growth stops early
   B. Development is uniform
   C. Development is continuous
   D. Only physical growth

4. The direction of development from head to toe is known as cephalocaudal development.
   A. Proximodistal B. General to specific
   C. Simple to complex D. Cephalocaudal

5. Which factor most influences growth and development in children?
   A. Nutrition B. Climate
   C. Religion D. Language

6. The average birth weight of a newborn is about ____ kg.
   A. 2.0 B. 2.5
   C. 3.0 D. 3.5

7. Development proceeds from simple to complex patterns.
   A. True B. False
   C. Only in adults D. Only mental

8. Which stage of development is characterized by rapid physical growth in infancy?
   A. Adolescence B. Infancy
   C. Childhood D. Old age

9. Which aspect of development involves learning to think and reason?
   A. Physical B. Social
   C. Cognitive D. Emotional

10. The development of skills from central to peripheral parts is known as proximodistal development.
    A. Cephalocaudal B. Sequential
    C. Continuous D. Proximodistal

11. The age at which a child usually doubles birth weight is about ______ months.
    A. 3 B. 5
    C. 6 D. 9

12. Growth is influenced by both genetic and environmental factors.
    A. True B. False
    C. Only genetic D. Only environment

13. Which of the following is a milestone of development in infancy?
    A. Walking at 1 month
    B. Talking at 2 months
    C. Sitting without support
    D. Reading

14. Which factor can negatively affect growth in children?
    A. Good nutrition B. Proper care
    C. Exercise D. Malnutrition

15. Which development domain involves relationships and interactions?
    A. Physical B. Cognitive
    C. Social D. Motor

16. Match the stages of development with age groups.

Column I	Column II
A. Infancy	1. 1–3 years
B. Toddler	2. 6–12 years
C. Preschool	3. Birth–1 year
D. School age	4. 3–6 years

   A. A-3, B-1, C-4, D-2 B. A-1, B-3, C-2, D-4
   C. A-2, B-4, C-3, D-1 D. A-4, B-2, C-1, D-3

17. The term growth monitoring refers to regular measurement of ______ in children.

A. Blood pressure B. Height and weight
C. Pulse D. Temperature

18. Assertion I: Growth and development are interrelated processes.

Assertion II: Growth occurs without development.

A. Both statements are correct
B. I is correct, II is incorrect
C. Both are incorrect
D. I is incorrect, II is correct

19. Assertion I: Nutrition plays a key role in growth.

Assertion II: Nutrition has no effect on development.

A. Both statements are correct
B. I is correct, II is incorrect
C. Both are incorrect
D. I is incorrect, II is correct

20. Growth charts are used to assess the physical growth of children over time.

A. True B. False
C. Only for adults D. Only for sick children

21. A neonate is defined as a baby within ______ days of birth.

A. 14 B. 21
C. 28 D. 30

22. The Apgar score is assessed at ______ and 5 minutes after birth.

A. 1 minute B. 2 minutes
C. 3 minutes D. 4 minutes

23. Which parameter is included in the Apgar scoring system?

A. Weight B. Length
C. Heart rate D. Temperature

24. The normal respiratory rate of a newborn is about 40–60 breaths per minute.

A. 20–30 B. 30–40
C. 60–80 D. 40–60

25. The normal birth weight of a neonate ranges from ______ kg.

A. 1–2 B. 2.5–3.5
C. 3–4 D. 4–5

26. Which of the following is the most important immediate care of the newborn?

A. Bathing B. Feeding
C. Drying and warming D. Immunization

27. The normal heart rate of a newborn is about ______ beats per minute.

A. 80–100 B. 100–120
C. 120–160 D. 160–180

28. Which reflex is present at birth in a normal newborn?

A. Gag reflex B. Corneal reflex
C. Moro reflex D. Knee reflex

29. Early initiation of breastfeeding helps in improving neonatal survival.

A. True B. False
C. Only for mothers D. Only for sick babies

30. The first milk produced after delivery is called ______.

A. Mature milk B. Formula milk
C. Colostrum D. Artificial milk

31. Which vitamin is commonly given to newborns to prevent bleeding disorders?

A. Vitamin A B. Vitamin C
C. Vitamin D D. Vitamin K

32. Thermoregulation is important in newborns because they cannot regulate their body temperature effectively.

A. True B. False
C. Only in adults D. Only in preterm

33. The condition of yellow discoloration of skin in newborn is called ______.

A. Cyanosis B. Pallor
C. Jaundice D. Anemia

34. Which method is used for maintaining warmth in low birth weight babies?

A. Phototherapy B. Kangaroo mother care
C. Oxygen therapy D. Ventilation

35. The average length of a newborn is about ______ cm.

A. 40 B. 45
C. 50 D. 60

36. Which complication is commonly seen in preterm babies?

A. Hypertension B. Obesity
C. Respiratory distress D. Diabetes

37. The umbilical cord normally falls off within 1–2 weeks after birth.

A. True B. False
C. Only after 1 month D. Only in hospital

38. The newborn is classified as low birth weight if weight is less than ______ kg.

A. 1.5 B. 2.0
C. 2.5 D. 3.0

39. Which of the following is an essential component of immediate newborn care?

A. Bathing B. Dressing
C. Delayed feeding D. Airway maintenance

40. Exclusive breastfeeding is recommended for the first 6 months of life.

A. True B. False
C. Only for 3 months D. Only for 1 month

41. Match the neonatal reflexes with their characteristics.

Column I	Column II
A. Moro reflex	1. Turning head to stimulus
B. Rooting reflex	2. Startle response
C. Sucking reflex	3. Holding object
D. Grasp reflex	4. Feeding reflex

A. A-2, B-1, C-4, D-3 B. A-1, B-2, C-3, D-4
C. A-3, B-4, C-1, D-2 D. A-4, B-3, C-2, D-1

42. The first stool passed by a newborn is called _____.

A. Urine B. Milk stool
C. Meconium D. Feces

43. Match the neonatal conditions with their meanings.

Column I	Column II
A. Cyanosis	1. Yellow skin
B. Jaundice	2. Blue discoloration
C. Apnea	3. Low body temperature
D. Hypothermia	4. Absence of breathing

A. A-2, B-1, C-4, D-3 B. A-1, B-3, C-2, D-4
C. A-3, B-2, C-1, D-4 D. A-4, B-1, C-2, D-3

44. Which sign indicates good health in a newborn?

A. Weak cry B. Poor feeding
C. Active movement D. Cyanosis

45. Assertion I: Early breastfeeding is beneficial for newborn.

Assertion II: Colostrum should be discarded.

A. Both are correct B. I is correct, II is incorrect
C. Both are incorrect D. I is incorrect, II is correct

46. Assertion I: Newborns are prone to hypothermia.

Assertion II: They have poor temperature regulation.

A. Both are correct B. I is correct, II is incorrect
C. Both are incorrect D. I is incorrect, II is correct

47. Assertion I: Vitamin K is given to prevent bleeding.

Assertion II: Newborns have low vitamin K levels.

A. Both are correct B. I is correct, II is incorrect
C. Both are incorrect D. I is incorrect, II is correct

48. Proper hygiene is essential in neonatal care to prevent infections.

A. True B. False
C. Only in hospital D. Only in NICU

49. The normal head circumference of a newborn is about ______ cm.

A. 25 B. 30
C. 35 D. 40

50. Newborn screening helps in early detection of certain congenital disorders.

A. True B. False
C. Only for adults D. Only for mothers

51. IMNCI stands for Integrated Management of Neonatal and ______ Illness.

A. Nutritional B. Childhood
C. Communicable D. Chronic

52. Which of the following age groups is covered under IMNCI strategy?

A. Only neonates B. Only adults
C. 0–5 years children D. Only adolescents

53. IMNCI approach focuses on improving case management skills of health workers.

A. True B. False
C. Only hospital care D. Only diagnosis

54. The IMNCI guidelines classify illnesses into different ______ for management.

A. Levels B. Categories
C. Phases D. Groups

55. Which of the following is a key component of IMNCI strategy?

A. Surgery B. Radiology
C. Laboratory work D. Community participation

56. IMNCI uses color coding such as pink, yellow, and green for classification of illness.

A. True B. False
C. Only red D. Only blue

57. The pink color in IMNCI indicates _____ condition.

A. Mild B. Moderate
C. No illness D. Severe

58. Which of the following conditions is considered a danger sign in IMNCI?

A. Mild fever B. Normal feeding
C. Convulsions D. Normal activity

59. The presence of chest indrawing in a child indicates severe respiratory illness.

A. True B. False
C. Only mild illness D. Only chronic disease

60. IMNCI emphasizes early identification and referral of serious cases.

A. True B. False
C. Only treatment D. Only diagnosis

61. The IMNCI chart booklet is used by health workers for ______ of illness.

A. Treatment B. Diagnosis
C. Classification D. Prevention

62. Which symptom is assessed in IMNCI for diarrheal disease?

A. Headache B. Vomiting
C. Dehydration D. Cough

63. The yellow color in IMNCI classification indicates moderate illness requiring treatment.

A. Mild illness B. No illness
C. Severe illness D. Moderate illness

64. Feeding practices are an important part of IMNCI counseling.

A. True B. False
C. Only for adults D. Only for sick children

65. Match the IMNCI color codes with their meanings.

Column I	Column II
A. Pink	1. Home care
B. Yellow	2. Severe illness
C. Green	3. Moderate illness
D. Red	4. Not used

A. A-2, B-3, C-1, D-4 B. A-1, B-2, C-3, D-4
C. A-3, B-1, C-2, D-4 D. A-4, B-2, C-3, D-1

66. Which of the following is assessed under IMNCI for respiratory illness?

A. Pulse rate B. Blood pressure
C. Fast breathing D. Temperature only

67. IMNCI includes both preventive and curative aspects of care.

A. True B. False
C. Only curative D. Only preventive

68. The main aim of IMNCI is to reduce child ______ and morbidity.

A. Disability B. Mortality
C. Infection D. Malnutrition

69. **Assertion I:** IMNCI improves child survival.
Assertion II: IMNCI focuses only on hospital-based care.

A. Both are correct B. I is correct, II is incorrect
C. Both are incorrect D. I is incorrect, II is correct

70. **Assertion I:** Early referral is important in severe illness.
Assertion II: Delay in referral can increase risk of complications.

A. Both are correct B. I is correct, II is incorrect
C. Both are incorrect D. I is incorrect, II is correct

71. Measles is caused by a ______.

A. Bacteria B. Fungus
C. Parasite D. Virus

72. Which of the following is a symptom of measles?

A. Rash B. Chest pain
C. Paralysis D. Jaundice

73. Which disease is prevented by DPT vaccine?

A. Measles B. Polio
C. Diphtheria D. Hepatitis

74. The causative organism of tuberculosis is ______.

A. Virus B. Bacteria
C. Fungus D. Parasite

75. Which of the following is a complication of measles?

A. Diabetes B. Hypertension
C. Asthma D. Pneumonia

76. Chickenpox is a highly contagious viral disease.

A. True B. False
C. Only bacterial D. Only fungal

77. Which disease is caused by Mycobacterium tuberculosis?

A. Measles B. Tuberculosis
C. Polio D. Dengue

78. The causative agent of malaria is ______.

A. Virus B. Bacteria
C. Protozoa D. Fungus

79. Which disease is transmitted by Aedes mosquito?

A. Malaria B. Typhoid
C. Dengue D. Cholera

80. Which of the following is a sign of dehydration in children?

A. Sunken eyes B. High BP
C. Normal skin D. Increased urine

81. Oral rehydration solution is used to treat ______.

A. Fever B. Dehydration
C. Infection D. Cough

82. Which disease is caused by poliovirus?

A. Measles B. Tuberculosis
C. Chickenpox D. Poliomyelitis

83. Polio mainly affects which system?

A. Respiratory B. Digestive
C. Nervous D. Circulatory

84. Immunization protects children from many infectious diseases.

A. True B. False
C. Only adults D. Only elderly

85. The vaccine given at birth for tuberculosis is ______.

A. OPV B. BCG
C. DPT D. MMR

86. Which disease causes severe diarrhea in children?
A. Asthma B. Cholera
C. Cancer D. Diabetes

87. Which vitamin deficiency causes rickets?
A. Vitamin A B. Vitamin C
C. Vitamin D D. Vitamin K

88. Which disease is caused by Bordetella pertussis?
A. Measles B. Whooping cough
C. TB D. Polio

89. The inflammation of tonsils is called ______.
A. Pharyngitis B. Tonsillitis
C. Laryngitis D. Bronchitis

90. Which of the following is a complication of untreated diarrhea?
A. Obesity B. Hypertension
C. Diabetes D. Dehydration

91. Pneumonia affects which organ?
A. Heart B. Liver
C. Lungs D. Kidney

92. Pneumonia can be caused by bacteria, viruses, or fungi.
A. True B. False
C. Only bacteria D. Only virus

93. The inflammation of the middle ear is called ______.
A. Sinusitis B. Otitis media
C. Rhinitis D. Bronchitis

94. Which of the following is a symptom of pneumonia?
A. Cough B. Rash
C. Paralysis D. Blindness

95. Which disease is prevented by measles vaccine?
A. Polio B. TB
C. Measles D. Diphtheria

96. Which disease is transmitted through contaminated water?
A. Dengue B. Cholera
C. Measles D. TB

97. The causative agent of typhoid is ______.
A. Virus B. Salmonella
C. Protozoa D. Fungus

98. Which of the following is a complication of tuberculosis?
A. Diabetes B. Cancer
C. Hypertension D. Lung damage

99. Which disease is caused by deficiency of iodine?
A. Rickets B. Scurvy
C. Goitre D. Anemia

100. Handwashing helps in preventing infectious diseases in children.
A. True B. False
C. Only adults D. Only hospitals

101. The deficiency of vitamin A causes ______.
A. Night blindness B. Rickets
C. Scurvy D. Beriberi

102. Which disease affects red blood cells in children?
A. Diabetes B. Anemia
C. Hypertension D. Cancer

103. Which disease is caused by rubella virus?
A. Measles B. Chickenpox
C. Rubella D. Polio

104. Which of the following is a sign of malnutrition?
A. Normal weight B. Good appetite
C. Stunted growth D. Strong immunity

105. Balanced diet is essential for growth and development of children.
A. True B. False
C. Only adults D. Only infants

106. Which of the following is a complication of severe malnutrition?
A. Obesity B. Diabetes
C. Hypertension D. Growth failure

107. Which disease is caused by deficiency of vitamin C?
A. Rickets B. Scurvy
C. Beriberi D. Pellagra

108. The condition of reduced hemoglobin in blood is called ______.
A. Diabetes B. Hypertension
C. Anemia D. Cancer

109. Which disease is prevented by oral polio vaccine?
A. Measles B. TB
C. Polio D. Dengue

110. Early diagnosis and treatment can prevent complications of childhood diseases.
A. True B. False
C. Only severe cases D. Only adults

111. The fear of darkness in children is called ______.
A. Phobia B. Anxiety
C. Fear D. Depression

112. Bedwetting in children is medically termed as enuresis.
A. True B. False
C. Only daytime D. Only adults

113. Which of the following is a common behavioral problem in children?

A. Hypertension B. Diabetes
C. Temper tantrums D. Cancer

114. Thumb sucking in young children is considered a normal behavior up to a certain age.

A. Always abnormal B. Always harmful
C. Only in adults D. Normal behavior

115. Excessive fear or anxiety without clear reason is called ______.

A. Anger B. Phobia
C. Habit D. Interest

116. Which of the following is a common sleep problem in children?

A. Insomnia B. Hypertension
C. Diabetes D. Asthma

117. Nail biting is considered a habit disorder in children.

A. True B. False
C. Only in adults D. Only in infants

118. The inability to control urination at night is called ______.

A. Dysuria B. Enuresis
C. Polyuria D. Hematuria

119. Which of the following is an emotional problem in children?

A. Fever B. Infection
C. Anxiety D. Fracture

120. Good parenting helps in preventing behavioral problems in children.

A. True B. False
C. Only for school D. Only for hospital

121. The repeated act of hair pulling is called ______.

A. Depression B. Trichotillomania
C. Anxiety D. Fear

122. Which of the following is an example of a habit disorder?

A. Fever B. Infection
C. Injury D. Nail biting

123. Behavioral problems in children may arise due to environmental and emotional factors.

A. True B. False
C. Only genetic D. Only physical

124. Which of the following is a sign of anxiety in children?

A. Calmness B. Relaxation
C. Normal sleep D. Restlessness

125. Parental neglect can lead to behavioral problems in children.

A. True B. False
C. Only in adults D. Only in schools

126. Which approach is useful in managing behavioral problems?

A. Punishment B. Counseling
C. Ignoring D. Isolation

127. The inability to concentrate or remain still is called ______.

A. Anxiety B. Hyperactivity
C. Depression D. Fear

128. Consistent discipline helps in correcting behavioral problems.

A. True B. False
C. Only punishment D. Only reward

129. Which of the following is a method to manage temper tantrums?

A. Encouragement B. Calm approach
C. Ignoring behavior D. Rewarding anger

130. Early identification of behavioral problems helps in effective management.

A. True B. False
C. Only late D. Only severe cases

EXPLANATORY ANSWERS

1. **A:** Growth refers to increase in size. It includes height and weight. It is measurable.

2. **C:** Development involves functional changes. It includes skills and abilities. It is qualitative.

3. **C:** Development occurs throughout life. It is gradual. It is sequential.

4. **D:** Development proceeds head to toe. Head develops first. Then lower parts.

5. **A:** Nutrition affects growth. It supports development. Poor nutrition delays growth.

6. **C:** Average birth weight is around 3 kg. It varies slightly. It indicates health.

7. **A:** Development progresses simple to complex. Skills become refined. It is orderly.

8. **B:** Infancy shows rapid growth. Physical changes are fast. It is critical stage.

9. **C:** Cognitive development includes thinking. It involves reasoning. It affects learning.

10. **D:** Development proceeds center to extremities. Trunk develops first. Then limbs.

11. B: Birth weight doubles by 5 months. It triples by one year. It indicates normal growth.

12. A: Both heredity and environment influence growth. Nutrition, health also matter. It is multifactorial.

13. C: Sitting is milestone. It occurs around 6 months. It indicates development.

14. D: Malnutrition impairs growth. It causes delays. It affects health.

15. C: Social development includes relationships. It involves interaction. It affects behaviour.

16. A: Infancy birth-1, toddler 1-3, preschool 3-6, school age 6-12. These are stages of development.

17. B: Growth monitoring measures growth. It tracks progress. It detects problems.

18. B: Growth and development are linked. Growth alone not enough. Second statement is incorrect.

19. B: Nutrition is essential. It affects development. Second incorrect.

20. A: Growth charts track growth. They compare standards. They help assessment.

21. C: Neonate is first 28 days. It is critical period. Requires special care.

22. A: Apgar is at 1 and 5 min. It assesses condition. It guides care.

23. C: Apgar includes HR, respiration, tone. It assesses vitality.

24. D: Normal RR is 40–60. It indicates breathing status.

25. B: Normal weight range. Indicates healthy baby.

26. C: Prevents hypothermia. Essential immediately.

27. C: Normal HR range. Indicates circulation.

28. C: Present at birth. Indicates CNS function.

29. A: Breastfeeding improves survival. Provides immunity.

30. C: First milk rich in antibodies. Protects baby.

31. D: Prevents bleeding. Newborn has low stores.

32. A: Newborns lose heat easily. Need warmth.

33. C: Yellow skin due to bilirubin. Common in newborns.

34. B: Skin-to-skin keeps warm. Helps growth.

35. C: Average length. Indicates normal growth.

36. C: Preterms have immature lungs. Need support.

37. A: Cord falls in 1–2 weeks. Normal process.

38. C: LBW <2.5 kg. High risk. Needs care.

39. D: First priority. Ensures breathing.

40. A: Exclusive breastfeeding 6 months. Improves health.

41. A: Reflexes indicate development. Important for assessment.

42. C: First stool. Dark green. Normal finding.

43. A: Cyanosis blue, jaundice yellow, apnea no breathing, hypothermia cold.

44. C: Indicates good health. Shows vitality.

45. B: Colostrum beneficial. Should not discard.

46. A: Newborns lose heat. Poor regulation.

47. A: Vitamin K prevents bleeding. Low at birth.

48. A: Hygiene prevents infection. Essential care.

49. C: Normal head size. Indicates brain growth.

50. A: Screening detects disorders early. Improves outcomes.

51. B: IMNCI stands for Integrated Management of Neonatal and Childhood Illness. It focuses on under-five children. It improves survival.

52. C: IMNCI covers children below 5 years. This age group is most vulnerable. It reduces mortality.

53. A: IMNCI improves health worker skills. It enhances case management. It ensures proper care.

54. B: IMNCI classifies illnesses. It helps treatment decisions. It simplifies care.

55. D: IMNCI involves community. It improves awareness. It supports prevention.

56. A: IMNCI uses color coding. It helps classification. It guides treatment.

57. D: Pink indicates severe illness. It needs urgent referral. It is critical.

58. C: Convulsions are danger signs. They indicate severe illness. Immediate care needed.

59. A: Chest indrawing shows severe pneumonia. It requires urgent care. It is danger sign.

60. A: Early identification is key. Referral prevents complications. It saves lives.

61. C: Chart booklet helps classification. It guides management. It standardizes care.

62. C: Dehydration is key in diarrhea. It indicates severity. It guides treatment.

63. D: Yellow indicates moderate illness. It requires treatment. It may not need referral.

64. A: Feeding advice is important. It prevents malnutrition. It supports recovery.

65. A: Pink severe, yellow moderate, green home care. Red not used. It guides management.

66. C: Fast breathing indicates pneumonia. It is important sign. It needs attention.

67. A: IMNCI includes prevention and treatment. It is holistic. It improves health.

68. B: IMNCI reduces deaths. It improves survival. It also reduces illness.

69. B: IMNCI improves survival. It includes community care. Not only hospital.

70. A: Early referral is essential. Delay worsens condition. It increases risk.

71. D: Measles is caused by virus. It spreads easily. It causes rash and fever.

72. A: Rash is common symptom. It appears after fever. It spreads over body.

73. C: DPT protects against diphtheria. It also prevents pertussis and tetanus.

74. B: TB is bacterial infection. It spreads via air. It affects lungs.

75. D: Measles can lead to pneumonia. It is serious. Needs treatment.

76. A: Chickenpox is viral. It spreads easily. It causes rash.

77. B: TB caused by bacteria. It affects lungs. It spreads via air.

78. C: Malaria is protozoal. Spread by mosquito. It causes fever.

79. C: Dengue spread by Aedes mosquito. It causes fever. It is viral.

80. A: Dehydration shows sunken eyes. Also dry mouth. Needs ORS.

81. B: ORS replaces fluids. Prevents dehydration. Saves life.

82. D: Polio caused by virus. It affects nerves. Causes paralysis.

83. C: Polio damages nerves. Causes weakness. Affects movement.

84. A: Immunization prevents diseases. Protects children. Improves health.

85. B: BCG protects TB. Given at birth. Prevents severe forms.

86. B: Cholera causes diarrhea. Leads dehydration. Needs ORS.

87. C: Deficiency causes rickets. Bones become weak. Growth affected.

88. B: Caused by bacteria. Causes severe cough. Vaccination prevents.

89. B: Tonsils inflamed. Causes sore throat. Infection common.

90. D: Diarrhea causes fluid loss. Leads dehydration. Dangerous.

91. C: Pneumonia affects lungs. Causes cough. Breathing difficulty.

92. A: Pneumonia has many causes. It can be viral or bacterial. Treatment varies.

93. B: Middle ear infection. Causes pain. Common in children.

94. A: Pneumonia causes cough. Also fever. Needs treatment.

95. C: Vaccine prevents measles. Reduces complications. Saves lives.

96. B: Water-borne disease. Due to contamination. Causes diarrhea.

97. B: Typhoid caused by Salmonella. Spread by food. Causes fever.

98. D: TB damages lungs. Causes complications. Needs treatment.

99. C: Iodine deficiency enlarges thyroid. Causes goitre. Affects metabolism.

100. A: Handwashing prevents infection. Reduces disease spread. Essential hygiene.

101. A: Vitamin A deficiency affects vision. Causes blindness. Needs supplementation.

102. B: Low hemoglobin. Causes weakness. Needs iron.

103. C: Viral disease. Causes rash. Vaccination prevents.

104. C: Malnutrition affects growth. Causes stunting. Needs nutrition.

105. A: Balanced diet supports growth. Provides nutrients. Prevents disease.

106. D: Malnutrition affects growth. Delays development. Needs care.

107. B: Vitamin C deficiency. Causes bleeding gums. Weakness.

108. C: Low hemoglobin. Causes fatigue. Needs treatment.

109. C: OPV prevents polio. Protects nerves. Prevents paralysis.

110. A: Early treatment prevents complications. Improves outcomes. Reduces mortality.

111. B: Phobia is irrational fear. It may occur in children. Needs reassurance.

112. A: Enuresis is bedwetting. Common in children. Often resolves.

113. C: Common in toddlers. Due to frustration. Needs management.

114. D: Thumb sucking normal in early age. Becomes concern later. Needs guidance.

115. B: Excess fear without reason. Affects behavior. Needs support.

116. A: Sleep problem. Causes irritability. Needs routine.

117. A: Nail biting is habit disorder. Due to stress. Needs correction.

118. B: Bedwetting condition. Common in children. Needs support.

119. C: Emotional problem. Causes stress. Needs care.

120. A: Good parenting prevents problems. Provides support. Builds confidence.

121. B: Hair pulling disorder. Due to stress. Needs therapy.

122. D: Habit disorder. Linked with anxiety. Needs control.

123. A: Behavior affected by environment. Also emotions. Needs care.

124. D: Anxiety causes restlessness. Affects behavior. Needs attention.

125. A: Neglect affects child. Causes problems. Needs care.

126. B: Helps understanding. Provides support. Improves behavior.

127. B: Child cannot sit still. Needs management. May need therapy.

128. A: Discipline guides behavior. Consistency important. Avoid harshness.

129. B: Calm handling effective. Reduces tantrums. Helps control.

130. A: Early detection helps. Prevents complications. Improves outcome.

13. Mental Health Nursing

1. Mental health is defined as a state of well-being in which an individual realizes his abilities and can cope with normal stresses.

A. True B. False
C. Only physical health D. Only emotional health

2. Mental health includes emotional, psychological, and ______ well-being of an individual.

A. Physical B. Social
C. Spiritual D. Cultural

3. Which of the following is a characteristic of good mental health?

A. Isolation B. Anxiety
C. Adjustment D. Aggression

4. Mental illness affects thinking, mood, and behavior of an individual.

A. Only thinking B. Only mood
C. Only behavior D. All of these

5. The ability to cope with stress is an important aspect of ______ health.

A. Physical B. Mental
C. Social D. Emotional

6. Which of the following factors can influence mental health?

A. Genetics B. Environment
C. Social support D. All of these

7. Mental health problems may arise due to biological, psychological, and ______ factors.

A. Social B. Economic
C. Physical D. Cultural

8. Which of the following is a sign of poor mental health?

A. Happiness B. Stability
C. Irritability D. Adjustment

9. Stress is a normal response of the body to challenging situations.

A. Only abnormal B. Only disease
C. Only mental illness D. Normal response

10. The ability to maintain good relationships is an indicator of ______ mental health.

A. Poor B. Good
C. Severe D. Chronic

11. Mental health promotion focuses on improving well-being and preventing mental illness.

A. True B. False
C. Only treatment D. Only diagnosis

12. Which of the following is an example of a coping strategy?

A. Avoidance B. Substance abuse
C. Problem solving D. Aggression

13. Mental hygiene refers to the maintenance of ______ health.

A. Physical B. Mental
C. Emotional D. Social

14. Match the components of mental health with their meanings.

Column I	Column II
A. Emotional health	1. Interaction with others
B. Social health	2. Thinking and reasoning
C. Psychological health	3. Feeling and emotions
D. Physical health	4. Body functions

A. A-3, B-1, C-2, D-4 B. A-2, B-3, C-1, D-4
C. A-1, B-2, C-3, D-4 D. A-4, B-3, C-2, D-1

15. Assertion I: Mental health is important for overall well-being.

Assertion II: Mental health has no effect on physical health.

A. Both are correct B. I is correct, II is incorrect
C. Both are incorrect D. I is incorrect, II is correct

16. Therapeutic communication is a purposeful use of communication to promote ______.

A. Conflict B. Illness
C. Stress D. Healing

17. Which of the following is an important technique of therapeutic communication?

A. Ignoring B. Judging
C. Active listening D. Arguing

18. Therapeutic communication is used mainly to help patients express feelings and concerns.

A. Only diagnosis B. Only treatment
C. Only observation D. Expression of feelings

19. The process of understanding the message of the patient is called ______.

A. Encoding B. Feedback
C. Listening D. Speaking

20. Empathy is the ability to understand and share the feelings of another person.

A. True B. False
C. Only sympathy D. Only advice

21. Non-verbal communication includes gestures, facial expressions, and ______.

A. Writing B. Speaking
C. Listening D. Body language

22. Which of the following is a barrier to effective communication?

A. Clarity B. Feedback
C. Noise D. Understanding

23. Maintaining eye contact during communication shows interest and attentiveness.

A. True B. False
C. Only in children D. Only in adults

24. Which of the following is a therapeutic communication technique?

A. Giving orders B. Changing topic
C. Ignoring patient D. Encouraging expression

25. Silence is used in communication to give the patient time to ______.

A. Sleep B. Think
C. Ignore D. Speak

26. Open-ended questions help the patient to express feelings freely.

A. True B. False
C. Only closed answers D. Only yes/no

27. Which of the following is a non-therapeutic communication technique?

A. Clarifying B. Reflecting
C. Giving advice D. Summarizing

28. Therapeutic communication helps in building ______ between nurse and patient.

A. Conflict B. Fear
C. Anger D. Trust

29. Match the communication techniques with their meanings.

Column I	Column II
A. Clarifying	1. Restating main points
B. Reflecting	2. Repeating patient's ideas
C. Summarizing	3. Seeking explanation
D. Silence	4. Allowing time

A. A-3, B-2, C-1, D-4 B. A-2, B-1, C-4, D-3
C. A-1, B-3, C-2, D-4 D. A-4, B-2, C-3, D-1

30. **Assertion I:** Therapeutic communication improves patient care.

Assertion II: Communication has no role in nursing practice.

A. Both are correct B. I is correct, II is incorrect
C. Both are incorrect D. I is incorrect, II is correct

31. Schizophrenia is a severe mental disorder affecting ______, perception, and behavior.

A. Vision B. Hearing
C. Thinking D. Speech

32. Schizophrenia is characterized by disturbances in thought, perception, and behavior.

A. True B. False
C. Only behavior D. Only thought

33. Which of the following is a positive symptom of schizophrenia?

A. Social withdrawal B. Lack of motivation
C. Hallucinations D. Flat affect

34. Delusions are false beliefs that are firmly held despite evidence to the contrary.

A. Perception B. Emotion
C. Behavior D. False beliefs

35. The hearing of voices without external stimulus is called ______.

A. Illusion B. Delusion
C. Hallucination D. Fantasy

36. Negative symptoms of schizophrenia include lack of emotion and social withdrawal.

A. True
B. False
C. Only positive symptoms
D. Only physical symptoms

37. Which of the following is a negative symptom of schizophrenia?

A. Hallucination B. Delusion
C. Agitation D. Apathy

38. Which neurotransmitter is commonly associated with schizophrenia?

A. Serotonin B. GABA
C. Dopamine D. Acetylcholine

39. Disorganized thinking is also called ______ disorder in schizophrenia.

A. Mood B. Behavior
C. Thought D. Memory

40. Schizophrenia usually affects young adults.

A. True B. False
C. Only children D. Only elderly

41. Which of the following is a type of schizophrenia characterized by disorganized speech and behavior?

A. Paranoid B. Catatonic
C. Residual D. Disorganized

42. Antipsychotic drugs are used in the treatment of schizophrenia.

A. True B. False
C. Only antibiotics D. Only sedatives

43. The lack of emotional expression in schizophrenia is called ______ affect.

A. Blunted B. Flat
C. Restricted D. Elevated

44. Which of the following is a symptom of catatonic schizophrenia?

A. Excess movement B. Hallucinations
C. Delusions D. Immobility

45. Which of the following is a cognitive symptom of schizophrenia?

A. Fever B. Pain
C. Impaired memory D. Rash

46. Family support plays an important role in the management of schizophrenia.

A. True B. False
C. Only medication D. Only hospital care

47. The inability to initiate and persist in goal-directed activity is called ______.

A. Agitation B. Anxiety
C. Depression D. Avolition

48. Which of the following is a key nursing intervention in schizophrenia?

A. Isolation B. Punishment
C. Ignoring patient D. Establishing trust

49. Social skills training is helpful in rehabilitation of patients with schizophrenia.

A. True B. False
C. Only medication D. Only rest

50. Early diagnosis and treatment improve the prognosis of schizophrenia.

A. True B. False
C. Only severe cases D. Only chronic cases

51. Depression is a mood disorder characterized by persistent feelings of ______ and loss of interest.

A. Happiness B. Excitement
C. Sadness D. Energy

52. Which of the following is a symptom of depression?

A. Increased appetite B. High energy
C. Loss of interest D. Excess sleep

53. Mania is characterized by elevated mood, increased activity, and ______ behavior.

A. Slow B. Withdrawn
C. Normal D. Hyperactive

54. Bipolar disorder involves episodes of depression and mania.

A. Only depression
B. Only mania
C. Only anxiety
D. Both depression and mania

55. Depression can affect sleep, appetite, and energy levels of a person.

A. True B. False
C. Only sleep D. Only appetite

56. A person with depression may experience feelings of ______ and worthlessness.

A. Joy B. Hope
C. Happiness D. Guilt

57. Which of the following is a feature of mania?

A. Low mood B. Fatigue
C. Increased activity D. Sleepiness

58. Antidepressant drugs are used in the treatment of depression.

A. True B. False
C. Only sedatives D. Only antibiotics

59. Which of the following is a symptom of mania?

A. Low energy B. Slow speech
C. Withdrawal D. Excessive talkativeness

60. Mood disorders involve disturbances in ______ of a person.

A. Memory B. Thinking
C. Behavior D. Mood

61. Which neurotransmitter is associated with mood disorders?

A. Calcium B. Sodium
C. Serotonin D. Potassium

62. Electroconvulsive therapy is used in severe depression.

A. True B. False
C. Only anxiety D. Only stress

63. Lack of pleasure in daily activities is called ______ in depression.

A. Euphoria B. Mania
C. Anxiety D. Anhedonia

64. Match the mood disorders with their characteristics.

Column I	Column II
A. Depression	1. Chronic mild depression
B. Mania	2. Elevated mood
C. Bipolar disorder	3. Alternating mood states
D. Dysthymia	4. Low mood

A. A-4, B-2, C-3, D-1 B. A-2, B-3, C-4, D-1
C. A-1, B-4, C-2, D-3 D. A-3, B-1, C-4, D-2

65. Assertion I: Early treatment of mood disorders improves outcomes.

Assertion II: Mood disorders have no effect on daily functioning.

A. Both are correct B. I is correct, II is incorrect
C. Both are incorrect D. I is incorrect, II is correct

66. Anxiety disorder is characterized by excessive ______ and worry.

A. Happiness B. Anger
C. Fear D. Pleasure

67. Which of the following is a type of neurotic disorder?

A. Schizophrenia B. Mania
C. Anxiety disorder D. Delusion

68. Phobia is an irrational fear of a specific object or situation.

A. True B. False
C. Only normal fear D. Only temporary fear

69. Which of the following is a common symptom of anxiety disorder?

A. Happiness B. Relaxation
C. Calmness D. Restlessness

70. Obsessive thoughts are repeated and unwanted ______ in the mind.

A. Actions B. Ideas
C. Feelings D. Behaviors

71. Compulsions are repetitive behaviors performed to reduce anxiety.

A. True B. False
C. Only thoughts D. Only emotions

72. Which of the following is an example of obsessive-compulsive disorder?

A. Delusion
B. Hallucination
C. Repeated hand washing
D. Depression

73. Panic disorder is characterized by sudden episodes of intense ______.

A. Joy B. Happiness
C. Relaxation D. Fear

74. Which of the following is a treatment for neurotic disorders?

A. Surgery B. Isolation
C. Ignoring symptoms D. Psychotherapy

75. Relaxation techniques can help in managing anxiety disorders.

A. True B. False
C. Only medication D. Only surgery

76. Substance abuse refers to the harmful or hazardous use of ______ substances.

A. Food B. Water
C. Drugs D. Vitamins

77. Which of the following is an example of substance abuse?

A. Balanced diet B. Exercise
C. Alcohol use D. Meditation

78. Substance abuse can lead to physical and psychological dependence.

A. True B. False
C. Only physical D. Only psychological

79. Which of the following is a common effect of substance abuse?

A. Improved memory B. Better health
C. Increased immunity D. Dependence

80. Withdrawal symptoms occur when a person stops taking ______ substances.

A. Healthy B. Required
C. Nutritional D. Addictive

81. Substance abuse can affect social and occupational functioning.

A. True B. False
C. Only physical health D. Only mental health

82. Which of the following is a depressant substance?

A. Nicotine B. Caffeine
C. Alcohol D. Cocaine

83. Long-term use of substances can cause ______ damage to organs.

A. Temporary B. Minor
C. Reversible D. Permanent

84. Match the substances with their types.

Column I	Column II
A. Alcohol	1. Opioid
B. Cocaine	2. Stimulant
C. Morphine	3. Depressant
D. Nicotine	4. Addictive stimulant

A. A-3, B-2, C-1, D-4 B. A-2, B-1, C-3, D-4
C. A-1, B-3, C-2, D-4 D. A-4, B-2, C-3, D-1

85. Assertion I: Substance abuse can lead to addiction.

Assertion II: Addiction has no effect on health.

A. Both are correct B. I is correct, II is incorrect
C. Both are incorrect D. I is incorrect, II is correct

86. Personality disorders are characterized by long-term patterns of behavior that differ from ______ expectations.

A. Personal B. Cultural
C. Social D. Individual

87. Which of the following is a type of personality disorder?

A. Depression B. Anxiety
C. Antisocial personality D. Schizophrenia

88. Personality disorders affect thinking, emotions, and behavior of an individual.

A. True B. False
C. Only emotions D. Only behavior

89. Which of the following is a characteristic of antisocial personality disorder?

A. Empathy B. Responsibility
C. Carefulness D. Lack of remorse

90. Borderline personality disorder is associated with unstable ______ and relationships.

A. Behavior B. Mood
C. Memory D. Intelligence

91. Personality disorders usually begin in adolescence or early adulthood.

A. True B. False
C. Only childhood D. Only old age

92. Which of the following is a feature of paranoid personality disorder?

A. Trust B. Cooperation
C. Suspiciousness D. Confidence

93. Narcissistic personality disorder involves an exaggerated sense of ______.

A. Fear B. Guilt
C. Anxiety D. Self-importance

94. Match the personality disorders with their characteristics.

Column I	Column II
A. Antisocial	1. Suspiciousness
B. Borderline	2. Lack of remorse
C. Paranoid	3. Unstable relationships
D. Narcissistic	4. Grandiosity

A. A-2, B-3, C-1, D-4 B. A-3, B-2, C-4, D-1
C. A-1, B-4, C-2, D-3 D. A-4, B-1, C-3, D-2

95. Assertion I: Personality disorders are long-standing patterns of behavior.

Assertion II: Personality disorders do not affect relationships.

A. Both are correct B. I is correct, II is incorrect
C. Both are incorrect D. I is incorrect, II is correct

96. A psychiatric emergency is a situation that requires immediate ______ intervention.

A. Routine B. Delayed
C. Planned D. Urgent

97. Which of the following is considered a psychiatric emergency?

A. Mild anxiety B. Normal stress
C. Suicide attempt D. Mild sadness

98. Psychiatric emergencies can be life-threatening if not managed properly.

A. True B. False
C. Only physical D. Only emotional

99. Which of the following is the priority in managing an aggressive patient?

A. Ignoring B. Punishment
C. Isolation D. Safety

100. The act of harming oneself intentionally is called ______ behavior.

A. Aggressive B. Violent
C. Social D. Self-harm

101. Early recognition of psychiatric emergencies helps in better management.

A. True B. False
C. Only treatment D. Only diagnosis

102. Which of the following is a symptom of acute psychosis?

A. Calm behavior B. Normal thinking
C. Hallucinations D. Stable mood

103. Overdose of drugs can lead to ______ emergency.

A. Physical B. Social
C. Emotional D. Medical

104. Match the emergencies with their management.

Column I	Column II
A. Suicide attempt	1. Calm reassurance
B. Aggression	2. Immediate medical care
C. Overdose	3. Safety measures
D. Panic attack	4. Crisis intervention

A. A-4, B-3, C-2, D-1 B. A-2, B-4, C-1, D-3
C. A-1, B-2, C-3, D-4 D. A-3, B-1, C-4, D-2

105. Assertion I: Immediate care is important in psychiatric emergencies.

Assertion II: Delay in treatment has no consequences.

A. Both are correct B. I is correct, II is incorrect
C. Both are incorrect D. I is incorrect, II is correct

106. Mental health care services are governed by ______ provisions to protect patient rights.

A. Social B. Ethical
C. Medical D. Legal

107. Which of the following is a right of a mentally ill patient?

A. Isolation B. Neglect
C. Right to treatment D. Punishment

108. Confidentiality is an important principle in mental health care.

A. True B. False
C. Only legal D. Only social

109. Which of the following is an important aspect of community mental health?

A. Hospitalization only B. Isolation of patient
C. Medication only D. Rehabilitation

110. Informed consent means taking permission from the patient before treatment.

A. True B. False
C. Only family consent D. Only legal form

111. Community mental health focuses on prevention and promotion of mental well-being.

A. True B. False
C. Only treatment D. Only hospital care

112. Which of the following is a role of a nurse in community mental health?

A. Ignoring patient B. Providing care
C. Punishment D. Isolation

113. Match the legal terms with their meanings.

Column I	Column II
A. Confidentiality	1. Permission for treatment
B. Consent	2. Failure to provide care
C. Negligence	3. Privacy of information
D. Rights	4. Legal entitlements

A. A-3, B-1, C-2, D-4 B. A-1, B-2, C-3, D-4
C. A-2, B-3, C-1, D-4 D. A-4, B-1, C-3, D-2

114. Assertion I: Community mental health services reduce stigma.

Assertion II: Mental illness should be hidden from society.

A. Both are correct B. I is correct, II is incorrect
C. Both are incorrect D. I is incorrect, II is correct

115. Rehabilitation helps mentally ill patients to reintegrate into society.

A. True B. False
C. Only hospital care D. Only medication

EXPLANATORY ANSWERS

1. **A:** Mental health includes coping ability. It helps manage stress. It is essential for well-being.
2. **B:** Mental health includes social well-being. It affects relationships. It influences functioning.
3. **C:** Good mental health shows adjustment. It reflects stability. It promotes harmony.
4. **D:** Mental illness affects thoughts, mood, behaviour. It impacts functioning. Needs care.
5. **B:** Coping with stress is mental function. It reflects resilience. Important for stability.
6. **D:** Mental health influenced by many factors. Includes biological and social. It is multifactorial.
7. **A:** Social factors affect mental health. Include family and environment. Important role.
8. **C:** Irritability shows poor mental health. Indicates stress. Needs attention.
9. **D:** Stress is natural reaction. Helps adaptation. Excess causes harm.
10. **B:** Good mental health shows relationships. It improves functioning. It indicates stability.
11. **A:** Promotion prevents illness. It improves well-being. Important for health.
12. **C:** Healthy coping includes solving problems. It reduces stress. Improves outcomes.
13. **B:** Mental hygiene maintains mental health. Prevents illness. Promotes well-being.
14. **A:** Emotional feelings, social interaction, psychological thinking, physical body. These are components of mental health.

15. B: Mental health affects physical health. They are linked. Second statement is incorrect.

16. D: Therapeutic communication aims at healing. It helps patient express feelings. It builds trust.

17. C: Active listening involves full attention. It improves understanding. It is essential skill.

18. D: It helps patients share emotions. It reduces anxiety. It supports care.

19. C: Listening means understanding message. It is important skill. It ensures clarity.

20. A: Empathy helps understanding feelings. It builds rapport. It improves communication.

21. D: Non-verbal communication includes gestures. It conveys emotions. It supports verbal message.

22. C: Noise disturbs communication. It reduces clarity. It acts as barrier.

23. A: Eye contact shows attention. It builds trust. It improves interaction.

24. D: Encouraging expression helps patient speak. It improves communication. It is therapeutic.

25. B: Silence allows thinking. It gives time. It supports expression.

26. A: Open questions promote expression. They encourage sharing. They improve communication.

27. C: Giving advice is non-therapeutic. It limits expression. It affects relationship.

28. D: Communication builds trust. It strengthens relationship. It improves care.

29. A: Clarifying seeks explanation. Reflecting repeats, summarizing main points, silence allows time.

30. B: Communication is essential. It improves care. Second statement is incorrect.

31. C: Schizophrenia affects thinking and perception. It disturbs reality. It alters behavior.

32. A: It involves thought and perception. Behavior changes occur. It is major disorder.

33. C: Hallucinations are false perceptions. Common symptom. Seen in schizophrenia.

34. D: Delusions are fixed beliefs. Not based on reality. Resist correction.

35. C: Hearing voices is hallucination. No external stimulus. Common symptom.

36. A: Negative symptoms include apathy. Social withdrawal occurs. Emotional expression reduces.

37. D: Apathy is lack of interest. It is negative symptom. Affects functioning.

38. C: Dopamine imbalance involved. Leads to symptoms. Important in pathophysiology.

39. C: Thought disorder affects thinking. Leads to disorganized speech. Seen in schizophrenia.

40. A: Usually begins in youth. Common in young adults. Affects functioning.

41. D: Disorganized type shows speech disturbance. Behavior is disorganized. Needs care.

42. A: Antipsychotics reduce symptoms. They act on neurotransmitters. Essential treatment.

43. B: Flat affect means no emotion. Expression reduced. Seen in schizophrenia.

44. D: Catatonia shows immobility. Patient may be rigid. Severe condition.

45. C: Cognitive symptoms include memory issues. Affect thinking. Reduce function.

46. A: Family support helps recovery. Improves compliance. Reduces relapse.

47. D: Avolition is lack of motivation. Affects activity. Common negative symptom.

48. D: Trust builds relationship. Helps communication. Improves care.

49. A: Training improves skills. Helps reintegration. Supports recovery.

50. A: Early treatment improves outcome. Reduces severity. Prevents complications.

51. C: Depression shows persistent sadness. It reduces interest. It affects daily life.

52. C: Loss of interest is key symptom. It reduces activity. It affects life.

53. D: Mania shows high activity. Person is energetic. Behavior becomes excessive.

54. D: Bipolar includes both phases. Mood fluctuates. Needs treatment.

55. A: Depression affects body functions. Sleep and appetite change. Energy reduces.

56. D: Depressed person feels guilt. Also worthlessness. It affects mental state.

57. C: Mania increases activity. Person becomes energetic. Sleep reduces.

58. A: Antidepressants treat depression. They act on neurotransmitters. Improve mood.

59. D: Mania leads to excessive talking. Speech becomes rapid. It reflects excitement.

60. D: Mood disorders affect emotions. They disturb feelings. Impact behavior.

61. C: Serotonin imbalance seen. It affects mood. Important neurotransmitter.

62. A: ECT used in severe depression. Works quickly. Used in emergencies.

63. D: Anhedonia is loss of pleasure. Common in depression. Affects interest.

64. A: Depression low mood, mania high mood, bipolar alternating, dysthymia chronic mild depression.

65. B: Mood disorders affect functioning. Early treatment helps. Second statement wrong.

66. C: Anxiety disorder involves excessive fear. It is persistent. It affects functioning.

67. C: Anxiety disorders are neurotic. They include phobia. They affect behavior.

68. A: Phobia is irrational fear. It may be specific. It causes avoidance.

69. D: Anxiety causes restlessness. It leads to tension. Affects daily life.

70. B: Obsessions are unwanted thoughts. They repeat. Cause distress.

71. A: Compulsions are actions. They reduce anxiety. They are repetitive.

72. C: OCD includes repetitive acts. It relieves anxiety. It is disorder.

73. D: Panic causes intense fear. Sudden onset. May include physical symptoms.

74. D: Therapy helps manage anxiety. It improves coping. It is effective.

75. A: Relaxation reduces anxiety. It calms mind. Helps control symptoms.

76. C: Substance abuse involves harmful drug use. It affects health. It leads to dependence.

77. C: Alcohol abuse is common. It leads to addiction. It harms health.

78. A: Substance abuse causes dependence. It affects body and mind. It needs treatment.

79. D: Dependence is key effect. Person cannot stop use. It causes harm.

80. D: Withdrawal occurs when addictive drugs stop. Symptoms appear. It causes distress.

81. A: Substance abuse affects social life. It reduces performance. It causes problems.

82. C: Alcohol is depressant. It slows CNS. Affects coordination.

83. D: Long use damages organs. Effects may be irreversible. It harms body.

84. A: Alcohol depressant, cocaine stimulant, morphine opioid, nicotine addictive stimulant.

85. B: Addiction harms health. It affects body and mind. Second statement is incorrect.

86. B: Personality disorders deviate from cultural norms. Behavior becomes maladaptive. It affects functioning.

87. C: It is a type of personality disorder. It involves disregard for others. It affects behavior.

88. A: Personality disorders affect thoughts and emotions. Behavior is also disturbed. It impacts life.

89. D: Antisocial individuals lack guilt. They ignore rights of others. Behavior is harmful.

90. B: Borderline disorder shows mood instability. Relationships are affected. Emotional control poor.

91. A: Begins in adolescence. Continues in adulthood. It is long term.

92. C: Paranoid disorder shows mistrust. Person doubts others. Relationships affected.

93. D: Narcissistic disorder shows grandiosity. Person feels superior. Needs admiration.

94. A: Antisocial lacks remorse, borderline unstable, paranoid suspicious, narcissistic grandiose.

95. B: Disorders affect relationships. They disturb functioning. Second statement wrong.

96. D: Psychiatric emergencies need immediate care. Delay can worsen condition. Quick response is essential.

97. C: Suicide attempt is serious emergency. Needs urgent care. Risk of death is high.

98. A: Emergencies can be fatal. Without care, risk increases. Early management is important.

99. D: Safety is priority. Protect patient and others. Prevent harm.

100. D: Self-harm is intentional injury. Seen in psychiatric conditions. Needs intervention.

101. A: Early detection helps treatment. Prevents complications. Improves outcome.

102. C: Psychosis involves hallucinations. Reality is disturbed. Needs treatment.

103. D: Overdose leads to medical emergency. It affects body systems. Requires urgent care.

104. A: Suicide crisis intervention, aggression safety, overdose medical care, panic reassurance.

105. B: Immediate care prevents harm. Delay worsens condition. Second statement is wrong.

106. D: Mental health care is governed by laws. It protects patient rights. It ensures safe practice.

107. C: Patients have legal rights. They deserve proper care. Treatment must be provided.

108. A: Confidentiality protects privacy. It builds trust. It is ethical duty.

109. D: Community care includes rehab. It helps reintegration. Improves independence.

110. A: Consent is required. Patient must agree. It is legal requirement.

111. A: Community care prevents illness. Promotes mental health. Reduces stigma.

112. B: Nurse plays important role. Provides support. Educates patients.

113. A: Confidentiality privacy, consent permission, negligence failure, rights legal entitlements.

114. B: Community care reduces stigma. Hiding illness is harmful Awareness needed.

115. A: Rehabilitation improves functioning. Helps social adjustment. Supports independence.

14. Nursing Research & Statistics

1. Research is a systematic process of collecting and analyzing ______ to answer questions.
A. Data B. Ideas
C. Opinions D. Thoughts

2. The first step of research process is identifying the problem.
A. True B. False
C. Only analysis D. Only conclusion

3. Which of the following is a step in the research process?
A. Guessing B. Ignoring data
C. Literature review D. Random action

4. Research helps in improving nursing practice and patient care.
A. Only theory B. Only data
C. Only observation D. Improvement of care

5. The process of gathering information from various sources is called ______ review.
A. Data B. Sample
C. Variable D. Literature

6. A research problem should be clear, specific, and researchable.
A. True B. False
C. Only broad D. Only vague

7. A ______ is a tentative answer to the research question.
A. Conclusion B. Data
C. Result D. Hypothesis

8. Which of the following is a characteristic of good research?
A. Bias B. Accuracy
C. Confusion D. Guessing

9. Which type of research is conducted to explore new ideas?
A. Experimental B. Descriptive
C. Exploratory D. Analytical

10. Research requires careful planning and systematic approach.
A. True B. False
C. Only observation D. Only experiment

11. Which of the following is a purpose of research?
A. To confuse B. To mislead
C. To ignore data D. To generate knowledge

12. The process of organizing collected data is called ______
A. Sampling B. Collection
C. Reporting D. Analysis

13. Validity refers to the accuracy of the research findings.
A. True B. False
C. Only reliability D. Only bias

14. Reliability refers to consistency of results in research.
A. True B. False
C. Only validity D. Only data

15. Which of the following improves reliability of research?
A. Bias B. Error
C. Repetition D. Guessing

16. Which of the following is an ethical principle in research?
A. Harm to subjects B. Confidentiality
C. Bias D. Ignoring consent

17. In research, the group selected for study is called ______
A. Data B. Population
C. Variable D. Sample

18. Match the research terms with their meanings.

Column I	Column II
A. Hypothesis	1. Information collected
B. Sample	2. Selected group
C. Variable	3. Measurable factor
D. Data	4. Tentative answer

A. A-4, B-2, C-3, D-1 B. A-2, B-3, C-4, D-1
C. A-3, B-1, C-2, D-4 D. A-1, B-4, C-3, D-2

19. **Assertion I:** Research is essential for evidence-based practice.
Assertion II: Research has no role in nursing practice.
A. Both are correct B. I is correct, II is incorrect
C. Both are incorrect D. I is incorrect, II is correct

20. Research findings help in improving quality of healthcare services.
A. True B. False
C. Only theory D. Only experiment

21. A research problem should be clearly defined and ______ in nature.
A. Vague B. Broad
C. General D. Specific

22. A good research problem should be feasible and researchable.
A. True B. False
C. Only theoretical D. Only practical

23. A hypothesis is a ______ answer to the research problem.
A. Final B. Definite
C. Proven D. Tentative

24. Which of the following is a characteristic of a good hypothesis?
A. Complex B. Vague
C. Not testable D. Testable

25. The research problem guides the entire research study.
A. True B. False
C. Only data D. Only results

26. A null hypothesis states that there is no ______ between variables.
A. Relation B. Difference
C. Effect D. Association

27. Which type of hypothesis predicts a relationship between variables?
A. Null hypothesis B. Simple hypothesis
C. Research hypothesis D. Statistical hypothesis

28. Match the research terms with their meanings.

Column I	Column II
A. Research problem	1. Measurable factor
B. Hypothesis	2. Purpose of study
C. Variable	3. Question to be answered
D. Objective	4. Tentative statement

A. A-3, B-4, C-1, D-2 B. A-2, B-3, C-4, D-1
C. A-1, B-2, C-3, D-4 D. A-4, B-1, C-2, D-3

29. **Assertion I:** Hypothesis helps in guiding research.
Assertion II: Hypothesis is not required in research.
A. Both are correct B. I is correct, II is incorrect
C. Both are incorrect D. I is incorrect, II is correct

30. A research hypothesis should be clear, concise, and testable.
A. True B. False
C. Only theoretical D. Only descriptive

31. Research design is the plan or ______ for conducting a study.
A. Method B. Structure
C. Approach D. Blueprint

32. Research design helps in answering research questions effectively.
A. True B. False
C. Only data D. Only results

33. Which of the following is a type of research design?
A. Random B. Biased
C. Experimental D. Illogical

34. Experimental research design involves manipulation of variables.
A. Only observation B. Only survey
C. Only analysis D. Manipulation

35. In research, control group is used for ______ purpose.
A. Comparison B. Observation
C. Measurement D. Analysis

36. Descriptive research design describes characteristics of a population.
A. True B. False
C. Only experimental D. Only analytical

37. Which research design studies relationships between variables?
A. Descriptive B. Correlational
C. Experimental D. Historical

38. Which design is used to establish cause-effect relationship?
A. Descriptive B. Observational
C. Experimental D. Survey

39. In research, a variable is a ______ that can be measured.
A. Idea B. Concept
C. Factor D. Value

40. Pilot study is conducted before the main research study.
A. True B. False
C. Only after study D. Only for analysis

41. Which of the following is a non-experimental research design?

A. Experimental B. Quasi-experimental
C. Survey D. Clinical trial

42. Randomization is used to reduce bias in research.

A. Only error B. Only variation
C. Only observation D. Bias reduction

43. Sampling is selecting a group from a population.

A. True B. False
C. Only analysis D. Only reporting

44. A ______ study is conducted to test feasibility of research design.

A. Main B. Final
C. Pilot D. Sample

45. Which of the following is a qualitative research design?

A. Experimental B. Survey
C. Phenomenological D. Analytical

46. Which research design is used to collect data at a single point in time?

A. Longitudinal B. Experimental
C. Cross-sectional D. Case study

47. Control of extraneous variables improves validity of research.

A. True B. False
C. Only reliability D. Only bias

48. Which design follows subjects over a period of time?

A. Cross-sectional B. Survey
C. Experimental D. Longitudinal

49. Research design should be flexible and appropriate for the study.

A. True B. False
C. Only fixed D. Only rigid

50. Validity of research depends on proper ______ of study.

A. Planning B. Execution
C. Design D. Analysis

51. Match the research designs with their characteristics.

Column I	Column II
A. Experimental	1. Study over time
B. Descriptive	2. Cause-effect relationship
C. Correlational	3. Describes characteristics
D. Longitudinal	4. Relationship between variables

A. A-2, B-3, C-4, D-1 B. A-3, B-2, C-1, D-4
C. A-4, B-1, C-2, D-3 D. A-1, B-4, C-3, D-2

52. Assertion I: Research design guides the study.

Assertion II: Research design has no role in data collection.

A. Both are correct
B. I is correct, II is incorrect
C. Both are incorrect
D. I is incorrect, II is correct

53. A good research design ensures validity and reliability of results.

A. True B. False
C. Only validity D. Only reliability

54. Which of the following is essential for good research design?

A. Bias B. Confusion
C. Planning D. Guessing

55. Research design should match the objectives of the study.

A. True B. False
C. Only theory D. Only data

56. Sampling is the process of selecting a ______ from a population.

A. Variable B. Data
C. Sample D. Group

57. Which of the following is a probability sampling method?

A. Convenience sampling
B. Purposive sampling
C. Random sampling
D. Quota sampling

58. A sample should represent the characteristics of the population.

A. Only part
B. Only data
C. Only group
D. Represent population

59. The total group from which a sample is drawn is called ______.

A. Sample B. Variable
C. Population D. Data

60. Sampling reduces the time and cost of research.

A. True B. False
C. Only cost D. Only time

61. Which sampling method is based on chance?

A. Non-probability B. Purposive
C. Probability D. Judgmental

62. Convenience sampling involves selecting subjects easily available.

A. True B. False
C. Only random D. Only systematic

63. Which of the following is a non-probability sampling method?

A. Random B. Stratified
C. Systematic D. Purposive

64. Sampling error occurs due to ______ selection of sample.

A. Accurate B. Proper
C. Random D. Improper

65. Larger sample size increases accuracy of research findings.

A. True B. False
C. Only bias D. Only error

66. Which sampling method divides population into subgroups?

A. Simple random B. Systematic
C. Stratified D. Cluster

67. Systematic sampling selects every *n*th element from population.

A. True B. False
C. Only cluster D. Only purposive

68. The process of dividing population into groups is called ______ sampling.

A. Random B. Cluster
C. Stratified D. Systematic

69. Match the sampling methods with their characteristics.

Column I	Column II
A. Random sampling	1. Easy selection
B. Stratified sampling	2. Based on chance
C. Cluster sampling	3. Divided groups
D. Convenience sampling	4. Group selection

A. A-2, B-3, C-4, D-1 B. A-3, B-4, C-1, D-2
C. A-1, B-2, C-3, D-4 D. A-4, B-1, C-2, D-3

70. Assertion I: Sampling helps in generalizing results.

Assertion II: Sampling has no importance in research.

A. Both are correct B. I is correct, II is incorrect
C. Both are incorrect D. I is incorrect, II is correct

71. Data collection is the process of gathering ______ for research study.

A. Ideas B. Concepts
C. Information D. Opinions

72. Data collection is an important step in research process.

A. True B. False
C. Only analysis D. Only conclusion

73. Primary data are collected directly from ______ sources.

A. Books B. Articles
C. Subjects D. Records

74. Which of the following is a method of data collection?

A. Guessing B. Estimation
C. Prediction D. Interview

75. Observation method involves watching and recording behavior.

A. True B. False
C. Only experiment D. Only survey

76. Questionnaire is a tool used to collect ______ from respondents.

A. Data B. Results
C. Findings D. Conclusions

77. Which of the following is a primary data collection method?

A. Books B. Journals
C. Interview D. Reports

78. Match the data collection methods with their characteristics.

Column I	Column II
A. Interview	1. Watching behavior
B. Observation	2. Asking questions
C. Questionnaire	3. Written responses
D. Records	4. Existing data

A. A-2, B-1, C-3, D-4 B. A-1, B-2, C-4, D-3
C. A-3, B-4, C-2, D-1 D. A-4, B-3, C-1, D-2

79. Assertion I: Data collection should be accurate and reliable.

Assertion II: Incorrect data can affect research results.

A. Both are correct
B. I is correct, II is incorrect
C. Both are incorrect
D. I is incorrect, II is correct

80. Secondary data are collected from existing sources like books and records.

A. True B. False
C. Only primary D. Only survey

81. Data analysis is the process of organizing and interpreting ______.

A. Ideas B. Variables
C. Data D. Samples

82. Data analysis helps in drawing conclusions from research.

A. True B. False
C. Only data D. Only sampling

83. Quantitative data are analyzed using ______ methods.

A. Descriptive B. Observational
C. Statistical D. Experimental

84. Which of the following is a step in data analysis?

A. Guessing B. Ignoring data
C. Skipping steps D. Interpretation

85. Data analysis helps in understanding patterns and relationships.

A. True B. False
C. Only values D. Only variables

86. Qualitative data analysis involves _____ of information.

A. Measurement B. Calculation
C. Coding D. Testing

87. Which of the following is a tool for data analysis?

A. Interview B. Questionnaire
C. Statistical software D. Observation

88. Match the data analysis terms with their meanings.

Column I	Column II
A. Mean	1. Middle value
B. Median	2. Most frequent value
C. Mode	3. Difference between values
D. Range	4. Average value

A. A-4, B-1, C-2, D-3 B. A-1, B-2, C-3, D-4
C. A-2, B-3, C-4, D-1 D. A-3, B-4, C-1, D-2

89. Assertion I: Data analysis is essential for interpretation of results.

Assertion II: Data analysis has no role in research.

A. Both are correct B. I is correct, II is incorrect
C. Both are incorrect D. I is incorrect, II is correct

90. Graphs and charts are used to present analyzed data effectively.

A. True B. False
C. Only tables D. Only text

91. Statistics is the science of collecting, analyzing, and interpreting ______.

A. Ideas B. Opinions
C. Data D. Thoughts

92. Statistics helps in summarizing large amounts of data.

A. True B. False
C. Only small data D. Only theory

93. Which of the following is a measure of central tendency?

A. Range B. Variance
C. Mean D. Deviation

94. Mean is calculated by dividing sum of values by number of observations.

A. Median B. Mode
C. Range D. Mean

95. The most frequently occurring value in a dataset is called ______.

A. Mean B. Median
C. Mode D. Range

96. Median is the middle value of a dataset arranged in order.

A. True B. False
C. Only mean D. Only mode

97. The difference between highest and lowest value is called ______.

A. Mean B. Median
C. Range D. Mode

98. Which of the following represents dispersion of data?

A. Mean B. Median
C. Standard deviation D. Mode

99. Standard deviation shows variability in data.

A. True B. False
C. Only mean D. Only median

100. The arithmetic average of data is called ______.

A. Median B. Mode
C. Range D. Mean

101. Which of the following is a graphical representation of data?

A. Table B. List
C. Text D. Histogram

102. Frequency distribution shows how often values occur.

A. True B. False
C. Only mean D. Only median

103. Data can be classified into ______ and qualitative types.

A. Primary B. Secondary
C. Quantitative D. Sample

104. Pie chart represents data in circular form.

A. True B. False
C. Only bar D. Only line

105. Which measure is least affected by extreme values?

A. Mean B. Range
C. Median D. Mode

106. Variance is the square of standard deviation.

A. True B. False
C. Only mean D. Only range

107. In statistics, data arranged in order is called ______ series.

A. Nominal B. Interval
C. **Ordinal** D. **Ratio**

108. Bar diagram is used to compare different categories of data.

A. True B. False
C. Only pie D. Only line

109. A ______ graph is used to show trends over time.

A. Bar B. Pie
C. Histogram D. Line

110. Which of the following is used to measure variability?

A. Mean B. Median
C. Mode D. Range

111. Statistical analysis helps in decision making.

A. True B. False
C. Only theory D. Only data

112. A group of data values is called a ______ set.

A. Data B. Sample
C. Value D. Variable

113. Histogram is used for continuous data representation.

A. True B. False
C. Only discrete D. Only nominal

114. Which of the following is a type of data?

A. Mean B. Median
C. Qualitative D. Range

115. Graphs make data easy to understand.

A. True B. False
C. Only tables D. Only numbers

116. The middle value of data is called ______.

A. Mean B. Mode
C. Range D. Median

117. Statistics is widely used in research and healthcare.

A. True B. False
C. Only education D. Only economy

118. Which measure represents the spread of data?

A. Mean B. Median
C. Mode D. Standard deviation

119. The number of times a value occurs is called ______.

A. Mean B. Range
C. Mode D. Frequency

120. Match the statistical terms with their meanings.

Column I	Column II
A. Mean	1. Most frequent value
B. Median	2. Middle value
C. Mode	3. Difference of values
D. Range	4. Average

A. A-4, B-2, C-1, D-3 B. A-2, B-3, C-4, D-1
C. A-3, B-4, C-2, D-1 D. A-1, B-2, C-3, D-4

121. Research utilization refers to applying research findings into ______ practice.

A. Theory B. Education
C. Clinical D. Social

122. Research utilization helps in improving patient care and outcomes.

A. True B. False
C. Only theory D. Only research

123. Evidence-based practice is based on best available ______ and clinical expertise.

A. Data B. Opinion
C. Evidence D. Experience

124. Which of the following is a benefit of research utilization?

A. Confusion B. Delay
C. Error D. Improved care

125. Nurses should use research findings in clinical practice.

A. True B. False
C. Only education D. Only management

126. Barriers to research utilization include lack of ______ and resources.

A. Knowledge B. Skill
C. Interest D. Time

127. Which of the following is an example of evidence-based practice?

A. Guessing
B. Tradition
C. Using research findings
D. Ignoring evidence

128. Match the terms with their meanings.

Column I	Column II
A. Research utilization	1. Application of research
B. Evidence-based practice	2. Use of best evidence
C. Clinical practice	3. Patient care
D. Knowledge	4. Information

A. A-1, B-2, C-3, D-4 B. A-2, B-1, C-4, D-3
C. A-3, B-4, C-1, D-2 D. A-4, B-3, C-2, D-1

129. **Assertion I:** Research utilization improves quality of care.

Assertion II: Research findings should not be used in practice.

A. Both are correct B. I is correct, II is incorrect
C. Both are incorrect D. I is incorrect, II is correct

130. Continuous research helps in updating nursing knowledge.

A. True B. False
C. Only education D. Only practice

EXPLANATORY ANSWERS

1. **A:** Research involves collecting data. It helps answer questions. It is systematic.
2. **A:** Identifying problem is first step. It guides research. It defines focus.
3. **C:** It reviews existing knowledge. It helps understanding. It guides study.
4. **D:** Research improves practice. It enhances care. It is useful.
5. **D:** Literature review collects information. It analyzes studies. It provides base.
6. **A:** Problem must be clear. It should be specific. It guides research.
7. **D:** Hypothesis is assumption. It is tested. It guides study.
8. **B:** Good research is accurate. It is reliable. It avoids bias.
9. **C:** Exploratory research explores ideas. It is initial step. It generates insights.
10. **A:** Research needs planning. It must be systematic. It ensures validity.
11. **D:** Research creates knowledge. It improves practice. It answers questions.
12. **D:** Data analysis organizes data. It interprets results. It draws conclusions.
13. **A:** Validity ensures accuracy. It measures what intended. It is important.
14. **A:** Reliability ensures consistency. Results remain same. It improves trust.
15. **C:** Repetition increases reliability. Results become consistent. It reduces error.
16. **B:** Ethics protect subjects. Privacy maintained. It builds trust.
17. **D:** Sample is selected group. It represents population. Used in study.
18. **A:** Hypothesis answer, sample group, variable factor, data information.
19. **B:** Research supports practice. It improves care. Second is wrong.
20. **A:** Research improves quality. It enhances care. It is essential.
21. **D:** Research problem must be specific. It gives direction. It makes study focused.
22. **A:** Problem should be feasible. It must be researchable. It ensures success.
23. **D:** Hypothesis is tentative answer. It is tested. It guides research.
24. **D:** Good hypothesis must be testable. It can be verified. It improves study.
25. **A:** Problem guides research. It defines objectives. It directs process.
26. **D:** Null hypothesis states no association. It is tested. It is statistical.
27. **C:** It predicts relationship. It is tested. It supports study.
28. **A:** Problem is question, hypothesis statement, variable factor, objective purpose.
29. **B:** Hypothesis guides study. It is important. Second statement is wrong.
30. **A:** Hypothesis must be clear. It must be concise. It should be testable.
31. **D:** Research design is a blueprint. It guides study. It provides structure.
32. **A:** Design helps answer questions. It ensures clarity. It improves results.
33. **C:** Experimental design tests variables. It shows cause-effect. It is important.
34. **D:** Experimental design involves manipulation. Variables are controlled. It tests effects.
35. **A:** Control group used for comparison. It helps evaluate results. It improves validity.
36. **A:** Descriptive design describes data. It studies characteristics. It is simple.
37. **B:** It studies relationships. No manipulation. Shows association.
38. **C:** Experimental shows cause-effect. It controls variables. It is scientific.
39. **C:** Variable is measurable factor. It changes. It affects results.
40. **A:** Pilot study tests feasibility. It helps planning. It improves design.
41. **C:** Survey is non-experimental. It collects data. No manipulation.
42. **D:** Randomization reduces bias. It ensures fairness. It improves validity.
43. **A:** Sampling selects group. Represents population. It is important.
44. **C:** Pilot study tests design. It improves research. It identifies issues.
45. **C:** It is qualitative design. Studies experiences. Focus on meaning.
46. **C:** Data collected once. It is quick. No follow-up.
47. **A:** Controlling variables improves validity. It reduces bias. It strengthens results.
48. **D:** It studies over time. Tracks changes. Provides detailed data.
49. **A:** Design should be flexible. It adapts needs. It improves research.

50. C: Good design ensures validity. It supports structure. It improves outcome.

51. A: Experimental cause-effect, descriptive describes, correlational relation, longitudinal time.

52. B: Design guides study. It affects data. Second statement wrong.

53. A: Design ensures quality. It improves reliability. It supports validity.

54. C: Planning is essential. It avoids errors. It improves design.

55. A: Design must match objectives. It ensures relevance. It improves study.

56. C: Sampling selects a sample. It represents population. It saves time.

57. C: Random method uses chance. It reduces bias. It is probability method.

58. D: Sample must reflect population. It ensures validity. It improves results.

59. C: Population is total group. Sample is drawn from it. It is important.

60. A: Sampling saves time. It reduces cost. It makes research feasible.

61. C: Probability sampling uses chance. It ensures fairness. It reduces bias.

62. A: Convenience sampling selects easily available subjects. It is simple. It is quick.

63. D: Purposive sampling is non-probability. It is based on judgment. It is selective.

64. D: Improper sampling leads to error. It reduces accuracy. It affects results.

65. A: Large sample increases accuracy. It represents population. It reduces error.

66. C: Stratified divides population. Ensures representation. Improves accuracy.

67. A: Systematic sampling selects nth element. It is simple. It is structured.

68. C: Stratified sampling divides groups. It improves representation. It is useful.

69. A: Random chance, stratified groups, cluster group selection, convenience easy.

70. B: Sampling helps generalization. It is important. Second is wrong.

71. C: Data collection gathers information. It supports research. It helps analysis.

72. A: Data collection is essential. It provides base. It affects results.

73. C: Primary data collected from subjects. It is original. It is reliable.

74. D: Interview collects data directly. It is interactive. It provides **detailed information.**

75. A: Observation records behavior. It is direct method. It is useful.

76. A: Questionnaire collects data. It is structured. It is widely used.

77. C: Interview is primary method. It collects original data. It is direct.

78. A: Interview questions, observation watching, questionnaire written, records existing.

79. A: Data must be accurate. Wrong data affects results. It reduces validity.

80. A: Secondary data from records. It is already available. It saves time.

81. C: Data analysis organizes data. It interprets results. It gives meaning.

82. A: Analysis leads to conclusions. It explains findings. It supports decisions.

83. C: Quantitative data uses statistics. It involves numbers. It is measurable.

84. D: Interpretation explains results. It gives meaning. It is final step.

85. A: Analysis identifies patterns. It shows relationships. It helps understanding.

86. C: Qualitative data uses coding. It organizes data. It helps interpretation.

87. C: Software analyzes data. It processes numbers. It gives results.

88. A: Mean average, median middle, mode frequent, range difference.

89. B: Analysis is essential. It gives meaning. Second is wrong.

90. A: Graphs present data. They simplify understanding. They show trends.

91. C: Statistics deals with data. It collects and analyzes. It interprets results.

92. A: Statistics summarizes data. It simplifies information. It helps understanding.

93. C: Mean is central tendency. It shows average. It represents data.

94. D: Mean is sum divided by number. It shows average. It is common.

95. C: Mode is most frequent value. It shows repetition. It is useful.

96. A: Median is middle value. It divides data. It is stable.

97. C: Range shows difference. It measures spread. It is simple.

98. C: It measures dispersion. It shows variability. It is important.

99. A: Standard deviation shows spread. It indicates variability. It is useful.

100. D: Mean is average. It is widely used. It summarizes data.

101. D: Histogram shows data graphically. It is visual. It helps analysis.

102. A: Frequency shows occurrence. It counts values. It is basic.

103. C: Data types include quantitative. It is numerical. It is measurable.

104. A: Pie chart shows proportions. It is circular. It is simple.

105. C: Median unaffected by extremes. It is stable. It is useful.

106. A: Variance is square of SD. It measures spread. It is important.

107. C: Ordered data is ordinal. It shows rank. It is sequence.

108. A: Bar diagram compares categories. It is visual. It is simple.

109. D: Line graph shows trends. It shows time changes. It is useful.

110. D: Range measures spread. It is simple. It shows variation.

111. A: Statistics aids decisions. It supports analysis. It is useful.

112. A: Data set is group. It contains values. It is analyzed.

113. A: Histogram shows continuous data. It is graphical. It is useful.

114. C: Data types include qualitative. It is descriptive. It is non-numeric.

115. A: Graphs simplify data. They improve understanding. They show patterns.

116. D: Median is middle value. It divides data. It is stable.

117. A: Statistics used widely. It helps research. It improves care.

118. D: It measures spread. It shows variation. It is important.

119. D: Frequency shows occurrence. It counts values. It is basic.

120. A: Mean average, median middle, mode frequent, range difference.

121. C: Research utilization applies findings. It improves clinical practice. It enhances care.

122. A: It improves outcomes. It ensures quality care. It supports evidence.

123. C: Evidence-based practice uses evidence. It improves decisions. It ensures care quality.

124. D: Utilization improves care. It reduces errors. It enhances outcomes.

125. A: Nurses should apply research. It improves practice. It supports care.

126. D: Lack of time is barrier. It limits application. It affects practice.

127. C: Evidence-based practice uses research. It improves decisions. It ensures quality.

128. A: Utilization application, evidence best practice, clinical care, knowledge information.

129. B: Research improves care. It should be used. Second statement wrong.

130. A: Research updates knowledge. It improves practice. It enhances care.

15. Midwifery & Obstetrical Nursing

1. Antenatal care refers to care provided to a woman during ______ period.

A. Childhood B. Postnatal
C. Pregnancy D. Neonatal

2. Antenatal care helps in early detection of complications.

A. True B. False
C. Only after delivery D. Only in hospital

3. Which of the following is a sign of pregnancy?

A. Fever B. Headache
C. Amenorrhea D. Pain

4. The average duration of pregnancy is about ______.

A. 30 weeks B. 35 weeks
C. 45 weeks D. 40 weeks

5. The first visit for antenatal care should be within ______ trimester.

A. First B. Second
C. Third D. Last

6. Regular antenatal check-ups are important for maternal and fetal health.

A. True B. False
C. Only fetus D. Only mother

7. The expected date of delivery is calculated using ______ formula.

A. Simpson B. Naegele's
C. Boyle's D. Newton's

8. Which of the following is a probable sign of pregnancy?

A. Vomiting
B. Nausea
C. Positive pregnancy test
D. Amenorrhea

9. The normal hemoglobin level in pregnancy should be above ______ g/dl.

A. 8 B. 9
C. 10 D. 11

10. Which of the following is a danger sign during pregnancy?

A. Mild nausea B. Weight gain
C. Normal BP D. Vaginal bleeding

11. Iron and folic acid supplements are given during pregnancy.

A. True B. False
C. Only after delivery D. Only anemia

12. The number of fetal movements felt by mother is called ______.

A. Labor B. Quickening
C. Delivery D. Contraction

13. Which of the following is a component of antenatal care?

A. Surgery B. Counseling
C. Examination D. All of these

14. Which nutrient is essential to prevent anemia in pregnancy?

A. Calcium B. Protein
C. Iron D. Vitamin D

15. Tetanus toxoid vaccine is given during ______ period.

A. Childhood B. Pregnancy
C. Adolescence D. Old age

16. Which of the following is used to monitor fetal growth?

A. BP B. Pulse
C. Weight D. Fundal height

17. Blood pressure monitoring is important during pregnancy.

A. True B. False
C. Only after delivery D. Only labor

18. The increase in blood volume during pregnancy is about ______ percent.

A. 10 B. 20
C. 30 D. 50

19. Which of the following is a minor disorder of pregnancy?

A. Hemorrhage B. Eclampsia
C. Nausea D. Diabetes

20. Which of the following is a sign of fetal well-being?

A. No movement B. Bleeding
C. Active movements D. Pain

21. Balanced diet is essential during pregnancy.

A. True B. False
C. Only protein D. Only fat

22. The normal weight gain during pregnancy is about ______ kg.

A. 5 B. 8
C. 10 D. 12

23. Which of the following is a complication of pregnancy?

A. Vomiting B. Fatigue
C. Backache D. Hypertension

24. Urine test is done during antenatal visits.

A. True B. False
C. Only blood test D. Only scan

25. The position of fetus in uterus is called ______.

A. Lie B. Attitude
C. Position D. Presentation

26. Which of the following is important advice during pregnancy?

A. Smoking B. Alcohol
C. Balanced diet D. Stress

27. Which of the following is a risk factor in pregnancy?

A. Young age B. Nutrition
C. Advanced age D. Exercise

28. Antenatal education prepares mother for labor.

A. True B. False
C. Only after birth D. Only hospital

29. Which of the following is a danger sign of pregnancy?

A. Mild headache B. Normal swelling
C. Weight gain D. Severe headache

30. Match the antenatal care components with their purposes.

Column I	Column II
A. Iron tablets	1. Prevent anemia
B. TT vaccine	2. Detect fetal growth
C. Ultrasound	3. Prevent tetanus
D. BP check	4. Detect hypertension

A. A-1, B-3, C-2, D-4 B. A-3, B-1, C-4, D-2
C. A-2, B-4, C-1, D-3 D. A-4, B-2, C-3, D-1

31. Fertilization occurs when sperm meets ______ in the fallopian tube.

A. Embryo B. Fetus
C. Ovum D. Placenta

32. Pregnancy is divided into three trimesters.

A. True B. False
C. Only two D. Only four

33. Which hormone maintains pregnancy?

A. Estrogen B. Progesterone
C. Progesterone D. Oxytocin

34. The first trimester lasts up to 12 weeks of pregnancy.

A. 8 weeks B. 10 weeks
C. 16 weeks D. 12 weeks

35. The organ that connects mother and fetus is called ______.

A. Uterus B. Placenta
C. Cord D. Embryo

36. Placenta helps in exchange of nutrients and waste.

A. True B. False
C. Only oxygen D. Only blood

37. The developing baby in uterus after 8 weeks is called ______.

A. Embryo B. Zygote
C. Fetus D. Ovum

38. Which hormone is responsible for uterine contractions?

A. Estrogen B. Progesterone
C. Oxytocin D. HCG

39. Fundal height increases with advancing pregnancy.

A. True B. False
C. Only early D. Only late

40. The fertilized ovum implants in the ______ of uterus.

A. Cervix B. Fundus
C. Endometrium D. Vagina

41. Quickening is usually felt around 18–20 weeks of pregnancy.

A. 10 weeks B. 12 weeks
C. 25 weeks D. 18–20 weeks

42. Which of the following is a physiological change in pregnancy?

A. Decreased blood volume
B. Increased BP
C. Increased blood volume
D. Decreased weight

43. Breast changes occur during pregnancy to prepare for lactation.

A. True B. False
C. Only after birth D. Only disease

44. The fetal heartbeat can be heard around ______ weeks.

A. 6 B. 10
C. 20 D. 12

45. Which of the following is a probable sign of pregnancy?

A. Nausea B. Amenorrhea
C. Fetal heartbeat D. Fatigue

46. Weight gain is a normal change during pregnancy.

A. True B. False
C. Only abnormal D. Only disease

47. The process of cell division after fertilization is called ______.

A. Growth B. Cleavage
C. Development D. Implantation

48. Which of the following is an important function of amniotic fluid?

A. Nutrition only B. Protection only
C. Oxygen supply D. Protection of fetus

49. Match the pregnancy terms with their meanings.

Column I	Column II
A. Zygote	1. After 8 weeks
B. Embryo	2. Fertilized ovum
C. Fetus	3. Before 8 weeks
D. Placenta	4. Exchange organ

A. A-2, B-3, C-1, D-4 B. A-3, B-2, C-4, D-1
C. A-1, B-4, C-2, D-3 D. A-4, B-1, C-3, D-2

50. **Assertion I:** Pregnancy involves physiological changes.
Assertion II: Pregnancy has no effect on body systems.

A. Both are correct
B. I is correct, II is incorrect
C. Both are incorrect
D. I is incorrect, II is correct

51. The process of childbirth is called ______.

A. Pregnancy B. Labor
C. Delivery D. Conception

52. Labor is divided into three stages.

A. True B. False
C. Only two D. Only four

53. Which hormone is responsible for uterine contractions during labor?

A. Progesterone B. Estrogen
C. Oxytocin D. HCG

54. The first stage of labor begins with onset of contractions.

A. Expulsion B. Placenta
C. Recovery D. Dilation

55. The opening of cervix during labor is called ______.

A. Effacement B. Dilation
C. Contraction D. Delivery

56. Cervical dilation is measured in centimeters.

A. True B. False
C. Only mm D. Only inches

57. The stage from full dilation to birth of baby is called ______ stage.

A. First B. Second
C. Third D. Fourth

58. Which stage of labor involves delivery of placenta?

A. First B. Second
C. Third D. Fourth

59. The regular uterine contractions help in ______ of baby.

A. Growth B. Descent
C. Rotation D. Delivery

60. The normal duration of first stage of labor is about 12 hours in primigravida.

A. 6 hours B. 8 hours
C. 10 hours D. 12 hours

61. Fetal heart rate monitoring is important during labor.

A. True
B. False
C. Only after delivery
D. Only before labor

62. The part of fetus that comes first during birth is called ______.

A. Lie B. Position
C. Presentation D. Attitude

63. Which of the following is the normal presentation?

A. Breech B. Shoulder
C. Cephalic D. Face

64. Pain during labor is due to uterine contractions.

A. True B. False
C. Only fetus D. Only mother

65. The stretching of cervix during labor causes ______.

A. Relaxation B. Pain
C. Growth D. Expansion

66. Which of the following indicates true labor?

A. Irregular pain B. No dilation
C. False pain D. Regular contractions

67. False labor pains do not lead to cervical dilation.

A. True B. False
C. Only first stage D. Only second stage

68. The position of fetus in uterus is called ______.
A. Attitude B. Lie
C. Position D. Presentation

69. The second stage of labor ends with birth of baby.
A. True B. False
C. Only placenta D. Only dilation

70. Which of the following is a sign of labor?
A. No pain B. No contraction
C. Cervical dilation D. No movement

71. The bag of membranes rupturing is called ______.
A. Bleeding B. Water break
C. Rupture D. Discharge

72. Amniotic fluid protects the fetus during labor.
A. True B. False
C. Only before labor D. Only after labor

73. Which of the following is a complication during labor?
A. Normal pain B. Regular contractions
C. Mild discomfort D. Prolonged labor

74. Episiotomy is an incision made during delivery.
A. True B. False
C. Only surgery D. Only placenta

75. The time between contractions is called ______.
A. Interval B. Duration
C. Intensity D. Frequency

76. Frequency of contractions increases during labor.
A. True B. False
C. Only early D. Only late

77. Which of the following helps in monitoring labor progress?
A. X-ray B. MRI
C. Partograph D. CT scan

78. The descent of fetus occurs during labor.
A. True B. False
C. Only before D. Only after

79. Which of the following is a function of uterus in labor?
A. Nutrition B. Protection
C. Contraction D. Respiration

80. Match the stages of labor with their events.

Column I	Column II
A. First stage	1. Placenta delivery
B. Second stage	2. Baby delivery
C. Third stage	3. Cervical dilation
D. Fourth stage	4. Recovery

A. A-3, B-2, C-1, D-4 B. A-2, B-1, C-4, D-3
C. A-1, B-4, C-3, D-2 D. A-4, B-3, C-2, D-1

81. Assertion I: True labor leads to cervical dilation.
Assertion II: False labor causes cervical dilation.
A. Both are correct B. I is correct, II is incorrect
C. Both are incorrect D. I is incorrect, II is correct

82. Which of the following is a sign of fetal distress?
A. Normal heart rate B. Regular contractions
C. Movement D. Abnormal heart rate

83. The instrument used to listen fetal heart is ______.
A. Stethoscope B. Fetoscope
C. Doppler D. Monitor

84. Active management of labor reduces complications.
A. True B. False
C. Only drugs D. Only surgery

85. Labor ends with delivery of placenta.
A. True B. False
C. Only baby D. Only cervix

86. Postnatal period refers to the time after ______.
A. Pregnancy B. Labor
C. Delivery D. Conception

87. The postnatal period lasts for about 6 weeks after delivery.
A. True B. False
C. Only 2 weeks D. Only 10 weeks

88. Which hormone is responsible for milk production?
A. Estrogen B. Progesterone
C. Prolactin D. Oxytocin

89. Which of the following is an important postnatal care activity?
A. Ignoring mother B. No check-up
C. Only rest D. Monitoring vitals

90. The first milk produced after delivery is called ______.
A. Colostrum B. Milk
C. Secretion D. Fluid

91. Breastfeeding should be initiated within one hour of birth.
A. True B. False
C. Only after 1 day D. Only after discharge

92. The uterus returns to normal size by a process called ______.
A. Evolution B. Involution
C. Contraction D. Regression

93. Which of the following is a sign of postnatal infection?
A. Normal temperature B. Good appetite
C. Fever D. Sleep

94. Lochia is the vaginal discharge after delivery.

A. True B. False
C. Only blood D. Only mucus

95. Which of the following is a complication in postnatal period?

A. Breastfeeding B. Rest
C. Exercise D. Hemorrhage

96. Postnatal exercises help in recovery of mother.

A. True B. False
C. Only baby D. Only doctor

97. The emotional changes after delivery are called ______.

A. Depression B. Baby blues
C. Anxiety D. Stress

98. Match the postnatal terms with their meanings.

Column I	Column II
A. Lochia	1. Milk production
B. Colostrum	2. Vaginal discharge
C. Involution	3. Uterus shrinking
D. Lactation	4. First milk

A. A-2, B-4, C-3, D-1 B. A-3, B-2, C-1, D-4
C. A-1, B-3, C-4, D-2 D. A-4, B-1, C-2, D-3

99. Balanced diet is essential in postnatal period.

A. True B. False
C. Only baby D. Only milk

100. Which nutrient is important for lactating mothers?

A. Fat B. Sugar
C. Protein D. Salt

101. **Assertion I:** Breastfeeding strengthens mother-child bond.

Assertion II: Breastfeeding has no benefits for baby.

A. Both are correct
B. I is correct, II is incorrect
C. Both are incorrect
D. I is incorrect, II is correct

102. Which of the following helps prevent infection in postnatal period?

A. Poor hygiene B. No care
C. Ignoring wounds D. Cleanliness

103. Match the care practices with their purposes.

Column I	Column II
A. Breastfeeding	1. Prevent infection
B. Hygiene	2. Strength recovery
C. Nutrition	3. Baby feeding
D. Exercise	4. Energy supply

A. A-3, B-1, C-4, D-2 B. A-1, B-2, C-3, D-4
C. A-2, B-4, C-1, D-3 D. A-4, B-3, C-2, D-1

104. The normal color of lochia changes from red to ______ over time.

A. White B. Yellow
C. Pink D. Green

105. **Assertion I:** Postnatal care is essential for mother and baby.

Assertion II: Postnatal care is not required after delivery.

A. Both are correct B. I is correct, II is incorrect
C. Both are incorrect D. I is incorrect, II is correct

106. A newborn baby is called a ______.

A. Infant B. Child
C. Neonate D. Fetus

107. Neonatal period lasts for 28 days after birth.

A. True B. False
C. Only 7 days D. Only 1 year

108. Which of the following is a normal birth weight of a newborn?

A. 1 kg B. 1.5 kg
C. 2.5–3.5 kg D. 5 kg

109. The first breath of a newborn is essential for survival.

A. Only after hours B. Not required
C. Optional D. Essential

110. The process of assessing newborn immediately after birth is called ______ score.

A. APGAR B. Silverman
C. Ballard D. Bishop

111. The normal respiratory rate of newborn is 40–60 per minute.

A. True B. False
C. Only 20 D. Only 80

112. Which of the following helps maintain body temperature of newborn?

A. Cold exposure B. Wet skin
C. Warm environment D. No clothing

113. The umbilical cord is cut and tied after ______.

A. Delivery B. Cry
C. Birth D. Feeding

114. Which of the following is given to newborn to prevent infection?

A. Antibiotic B. Vaccine later
C. None D. Vitamin K

115. Early breastfeeding provides immunity to newborn.

A. True B. False
C. Only milk D. Only food

116. The yellow discoloration of skin in newborn is called ______.

A. Cyanosis B. Jaundice
C. Anemia D. Pallor

117. Newborn should be kept warm immediately after birth.

A. True B. False
C. Only later D. Only day

118. Which of the following is a reflex in newborn?

A. Walking B. Running
C. Moro reflex D. Speaking

119. The cord stump falls off within 7–10 days.

A. True B. False
C. Only 1 day D. Only 20 days

120. Which of the following is an essential newborn care?

A. Cold bath B. No feeding
C. Delay care D. Clean cord care

121. The body temperature of newborn should be maintained at ______.

A. 30°C B. 34°C
C. 36.5–37.5°C D. 40°C

122. Kangaroo mother care helps in maintaining warmth.

A. True B. False
C. Only feeding D. Only rest

123. Which of the following is a sign of healthy newborn?

A. Weak cry B. Poor feeding
C. Active movement D. Cyanosis

124. Immunization starts soon after birth.

A. True B. False
C. Only later D. Only school

125. Which of the following is given at birth?

A. OPV later B. Measles
C. BCG D. None

126. Match the newborn reflexes with their meanings.

Column I	Column II
A. Moro reflex	1. Searching for nipple
B. Rooting reflex	2. Holding objects
C. Sucking reflex	3. Startle response
D. Grasp reflex	4. Feeding action

A. A-3, B-1, C-4, D-2 B. A-1, B-2, C-3, D-4
C. A-2, B-3, C-1, D-4 D. A-4, B-3, C-2, D-1

127. The first stool passed by newborn is called ______.

A. Urine B. Stool
C. Meconium D. Feces

128. Which of the following is a danger sign in newborn?

A. Active cry B. Good feeding
C. Normal color D. Poor feeding

129. **Assertion I:** Early breastfeeding improves immunity.
Assertion II: Colostrum has no benefits.

A. Both are correct B. I is correct, II is incorrect
C. Both are incorrect D. I is incorrect, II is correct

130. Proper newborn care reduces neonatal mortality.

A. True B. False
C. Only hospital D. Only drugs

131. A high-risk pregnancy is one in which there is increased risk to ______ or baby.

A. Family B. Doctor
C. Mother D. Society

132. High-risk pregnancy requires special care and monitoring.

A. True B. False
C. Only delivery D. Only baby

133. Which of the following is a risk factor for pregnancy?

A. Young age
B. Normal diet
C. Advanced maternal age
D. Exercise

134. Pregnancy below 18 years is considered high risk.

A. Only normal B. Safe
C. Average D. High risk

135. A pregnant woman with ______ may develop complications.

A. Anemia B. Nutrition
C. Exercise D. Rest

136. Hypertension in pregnancy can lead to complications.

A. True B. False
C. Only normal D. Only safe

137. Which of the following is a medical condition causing high-risk pregnancy?

A. Health B. Fitness
C. Diabetes D. Exercise

138. Which of the following is a sign of pre-eclampsia?

A. Low BP B. Normal urine
C. Edema D. Appetite

139. Severe headache in pregnancy may indicate ______.

A. Normal B. Weakness
C. Danger D. Fatigue

140. Multiple pregnancy increases risk of complications.

A. True B. False
C. Only single D. Only normal

141. Which of the following is a complication of high-risk pregnancy?

A. Normal delivery B. Good health
C. Balanced diet D. Preterm labor

142. Lack of antenatal care increases ______ in pregnancy.
A. Safety B. Health
C. Risk D. Comfort

143. Which of the following is a risk factor?
A. Good nutrition B. Exercise
C. Smoking D. Sleep

144. Anemia during pregnancy can affect fetal growth.
A. True B. False
C. Only mother D. Only placenta

145. Which of the following is a complication of diabetes in pregnancy?
A. Low weight B. No growth
C. Large baby D. Weakness

146. A pregnant woman with high BP needs ______ monitoring.
A. Less B. Normal
C. Close D. No

147. Which condition leads to convulsions in pregnancy?
A. Anemia B. Diabetes
C. Eclampsia D. Fever

148. Regular antenatal visits help in detecting complications early.
A. True B. False
C. Only late D. Only delivery

149. Bleeding during pregnancy is a ______ sign.
A. Normal B. Mild
C. Danger D. Routine

150. Which of the following requires immediate attention in pregnancy?
A. Mild nausea B. Sleep
C. Rest D. Severe bleeding

151. Match the conditions with their effects.

Column I	Column II
A. Anemia	1. High blood sugar
B. Hypertension	2. Low hemoglobin
C. Diabetes	3. High blood pressure
D. Infection	4. Risk to fetus

A. A-2, B-3, C-1, D-4 B. A-1, B-2, C-3, D-4
C. A-3, B-4, C-2, D-1 D. A-4, B-1, C-3, D-2

152. Good nutrition reduces complications in pregnancy.
A. True B. False
C. Only after D. Only baby

153. A woman with history of complications needs ______ care.
A. Routine B. Less
C. Special D. No

154. Which of the following increases risk in pregnancy?
A. Balanced diet B. Exercise
C. Alcohol intake D. Rest

155. **Assertion I:** High-risk pregnancy needs special care.
Assertion II: All pregnancies have equal risk.
A. Both are correct B. I is correct, II is incorrect
C. Both are incorrect D. I is incorrect, II is correct

156. Abnormal labor is also known as ______ labor.
A. Normal B. Easy
C. Difficult D. Routine

157. Abnormal labor deviates from the normal process of labor.
A. True B. False
C. Only normal D. Only routine

158. Which of the following is a cause of abnormal labor?
A. Good nutrition B. Normal pelvis
C. Malpresentation D. Exercise

159. Prolonged labor is a type of abnormal labor.
A. Short labor B. Easy labor
C. Normal labor D. Prolonged labor

160. Weak uterine contractions are called ______.
A. Hypertonic B. Hypotonic
C. Normal D. Strong

161. Obstructed labor occurs due to failure of descent of fetus.
A. True B. False
C. Only early D. Only late

162. Which of the following is a complication of abnormal labor?
A. Normal delivery B. Good health
C. Fetal distress D. Recovery

163. Which of the following is a malpresentation?
A. Cephalic B. Vertex
C. Breech D. Occipital

164. The excessive uterine contractions are called ______ labor.
A. Hypotonic B. Normal
C. Hypertonic D. Weak

165. Which condition may require cesarean section?
A. Normal labor B. Good contraction
C. Normal presentation D. Obstructed labor

166. Fetal distress can occur in abnormal labor.
A. True B. False
C. Only normal D. Only safe

167. Match the types of labor with their features.

Column I	Column II
A. Prolonged labor	1. Slow progress
B. Obstructed labor	2. No descent
C. Precipitate labor	3. Very fast labor
D. Hypotonic labor	4. Weak contractions

A. A-1, B-2, C-3, D-4 B. A-2, B-1, C-4, D-3
C. A-3, B-4, C-1, D-2 D. A-4, B-3, C-2, D-1

168. Labor lasting more than ______ hours is considered prolonged.
A. 6 B. 12
C. 24 D. 48

169. **Assertion I:** Abnormal labor increases maternal risk.
Assertion II: Abnormal labor has no effect on baby.
A. Both are correct B. I is correct, II is incorrect
C. Both are incorrect D. I is incorrect, II is correct

170. Which of the following is a sign of fetal distress?
A. Normal heart rate B. Active movement
C. Abnormal heart rate D. Strong cry

171. Precipitate labor is very rapid labor.
A. True B. False
C. Only slow D. Only delayed

172. Which of the following is a complication of obstructed labor?
A. Easy delivery B. No risk
C. Recovery D. Uterine rupture

173. The abnormal position of fetus is called ______.
A. Presentation B. Position
C. Malposition D. Attitude

174. Match the complications with their causes.

Column I	Column II
A. Fetal distress	1. Prolonged labor
B. Uterine rupture	2. Obstructed labor
C. Infection	3. Poor hygiene
D. Hemorrhage	4. Blood loss

A. A-1, B-2, C-3, D-4 B. A-2, B-1, C-4, D-3
C. A-3, B-4, C-1, D-2 D. A-4, B-3, C-2, D-1

175. **Assertion I:** Timely management prevents complications in abnormal labor.
Assertion II: Abnormal labor does not require medical care.
A. Both are correct B. I is correct, II is incorrect
C. Both are incorrect D. I is incorrect, II is correct

176. Postnatal complications occur after ______ period.
A. Pregnancy B. Labor
C. Delivery D. Conception

177. Postnatal complications can affect both mother and baby.
A. True B. False
C. Only mother D. Only baby

178. Which of the following is a postnatal complication?
A. Breastfeeding B. Rest
C. Infection D. Exercise

179. Postpartum hemorrhage is a serious complication after delivery.
A. Mild condition B. Normal change
C. Recovery phase D. Serious complication

180. Excessive bleeding after delivery is called ______ hemorrhage.
A. Antepartum B. Intrapartum
C. Postpartum D. Internal

181. Match the complications with their features.

Column I	Column II
A. Hemorrhage	1. Breast inflammation
B. Infection	2. Excessive bleeding
C. Mastitis	3. Emotional disturbance
D. Depression	4. Fever

A. A-2, B-4, C-1, D-3 B. A-1, B-2, C-3, D-4
C. A-3, B-1, C-4, D-2 D. A-4, B-3, C-2, D-1

182. Breast infection after delivery is called ______.
A. Mastitis B. Sepsis
C. Fever D. Infection

183. Which of the following is a sign of infection?
A. Normal temperature B. Good appetite
C. Fever D. Sleep

184. Which of the following is a psychological complication after delivery?
A. Recovery B. Exercise
C. Feeding D. Depression

185. **Assertion I:** Early detection prevents postnatal complications.
Assertion II: Postnatal complications do not require treatment.
A. Both are correct B. I is correct, II is incorrect
C. Both are incorrect D. I is incorrect, II is correct

186. Oxytocin is used to induce ______ during labor.
A. Sleep B. Relaxation
C. Contractions D. Growth

187. Drugs are used in obstetrics to manage labor and complications.
A. True B. False
C. Only surgery D. Only rest

188. Which of the following drug is used to prevent hemorrhage?

A. Insulin B. Antibiotic
C. Oxytocin D. Vitamin

189. Magnesium sulfate is used to control convulsions in eclampsia.

A. Fever B. Pain
C. Bleeding D. Convulsions

190. The drug used to increase uterine contractions is called ______.

A. Tocolytic B. Sedative
C. Uterotonic D. Analgesic

191. Match the drugs with their uses.

Column I	Column II
A. Oxytocin	1. Treat infection
B. Magnesium sulfate	2. Increase Hb
C. Iron	3. Control convulsions
D. Antibiotics	4. Induce labor

A. A-4, B-3, C-2, D-1 B. A-3, B-4, C-1, D-2
C. A-2, B-1, C-4, D-3 D. A-1, B-2, C-3, D-4

192. Which of the following drug is used to treat anemia in pregnancy?

A. Calcium B. Vitamin C
C. Iron D. Protein

193. Tocolytic drugs are used to stop uterine contractions.

A. True B. False
C. Only increase D. Only induce

194. Which of the following drug is used to relieve labor pain?

A. Antibiotic B. Iron
C. Vaccine D. Analgesic

195. Assertion I: Proper drug use reduces complications.
Assertion II: Drugs should be used without prescription.

A. Both are correct B. I is correct, II is incorrect
C. Both are incorrect D. I is incorrect, II is correct

196. Family welfare aims at improving the ______ of family.

A. Economy B. Education
C. Health D. Society

197. Family planning helps in spacing of children.

A. True B. False
C. Only limit D. Only delay

198. Which method prevents pregnancy temporarily?

A. Sterilization B. Surgery
C. Condom D. Removal

199. Which method is permanent contraception?

A. Condom B. Pills
C. IUCD D. Sterilization

200. Oral contraceptive pills contain ______ hormones.

A. One B. Two
C. Three D. Four

201. IUCD is inserted into uterus to prevent pregnancy.

A. True B. False
C. Only injection D. Only tablet

202. The copper-T device is placed inside the ______.

A. Cervix B. Ovary
C. Uterus D. Vagina

203. Which method provides protection against STDs?

A. Pills B. IUCD
C. Condom D. Sterilization

204. Family planning reduces maternal mortality.

A. True B. False
C. Only child D. Only family

205. Which method is used after childbirth to avoid pregnancy?

A. Surgery B. Exercise
C. Rest D. Lactational amenorrhea

206. Match the methods with their types.

Column I	Column II
A. Condom	1. Barrier method
B. IUCD	2. Hormonal method
C. Sterilization	3. Permanent method
D. Pills	4. Intrauterine method

A. A-1, B-4, C-3, D-2 B. A-2, B-3, C-1, D-4
C. A-3, B-1, C-4, D-2 D. A-4, B-2, C-3, D-1

207. Vasectomy is a surgical method for ______.

A. Women B. Children
C. Men D. Doctors

208. Tubectomy is done in females for permanent contraception.

A. True B. False
C. Only men D. Only child

209. Emergency contraceptive pills are taken within ______ hours.

A. 24 B. 48
C. 72 D. 96

210. Which of the following is a natural method of contraception?

A. Pills B. IUCD
C. Safe period D. Injection

211. Family welfare includes maternal and child health services.

A. True B. False
C. Only mother D. Only child

212. The ideal gap between two children is ______ years.

A. 1 B. 2
C. 3 D. 5

213. Which of the following is a benefit of family planning?

A. Overpopulation B. Poor health
C. Disease D. Healthy family

214. **Assertion I:** Family planning helps control population.
Assertion II: Family planning increases maternal risk.

A. Both are correct B. I is correct, II is incorrect
C. Both are incorrect D. I is incorrect, II is correct

215. The failure of condom may lead to ______ pregnancy.

A. Planned B. Safe
C. Unwanted D. Delayed

216. Which method involves periodic abstinence?

A. Pills B. IUCD
C. Rhythm method D. Surgery

217. Match the programs with their focus.

Column I	Column II
A. MCH	1. Child protection
B. RCH	2. Maternal care
C. Family planning	3. Population control
D. Immunization	4. Disease prevention

A. A-2, B-1, C-3, D-4 B. A-1, B-2, C-4, D-3
C. A-3, B-4, C-1, D-2 D. A-4, B-3, C-2, D-1

218. The use of IUCD prevents ______ of ovum.

A. Formation B. Fertilization
C. Growth D. Implantation

219. Which of the following is a long-term contraceptive method?

A. Condom B. Pills
C. Injection D. IUCD

220. **Assertion I:** Family welfare improves quality of life.
Assertion II: Family welfare has no role in health.

A. Both are correct
B. I is correct, II is incorrect
C. Both are incorrect
D. I is incorrect, II is correct

EXPLANATORY ANSWERS

1. **C:** Antenatal care is during pregnancy. It ensures maternal and fetal health. It prevents complications.
2. **A:** Early detection prevents problems. It improves outcomes. It ensures safety.
3. **C:** Missed periods indicate pregnancy. It is early sign. Needs confirmation.
4. **D:** Pregnancy lasts about 40 weeks. It is normal duration. It ends with delivery.
5. **A:** Early visit important. It helps detection. It improves care.
6. **A:** Check-ups monitor health. They prevent complications. They ensure safety.
7. **B:** Formula estimates due date. It is commonly used. It is simple.
8. **C:** Confirms pregnancy. It detects hormone. It is reliable.
9. **D:** Hb should be above 11. Prevents anemia. Ensures oxygen supply.
10. **D:** Bleeding is danger sign. Needs immediate care. It may be serious.
11. **A:** Supplements prevent anemia. Support growth. Essential care.
12. **B:** Fetal movement felt. It is important sign. Indicates life.
13. **D:** Antenatal includes care. It involves examination. It includes counseling.
14. **C:** Iron prevents anemia. Supports RBCs. Important in pregnancy.
15. **B:** TT prevents tetanus. Protects mother and baby. It is essential.
16. **D:** It measures growth. Indicates fetal development. It is important.
17. **A:** BP detects complications. Prevents hypertension. Important monitoring.
18. **D:** Blood volume increases. Supports fetus. Maintains circulation.
19. **C:** It is minor issue. Common in pregnancy. Usually temporary.
20. **C:** Movement shows well-being. Indicates healthy fetus. Important sign.
21. **A:** Balanced diet needed. Supports growth. Prevents deficiencies.
22. **D:** Weight gain about 10–12 kg. It is normal. Indicates growth.
23. **D:** It is complication. It can be dangerous. Needs monitoring.
24. **A:** Urine test checks sugar. Detects infection. Important screening.
25. **C:** Position describes fetal relation. It is important. Helps delivery.

26. **C:** Diet supports health. Prevents deficiency. Ensures growth.

27. **C:** Risk increases with age. Complications more. Needs care.

28. **A:** Education prepares mother. Reduces anxiety. Improves outcome.

29. **D:** It indicates hypertension. Needs attention. It is danger sign.

30. **A:** Iron anemia, TT tetanus, USG growth, BP hypertension.

31. **C:** Fertilization occurs with ovum. It forms zygote. It begins pregnancy.

32. **A:** Pregnancy divided into trimesters. Each has stages. It helps monitoring.

33. **C:** Progesterone maintains pregnancy. It supports uterus. It prevents contractions.

34. **D:** First trimester ends at 12 weeks. It is early phase. Important development.

35. **B:** Placenta connects mother and fetus. It supplies nutrients. Removes waste.

36. **A:** Placenta exchanges oxygen. It supplies nutrients. Removes waste.

37. **C:** After 8 weeks called fetus. Organs develop. Growth continues.

38. **C:** Oxytocin causes contractions. It helps labor. It is important hormone.

39. **A:** Fundal height increases. It indicates growth. It helps assessment.

40. **C:** Implantation occurs in endometrium. It supports embryo. It provides nutrients.

41. **D:** Quickening felt at 18–20 weeks. It indicates fetal movement. Important sign.

42. **C:** Blood volume increases. Supports fetus. Maintains circulation.

43. **A:** Breast prepares for feeding. Hormones act. Lactation possible.

44. **D:** Fetal heart heard early. Indicates life. Important sign.

45. **C:** Positive sign. Confirms pregnancy. Indicates living fetus.

46. **A:** Weight gain normal. Supports growth. Indicates health.

47. **B:** Cleavage is cell division. It forms embryo. It is early stage.

48. **D:** Fluid protects fetus. Cushions movement. Prevents injury.

49. **A:** Zygote fertilized, embryo early, fetus later, placenta exchange.

50. **B:** Pregnancy changes body. Many systems affected. Second is wrong.

51. **B:** Labor is childbirth process. It includes stages. It ends with delivery.

52. **A:** Labor has stages. It includes dilation, expulsion, placenta. It is systematic.

53. **C:** Oxytocin causes contractions. It stimulates uterus. It aids delivery.

54. **D:** First stage involves dilation. Cervix opens. It prepares for birth.

55. **B:** Dilation opens cervix. It allows baby passage. It is measured.

56. **A:** Dilation measured in cm. It indicates progress. It is important.

57. **B:** Second stage ends with baby. It follows dilation. It is active phase.

58. **C:** Placenta delivered. It follows baby. It completes labor.

59. **B:** Contractions help descent. Baby moves down. It aids delivery.

60. **D:** Primigravida takes longer. Around 12 hours. It is normal.

61. **A:** Monitoring detects distress. Ensures safety. Important care.

62. **C:** Presentation is presenting part. It leads delivery. It is important.

63. **C:** Head presentation normal. It is safest. It is common.

64. **A:** Pain due to contractions. It increases. It helps progress.

65. **B:** Cervical stretching causes pain. It indicates progress. It is normal.

66. **D:** True labor regular. Leads dilation. It is progressive.

67. **A:** False labor irregular. No dilation. It subsides.

68. **C:** Position relates fetus. It affects delivery. It is important.

69. **A:** Second stage ends with baby. It is delivery stage. Important phase.

70. **C:** Dilation shows labor. It indicates progress. It is sign.

71. **B:** Membrane rupture releases fluid. It indicates labor. Important sign.

72. **A:** Fluid protects fetus. Cushions during labor. Prevents injury.

73. **D:** It is complication. Needs care. May harm mother and baby.

74. **A:** Episiotomy is incision. It aids delivery. Prevents tearing.

75. **A:** Interval is time between contractions. It is monitored. It shows progress.

76. **A:** Contractions increase. Frequency rises. It shows progress.

77. **C:** It monitors labor. Tracks progress. It helps decisions.

78. **A:** Descent occurs. Baby moves down. It is essential.

79. **C:** Uterus contracts. It pushes baby. It aids delivery.

80. **A:** First dilation, second baby, third placenta, fourth recovery.

81. **B:** True labor causes dilation. False does not. Second is wrong.

82. **D:** Indicates distress. Needs attention. It is serious.

83. **B:** Used for fetal heart. It detects beats. It is simple tool.

84. **A:** Active management prevents complications. Improves outcome. Ensures safety.

85. **A:** Labor ends after placenta. It completes process. It is final stage.

86. C: Postnatal period starts after delivery. It lasts about 6 weeks. It involves recovery.

87. A: It is about 6 weeks. Body returns to normal. It is important phase.

88. C: Prolactin produces milk. It acts on breast. It supports lactation.

89. D: Monitoring ensures safety. Detects complications. It is essential.

90. A: First milk is colostrum. It is rich in antibodies. It protects baby.

91. A: Early feeding important. It improves bonding. It provides immunity.

92. B: Uterus shrinks. It returns to normal. It is natural process.

93. C: Fever indicates infection. Needs attention. It is warning sign.

94. A: Lochia is discharge. It changes color. It indicates recovery.

95. D: It is serious complication. Needs immediate care. It may be fatal.

96. A: Exercises improve recovery. They strengthen muscles. They promote health.

97. B: Emotional changes common. Temporary mood swings. Needs support.

98. A: Lochia discharge, colostrum first milk, involution shrink, lactation milk.

99. A: Diet supports recovery. Provides energy. Helps lactation.

100. C: Protein aids repair. Supports milk production. It is essential.

101. B: Breastfeeding beneficial. It improves bonding. Second wrong.

102. D: Hygiene prevents infection. It protects mother. It ensures recovery.

103. A: Feeding baby, hygiene prevents infection, nutrition energy, exercise recovery.

104. A: Lochia changes color. Red to white. Indicates healing.

105. B: Postnatal care essential. It prevents complications. Second wrong.

106. C: Neonate is newborn up to 28 days. It is critical period. Needs care.

107. A: Neonatal period is 28 days. It is early life. Needs monitoring.

108. C: Normal weight range. Indicates healthy baby. Important indicator.

109. D: First breath starts respiration. Oxygen supply begins. Life depends on it.

110. A: APGAR assesses newborn. It checks condition. It is immediate score.

111. A: Normal RR is 40–60. It is higher than adult. It is normal.

112. C: Warmth prevents hypothermia. It maintains temperature. Essential care.

113. C: Cord cut after birth. It separates baby. It is routine.

114. D: Prevents bleeding. It is given at birth. It is essential.

115. A: Breastfeeding gives antibodies. It protects baby. It improves immunity.

116. B: Yellow color due to bilirubin. Common in newborn. Needs monitoring.

117. A: Warmth prevents hypothermia. It is essential. Newborn cannot regulate temperature.

118. C: It is startle reflex. Present at birth. Indicates normal CNS.

119. A: Cord falls in 7–10 days. It is natural. Needs care.

120. D: Prevents infection. Keeps area dry. Essential practice.

121. C: Normal temperature range. Maintains health. Prevents hypothermia.

122. A: KMC provides warmth. It improves bonding. It helps growth.

123. C: Active baby is healthy. Good tone. Normal sign.

124. A: Immunization starts early. Protects baby. Prevents diseases.

125. C: BCG given at birth. Prevents TB. It is routine.

126. A: Moro startle, rooting search, sucking feeding, grasp hold.

127. C: First stool is meconium. It is dark green. It is normal.

128. D: It is danger sign. Indicates illness. Needs attention.

129. B: Breastfeeding improves immunity. Colostrum beneficial. Second wrong.

130. A: Proper care reduces deaths. Improves survival. Ensures health.

131. C: High-risk affects mother and baby. It needs monitoring. It prevents complications.

132. A: Special care required. It reduces risk. It improves outcome.

133. C: Age increases risk. Complications more likely. Needs monitoring.

134. D: Teenage pregnancy risky. Body not mature. Complications possible.

135. A: Anemia reduces oxygen. Affects fetus. Causes complications.

136. A: Hypertension dangerous. Leads to complications. Needs control.

137. C: Diabetes increases risk. Affects fetus. Needs management.

138. C: Edema is sign. Seen in preeclampsia. Needs attention.

139. C: Headache may indicate complication. Needs evaluation. It is warning.

140. A: Multiple pregnancy increases risk. More complications. Needs care.

141. D: It is complication. Leads to early birth. Needs care.

142. C: Lack of care increases risk. Complications go unnoticed. Dangerous.

143. C: Smoking harmful. Affects fetus. Increases risk.

144. A: Anemia affects growth. Reduces oxygen. Causes problems.

145. C: Diabetes leads to macrosomia. Difficult delivery. Needs monitoring.

146. C: High BP needs close monitoring. Prevents complications. Ensures safety.

147. C: Causes convulsions. It is severe. Needs emergency care.

148. A: Visits detect issues. Prevent complications. Improve outcome.

149. C: Bleeding serious sign. Needs immediate care. It is risky.

150. D: It is emergency. Needs immediate care. It is life-threatening.

151. A: Anemia low Hb, hypertension BP, diabetes sugar, infection risk.

152. A: Nutrition supports health. Prevents deficiency. Reduces risk.

153. C: High-risk needs special care. Close monitoring needed. Prevents complications.

154. C: Alcohol harmful. Affects fetus. Causes defects.

155. B: High-risk needs care. All pregnancies not equal risk. Second wrong.

156. C: Abnormal labor is difficult. It deviates from normal. Needs management.

157. A: It differs from normal. Progress is affected. It needs attention.

158. C: Malpresentation causes difficulty. It affects delivery. Leads to complications.

159. D: Long labor abnormal. It increases risk. Needs intervention.

160. B: Weak contractions hypotonic. Slow progress. Needs support.

161. A: Obstruction prevents descent. Labor stops. It is serious.

162. C: Baby may suffer. Oxygen reduced. Needs urgent care.

163. C: Breech is abnormal. Head not first. Difficult delivery.

164. C: Excess contractions hypertonic. Painful. May cause distress.

165. D: Obstruction prevents delivery. Surgery needed. Prevents complications.

166. A: Distress common. Due to poor oxygen. Needs monitoring.

167. A: Prolonged slow, obstructed no descent, precipitate fast, hypotonic weak.

168. C: Labor >24 hours prolonged. It is abnormal. Needs management.

169. B: Risk increases. Baby also affected. Second wrong.

170. C: Indicates distress. Needs immediate care. Important sign.

171. A: Precipitate is rapid. Very fast labor. May cause injury.

172. D: Serious complication. Due to obstruction. Life-threatening.

173. C: Abnormal position affects labor. Causes difficulty. Needs care.

174. A: Distress prolonged, rupture obstruction, infection hygiene, hemorrhage blood loss.

175. B: Management prevents risk. Care essential. Second wrong.

176. C: Postnatal complications occur after delivery. It is postpartum period. Needs monitoring.

177. A: Both mother and baby affected. Complications may arise. Care is needed.

178. C: Infection is common complication. Needs treatment. It can be serious.

179. D: Hemorrhage is severe. It causes blood loss. Needs urgent care.

180. C: Bleeding after delivery called postpartum hemorrhage. It is dangerous. Needs care.

181. A: Hemorrhage bleeding, infection fever, mastitis breast, depression emotional.

182. A: Breast infection causes pain. It affects feeding. Needs treatment.

183. C: Fever indicates infection. It is warning sign. Needs evaluation.

184. D: Postnatal depression affects mood. Needs support. It is common.

185. B: Early detection prevents issues. Treatment is necessary. Second wrong.

186. C: Oxytocin induces contractions. It helps labor progress. It is commonly used.

187. A: Drugs manage labor. They prevent complications. They support delivery.

188. C: Oxytocin reduces bleeding. It contracts uterus. Prevents hemorrhage.

189. D: Magnesium sulfate controls seizures. Used in eclampsia. It is essential.

190. C: Uterotonics increase contractions. They aid labor. They prevent bleeding.

191. A: Oxytocin labor, $MgSO_4$ convulsions, iron Hb, antibiotics infection.

192. C: Iron treats anemia. It increases hemoglobin. It is essential.

193. A: Tocolytics reduce contractions. They delay labor. Used in preterm.

194. D: Analgesics relieve pain. Used in labor. Provide comfort.

195. B: Drugs must be prescribed. Proper use prevents complications. Second is wrong.

196. C: Family welfare improves health. It ensures well-being. It supports family.

197. A: It helps spacing. Prevents early pregnancy. Improves health.

198. C: Condom is temporary. Prevents pregnancy. Protects from STDs.

199. D: Sterilization permanent. It stops fertility. It is surgical.

200. B: Pills contain hormones. Prevent ovulation. Used for contraception.

201. A: IUCD placed in uterus. Prevents fertilization. Long-term method.

202. C: Device inserted in uterus. It prevents implantation. It is effective.

203. C: Condom prevents STDs. Also prevents pregnancy. It is barrier.

204. A: Planning reduces risk. Improves maternal health. Prevents complications.

205. D: Breastfeeding delays ovulation. It prevents pregnancy. Temporary method.

206. A: Condom barrier, IUCD intrauterine, sterilization permanent, pills hormonal.

207. C: Vasectomy in males. It blocks sperm. It is permanent.

208. A: Tubectomy female sterilization. Prevents pregnancy. It is permanent.

209. C: Emergency pills taken early. Prevent pregnancy. Time is important.

210. C: Natural method. Avoids fertile days. Prevents conception.

211. A: Family welfare includes care. Supports mother and child. Improves health.

212. C: Gap improves health. Allows recovery. Reduces risk.

213. D: Planning improves health. Reduces risk. Supports well-being.

214. B: Planning controls population. Reduces risk. Second wrong.

215. C: Failure leads to unwanted pregnancy. Needs awareness. Prevention needed.

216. C: Based on cycle. Avoids fertile period. Natural method.

217. A: MCH maternal, RCH child, planning population, immunization disease.

218. D: IUCD prevents implantation. Stops pregnancy. It is effective.

219. D: IUCD long-term. Works for years. Reversible method.

220. B: Welfare improves life. Supports health. Second wrong.

16. Management of Nursing Services & Education

1. Management is the process of planning, organizing, directing, and ______.

A. Staffing B. Controlling
C. Controlling D. Leading

2. Management aims at achieving organizational goals effectively.

A. False B. Only planning
C. Only directing D. True

3. The function of arranging resources is called ______.

A. Planning B. Directing
C. Organizing D. Staffing

4. Which of the following is a principle of management?

A. Confusion B. Delay
C. Unity of command D. Ignorance

5. Assertion I: Management ensures efficient use of resources.

Assertion II: Management has no role in achieving goals.

A. Both are correct B. I is correct, II is incorrect
C. Both are incorrect D. I is incorrect, II is correct

6. The first step of management process is ______.

A. Organizing B. Directing
C. Planning D. Controlling

7. Planning involves setting goals and deciding actions.

A. False B. Only organizing
C. Only directing D. True

8. Directing involves guiding and ______ employees.

A. Ignoring B. Punishing
C. Motivating D. Controlling

9. Which of the following is a function of management?

A. Sleeping B. Avoiding
C. Staffing D. Ignoring

10. Assertion I: Controlling compares actual performance with standards.

Assertion II: Controlling has no role in management.

A. Both are correct B. I is correct, II is incorrect
C. Both are incorrect D. I is incorrect, II is correct

11. Organizational behavior studies the behavior of ______ in organization.

A. Machines B. Systems
C. Individuals D. Buildings

12. Good organizational behavior improves teamwork and performance.

A. False B. Only conflict
C. Only rules D. True

13. Which of the following influences behavior in organization?

A. Environment B. Leadership
C. Motivation D. All of these

14. Motivation improves efficiency of employees.

A. True B. False
C. Only rules D. Only structure

15. Assertion I: Organizational behavior helps in understanding employees.

Assertion II: Organizational behavior has no effect on productivity.

A. Both are correct B. I is correct, II is incorrect
C. Both are incorrect D. I is incorrect, II is correct

16. Nursing education prepares students for ______ practice.

A. Theory B. Research
C. Clinical D. Teaching

17. Teaching methods help in effective learning of students.

A. True B. False
C. Only exam D. Only theory

18. Which of the following is a method of teaching?

A. Ignoring B. Sleeping
C. Punishment D. Lecture

19. Evaluation helps to assess learning outcomes.

A. True B. False
C. Only teaching D. Only theory

20. **Assertion I:** Nursing education improves skills and knowledge.

Assertion II: Education has no role in patient care.

A. Both are correct
B. I is correct, II is incorrect
C. Both are incorrect
D. I is incorrect, II is correct

EXPLANATORY ANSWERS

1. **C:** Management includes controlling. It ensures goals. It monitors performance.
2. **D:** Management achieves goals. It improves efficiency. It guides organization.
3. **C:** Organizing arranges resources. It structures work. It ensures coordination.
4. **C:** One boss principle. Avoids confusion. Improves discipline.
5. **B:** Management uses resources. Achieves goals. Second is wrong.
6. **C:** Planning is first step. It sets objectives. It guides actions.
7. **D:** Planning defines goals. It decides methods. It directs activities.
8. **C:** Directing motivates workers. It guides them. It improves performance.
9. **C:** Staffing selects people. It assigns jobs. It supports management.
10. **B:** Controlling monitors work. It corrects errors. Second is wrong.
11. **C:** Organizational behavior studies people. It focuses on actions. It improves management.
12. **D:** Good behavior improves teamwork. It increases efficiency. It enhances productivity.
13. **D:** Behavior influenced by factors. Includes leadership and environment. It is complex.
14. **A:** Motivation improves performance. It increases efficiency. It boosts morale.
15. **B:** OB improves understanding. It affects productivity. Second is wrong.
16. **C:** Nursing education prepares for practice. It builds skills. It improves care.
17. **A:** Teaching methods enhance learning. They improve understanding. They guide students.
18. **D:** Lecture is teaching method. It delivers knowledge. It is common.
19. **A:** Evaluation measures learning. It checks progress. It improves teaching.
20. **B:** Education improves skills. It supports patient care. Second is wrong.

REASONING

1. SEMANTIC ANALOGY

In Analogy Tests, the relationship between two given words is established and then applied to the other words. The type of relationship may vary, so while attempting such questions the first step is to identify the type of relationship, which can be any one of the following.

EXERCISE

Directions : *In the questions given below one term is missing. Based on the relationship of the two given words find the missing term from the given options.*

1. HUNGER : FOOD : : THIRST : ?
A. Water B. Drink
C. Tea D. Coffee

2. HUNTER : GUN : : WRITER : ?
A. Book B. Pen
C. Poem D. Page

3. WOOL : SHEEP : : SILK : ?
A. Saree B. String
C. Silkworm D. Moth

4. FOOD : STOMACH : : FUEL : ?
A. Engine B. Automobile
C. Rail D. Aeroplane

5. WATER : SAND : : OCEAN : ?
A. Island B. River
C. Desert D. Waves

6. ADULT : BABY : : FLOWER : ?
A. Seed B. Bud
C. Fruit D. Butterfly

7. WRITER : READER : : PRODUCER : ?
A. Creator B. Contractor
C. Creature D. Consumer

8. ENTRANCE : EXIT : : LOYALTY : ?
A. Treachery B. Patriotism
C. Fidelity D. Reward

9. MOTHER : MATERNAL : : FATHER : ?
A. Eternal B. Detrimental
C. Paternal D. Formidable

10. PEARL : NECKLACE : : FLOWER : ?
A. Plant B. Garden
C. Petal D. Bouquet

11. ALPHABET : WORD : : WORD : ?
A. Sound B. Music
C. Sentence D. Dictionary

12. LIFE : DEATH : : HOPE : ?
A. Cry B. Pain
C. Despair D. Sad

13. GOOD : BAD : : VIRTUE : ?
A. Blame B. Sin
C. Despair D. Vice

14. BIRD : FLY : : SNAKE : ?
A. Timid B. Clatter
C. Crawl D. Hole

15. CAT : MOUSE : : BIRD : ?
A. Cage B. Trap
C. Eagle D. Worm

16. STATE : EXILE
A. Police : Arrest
B. Judge : Convict
C. Constitution : Amendment
D. Church : Excommunicate

17. CAPRICIOUSNESS : RELIABILITY
A. Extemporaneous : Predictability
B. Unreliable : Inhuman
C. Tenacious : Practicality
D. Arbitrary : Whimsical

18. LOATH : COERCION
A. Detest : Caressing
B. Irritate : Caressing
C. Irate : Antagonism
D. Reluctant : Persuasion

19. SCALES : FISH
A. Lady : Dress B. Tree : Leaves
C. Bird : Feather D. Skin : Man

20. TREE : SAPLING
A. Hut : Mansion
B. Giant : Dwarf
C. Horse : Foal
D. Ant : Elephant

21. CHALK : BLACKBOARD
A. Door : Handle B. Table : Chair
C. Ink : Paper D. Type : Paint

22. PRIMEVAL : MEDIEVAL
A. Dinosaur : Dragon
B. Gorilla : Soldier
C. Evolution : Revelation
D. Thorn : Rose

23. TRILOGY : NOVEL
A. Rice : Husk B. Milk : Cream
C. Fabric : Weaving D. Serial : Episode

24. PEDANT : ERUDITION
A. Prude : Modesty
B. Blunt : Politician
C. Diplomats : Tactless
D. Enemy : Friendly

25. FURY : IRE
A. Convulsion : Spasm
B. Amusement : Happiness
C. Joke : Laugh
D. Dispassion : Emotion

EXPLANATORY ANSWERS

1. (A) : Hunger is satiated by food, thirst by water.

2. (B) : Weapon of a hunter is a gun, weapon of a writer is a pen.

3. (C) : Wool is obtained from sheep, silk is obtained from silkworm.

4. (A) : Food is consumed in stomach, fuel is consumed in engine.

5. (C) : The related words are near opposites.

6. (B) : The youngone of an adult is a baby and that of a flower is a bud.

7. (D) : A writer aims to please the readers by his writings, a producer aims to please the consumers by his products.

8. (A) : The related words are opposites.

9. (C) : Relations on the mother's side are maternal and on the father's side paternal.

10. (D) : Many pearls make a necklace, many flowers make a bouquet.

11. (C) : More than one alphabet make a word, more than one word make a sentence.

12. (C) : The related words are opposites.

13. (D) : The related words are opposites.

14. (C) : Birds fly, snakes crawl.

15. (D) : Cat chases the mouse, bird chases the worm.

16. (D) : Punishment of leaving the State is exile, punishment of leaving the Church is excommunication.

17. (C) : The related words are antonyms.

18. (D) : Loathing is the result of constant coersion, reluctance is the result of constant persuasion.

19. (D) : Covering of the fish is scales, covering of man is skin.

20. (C) : Young tree is a sapling, young horse is a foal.

21. (C) : Chalk is used to write on blackboard, ink is used to write on paper.

22. (A) : The related words represent almost the same time period and answer option represents almost the same sized creatures.

23. (D) : Trilogy is section of a novel, episode is a section of a serial.

24. (A) : The related words are synonyms.

25. (B) : Fury causes ire, amusement causes happiness.

✤✤✤✤✤

2. SYMBOLIC OPERATION

Questions in these category are easy to attempt. Candidates must be quick in substituting symbols and calculations. The common pattern of questions asked are given below.

EXERCISE

1. If "+" means "–"; "–" means "×"; "×"means "÷" and "÷" means "+", then
$15 \times 5 \div 10 + 5 - 3 = ?$
A. 9.5 B. 0
C. –2 D. 24

2. If "+" means "×"; "–" means "÷"; "÷"means "+" and "×" means "–", then what will be the value of
$20 \div 40 - 4 \times 5 + 6 = ?$
A. 60 B. 1.67
C. 150 D. 0

3. If × stands for addition, < for subtraction, + stands for division, > for multiplication, – stands for equal to, ÷ for greater than, and = stands for less than, state which of the following is true?
A. $5 \times 3 < 7 \div 8 + 4 \times 1$
B. $3 \times 4 > 2 - 9 + 3 < 3$
C. $5 > 2 + 2 = 10 < 4 \times 8$
D. $3 \times 2 < 4 \div 16 > 2 + 4$

4. If → stands for subract, ← stands for add, ↑↑ stands for multiply, ↓↓ stands for divide, ↔ stands for greater than, ⟷ stands for equal to, then which of the following alternatives is true?
A. 4 ← 6 ↑↑ 2 ⟷ 3 → 12 ← 12
B. 10 ↓↓ 5 ↑↑ 5 ⟷ 9 → 3 ← 4
C. 15 ↑↑ 2 → 5 ⟷ 12 ↓↓ 4 ← 3
D. 13 ↓↓ 13 ← 1 ↔ 20 → 5 ↑↑ 2

5. If Δ denotes =; + denotes >, – denotes <, □ denotes ≠, × denotes > and ÷ denotes < then a + b – c denotes
A. b Δ c □ a B. b □ a ÷ c
C. a ÷ b × c D. b – a + c

6. If '✱' denotes '×', 'Δ' denotes '÷', '□' denotes '–', '●' denotes '+', 'α' denotes '=' and 'β' denotes ≠, then which of the following euations is correct?
A. 2 □ 10 ✱ 4 Δ 5 α 5 ● 12 Δ 6
B. 27 Δ 9 ● 6 β 3 ✱ 6 □ 9
C. 4 Δ 2 ✱ 0 α 7 Δ 1 ✱ 0
D. 5 ● 6 Δ 3 □ 2 α 8 Δ 4 ✱ 3

7. If ↓ stands for '÷', ↑ stands for '×', → stands for '+' and ← stands for '–', then
25 ↓ 5 → 3 ↑ 6 ← 8 = ?
A. 9 B. 12
C. 16 D. 15

8. If the + and × signs of the following equations are interchanged, which will be the correct equation?
A. $7 \times 5 + 3 = 20$ B. $4 + 9 \times 1 = 42$
C. $6 \times 5 + 8 = 46$ D. $2 + 11 \times 4 = 28$

9. If '+' stands for multiplication, '×' stands for addition, '÷' stands for subtraction and '–' stands for division, then what will be the result of the following equation?
$7 \times 4 \div 10 \times 2 + 5 = ?$
A. 7 B. 0
C. 11 D. 15

10. If 'A' means '÷', 'B' means '+', 'C' means '×' and 'D' means '–', then
12 C 4 A 24 D 10 B 1 = ?
A. $11\frac{1}{3}$ B. 23
C. –7 D. $16\frac{4}{5}$

EXPLANATORY ANSWERS

1. (C) : $15 \div 5 + 10 - 5 \times 3$
$3 + 10 - 15 = -2$

2. (D) : $20 + 40 \div 4 - 5 \times 6$
$20 + 10 - 30 = 0$

3. (C) : A. $5 + 3 - 7 > 8 \div 4 + 1$
$1 > 3$
B. $3 + 4 \times 2 = 9 \div 3 - 3$
$11 = 0$

C. $5 \times 2 \div 2 < 10 - 4 + 8$

$5 < 14$

D. $3 + 2 - 4 > 16 \times 2 \div 4$

$1 > 8$

4. (B) : A. $4 + 6 \times 2 = 3 - 12 + 12$

$16 = 3$

B. $10 \div 5 \times 5 = 9 - 3 + 4$

$10 = 10$

C. $15 \times 2 - 5 = 12 \div 4 + 3$

$25 = 6$

D. $13 \div 13 + 1 > 20 - 5 \times 2$

$2 > 10$

5. (D) : What is given is a > b < c

The equations are :

A. $b = c \neq a$ which is wrong

B. $b \neq a < c$ which is wrong

C. $a < b > c$ which is wrong

D. $b < a > c$ which is correct

Therefore, (*d*) is the answer.

6. (C) : The solved equations will be :

A. $2 - 10 \times 4 \div 5 = 5 + 12 \div 6$

$2 - 8 = 5 + 2$

$-6 = 7$ which is wrong

B. $27 \div 9 + 6 \neq 3 \times 6 - 9$

$3 + 6 \neq 18 - 9$

$9 \neq 9$ which is wrong

C. $4 \div 2 \times 0 = 7 \div 1 \times 0$

$2 \times 0 = 7 \times 0$

$0 = 0$ which is correct

D. $5 + 6 \div 3 - 2 = 8 \div 4 \times 3$

$5 = 6$ which is wrong

7. (D) : $25 \div 5 + 3 \times 6 - 8$

$5 + 18 - 8 = 15$

8. (C) : After interchanging the signs the equations are :

A. $7 + 5 \times 3 = 22$ which is wrong

B. $4 \times 9 + 1 = 37$ which is wrong

C. $6 + 5 \times 8 = 46$ which is correct

D. $2 \times 11 + 4 = 26$ which is wrong

9. (C) : $7 + 4 - 10 + 2 \times 5$

$7 + 4 - 10 + 10 = 11$

10. (C) : $12 \times 4 \div 24 - 10 + 1$

$2 - 10 + 1 = -7$

✤✤✤✤✤

3. NUMBER ANALOGY

In number analogy also, the relationship between the given numbers is detected and then applied to the second part to find the missing numbers. This relationship between the numbers can be based on any of the following patterns : *(i)* numbers can be odd/even/prime numbers; *(ii)* numbers can be multiples of one number; *(iii)* numbers can be squares/cubes of different numbers; *(iv)* some numbers can be added to/subtracted from/multiplied to/divided into the first number to get the second number; *(v)* the second number can be the sum/product/difference of the digits of first number; and *(vi)* combinations of any mathematical calculations given above can apply to the relationship between the two given numbers.

EXERCISE

Directions : *In the following questions, select the number from the given options which follows the same relationship as shared between the first two numbers.*

1. 1 : 11 : : 2 : ?
A. 20 B. 22
C. 24 D. 44

2. $\frac{1}{7} : \frac{1}{14} :: \frac{1}{9} : ?$
A. $\frac{1}{88}$ B. $\frac{1}{80}$
C. $\frac{1}{81}$ D. $\frac{1}{18}$

3. 0.16 : 0.0016 : : 1.02 : ?
A. 10.20 B. 0.102
C. 0.0102 D. 1.020

4. 663 : 884 : : 221 : ?
A. 332 B. 554
C. 773 D. 442

5. 16 : 0.16 : : ?
A. 2 : 0.02
B. 7 : 0.007
C. 1.3 : 0.13
D. 0.01 : 0.001

6. $3 : \frac{1}{3} :: ?$
A. 6 : 12
B. 5 : 2/15
C. 8 : 1/8
D. 9 : 27

7. 65 : 13 : : 180 : ?
A. 93 B. 36
C. 133 D. 102

8. 125 : 27 : : 343 : ?
A. 729 B. 64
C. 216 D. 512

9. 357 : 73 : : ?
A. 429 : 94
B. 201 : 21
C. 138 : 38
D. 93 : 39

10. 731 : 902 : : 655 : ?
A. 646 B. 800
C. 793 D. 556

11. 162 : 9 : : 310 : ?
A. 33 B. 27
C. 16 D. 4

12. 13 : 17 : : 15 : ?
A. 19 B. 11
C. 21 D. 16

13. 225 : 15 : : 256 : ?
A. 26 B. 16
C. 20 D. 28

14. 46 : 48 : : 54 : ?
A. 59 B. 40
C. 67 D. 62

15. 33 : 36 : : 21 : ?
A. 9 B. 18
C. 25 D. 32

EXPLANATORY ANSWERS

1. (B) : The first number is repeated to obtain the second number.

2. (D) : The first fraction is multiplied by half to obtain the second fraction.

$\frac{1}{7} : \frac{1}{14} :: \frac{1}{9} : \frac{1}{18}$

$\times \frac{1}{2}$ $\quad$ $\times \frac{1}{2}$

3. (C) : The decimals are divided by 100.

0.16 : 0.0016 :: 1.02 : 0.0102

÷ 100 $\quad$ ÷ 100

4. (D) : The digits at tens and hundreds place is same but the digit at the units place is half the other identical digits.

663 : 884 :: 221 : 442

5. (A) : Of the two related numbers, the second number is the result of first number divided by 100.

16 : 0.16 :: 2 : 0.02

÷ 100 $\quad$ ÷ 100

6. (C) : Of the two related numbers, the second number is the part fraction of the first number, *i.e.* 3 is related to one-third $\left(\frac{1}{3}\right)$. Similarly, 8 will be related to one-eighth $\left(\frac{1}{8}\right)$.

7. (B) : The first number is divided by 5 to get the second number.

65 : 13 :: 180 : 36

÷ 5 $\quad$ ÷ 5

8. (A) : The numbers are cubes of different odd numbers.

125 : 27 :: 343 : 729

↓ ↓ ↓ ↓

5^3 $\quad$ 3^3 $\quad$ 7^3 $\quad$ 9^3

9. (A) : The central digit of the first number is left out and the corner digits written in reverse order to get the second number.

357 : 73 :: 429 : 94

10. (A) : The sum of the digits of both the numbers is same.

$731 : 902 \rightarrow 7+3+1$

$= 9+0+2$ *i.e.* $11 = 11$

$655 : 646 \rightarrow 6+5+5$

$= 6+4+6$ *i.e.* $16 = 16$

11. (D) : The sum of the digits of the first number is the second number.

162 : 9 :: 310 : 4

$1+6+2$ $\quad$ $3+1+0$

12. (A) : First number plus 4 gives the second number.

13 : 17 :: 15 : 19

+4 $\quad$ +4

13. (B) : The root of first number is the second number.

225 : 15 :: 256 : 16

$\sqrt{225}$ $\quad$ $\sqrt{256}$

14. (B) : The product of the digits of first number is multiplied by 2 to get the second number.

46 : 48 :: 54 : 40

$(4 \times 6)\, 2$ $\quad$ $(5 \times 4)\, 2$

15. (A) : The square of the sum of the digits of the first number is the second number.

33 : 36 :: 21 : 9

$(3+3)^2$ $\quad$ $(2+1)^2$

✤ ✤ ✤ ✤ ✤

4. TRENDS

This type of questions are asked to assess the thinking pattern or mental trends of the candidate. These are simple questions but should be answered honestly and carefully.

EXERCISE

Directions : *In the questions given below four alternatives have been given below each one of them. You have to select the right alternative according to your mind and mark it in your answer sheet.*

1. I like pre-defined rules and regulations.

A. Sometimes B. No
C. Yes D. No idea

2. I found a purse full of money in college premise. I:

A. donated the amount among poor
B. gave it to the principal
C. offered it at temple
D. None of these

3. I am punctual regarding.

A. going to bed B. time
C. meals D. dating

4. I was travelling on a boat which capsized. Firstly, I:

A. rescued others B. saved myself
C. closed my eyes D. cursed my luck

5. When someone asks you for help in odd situations then:

A. you give him/her all possible help
B. you promise him/her help
C. you do not help him/her
D. you turn a deaf ear

6. In case my wristwatch is out of order, I:

A. would try to repair it myself
B. would give it to watchmaker
C. would buy a new watch
D. would throw it away

7. Often I change my opinion in the last moment.

A. Yes B. No
C. Sometimes D. No idea

8. Generally I am extrovert and well behaved.

A. Yes B. No
C. Sometimes D. No idea

9. I like to use new technique of work.

A. Yes B. No
C. Sometimes D. No idea

10. When someone considers you wrong then:

A. you do not react
B. you consider him/her wrong
C. you try to ward off the misunderstanding on proper occasion.
D. you pick a fight

11. The secret of my success is:

A. hard labour
B. awakening in night
C. gossiping
D. luck

12. If you are a female and you are talking with a male:

A. You hide your age
B. You are afraid
C. You talk without hesitation
D. You avoid talks

13. I do like rules and regulations.

A. Yes B. No
C. Sometimes D. No idea

14. Excellent ideas come to my mind:

A. while working alone
B. while working in a group
C. while in sleep
D. while in bathroom

15. Whenever my little baby cries loudly, then I

A. beat him/her
B. feed milk to him/her
C. make him/her sleep
D. ask my husband to handle him/her

16. When I see a mad person, I :
A. approach towards him/her
B. maintain distance from him/her
C. throw stone at him/her
D. start laughing at him/her

17. While driving my car I offer lift to people who ask for lift.
A. Always
B. Sometimes
C. Never
D. If she is a girl

18. When someone tries to convince you then:
A. You get convinced
B. You do not get convinced
C. You hear him/her passionately
D. You turn a deaf ear

19. Whenever someone knocks on my closed door then firstly I
A. open the door
B. peep through the lens fitted in the door
C. do not open the door
D. yell at him/her

20. I speak to others about my expectation and dreams.
A. Rarely B. Often
C. Sometimes D. Never

21. Any dispute can be solved by :
A. quarrelling B. court
C. dialogue D. money

22. When I do any foolish work then :
A. I feel ashamed
B. I feel proud of myself
C. Nothing happens
D. I weep

23. If I were correspondent of any newspaper then I would write on the following subject :
A. Cinema and theatre
B. Political events
C. Sports
D. Stock market

24. If I were not human being then :
A. I wish to be a bird B. I wish to be a horse
C. I wish to be God D. Can't say

25. Suppose, you have worn a new shirt and your friend passed a comment that it is not looking good on you. You :
A. will change the shirt immediately
B. will take it lightly as it is your style
C. will not change the shirt but feel offended
D. will start quarrelling

ANSWERS

1	2	3	4	5	6	7	8	9	10
C	B	B	B	A	B	B	A	A	C
11	**12**	**13**	**14**	**15**	**16**	**17**	**18**	**19**	**20**
A	C	A	A	B	B	B	A	B	A
21	**22**	**23**	**24**	**25**					
C	A	C	A	B					

✤✤✤✤✤

5. FIGURAL ANALOGY

EXERCISE

TYPE-I

Directions (Qs. 1-15): *The second figure in the first unit of the Problem Figures bears a certain relationship to the first figure. Similarly, one of the figures in the Answer Figures bears the same relationship to the first figures in the second unit of the Problem Figures. Locate the figure which would fit the questions marks.*

Problem Figures | **Answer Figures**

1. 
1 2 3 4

(A) (B) (C) (D) (E)

2. 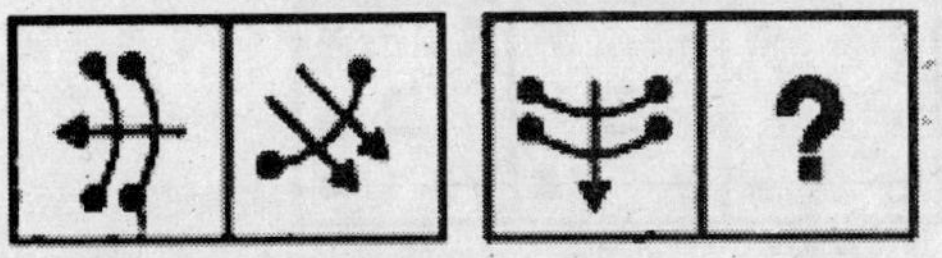
1 2 3 4

(A) (B) (C) (D) (E)

3. 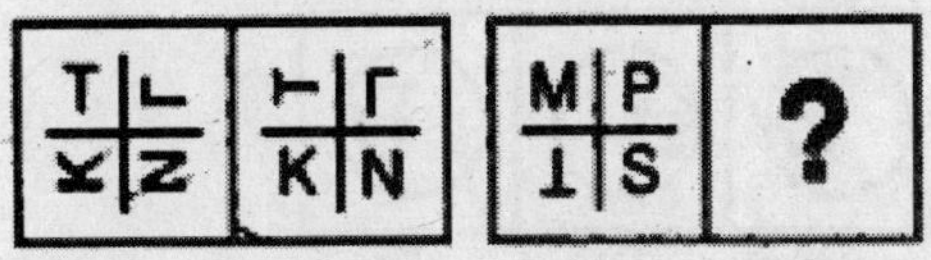
1 2 3 4
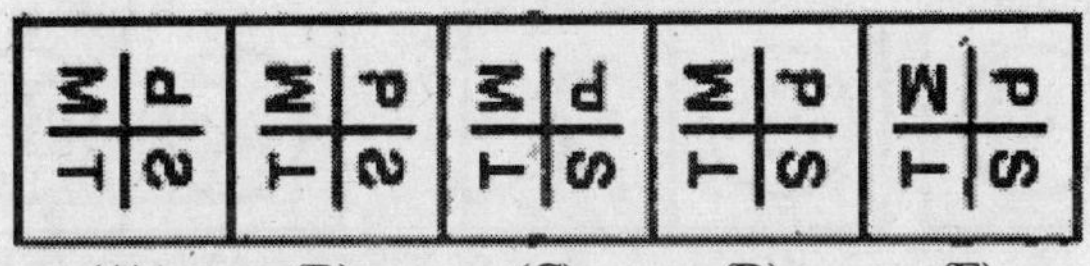
(A) (B) (C) (D) (E)

4. 
1 2 3 4

(A) (B) (C) (D) (E)

5. 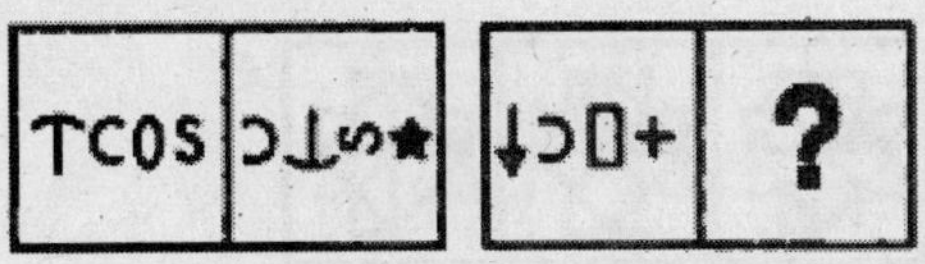
1 2 3 4
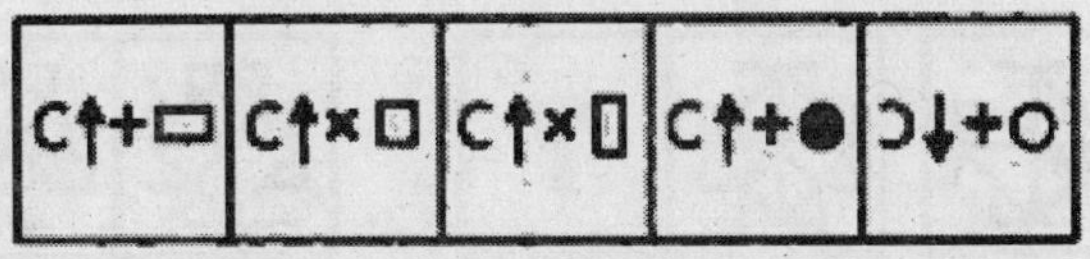
(A) (B) (C) (D) (E)

6. 
1 2 3 4

(A) (B) (C) (D) (E)

7. 
1 2 3 4
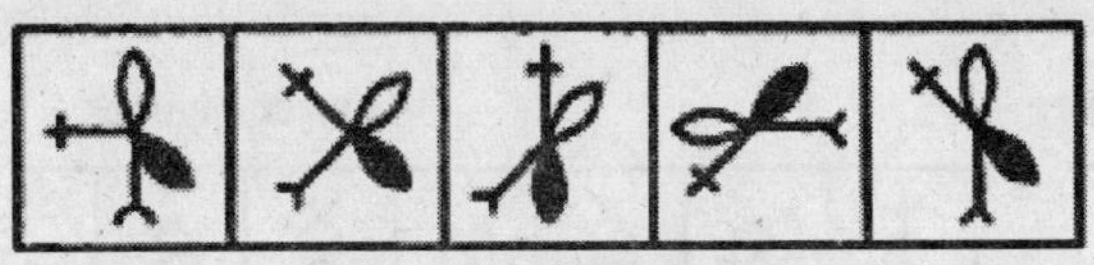
(A) (B) (C) (D) (E)

Problem Figures **Answer Figures**

8. 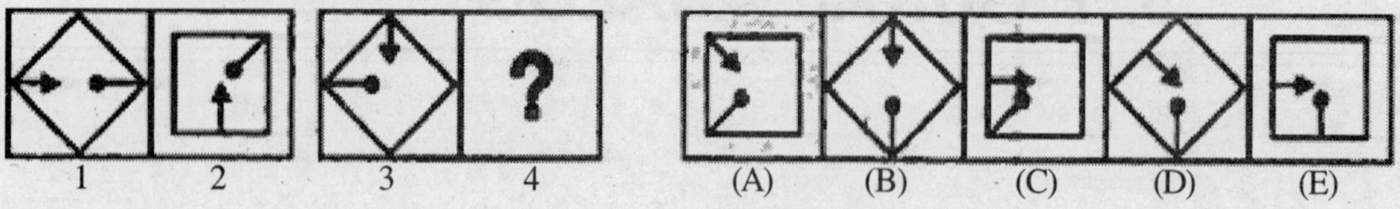

9. 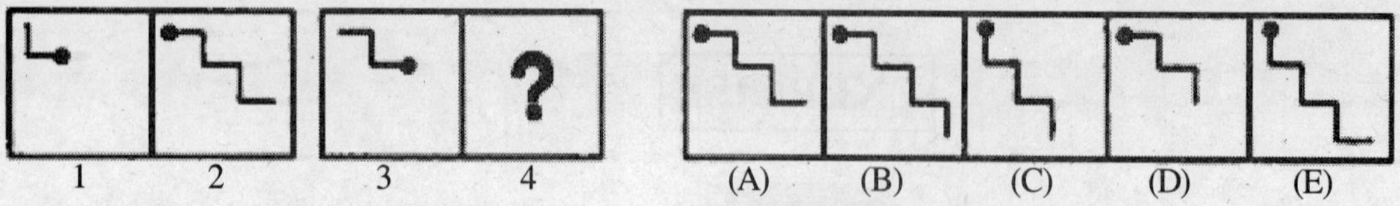

10. 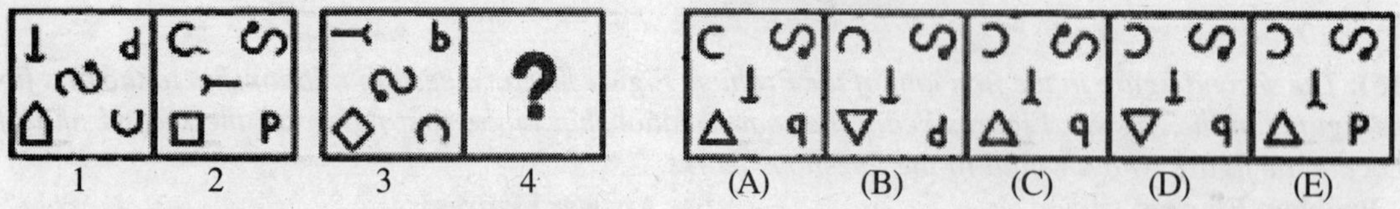

11. 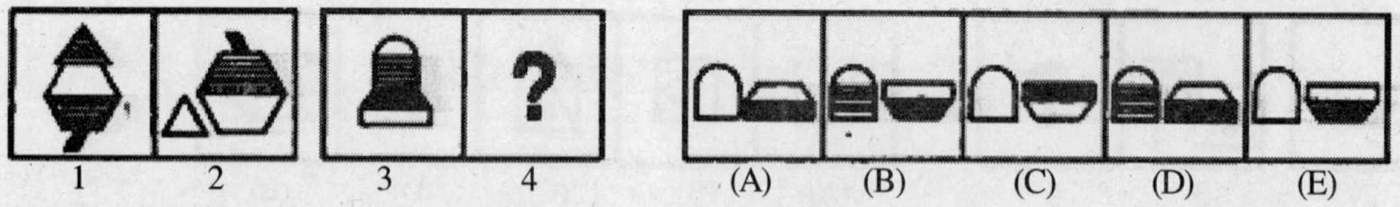

12. 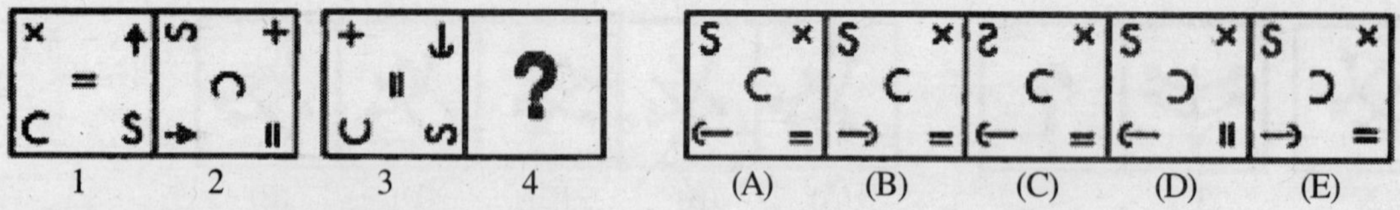

13. 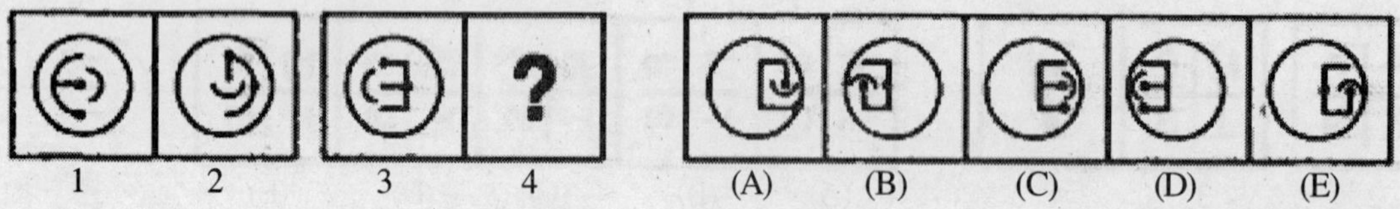

14. 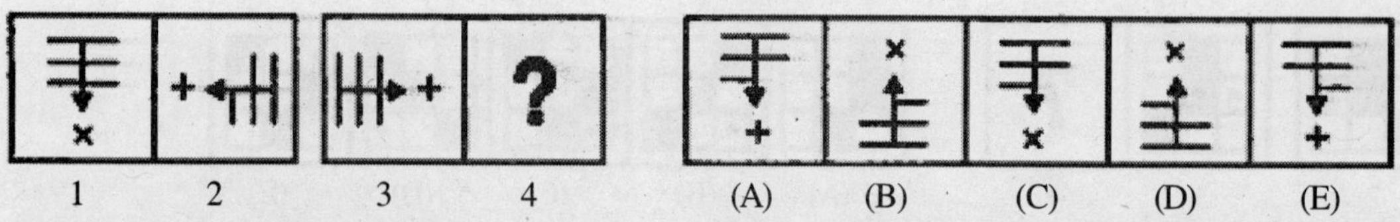

15. 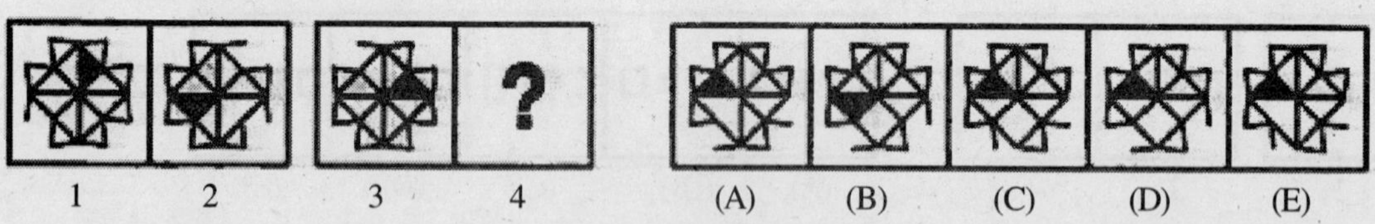

TYPE-II

Directions (Qs. 16–30): *In each of the following questions, a related pair of figures is followed by five numbered pairs of figures. Select the pair that has a relationship* ***similar*** *to that in the unnumbered pair.*

Problem Figure **Answer Figures**

16. 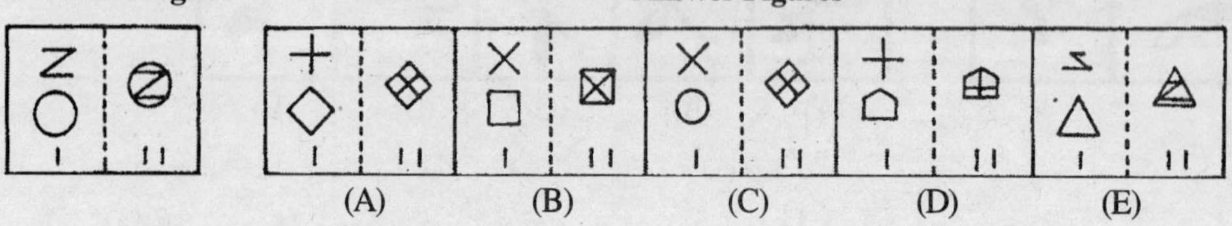

Problem Figure **Answer Figures**

17.

(A) (B) (C) (D) (E)

18.

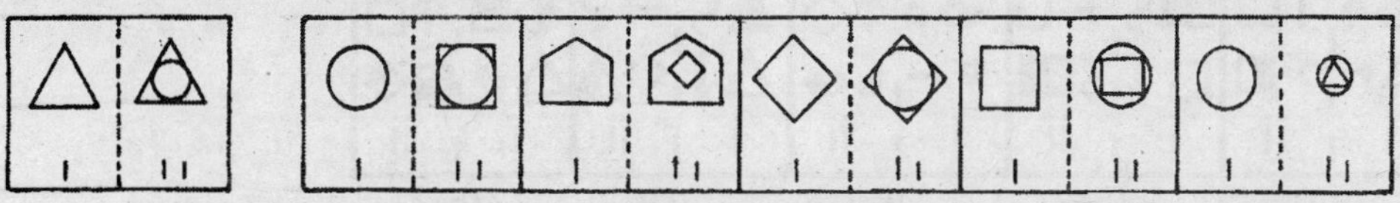

(A) (B) (C) (D) (E)

19.

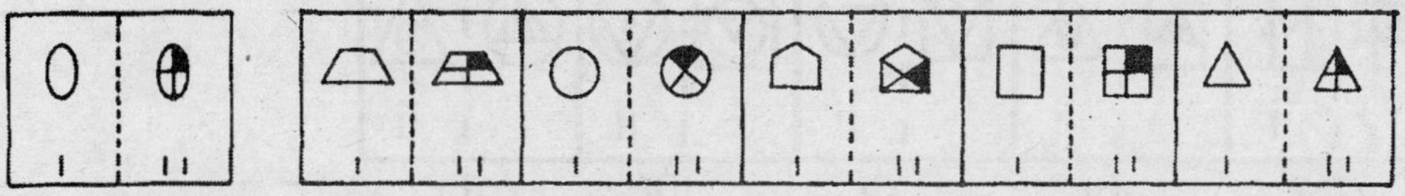

(A) (B) (C) (D) (E)

20.

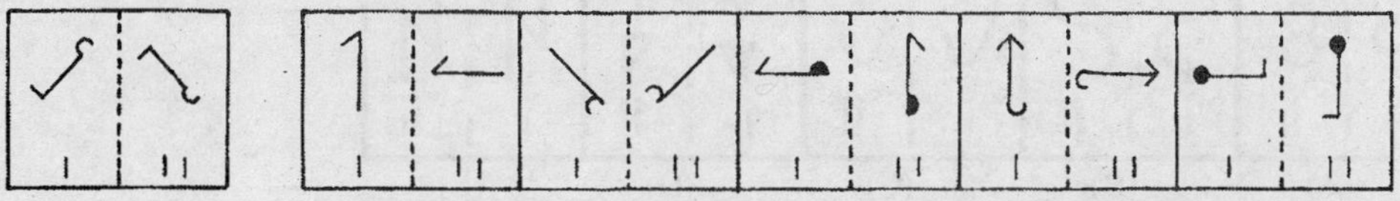

(A) (B) (C) (D) (E)

21.

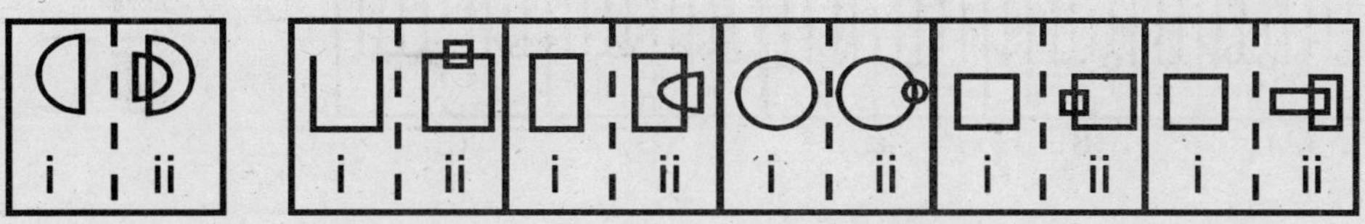

(A) (B) (C) (D) (E)

22.

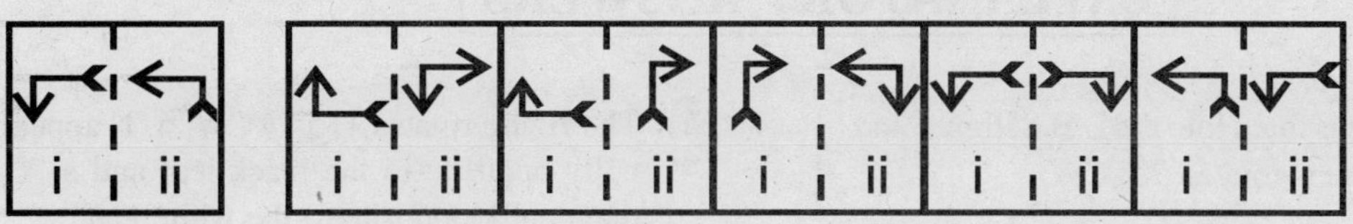

(A) (B) (C) (D) (E)

23.

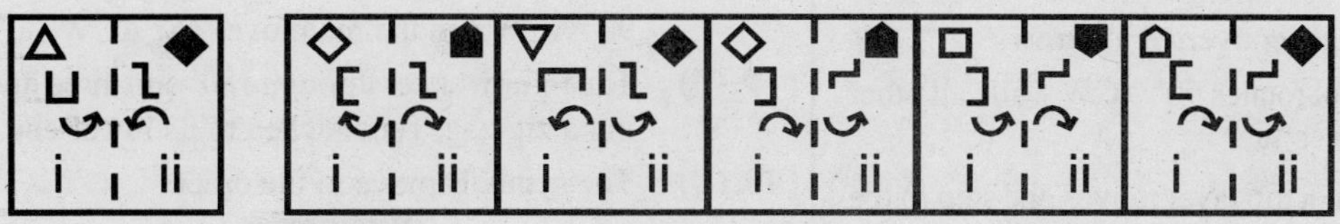

(A) (B) (C) (D) (E)

24.

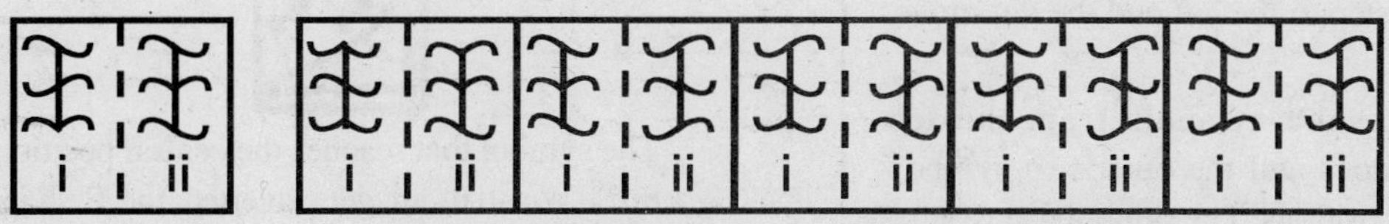

(A) (B) (C) (D) (E)

25.

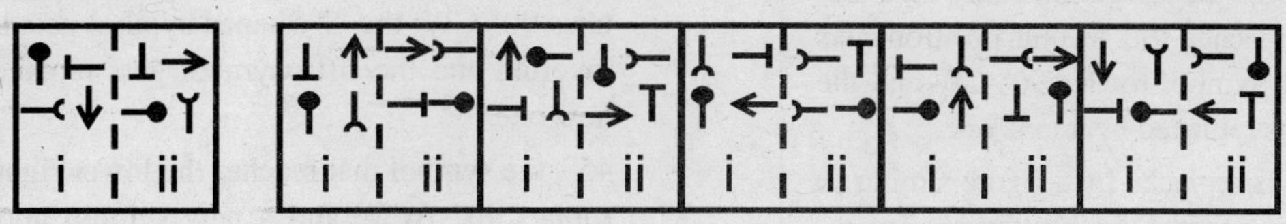

(A) (B) (C) (D) (E)

26. 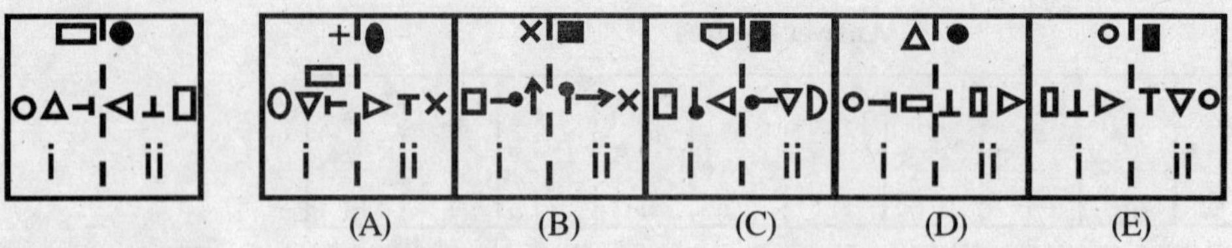

27. 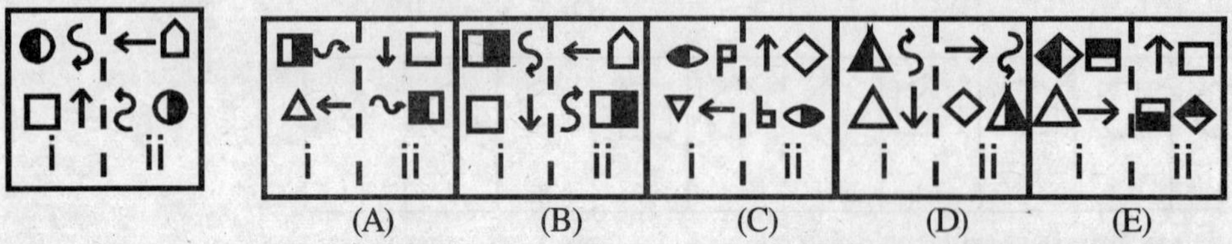

28. 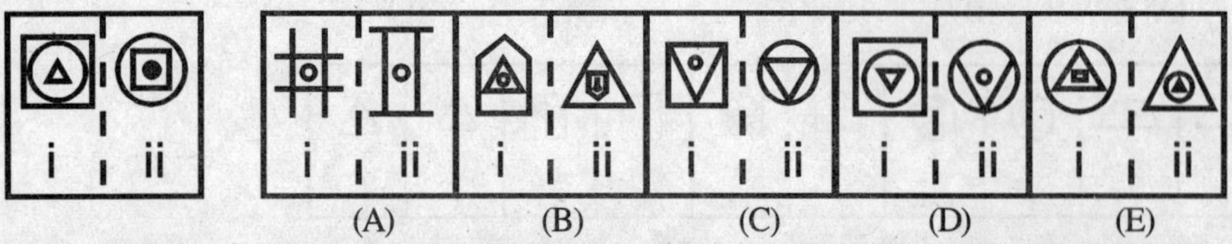

29. 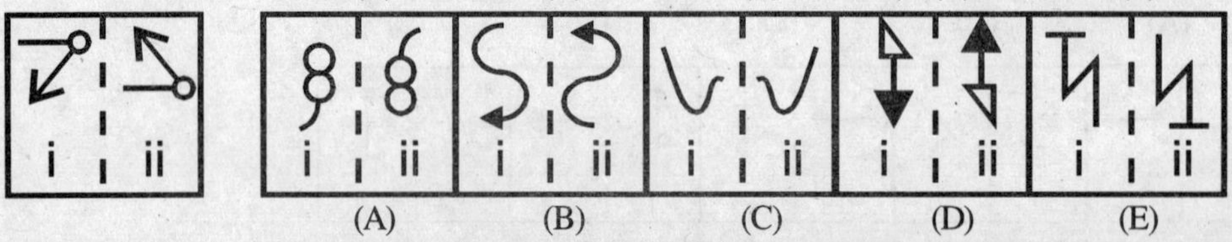

30. 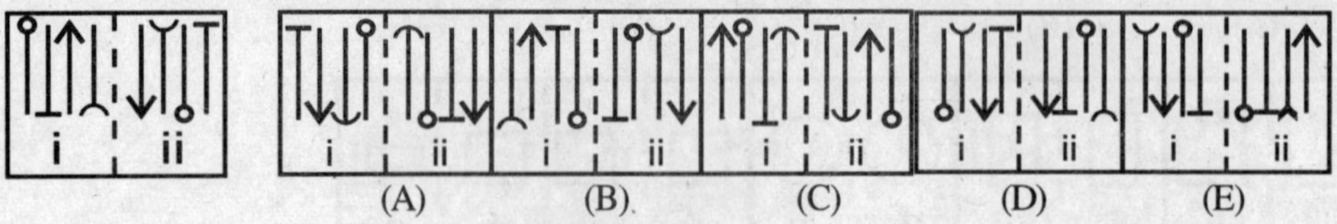

EXPLANATORY ANSWERS

1. (B) : The R.H.S. figure is fitted into the L.H.S. figure and the resulting figure is rotated 90° CW.

2. (B) : The figure rotates 45° ACW, the arrow changes to a curved line with dotted ends and the curved lines with dotted ends get converted to arrows.

3. (D) : The top left symbol rotates 90° ACW while all other symbols rotate 90° CW.

4. (E) : The black portion in top layer moves one step to the right; the black portions in the middle and the lower layers move one step to the left and the dot moves one step upwards.

5. (D) : The first and second symbols from the left interchange positions and the other two symbols also interchange positions. The symbol that reaches the first position from the left gets laterally inverted; the symbol that reaches the second position gets inverted, the third symbol rotates 90° CW and the fourth symbol gets replaced by a new one.

6. (D) : The single figure is replaced by a figure similar to the double figures and the double figures are replaced by figures similar to the single figure.

7. (E) : The figure rotates 135° ACW; a 'T' appears diagonally opposite to the black leaf and a 'Y' appears diagonally opposite to the white leaf.

8. (C) : The square rotates through 45°. The arrow moves 90° ACW and the pin moves 45° ACW.

9. (B) : The figure rotates through 180° and three lines forming a zig-zag, get attached to its lower end.

10. (D) : The symbols move in the order

The symbol that reaches the central position rotates 90° CW and its arc gets inverted; the 'P' shaped symbol rotates through 180°; the 'C' shaped symbol rotates 90° CW; the 'S' Shaped symbol gets laterally inverted and the fifth symbol gets replaced by a new one.

45°, the symbol that reaches the lower right corner rotates 90° ACW and a new symbol appears in middle-left position.

11. (E) : The upper and the lower parts of the figure get separated. Shading is removed from the upper part and the lower part is inverted. The two parts are then placed side by side.

12. (A) : The symbols move in the order

The symbol that reaches the top-left corner rotates 90° ACW; the symbol in the top-right corner rotates through 45°; the symbols in the lower-left corner and in the central positions rotates 90° CW and the symbol that reaches the lower-right corner rotates through 90°.

13. (E) : The figure gets laterally inverted. The dot on the larger arc, the pin and the small arc rotate 90° ACW. Also, the pin gets inverted.

14. (C) : The figure rotates 90° CW. One half of one of the lines on the arrow is lost. The figure in front of the arrowhead rotates through 45°.

15. (D) : The missing line segment in the first figure is replaced in second. Then moving ACW, the third line segment is removed along the two next consecutive sides of the square. Shaded portion in the first figure moves three steps ACW. Similarly, the third figure gives figure (*d*).

16. (B) : The uppermost design enters into innerside side of the lower design from Ist figure to the IInd figure.

17. (A) : In element I to II upper left design comes at lower right rotating 135° C.W. Middle design goes to upper left and rotates 90° CW. While lower right design goes to middle and it also rotates 90° C.W. The same changes occur in option (*a*).

18. (E) : In element I to II and ellipse is put in the triangle. Similarly in option E a triangle is put in the ellipse.

19. (D) : From first figure to IInd figure, design is divided into four equal parts and right side of the upper portion becomes shaded.

20. (E) : From Ist figure to IInd figure, design is reversed after moving 90° anticlockwise direction.

21. (D) : The figure in the first part is laterally inverted and a similar but smaller design is placed on its left side in the second part.

22. (E) : The element in first part is moved by 90° and the places of short and long line segments are interchanged.

23. (C) : The number of sides making the top left figure is increased by one and a new figure is made, shaded and moved to the top right position. The element in the centre is turned 90° anticlockwise and the small line on the other side is turned by 180°. The element in the bottom right is turned upside down and moved to the bottom left position.

24. (A) : The direction of both arcs on the top, are on the middle right and arc on the bottom left in first part are turned to the other side in the second part.

25. (B) : From part one to part two, the element in the top left is turned 90° clockwise and the other three 90° anticlockwise, also the elements are moved one step anticlockwise.

26. (B) : From part one to part two, the top right element is turned by 90° and moved down, the lower right and middle elements are turned 90° clockwise and 90° anticlockwise respectively and moved to the left and the lower left element is shaded and moved up.

27. (A) : All the four elements exchange place diagonally and in doing so the top left element is laterally inverted, the top right element is horizontally inverted, the bottom right element is turned 90° anticlockwise and the number of lines making the element in bottom left is increased by one.

28. (E) : The innermost figure is removed and the new innermost figure also encloses the other two figures. The innermost and smallest figure is then shaded.

29. (B) : The design in the first part is horizontally inverted in the second.

30. (B) : All the elements in the first part are turned upside down and then 1st, 2nd, 3rd and 4th positioned elements become 3rd, 4th, 1st and 2nd elements in the second part.

✤ ✤ ✤ ✤ ✤

6. SPACE ORIENTATION

In these type of questions, a template or a layout of a cube, dice or a box is given, which can be folded to produce different patterns. To solve these questions what is required is a clear study of the given layout and the selection of one figure, from the alternative patterns which can be made from the given layout. To attempt such problems understand the unfolded patterns given below:

Layout 1.

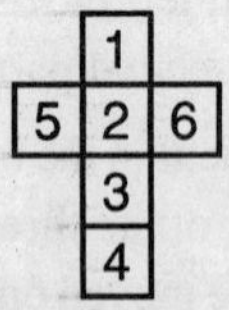

or

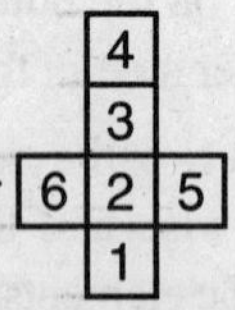

The opposite sides are :

1—3, 2 — 4 and 5 — 6

Layout 2.

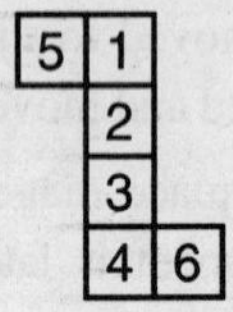

or

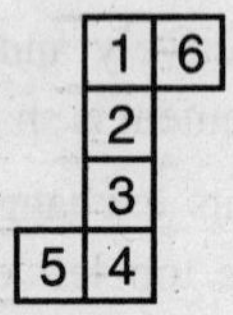

The opposite sides are :

1 — 3, 2 — 4 and 5 — 6

Layout 3.

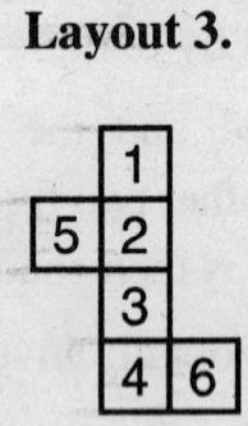

or

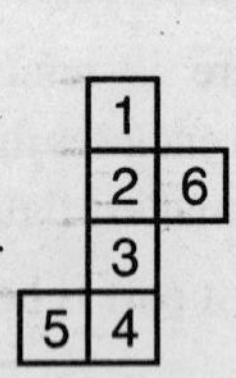

The opposite sides are :

1 — 3, 2 — 4 and 5 — 6.

Layout 4.

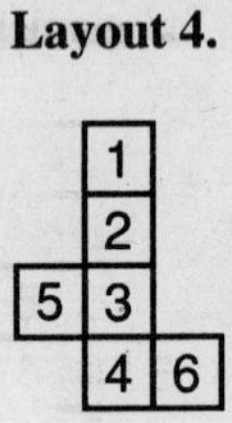

or

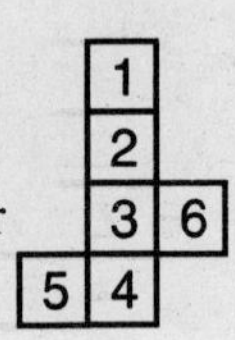

The opposite sides are :

1 — 3, 2 — 4 and 5 — 6

Layout 5.

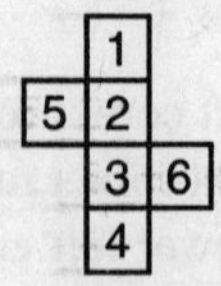

or

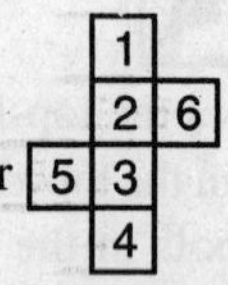

The opposite sides are :

1 — 3, 2 — 4 and 5 — 6

Layout 6.

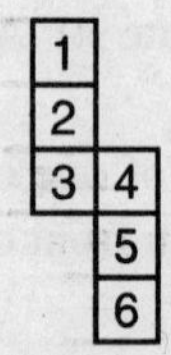

or

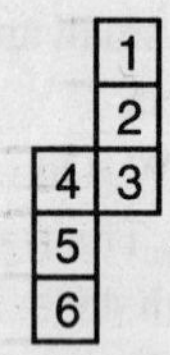

The opposite sides are :

1 — 3, 2 — 5 and 4 — 6

Layout 7.

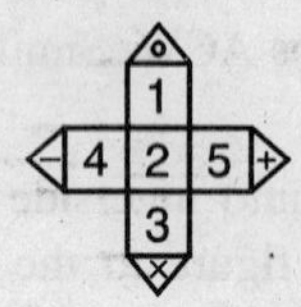

The opposite sides are :

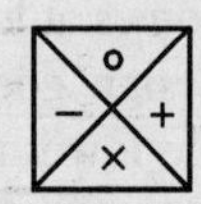 — 2, 1 — 3 and 4 — 5. Here, side 6 is divided into four parts.

Layout 8.

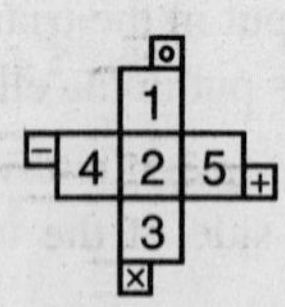

The opposite sides are

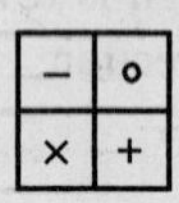 — 2, 1 — 3 and 4 — 5. Here, side 6 is divided into four parts.

Observe from the above layouts that all sides except the opposite side are adjacent sides. Also keep in mind that the three visible sides of the option figures are one of the opposite sides of each opposite pair.

EXERCISE

Directions : *The figure is folded to produce different box patterns. Study the pattern to know if they can be produced from given figure and select the answer from the alternatives.*

1.

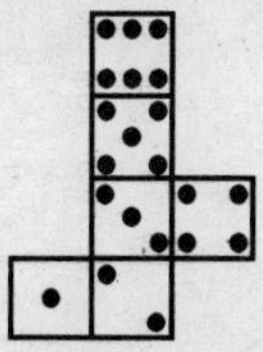

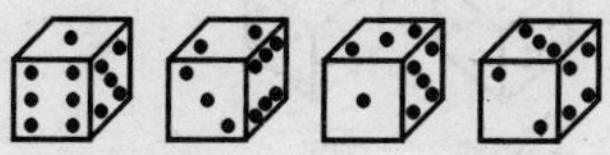

A B C D

2.

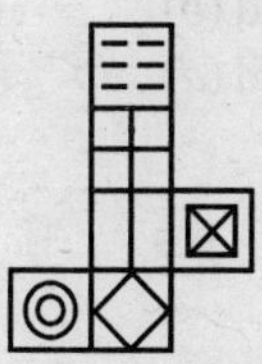

A B C D

3.

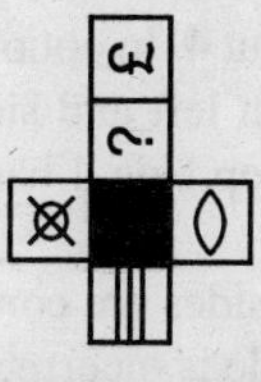

A B C D

4.

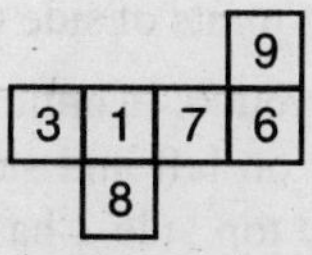

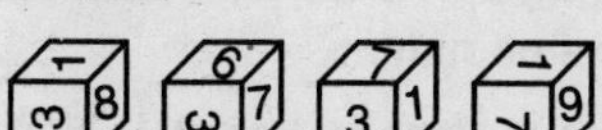

A B C D

5.

A B C D

6.

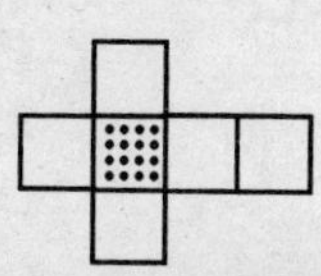

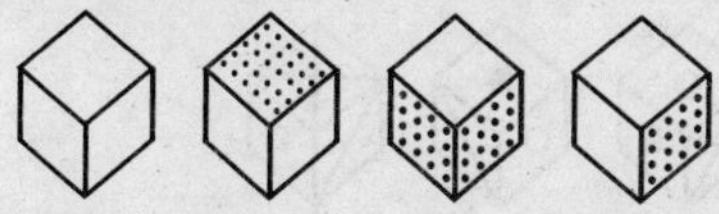

(*a*) (*b*) (*c*) (*d*)

A. (*a*), (*b*) and (*d*) B. (*b*) and (*d*)
C. (*b*), (*c*) and (*d*) D. (*a*) and (*d*)

7.

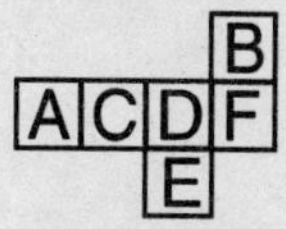

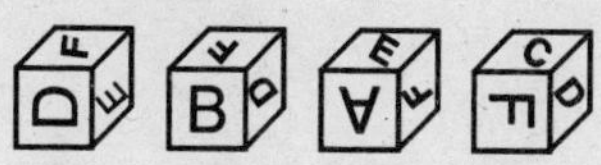

(*a*) (*b*) (*c*) (*d*)

A. (*a*) and (*b*) B. (*a*) and (*d*)
C. (*b*) and (*c*) D. All four

8.

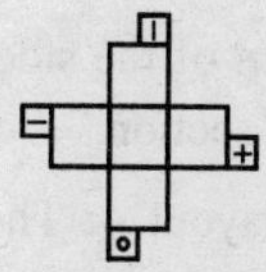

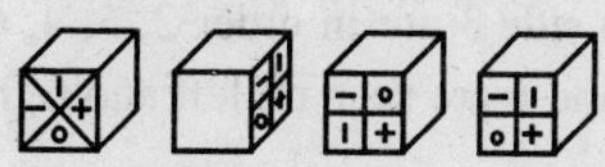

(*a*) (*b*) (*c*) (*d*)

A. (*b*) and (*d*) B. (*a*) and (*d*)
C. (*b*) and (*c*) D. C and (*d*)

9.

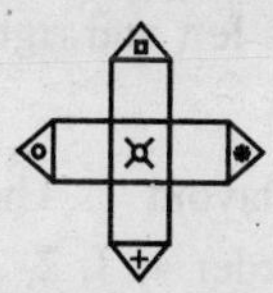

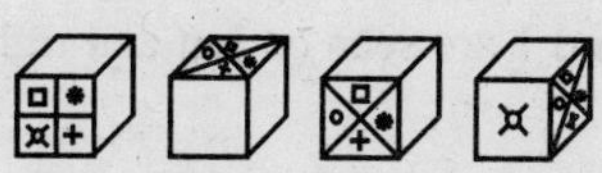

(*a*) (*b*) (*c*) (*d*)

A. (*a*) and (*c*) B. (*b*) and (*c*)
C. (*b*) and (*d*) D. A and (*d*)

10.

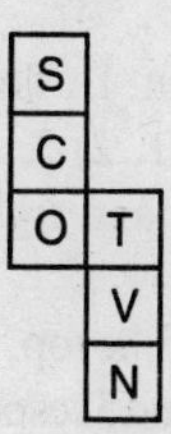

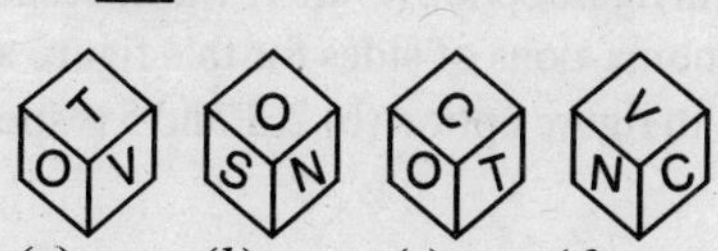

(*a*) (*b*) (*c*) (*d*)

A. (*b*) and (*c*) B. (*a*) and (*d*)
C. (*a*) and (*c*) D. All four

11.

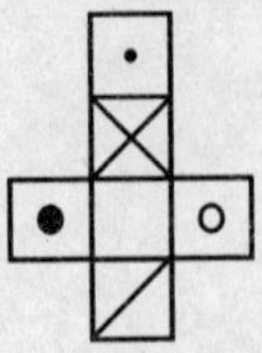

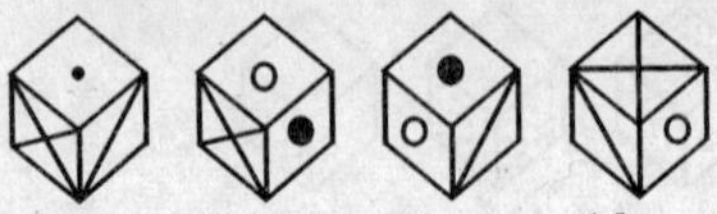

(*a*) (*b*) (*c*) (*d*)

A. (*a*) and (*d*) B. (*b*), C and (*d*)
C. All four D. None of the above

12.

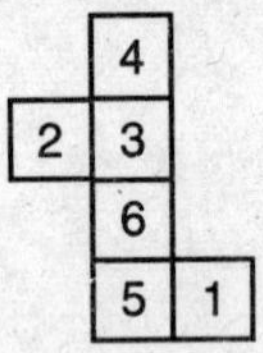

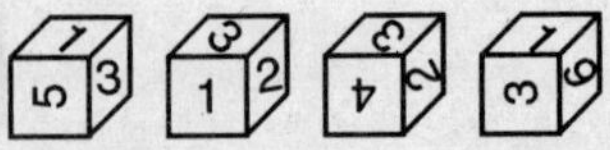

(*a*) (*b*) (*c*) (*d*)

A. (*a*) and (*c*) B. (*c*) and (*d*)
C. (*b*) and (*c*) D. (*b*) and (*d*)

13.

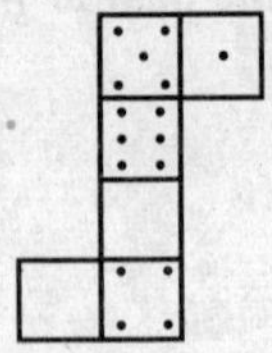

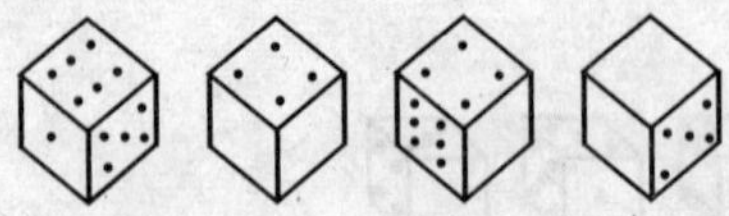

(*a*) (*b*) (*c*) (*d*)

A. (*a*) and (*c*) B. (*a*) and (*b*)
C. (*b*) and (*c*) D. (*b*) and (*d*)

EXPLANATORY ANSWERS

All answers are based on number pattern of the sides as in the layout given in the beginning of this section.

1. (D) : The given figure is same as layout 4. The sides adjacent to top side 3 are in order 2, 5, 4, 6 — of these sides, 4 and 6 are seen on left and right sides respectively.

2. (B) : The given figure is same as layout 4. The sides adjacent to top side 5 are in order 4, 3, 2, 1 —of these sides 1 and 4 are seen on left and right sides respectively.

3. (D) : The given figure is same as layout 1. The sides adjacent to top side 5 are in order 4, 3, 2, 1 — of these sides 2 and 1 are seen on left and right sides respectively.

4. (A) : The given figure is same as layout 3. The sides adjacent to top side 2 are in order 1, 5, 3, 6 — of these sides 1 and 5 are seen on left and right sides respectively.

5. (C) : The given figure is same as layout 1. The sides adjacent to top side 6 are in order 1, 2, 3, 4 — of these sides 2 and 3 are seen on left and right sides respectively.

6. (A) : The given figure is same as layout 1. The top, left and right sides in figure option (a) are 1, 4 and 5 respectively (other combina-tions of sides for this figure are also possible); in figure option (b) 2, 1 and 5 respectively (other combination of sides for this figure are also possible; and in figure option (d) 1, 5 and 2 respectively (other combinations of sides for this figure are also possible).

7. (A) : The given figure is same as layout 4. In option figure (a) the top side 4 has side 3 on left and side 5 on right. In option figure (b) the top side 4 has side 6 on its left and side 3 on right.
Note : in option figure (c) the sides are correct but the printing of letter on right side is incorrect.

8. (A) : The given figure is same as layout 8. Option figures (b) and (d) contain the correct joints of side 6.

9. (B) : The given figure is same as layout 7. Option figures (a) and (c) contain the correct joints of side 6.

10. (C) : The given figure is same as layout 6. In option figure (a) the top side 4 has side 3 on left and side 5 on right. In option figure (c) the top side 2 has side 3 on left and side 4 on right.

11. (D) : The given figure is same as layout 1. None of the figure options can be made from the given figure.

12. (B) : The given figure is same as layout 3. In option figure (c) the top side 2 has side 1 on left and side 5 on right. In option figure (d) the top side 6 has side 2 on left and side 3 on right.

13. (B) : The given figure is same as layout 2. In option figure (a) the top side 2 has side 6 on left and side 1 on right. In option figure (b) the top side 4 has side 3 on left and side 5 on right.

✤✤✤✤✤

7. SEMANTIC CLASSIFICATION

In this type of classification, four words are given out of which three are almost same in matter or meaning and only one word is different from the common three. One has to find out the word which is different from the rest.

EXERCISE

Directions : *In each of the following questions, three words are alike in some manner. Spot the odd one out.*

1. A. Green B. Red C. Colour D. Orange

2. A. Stable B. Hole C. Canoe D. Sty

3. A. Nose B. Eyes C. Skin D. Teeth

4. A. Venus B. Moon C. Pluto D. Mars

5. A. Happy B. Gloomy C. Lively D. Cheerful

Directions : *Three of the following four in each question are alike in a certain way and so form a group. Select the group of letters that does not belong to that group.*

6. A. ACE B. LOR C. GIK D. VXZ

7. A. TSR B. LKJ C. PQO D. HGF

8. A. EF LM B. KJ SR C. XW HG D. ED YX

9. A. JOPK B. BOPC C. QOPR D. TOPS

10. A. DfH B. MoQ C. UwY D. lnO

Directions : *In each of the following questions, there are four options. Three numbers, in these options, are alike in certain manner. Only one number does not fit in. Choose the one which is different from the rest.*

11. A. 1948 B. 2401 C. 966 D. 1449

12. A. 182 B. 169 C. 130 D. 158

13. A. 129 B. 130 C. 131 D. 132

14. A. 3215 B. 9309 C. 4721 D. 2850

15. A. 1776 B. 2364 C. 1976 D. 3776

Directions : *In the following questions select the pair which is different from the other three.*

16. A. Chair - Furniture
B. Shirt - Garment
C. Necklace - Jewellery
D. Bogie - Engine

17. A. Crayon - Paper B. Pencil - Lead C. Pen - Ink D. Brush - Paint

18. A. War - Peace B. Real - Natural C. Premiere - First D. Wrath - Anger

19. A. Finger - Thimble B. Head - Cap C. Waist - Tiara D. Foot - Shoe

20. A. Day - Night B. Clever - Foolish C. Clear - Blurred D. Arrive - Come

Directions : *In the following questions, which of the following pair of letters is different from the other three?*

21. A. FGH - HIJ B. PQR - RST C. MNO - OPQ D. CDE - DEF

22. A. JuM - jUm B. iLo - Ilo C. PSa - psA D. ZeX - zEx

23. A. NQT - JMP B. CFI - RUX C. ADG - FGH D. SVY - ORU

24. A. DXD - XDX B. KUK - UKU C. FHF - EHE D. RSR - SRS

25. A. AYT - BZU B. FNG - EMF C. RWO - QVN D. HJD - GIC

EXPLANATORY ANSWERS

1. (C) : All others are types of colour.

2. (C) : Canoe is a boat. Others are resting places of birds/ animals.

3. (D) : All others are sense organs.

4. (B) : All others are planets.

5. (B) : All others are expressions of joy.

6. (B) : The sequence in each group is +2. Only option (*b*) has sequence in +3, *i.e.,*

ABCDE (+2 +2) LMNOPQR (+3 +3)

GHIJK (+2 +2) VWXYZ (+2 +2)

7. (C) : The sequence of alphabet in each group is in reverse order. Only option (*c*) has sequence in disturbed order.

8. (A) : Two consecutive alphabet in each group are in reverse sequence (–1), *i.e.,*

KJ (–1) SR (–1); XW (–1) HG (–1); ED (–1) YX (–1)

Only in option (*a*) the sequence is in natural order (+1), *i.e.,*

E F (+1) L M (+1)

9. (D) : In each group, letters 'OP' are common. The two corner alphabet are in natural order (+1); *i.e.,*

JOPK (+1); BOPC (+1); QOPR (+1)

Only in option (*d*) they are in reverse order (–1); *i.e.,*

TOPS (–1)

10. (D) : In other groups, only the alphabet in the centre is of lower case. In this option letter 'L' on the left is also in lower case.

11. (A) : Other numbers are divisible by 7.

12. (D) : Other numbers are multiples of 13.

13. (C) : 131 is a prime number.

14. (B) : In other numbers, no digit is repeated.

15. (B) : In other numbers, the last two digits are same.

16. (D) : Bogie is a part of train which is a type of conveyance. Chair, Shirt and Necklace are types of furniture, garment and jewellery respectively.

17. (A) : The medium used for writing with pencil is lead, with pen it is ink and with brush, it is paint. With crayon it should be wax.

18. (A) : The pair of words are opposite. Other pairs are synonyms.

19. (C) : Tiara is worn on the head.

20. (D) : Other words are opposite to each other.

21. (D) : In all other groups, the letters are in natural series and the last letter of first part is the first letter of the second part.

22. (B) : In all other groups, only the vowel is in lower case in the first part and in second part the case is reversed.

23. (C) : In all other groups, the letters jump two letters in between them.

24. (C) : In all other groups, the single letter in first part is repeated in the second and vice versa.

25. (A) : In all other groups, the letters in the first part are one step forward than the corresponding letters in the second part.

✤ ✤ ✤ ✤ ✤

8. OBSERVATION

In this type of reasoning a statement is followed by inferences drawn from it. From these inferences only one definitely follows which is the hidden proposition of the sentence and it is the right answer to the question.

EXERCISE

Directions : *In each question one or more statements are given followed by various inferential conclusions. The inferential conclusion which can be drawn, without assuming anything in addition to the information given, is the correct answer.*

1. Unless you have atleast two years work experience, you stand limited chance to be selected for the job. This is reflected in the selections of about last eight years.

A. Minimum stipulation of two years' work experience is made very clear to everybody aspiring for the job.

B. Most applicants have much more than two years' work experience.

C. Prior work experience is considered an important advantage in performing the job.

D. If you have more than two years' work experience, you are bound to be selected.

2. Some sutdents, who get only average marks in school, become highly successful later in their profession though these are only exceptions.

A. There is no link whatsoever between academic performance and success in the profession.

B. There are other exceptions also— like good school performance but utter failure otherwise.

C. Only those who perform well in school are given good jobs.

D. Some students under-perform during school years.

3. Various offices of an organisation are usually connected by an internal telephone system called INTERCOM.

A. PBX is manually operated and controlled by an operator.

B. A good internal communication system is essential for dealing with inter-departmental business.

C. Communication made over the intercom can be kept secret.

D. A maximum of 10 pins can be connected together in the intercom between a distance of 3000 meters.

4. High rate of population growth is linked closely with the fact of dwindling area under forest cover.

A. Forests are inimical to human growth.

B. There is less danger to human population from wild animals.

C. Decreasing space of forest cover acts as incentive for humans to reproduce at a faster rate.

D. Population growth leads to demand for more land.

5. Word Processors are screen-based systems in which the typed matter is displayed on a screen.

A. The text can be stored on hard disc, floppy disc for subsequent amendment or printing.

B. It is manually and electrically operated.

C. Editing is possible by inserting new material or deleting unwanted material.

D. It holds data in memory for future use.

6. The least technological development in the field of copying is photo-copying system.

A. It does not have capacity to reduce or enlarge the script of photograph.

B. It is an electrically-operated machine which produces an image of the original copy.

C. Every copy produced looks as original, impressive and attractive.

D. It is fast, easy to operate and cheaper and elegant in producing copies.

7. The population of big cities is increasing day by day but the civic amenities and support services are the same and not expanding.

A. Birth rate is higher in cities as compared to villages.
B. The cities are dying.
C. If civic services are improved, the rate of population growth would further increase.
D. More and more people are using services which have limited capacity.

8. Women being poorly educated, 33 per cent reservation for women in legislative bodies will mean rule by the poorly educated over the educated people.
A. Uneducated women are elected by uneducated women.
B. 33 per cent of the elected women will be uneducated.
C. The number of uneducated persons in the legislative bodies will rise significantly.
D. Educated persons will loose voice in the legislature.

9. Fax machine uses telephone to transmit any form of written or printed matter, diagrams, photographs from one location to another.
A. It is a method of editing, amending and printing of any document.
B. Equipments have to be on both receiving and sending ends.
C. This machine is known as Fascimile Telegraphy.
D. It can send copy of document to long distances by combining the speed of telephone with the reproduction facility of the office copier.

ANSWERS

1	2	3	4	5	6	7	8	9
C	D	C	D	B	A	D	D	A

✤✤✤✤✤

9. RELATIONSHIP CONCEPT

While attempting questions on blood relations, one should be clear of all the relation patterns that can exist between any two individuals. These type of questions are given mainly to test one's relationship ability.

Very well-known relations are :

Mother	Grandmother	Father	Grandfather	Son	Grandson
Daughter	Granddaughter	Brother	Brother-in-law	Sister	Sister-in-law
Niece	Father-in-law	Nephew	Mother-in-law	Uncle	Son-in-law
Aunt	Daughter-in-law	Husband	Cousin	Wife	

The patterns of some relationships which help in solving questions in these tests are :

Father's *or* Mother's Father	—	Grandfather (Paternal *or* Maternal)
Father's *or* Mother's Mother	—	Grandmother (Paternal *or* Maternal)
Father's *or* Mother's Son	—	Brother
Father's *or* Mother's Daughter	—	Sister
Father's Brother	—	Paternal Uncle
Father's Sister	—	Paternal Aunt
Mother's Brother	—	Maternal Uncle
Mother's Sister	—	Maternal Aunt
Uncle *or* Aunt's Son *or* Daughter	—	Cousin
Son's Wife	—	Daughter-in-law
Daughter's Husband	—	Son-in-law
Husband's *or* Wife's Brother	—	Brother-in-law
Husband's *or* Wife's Sister	—	Sister-in-law
Brother's Wife	—	Sister-in-law
Sister's Husband	—	Brother-in-law
Brother's Son	—	Nephew
Brother's Daughter	—	Niece

EXERCISE

Directions : *In each of the following questions keenly study the relationship mentioned between the persons, and then from the given options select the right relationship as the answer.*

1. A lady said, "The person standing there is my grandfather's only son's daughter". How is the lady related to the standing person?

A. Sister B. Mother
C. Aunt D. Cousin

2. Ajay is the brother of Vijay. Mili is the sister of Ajay. Sanjay is the brother of Rahul and Mehul is the daughter of Vijay. Who is Sanjay's Uncle?

A. Rahul
B. Ajay
C. Mehul
D. Data inadequate

3. A man introduced the boy coming with him as "He is son of the father of my wife's daughter". What relation did the boy bear to the man?

A. Son-in-law B. Son
C. Brother D. Father

4. If Amit's father is Billoo's father's only son and Billoo has neither a brother nor a daughter, what is the relationship between Amit and Billoo?

A. Uncle — Nephew B. Father — Daughter
C. Father — Son D. Cousins

5. Pointing to a woman in the photograph a man said, "She is the daughter of my grand-mother's only son." How is the woman related to the man?

A. Mother B. Daughter
C. Sister-in-law D. Sister

6. Pointing to a photograph, a woman said, "She is the only daughter of my mother's father." How is the woman related to the person in the photograph?

A. Mother
B. Grandmother
C. Daughter
D. Cannot be determined

7. Ram is the brother of Shyam and Mahesh is the father of Ram. Jagat is the brother of Priya and Priya is daughter of Shyam. Who is the uncle of Jagat ?

A. Shyam
B. Mahesh
C. Ram
D. Data insufficient

8. Introducing a man, a woman said, "His wife is the only daughter of my father". How is the man related to the woman?

A. Husband B. Father
C. Father-in-law D. Brother

9. If Maya is the only daughter of Richa's grandmother's brother, how is Maya's daughter related to Richa?

A. Niece B. Cousin
C. Aunt D. Mother

10. Pointing to a woman, a man said, "Her husband's mother is the wife of my father's only son". How is the man related to the woman?

A. Son B. Brother-in-law
C. Uncle D. Father-in-law

EXPLANATORY ANSWERS

1. (A) :

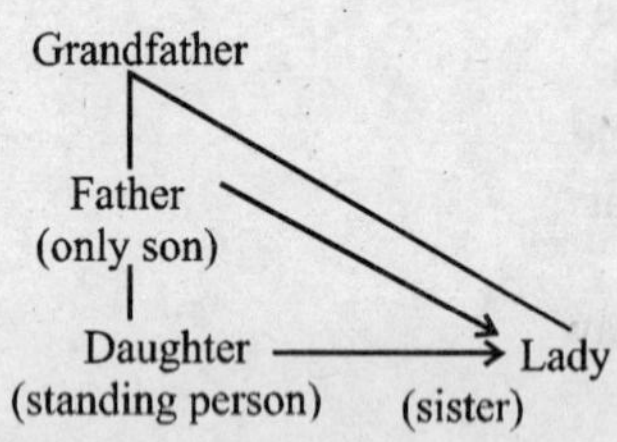

Lady's grandfather's son is lady's father and father's daughter will only be lady's sister.

2. (D) :

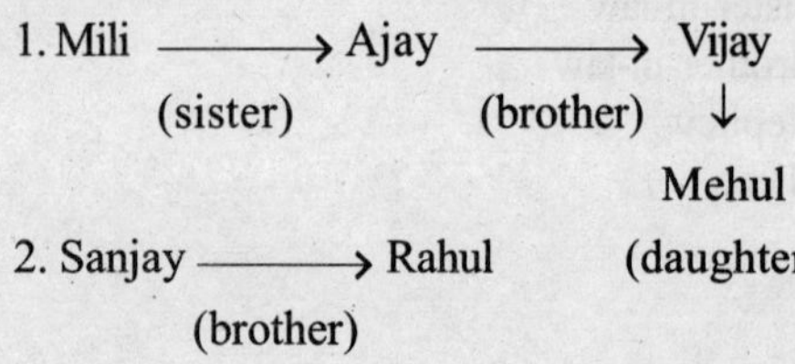

There are two sets of relationship. Information given is incomplete and no relation can be established between the two sets.

3. (B) : The relationship chart based on problem is :

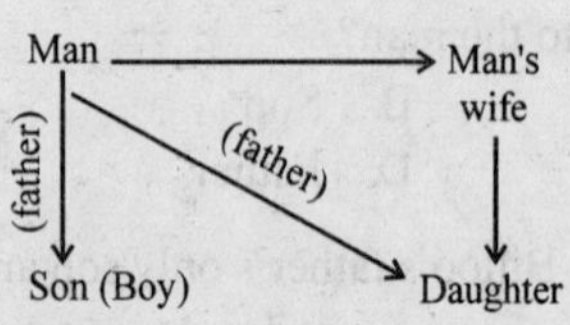

'Father of the man's wife's daughter' is the man himself and the boy in question is the man's son.

4. (C) : The relationship chart based on problem is :

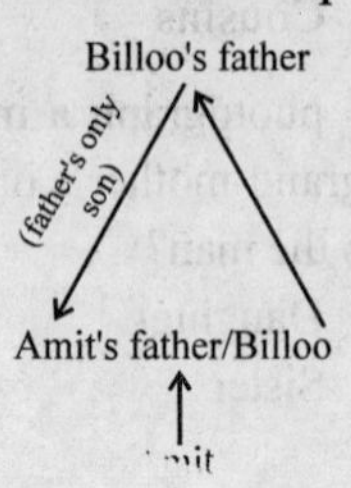

Amit's father is Billoo's father's only son means Billoo is the only son in question also, he is the father of Amit. It must be noted that Billoo has no brother which means he is single and also, when he has no daughter, Amit is his only son.

5. (D) :

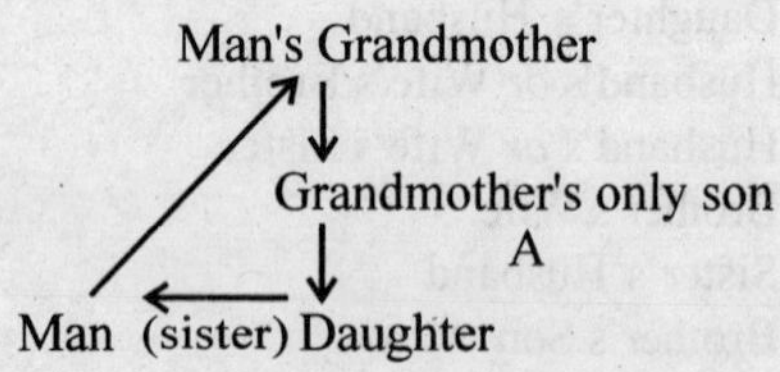

'My grandmother's only son' is the father of the man, and 'daughter of my grandmother's only son' is the sister of the man.

6. (C) :

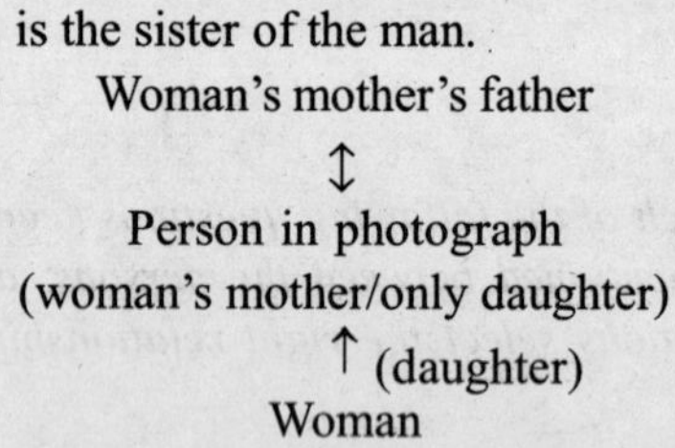

'Only daughter of my mother's father' is the person in the photograph and she is also the mother of the woman. So, the woman is the daughter of the person in the photograph.

7. (C) :

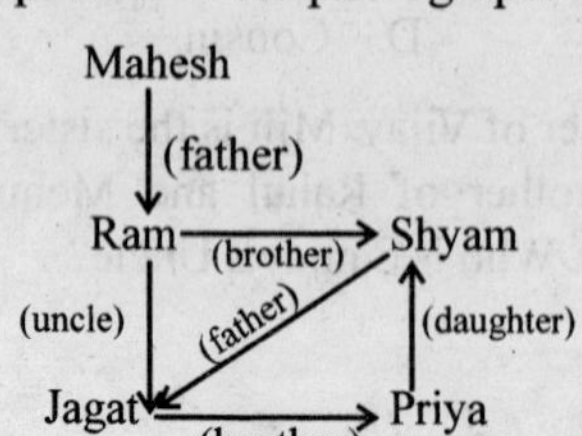

Jagat is brother of Priya and Priya is daughter of Shyam. So, Shyam is also the father of Jagat. Ram is the brother of Shyam. So, Jagat's father's brother Ram is the uncle of Jagat.

8. (A) :

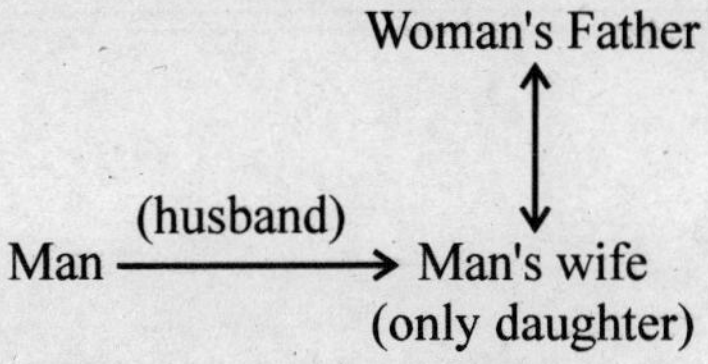

'Only daughter of my father' is the woman herself and the man is her husband.

9. (B) :

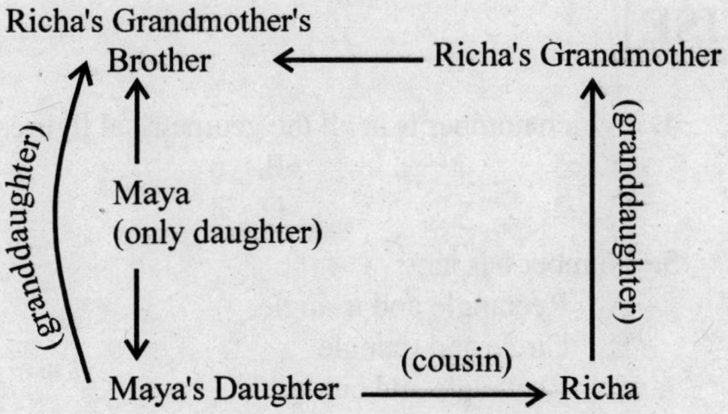

Both Maya's Daughter and Richa are grand-daughters of a brother and a sister respectively. So, Maya's daughter is the cousin of Richa.

10. (D) :

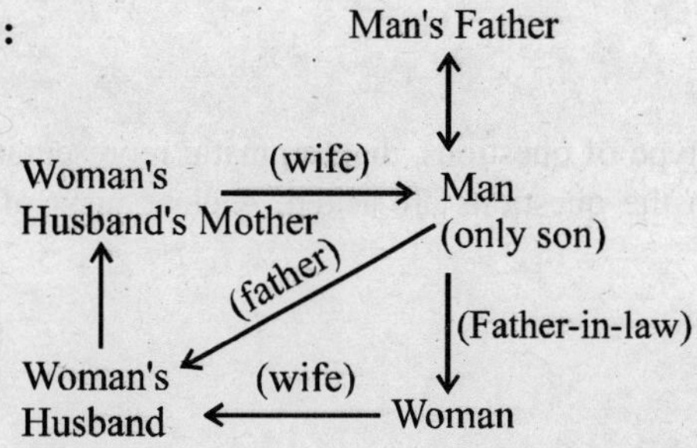

'My father's only son' is the man himself. 'Her husband's mother' is the wife of the man and so the man is the father of the woman's husband. As the woman is the wife of man's son, the man is the father-in-law of the woman.

✤ ✤ ✤ ✤ ✤

10. VENN DIAGRAMS

In these type of questions, diagrammatic representation presents a logical illustration of particular class or statements based on which the questions are asked. A clear view of the diagram makes the concepts clear for attempting such questions.

EXERCISE

1. What is the number which is common to only two geometrical figures?

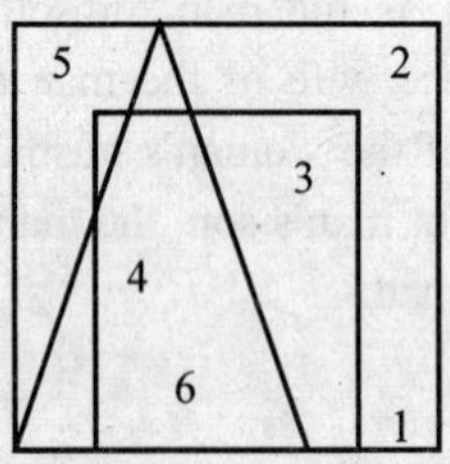

A. 4 B. 3
C. 5 D. 2

Directions (Qs. 2 and 3) : *In the following diagram, rectangle represents Hindi Announcers, circle represents English Announcers, square represents French Announcers, and triangle represents German Announcers.*

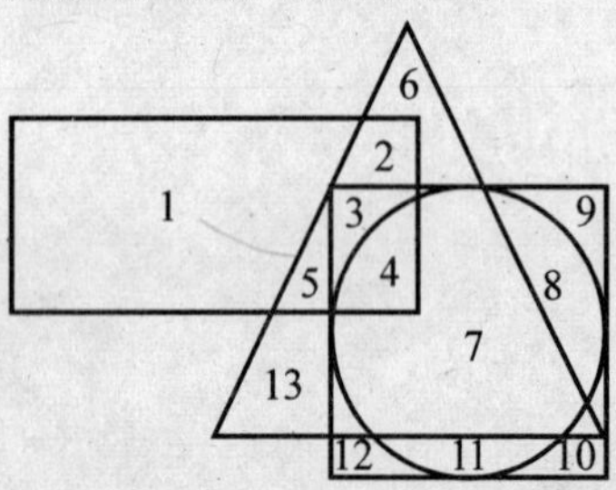

2. Which area represents those announcers who can present programmes in Hindi, French and German only?
A. 1 B. 2
C. 3 D. 4

3 Which area represents those announcers who can present programmes in French and English only?
A. 7 B. 9
C. 11 D. 13

Directions (Qs. 4 and 5) : *Study the diagram to answer these questions.*

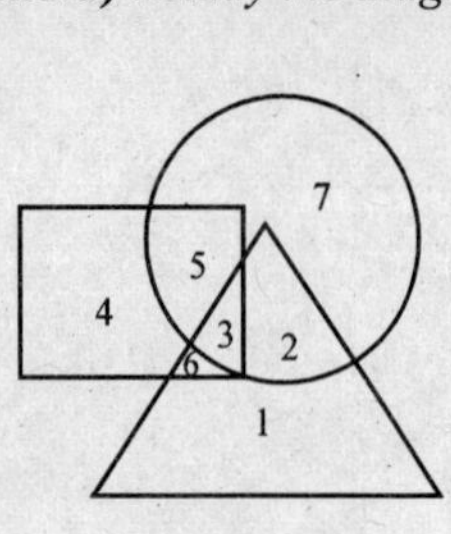

4. Which number is in all the geometrical figures?
A. 5 B. 6
C. 2 D. 3

5. Number 6 is in :
A. Rectangle and triangle
B. Circle and traingle
C. Rectangle and circle
D. Rectangle only

Directions (Qs. 6 to 9) : *In the following diagram*

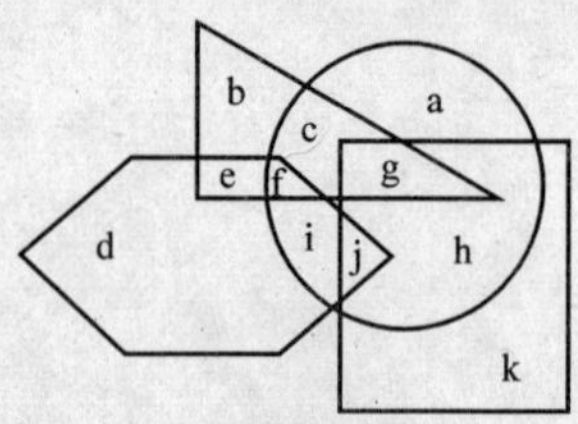

The Circle represents players
The Triangle represents outdoor games
The Hexagon represents indoor games and
The Square represents national level players
Study the diagram and answer the questions given below :

6. The letter in the section representing the players who play indoor games at national level is :
A. f B. i
C. j D. g

7. The letter representing the section of outdoor as well as indoor game players who do not play at the national level is :
A. c B. f
C. e D. i

8. The section representing national level players who do not play either outdoor or indoor games but still come under the category of players is :
A. k B. g
C. c D. h

9. Persons who play outdoor games but do not come under the category of players are represented in the section marked :
A. b B. c
C. a D. d

Direction (Q. 10) : *Study the diagram given below.*

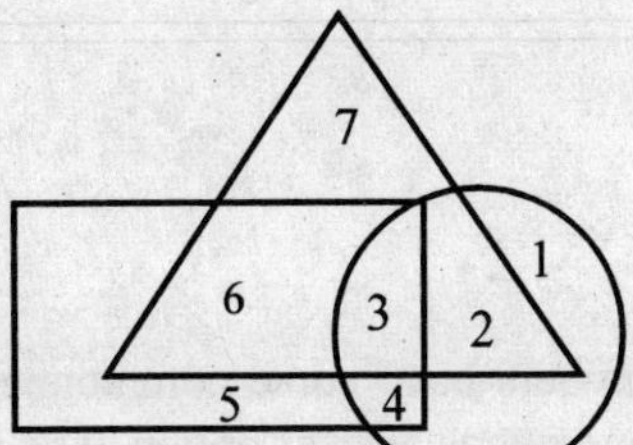

A college provides three different activities, students union represented by triangle, literary society represented by rectangle and social service league represented by circle.

10. Those who take part in both literary society and social service league but not in students union are represented by :

A. 3 & 4 B. 5 & 6
C. 5 & 1 D. 4

EXPLANATORY ANSWERS

1. (B) :

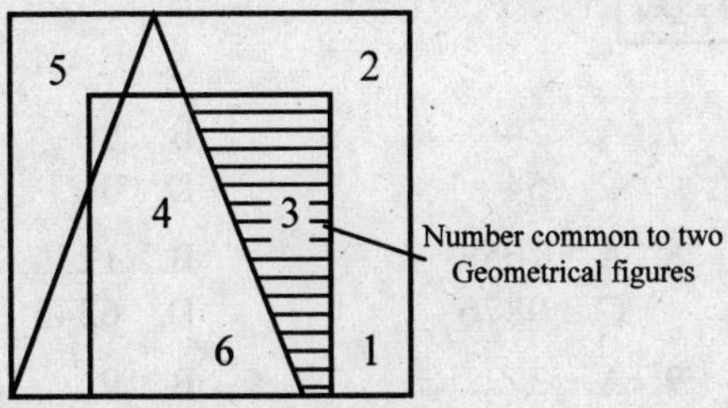

Note : Numbers 4 and 6 are common to all three geometrical figures.

2. (C):

3. (C):

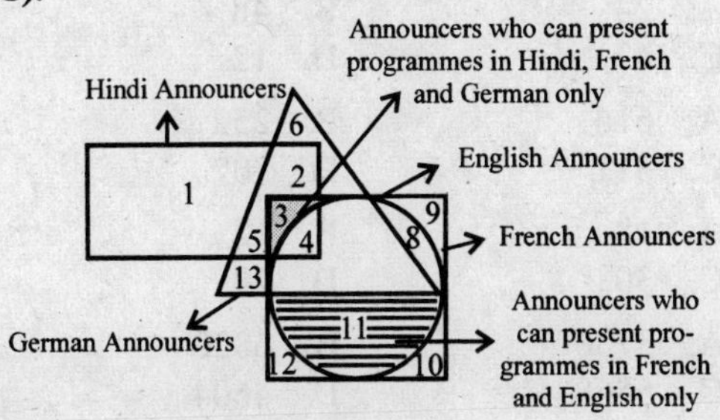

4. (D), **5. *(a)* :**

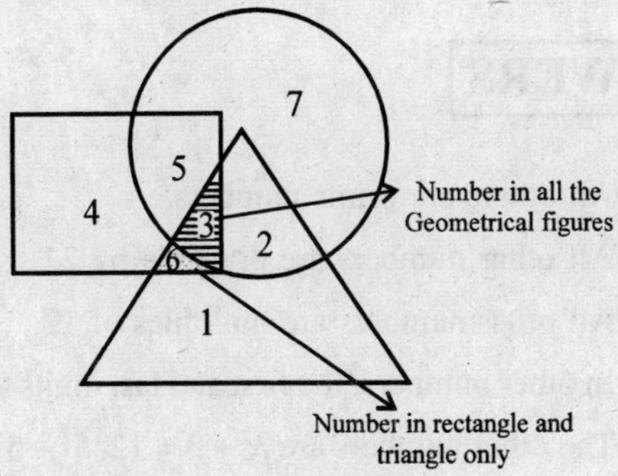

6. (C), **7. (B),** **8. (D),** **9. (A) :**

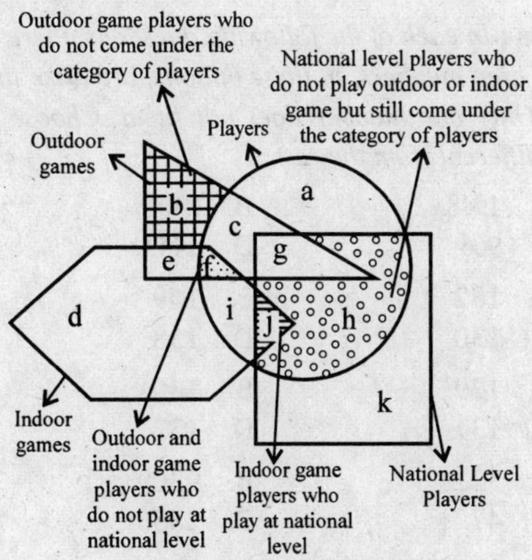

10. (D)

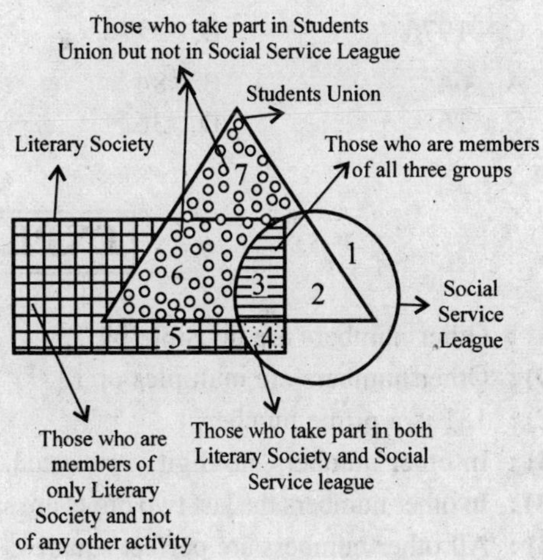

✤ ✤ ✤ ✤ ✤

11. NUMBER CLASSIFICATION

In this type of classification, different numbers are given as options. These numbers have some commonness; except one which is the odd one. One has to identify the similarity and then strike the odd one out as answer option. The number can be odd/even/consecutive, prime numbers, multiple of some number, single, square or cubes of different numbers, plus/minus of some other number or combinations of any mathematical calculation.

EXERCISE

Directions : *In each of the following questions, there are four options. Three numbers, in these options, are alike in certain manner. Only one number does not fit in. Choose the one which is different from the rest.*

1. A. 1948 B. 2401 C. 966 D. 1449

2. A. 182 B. 169 C. 130 D. 158

3. A. 129 B. 130 C. 131 D. 132

4. A. 3215 B. 9309 C. 4721 D. 2850

5. A. 1776 B. 2364 C. 1976 D. 3776

6. A. 64 B. 84 C. 16 D. 36

7. A. 24 B. 90 C. 54 D. 36

8. A. 7658 B. 1234 C. 9876 D. 6543

9. A. 3 B. 9 C. 5 D. 7

10. A. 6450 B. 1776 C. 2392 D. 3815

11. A. 24 B. 48 C. 42 D. 12

12. A. 616 B. 252 C. 311 D. 707

13. A. 18 B. 12 C. 30 D. 20

14. A. 3730 B. 6820 C. 5568 D. 4604

EXPLANATORY ANSWERS

1. (A) : Other numbers are divisible by 7.

2. (D) : Other numbers are multiples of 13.

3. (C) : 131 is a prime number.

4. (B) : In other numbers, no digit is repeated.

5. (B) : In other numbers the last two digits are same.

6. (B) : All other numbers are perfect squares.

7. (A) : In other numbers, the sum of both the digits is 9.

8. (A) : In others, the digits are consecutive in natural or reverse series.

9. (B) : All others are prime numbers.

10. (D) : All other numbers are divisible by 2.

11. (C) : All other numbers are multiples of 12.

12. (C) : In other numbers, the first and last digits are same.

13. (A) : The other numbers are $3^2 + 3 = 12$, $5^2 + 5 = 30$, $4^2 + 4 = 20$, $6^2 + 6 = 42$

14. (B) : In all other numbers, two digits are same.

✤ ✤ ✤ ✤ ✤

12. DRAWING INFERENCES

Questions on this type of reasoning have become quite common in competitive examinations. In this test, instead of a statement or proposition, a passage is given which is a congregation of many propositions coupled with arguments. Some inferences are given followed by the passage. The candidate has to decide whether the given inference follows, or does not follow in the light of the given passage.

EXERCISE

Directions : *Below are given some passages followed by several possible inferences which can be drawn from the facts stated in each passage. You have to examine each inference separately in the context of the passage and decide upon its degree of truth or falsity.*

Mark Answers	If you think...
A. "Definitely True"	the inference properly follows from the statement of facts given.
B. "Probably True"	the inference may be true in the light of the facts given but not definitely true.
C. "Data Inadequate"	from the facts given it cannot be said whether the inference is likely to be true or false.
D. "Probably False"	the inference is probably false in the light of the facts given though not definitely false.
E "Definitely False"	the inference cannot possibly be drawn from the facts given or it contradicts the given facts.

PASSAGE-1

Indian granite industry is in peril in the absence of a uniform policy from the state governments, despite the thrust given by liberalisation policies of the union government. Compared to the remarkable progress in the field during the last three years, the absence of matching policies by state governments had put granite quarry owners and others involved in the industry on the verge of collapse in the international market. The policies differed from state to state, had created problems as far as loyalty, dead rent and duration of lease were concerned.

1. Each state having granite quarry has set up its own rules which are contrary to the interest of the industry.

2. Till three years ago, granite production in India was not profitable.

3. The granite production is largely controlled by individuals.

4. The granite produced in India does not match with the quality of international level.

5. The union government's liberalisation policy became applicable to granite industry only during the last three years.

PASSAGE-2

Steel production has always been burdened with costs much higher than in comparable plants overseas. On the one hand custom duty on almost all steel imports has been reduced, on the other excise duty has been raised. Domestic steel products are now uncompetitive which in turn has led to the demand that both the custom and excise rates should be reviewed to prevent sickness in the industry.

6. The steel industry in general is making losses as a fall out of the government policy.

7. The cost of production of steel in other countries is less than that in India.

8. India can compete with the foreign countries in re gard to the price of steel with a favourable government policy.

9. Foreign steel has become cheaper comparative to domestic steel.

10. The government is considering lowering of excise duty on steel products.

EXPLANATORY ANSWERS

1. (A) : The policies differed from state to state.

2. (C) : Remarkable progress during the last three years is mentioned in the paragraph but nothing suggests that the production was not profitable.

3. (A) : There is absence of a uniform policy from the state Governments.

4. (C) : According to the paragraph, absence of matching policies had put the quarry owners and others involved in the industry on the verge of collapse in the international market. Nothing is mentioned about the granite quality produced in India or of the international level.

5. (E) : The inference does not relate to the facts given in the statement.

6. (D) : Government policy alone may not be responsible for the losses. Cost or quality factor may also be responsible.

7. (C) : The paragraph mentions that steel production in India has always been burdened with costs much higher than in comparable plants overseas. But nowhere in the paragraph it is mentioned that the cost of production of steel is less in other countries.

8. (A) : If the government reviews its policy, India can definitely compete with the foreign countries in regard to the steel price.

9. (A) : Customs duty on almost all steel products has been reduced.

10. (B) : There is a demand that both the customs and excise rates should be reviewed.

✤ ✤ ✤ ✤ ✤

13. FIGURAL CLASSIFICATION

In this type of reasoning, a set of five figures are given. Out of them, four figures are similar in a certain way or following a certain logic and so form a group. You have to choose one of the figures which does not belong to that group.

EXERCISE

Directions (Qs. 1–10) : *In each question below five figures are given. Four are similar in a certain way and so form a group. The question is— which one of the figures* ***does not*** *belong to that group?*

1. 

(A) (B) (C) (D) (E)

2. 

(A) (B) (C) (D) (E)

3. 

(A) (B) (C) (D) (E)

4. 

(A) (B) (C) (D) (E)

5. 

(A) (B) (C) (D) (E)

6. 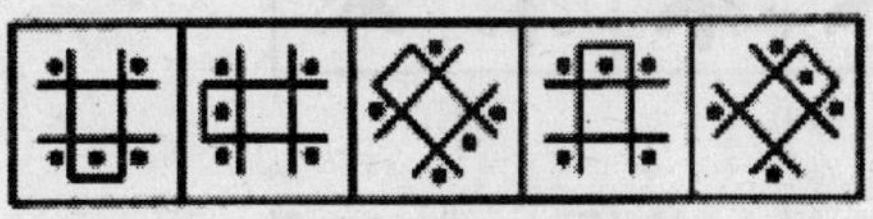

(A) (B) (C) (D) (E)

7. 

(A) (B) (C) (D) (E)

8. 

(A) (B) (C) (D) (E)

9. 

(A) (B) (C) (D) (E)

10. 

(A) (B) (C) (D) (E)

Directions (Qs. 11–20) : *In each of the following questions, in four out of the five figures, element I is related to element II in the same particular way. Find out the figure in which the element I is* ***not*** *so related to element II.*

11. 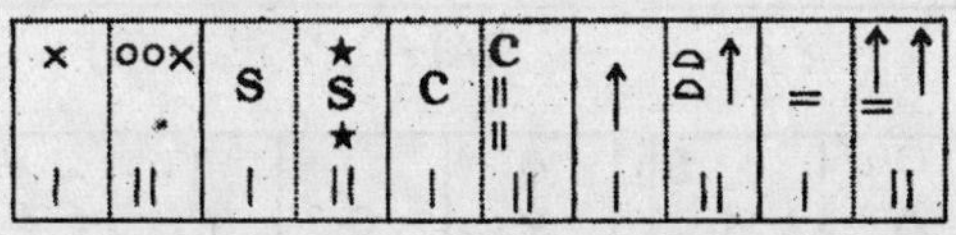

(A) (B) (C) (D) (E)

12. 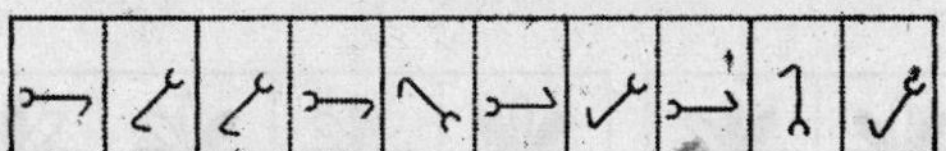

(A) (B) (C) (D) (E)

13. 

(A) (B) (C) (D) (E)

14. 

(A) (B) (C) (D) (E)

15.

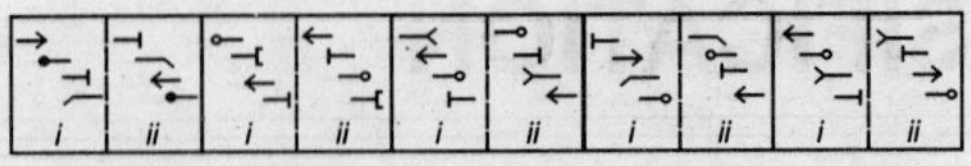

(A) (B) (C) (D) (E)

16.

(A) (B) (C) (D) (E)

17.

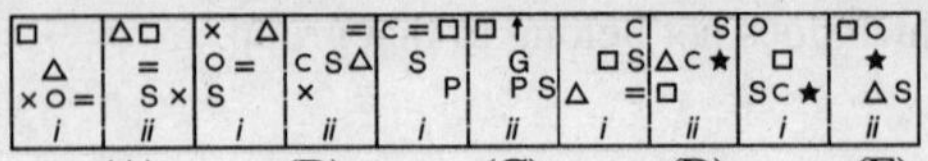

(A) (B) (C) (D) (E)

18.

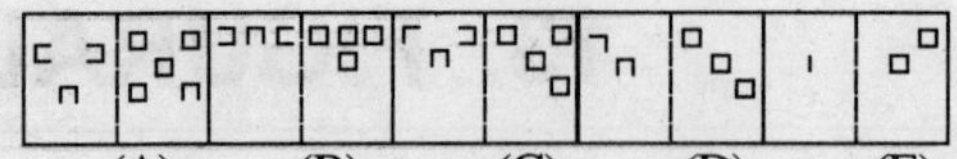

(A) (B) (C) (D) (E)

19.

(A) (B) (C) (D) (E)

20.

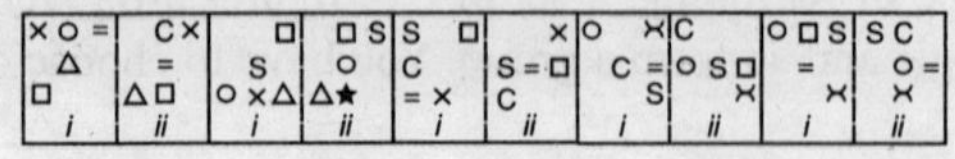

(A) (B) (C) (D) (E)

Directions (Qs. 21–30) : *In each of the following questions, a related pair of figures (unnumbered) is followed by five numbered pairs of figures. Out of these five, four have relationship similar to that in the unnumbered pair. Only one pair of figures does not have similar relationship. Select that pair of figures which does not have a similar relationship to that in the unnumbered pair. Number of that pair is your answer.*

21.

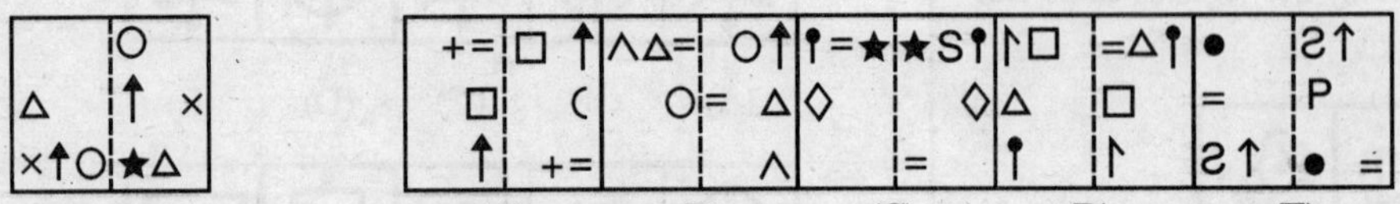

(A) (B) (C) (D) (E)

22.

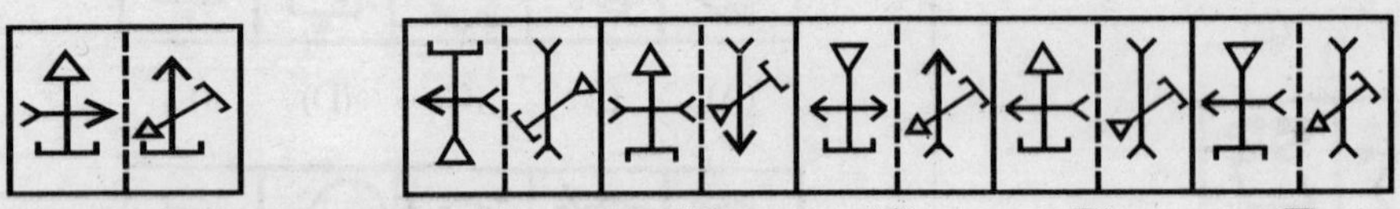

(A) (B) (C) (D) (E)

23.

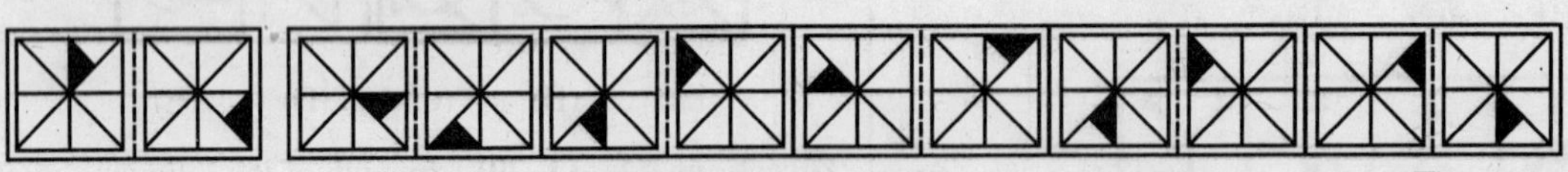

(A) (B) (C) (D) (E)

24.

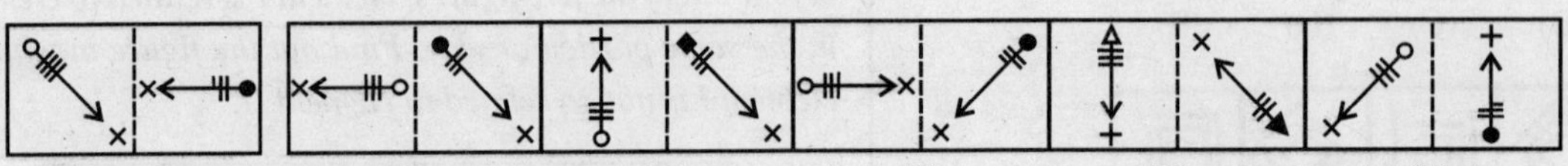

(A) (B) (C) (D) (E)

25.

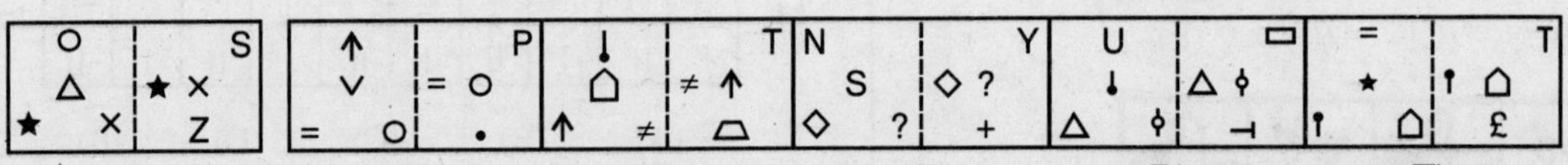

(A) (B) (C) (D) (E)

26.

(A) (B) (C) (D) (E)

27.

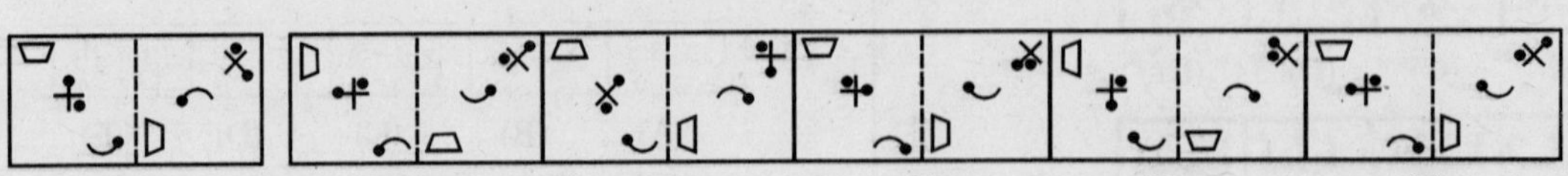

(A) (B) (C) (D) (E)

28.

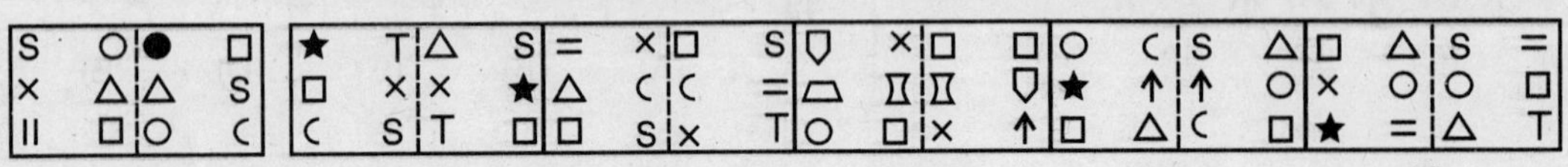

(A) (B) (C) (D) (E)

29. 

(A) (B) (C) (D) (E)

30. 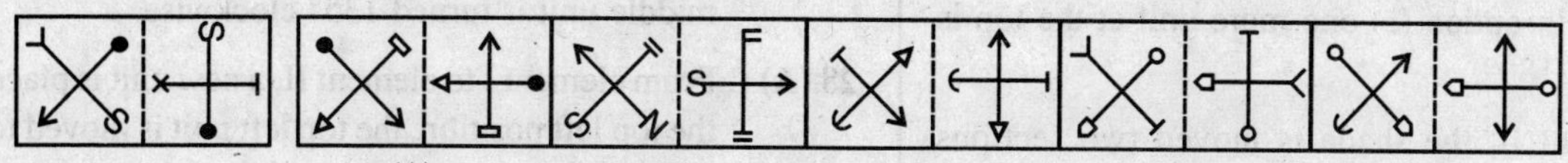

(A) (B) (C) (D) (E)

EXPLANATORY ANSWERS

1. (D) : In all other figures, the arrow and the + sign lie towards the black end of the main figure.

2.(A) : The pins, equal in number of sides in the main figure are attached to the midpoint of a side of the main figure in case of figures (*b*), (*c*), (*d*) and (*e*). In figure (*a*), these pins are attached to a vertex of the main figure.

3.(C) : In all other figures, the dot appears in the angle formed between the arrow and the pin.

4.(A) : All other figures can be rotated into each other. (In each figure except figure (*a*), the middle element is obtained by rotating the outer element through 90° CW and the inner element is obtained by rotating the middle element through 90° CW).

5.(C) : All other figures have at least one line of symmetry.

6.(C) : All other figures can be rotated into each other.

7.(E) : In each one of the other four figures, four arcs are curved towards the left and four other arcs are curved towards the right.

8.(C) : All other figures can be rotated into each other.

9.(D) : In all other figures, the number of dots outside the main figure is one more than the number of dots inside the main figure.

10.(A) : In all other figures, one of the dots lies outside the triangle as well as the circle.

11.(E) : Except in figure (*b*), in all other figures, from element I to II two new designs are added in one side of the main design.

12.(C) : In each figure from element I to II the main design rotates through 135° clockwise or anticlockwise. Except in figure (*c*), in all other figures, the smaller line segment moves to other side from element I to II.

13.(A) : In all other figures the element II can be obtained by the lateral inversion of the element I. In figure (*a*), the lower design has not been inverted.

14.(B) : In figure (*b*), the small segment is on the same side as that of the half shaded circle in both the elements.

15.(D) : The first design is inverted and moved to third place, the second design is moved to the fourth place, third design to the first place and fourth design is inverted and moved to the second place. Option (*d*) violates this.

16.(B) : In all other options the top-left element is moved to the centre with 90° clockwise rotation. Here, it is rotated anticlockwise.

17.(D) : All the designs are shifted in a set pattern one behind the other. The fourth design in all others is changed and placed in the last. Here, the fifth and last designs are changed.

18.(A) : In all other pair of figures, all incomplete squares in the first elements are completed and an extra square is added in the second element.

19.(A) : From element I to element II, the 'S' shape is turned 90° clockwise and moved down, the double arrow shape '⇒' is turned 90° clockwise and moved to the right, the two parallel lines one turned by 90°; one parallel line is added and all three lines are moved up, the line with a dot is turned 90° clockwise and moved to the centre and the 'C' shape in the centre is turned by 180° and moved to top left position. Here, the double arrow is turned anticlockwise.

20.(C) : Starting from one unit, all units are moved in a set pattern, the places of last two units moved are interchanged and the last unit is then made new. Here, no changes are made in the last two units.

21.(D) : From element I to element II clockwise the first unit is moved 2 steps forward, the second unit 1 step forward, the third unit 2½ steps forward and the fourth unit 3 steps forward. In option (*d*) the third unit violates the rule.

22.(E) : From element I to element II, the horizontal bar is turned 135° anticlockwise and the unit at the lower end is turned by 180°. The vertical bar is turned 90° anticlockwise and the unit at the lower end is turned by 180°. In option (*e*) one more unit at the top is turned by 180°.

23.(E) : In element II, the shade is moved two sections clockwise and shifted from the centre to the base. In option (*e*) it is not so.

24.(A) : In element II, the arrow is turned 135° clockwise. In option (*a*) it is turned anticlockwise.

25.(B) : From element I to element II, the bottom right unit and bottom left unit are moved to the centre and middle left position respectively. The other two units are removed and two new elements are placed in the top right and bottom centre position respectively. In option (*b*) the placement of bottom right and left elements is not right.

26.(C) : In element II, the shades are shifted one petal clockwise. In option (*c*) one of the shades is not moved.

27.(B) : From element I to element II, the unit on the top left is turned 90° anticlockwise and moved to the bottom right corner position, the unit in the centre is turned 135° anticlockwise and moved to the top right position, and the unit in the bottom right is turned by 180° and moved to the centre. In option (*b*), the middle unit is turned 135° clockwise.

28.(A) : From element I to element II, a new unit is placed in the top left position, the top left unit is moved to the middle right position, the middle right unit is moved to the left position, the middle left unit is replaced by a new unit and placed in bottom right position, the bottom right unit is moved to the top right position, and the top right unit is moved diagonally to replace the bottom left unit. In option (*a*), the middle left unit is not changed when moved to the bottom right position.

29.(E) : From element I to element II starting anticlockwise, the first and second units are moved 1½ steps clockwise respectively, the third unit ½ step anticlockwise, the fourth unit 2 steps clockwise, and a new unit is placed ahead of the first unit. Option (*e*) violates the rules.

30.(E) : In element II, the cross is turned 135° clockwise and then the positions of left and top units on the cross are interchanged. In option (*e*) it is not so.

✤✤✤✤✤

14. PUNCHED HOLE PATTERN– FOLDING & UNFOLDING

These type of questions are based on a piece of paper which is folded and cut or punched in a particular manner. One of the option figures either resembles the pattern that would be formed when the paper is unfolded or resembles the form in which the paper is folded and cut or punched.

EXERCISE

Directions (Qs. 1-5) : *In each one of the following problems, a square transparent sheet with a pattern is given. Figure out from amongst the four alternatives as to how the pattern would appear when the transparent sheet is folded at the dotted line.*

1. 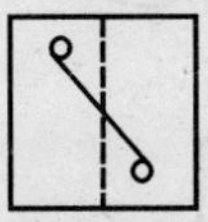

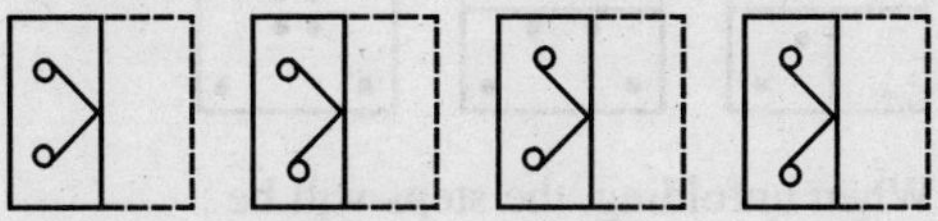

(A) (B) (C) (D)

2. 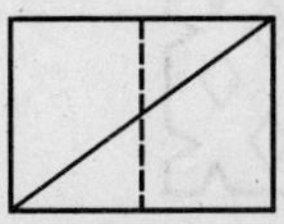

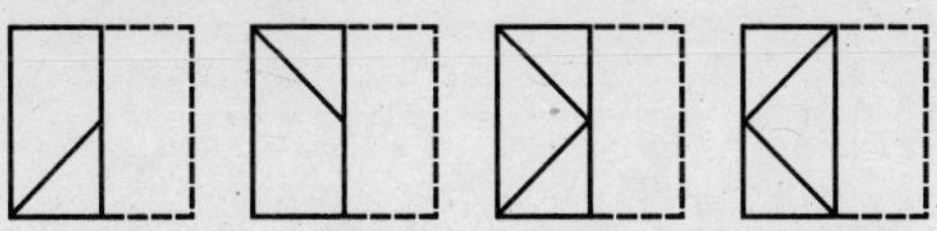

(A) (B) (C) (D)

3. 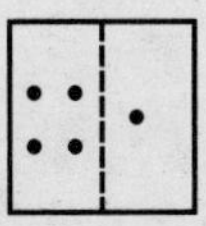

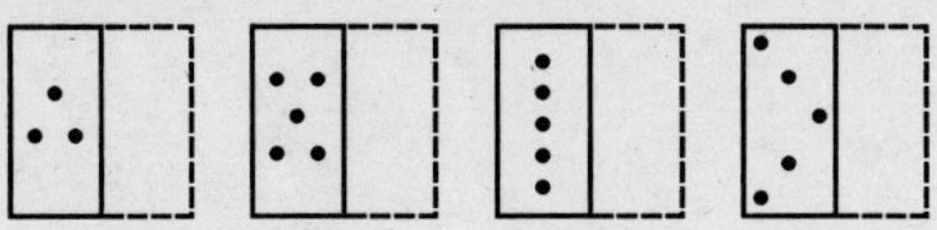

(A) (B) (C) (D)

4. 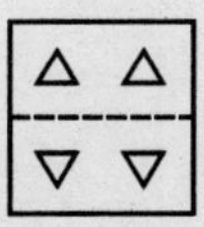

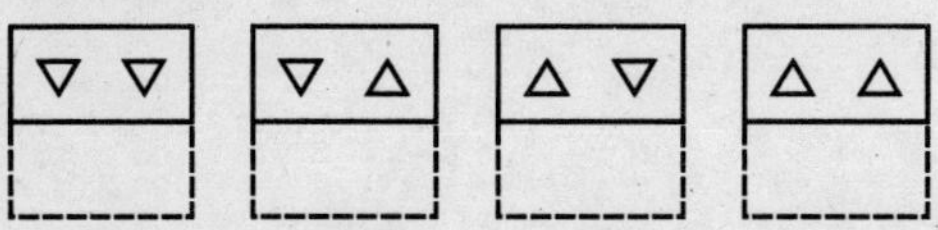

(A) (B) (C) (D)

5. 

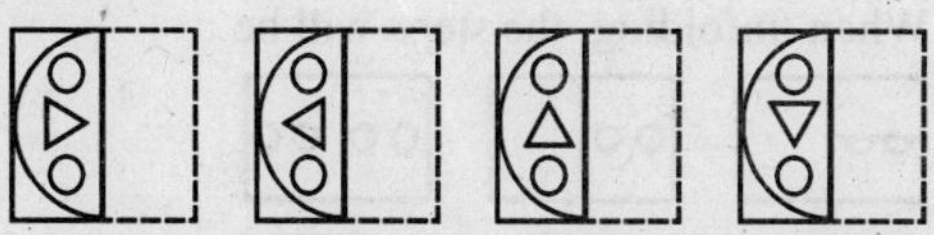

(A) (B) (C) (D)

Directions (Qs. 6-11) : *In each of the following questions a piece of paper has been folded and then punched. From the given options figure out the correct response which shows how it will appear when opened.*

6. 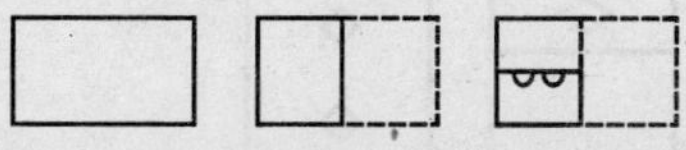

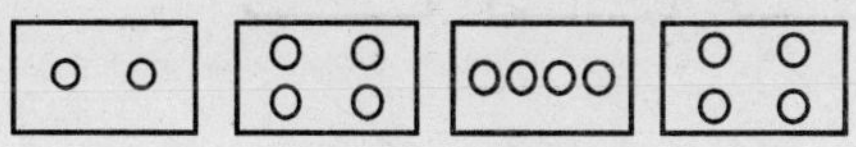

(A) (B) (C) (D)

7. 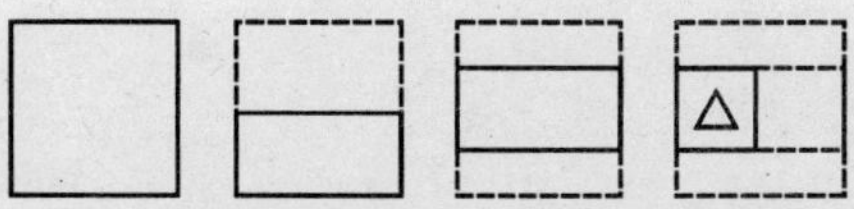

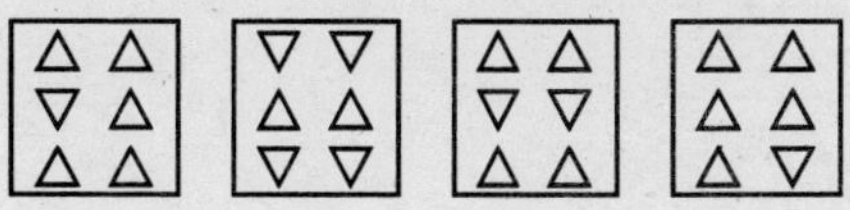

(A) (B) (C) (D)

8. 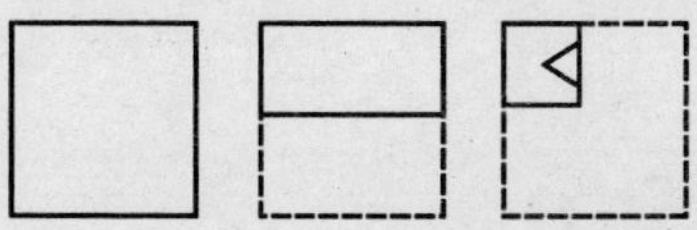

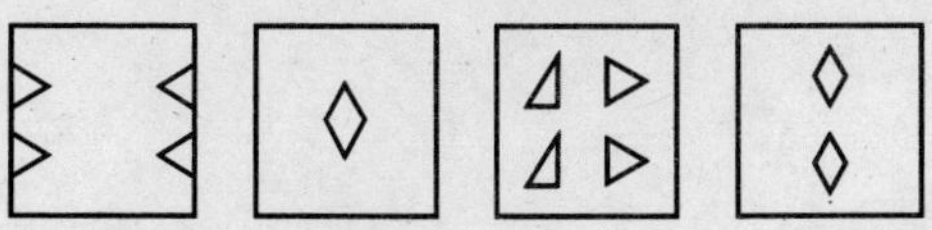

(A) (B) (C) (D)

9.

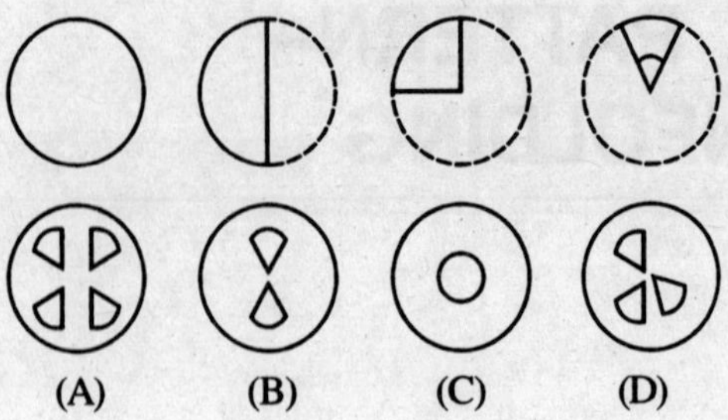

10.

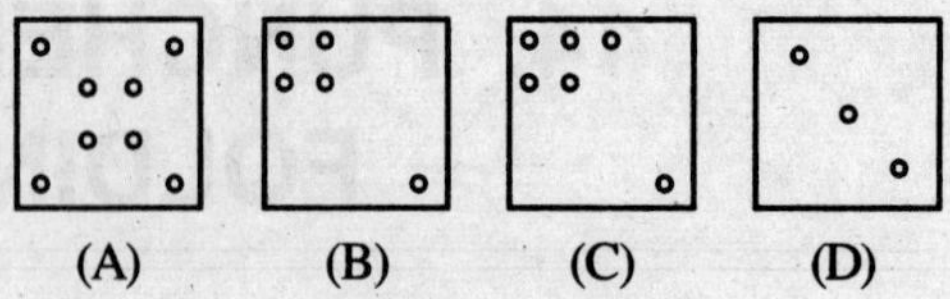

11.

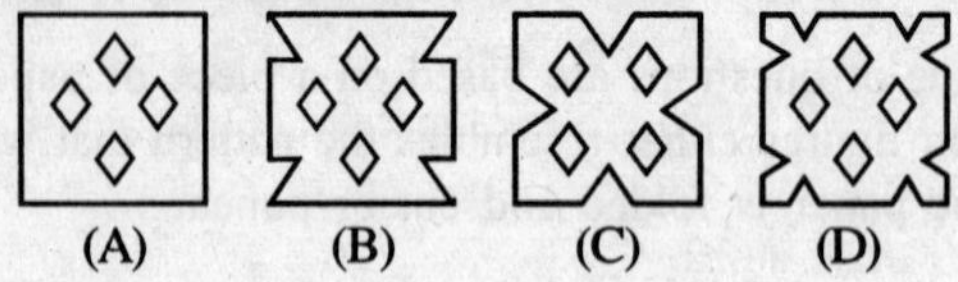

EXPLANATORY ANSWERS

1. (D) **2. (C)**
3. (B) **4. (D)**
5. (B)

6. (C) : When unfolding, the steps will be :

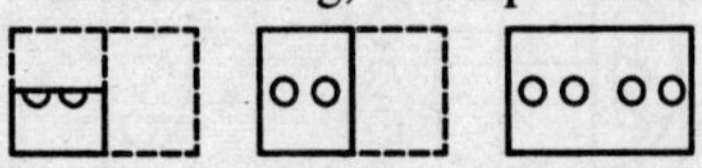

7. (B) : When unfolding, the steps will be :

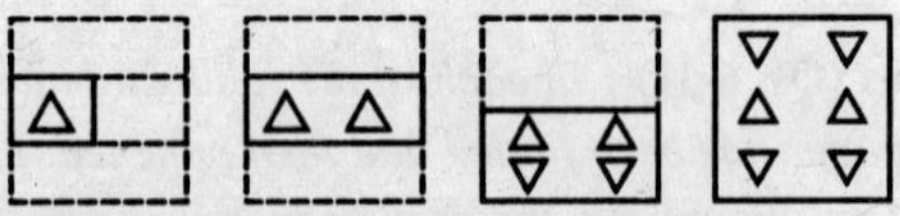

8. (D) : When unfolding, the steps will be :

9. (C) : When unfolding, the steps will be :

10. (A) : When unfolding, the steps will be :

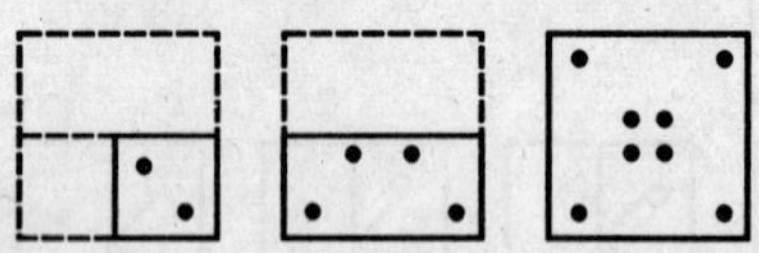

11. (D) : When unfolding, the steps will be :

✤✤✤✤✤

15. SEMANTIC SERIES

In letter series, the letters follow a definite order. The given series of letters can be in natural order or in reverse order or combination of both. The letters may be skipped or repeated or consecutive. The given series may be single or may even comprise of two different series merged at alternate positions. While attempting questions on letter series one should note the pattern of alphabet series.

Alphabets in natural series are :

A	B	C	D	E	F	G	H	I	J	K	L	M	N	O	P	Q	R	S	T	U	V	W	X	Y	Z
↓				↓					↓					↓					↓					↓	
1st				5th					10th					15th					20th					25th	

Alphabets in reverse series are :

Z	Y	X	W	V	U	T	S	R	Q	P	O	N	M	L	K	J	I	H	G	F	E	D	C	B	A
↓				↓					↓					↓					↓					↓	
1st				5th					10th					15th					20th					25th	

Note : On reaching Z, the series restarts from A and on reaching A, it restarts from Z.

EXERCISE

Directions : *In each of the following series determine the order of the letters. Then from the given options select the one which will complete the given series.*

1. B Y C X D W E ?
A. S B. T
C. U D. V

2. B A F E J I P O ? U
A. V B. T
C. S D. Q

3. B A D C ? H G J I
A. EF B. FE
C. FG D. DF

4. ADG, XVT, BEH, WUS, ?
A. VTR B. CFI
C. DFJ D. STU

5. GMSY, IOUA, KQWC, ?
A. MSYE B. NSYE
C. MTYE D. MSYF

6. ADG, GJM, ?, SVY
A. MPS B. MQR
C. MQS D. SPM

7. XYZ, UVW, ?, OPQ
A. RST B. STU
C. QRS D. TUV

8. JOBS, KMEO, LKHK, ?, NGNC
A. MJLH B. LIKG
C. MIKG D. MNGM

9. AZ, GT, MN, ?, YB
A. KF B. TS
C. RX D. SH

10. BMY, DNW, FOU, ?
A. HPT B. HPS
C. HQS D. GPS

11. AZ, CX, EV, ?
A. HU B. GS
C. GT D. HT

12. DMP, FLN, HKL, JJJ, ?
A. MIH B. III
C. LIH D. MII

13. ECA, JHF, OMK, ?, YWU
A. TRP B. LNP
C. QPN D. RPT

14. ABP, CDQ, EFR, ?
A. GHS B. HGS
C. GHR D. GHT

15. BEH, KNQ, TWZ, ?
A. IJL B. BDF
C. CFI D. ADG

EXPLANATORY ANSWERS

1. (D) : There are two alternate series.

+1 +1 +1

B Y C X D W E V

–1 –1 –1

Series I : BCDE (natural order)

Series II : YXWV (reverse order)

2. (A) : Each vowel (AEIOU) is preceded by the letter that comes next to it in the natural alphabetical series.

B A F E J I P O V U

3. (B) : The letters in natural series are divided into sections of two letters each. The letters in each section are written backward.

BA DC FE HG JI

4. (B) : There are two alternate series.

ADG XVT BEH WUS CFI

Series I : ADG BEH CFI

+1 +1
+1 +1
+1 +1

Series II : XVT WUS

–1
–1
–1

5. (A) : The series is formed by moving each letter two steps forward from one group to the next.

GMSY IOUA KQWC MSYE

+2 +2 +2
+2 +2 +2
+2 +2 +2
+2 +2 +2

(The series restarts from A on reaching Z)

6. (A) : In each group of three letters the alphabet is in the succession of +3. The next group begins with the last alphabet of the previous group.

A D G G J M M P S S V Y

+3 +3 +3 +3 +3 +3 +3 +3

7. (A) : The alphabet from one group to the next are in recession of –3, *i.e.*,

XYZ UVW RST OPQ

–3 –3 –3
–3 –3 –3
–3 –3 –3

8. (C) : The alphabets in each group follow the pattern +1, –2, +3 and –4 respectively from one group to the next group.

JOBS KMEO LKHK MIKG NGNC

+1 +1 +1 +1
–2 –2 –2 –2
+3 +3 +3 +3
–4 –4 –4 –4

9. (D) : The letters in one group correspond to the letters in the next group in the manner +6, –6 respectively, *i.e.,*

AZ GT MN SH YB

+6 +6 +6 +6
–6 –6 –6 –6

10. (B) : The letters in one group correspond to the letters in the next group in the manner +2, +1, –2 respectively, *i.e.,*

BMY DNW FOU HPS

+2 +2 +2
+1 +1 +1
–2 –2 –2

11. (C) : The letters in each group correspond to the letters in the next group in the manner +2, –2 respectively, *i.e.,*

AZ CX EV GT

+2 +2 +2
–2 –2 –2

12. (C) : The alphabets in each group correspond to the alphabets in the next group in the manner +2, –1, –2 respectively, *i.e.,*

DMP FLN HKL JJJ LIH

+2 +2 +2 +2
–1 –1 –1 –1
–2 –2 –2 –2

13. (A) : The alphabets in each group are moved five steps forward, *i.e.,*

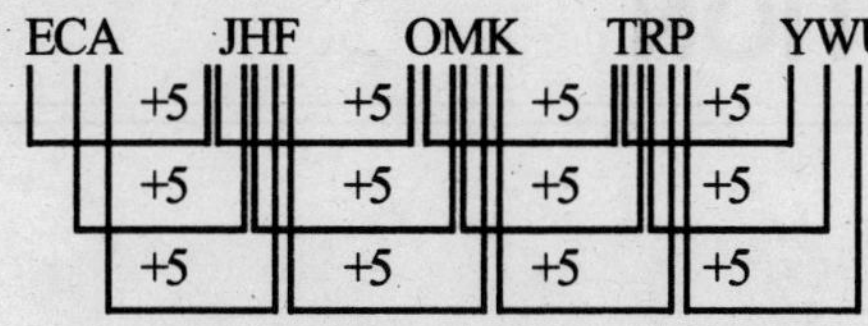

14. (A) : The letters in one group correspond to the letters in the next group in the manner +2, +2, +1 respectively, *i.e.,*

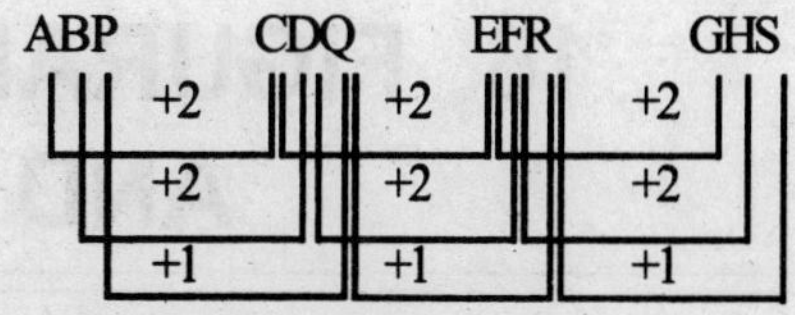

15. (C) : All the letters in each group are moved nine steps forward.

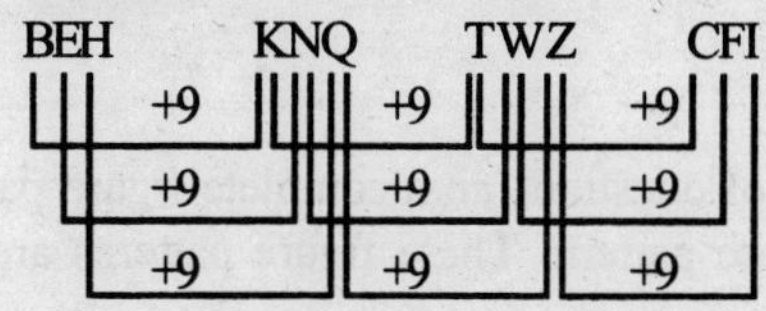

✤ ✤ ✤ ✤ ✤

16. FIGURAL PATTERN FOLDING AND COMPLETION

In these type of questions an incomplete figure pattern is given followed by alternative figures of which one will complete the given figure pattern. These figure patterns are mainly based on symmetries.

EXERCISE

Directions : *In each question, which one of the alternative figures will complete the given figure pattern?*

1. Pattern 

Alternative figures

(A) (B) (C) (D)

2. Pattern 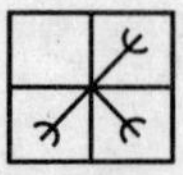

Alternative figures

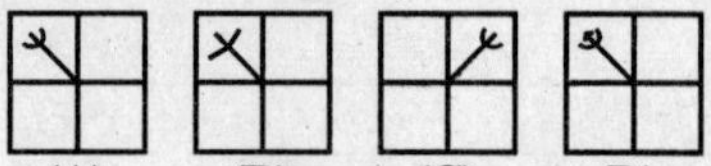

(A) (B) (C) (D)

3. Pattern 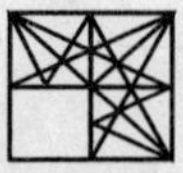

Alternative figures

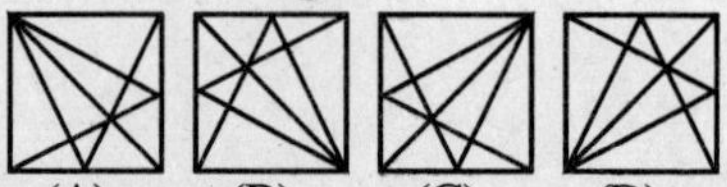

(A) (B) (C) (D)

4. Pattern 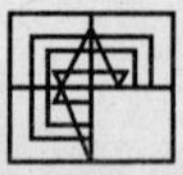

Alternative figures

(A) (B) (C) (D)

5. Pattern 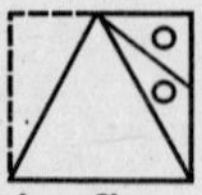

Alternative figures

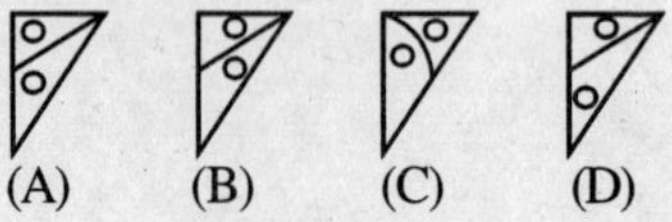

(A) (B) (C) (D)

6. Pattern 

Alternative figures

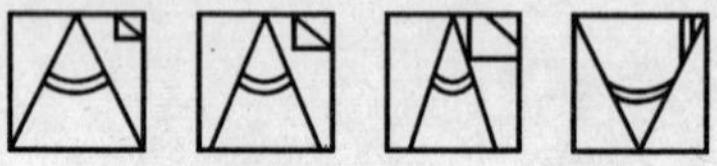

(A) (B) (C) (D)

7. Pattern 

Alternative figures

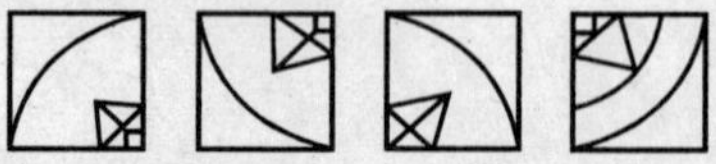

(A) (B) (C) (D)

8. Pattern 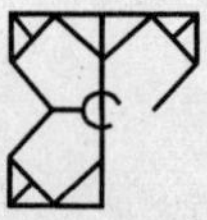

Alternative figures

(A) (B) (C) (D)

9. Pattern 

Alternative figures

(A) (B) (C) (D)

10. Pattern 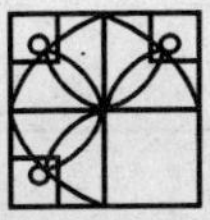

Alternative figures

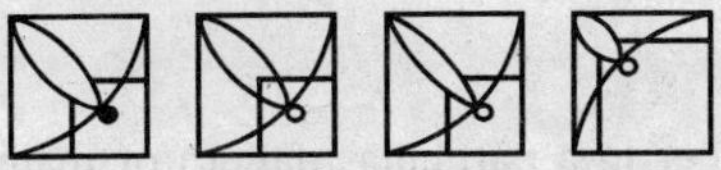

(A) (B) (C) (D)

11. Pattern 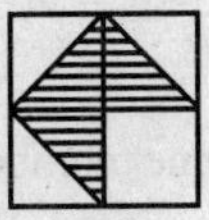

Alternative figures

(A) (B) (C) (D)

12. Pattern 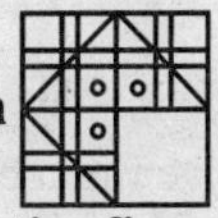

Alternative figures

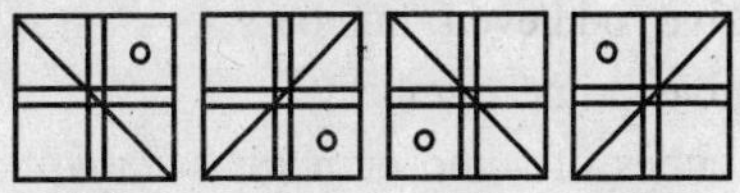

(A) (B) (C) (D)

EXPLANATORY ANSWERS

All the completed figures will look like this:

1. (B) : 

2. (A) : 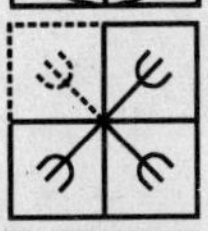

3. (D) : 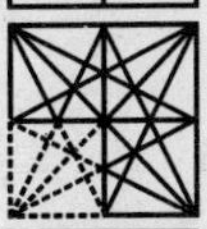

4. (D) : 

5. (A) : 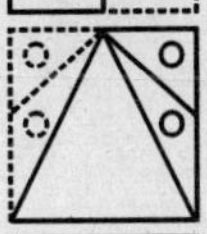

6. (A) : 

7. (B) : 

8. (C) : 

9. (A) : 

10. (B) : 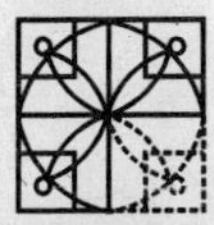

11. (A) : 

12. (D) : 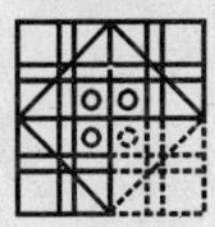

✤ ✤ ✤ ✤ ✤

17. NUMBER SERIES

In this type of series, the set of given numbers in a series are related to one another in a particular pattern or manner. The relationship between the numbers may be

(*i*) consecutive odd/even numbers;
(*ii*) consecutive prime numbers;
(*iii*) squares/cubes of some numbers with/without variation of addition or subtraction of some number;
(*iv*) sum/product/difference of preceding numbers;
(*v*) addition/subtraction/multiplication/division by some number; and
(*vi*) many more combinations of the relationships given above.

EXERCISE

Directions : *In the following questions, select the number(s) from the given options for completing the given series.*

1. 7776, 1296, 216, 36, 6, ?
A. 6 B. 0
C. 3 D. 1

2. 29282, 2662, 242, 22, ?
A. 1 B. 2
C. 0 D. 11

3. 1, 2, 2, 4, 16, ?, 65536
A. 276 B. 64
C. 256 D. 198

4. 3, 5, 9, 15, 23, ?, 45
A. 37 B. 35
C. 31 D. 33

5. 7, 21, 35, 49, 63, ?
A. 70 B. 77
C. 81 D. 108

6. 10, 14, 23, 39, 64, ?, 149
A. 78 B. 128
C. 103 D. 100

7. 6, 24, 29, 116, 121, ?, 489
A. 468 B. 484
C. 243 D. 363

8. 5, 50, 45, 450, 445, ?, 4445
A. 4450 B. 4600
C. 4550 D. 4500

9. 6.25, 9, 12.25, 16, 20.25, 25, 30.25?
A. 36 B. 32
C. 28.25 D. 40.25

10. 243, 5, 81, 15, 27, 45, 9, ?
A. 5 B. 15
C. 135 D. 27

11. 2, 7, 14, 23, ?, 47
A. 31 B. 38
C. 28 D. 34

12. 0, 1, 8, 27, 64, ?
A. 125 B. 128
C. 256 D. 121

13. 37, 47, 58, ?, 79, 95
A. 71 B. 69
C. 68 D. 67

14. 4, –8, 14, –22, 32, ?
A. –44 B. 42
C. –42 D. 44

15. 6, 7, 9, 11, 15, 15, 24, 19, ?
A. 32 B. 34
C. 36 D. 37

EXPLANATORY ANSWERS

1. (D) : The numbers in this sequence are divided by 6 each time.

2. (B) : The numbers in the series are divided by 11 at each step.

3. (C) : The number in the series is product of all the numbers preceding it.

1 2 2 4 16 256 65536

(1×2)

(1×2×2)

(1×2×2×4)

(1×2×2×4×16)

(1×2×2×4×16×256)

4. (D) : The difference between consecutive numbers increases by 2 at each step.

3 5 9 15 23 33 45

+2 +4 +6 +8 +10 +12

5. (B) : The series is multiplication of 7 by odd numbers starting from 3.

7 21 35 49 63 77

× 3

× 5

× 7

× 9

× 11

6. (D) : The number plus the square of numbers in natural order starting from 2 gives the next number in the series.

10 14 23 39 64 100 149

$+2^2$ $+3^2$ $+4^2$ $+5^2$ $+6^2$ $+7^2$

7. (B) : The sequence in the series is ×4, +5, which is repeated.

8. (A) : The sequence in the series is ×10, –5, which is repeated.

9. (A) : There are two alternate series :

+6 +8 +10

6.25 9 12.25 16 20.25 25 30.25 36

+7 +9 +11

Series I : 6.25, 12.25, 20.25, 30.25 (sequence is +6, +8, +10)

Series II : 9, 16, 25, 36 (sequence is +7, +9, +11)

10. (C) : There are two alternate series :

÷3 ÷3 ÷3

243 5 81 15 27 45 9 135

×3 ×3 ×3

Series I : 243, 81, 27, 9 (division by 3)

Series II : 5, 15, 45, 135 (multiplication by 3)

11. (D) : The difference between two consecutive numbers is increasing by 2 starting from 5.

2 7 14 23 34 47

+5 +7 +9 +11 +13

12. (A) : The numbers are cubes of numbers in natural order.

13. (A) : The sum of the digits of the number is added to the number to obtain the next number in the series.

37 47 58 71 79 95

+(3+7) +(4+7) +(5+8) +(7+1) +(7+9)

14. (A) : Alternate numbers are marked positive and negative, but the difference between their magnitude increases by 2 at each step.

4 – 8 14 – 22 32 – 44

4 6 8 10 12

15. (C) : There are two alternate series :

+3 +6 +9 +12

6 7 9 11 15 15 24 19 36

+4 +4 +4

Series I : 6, 9, 15, 24, 36 (sequence is +3, +6, +9, +12)

Series II : 7, 11, 15, 19 (addition of 4 at each step).

✤ ✤ ✤ ✤ ✤

18. EMBEDDED FIGURES

In these type of questions a figure form is given followed by alternative figures. In one of these figure options the given form is embedded. Practice of visualisation comes handy in attempting such easy questions.

EXERCISE

Directions (Qs. 1 to 6) : *In the questions given below a figure is given. From the given alternatives select the one in which the given figure is embedded.*

1. 

(A) (B) (C) (D)

2. 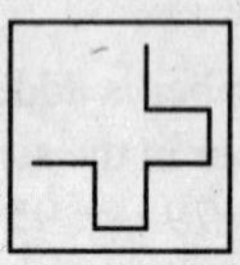

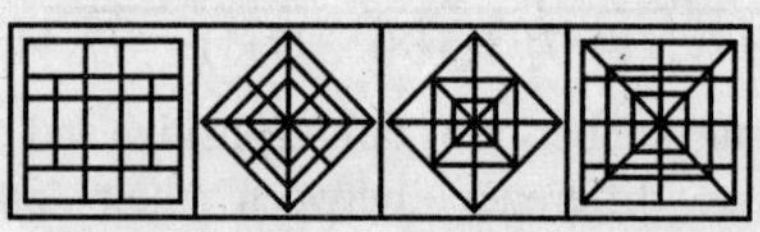

(A) (B) (C) (D)

3. 

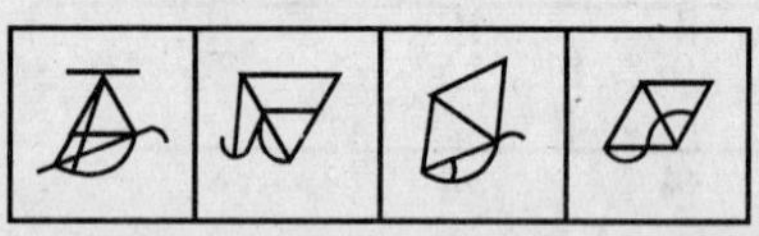

(A) (B) (C) (D)

4. 

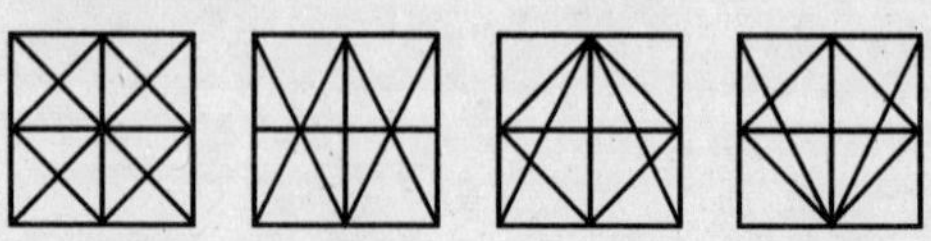

(A) (B) (C) (D)

5. 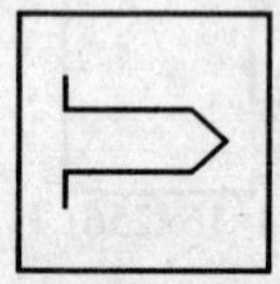

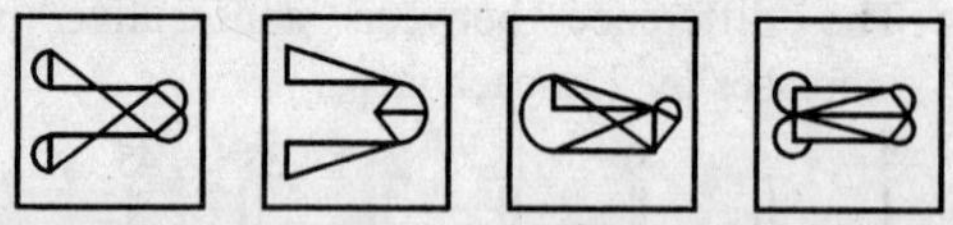

(A) (B) (C) (D)

6. 

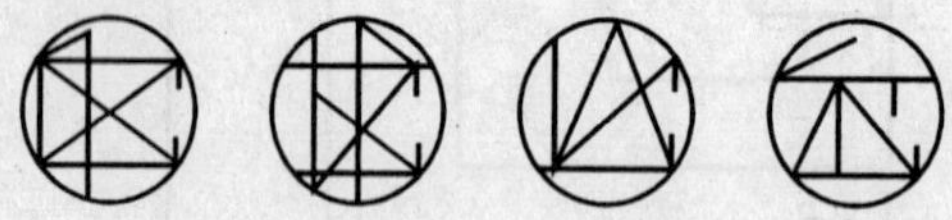

(A) (B) (C) (D)

Directions (Qs. 7 to 10) : *In each question given below find the figure form which is embedded in the given pattern.*

7. 

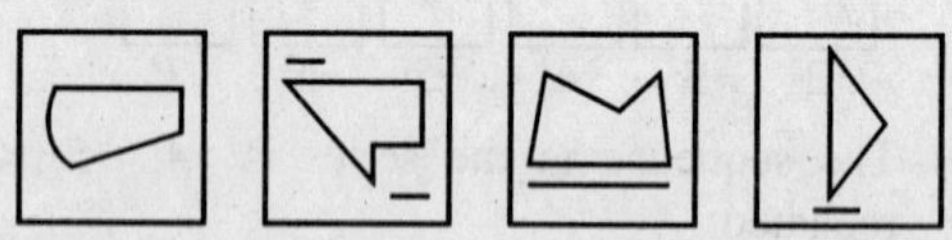

(A) (B) (C) (D)

8. 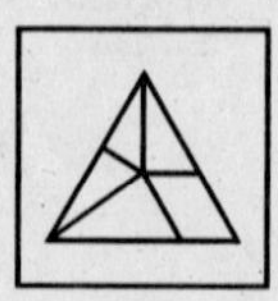

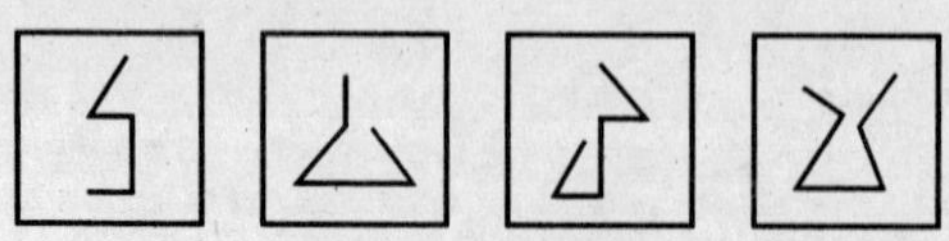

(A) (B) (C) (D)

9. 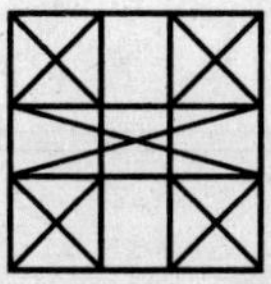

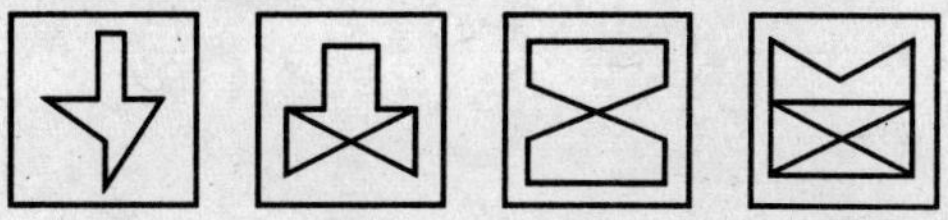

(A) (B) (C) (D)

10. 

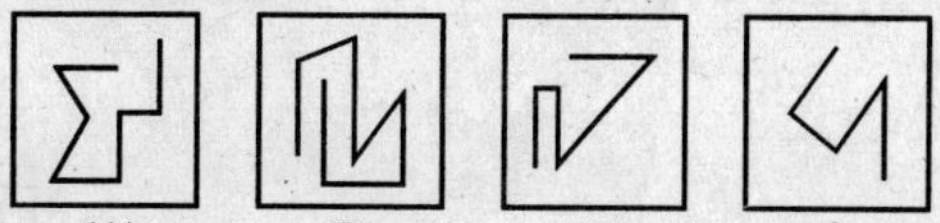

(A) (B) (C) (D)

EXPLANATORY ANSWERS

1. (A) : 

2. (A) : 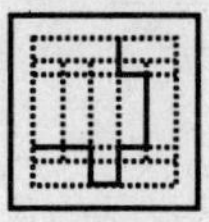

3. (D) : 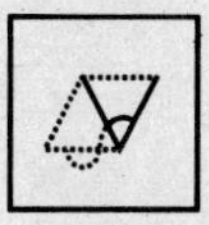

4. (B) : 

5. (A) : 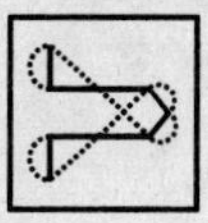

6. (B) : 

7. (D) : 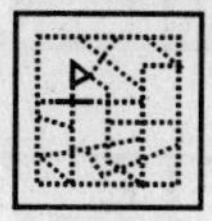

8. (B) : 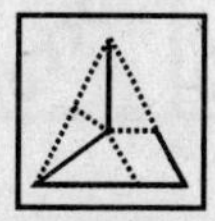

9. (C) : 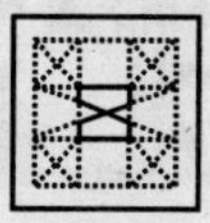

10. (D) : 

✤✤✤✤✤

19. FIGURAL SERIES

EXERCISE

Directions (Qs. 1–10) : *In each of the following questions which one of the five answer figures given below should come after the problem figures if the sequence are continued?*

Problem Figures | **Answer Figures**

1.  

(A) (B) (C) (D) (E)

2.  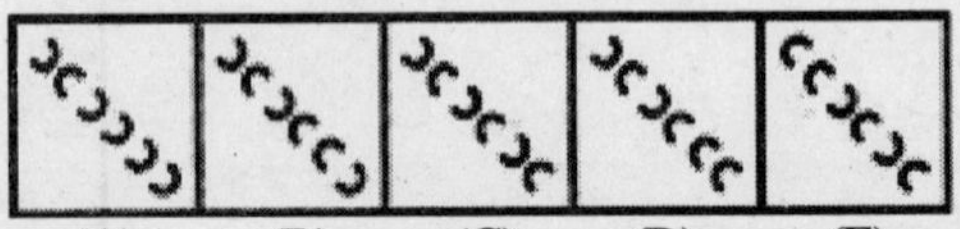

(A) (B) (C) (D) (E)

3. 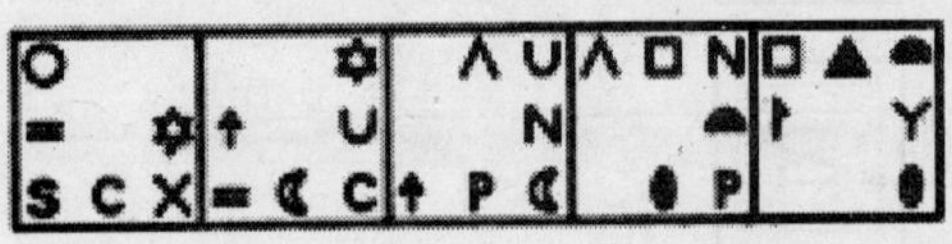 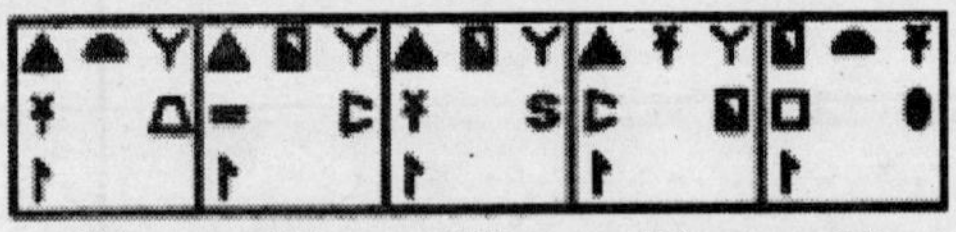

(A) (B) (C) (D) (E)

4.  

(A) (B) (C) (D) (E)

5.  

(A) (B) (C) (D) (E)

6.  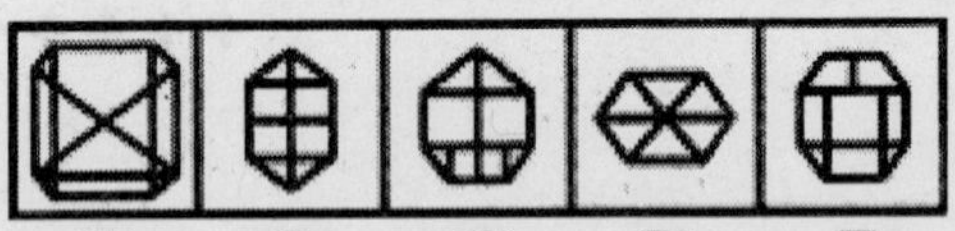

(A) (B) (C) (D) (E)

7.  

(A) (B) (C) (D) (E)

8. 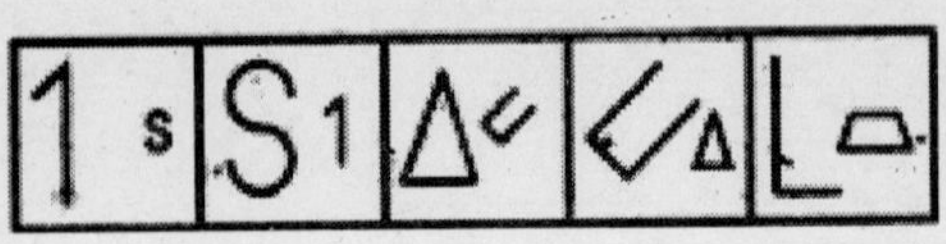 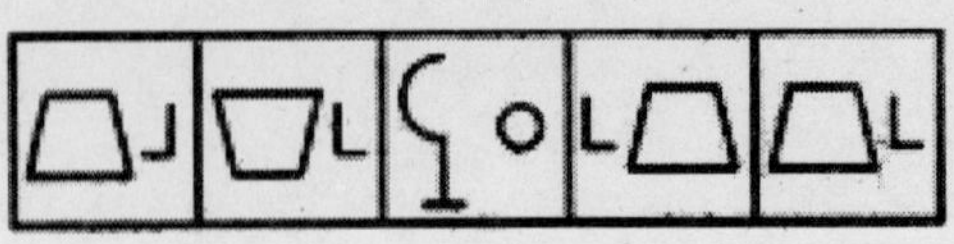

(A) (B) (C) (D) (E)

Problem Figures | **Answer Figures**

9. 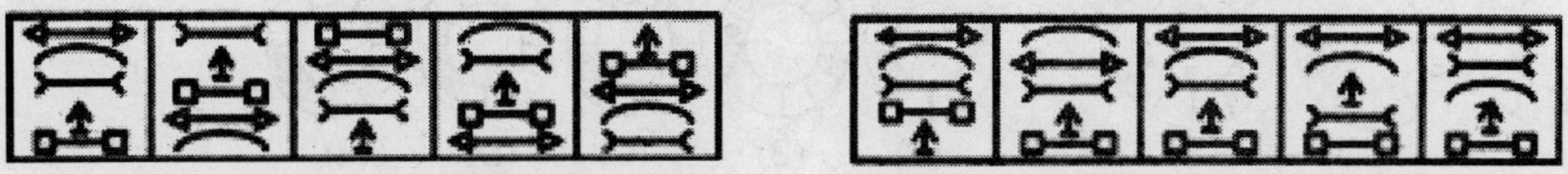

(A) (B) (C) (D) (E)

10. 

(A) (B) (C) (D) (E)

Directions (Qs. 11-20) : *In each of these questions, a series begins with an unmarked figure on the extreme left in the row of figures. One and only one of the five lettered figures in the series does not fit into the series. The two unmarked figures, one on the extreme left and the other on the extreme right fit into the series. Take as many aspects into account as possible of the figures in the series and find out the one and only of the five marked figures which does not fit into the series. The letter of that figure is the answer.*

11. 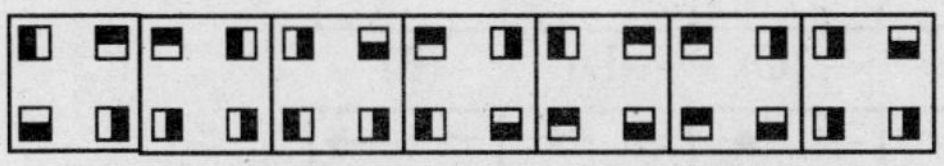

(A) (B) (C) (D) (E)

12. 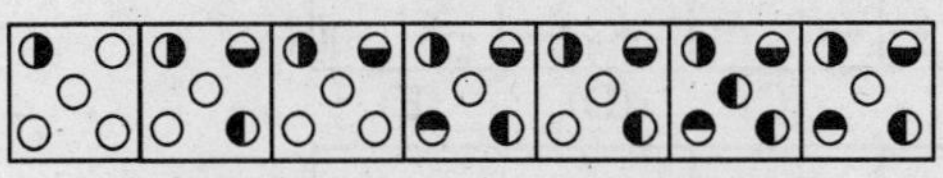

(A) (B) (C) (D) (E)

13. 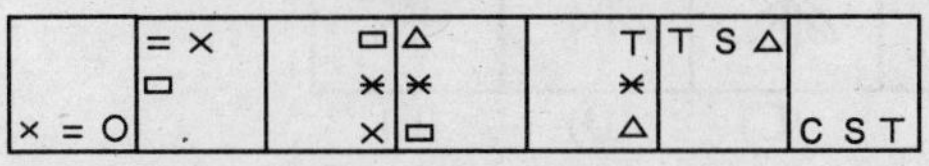

(A) (B) (C) (D) (E)

14. 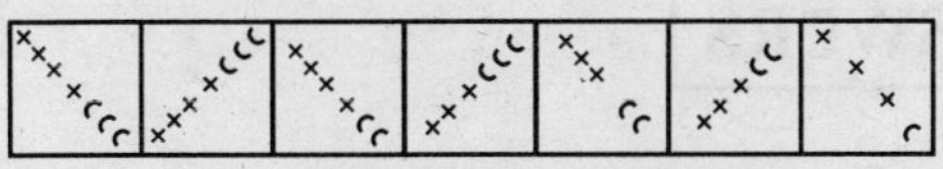

(A) (B) (C) (D) (E)

15. 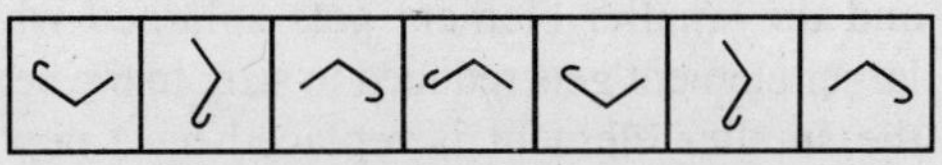

(A) (B) (C) (D) (E)

16. 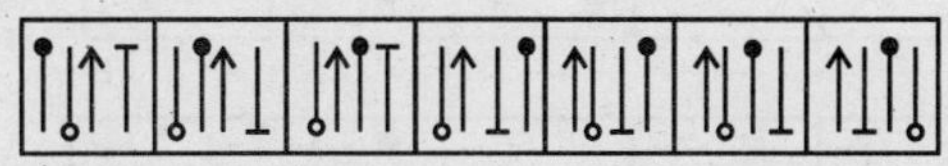

(A) (B) (C) (D) (E)

17. 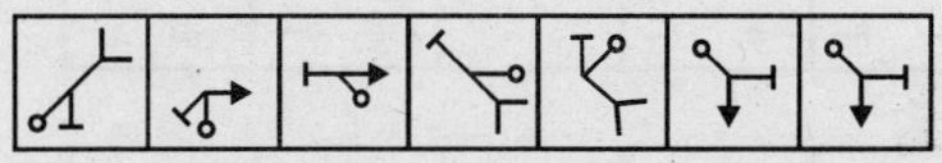

(A) (B) (C) (D) (E)

18. 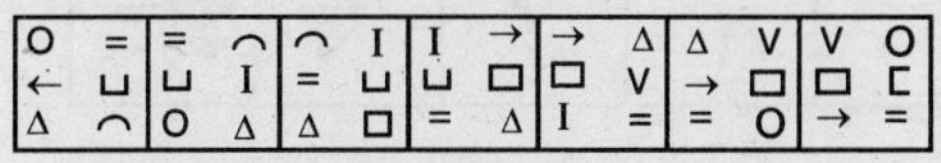

(A) (B) (C) (D) (E)

19. 

(A) (B) (C) (D) (E)

20. 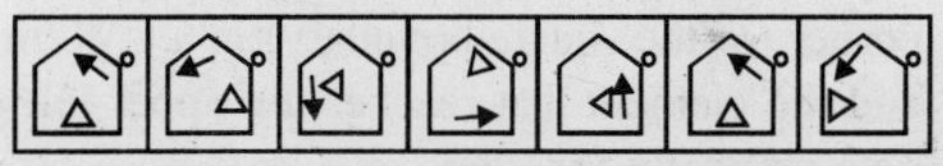

(A) (B) (C) (D) (E)

Directions (Qs. 21–30) : *Each of the following questions consist of problem figures followed by answer figures. Select a figure from amongst the answer figures which will continue the same series or pattern as established by the problem figures.*

Problem Figures | **Answer Figures**

21. 

(A) (B) (C) (D)

22. 

(A) (B) (C) (D) (E)

23. 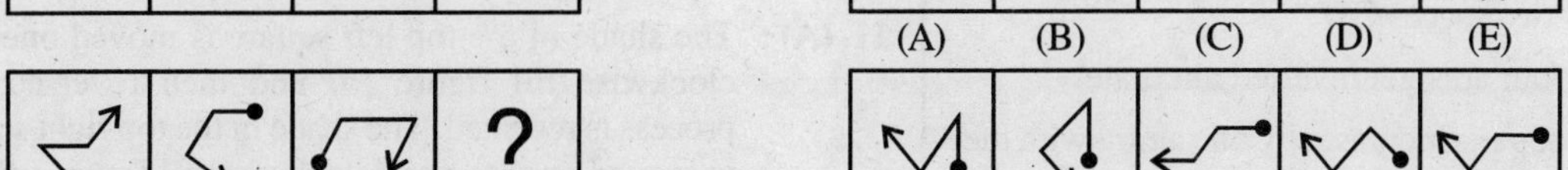

(A) (B) (C) (D) (E)

24. 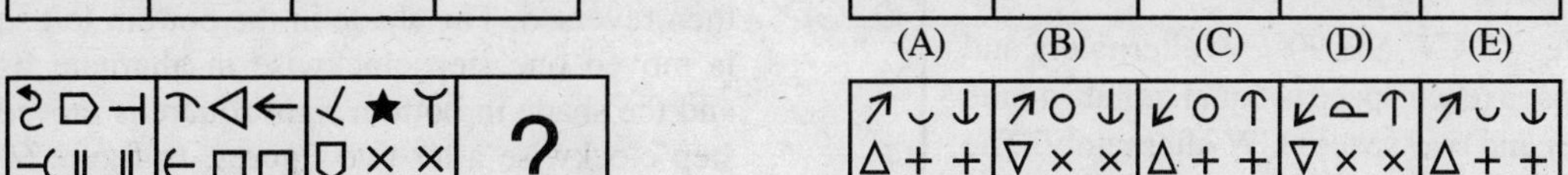

(A) (B) (C) (D) (E)

25. 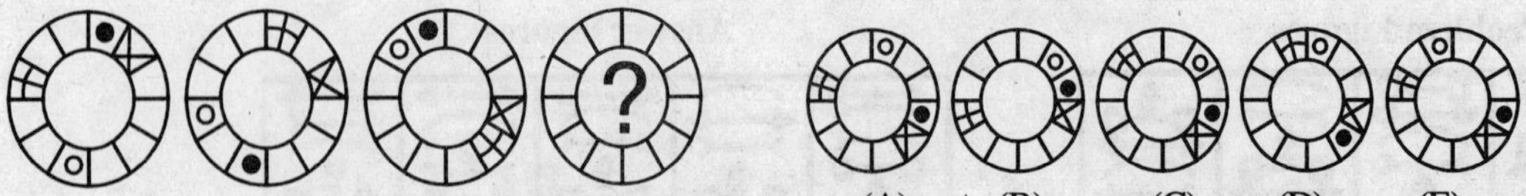

(A) (B) (C) (D) (E)

26. 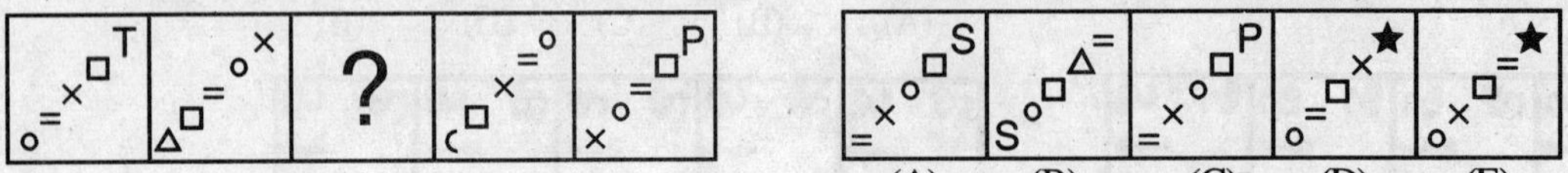

(A) (B) (C) (D) (E)

27. 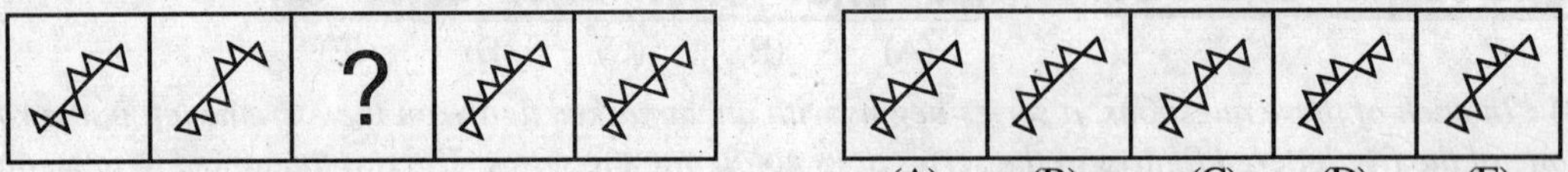

(A) (B) (C) (D) (E)

28. 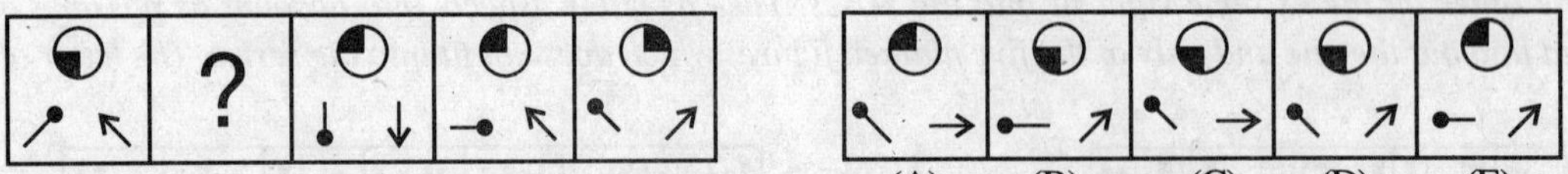

(A) (B) (C) (D) (E)

29. 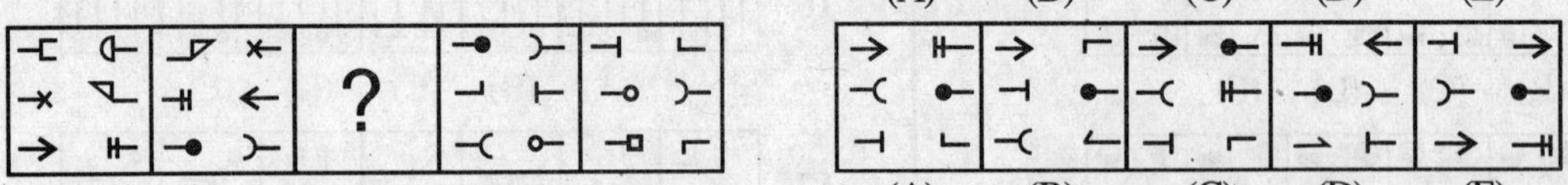

(A) (B) (C) (D) (E)

30. 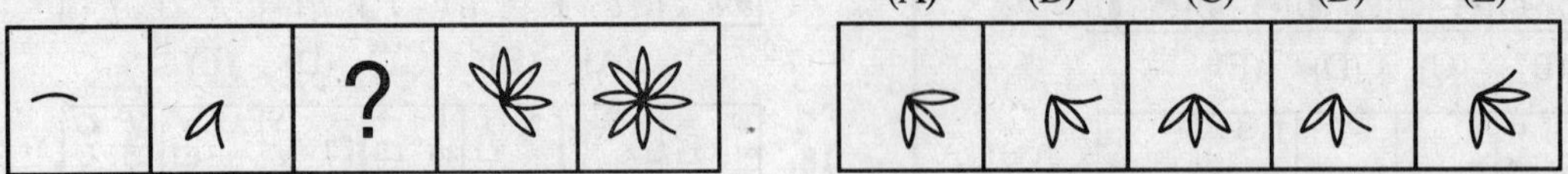

(A) (B) (C) (D) (E)

EXPLANATORY ANSWERS

1. (D) : In each step, all the elements move to the adjacent corner (of the square boundary) in a CW direction and the element that reaches the upper-left corner gets vertically inverted.

2. (C) : We can label the arcs as shown . The arcs get inverted in the sequence (1 & 2), (3, 4 & 5), (6 & 1), (2, 3 & 4), (5 & 6), ...

3. (D) : All the elements move half-a-side of the square boundary in ACW direction in each step. Also, first, third and fifth elements are replaced by new elements in one step and second, fourth and sixth elements are replaced by new elements in the next step. The two steps are repeated alternately.

4. (A) : In each step, the dot moves one space CW and the arrow moves two spaces CW.

5. (C) : One arc and four arcs get inverted alternately.

6. (E) : The number of parts increases by one along with the number of sides in the figure.

7. (C) : The pin rotates 45°CW and 90°CW alternately and moves one space (each space is equal to half-a-side of the square) and two spaces CW alternately. The arrow rotates 90°ACW and 45°ACW alternately and moves two spaces and one space.

8. (E) : In one step, the two elements interchange positions and the smaller element gets enlarged while the larger element gets reduced in size. In the next step, the smaller element is replaced by a new small element and the larger element is replaced by a new large element.

9. (C) : In each step, the elements move in the order .

10. (B) : The upper-left element gets laterally inverted in first, third, fifth. .... steps; the upper-right element gets rotated through 180° is first, fourth, seventh,.... steps; the lower-left element gets laterally inverted in second, fourth, sixth, ... steps; the lower-right element gets rotated through 180° in third, sixth,... steps and the pin at the middle-right position gets laterally inverted in every second step.

11. (A) : The shade in the top left square is moved one step clockwise till figure *(b)* and then reversed, the process is repeated. The shade in the top right square is moved one step anticlockwise till figure *(d)* and then reversed. The shade in the bottom left square is moved one step clockwise in alternate figures and the shade in bottom right square is moved one step clockwise after two figures. In figure *(a)* the rule is isolated by the shade in the bottom left square.

12. (E) : In alternate figures a new circle is shaded clockwise. The pattern of the shade is also moved clockwise. In figure *(e)* right half of the circle in the centre should have been shaded.

13. (A) : The three elements are placed either horizontally or vertically. In option *(a)* neither of the placements can be applied.

14. (C) : The placement of elements is same in alternate figures. The number and type of elements is same in two subsequent figures. In this manner, figure *(c)* should have four crosses and two C shapes.

15. (C) : The element is moved one step anticlockwise and the arc at one end is turned outside and inside alternately. In figure *(c)* the element should be on the right side with the arc turned outside on the top side.

16. (E) : The left most element, line segment with the dot is moved one step towards right till figure *(c)* where it reaches the extreme right position. This process is repeated from figure *(d)* where the element on the extreme left, line segment with a circle, is moved. In figure *(e)* the placement of the elements does not follow the rule of the series.

17. (E) : The 'T' line is rotated 45° clockwise and the line with the circle 45° anticlockwise. The 'Y' shape and the arrow are repeated twice after two figures. In option *(e)*, the 'T' shape and the line with the circle are rotated by 90°.

18. (E) : First the elements in the four corners are moved one step anticlockwise, next the four elements from the top are moved one step anticlockwise and then the four elements from the bottom are moved one step anticlockwise. Of the remaining two elements, the one on the left is made new each time and then their places are interchanged. This process is repeated from figure *(d)*. In option 'E' open square should have been in place of circle to continue the series.

19. (A) : At each step the outermost figure is removed and a new figure is placed right in the centre of other two figures. In option *(a)* the triangle is turned upside down, which violates the rule of the series.

20. (A) : The arrow is moved one step anticlockwise and the triangle one step clockwise. In figure *(a)* the triangle should have been on the left side of the figure.

21. (A) : The places of star, circle and square are moved one step clockwise at each step.

22. (E) : The elements in the four quadrants are moved one step clockwise and the elements at the ends of the cross are moved one step anticlockwise in this series.

23. (A) : In alternate figures, the line with the dot is turned 90° clockwise and the arrow 180° clockwise.

24. (E) : In alternate figures, the element in the top left position is horizontally inverted and moved one and half steps anticlockwise, the top middle element is turned 90° clockwise and moved one step anticlockwise, the top right element is turned 135° clockwise and moved one step anticlockwise, the element at the bottom is replaced by a new element and moved to the top middle position, and the two identical elements are replaced by two new identical elements.

25. (A) : The cross and the circle move one and two steps clockwise respectively (at each step), the plus moves 3, 4 and 5 steps clockwise, and the dot 6, 5 and 4 steps clockwise.

26. (A) : At first step, the fifth or the bottom most element is moved to the second place from top, the second element moved to the fourth place, the fourth element is moved to the third place, the third element is moved to the first or the topmost place and the element on the top, which is made new, is moved to the last or the fifth place. At second step i.e., from second problem figure to third problem figure the above process is reversed. The bottom most element is the first and the top most element is the last or fifth. Hereafter, the process is repeated from the beginning. Option *(a)* is the right answer.

27. (C) : Starting from the bottom, one triangle is moved to the opposite side at each step in upward order. Option *(c)* fits into the question marked space.

28. (C) : The shade inside the circle is rotated clockwise in alternate figures; the line segment with a dot is rotated 135° clockwise in alternate figures and the arrow is rotated 135° anticlockwise in alternate figures. By this process answer figure *(c)* completes the series.

29. (A) : At each step the elements are moved diagonally upward and then laterally inverted, and the top two elements are made new and placed at the bottom line. By this process, option figure *(a)* completes the series.

30. (A) : The number of arcs making the petals of the flower are increased by one, one and half, two, two and half respectively at each step. Also, the flower is turned 45° anticlockwise. By this process, option *(a)* is the right answer.

✤✤✤✤✤

20. CRITICAL THINKING

In this type of reasoning, a statement is given and assumptions are drawn from it. An assumption is something assumed, supposed and taken for granted. The implicity of the two assumptions is in question. The implication means the hidden meaning, something which is derived from and as such based upon the statement.

EXERCISE

Directions (Qs. 1 to 6): *In each question below are given two statements followed by two conclusions numbered I and II. You have to take the two given statements to be true even if they seem to be at variance from commonly known facts and then decide which of the given conclusions logically follows from the two given statements, disregarding commonly known facts. Read both the statements and—*

Give answer (A) if only conclusion I follows; give answer (B) if only conclusion II follows; give answer (C) if either I or II follows; give answer (D) if neither I nor II follows and give answer (E) if both I and II follows.

1. *Statements* *I*: All tomatoes are red.
II: All grapes are tomatoes.
Conclusions *I*: All grapes are red.
II: Some tomatoes are grapes.

2. *Statements* *I*: All painters are smiling.
II: Some authors are painters.
Conclusions *I*: All smiling authors are painters.
II: Some authors are smiling.

3. *Statements* *I*: All peons in this office are efficient.
II: Ramu is not efficient.
Conclusions *I*: Ramu is not peon in this office.
II: Ramu should be more efficient.

4. *Statements* *I*: All weavers are hard working.
II: No hard working men are foolish.
Conclusions *I*: No weavers are foolish.
II: Some foolish are weavers.

5. *Statements* *I*: All fishes are cars.
II: All cars are vegetables.
Conclusions *I*: Some vegetables are cars.
II: Some vegetables are fishes.

6. *Statements* *I*: Some dogs are pups.
II: All horses are pups.

Directions (Qs. 7 to 9): *In each question below is given a statement followed by three assumptions number I, II and III. An assumption is something supposed or taken for granted. You have to consider the statement along with the assumptions and decide which of the assumptions is implicit in the statement. Then decide which of the alternatives is the correct answer.*

7. *Statement :*

"Use Riya Cold Cream for fair complexion"—an advertisement.

Assumptions :

I. People like to use cream for fair complexion.
II. People are easily fooled.
III. People respond to advertisements.

A. Only I is implicit.
B. Only II is implicit.
C. Only I and III are implicit.
D. Only I and II are implicit.
E. All are implicit.

8. *Statement :*

"Slogans against smoking in office should be put on the notice board"—an employee in an office suggests.

Assumptions :

I. The employee felt that his suggestion will be considered.
II. People smoke in the office.
III. Some people will stop smoking after reading the slogans.

A. Only I is implicit.
B. Only I and II are implicit.
C. Only II and III are implicit.
D. None is implicit.
E. All are implicit.

9. *Statement :*

"I want to present him a book on techniques of yoga on his birthday"—A tells B.

Assumptions :

I. A and B will be invited for the birthday celebrations.
II. The person to whom the book is to be presented, is not keeping good health.
III. Book is the best gift for birthdays.

A. Only I and II are implicit.
B. Only II and III are implicit.
C. Only I and III are implicit.
D. None is implicit.
E. All are implicit

EXPLANATORY ANSWERS

1. (E) : When all tomatoes are red and all grapes are tomatoes, then all grapes are also red. When all grapes are tomatoes, then some tomatoes must be grapes. Therefore, both conclusions I and II are correct.

2. (B) : When all painters are smiling and some authors are painters, then some authors are smiling. Therefore, only conclusion II is correct.

3. (A) : When all the peons of the office are efficient, then Ramu cannot be a peon in this office. Therefore, only conclusion I is correct.

4. (A) : When all weavers are hardworking and no hardworking men are foolish, then no weavers are foolish. Therefore, only conclusion I is correct.

5. (E) : When all fishes are cars and all cars are vegetables, then all fishes will naturally be vegetables. This means that some vegetables are fishes. And when all cars are vegetables, then some vegetables will be cars naturally. Therefore, both the conclusions I and II are correct.

6. (D) : No relationship can be established between the two statements. There-fore, neither conclusion I nor conclusion II is correct.

7. (C) : The advertisement itself denotes that people like to use cream for fair complexion and they do respond to advertisements. Advertisements are for awareness of the product not for fooling people.

8. (E) : Suggestion for putting up the notice is made because some people must be smoking in office. Notice board is read by people in office and some may stop smoking after reading the slogans.

9. (C) : According to A presents are best gifts for birthdays and when A has bought the book he expects to be invited for the birthday celebration. Nothing is mentioned about health of the birthday person.

✤✤✤✤✤

21. PROBLEM SOLVING

Number problems consists of number sequences, problems with algebraic expressions, mathematical calculations and other compatiable problems.

EXERCISE

1. How many 6's are there in the following series of numbers which are preceded by 7 but not immediately followed by 9?

6 7 9 5 6 9 7 6 8 7 6 7 8 6 9 4 6 7 7 6 9 5 7 6 3

A. One B. Two
C. Three D. Four

2. In a chess tournament each of six players will play every other player exactly once. How many matches will be played during the tournament?

A. 12 B. 15
C. 30 D. 36

3. How many 4's are there in the following series which are preceded by 7, but are not preceded by 8?

3 4 5 7 4 3 7 4 8 5 4 3 7 4 9 8 4 7 2 7 4 1 3 6

A. 1 B. 2
C. 3 D. 4

4. How many even numbers are there in the following series of numbers, each of which is immediately preceded by an odd number, but not immediately followed by an even number?

5 3 4 8 9 7 1 6 5 3 2 9 8 4 3 5

A. Nil B. 1
C. 2 D. 3

5. If all the numbers from 1 to 51 which are exactly divisible by 3 are arranged in descending order, which of the following numbers will come at the seventh and tenth places from the top?

A. 33 & 27 B. 33 & 21
C. 21 & 30 D. 33 & 24

6. Nitin was counting down from 32. Shasank was counting upwards, the numbers starting from 1 and he was calling out only the odd numbers. Which common number will they call out at the same time if they were calling out at the same speed?

A. 21
B. 22
C. 19
D. They will not call out the same number

7. In the following list of numerals, how many 3s are followed by 3, but NOT preceded by 3?

2 4 6 3 3 1 5 7 8 3 3 3 4 6 2 3 3 3 3 9 7 2 3

A. 1 B. 2
C. 3 D. 4

8. If in a given number 5 8 9 4 3 2 7 6 1 4, we interchange the first and the second digits, the third and the fourth, the fifth and the sixth and so on, then counting from the right end, which digit will be sixth?

A. 3 B. 2
C. 4 D. 5

9. Aparna cuts a cake into two halves and cuts one-half into smaller pieces of equal size. Each of the small pieces is twenty grams in weight. If she has seven pieces of the cake in all with her, how heavy was the original cake?

A. 140 grams B. 280 grams
C. 240 grams D. 120 grams

10. In the following number sequence how many such even numbers are there which are exactly divisible by its immediate preceding number but not exactly divisible by its immediate following number?

3 8 4 1 5 7 2 8 3 4 8 9 3 9 4 2 1 5 8 2

A. Two B. Three
C. Four D. More than four

11. How many 7s are there in the following series which are not immediately followed by 3 but immediately preceded by 8?

8 9 8 7 6 2 2 6 3 2 6 9 7 3 2 8 7 2 7 7 8 7 3 7 7 9 4

A. Nil B. One
C. Two D. Three

12. How many 9's are there in the following sequence which are neither preceded by 6 nor immediately followed by 3?

9 3 8 6 9 9 5 9 3 7 8 9 9 9 3 9 6 3 9

A. One B. Two
C. Three D. Four

13. If a number is five times as great as another number which is four less than forty, then the number is :

A. 220 B. 180
C. 144 D. 200

14. If 2/3rd of a number is 96, what will be the 3/4th of that number?

A. 108 B. 198
C. 128 D. 48

15. If such numbers which are divisible by 5, and also those which have 5 as one of the digits are eliminated from the numbers 1 to 60, how many numbers would remain?

A. 53 B. 47
C. 40 D. 45

16. How many 8's are there in the following number series which are exactly divisible by its immediately preceding and also exactly divisible by immediately succeeding numbers?

8 2 4 5 1 7 2 8 4 8 4 2 2 8 2 6 9 8 4 5 4 8

3 2 8 4 3 1 8 3

A. 1 B. 2
C. 3 D. 4

17. Jagan was to either get one-seventh of a milk chocolate or one-fourteenth of a bigger fruit chocolate. Which chocolate would give him the larger piece if the fruit chocolate is three times as large as the milk chocolate?

A. Milk chocolate
B. Fruit chocolate
C. The pieces will be of the same size
D. Information inadequate

18. How many such 3's are there in the following number sequence which are immediately preceded by an odd number and immediately followed by an even number?

5 3 8 9 4 3 7 2 3 8 1 3 8 4 2 3 5 7 3 4 2 3 6

A. One B. Two
C. Three D. Four

19. Count each 7 which is not immediately preceded by 5 but is immediately followed by either 2 or 3. How many such 7's are there?

5 7 2 6 5 7 3 8 3 7 3 2 5 7 2 7 3 4 8 2 6 7 8

A. 2 B. 3
C. 4 D. 5

20. A number is four less than two times the other number. If their difference is 21, what is the greater number?

A. 50 B. 46
C. 31 D. 21

EXPLANATORY ANSWERS

1. (C) : $679569\underset{1}{\underline{768}}\underset{2}{\underline{767}}8694677695\underset{3}{\underline{763}}$

2. (B) : When all the players have to play with each other then the method of calculating the number of matches to be played is $\frac{n(n-1)}{2}$ where *'n'* is the number of players playing the match. So, the number of matches played will be :
$(6 \times 5) \div 2 = 30 \div 2 = 15$

3. (D) : $345\underset{1}{\underline{74}}3\underset{2}{\underline{74}}8543\underset{3}{\underline{74}}98472\underset{4}{\underline{74}}136$

4. (C) : $534897\underset{1}{\underline{165}}\underset{2}{\underline{329}}8435$

5. (D) : The numbers divisible by 3 in descending order are:
51, 48, 45, 42, 39, 36, $\underset{7th}{\underline{33,}}$ 30, 27, $\underset{10th}{\underline{24,}}$ 21,
18, 15, 12, 9, 6, 3.

6. (D) : When Nitin is on count 22, Shasank is on 21 and when Nitin is on count 21, Shasank is on 23.

7. (C) : $246\underset{1}{\underline{33}}1578\underset{2}{\underline{33}}3462\underset{3}{\underline{33}}339723$

8. (B) : The new number after interchanging the digits is :
8549236741
↑___|
6th

9. (C) : There is one bigger piece and six smaller pieces. One small piece weighs 20 gm. Total weight of six smaller speices is 120 gm.
∴ Weight of the bigger piece = 120 gm
∴ Weight of the original cake = 240 gm

10. (A) : $384157\underset{1}{\underline{28}}3\underset{2}{\underline{48}}939421582$

11. (C) : 8987622632697328727787377 94

1 2

12. (D) : 9 3 8 6 9 9 5 9 3 7 8 9 9 9 3 9 6 3 9

1 2 3 4

13. (B) : Number four less than forty is $40 - 4 = 36$
Five times the number is $= 36 \times 5 = 180$

14. (A) : If the number is x, then

$$\frac{2}{3}x = 96$$

$$x = \frac{96 \times 3}{2} = 144$$

$\frac{3}{4}$ th of the number is $144 \times \frac{3}{4} = 108$

15. (C) : The eliminated twenty numbers are : 5, 10, 15, 20, 25, 30, 35, 40, 45 and 50 to 60. The remaining numbers are $60 - 20 = 40$.

16. (D) : 8 2 4 5 1 7 2 8 4 8 4 2 2 8 2 6 9 8 4 5 4 8 3 2 8 4 3 1 8 3

1 2 3 4

17. (B) : If fruit chocolate (F) is equal to three times as milk chocolate (M) then —

$$F = 3\,M$$

or

$$\frac{F}{M} = 3$$

$$\therefore \quad \frac{1/14\,F}{1/7\,M} = \frac{3/14}{1/7}$$

When $3/14 > 1/7$, then F (Fruit chocolate) will give him the larger piece.

18. (C) : 5 3 8 9 4 3 7 2 3 8 1 3 8 4 2 3 5 7 3 4 2 3 6

1 2 3

19. (A) : 5 7 2 6 5 7 3 8 3 7 3 2 5 7 2 7 3 4 8 2 6 7 8

1 2

20. (B) : If smaller number is x, then

$$(2x - 4) - x = 21$$

$$2x - x = 21 + 4$$

$$x = 25$$

The greater number is

$$(25 \times 2) - 4 = 46$$

✤ ✤ ✤ ✤ ✤

22. EMOTIONAL INTELLIGENCE

Emotional intelligence (EI) refers to the ability to perceive, control, and evaluate emotions. Emotional intelligence (EI) is the area of cognitive ability involving traits and social skills that facilitate interpersonal behaviour. Intelligence can be broadly defined as the capacity for goal-oriented adaptive behaviour; emotional intelligence focuses on the aspects of intelligence that govern self-knowledge and social adaptation.

Emotional Intelligence that is also called Emotional Intelligence Quotient or (EQ) narrates the capability, capacity, or deftness to understand. It evaluates and manages one's emotions.

EXERCISE

Directions: *Answer the following questions by selecting the appropriate option.*

1. In my group of friends, I am generally aware of how each person feels about the other people in our social circle.
A. Strongly Agree B. Agree
C. Disagree D. Strongly Disagree

2. When I am upset, I can usually pinpoint exactly why I am distressed.
A. Strongly Agree B. Agree
C. Disagree D. Strongly Disagree

3. While there are some things that I would like to change, I generally like who I am.
A. Strongly Agree B. Agree
C. Disagree D. Strongly Disagree

4. When I make mistakes, I often berate and criticize myself and my abilities.
A. Often B. Sometimes
C. Rarely D. Almost Never

5. I feel uncomfortable in emotionally charged situations.
A. Strongly Agree B. Agree
C. Disagree D. Strongly Disagree

6. I tend to avoid confrontations. When I am involved in a confrontation, I become extremely anxious.
A. Strongly Agree B. Agree
C. Disagree D. Strongly Disagree

7. I am generally aloof and detached until I really get to know a person.
A. Strongly Agree B. Agree
C. Disagree D. Strongly Disagree

8. I tend to overreact to minor problems.
A. Often B. Sometimes
C. Rarely D. Almost Never

9. I feel confident about my own skills, talents, and abilities.
A. Strongly Agree B. Agree
C. Disagree D. Strongly Disagree

10. I would describe myself as a good judge of character.
A. Strongly Agree B. Agree
C. Disagree D. Strongly Disagree

11. When I am facing an unpleasant task, I tend to:
A. Make a plan and work on it a little each day
B. Get it over with as soon as possible
C. Put it off until the last minute
D. Don't do it at all

12. During a heated argument, I am more likely to:
A. Stop the fight and agree to a short break before resuming the discussion.
B. Shut down and stop responding to the other person.
C. Give in and apologize in order to quickly end the argument.
D. Start insulting the other person.

13. When making an important decision, I tend to:
A. Follow my instincts
B. Rely on direction from other people
C. Go with the easiest option
D. Guess randomly

14. Which of the following statements best describes you?
A. I have an easy time making friends and getting to know new people.
B. I get along well with others, but I have to really get to know someone before they become a true friend.

C. I find it difficult to meet people and make friends.
D. I cannot make friends.

15. You have invested a lot of time and energy into a project for one of your classes. While you feel confident about your work, your instructor gives you a C+ on the project. How do you deal with this situation?
A. Decide the class is stupid and stop putting forth your best efforts.
B. Berate and criticize your own work.
C. Confront the instructor and ask for a better grade.
D. Think about ways you could improve the project and apply these ideas to future schoolwork.

16. One of your best friends has suffered a miscarriage. How do you respond?
A. Allow your friend to express her feelings and offer your support.
B. Spend time with her, but avoid talking about her loss.
C. Convince her to go out with some friends to get her mind off it.
D. Give her some time to herself.

17. One of your co-workers has a habit that annoys you. The problem seems to be getting worse each day. How do you respond?
A. Tell your co-worker what is bothering you.
B. Make a complaint about the behaviour to your supervisor.
C. Talk about your co-worker behind his back.
D. Suffer in silence.

18. You've been feeling stressed out at work and haven't finished projects as quickly as you should. When your boss suddenly assigns you another large project, how do you feel?
A. Anxious about getting all the work done.
B. Overwhelmed by the task before you.
C. Angry that your boss hasn't noticed how overworked you are.
D. Depressed and sure that you can never finish it all.

19. If I am scheduled to meet a loved one at a certain time and that person is late, I get worried and eventually start to panic:
A. Frequently B. Sometimes
C. Rarely D. Never

20. Others do not want to spend time with me in public because my behaviour embarrasses them.
A. Frequently B. Sometimes
C. Rarely D. Never

21. I prevent being in situations where I need to show compassion and affection because I feel uncomfortable comforting others.
A. Frequently B. Sometimes
C. Rarely D. Never

22. When I am angry, I do not care about what I say or do and end up saying and doing things I regret later and need to apologize for.
A. Frequently B. Sometimes
C. Rarely D. Never

23. I feel frequently depressed and unhappy without really knowing why.
A. Frequently B. Sometimes
C. Rarely D. Never

24. If others point out my mistakes or give me negative feedback about myself, I feel ashamed, embarrassed and then become offensive and angry.
A. Frequently
B. Sometimes
C. Rarely
D. Never

25. Crying makes me feel better so I frequently cry when I am angry, ashamed, or embarrassed.
A. Frequently B. Sometimes
C. Rarely D. Never

ANSWERS

1	2	3	4	5	6	7	8	9	10
B	B	A	B	D	D	C	D	A	B
11	**12**	**13**	**14**	**15**	**16**	**17**	**18**	**19**	**20**
A	A	A	A	D	A	A	A	C	D
21	**22**	**23**	**24**	**25**					
D	D	D	D	D					

✤✤✤✤✤

23. ARITHMETICAL REASONING

EXERCISE

Directions (1–5) : *The following questions are based on the information given below :*

Data of 450 candidates, who took part in an examination in Social Science, Mathematics and Science is given below:

Passed in all the subject	167
Failed in all the subject	60
Failed in Mathematics	199
Failed in Social Science	175
Failed in Science	191
Passed in Science only	52
Passed in Mathematics only	48
Passed in Social Science only	62

1. How many passed in at least one subject?
A. 450 B. 390
C. 304 D. 167

2. How many failed in two subjects only?
A. 56 B. 61
C. 152 D. 162

3. How many passed in Mathematics and at least in one more subject?
A. 210 B. 203
C. 170 D. 94

4. How many failed in Social Science only?
A. 15 B. 21
C. 30 D. 42

5. How many failed in one subject only?
A. 152 B. 144
C. 61 D. 56

6. A, B, C, D and E play a game of cards. A says to B, "If you give me three cards, you will have as many as E has and if I give you three cards, you will have as many as D has." A and B together have 10 cards more than what D and E together have. If B has two cards more than what C has and the total number of cards be 133, how many cards does B have?
A. 22 B. 35
C. 25 D. 23

7. A bus starts from city X. The number of women in the bus is half of the number of men. In the city Y, 10 men left the bus and five women entered. Now, number of men and women is equal. In the beginning, how many passenger entered the bus?
A. 15 B. 30
C. 36 D. 45

8. I have a few sweets to be distributed. If I keep 2, 3 or 4 in a pack, I am left with one sweet. If I keep 5 in a pack, I am left with none. What is the minimum number of sweets I can have to pack and distributed?
A. 25 B. 37
C. 54 D. 65

9. A, B, C, D and E play a game of cards. A says to B, "If you give me 3 cards, you will have as many as I have at this moment while if D takes 5 cards from you, he will have as many as E has", A and C together have twice as many cards as E has B and D together also have the same number of cards as A and C taken together. I all together they have 150 cards, how many cards has C got?
A. 28 B. 29
C. 31 D. 35

EXPLANATORY ANSWERS

1. (B) : Candidates passed at least in one subject = (Candidates passed in only one subjects) + (Candidates passed in only two subjects) + (Candidates passed in only all subjects).

(Candidates failed in only two subjects) + (Candidates failed in only one subject) + (Candidates passed in all the subject)
= 162 + 61 + 167 = 390.

2. (D) : Candidates failed in two subjects only
= Candidates passed in one subjects only
= 62 + 48 + 52
= 162.

3. (B) : Candidates failed in science only
= 191 – (62 + 60 + 48)
= 21

Candidates failed in one social science only = 15
Therefore, candidates passed in maths and at least one more subject
= (21 + 15 + 167)
= 203

4. (A) : Candidates failed in social science only = (candidates failed in social science) – (candidates failed in all subjects + candidates passed in science only + candidates passed in maths only)
= 175 – (60 + 52 + 48)
= 175 – 160
= 15.

5. (C) : Candidates failed in one subject only
= (total number of candidates) – (candidates passed in all subjects + candidates failed in all the subjects + candidates passed in one subject only)
= 450 – (167 + 60 + 62 + 48 + 52)
= 450 – 389
= 61.

6. (C) : From the questions, we have
B – 3 = E ...... (i)
B + 3 = D ...... (ii)
A + B = D + E + 10 ...... (iii)
B = C + 2 ...... (iv)
A + B + C + D + E = 133 ...... (v)
From (i) and (ii)
B – E = D – B ⇒ E + D = 2 B ...... (vi)
From (iii) and (vi)
A + B = 2B + 10 ⇒ B = A – 10
or, A = B + 10 ...... (vii)
From (v), (vi), (iv) and (vii) we have
(B + 10) + (B) + (B – 2) + 2B = 133
5B = 133 – 8
= 125
= 25.

7. (D) : In the city X let the number of men be x

Then the number of women be $\frac{x}{2}$.

In the city y, $x - 10 = \frac{x}{2} + 5$

or, $\frac{x}{2} = 15$ or, $x = 30$ and $y = 15$.

Therefore, total number of passenger at the beginning were 30 + 15 = 45.

8. (A) : The required number will be obtained by taking LCM of 2, 3 and 4 and adding 1 into it. The number so obtained is 25.

9. (A) : From the questions it is clear that
B – 3 = A ...... (1)
D + 5 = E ...... (2)
A + C = 2 E ...... (3)
A + C = B + D ...... (4)
A + B + C + D + E = 150 ...... (5)
From (3), (4) and (5) we get
5E = 150
∴ E = 30
Now from (2) D = 30 – 5 = 25
and from (4) A = 32
Now from (3) 32 + C = 2 × 30
C = 60 – 32 = 28.

✤ ✤ ✤ ✤ ✤

24. WORD BUILDING

These are spellings, word order and dictionary related questions. The candidate is given a word and asked to select the word that can/cannot be formed from its spellings. He/she may be asked to decide the meaningful order of the given words. He/she may also be asked to arrange the given words in the sequence in which they occur in the dictionary.

EXERCISE

Directions (Qs. No. 1 to 12): *From the given alternatives select the word which **cannot** be formed using the letters of the given word.*

1. REPUBLICAN
A. CLIP B. PURE
C. ANKLE D. BANE

2. ESTRANGE
A. GENERATE B. SERGEANT
C. REAGENTS D. GREAT

3. DETERMINATION
A. DETENTION B. DESTINATION
C. TERMINATE D. DOMINATE

4. CHRISTMAS
A. CHRIST B. SMART
C. CRUST D. HARM

5. LEGALIZATION
A. ALERT B. ALEGATION
C. GALLANT D. NATAL

6. CHARACTER
A. CRATE B. CHARTER
C. HEARTY D. TRACER

7. ADMINISTRATION
A. Station B. Minister
C. Ration D. Mind

8. ORGANISATION
A. ORGAN B. ORGANISE
C. NATION D. ORATION

9. PERAMBULATOR
A. RAMPANT B. LABOUR
C. MARBLE D. RAMBLE

10. POSSESSION
A. SESSION B. POSE
C. POISE D. OBSESS

11. PRINTINGS
A. SAINT B. PRINT
C. STING D. RINGS

12. QUALIFICATION
A. LIAR B. FIAT
C. LION D. FICTION

13. From the given alternatives select the word which can be formed using the letters given in the word.

ULTRANATIONALISM
A. ULTRAMONTANE
B. ULTRAMODERN
C. ULTRAIST
D. ULULATE

14. A meaningful word starting with R is made from the first, second, fourth, fifth and eighth letters of the word CREATIVE. Which of the following is the middle letter of the word?
A. E B. T
C. C D. A

Directions (Qs. No. 15 to 18): *Which one of the given responses would be a meaningful order of the following words?*

15. 1. Amoeba 2. Oyster
3. Worm 4. Cow
A. 1, 3, 2, 4 B. 1, 2, 3, 4
C. 4, 3, 2, 1 D. 3, 2, 4, 1

16. 1. Birth 2. Death
3. Childhood 4. Infancy
5. Adolescence 6. Adulthood
7. Old age
A. 2, 6, 7, 5, 4, 3, 1
B. 1, 4, 3, 5, 6, 7, 2
C. 1, 4, 3, 6, 5, 7, 2
D. 2, 7, 6, 4, 5, 3, 1

17. 1. Police 2. Punishment
3. Crime 4. Judge
4. Judgement
A. 3, 1, 2, 4, 5 B. 1, 2, 4, 3, 5
C. 5, 4, 3, 2, 1 D. 3, 1, 4, 5, 2

18. 1. Orange 2. Indigo
3. Red 4. Blue
5. Green 6. Yellow
7. Violet
A. 7, 2, 4, 5, 6, 1, 3
B. 7, 2, 4, 6, 5, 1, 3
C. 7, 2, 6, 4, 5, 1, 3
D. 7, 2, 6, 4, 1, 5, 3

Directions (Qs. No. 19 to 24): *Arrange the given words in the sequence in which they occur in the dictionary.*

19. 1. Clone 2. Climate
3. Clutter 4. Create
5. Clapped
A. 52143 B. 51234
C. 52134 D. 53124

20. 1. Lasted 2. Loop
3. Lake 4. Litter
5. Listed
A. 31542 B. 31254
C. 31245 D. 31452

21. 1. Intricate 2. Interview
3. Intransigent 4. Interrogation
5. Intravenous
A. 2, 4, 5, 3, 1 B. 5, 3, 1, 2, 4
C. 4, 2, 3, 5, 1 D. 3, 5, 2, 1, 4

22. 1. Forge 2. Forget
3. Forgo 4. Forgive
5. Format
A. 1, 2, 4, 3, 5 B. 5, 2, 4, 3, 1
C. 1, 4, 3, 2, 5 D. 3, 4, 5, 2, 1

23. 1. Forecast 2. Forget
3. Foreign 4. Forsook
5. Force
A. 3, 5, 1, 2, 4 B. 5, 1, 3, 2, 4
C. 5, 1, 3, 4, 2 D. 5, 1, 2, 3, 4

24. 1. Fenestration 2. Feather
3. Feed head 4. Feature
5. Feminine
A. 2, 4, 3, 5, 1 B. 4, 2, 3, 1, 5
C. 2, 4, 1, 5, 3 D. 4, 2, 3, 5, 1

25. Arrange the given words in the sequence in which they occur in the Dictionary and locate the last word.
A. Frankenstein B. Frankincense
C. Frankalmoign D. Frauendienst

ANSWERS

1	2	3	4	5	6	7	8	9	10
C	A	B	C	A	C	B	B	A	D
11	**12**	**13**	**14**	**15**	**16**	**17**	**18**	**19**	**20**
A	A	C	D	A	B	D	A	C	D
21	**22**	**23**	**24**	**25**					
C	A	B	A	D					

✤✤✤✤✤

25. SOCIAL INTELLIGENCE

Questions on social intelligence are asked to assess the common sense of the candidate in various social situations.

EXERCISE

Directions : *Each of the following questions is followed by four alternatives. Select the most appropriate answer.*

1. In the examination hall, you find that your question paper is too tough to be answered satisfactorily by you. The best thing you can do is:

A. try cheating from your neighbouring candidate.
B. leave the paper and walk out.
C. try attempting those questions first of which you know something.
D. complain to the examiner about the toughness of the question paper.

2. Your best friend is annoyed with you for certain reasons. You will :

A. try your best to reason out your friend's annoyance.
B. go out and make new friends.
C. show indifference.
D. remind the friend of your good friendship.

3. You were invited to a party, but on the day of the party you are informed that the party has been cancelled. You will :

A. try to find out the reason for its cancellation.
B. decide that you will never go to that place ever again.
C. not discuss the matter with anyone.
D. hold the party at your place instead.

4. You find that the cooking gas cylinder is leaking. The first thing you would do is :

A. switch off the light.
B. close the knob of the cylinder.
C. call the fire brigade for help.
D. alert all the members at home.

5. While returning home from a far away place you find that your pocket has been picked. You will :

A. try to hitch-hike to home.
B. hire a taxi and pay on reaching home.
C. go to the nearest police station and lodge an FIR.
D. call home and ask someone to pick you from the place you made the phone call.

6. Your friend has not invited you to his marriage party, you will :

A. ignore the whole affair.
B. send him your best wishes.
C. attend the ceremony.
D. hold it against him.

7. You are interviewed for a new job. Which of the following questions is most important to you?

A. Remuneration you will be paid.
B. Opportunities for promotion.
C. Scope to develop your ideas and use them to improve the working of the organisation.
D. All the above are equally important.

ANSWERS

1	2	3	4	5	6	7
C	A	A	B	B	B	D

✤✤✤✤✤

26. CODING AND DECODING

Coding is a secretive language which is used to change the representation of the actual term/word/value. This coded language can be framed by *(i)* moving the letters one or more steps forward or backward; *(ii)* substituting numbers for letters and vice–versa; *(iii)* writing the letters of the given word in reverse order in part or in whole; and *(iv)* replacing the letters in their natural series by the same positioned letters in their reverse series.

There is variety in ways of coding. Coding language is not only for words and numbers but also for hiding a group of words, statements or even sentences. This form of coding pattern may appear to be confusing but after solving only a few questions it is very easy to understand. Questions based on this coding pattern require no moving of steps or straining efforts of calculations, but only quick tallying or comparing ability. The codes can be letters or numbers.

EXERCISE

Directions : *In the following questions select the right option which indicates the correct code for the word or letter given in the question.*

1. If MUSK is coded as 146816, then ZERO will be coded as :

A. 113811 B. 122912
C. 15915 D. 2651815

2. If BAD is coded as 7, HIS as 9, LOW will be coded as:

A. 50 B. 8
C. 23 D. 5

3. In a certain code LIBERATE is written as 56403170, TRIBAL will be written in the same code as :

A. 734615 B. 736415
C. 136475 D. 034615

4. In certain military code, SYSTEM is written as SYSMET, and NEARER as AENRER, what will be the code for FRACTION?

A. CRAFNOIT B. FRCAITNO
C. CARFNOIT D. FRACNOIT

5. If CRUDE is written as BSTED, then MOIST will be coded as :

A. NNJRU B. LNHRS
C. NPJTU D. LPHTS

6. In a certain code ALPACA is written as ACAPLA. How will ANIMAL be written in that code?

A. LAMINA B. ALAMIN
C. LAMNIA D. AAMLIN

7. In a certain code FINGER is written as DGLECP. What will be the code for KIDNEY?

A. IGBLCW B. IGCLBW
C. IBCGLE D. IGBKCV

8. In a certain code QUESTION is written as NXBVQLLQ. How will REPLY be coded?

A. YHMOV B. OBMVI
C. VHSOB D. OHMOV

9. If in a certain code SKEW is coded as PNCY, then what will JXQV will stand for?

A. MUTS B. MUST
C. MTSU D. STUM

10. In a certain code LONDON is written as MPOEPO. What will IVOHSZ mean in the same code?

A. HUNGRY B. HUNDRY
C. GRUNHY D. HONDUS

11. In a certain code language 8514 is a code for HEAD, 3945 for RIDE and 057 for BEG. What will be the code for GRADE?

A. 71345 B. 73415
C. 74135 D. 73145

12. If MOTHERLAND is coded as 9501623748, how will DREAM be coded?

A. 82697 B. 86297
C. 82769 D. 82679

13. If OATH is coded in a certain language as TEYL, then how will WORD be coded?

A. BWRH B. HRWB
C. BSWH D. CSXI

EXPLANATORY ANSWERS

1. (B) : The coded number signifies the position of the alphabet in its reverse order of the alphabetical series (ZYXW...)

M U S K → MUSK
↓ ↓ ↓ ↓
14th 6th 8th 16th → 146816

Similarly,

Z E R O → ZERO
↓ ↓ ↓ ↓
1st 22nd 9th 12th → 122912

2. (D) : The coded number is the sum of number digits signifying the position of the alphabet in the natural order.

B A D
↓ ↓ ↓
2nd 1st 4th *i.e.,* $2+1+4 = 7$

Similarly,

H I S
↓ ↓ ↓
8th 9th 19th *i.e.,* $8+9+19 = 36$
further, $3+6 = 9$

Also,

L O W
↓ ↓ ↓
12th 15th 23rd *i.e.,* $12+15+23 = 50$
further, $5+0 = 0$

3. (B) : The letters of the word TRIBAL are picked from LIBERATE. So will be the coded numbers.

L I B E R A T E → given word
5 6 4 0 3 1 7 0 → codes

Similarly,

T R I B A L → word to be coded
7 3 6 4 1 5 → answer codes

4. (C) : The word is divided into two equal parts and the letters of each part are written in reverse order.

Similarly,

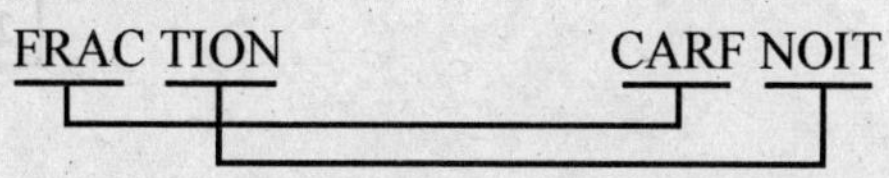

5. (D) : The code is formed by moving the letters one step backwards and one step forward alternately.

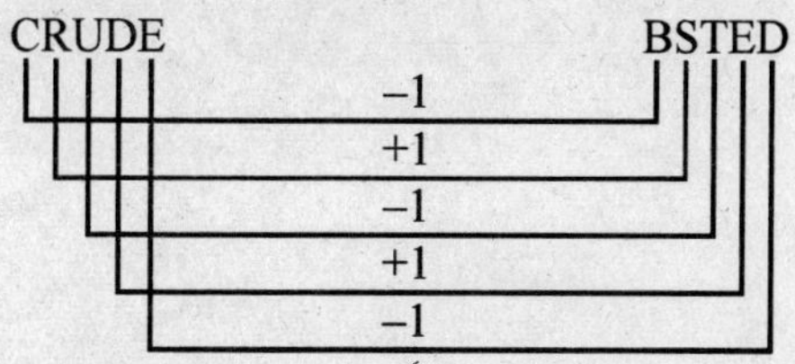

Similarly,

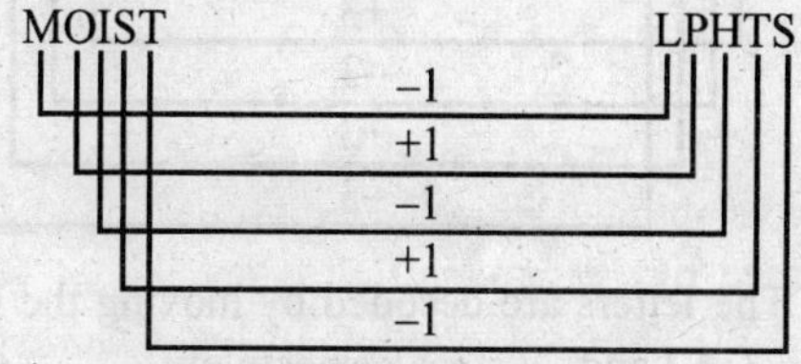

6. (A) : The letters of the word are written backwards.

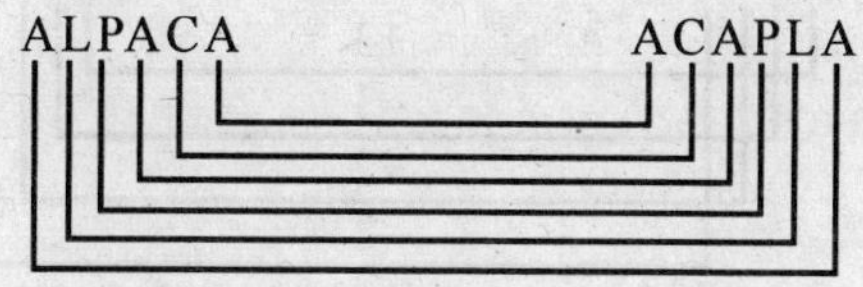

Similarly,

7. (A) : The word is coded by moving the letters two steps backwards.

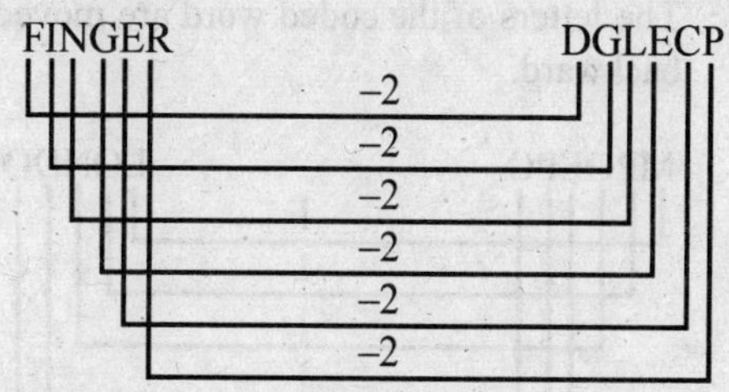

Similarly,

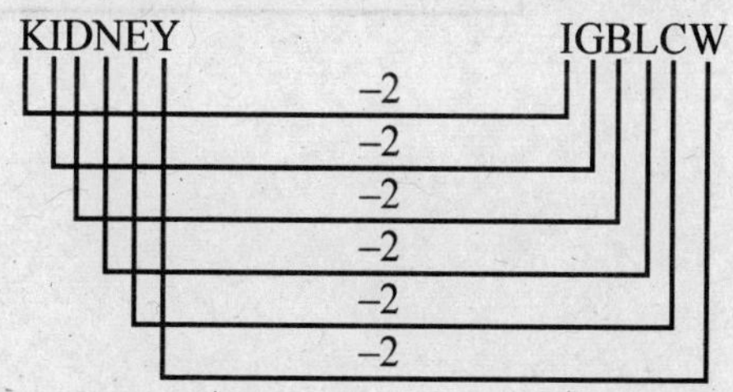

8. (D) : The letters of the word are coded by moving three steps backward and three steps forward alternately.

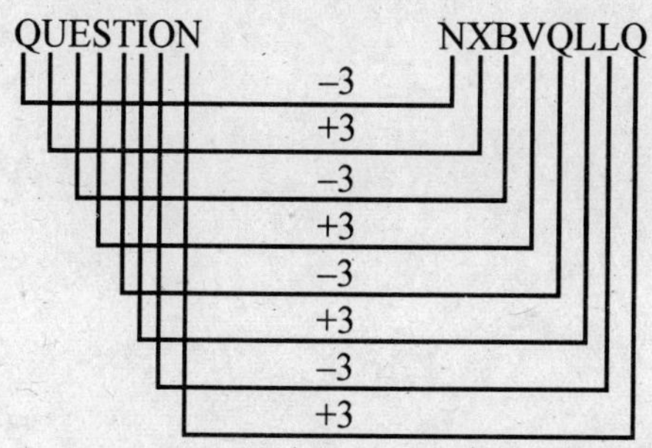

Similarly,

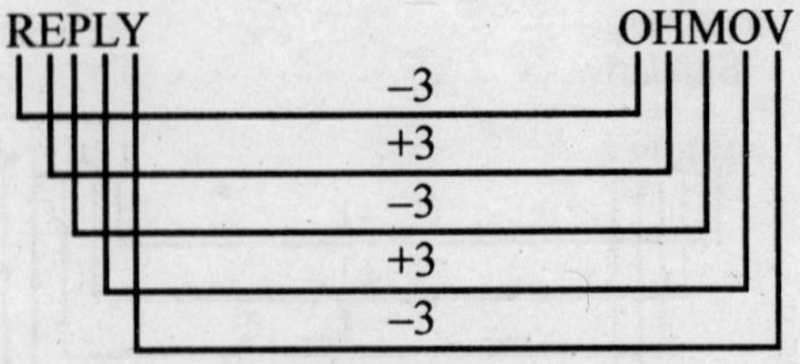

9. (B) : The letters are decoded by moving the letters +3, –3, +2 and –2 steps respectively.

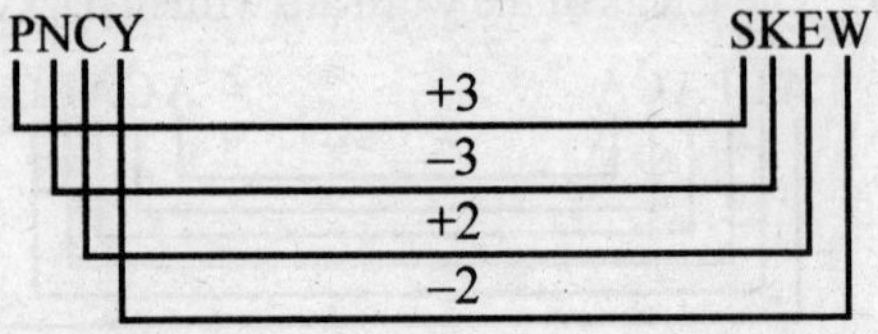

Similarly,

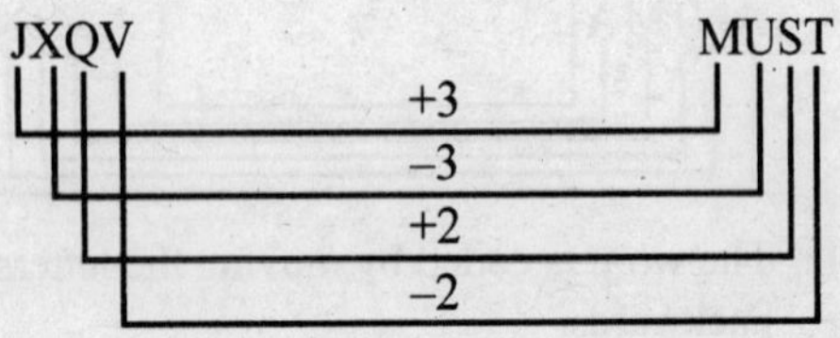

10. (A) : The letters of the coded word are moved one step backward.

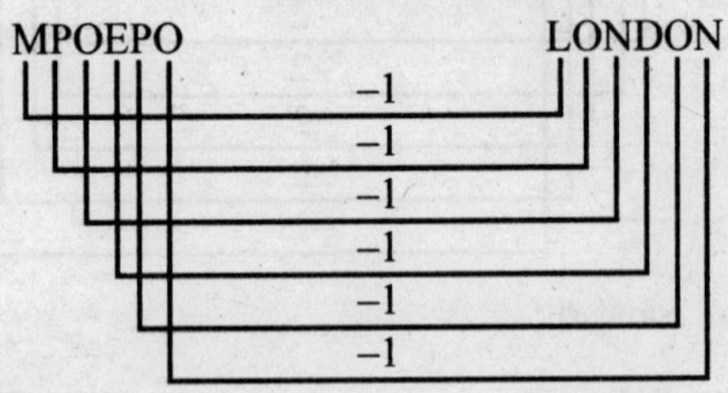

Similarly,

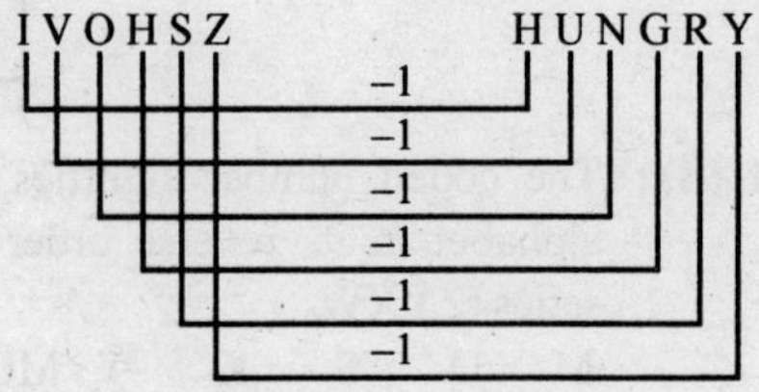

11. (D) : The word GRADE is framed by letters in the given words. So, in order to find the code for GRADE select the respective number codes.

H E A D R I D E B E G → letters
8 5 1 4 3 9 4 5 0 5 7 → codes

So,

G R A D E →letters
7 3 1 4 5 →answer codes

12. (D) : The letters of the word are coded by numbers. So to find the code for DREAM select the respective numbers.

M O T H E R L A N D → letters
9 5 0 1 6 2 3 7 4 8 → codes

So, D R E A M → letters
8 2 6 7 9 → answer codes

13. (C) : The letters are coded by moving five and four steps forward alternately.

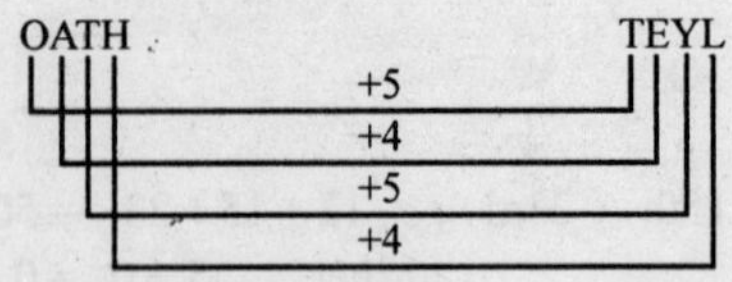

Similarly,

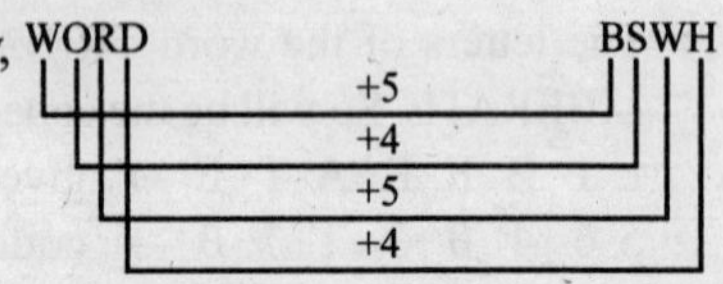

✤ ✤ ✤ ✤ ✤

QUANTITATIVE ABILITY

1. NUMBER SYSTEM

The development of the number system started with natural numbers. These are generally known as counting numbers.

Natural Numbers

Numbers which start from 1 are known as natural numbers. It is denoted by N. The smallest natural number is 1. It is written as,

$$N = \{1, 2, 3, ..., \infty\}$$

Whole Numbers

A number which starts from zero (0) is known as whole number. It is denoted by W. It is written as,

$$W = \{0, 1, 2, 3, ..., \infty\}$$

Integers

Natural numbers along with 0 and their negatives are known as integers. It is denoted by I. It is written as,

$$I = \{..., -4, -3, -2, -1, 0, 1, 2, 3, 4, ...\}$$

Even Numbers

A number which is divisible by 2 is known as even numbers.

Such as, 2, 4, 6, 10, 12, 128, 432 etc.

Odd Numbers

A number which is not divisible by 2 is known as odd numbers:

Such as, 1, 3, 5, 7, 9, 11, 13, 21, 29, 123 etc.

Prime Numbers

A number which is divided by itself is known as prime numbers. The smallest prime number is 2.

Such as, 2, 3, 5, 7, 11, 13, 17, 19, 23, ... etc.

Composite Numbers

A number which is divided by itself and others also is known as composite numbers. The smallest composite number is 4.

Such as, 4, 6, 8, 9, 10, 12, 14, 15, 16, 18, ... etc.

There are 25 prime numbers between 1 to 100.

Such as, 2, 3, 5, 7, 11, 13, 17, 19, 23, 29, 31, 37, 41, 43, 47, 53, 59, 61, 67, 71, 73, 79, 83, 89, 97.

Test, whether a given number is prime or composite: If we want to test any number more than 100, whether it is prime or not, take an integer larger than the approximate square root of that number. Let it be x. Test the divisibility of the given number by every prime number less than x. If it is not divisible by any of them, then it is prime; otherwise it is composite number.

EXAMPLE: Which of the following numbers are prime numbers?

(*i*) 421 (*ii*) 671

SOLUTION:

(*i*) The square root of 421 is nearly 21.
Prime numbers less than 21 are 2, 3, 5, 7, 11, 13, 17, 19.
Clearly, 421 is not divisible by any of them. So, 421 is a prime number.

(*ii*) The square root of 671 is nearly 26.
Prime numbers less than 26 are 2, 3, 5, 7, 11, 13, 17, 19, 23.
Out of these, 671 is divisible by 11.
So, 671 is not a prime number. Hence it is composite number.

The formulae given below are quite useful for quick multiplication:

(*i*) $(a+b)^2 = a^2 + 2ab + b^2$

(*ii*) $(a-b)^2 = a^2 - 2ab + b^2$

(*iii*) $a^2 - b^2 = (a+b)(a-b)$

(*iv*) $a^2 + b^2 = (a+b)^2 - 2ab$

(*v*) $(a+b)^3 = a^3 + b^3 + 3ab(a+b)$

(*vi*) $(a-b)^3 = a^3 - b^3 - 3ab(a-b)$

(*vii*) $a^3 + b^3 = (a+b)(a^2 - ab + b^2)$

(*viii*) $a^3 - b^3 = (a-b)(a^2 + ab + b^2)$

EXAMPLE: Simplify the following.

(*i*) $\dfrac{348 \times 348 \times 348 + 252 \times 252 \times 252}{348 \times 348 - 348 \times 252 + 252 \times 252}$

(*ii*) $\dfrac{261 \times 261 \times 261 - 77 \times 77 \times 77}{261 \times 261 + 261 \times 77 + 77 \times 77}$

SOLUTION:

(*i*) $\dfrac{348 \times 348 \times 348 + 252 \times 252 \times 252}{348 \times 348 - 348 \times 252 + 252 \times 252}$

Let $348 = a$

and $252 = b$

$\therefore$ Given expression is written as

$$\frac{a \times a \times a + b \times b \times b}{a \times a - a \times b + b \times b} = \frac{a^3 + b^3}{a^2 - ab + b^2}$$

$$= \frac{(a+b)(a^2-ab+b^2)}{(a^2-ab+b^2)} = a+b$$

$= 348 + 252 = 600.$

(ii) $\frac{261 \times 261 \times 261 - 77 \times 77 \times 77}{261 \times 261 + 261 \times 77 + 77 \times 77}$

Let $261 = a$

and $77 = b$

$$\therefore \quad \frac{a^3-b^3}{a^2+ab+b^2} = \frac{(a-b)(a^2+ab+b^2)}{(a^2+ab+b^2)} = a-b$$

$\therefore \quad 261 - 77 = 184.$

If we divide a given number by another number, then

Dividend = (Divisor × Quotient) + Remainder

EXAMPLE: On dividing 18254 by a certain number, the quotient is 289 and the remainder is 47. Find the divisor.

SOLUTION: Here, Dividend = 18254

quotient = 289

remainder = 47

$$\therefore \quad \text{Divisor} = \frac{\text{Dividend} - \text{Remainder}}{\text{Quotient}}$$

$$= \frac{18254-47}{289} = \frac{18207}{289} = 63$$

Hence, divisor = 63.

EXAMPLE: What least number must be subtracted from 862 to get a number exactly divisible by 31?

SOLUTION: On dividing 862 by 31, the remainder obtained is 25.

Hence, the required number = 25.

MULTIPLE CHOICE QUESTIONS

1. The face value of 8 in the numeral 458926 is:

A. 8000 B. 8
C. 1000 D. 458000

2. $106 \times 106 + 94 \times 94 = x$, the value of x is:

A. 21032 B. 20032
C. 23032 D. 20072

3. If $m \times 48 = 173 \times 240$ then the value of m is:

A. 545 B. 685
C. 865 D. 495

4. $\left(1-\frac{1}{3}\right)\left(1-\frac{1}{4}\right)\left(1-\frac{1}{5}\right)...\left(1-\frac{1}{n}\right) = x$

then the value of x is:

A. $\frac{1}{n}$ B. $\frac{2}{n}$
C. $\frac{2(n-1)}{n}$ D. $\frac{2}{n(n+1)}$

5. When simplified the product

$\left(2-\frac{1}{3}\right)\left(2-\frac{3}{5}\right)\left(2-\frac{5}{7}\right)...\left(2-\frac{997}{999}\right)$ is equal to:

A. $\frac{5}{999}$ B. $\frac{1001}{999}$
C. $\frac{1001}{3}$ D. None of these

6. Which number should replace both the asterisks in $\left(\frac{*}{21}\right)\times\left(\frac{*}{189}\right) = 1$?

A. 21 B. 63
C. 3969 D. 147

7. In a division sum, the divisor is 12 times the quotient and 5 times the remainder. If the remainder be 48, then the dividend is:

A. 240 B. 576
C. 4800 D. 4848

8. What least number must be subtracted from 1294 so that the remainder when divided by 9, 11, 13 will leave in each case the same remainder 6?

A. 0 B. 1
C. 2 D. 3

9. If $\sqrt{\left(1+\frac{27}{169}\right)} = \left(1+\frac{x}{13}\right)$, then the value of x is:

A. 1 B. 3
C. 5 D. 7

10. If $\frac{x}{y} = \frac{3}{4}$, then the value of $\left(\frac{6}{7}+\frac{y-x}{y+x}\right)$ equals:

A. $\frac{5}{7}$ B. $1\frac{1}{7}$
C. 1 D. 2

11. The largest natural number by which the product of three consecutive even natural numbers is always divisible, is:

A. 16 B. 24
C. 48 D. 96

12. The least number of five digits which is exactly divisible by 12, 15 and 18 is:

A. 10080 B. 10800
C. 18000 D. 81000

13. The least number which when divided by 8, 9, 12, 16 and 20 leaves the same remainder 1 in each case is:

A. 712 B. 271
C. 721 D. 720

14. The value of 0.8693 + 0.092 + 0.87 + 0.4 equals:
A. 2.3213 B. 2.2331
C. 3.2313 D. 2.2313

15. The prime numbers between 1 to 50 are:
A. 8 B. 12
C. 15 D. 10

16. If $\frac{a}{b}=\frac{4}{3}$, then $\frac{3a+2b}{3a-2b}$ equals:
A. 6 B. 3
C. 5 D. –1

17. If $\sqrt{3^n} = 81$, then n equals:
A. 2 B. 4
C. 6 D. 8

18. If $\sqrt{\frac{x}{196}}=\frac{72}{56}$, then x equals:
A. 18 B. 14
C. 324 D. 212

19. If $a \times 48 = 173 \times 240$, then the value of a is:
A. 545 B. 685
C. 865 D. 495

20. If $\frac{80}{x}=\frac{x}{20}$, then the value of x is:
A. 40 B. 400
C. 800 D. 1600

ANSWERS

1	2	3	4	5	6	7	8	9	10
B	D	C	B	C	B	D	B	A	C
11	**12**	**13**	**14**	**15**	**16**	**17**	**18**	**19**	**20**
C	A	C	D	C	B	D	C	C	A

EXPLANATORY ANSWERS

1. The face value of 8 in the numeral 458926 is 8.

2. $106 \times 106 + 94 \times 94 = x$

$$\Rightarrow (106)^2 + (94)^2 = x$$
$$\Rightarrow (100+6)^2 + (100-6)^2 = x$$
$$\Rightarrow 10000 + 1200 + 36 + 10000 - 1200 + 36 = x$$
$$\Rightarrow 20072 = x$$
$$\Rightarrow x = 20072.$$

3. $\because m = \frac{173 \times 240}{48} = 865.$

4. $\left(1-\frac{1}{3}\right)\left(1-\frac{1}{4}\right)\left(1-\frac{1}{5}\right)...\left(1-\frac{1}{n}\right) = x$

$$\because \quad 1-\frac{1}{3} = \frac{3-1}{3} = \frac{2}{3}$$
$$1-\frac{1}{4} = \frac{4-1}{4} = \frac{3}{4}$$
$$1-\frac{1}{5} = \frac{5-1}{5} = \frac{4}{5}$$
$$\vdots$$
$$1-\frac{1}{n} = \frac{n-1}{n}$$
$$\therefore \frac{2}{3}\times\frac{3}{4}\times\frac{4}{5}\times...\times\frac{n-2}{n-1}\times\frac{n-1}{n} = \frac{2}{n}$$

5. $\left(2-\frac{1}{3}\right)\left(2-\frac{3}{5}\right)\left(2-\frac{5}{7}\right)...\left(2-\frac{997}{999}\right)$

$$2-\frac{1}{3} = \frac{6-1}{3} = \frac{5}{3}$$
$$2-\frac{3}{5} = \frac{10-3}{5} = \frac{7}{5}$$
$$2-\frac{5}{7} = \frac{14-5}{7} = \frac{9}{7}$$
$$2-\frac{997}{999} = \frac{1998-997}{999} = \frac{1001}{999}$$
$$\therefore \frac{5}{3}\times\frac{7}{5}\times\frac{9}{7}\times...\times\frac{999}{997}\times\frac{1001}{999} = \frac{1001}{3}$$

6. $\frac{*}{21}\times\frac{*}{189} = 1$

$$\frac{x^2}{21\times189} = 1$$
$$\Rightarrow x^2 = 21 \times 189 = 21 \times 21 \times 9$$
$$\Rightarrow x^2 = 21 \times 21 \times 3 \times 3$$
$$\Rightarrow x = 21 \times 3 = 63$$

7. Let quotient = Q and remainder = R
Then, divisor = 12Q = 5R
Now, R = 48
$\Rightarrow$ 12Q = 5 × 48 $\Rightarrow$ Q = 20
$\therefore$ Dividend = (20 × 240 + 48) = 4848

8. The number when divided by 9, 11, 13 leaving remainder 6 = (LCM of 9, 11, 13) + 6 = 1293
$\therefore$ Required number = (1294 – 1293) = 1

9. $\sqrt{\left(1+\frac{27}{169}\right)} = \left(1+\frac{x}{13}\right)$

$$\Rightarrow \quad \sqrt{\frac{169+27}{169}} = \frac{13+x}{13}$$

$$\Rightarrow \quad \sqrt{\frac{196}{169}} = \frac{x+13}{13}$$

$$\Rightarrow \quad \frac{14}{13} = \frac{x+13}{13}$$

$$\Rightarrow \quad x + 13 = 14$$

$$\Rightarrow \quad x = 1$$

10. $\because \frac{x}{y} = \frac{3}{4}$ then,

$$\frac{6}{7}+\frac{y-x}{y+x} = \frac{6}{7}+\frac{\frac{y}{y}-\frac{x}{y}}{\frac{y}{y}+\frac{x}{y}}$$

[Divide numerator and denominator by y.]

$$= \frac{6}{7}+\frac{1-\frac{3}{4}}{1+\frac{3}{4}} = \frac{6}{7}+\frac{\frac{1}{4}}{\frac{7}{4}}$$

$$= \frac{6}{7}+\frac{1}{7} = \frac{7}{7} = 1$$

11. It is $2 \times 4 \times 6 = 48$

12. Least number of 5 digits is 10000.

LCM of 12, 15, 18 is 180.

On dividing 10000 by 180, the remainder is 100.

$\therefore$ The least number $= 10000 + (180 - 100)$

$= 10080.$

13. Least number = (LCM of 8, 9, 12, 16, 20) + 1

2	8,	9,	12,	16,	20
2	4,	9,	6,	8,	10
2	2,	9,	3,	4,	5
3	1,	9,	3,	2,	5
	1,	3,	1,	2,	5

$\therefore$ LCM $= 2^4 \times 3^2 \times 5 = 720$

Hence, least number $= (720 + 1) = 721$.

14.

$$\begin{array}{r} 0.8693 \\ 0.092 \\ 0.87 \\ +\ 0.4 \\ \hline 2.2313 \\ \hline \end{array}$$

$\therefore$ The value of $0.8693 + 0.092 + 0.87 + 0.4 = 2.2313$.

15. The prime numbers between 1 to 50 are 2, 3, 5, 7, 11, 13, 17, 19, 23, 29, 31, 37, 41, 43, 47.

Hence, there are 15 prime numbers between 1 to 50.

16. $\because \quad \frac{a}{b} = \frac{4}{3}$

$$\therefore \quad \frac{3a+2b}{3a-2b} = \frac{\frac{3a}{b}+\frac{2b}{b}}{\frac{3a}{b}-\frac{2b}{b}}$$

[Divide numerator and denominator by b.]

$$= \frac{3\left(\frac{4}{3}\right)+2}{3\left(\frac{4}{3}\right)-2} = \frac{4+2}{4-2}$$

$$= \frac{6}{2} = 3.$$

17. $\because \sqrt{3^n} = 81 \quad \Rightarrow \quad 3^{\frac{n}{2}} = 3^4$

$$\Rightarrow \quad \frac{n}{2} = 4 \quad \Rightarrow \quad n = 8.$$

18. $\because \quad \sqrt{\frac{x}{196}} = \frac{72}{56} \Rightarrow \frac{x}{196} = \frac{72 \times 72}{56 \times 56}$

$$\Rightarrow \quad x = \frac{72 \times 72 \times 196}{56 \times 56}$$

$$\Rightarrow \quad x = 18 \times 18 = 324.$$

19. $\because \quad a \times 48 = 173 \times 240$

$$\Rightarrow \quad a = \frac{173 \times 240}{48}$$

$$= 173 \times 5 = 865$$

$\therefore$ The value of $a = 865$.

20. $\because \quad \frac{80}{x} = \frac{x}{20} \quad \Rightarrow \quad x^2 = 80 \times 20$

$$\Rightarrow \quad x^2 = 1600 \quad \Rightarrow \quad x = 40$$

Hence, the value of $x = 40$.

2. SIMPLIFICATION

Simplification means expressing in a simpler form. In order to simplify an expression we use the operations in the following order which is easily remembered as "BODMAS".
(*i*) Bracket (*ii*) Of (*iii*) Division (*iv*) Multiplication (*v*) Addition (*vi*) Subtraction.

'Of' means multiplication but it is operated even before division.

While removing brackets, first of all bar bracket '—' and after that small bracket '( )' is removed. Thereafter curley bracket '{ }' and at last square bracket '[ ]' is removed.

EXAMPLE: Simplify: $100 \div 25 \times 6 + 16 - 32$

SOLUTION: $100 \div 25 \times 6 + 16 - 32$

$= 4 \times 6 + 16 - 32$
$= 24 + 16 - 32$
$= 40 - 32 = 8$

EXAMPLE: Simplify: $54 + 24 \div 4 - 8 \times 5 + 4 \times 3$

SOLUTION: $54 + 24 \div 4 - 8 \times 5 + 4 \times 3$

$= 54 + 6 - 40 + 12$
$= 72 - 40 = 32$

EXAMPLE: Simplify: $10 - \left[6 - \left\{7 - \left(6 - \overline{8 - 5}\right)\right\}\right]$

SOLUTION: $10 - \left[6 - \left\{7 - (6 - 3)\right\}\right]$

$= 10 - [6 - \{7 - 3\}]$
$= 10 - [6 - 4] = 10 - 2 = 8.$

EXAMPLE: Simplify: $\dfrac{12 \times 12 \times 12 - 1 \times 1 \times 1}{12 \times 12 + 12 \times 1 + 1 \times 1}$

SOLUTION: Let $a = 12$ and $b = 1$

$$\therefore \frac{a \times a \times a - b \times b \times b}{a \times a + a \times b + b \times b} = \frac{a^3 - b^3}{a^2 + ab + b^2}$$

$$= \frac{(a - b)(a^2 + ab + b^2)}{(a^2 + ab + b^2)}$$

$$= a - b = 12 - 1 = 11$$

EXAMPLE: Simplify:

$$\frac{2.33 \times 2.33 \times 2.33 + 7.67 \times 7.67 \times 7.67}{2.33 \times 2.33 - 2.33 \times 7.67 + 7.67 \times 7.67}$$

SOLUTION: Let $a = 2.33$ and $b = 7.67$

$$\frac{a^3 + b^3}{a^2 - ab + b^2} = \frac{(a + b)(a^2 - ab + b^2)}{(a^2 - ab + b^2)} = (a + b)$$

$$= 2.33 + 7.67 = 10$$

MULTIPLE CHOICE QUESTIONS

1. $\dfrac{48 - 12 \times 3 + 9}{12 - 9 + 3}$ equals:

A. 3 B. 21
C. $\dfrac{7}{3}$ D. $\dfrac{1}{3}$

2. $\dfrac{69 - 14 \times 3 + 2}{9 \times 5 - (5)^2}$ equals:

A. 1.45 B. 2.75
C. 26.5 D. 265

3. If $\dfrac{17.28 \div x}{3.6 \times 0.2} = 2$ then, the value of x is:

A. 120 B. 1.20
C. 12 D. 0.12

4. $171 \div 19 \times 9$ equals:

A. 0 B. 1
C. 18 D. 81

5. $3120 \div 26 + 13 \times 30$ equals:

A. 2400 B. 3900
C. 536 D. None of these

6. $\dfrac{31}{10} \times \dfrac{3}{10} + \dfrac{7}{5} \div 20$ equals:

A. 0 B. 1
C. 100 D. $\dfrac{107}{200}$

7. The simplification of $1 + \dfrac{1}{2 + \dfrac{1}{1 - \dfrac{1}{3}}}$ yields the result:

A. $\dfrac{2}{7}$ B. $\dfrac{7}{9}$
C. $\dfrac{9}{7}$ D. $\dfrac{13}{7}$

8. The value of $1+\frac{1}{4\times 3}+\frac{1}{4\times 3^2}+\frac{1}{4\times 3^3}$ up to four places of decimals is:

A. 1.1202 B. 1.1203
C. 1.1204 D. None of these

9. $\dfrac{\frac{1}{2}\div 4+20}{\frac{1}{2}\times 4+20}$ equals:

A. $\frac{81}{88}$ B. $2\frac{3}{11}$
C. $\frac{161}{176}$ D. 1

10. $3\div\left[(8-5)\div\left\{(4-2)\div\left(2+\frac{8}{13}\right)\right\}\right]$ equals:

A. $\frac{13}{17}$ B. $\frac{68}{13}$
C. $\frac{17}{13}$ D. $\frac{13}{68}$

11. 10 – [9 – {8 – (7 – 6)}] – 5 is equal to:

A. –5 B. 1
C. 3 D. 9

12. $\dfrac{\frac{1}{5}\div\frac{1}{5}\text{ of }\frac{1}{5}}{\frac{1}{5}\text{ of }\frac{1}{5}\div\frac{1}{5}}$ is equal to:

A. 1 B. 5
C. $\frac{1}{5}$ D. 25

13. The value of $1+\dfrac{1}{1+\dfrac{1}{1+\frac{1}{9}}}$ is:

A. $\frac{29}{19}$ B. $\frac{10}{19}$
C. $\frac{29}{10}$ D. $\frac{10}{9}$

14. $\frac{3}{48}$ is what part of $\frac{1}{12}$?

A. $\frac{3}{7}$ B. $\frac{1}{12}$
C. $\frac{4}{3}$ D. None of these

15. How many $\frac{1}{8}$ s are there in $37\frac{1}{2}$?

A. 300
B. 400
C. 500
D. Cannot be determined

16. $\dfrac{885\times 885\times 885+115\times 115\times 115}{885\times 885+115\times 115-885\times 115}$ is equal to:

A. 115 B. 770
C. 885 D. 1000

17. The value of $\dfrac{9^2\times 18^4}{3^{16}}$ is:

A. $\frac{2}{3}$ B. $\frac{4}{9}$
C. $\frac{16}{81}$ D. $\frac{32}{243}$

18. $\left(1\frac{3}{5}-\frac{2}{3}\div\frac{12}{13}+\frac{7}{5}\times\frac{1}{3}\right)$ is equal to:

A. $1\frac{31}{90}$ B. $\frac{19}{30}$
C. $\frac{11}{30}$ D. 30

19. The value of $48\div 12\times\left(\frac{9}{8}\text{ of }\frac{4}{3}\div\frac{3}{4}\text{ of }\frac{2}{3}\right)$ is:

A. $1\frac{1}{3}$ B. $5\frac{1}{3}$
C. 3 D. 12

20. (20 ÷ 5) ÷ 2 + (16 ÷ 8) × 2 + (10 ÷ 5) × (3 ÷ 2) is equal to

A. 9 B. 12
C. 15 D. 18

ANSWERS

1	2	3	4	5	6	7	8	9	10
C	A	C	D	D	B	C	B	C	A
11	**12**	**13**	**14**	**15**	**16**	**17**	**18**	**19**	**20**
C	D	A	D	A	D	C	A	D	A

EXPLANATORY ANSWERS

1. $\dfrac{48-12\times 3+9}{12-9\div 3}=\dfrac{48-36+9}{12-3}=\dfrac{57-36}{9}=\dfrac{21}{9}=\dfrac{7}{3}.$

2. $\dfrac{69-14\times 3+2}{9\times 5-5^2}=\dfrac{69-42+2}{45-25}=\dfrac{71-42}{20}=\dfrac{29}{20}=1.45.$

3. $17.28 \div x = 2 \times 3.6 \times 0.2$

$$\Rightarrow \frac{17.28}{x} = 1.44 \Rightarrow 1.44\,x = 17.28$$

$$\Rightarrow \quad x = \frac{17.28}{1.44} = \frac{1728}{144} = 12.$$

4. $171 \div 19 \times 9 = 9 \times 9 = 81.$

5. $3120 \div 26 + 13 \times 30 = 120 + 390 = 510.$

6. $\frac{31}{10}\times\frac{3}{10}+\frac{7}{5}\div 20 = \frac{31}{10}\times\frac{3}{10}+\frac{7}{5}\times\frac{1}{20}$

$$= \frac{93}{100}+\frac{7}{100} = \frac{93+7}{100} = \frac{100}{100} = 1$$

7. $1+\cfrac{1}{2+\cfrac{1}{1-\cfrac{1}{3}}} = 1+\cfrac{1}{2+\cfrac{1}{\cfrac{3-1}{3}}}$

$$= 1+\cfrac{1}{2+\cfrac{1}{\cfrac{2}{3}}} = 1+\cfrac{1}{2+\cfrac{3}{2}} = 1+\cfrac{1}{\cfrac{7}{2}} = 1+\frac{2}{7} = \frac{9}{7}$$

8. $1+\frac{1}{4\times3}+\frac{1}{4\times3^2}+\frac{1}{4\times3^3}$

$$= 1+\frac{1}{12}+\frac{1}{36}+\frac{1}{108} = \frac{108+9+3+1}{108} = \frac{121}{108} = 1.1203$$

9. $\dfrac{\frac{1}{2}\div4+20}{\frac{1}{2}\times4+20} = \dfrac{\frac{1}{8}+20}{2+20} = \dfrac{\frac{1+160}{8}}{22} = \dfrac{161}{8\times22} = \dfrac{161}{176}$

10. $3\div\left[(8-5)\div\left\{(4-2)\div\left(2+\frac{8}{13}\right)\right\}\right]$

$$= 3\div\left[3\div\left\{2\div\frac{34}{13}\right\}\right] = 3\div\left[3\div\left\{2\times\frac{13}{34}\right\}\right]$$

$$= 3\div\left[3\div\frac{13}{17}\right] = 3\div\left[3\times\frac{17}{13}\right] = 3\div\frac{51}{13} = 3\times\frac{13}{51} = \frac{13}{17}$$

11. $10-[9-\{8-(7-6)\}]-5$
$= 10-[9-\{8-1\}]-5 = 10-[9-7]-5$
$= 10-2-5 = 10-7 = 3$

12. $\dfrac{\frac{1}{5}\div\frac{1}{5}\text{ of }\frac{1}{5}}{\frac{1}{5}\text{ of }\frac{1}{5}+\frac{1}{5}} = \dfrac{\frac{1}{5}\div\frac{1}{25}}{\frac{1}{25}\div\frac{1}{5}} = \dfrac{\frac{1}{5}\times\frac{25}{1}}{\frac{1}{25}\times\frac{5}{1}} = \dfrac{\frac{5}{1}}{\frac{1}{5}} = \frac{5}{1}\times\frac{5}{1} = 25$

13. $1+\cfrac{1}{1+\cfrac{1}{1+\cfrac{1}{9}}} = 1+\cfrac{1}{1+\cfrac{1}{\cfrac{10}{9}}}$

$$= 1+\cfrac{1}{1+\cfrac{9}{10}} = 1+\cfrac{1}{\cfrac{19}{10}} = 1+\frac{10}{19} = \frac{29}{19}$$

14. Let x of $\frac{1}{12} = \frac{3}{48}$

$$\Rightarrow \frac{x}{12} = \frac{3}{48} \Rightarrow 48x = 36$$

$$\Rightarrow \quad x = \frac{36}{48} = \frac{3}{4}.$$

15. Let n times $\frac{1}{8} = 37\frac{1}{2}$

$$\Rightarrow \frac{n}{8} = \frac{75}{2} \Rightarrow 2n = 8\times75$$

$$\Rightarrow \quad n = \frac{8\times75}{2} = 4\times75 = 300.$$

16. $\dfrac{885\times885\times885+115\times115\times115}{885\times885+115\times115-885\times115}$

Let $a = 885$ and $b = 115$

$$\therefore \text{ Given expression} = \frac{a^3+b^3}{a^2+b^2-ab}$$

$$= \frac{(a+b)(a^2+b^2-ab)}{(a^2+b^2-ab)} = a+b$$

$= 885 + 115 = 1000$

17. $\dfrac{9^2\times18^4}{3^{16}} = \dfrac{3^4\times(3\times6)^4}{3^{16}} = \dfrac{3^4\times3^4\times6^4}{3^{16}}$

$$= \frac{3^4\times3^4\times(3\times2)^4}{3^{16}} = \frac{3^4\times3^4\times3^4\times2^4}{3^{16}}$$

$$= \frac{3^{12}\times2^4}{3^{16}} = \frac{2^4}{3^4} = \frac{16}{81}$$

18. $\left(1\frac{3}{5}-\frac{2}{3}\div\frac{12}{13}+\frac{7}{5}\times\frac{1}{3}\right)$

$$= \frac{8}{5}-\frac{2}{3}\times\frac{13}{12}+\frac{7}{15} = \frac{8}{5}-\frac{13}{18}+\frac{7}{15} = \frac{144-65+42}{90}$$

$$= \frac{186-65}{90} = \frac{121}{90} = 1\frac{31}{90}$$

19. $48\div12\times\left(\frac{9}{8}\text{ of }\frac{4}{3}\div\frac{3}{4}\text{ of }\frac{2}{3}\right) = 48\div12\times\left(\frac{3}{2}\div\frac{1}{2}\right)$

$$= 48\div12\times\left(\frac{3}{2}\times\frac{2}{1}\right) = 48\div12\times3 = 4\times3 = 12$$

20. $(20\div5)\div2+(16\div8)\times2+(10\div5)\times(3\div2)$

$$= 4\div2+2\times2+2\times\frac{3}{2} = 2+4+3 = 9$$

3. H.C.F AND L.C.M

FACTORS

The numbers are said to be factors of a given number when they exactly divide that number.

Example: Factors of 15 are 1, 3, 5 and 15 because each of these completely divides 15.

Highest Common Factor

The HCF of two or more than two numbers is the greatest number that divides each of them exactly. The highest common factor is also known as Greatest Common Divisor or Greatest Common Measure.

EXAMPLE: Let us consider two numbers 24 and 36. All possible factors of 24 are 1, 2, 3, 4, 6, 8, 12 and 24. All possible factors of 36 are 1, 2, 3, 4, 6, 9, 12, 18 and 36. The common factors of 24 and 36 are 1, 2, 3, 4, 6, 12. The greatest factor among these common factors is 12.

Hence, 12 is the HCF of 24 and 36.

EXAMPLE: Let us consider two numbers 18 and 30.

Now, $18 = 2 \times 3 \times 3$

and $30 = 2 \times 3 \times 5$

The factors common to the two numbers are 2 and 3. Hence the required HCF = $2 \times 3 = 6$.

There are two methods of determining the HCF of two or more numbers.

(*i*) HCF by Factorization method

(*ii*) HCF by Division method.

HCF by Factorization Method

Express each one of the given number as the product of prime factors. Now choose common factors and take the product of these factors to obtain the required HCF.

EXAMPLE: Find the HCF of 126, 396 and 5400.

SOLUTION: $126 = 2 \times 3 \times 3 \times 7$

$396 = 2 \times 2 \times 3 \times 3 \times 11$

$5400 = 2 \times 2 \times 2 \times 3 \times 3 \times 3 \times 5 \times 5$

Common factors are 2, 3 and 3.

Hence, the HCF = $2 \times 3 \times 3 = 18$.

EXAMPLE: Find the HCF of 1056, 1584 and 2178.

SOLUTION: $1056 = 2^5 \times 3 \times 11$

$1584 = 2^4 \times 3^2 \times 11$

and $2178 = 2 \times 3^2 \times 11^2$

Hence, HCF = $(2 \times 3 \times 11) = 66$.

HCF by Division Method

Suppose we have to find the HCF of two given numbers. Divide the larger number by the smaller one. Now, divide the divisor by the remainder. Repeat the process of dividing the preceding divisor by the remainder last obtained till zero is obtained as remainder. The last divisor is the required HCF.

Suppose we have to find the HCF of three numbers. Then HCF of [(HCF of any two numbers) and (the third number)] gives the HCF of three given numbers.

Similarly, the HCF of more than three numbers may be obtained.

EXAMPLE: Find the HCF of 48, 168 and 324.

SOLUTION: Firstly, we find the HCF of 48 and 168.

```
48) 1 6 8 (3
  − 1 4 4
    -------
      2 4) 4 8 (2
           4 8
           ---
            0
```

Thus, HCF of 48 and 168 = 24.

Now, we find the HCF of 24 and 324.

```
24) 3 2 4 (13
  − 2 4
    -----
      8 4
    − 7 2
    -----
      1 2) 2 4 (2
           2 4
           ---
            0
```

Thus, the HCF of 48, 168 and 324 is 12.

Lowest Common Multiple

The LCM of two or more numbers is the lowest or least number which is exactly divisible by each of them. In other words, it is the lowest number which contains each of them as a factor.

LCM by Factorization

Resolve each one of the given numbers into a product of prime factors. Then LCM is the product of highest powers of all the factors.

EXAMPLE: Find the LCM of 72, 189 and 1026.

SOLUTION: $72 = 2^3 \times 3^2$

$189 = 3^3 \times 7$

and $1026 = 2 \times 3^3 \times 19$

$\therefore$ LCM = $2^3 \times 3^3 \times 7 \times 19$

$= 8 \times 27 \times 7 \times 19 = 28728$

EXAMPLE: Find the LCM of 12, 15, 20 and 54 by short cut method.

SOLUTION:

2	12, 15, 20, 54
2	6, 15, 10, 27
3	3, 15, 5, 27
5	1, 5, 5, 9
	1, 1, 1, 9

$\therefore$ LCM $= 2 \times 2 \times 3 \times 5 \times 9 = 540$

FORMULA

Product of two numbers = HCF × LCM.

$$\text{LCM} = \frac{\text{Product of numbers}}{\text{HCF}}$$

$$\text{HCF} = \frac{\text{Product of numbers}}{\text{LCM}}$$

$$\text{First number} = \frac{\text{LCM} \times \text{HCF}}{\text{2nd number}}$$

$$\text{2nd number} = \frac{\text{LCM} \times \text{HCF}}{\text{First number}}$$

HCF and LCM of Fractions

(i) $\text{HCF} = \frac{\text{HCF of numerators}}{\text{LCM of denominators}}$

(ii) $\text{LCM} = \frac{\text{LCM of numerators}}{\text{HCF of denominators}}$

EXAMPLE: Find the HCF and LCM of $\frac{3}{4}, \frac{6}{8}, \frac{15}{64}$ and $\frac{12}{32}$.

SOLUTION: $\text{HCF} = \frac{\text{HCF of 3, 6, 15, 12}}{\text{LCM of 4, 8, 64, 32}} = \frac{3}{64}$

$\text{LCM} = \frac{\text{LCM of 3, 6, 15, 12}}{\text{HCF of 4, 8, 64, 32}} = \frac{60}{4}$.

MULTIPLE CHOICE QUESTIONS

1. HCF of 1485 and 4356 is:
A. 189 B. 89
C. 99 D. 83

2. LCM of 18, 24, 42, 63 is:
A. 302 B. 604
C. 504 D. 404

3. Which of the following fractions is the greatest of all?

$$\frac{7}{8}, \frac{6}{7}, \frac{4}{5}, \frac{5}{6}$$

A. $\frac{6}{7}$ B. $\frac{4}{5}$
C. $\frac{5}{6}$ D. $\frac{7}{8}$

4. Which of the following is in ascending order?
A. $\frac{5}{7}, \frac{7}{8}, \frac{9}{11}$ B. $\frac{5}{7}, \frac{9}{11}, \frac{7}{8}$
C. $\frac{7}{8}, \frac{5}{7}, \frac{9}{11}$ D. $\frac{9}{11}, \frac{7}{8}, \frac{5}{7}$

5. HCF of three numbers is 12. If they be in the ratio 1 : 2 : 3, the numbers are:
A. 12, 24, 36 B. 10, 20, 30
C. 5, 10, 15 D. 4, 8, 12

6. The largest natural number which exactly divides the product of any four consecutive natural numbers is:
A. 6 B. 12
C. 24 D. 120

7. The traffic lights at three different road crossings change after every 48 seconds, 72 seconds and 108 seconds respectively. If they all change simultaneously at 8 : 20 : 00 hrs; then they will again change simultaneously at:
A. 8 : 27 : 12 hrs B. 8 : 27 : 24 hrs
C. 8 : 27 : 36 hrs D. 8 : 27 : 48 hrs

8. The HCF of two numbers is 16 and their LCM is 160. If one of the number is 32, then the other number is:
A. 48 B. 80
C. 96 D. 112

9. The HCF of two numbers is 12 and their difference is also 12. The numbers are:
A. 66, 78 B. 70, 82
C. 94, 106 D. 84, 96

10. The largest number which exactly divides 210, 315, 147 and 161 is:
A. 3 B. 7
C. 21 D. 4410

11. The least perfect square number which is divisible by 3, 4, 5, 6 and 8 is:
A. 900 B. 1200
C. 2500 D. 3600

12. The smallest number which is divisible by 12, 15, 20 and is a perfect square, is:
A. 400 B. 900
C. 1600 D. 3600

13. The sum of two numbers is 216 and their HCF is 27. The numbers are:
A. 54, 162 B. 108, 108
C. 27, 189 D. None of these

14. The HCF and LCM of two numbers are 44 and 264 respectively. If the first number is divided by 2, the quotient is 44. The other number is:
A. 33 B. 66
C. 132 D. 264

15. The number of prime factors in $2^{222} \times 3^{333} \times 5^{555}$ is:
A. 3 B. 1107
C. 1110 D. 1272

16. The number of prime factors in the expression $(6)^{10} \times (7)^{17} \times (11)^{27}$ is:
A. 54 B. 64
C. 71 D. 81

17. Three measuring rods are 64 cm, 80 cm and 96 cm in length. The least length of cloth that can be measured exact number of times using any one of the above rod is:
A. 0.96 m B. 19.20 m
C. 9.60 m D. 96.00 m

18. The product of two numbers is 1600 and their HCF is 5. The LCM of the numbers is:
A. 320 B. 1605
C. 1595 D. 8000

19. About the number of pairs which have 16 as their HCF and 136 as their LCM, we can definitely say that:
A. Only one such pair exists
B. Only two such pairs exist
C. Many such pairs exist
D. No such pair exist

20. The total number of prime factors of the product $(8)^{20} \times (15)^{24} \times (7)^{15}$ is:
A. 59 B. 98
C. 123 D. 138

21. The LCM of two numbers is 85 and their product is 1020. Their HCF will be:
A. 16 B. 27
C. 12 D. 22

22. HCF of 420, 315 and 462 is:
A. 24 B. 28
C. 27 D. 21

23. Two numbers are in the ratio of 8 : 15. If their HCF is 4, the numbers are:
A. 32 and 60 B. 16 and 30
C. 80 and 150 D. 64 and 120

24. Three bells ring respectively at an interval of 15 seconds, 20 seconds and 24 seconds. If they ring continuously for 12 minutes then how many times during this period, will they ring together?
A. 2 times B. 6 times
C. 5 times D. 3 times

ANSWERS

1	2	3	4	5	6	7	8	9	10
C	C	D	B	A	C	A	B	D	B
11	**12**	**13**	**14**	**15**	**16**	**17**	**18**	**19**	**20**
D	B	C	C	C	B	C	A	D	C
21	**22**	**23**	**24**						
C	D	A	B						

EXPLANATORY ANSWERS

1.
```
1485) 4 3 5 6 (2
      2 9 7 0
      -------
      1 3 8 6) 1 4 8 5 (1
               1 3 8 6
               -------
                 9 9) 1 3 8 6 (14
                        9 9
                        ---
                        3 9 6
                        3 9 6
                        -----
                          0
```

∴ HCF of 1485 and 4356 is 99.

2.

2	18,	24,	42,	63
3	9,	12,	21,	63
3	3,	4,	7,	21
7	1,	4,	7,	7
	1,	4,	1,	1

LCM of 18, 24, 42, 63 = $2 \times 3^2 \times 7 \times 4 = 504$.

3. $\frac{7}{8} = 0.875$

$\frac{6}{7} = 0.857$

$\frac{4}{5} = 0.8$

$\frac{5}{6} = 0.833$

Clearly, 0.875 is the greatest of all.

Hence, $\frac{7}{8}$ is the greatest of all.

4. $\frac{5}{7} = 0.714$

$\frac{7}{8} = 0.875$

$\frac{9}{11} = 0.818$

Now, $0.714 < 0.818 < 0.875$

Hence, $\frac{5}{7} < \frac{9}{11} < \frac{7}{8}$.

5. Let the numbers be x, $2x$ and $3x$.
Then, their HCF = x
According to the question, $x = 12$
$\therefore$ The numbers are 12, 24, 36.

6. $1 \times 2 \times 3 \times 4 = 24$
$\therefore$ Required number = 24.

7. LCM of 48, 72, 108 = 432
432 seconds = 7 min 12 seconds.
So, the next simultaneous change will take place at 8 : 27 : 12 hrs.

8. Other number = $\dfrac{\text{LCM} \times \text{HCF}}{\text{One number}}$

$= \dfrac{160 \times 16}{32} = 80$

Hence, other number = 80.

9. 12 is not the HCF of given options A, B and C.
Hence, D is correct answer.
In 84, 96, 12 is HCF of 84 and 96
Difference of 96 – 84 = 12
So, required numbers are 84 and 96.

10. HCF of 210, 315, 147 and 161 = 7
Hence, the required number = 7.

11.

2	3,	4,	5,	6,	8
2	3,	2,	5,	3,	4
3	3,	1,	5,	3,	2
	1,	1,	5,	1,	2

LCM of 3, 4, 5, 6, 8
$= 2 \times 2 \times 3 \times 5 \times 2$
Required number
$= (2 \times 2 \times 3 \times 3 \times 5 \times 5 \times 2 \times 2)$
$= 3600$

12. LCM of 12, 15 and 20 = 60
Hence, required number = $60 \times 15 = 900$.

13. HCF of 54, 162 = 54
HCF of 108, 108 = 108
HCF of 27, 189 = 27
Hence, required numbers are 27 and 189.

14. According to the question,
First number = $2 \times 44 = 88$

Other number = $\dfrac{\text{LCM} \times \text{HCF}}{\text{First number}}$

$= \dfrac{264 \times 44}{88} = 132$

15. The number of prime factors in the given product = (222 + 333 + 555) = 1110

16. 2, 3, 7, 11 are prime numbers in the given expression. The number of prime factors in the given expression (10 + 10 + 17 + 27) = 64

17. Required length = (LCM of 64, 80, 96) cm
= 960 cm = 9.60 m.

18. LCM = $\dfrac{\text{Product of numbers}}{\text{HCF}} = \dfrac{1600}{5} = 320$

19. HCF is always a factor of LCM. So no two numbers exist with HCF = 16 and LCM = 136.

20. Since 2, 3, 5, 7 are prime numbers and the given expression is $(2^3)^{20} \times (3 \times 5)^{24} \times (7)^{15}$

i.e. $2^{60} \times 3^{24} \times 5^{24} \times 7^{15}$, so the number of prime factors in the given expression
= (60 + 24 + 24 + 15) = 123

21. LCM of two numbers × HCF of the numbers
= Product of the numbers
$\therefore \quad 85 \times \text{HCF} = 1020$

$\text{HCF} = \dfrac{1020}{85} = 12$

22.

```
315) 420 (1
     315
     ---
     105) 315 (3
          315
          ---
           ×
```

Now HCF of 105 and 462.

```
105) 462 (4
     420
     ---
      42) 105 (2
           84
           ---
           21) 42 (2
               42
               --
                ×
```

$\therefore$ Required HCF = 21

23. Let the numbers be $8x$ and $15x$
LCM of $8x$ and $15x = 120x$

$\therefore \quad \text{HCF} = \dfrac{8x \times 15x}{120x}$

$4 = \dfrac{120x^2}{120x} = x$

$\therefore$ Numbers are $8 \times 4 = 32$ and $15 \times 4 = 60$

24. LCM of 15, 20 and 24 = 120
$\because$ 12 minutes = $12 \times 60 = 720$ seconds
$\therefore$ Number of times the bells will ring together 12 minutes = $\dfrac{720}{120} = 6$ times.

4. RATIO AND PROPORTION

RATIO

When comparison is made by dividing one quantity by another of the same kind, the result is called ratio. If a and b are two numbers, ratio of a to b is denoted by $a : b$ or $\frac{a}{b}$. Here a is called first term and b is called the second term. The first term is also called antecedent and the second term is also called consequent.

EXAMPLE: The ratio 3 : 10 represents $\frac{3}{10}$ with antecedent 3 and consequent 10.

The multiplication or division of each term of a ratio by a same non-zero number does not effect the ratio.

PROPORTION

Equality of two ratios is called proportion. If $a : b = c : d$, then a, b, c, d are called in proportion. In a proportion $a : b :: c : d$, then a and d are called extremes and b and c are called means.

Product of extremes = Product of means

Comparison of Ratio: Suppose $\frac{a}{b} > \frac{c}{d}$ then we say that $a : b > c : d$.

Compounded Ratio: The compound ratio of the ratios $a : b$, $c : d$ and $e : f$ is $ace : bdf$.

Duplicate Ratio: The duplicate ratio of $a : b$ is $a^2 : b^2$.

Triplicate Ratio: The triplicate ratio of $a : b$ is $a^3 : b^3$.

Sub-duplicate and Sub-triplicate Ratios

The sub-duplicate and sub-triplicate ratios of ratio $a : b$ are $a^{1/2} : b^{1/2}$ and $a^{1/3} : b^{1/3}$ respectively.

Mean Proportional: Mean proportional between a and b is $\sqrt{ab}$.

Third Proportional: The third proportional to a, b is the fourth proportional to a, b, b.

Fourth Proportional: If $a : b :: c : d$ is a proportion, then d is called the fourth proportional to a, b, c.

EXAMPLE: If A : B = 3 : 4 and B : C = 8 : 9 then find A : C.

SOLUTION: $A : B = 3 : 4 \Rightarrow \frac{A}{B} = \frac{3}{4}$

$B : C = 8 : 9 \Rightarrow \frac{B}{C} = \frac{8}{9}$

$\frac{A}{C} = \frac{A}{B} \times \frac{B}{C} = \frac{3}{4} \times \frac{8}{9} = \frac{2}{3}$

$\Rightarrow \quad A : C = 2 : 3$

EXAMPLE: If 15% of A is the same as 20% of B, then find A : B.

SOLUTION: Given : 15% of A = 20% of B

$\Rightarrow \quad \frac{15}{100} \times A = \frac{20}{100} \times B$

$\Rightarrow \quad 3A = 4B$

$\Rightarrow \quad \frac{A}{B} = \frac{4}{3}$

$\Rightarrow \quad A : B = 4 : 3$

EXAMPLE: A stick 1.4 m long casts a shadow 1.3 m long at the same time when a pole casts a shadow 5.2 m long. Find the length of the pole.

SOLUTION: Clearly, more is the length of shadow, more is the length of the object.

Let the length of the pole be x metres.

Then, $1.3 : 5.2 :: 1.4 : x$

$\Rightarrow \quad \frac{1.3}{5.2} = \frac{1.4}{x}$

$\Rightarrow \quad \frac{1}{4} = \frac{1.4}{x}$

$\Rightarrow \quad x = 1.4 \times 4 = 5.6$

Hence, the length of the pole is 5.6 m.

MULTIPLE CHOICE QUESTIONS

1. If A : B = 2 : 3 and B : C = 4 : 5, then C : A is equal to:

A. 15 : 8 B. 12 : 10
C. 8 : 5 D. 8 : 15

2. If 10% of x is the same as 20% of y, then $x : y$ is equal to:

A. 1 : 2 B. 2 : 1
C. 5 : 1 D. 10 : 1

3. The mean proportional to $6 + \sqrt{27}$ and $6 - \sqrt{27}$ is:

A. 3 B. 9
C. 10 D. $\sqrt{10}$

4. If $x : y = 9 : 11$, the value of $\frac{5x + 3y}{3x + 5y}$ is:

A. 45 : 55 B. 18 : 22
C. 37 : 41 D. 39 : 41

5. If $a + b : b + c : c + a = 6 : 7 : 8$ and $a + b + c = 14$, then the value of c is:

A. 14　　B. 7
C. 8　　D. 6

6. Two numbers are in the ratio 2 : 3. If 5 is added to each number, the ratio becomes 5 : 7. The bigger number is:

A. 30　　B. 40
C. 60　　D. 20

7. What should be added to each of the numbers 12, 30, 40 and 86, so that they are in proportion?

A. 6　　B. 4
C. –6　　D. –4

8. The ratio of males and females of a village is 5 : 3. If there are 800 males in the village, females are:

A. 240　　B. 480
C. 840　　D. 488

9. In a mixture of 60 litres, the ratio of ethanol to ether is 4 : 1. How much ether must be added to the mixture to make this ratio 2 : 1?

A. 10 litres　　B. 12 litres
C. 18 litres　　D. 24 litres

10. The proportion of zinc and copper in a brass piece is 4 : 5. How much zinc will be there in 180 kg of such a piece?

A. 40 kg　　B. 80 kg
C. 100 kg　　D. 120 kg

11. The prices of a scooter and a television set are in the ratio 3 : 2. If a scooter costs ₹ 6000 more than the television set, the price of the television set is:

A. ₹ 18000　　B. ₹ 12000
C. ₹ 10000　　D. ₹ 6000

12. The weight of a 13 metres long iron rod be 23.4 kg. The weight of 6 metres long of such rod will be:

A. 7.2 kg　　B. 12.4 kg
C. 10.8 kg　　D. 18 kg

13. The ratio between the ages of Gayatri and Savitri is 6 : 5 and the sum of their ages is 44 years. The ratio of their ages after 8 years will be:

A. 5 : 6　　B. 7 : 8
C. 8 : 7　　D. 14 : 13

14. Two numbers are such that the ratio between them is 3 : 5 but if each is increased by 10, the ratio between them becomes 5 : 7. The numbers are:

A. 3, 5　　B. 7, 9
C. 13, 22　　D. 15, 25

15. In a factory the ratio of male workers to female workers was 5 : 3. If the number of female workers was less by 40, the total number of workers in the factory was:

A. 100　　B. 500
C. 160　　D. 200

16. If $a : b = 2 : 3$, $b : c = 4 : 5$ and $c : d = 6 : 7$, then $a : d$ is equal to:

A. 2 : 7　　B. 7 : 8
C. 16 : 35　　D. 4 : 13

17. A bag contains one rupee, fifty paise and 25 paise coins in the ratio of 2 : 3 : 4. If the total amount is ₹ 180, the number of fifty paise coins is:

A. 120　　B. 60
C. 40　　D. 240

18. $\frac{3}{7}$ of $\frac{7}{8}$ of a number is equal to the 25% of 45% of another number. The ratio of first number and second number is:

A. 3 : 7　　B. 9 : 10
C. 3 : 10　　D. None of the above

19. The ratios of milk and water in four solutions are 1 : 2, 2 : 3, 3 : 2 and 7 : 8 respectively.
If their equal quantities are mixed together, then the ratio of milk and water in the new solution will be:

A. 13 : 15　　B. 7 : 9
C. 9 : 11　　D. 11 : 9

20. A number is divided into parts such that the sum of 5 times of the first part and 18 times of the second part is equal to 7 times of the number. The ratio of two parts is:

A. 5 : 7　　B. 9 : 8
C. 1 : 7　　D. 11 : 2

21. If $x : y :: 5 : 2$, then $8x + 9y : 8x + 2y$ is equal to:

A. 22 : 29　　B. 29 : 22
C. 31 : 29　　D. 21 : 29

22. If 76 is divided in to the ratios of 7, 5, 3 and 4, then the smallest part will be:

A. 14　　B. 18
C. 32　　D. 12

23. The sum of two numbers is 70 and their difference is 16. Ratio of these two numbers is:

A. 43 : 27　　B. 27 : 64
C. 43 : 16　　D. 25 : 64

24. Two numbers are in the ratio of 12 and 19. If the sum of these two numbers is 217, the value of smallest number is:

A. 81　　B. 64
C. 70　　D. 84

ANSWERS

1	2	3	4	5	6	7	8	9	10
A	B	A	D	D	A	A	B	B	B
11	**12**	**13**	**14**	**15**	**16**	**17**	**18**	**19**	**20**
B	C	C	D	C	C	A	C	C	D
21	**22**	**23**	**24**						
B	D	A	D						

EXPLANATORY ANSWERS

1. $\frac{A}{B} = \frac{2}{3}$ and $\frac{B}{C} = \frac{4}{5}$

$\Rightarrow \quad \frac{A}{B}\times\frac{B}{C} = \frac{2}{3}\times\frac{4}{5} \Rightarrow \frac{A}{C} = \frac{8}{15}$

$\Rightarrow \quad \frac{C}{A} = \frac{15}{8}$

Hence, $\quad C : A = 15 : 8.$

2. 10% of x = 20% of y

$\Rightarrow \quad \frac{10}{100}x = \frac{20}{100}y \Rightarrow \frac{x}{10} = \frac{y}{5}$

$\Rightarrow \quad \frac{x}{y} = \frac{10}{5} \quad \Rightarrow x : y = 2 : 1$

3. Mean proportional $= \sqrt{(6+\sqrt{27})(6-\sqrt{27})}$

$= \sqrt{36-27} = \sqrt{9} = 3$

4. $\because \quad \frac{x}{y} = \frac{9}{11}$

$\frac{5x+3y}{3x+5y} = \frac{\frac{5x}{y}+\frac{3y}{y}}{\frac{3x}{y}+\frac{5y}{y}} = \frac{5\left(\frac{x}{y}\right)+3}{3\left(\frac{x}{y}\right)+5}$

$= \frac{5\times\frac{9}{11}+3}{3\times\frac{9}{11}+5} = \frac{\frac{45+33}{11}}{\frac{27+55}{11}} = \frac{78}{82} = \frac{39}{41}$

Hence, the value of $\frac{5x+3y}{3x+5y} = \frac{39}{41}$.

5. Given : $a+b = 6x,\ b+c = 7x$

and $\quad c+a = 8x \quad$ ...(*i*)

and $\quad a+b+c = 14 \quad$ ...(*ii*)

Adding Eq. (*i*)

$a+b+b+c+c+a = 6x+7x+8x$

$\Rightarrow \quad 2(a+b+c) = 21x$

$\Rightarrow \quad 2\times 14 = 21x \quad$ [from Eq. (*ii*)]

$\Rightarrow \quad x = \frac{28}{21} = \frac{4}{3}$

$\therefore \quad a+b = 6x = 6\times\frac{4}{3} = 8$

$\because \quad a+b+c = 14 \Rightarrow c = 14-8 = 6$

6. Let the two numbers are a and b

According to the question,

$\frac{a}{b} = \frac{2}{3} \Rightarrow 3a = 2b \Rightarrow b = \frac{3a}{2}$

Now, $\quad \frac{a+5}{b+5} = \frac{5}{7} \Rightarrow 7a+35 = 5b+25$

$\Rightarrow \quad 7a-5b = -10$

$\Rightarrow \quad 7a-5\left(\frac{3a}{2}\right) = -10$

$\Rightarrow \quad 14a-15a = -20 \Rightarrow -a = -20$

$\Rightarrow \quad a = 20,\ b = 3\times\frac{20}{2} = 30$

Hence, the bigger number is 30.

7. Let x be added to each of the numbers.

Then, $(12+x) : (30+x) :: (40+x) : (86+x)$

$\Rightarrow \quad \frac{12+x}{30+x} = \frac{40+x}{86+x}$

$\Rightarrow (12+x)(86+x) = (30+x)(40+x)$

$\Rightarrow 12\times 86+12x+86x+x^2$

$= 30\times 40+30x+40x+x^2$

$\Rightarrow \quad 1032+98x = 1200+70x$

$\Rightarrow \quad 28x = 168 \Rightarrow x = 6$

8. Ratio of Males : Females = 5 : 3

$\Rightarrow \quad \frac{800}{x} = \frac{5}{3} \Rightarrow 5x = 3\times 800$

$\Rightarrow \quad x = \frac{3\times 800}{5} = 3\times 160 = 480$

Hence, number of females = 480.

9. Let ethanol = $4x$ and ether = $1x$

$4x+1x = 60 \Rightarrow 5x = 60 \Rightarrow x = 12$

Quantity of ethanol = 12×4 = 48 litres

Quantity of ether = 1×12 = 12 litres

Let m litres of ether be added to mixture to get the desired ratio. Then,

$\frac{48}{12+m} = \frac{2}{1} \quad \Rightarrow \quad 24+2m = 48$

$\Rightarrow \quad 2m = 24 \quad \Rightarrow \quad m = 12$

Hence, 12 litres of ether is to be added.

10. In 9 kg of brass, zinc = 4 kg

$\therefore$ In 180 kg of brass, zinc $= \frac{4}{9}\times 180 = 80$ kg.

11. Let the prices of a scooter and a television be ₹ $3x$ and $2x$ respectively.

According to the question,

$3x-2x = 6000 \Rightarrow x = 6000$

$\therefore$ Price of a television = 2×6000 = ₹ 12000.

12. Weight of 13 m long iron rod = 23.4 kg

Weight of 6 m long iron rod

$= \frac{23.4}{13}\times 6$ kg $= 1.8\times 6 = 10.8$ kg.

13. Let present age of Gayatri = $6x$ years and present age of Savitri = $5x$ years.

According to the question,

$6x+5x = 44 \Rightarrow 11x = 44 \Rightarrow x = 4$

Gayatri's age = 6×4 = 24 years

Savitri's age = 5×4 = 20 years

After 8 years their ages will be 32 years and 28 years.

Ratio of their ages after 8 years $= \frac{32}{28} = 8 : 7$.

14. Let numbers are x and y

$$\frac{x}{y} = \frac{3}{5}$$

$$\Rightarrow \quad 5x = 3y \Rightarrow x = \frac{3y}{5}$$

According to the question,

$$\frac{x+10}{y+10} = \frac{5}{7} \Rightarrow 7x + 70 = 5y + 50$$

$$\Rightarrow \quad 7x - 5y = -20$$

$$\Rightarrow \quad 7\left(\frac{3y}{5}\right) - 5y = -20$$

$$\Rightarrow \quad 21y - 25y = -100$$

$$\Rightarrow \quad 4y = 100 \Rightarrow y = 25$$

$$\therefore \quad x = \frac{3 \times 25}{5} = 15$$

Hence, numbers are 15 and 25.

15. Let the number of male and female workers be $5x$ and $3x$ respectively.

According to the question,

$5x - 3x = 40 \Rightarrow 2x = 40 \Rightarrow x = 20$

$\therefore$ Number of male $= 5 \times 20 = 100$

and number of female $= 3 \times 20 = 60$

Hence, total number of workers $= 100 + 60 = 160$.

16. $\frac{a}{b} = \frac{2}{3}$, $\frac{b}{c} = \frac{4}{5}$ and $\frac{c}{d} = \frac{6}{7}$

$$\therefore \frac{a}{d} = \frac{a}{b} \times \frac{b}{c} \times \frac{c}{d} = \frac{2}{3} \times \frac{4}{5} \times \frac{6}{7} = \frac{16}{35}$$

Hence, $a : d = 16 : 35$.

17. One rupee Fifty paise Twenty-five paise

$$2 \times 1 \; : \; 3 \times \frac{50}{100} \; : \; 4 \times \frac{25}{100}$$

$$2 \; : \; \frac{3}{2} \; : \; 1$$

$$4 \; : \; 3 \; : \; 2$$

Amount of fifty paise coins

$$= \frac{3}{4+3+2} \times 180$$

$$= \frac{3}{9} \times 180 = ₹\,60$$

$\therefore$ Number of fifty paise coins $= 60 \times 2 = 120$.

18. Let first number be x and second number be y.

$$\frac{3}{7} \times \frac{7}{8} x = \frac{25}{100} \times \frac{45}{100} \times y$$

$$\Rightarrow \quad \frac{3}{8} x = \frac{1}{4} \times \frac{9}{20} y \Rightarrow \frac{3x}{8} = \frac{9y}{80}$$

$$\Rightarrow \quad 240x = 72y \Rightarrow \frac{x}{y} = \frac{72}{240} = \frac{3}{10}$$

Hence, ratio of first number and second number $= 3 : 10$.

19. Required ratio

$$= \left(\frac{1}{1+2} + \frac{2}{2+3} + \frac{3}{3+2} + \frac{7}{7+8}\right)$$

$$: \left(\frac{2}{1+2} + \frac{3}{2+3} + \frac{2}{3+2} + \frac{8}{7+8}\right)$$

$$= \left(\frac{1}{3} + \frac{2}{5} + \frac{3}{5} + \frac{7}{15}\right) : \left(\frac{2}{3} + \frac{3}{5} + \frac{2}{5} + \frac{8}{15}\right)$$

$$= \left(\frac{1}{3} + \frac{5}{5} + \frac{7}{15}\right) : \left(\frac{2}{3} + \frac{5}{5} + \frac{8}{15}\right)$$

$$= \left(\frac{5+15+7}{15}\right) : \left(\frac{10+15+8}{15}\right)$$

$= 27 : 33 = 9 : 11$.

20. Let first part $= x$, second part $= y$

Then, $5x + 18y = 7(x + y)$

$\Rightarrow \quad 5x + 18y = 7x + 7y$

$\Rightarrow \quad 18y - 7y = 7x - 5x$

$\Rightarrow \quad 11y = 2x$

$$\Rightarrow \quad \frac{x}{y} = \frac{11}{2}$$

$\therefore$ The ratio of two parts is $11 : 2$.

21. $\because x : y :: 5 : 2$

$$\Rightarrow \quad \frac{x}{y} = \frac{5}{2}$$

$\Rightarrow \quad 2x = 5y \Rightarrow 8x = 20y$

$\Rightarrow \quad 8x + 9y = 20y + 9y = 29y$

and $\quad 8x + 2y = 20y + 2y = 22y$

$$\therefore \quad \frac{8x+9y}{8x+2y} = \frac{29y}{22y} = \frac{29}{22}$$

22. We have to divide 76 in the ratio of

$7 : 5 : 3 : 4$

Sum of proportionals $= 7 + 5 + 3 + 4 = 19$

$$\therefore \text{Smallest share} = \frac{3}{19} \times 76 = 12$$

23. Let numbers are x and y

According to the question,

$x + y = 70$ ...(*i*)

and $x - y = 16$ ...(*ii*)

Solving (*i*) and (*ii*) we get $x = 43$

and $y = 27$

$\therefore$ Ratio of the numbers $= 43 : 27$

24. Ratio of two numbers $= 12 : 19$

$$\therefore \text{Value of the smaller number} = \frac{12}{31} \times 217$$

$$= 84$$

5. PERCENTAGE

The word 'per cent' or 'percentage' means 'for every one hundred'. In other words, it gives an indication of rate per hundred.

It is denoted by the symbol %.

For example, 5% means 5 out of one hundred or $\frac{5}{100}$.

Remember:

(i) For converting a per cent into a fraction, divide it by 100.

(ii) For converting a fraction into a per cent, multiply it by 100.

(iii) For converting a per cent into a decimal, shift the decimal point two places to the left.

(iv) For converting one given quantity (x) as a percentage of another given quantity (y), find $\frac{x}{y}\times 100$.

(v) There is no unit of percentage.

Important Facts:

For quickly solving the problems related to percentage, remember following rules:

A. Of the given two numbers if the first is $x\%$ more than the second, then the second will be $\left(\frac{100\times x}{100+x}\right)\%$ less than the first.

B. Of the given two numbers if the first is $x\%$ less than the second, then the second will be $\left(\frac{100\times x}{100-x}\right)\%$ more than the first.

C. If two numbers are respectively $x\%$ and $y\%$ more than a third number, then the first number will be $\left(\frac{100+x}{100+y}\times 100\right)\%$ of the second.

D. If two numbers are respectively $x\%$ and $y\%$ less than a third number, then the first number will be $\left(\frac{100-x}{100-y}\times 100\right)\%$ of the second.

EXAMPLES

Example 1: The population of a town is 45000. $\frac{11}{18}$th of them are males and the rest females, 40% of the females are married. Find the number of married males.

Solution: Number of males

$$= \frac{11}{18}\times 45000 = 27500$$

$\therefore$ No. of females = 45000 − 27500 = 17500

Thus, No. of married females

= 40% of 17500 = 7000

$\Rightarrow$ The number of married males = 7000

Example 2: The population of a town is 40,000. If the population increases 20% every year, find the population after 3 years.

Solution: Population after 3 years

$$= 40000\left(1+\frac{20}{100}\right)^3$$

$$= 40000\times\frac{6}{5}\times\frac{6}{5}\times\frac{6}{5} = 69120$$

Example 3 : In an examination 60% of the candidates passed in English, 55% in Mathematics and 25% failed in both subjects. Find the pass percentage.

Solution: Those failing in mathematics

= 100 − 55 = 45%

Those failing in English

= 100 − 60 = 40%

Failing in both = 25%

Failing in one or both the subjects

= (45 + 40 − 25) = 60%

$\therefore$ Pass % = 100 − 60 = 40%

Example 4: Atul's marks in Science are 20 less than 60% of the total marks obtained by him in Science and Maths together. If his total marks are 250, what are his marks in Maths?

Solution: Marks obtained in Science = 60% of 250 − 20

$$= \frac{60}{100}\times 250 - 20 = 130$$

$\therefore$ Marks obtained in Maths = 250 − 130 = 120

MULTIPLE CHOICE QUESTIONS

1. If x is 90% of y, then what per cent of x is y?
   A. 90 B. 190
   C. 101.1 D. 111.1
2. The price of an article is cut by 10%. To restore it to the former value, the new price must be increased by:
   A. 10% B. $9\frac{1}{11}\%$
   C. $10\frac{1}{9}\%$ D. $11\frac{1}{9}\%$
3. The income of a broker remains unchanged though the rate of commission is increased from 4% to 5%. The percentage of slump business is:
   A. 8% B. 1%
   C. 12% D. 20%
4. 5% income of A is equal to 15% income of B and 10% income of B is equal to 20% income of C. If income of C is ₹ 2000, then total income of A, B and C is:
   A. ₹ 6000 B. ₹ 18000
   C. ₹ 20000 D. ₹ 14000
5. A student who secures 20% marks in an examination fails by 30 marks. Another student who secures 32% gets 42 marks more than those required to pass. The percentage of marks required to pass is:
   A. 20 B. 25
   C. 28 D. 30
6. In a college election, a candidate secured 62% of the votes and is elected by a majority of 144 votes. The total number of votes polled is:
   A. 600 B. 800
   C. 925 D. 1200
7. The price of an article has been reduced by 25%. In order to restore the original price, the new price must be increased by:
   A. $33\frac{1}{3}\%$ B. $11\frac{1}{9}\%$
   C. $9\frac{1}{11}\%$ D. $66\frac{2}{3}\%$
8. The price of cooking oil has increased by 25%. The percentage of reduction that a family should effect in the use of cooking oil so as not to increase the expenditure on this account is:
   A. 25% B. 30%
   C. 20% D. 15%
9. In 40% of the people read newspaper X, 50% read newspaper Y, and 10% read both the papers. What percentage of the people read neither newspaper?
   A. 10% B. 15%
   C. 18% D. 20%
10. The population of a town increases by 5% annually. If its population in 2008 was 138915, what it was in 2005?
    A. 110000
    B. 100000
    C. 120000
    D. 90000
11. The population of a village is 4500. $\frac{5}{9}$th of them are males and rest females. If 40% of the males are married, then the percentage of married female is :
    A. 35 B. 40
    C. 50 D. 60
12. A mixture of 40 litres of milk and water contains 10% water. How much water must be added to make water 20% in the new mixture?
    A. 10 litres B. 7 litres
    C. 5 litres D. 3 litres
13. If $z = \frac{x^2}{y}$ and x, y both are increased in value by 10%, then the value of z is :
    A. unchanged
    B. increased by 10%
    C. increased by 11%
    D. increased by 20%
14. If the price of a television set is increased by 25%, then by what percentage should the new price be reduced to bring the price back to original level?
    A. 15% B. 18%
    C. 25% D. 30%
15. A candidate needs 35% marks to pass. If he gets 96 marks and fails by 16 marks, then the maximum marks are :
    A. 250 B. 320
    C. 300 D. 425

ANSWERS

1	2	3	4	5	6	7	8	9	10
D	D	D	B	B	A	A	C	D	C
11	**12**	**13**	**14**	**15**					
C	C	B	B	B					

EXPLANATORY ANSWERS

1. $x = 90\%$ of $y \Rightarrow x = \frac{90}{100}y$

Required percentage $= \frac{y}{9y/10} = \frac{10}{9} \times 100$

$= 111.1\%$

2. Required percentage $= \frac{10}{100-10} \times 100$

$= \frac{10}{90} \times 100 = 11\frac{1}{9}\%$

8. Required reduction $= \left[\frac{r}{(100+r)} \times 100\right]$

$= \left(\frac{25}{125} \times 100\right)\% = 20\%$

9. Number of people read either one or both

$= 40 + 50 - 10 = 80\%$

Hence, number of people read neither newspaper

$= 100 - 80 = 20\%.$

12. Water $= 10/100 \times 40 = 4$ litres

Let x litres of water be added,

Then, $x + 4 = \frac{20}{100}(40 + x)$

$\Rightarrow \quad 5x + 20 = 40 + x \Rightarrow 4x = 20$

$\therefore \quad x = 5$ litres.

14. Required reduction $= \frac{25}{100+25} \times 100 = 20\%.$

6. SQUARE ROOTS

☛ Points To Remember

- A number n is a perfect square number, if $n = m^2$
- A perfect square number is never negative.
- A square number never ends in 2, 3, 7 or 8.
- The number of zeros at the end of a perfect square is even.
- The square of an even number is even.
- The square of an odd number is odd.
- There are no natural number p and q such that $p^2 = 2q^2$.
- A number m is a square root of n, if $n = m \times m = m^2$. Positive square root of n is written as $\sqrt{n}$.
- If p and q are perfect squares ($q \neq 0$), then

  (*i*) $\sqrt{p \times q} = \sqrt{p} \times \sqrt{q}$

  (*ii*) $\sqrt{\frac{p}{q}} = \frac{\sqrt{p}}{\sqrt{q}}$

- A perfect squares leaves remainder 0 or 1 on division by 3.

  The following table gives the possible remainders for some other prime divisors.

Divisor	Possible Remainders
3	0, 1
5	0, 1, 4
7	0, 1, 2, 4
11	0, 1, 3, 4, 5, 9
13	0, 1, 3, 4, 9, 10, 12

- The unit's digit of the square of a natural number is the unit's digit of the square of the digit at unit's place of the given natural number.

Unit's digit of the number	Unit's digit of the square of the number
0	0
1 or 9	1
2 or 8	4
3 or 7	9
4 or 6	6
5	5

- For every natural number n,

$$(n + 1)^2 - n^2 = (n + 1) + n$$

e.g.; $9^2 - 8^2 = 9 + 8 = 17$

$19^2 - 18^2 = 19 + 18 = 37$

- The square of a natural number n is equal to the sum of first n odd natural numbers.

e.g.; $2^2 = 1 + 3$

$4^2 = 1 + 3 + 5 + 7 = 16$

n^2 = Sum of first n odd natural numbers.

- A triplet (m, n, p) of three natural numbers m, n and p is called a pythagorean triplet if $m^2 + n^2 = p^2$
- The square root of a perfect square number can be obtained by :

  (*i*) the prime factorization. (*ii*) the division method.

- If n is not a perfect square, then $\sqrt{n}$ is not a rational number.
- Squares of natural numbers having all digits 1 have a following pattern:

$1^2 = 1$

$11^2 = 1\,\mathbf{2}\,1$

$111^2 = 1\,2\,\mathbf{3}\,2\,1$

$1111^2 = 1\,2\,3\,\mathbf{4}\,3\,2\,1$

$11111^2 = 1\,2\,3\,4\,\mathbf{5}\,4\,3\,2\,1$

$111111^2 = 1\,2\,3\,4\,5\,\mathbf{6}\,5\,4\,3\,2\,1$

⋮ ⋮ ⋮

$111111111^2 = 1\,2\,3\,4\,5\,6\,7\,8\,\mathbf{9}\,8\,7\,6\,5\,4\,3\,2\,1$

In this pattern the sum of the digits of every number on the right hand side is a perfect square at given below:

$1 + 2 + 1 = 4 = 2^2$

$1 + 2 + 3 + 2 + 1 = 9 = 3^2$

$1 + 2 + 3 + 4 + 3 + 2 + 1 = 16 = 4^2$

. . . .

$1 + 2 + 3 + 4 + 5 + 6 + 7 + 8 + 9 + 8 + 7 + 6 + 5 + 4 + 3 + 2 + 1 = 81 = 9^2$.

- Observe the following pattern

$11^2 = 121$
$101^2 = 10201$
$1001^2 = 1002001$
$10001^2 = 100020001$

- Observe the following pattern

$11^2 = 121$
$101^2 = 10201$
$10101^2 = 102030201$
$1010101^2 = 1020304030201$
$101010101^2 = 10203040504030201$

- **Short Cut Method to find Squares Column Method**

Using $(a + b)^2 = a^2 + 2ab + b^2$.

Make three columns: What is square of 86

$a = 8, b = 6$

Step	Column I (a^2)	Column II $2ab$	Column III b^2
I	$(8)^2 = 64$	$2 \times 8 \times 6 = 96$	$(6)^2 = 36$
II	64	96 + 3 99	**36**

Step	Column I (a^2)	Column II $2ab$	Column III b^2
III	64 + 9 **73**	**96** + 3 99	**36**

The bold digits give the required square $86^2 = 7396$.

Square Root

Square root of a given number is that number which is multiplied by itself is equal to the given number. For example, square root of 81 is 9 because
92 = 9 × 9 = 81.

Methods of Finding the square root

A. Prime Factorization Method

(*i*) Prime Factorization Method

(*ii*) Group the Factors in Paris

(*iii*) Take one number from each pair of factors and then multiply them together.

Example: Find the square root of 4761?

Solution: $4761 = \underbrace{23 \times 23} \times \underbrace{3 \times 3}$

$\therefore \quad \sqrt{4761} = 23 \times 3 = 69.$

B. Method of Division: This method is used when the number is large and the factors cannot be easily determined.

Example: Find the square root of 226576?

Solution:

```
          476
    4   226516
         16
   87    665
    7    609
  946    5676
    6    5676
           ×
```

$\sqrt[2]{226576} = 476.$

MULTIPLE CHOICE QUESTIONS

1. $\sqrt{53824} = ?$

A. 202 B. 232
C. 242 D. 332

2. The value of $\sqrt{10+\sqrt{25+\sqrt{108+\sqrt{154+\sqrt{255}}}}}$ is:

A. 4 B. 6
C. 8 D. 10

3. Evaluate : $\sqrt{41-\sqrt{21+\sqrt{19-\sqrt{9}}}}$.

A. 3 B. 5
C. 6 D. 6.4

4. $\left(\dfrac{\sqrt{625}}{11} \times \dfrac{14}{\sqrt{25}} \times \dfrac{11}{\sqrt{196}}\right)$ is equal to:

A. 5 B. 6
C. 8 D. 11

5. If $x * y = x + y + \sqrt{xy}$, the value of 6*24 is:

A. 41 B. 42
C. 43 D. 44

6. $\sqrt{\dfrac{25}{81} - \dfrac{1}{9}} = ?$

A. $\dfrac{2}{3}$ B. $\dfrac{4}{9}$
C. $\dfrac{16}{81}$ D. $\dfrac{25}{81}$

7. The value of $\sqrt{0.01}+\sqrt{0.81}+\sqrt{1.21}+\sqrt{0.0009}$ is:

A. 2.03
B. 2.1
C. 2.11
D. 2.13

8. If $\sqrt{18225} = 135$, then the value of $\left(\sqrt{182.25}+\sqrt{1.8225}+\sqrt{0.018225}+\sqrt{0.00018225}\right)$ is:

A. 1.49985 B. 14.9985
C. 149.985 D. 1499.85

9. If $\sqrt{3^n} = 729$, then the value of n is:

A. 6 B. 8
C. 10 D. 12

10. If $\sqrt{1+\frac{x}{169}}=\frac{14}{13}$, then x is equal to:

A. 1 B. 13
C. 27 D. None of these

11. If $\sqrt{1+\frac{55}{729}}=1+\frac{x}{27}$, then the value of x is:

A. 1 B. 3
C. 5 D. 7

12. The value of $\frac{\sqrt{80}-\sqrt{112}}{\sqrt{45}-\sqrt{63}}$ is:

A. $\frac{3}{4}$ B. $1\frac{1}{3}$
C. $1\frac{7}{9}$ D. $1\frac{3}{4}$

13. Given $\sqrt{2}=1.414$. The value of $\sqrt{8}+2\sqrt{32}-3\sqrt{128}+4\sqrt{50}$ is:

A. 8.426 B. 8.484
C. 8.526 D. 8.876

14. $\sqrt{\frac{0.081\times 0.324\times 4.624}{1.5625\times 0.0289\times 72.9\times 64}}$ is equal to:

A. 0.024 B. 0.24
C. 2.4 D. 24

15. The value of $\sqrt{\frac{(0.03)^2+(0.21)^2+(0.065)^2}{(0.003)^2+(0.021)^2+(0.0065)^2}}$ is:

A. 0.1 B. 10
C. 10^2 D. 10^3

16. The square root of $\left(7+3\sqrt{5}\right)\left(7-3\sqrt{5}\right)$ is:

A. $\sqrt{5}$ B. 2
C. 4 D. $3\sqrt{5}$

17. $\left(\sqrt{3}-\frac{1}{\sqrt{3}}\right)^2$ simplifies to:

A. $\frac{3}{4}$ B. $\frac{4}{\sqrt{3}}$
C. $\frac{4}{3}$ D. None of these

18. $\left(\sqrt{2}+\frac{1}{\sqrt{2}}\right)^2$ is equal to :

A. $2\frac{1}{2}$ B. $3\frac{1}{2}$
C. $4\frac{1}{2}$ D. $5\frac{1}{2}$

19. If $3a = 4b = 6c$ and $a + b + c = 27\sqrt{29}$, then $\sqrt{a^2+b^2+c^2}$ is:

A. $3\sqrt{29}$ B. 81
C. 87 D. None of these

20. The square root of $0.\overline{4}$ is:

A. $0.\overline{6}$ B. $0.\overline{7}$
C. $0.\overline{8}$ D. $0.\overline{9}$

ANSWERS

1	2	3	4	5	6	7	8	9	10
B	A	C	A	B	B	D	B	D	C
11	**12**	**13**	**14**	**15**	**16**	**17**	**18**	**19**	**20**
A	B	B	A	B	B	C	C	C	A

EXPLANATORY ANSWERS

1.

```
     2 | 53824 (232
       | 4
    43 | 138
       | 129
   462 |  924
       |  924
       |   ×
```

$\therefore \sqrt{53824}=232.$

2. Given exp. $=\sqrt{10+\sqrt{25+\sqrt{108+\sqrt{154+15}}}}$

$=\sqrt{10+\sqrt{25+\sqrt{108+\sqrt{169}}}}$

$=\sqrt{10+\sqrt{25+\sqrt{108+13}}}=\sqrt{10+\sqrt{25+\sqrt{121}}}$

$=\sqrt{10+\sqrt{25+11}}=\sqrt{10+\sqrt{36}}=\sqrt{10+6}=\sqrt{16}=4$

3. Given exp. = $\sqrt{41-\sqrt{21+\sqrt{19-3}}}$

$= \sqrt{41-\sqrt{21+\sqrt{16}}} = \sqrt{41-\sqrt{21+4}}$

$= \sqrt{41-\sqrt{25}} = \sqrt{41-5} = \sqrt{36} = 6$

4. Given exp. = $\frac{25}{11}\times\frac{14}{5}\times\frac{11}{14} = 5$

5. $6*24 = 6 + 24 + \sqrt{6\times24} = 30+\sqrt{144} = 30+12 = 42$

6. $\sqrt{\frac{25}{81}-\frac{1}{9}} = \sqrt{\frac{25-9}{81}} = \sqrt{\frac{16}{81}} = \frac{\sqrt{16}}{\sqrt{81}} = \frac{4}{9}$

7. Given exp.

$= \sqrt{\frac{1}{100}}+\sqrt{\frac{81}{100}}+\sqrt{\frac{121}{100}}+\sqrt{\frac{9}{10000}}$

$= \frac{1}{10}+\frac{9}{10}+\frac{11}{10}+\frac{3}{100}$

$= 0.1 + 0.9 + 1.1 + 0.03 = 2.13$

8. Given exp.

$= \sqrt{\frac{18225}{10^2}}+\sqrt{\frac{18225}{10^4}}+\sqrt{\frac{18225}{10^6}}+\sqrt{\frac{18225}{10^8}}$

$= \sqrt{\frac{18225}{10}}+\sqrt{\frac{18225}{10^2}}+\sqrt{\frac{18225}{10^3}}+\sqrt{\frac{18225}{10^4}}$

$= \frac{135}{10}+\frac{135}{100}+\frac{135}{1000}+\frac{135}{10000}$

$= 13.5 + 1.35 + 0.135 + 0.0135 = 14.9985$

9. $\sqrt{3^n} = 729 = 3^6 \Leftrightarrow \left(\sqrt{3^n}\right)^2 = (3^6)^2$

$\Leftrightarrow 3^n = 3^{12} \Leftrightarrow n = 12$

10. $\sqrt{1+\frac{x}{169}} = \frac{14}{13} \Rightarrow 1+\frac{x}{169} = \frac{196}{169}$

$\Rightarrow \frac{x}{169} = \left(\frac{196}{169}-1\right) = \frac{27}{169} \Rightarrow x = 27.$

11. $\sqrt{1+\frac{55}{729}} = 1+\frac{x}{27} \Rightarrow \sqrt{\frac{784}{729}} = \frac{27+x}{27} \Rightarrow \frac{28}{27} = \frac{27+x}{27}$

$\Rightarrow 27 + x = 28 \Rightarrow x = 1$

12. $\frac{\sqrt{80}-\sqrt{112}}{\sqrt{45}-\sqrt{63}} = \frac{\sqrt{16\times5}-\sqrt{16\times7}}{\sqrt{9\times5}-\sqrt{9\times7}}$

$= \frac{4\sqrt{5}-4\sqrt{7}}{3\sqrt{5}-3\sqrt{7}} = \frac{4\left(\sqrt{5}-\sqrt{7}\right)}{3\left(\sqrt{5}-\sqrt{7}\right)} = \frac{4}{3} = 1\frac{1}{3}$

13. Given exp.

$= \sqrt{4\times2}+2\sqrt{16\times2}-3\sqrt{64\times2}+4\sqrt{25\times2}$

$= 2\sqrt{2}+8\sqrt{2}-24\sqrt{2}+20\sqrt{2}$

$= 6\sqrt{2} = 6 \times 1.414 = 8.484$

14. Given exp. = $\sqrt{\frac{81\times324\times4624}{15625\times289\times729\times64}}$

$= \frac{9\times18\times68}{125\times17\times27\times8} = \frac{3}{125} = 0.024$

15. Given exp. = $\sqrt{\frac{(0.03)^2+(0.21)^2+(0.065)^2}{\left(\frac{0.03}{10}\right)^2+\left(\frac{0.21}{10}\right)^2+\left(\frac{0.065}{10}\right)^2}}$

$= \sqrt{\frac{100\ [(0.03)^2+(0.21)^2+(0.065)^2}{(0.03)^2+(0.21)^2+(0.065)^2}} = \sqrt{100} = 10$

16. $\sqrt{(7+3\sqrt{5})(7-3\sqrt{5})} = \sqrt{(7)^2-(3\sqrt{5})^2}$

$= \sqrt{49-45} = \sqrt{4} = 2$

17. $\left(\sqrt{3}-\frac{1}{\sqrt{3}}\right)^2 = \left(\sqrt{3}\right)^2+\left(\frac{1}{\sqrt{3}}\right)^2-2\times\sqrt{3}\times\frac{1}{\sqrt{3}}$

$= 3+\frac{1}{3}-2 = 1+\frac{1}{3} = \frac{4}{3}$

18. $\left(\sqrt{2}+\frac{1}{\sqrt{2}}\right)^2 = \left(\sqrt{2}\right)^2+\left(\frac{1}{\sqrt{2}}\right)^2+2\times\sqrt{2}\times\frac{1}{\sqrt{2}}$

$= 2+\frac{1}{2}+2 = 4+\frac{1}{2} = 4\frac{1}{2}$

19. $4b = 6c \Rightarrow b = \frac{3}{2}c$ and $3a = 4b$

$\Rightarrow \quad a = \frac{4}{3}b = \frac{4}{3}\left(\frac{3}{2}c\right) = 2c$

$a + b + c = 27\sqrt{29}$

$2c+\frac{3}{2}c+c = 27\sqrt{29}$

$\Rightarrow \quad \frac{9}{2}c = 27\sqrt{29} \Rightarrow c = 6\sqrt{29}$

$\therefore \sqrt{a^2+b^2+c^2}$

$= \sqrt{(a+b+c)-2(ab+bc+ca)}$

$= \sqrt{\left(27\sqrt{29}\right)^2-2\left(2c\times\frac{3}{2}c+\frac{3}{2}c\times c+c\times2c\right)}$

$= \sqrt{(729\times29)-2\left(3c^2+\frac{3}{2}c^2+2c^2\right)}$

$= \sqrt{(729\times29)-2\times\frac{13}{2}c^2} = \sqrt{(729\times29)-13\times\left(6\sqrt{29}\right)^2}$

$= \sqrt{29(729-468)} = \sqrt{29\times261} = \sqrt{29\times29\times9}$

$= 29 \times 3 = 87$

20. $\sqrt{0.\bar{4}} = \sqrt{\frac{4}{9}} = \frac{2}{3} = 0.666.... = 0.\bar{6}$.

7. AVERAGE

The sum of all the quantities of same kind divided by their number is called average (or mean) of those quantities.

FORMULAE

1. Average = $\left(\dfrac{\text{Sum of observations}}{\text{Number of observations}}\right)$
2. Sum of the first n natural numbers

   $= 1 + 2 + 3 + ... + n = \dfrac{n(n+1)}{2}$
3. Sum of the squares of the first n natural numbers

   $= 1^2 + 2^2 + ... + n^2 = \dfrac{n(n+1)(2n+1)}{6}$
4. Sum of the cubes of the first n natural numbers

   $= 1^3 + 2^3 + ... + n^3 = \left\{\dfrac{n(n+1)}{2}\right\}^2$
5. Sum of the first n odd numbers

   $= 1 + 3 + 5 + ... + (2n - 1) = n^2$
6. Distance between two stations P and Q is x km. A person covers the journey from P to Q at 'a' km/hr and returns back to P with a uniform speed of 'b' km/hr. Then the average speed of the person during the whole journey $= \dfrac{2ab}{a+b}$ km/hr.

Different kinds of mean or average:

A. Arithmetic mean

B. Geometric mean

C. Harmonic mean

A. Arithmetic Mean: It is most popularly used of all the averages. For example, average income, average profit, average mileage etc. As defined earlier, it is the sum total of all values of items divided by the total number of items. For detailed discussion we will confine ourselves to Arithmetic Mean only because this is the most relevant of all the average for us.

Let $x_1, x_2, x_3, ..., x_n$ be the n values of x.

Their average is denoted by $\bar{x}$ and given by

$$\bar{x} = \frac{\text{Sum of observations}}{\text{Total number of observations}}$$

or $$\bar{x} = \frac{x_1 + x_2 + x_3 + ... + x_n}{n}$$

B. Geometric Mean : For observations $x_1, x_2, x_3, ..., x_n$ the geometric mean denoted by G.M. is defined as:

$$\text{G.M.} = (x_1 . x_2 . x_3 ... x_n)^{1/n}$$

It is useful in calculating averages of ratios such as average population, growth rate, average percentage increase etc.

C. Harmonic Mean: It is defined as

$$\text{H.M.} = \frac{n}{\frac{1}{x_1} + \frac{1}{x_2} + ... + \frac{1}{x_n}}.$$

EXAMPLE: Find the average of first ten prime numbers.

SOLUTION: First ten prime numbers are 2, 3, 5, 7, 11, 13, 17, 19, 23 and 29.

$$\therefore \text{Average} = \frac{2+3+5+7+11+13+17+19+23+29}{10}$$

$$= \frac{129}{10} = 12.9$$

EXAMPLE: If x_1, x_2, x_3, x_4, x_5 are five consecutive odd numbers then find the average of these numbers.

SOLUTION: Since x_1 is the first odd number.

$$\therefore \quad x_2 = x_1 + 2$$
$$x_3 = x_2 + 2 = x_1 + 4$$
$$x_4 = x_3 + 2 = x_1 + 6$$
$$x_5 = x_4 + 2 = x_1 + 8$$

$$\therefore \text{Average} = \frac{x_1 + x_1 + 2 + x_1 + 4 + x_1 + 6 + x_1 + 8}{5}$$

$$= \frac{5x_1 + 20}{5} = \frac{5(x_1 + 4)}{5} = x_1 + 4$$

EXAMPLE: If the average of four consecutive even numbers is 27, then find the largest of these numbers.

SOLUTION: Let x be the first even number in the series of four consecutive even numbers.

$\therefore$ 2nd even number $= x + 2$

3rd even number $= x + 4$

4th even number $= x + 6$

$$\text{Average} = \frac{x + x + 2 + x + 4 + x + 6}{4}$$

$$\Rightarrow \quad 27 = \frac{4x + 12}{4}$$

$$\Rightarrow \quad 4x + 12 = 27 \times 4 = 108$$

$$\Rightarrow \quad 4x = 96 \Rightarrow x = 24$$

Largest number in this series is $x + 6$

i.e., $24 + 6 = 30$

EXAMPLE: The average of eight numbers is 14. The average of six of these numbers is 16. What is the average of the remaining two numbers?

SOLUTION: Sum of the eight numbers = $14 \times 8 = 112$

Sum of six of these eight numbers = $16 \times 6 = 96$

$\therefore$ Sum of the remaining two numbers = $112 - 96 = 16$

$\therefore$ Average of the remaining two numbers = $\frac{16}{2} = 8$

EXAMPLE: What is the average of first 30 multiples of 7?

SOLUTION: Required Average

$$= \frac{7+14+21+...+210}{30}$$

$$= \frac{7(1+2+3+...+30)}{30}$$

$$= \frac{7 \times 30(30+1)}{2 \times 30}$$

$$= \frac{7 \times 31}{2} = \frac{217}{2} = 108.5$$

EXAMPLE: The average of 11 results is 50. If the average of first six results is 49 and that of last six is 52, find the sixth result.

SOLUTION: Sum of 11 results = $11 \times 50 = 550$

Sum of first 6 results $6 \times 49 = 294$

Sum of last 6 results = $6 \times 52 = 312$

$\therefore$ 6th result = $294 + 312 - 550$

$= 56$

EXAMPLE: The average age of three boys is 15 years. If their ages are in the ratio 3 : 5 : 7. What is the age of the youngest boy?

SOLUTION: Let the ages of the three boys be $3x$, $5x$ and $7x$.

$$\text{Average age} = \frac{3x + 5x + 7x}{3} = 5x$$

and $5x = 15 \Rightarrow x = 3$

The age of the youngest boy = $3x = 3 \times 3 = 9$ years.

EXAMPLE: The average of 100 observations is 45. It was later found that two observations 19 and 31 were incorrectly recorded as 91 and 13. Find the correct average.

SOLUTION: Sum of 100 observations

$= 100 \times 45 = 4500$

New sum of 100 observations

$= 4500 + (19 + 31) - (91 + 13)$

$= 4500 + 50 - 104 = 4446$

$$\text{Correct average} = \frac{4446}{100} = 44.46$$

MULTIPLE CHOICE QUESTIONS

1. The average of first five multiples of 3 is:
A. 3 B. 9
C. 12 D. 15

2. The average of 25 results is 18, that of first 12 is 14 and of the last 12 is 17. Thirteenth result is:
A. 78 B. 85
C. 28 D. 72

3. Out of three numbers, the first is twice the second and is half of the third. If the average of the three numbers is 56, the three numbers in order are:
A. 48, 96, 24 B. 48, 24, 96
C. 96, 24, 48 D. 96, 48, 24

4. The sum of three numbers is 98. If the ratio between first and second be 2 : 3 and that between second and third be 5 : 8, then the second number is:
A. 30 B. 20
C. 58 D. 48

5. The average age of a committee of seven trustees is the same as it was 5 years ago; a young man having been substituted for one of them. The new man compared to the replaced old man, is younger in age by:
A. 5 years B. 7 years
C. 12 years D. 35 years

6. The average expenditure of a man for the first five months is ₹ 120 and for the next seven months is ₹ 130. His monthly average income if he saves ₹ 290 in that year, is:
A. ₹ 160 B. ₹ 170
C. ₹ 150 D. ₹ 140

7. The average salary of 20 workers in an office is ₹ 1900 per month. If the manager's salary is added, the average becomes ₹ 2000 per month. The manager's salary is:
A. ₹ 24000 B. ₹ 25200
C. ₹ 45600 D. None of these

8. The average temperature of first 3 days is 27°C and of the next 3 days is 29°C. If the average of the whole week is 28.5°C, the temperature of the last day is:
A. 31.5°C B. 10.5°C
C. 21°C D. 42°C

9. A cricketer scored 180 runs in the first test and 258 runs in the second. How many runs should he score in the third test so that his average score in the three tests would be 230 runs?
A. 219 B. 242
C. 334 D. None of these

10. The average of first five prime numbers is:

A. 5.0 B. 5.2

C. 5.6 D. 6.0

11. The average weight of 3 men A, B and C is 84 kg. Another man D joins the group and the average now becomes 80 kg. If another man E, whose weight is 3 kg more than that of D, replaces A, then average weight of B, C, D and E becomes 79 kg. The weight of A is:

A. 70 kg B. 72 kg

C. 75 kg D. 80 kg

12. The average age of A, B, C, D 5 years ago was 45 years. By including *x*, the present average of all the five is 49 years. The present age of *x* is:

A. 64 years B. 48 years

C. 45 years D. 40 years

13. The average height of 30 boys, out of a class of 50, is 160 cm. If the average height of the remaining boys is 165 cm, the average height of the whole class (in cm) is:

A. 161 B. 162

C. 163 D. 164

14. The average age of an adult class is 40 years. 12 new students with an average age of 32 years join the class, thereby decreasing the average of the class by 4 years. The original strength of the class was:

A. 10 B. 11

C. 12 D. 15

15. If *a, b, c, d, e* are five consecutive odd numbers, their average is:

A. $5(a+4)$ B. $\frac{abcde}{5}$

C. $5(a+b+c+d+e)$ D. None of these

16. Of the three numbers, second is twice the first and is also thrice the third. If the average of the three numbers is 44, the largest number is:

A. 24 B. 36

C. 72 D. 108

17. The average of 50 numbers is 38. If two numbers namely, 45 and 55 are discarded, the average of remaining number is:

A. 36.50 B. 37.00

C. 37.50 D. 37.52

18. The average height of 30 girls out of a class of 40 is 160 cm and that of the remaining girls is 156 cm. The average height of the whole class is:

A. 158 cm B. 158.5 cm

C. 159 cm D. 159.5 cm

19. The average of *n* numbers is *x*. If 36 is subtracted from any two numbers each, then new average is $(x - 8)$. The value of *n* is:

A. 6 B. 8

C. 9 D. 72

20. The average salary of male employees in a firm is ₹ 520 and that of female employees is ₹ 420. The mean salary of all the employees is ₹ 500. The percentage of female employees is:

A. 40% B. 30%

C. 25% D. 20%

ANSWERS

1	2	3	4	5	6	7	8	9	10
B	A	B	A	D	C	D	A	D	C
11	**12**	**13**	**14**	**15**	**16**	**17**	**18**	**19**	**20**
C	C	B	C	D	C	C	C	C	D

EXPLANATORY ANSWERS

1. Average $= \frac{3(1+2+3+4+5)}{5} = \frac{(3\times15)}{5} = 9$

2. Thirteenth result

$= [(25 \times 18) - (12 \times 14 + 12 \times 17)]$

$= [450 - (168 + 204)]$

$= 450 - 372 = 78.$

3. Let the numbers be $2x$, x and $4x$.

$$\text{Average} = \frac{2x+x+4x}{3} = \frac{7x}{3}$$

According to the question,

$$\frac{7x}{3} = 56$$

$\Rightarrow \quad 7x = 3 \times 56$

$\Rightarrow \quad x = \frac{3\times56}{7} = 24$

Hence, the numbers in order are 48, 24 and 96.

4. Let the numbers be *x, y, z*, then

$x + y + z = 98$

$\frac{x}{y} = \frac{2}{3}$ and $\frac{y}{z} = \frac{5}{8}$

$\therefore \quad x = \frac{2y}{3}$ and $z = \frac{8y}{5}$

So, $\frac{2y}{3} + y + \frac{8y}{5} = 98$

$\Rightarrow \quad \frac{10y+15y+24y}{15} = 98 \Rightarrow 49y = 15 \times 98$

$\Rightarrow \quad y = \frac{15\times98}{49} = 30$

5. During these five years, the total age would have increased by $(7 \times 5) = 35$ years.

But, it remains the same as it was 5 years ago.

$\therefore$ The new man is younger than the replaced old man by 35 years.

6. Total income for 12 months

$= ₹\ (120 \times 5 + 130 \times 7 + 290) = ₹\ 1800$

Average monthly income $= ₹\frac{1800}{12} = ₹150$

7. Total salary of 20 workers

$= 20 \times 1900 = ₹\ 38000$

Total salary of 20 workers and manager

$= 21 \times 2000 = ₹\ 42000$

Monthly salary of the manager

$= 42000 - 38000 = ₹\ 4000.$

8. Total temperature of first 3 days $= 27 \times 3 = 81°C$

Total temperature of next 3 days $= 29 \times 3 = 87°C$

Total temperature of 7 days

$= 28.5 \times 7 = 199.5°C$

Temperature of the last day

$= 199.5 - (81 + 87)$

$= 199.5 - 168 = 31.5°C$

9. Let runs he should score in third test be x :

Then, $\frac{180+258+x}{3} = 230$

$\Rightarrow \quad x = 690 - 438 = 252.$

10. Average $= \frac{2+3+5+7+11}{5} = \frac{28}{5} = 5.6.$

11. Weight of D $= (80 \times 4 - 84 \times 3)$ kg $= 68$ kg

Weight of E $= (68 + 3)$ kg $= 71$ kg

(B + C + D + E)'s weight $= (79 \times 4)$ kg $= 316$ kg

$\therefore$ (B + C)'s weight $= [316 - (68 + 71)]$ kg $= 177$ kg

Hence, A's weight $= [(84 \times 3) - 177]$kg $= 75$ kg

12. Total age of A, B, C and D 5 years ago

$= (45 \times 4)$ years $= 180$ years.

Total present age of A, B, C, D and x

$= (49 \times 5)$ years $= 245$ years.

Present age of A, B, C and D

$= (180 + 5 \times 4)$ years $= 200$ years.

$\therefore$ Present age of $x = 45$ years.

13. Total height of 30 boys $= 30 \times 160 = 4800$

Total height of 20 boys $= 20 \times 165 = 3300$

Total height of 50 boys $= 8100$

Average height of 50 boys $= \frac{8100}{50} = 162.$

14. $40x + 12 \times 32 = (12 + x) \times 36$

$\Rightarrow \quad 40x + 384 = 432 + 36x$

$\Rightarrow \quad 4x = 432 - 384 = 48$

$\Rightarrow \quad x = \frac{48}{4} = 12$

Hence, the original strength of the class was 12.

15. Average $= \frac{a+a+2+a+4+a+6+a+8}{5}$

$= \frac{5a+20}{5} = \frac{5(a+4)}{5} = a+4$

16. Let the numbers be x, $2x$ and $\frac{2x}{3}$.

Average $= \frac{x+2x+\frac{2x}{3}}{3}$

$\Rightarrow \quad \frac{11x}{9} = 44$

$\Rightarrow \quad x = \frac{44 \times 9}{11} = 36$

So, the numbers are 36, 72 and 24.

Hence, the largest one is 72.

17. Total of 50 numbers $= 50 \times 38 = 1900$

Average of 48 numbers $= \frac{1900-(45+55)}{48}$

$= \frac{1800}{48} = 37.50$

18. The average of the whole class

$= \frac{(30 \times 160 + 10 \times 156)}{40} = \frac{4800+1560}{40}$

$= \frac{6360}{40} = 159$ cm

19. $\frac{nx-36-36}{n} = x - 8$

$\Rightarrow \quad nx - 72 = nx - 8n$

$\Rightarrow \quad 8n = 72$

$\Rightarrow \quad n = 9$

20. Let the total employees be 100.

n_1 = number of females $= x$

n_2 = number of males $= 100 - x$

$\bar{x} = \frac{n_1\bar{x}_1 + n_2\bar{x}_2}{n_1 + n_2}$

$\Rightarrow \quad 500 = \frac{x \times 420 + (100-x) \times 520}{100}$

$\Rightarrow \quad 500 = \frac{42x + 5200 - 52x}{10}$

$\Rightarrow \quad 5000 = 5200 - 10x$

$\Rightarrow \quad 10x = 200$

$\Rightarrow \quad x = 20$ *i.e.*, 20%.

8. PROFIT AND LOSS

Cost Price (CP)

The price at which an article is purchased is called the cost price of the article.

Selling Price (SP)

The price at which an article is sold is called the selling price of the article.

Profit or Gain

If SP is greater than the CP, the seller is said to have a profit or gain.

Clearly, Gain = SP – CP

Loss

If SP is less than CP, the seller is said to have a loss.

Clearly, Loss = CP – SP

Profit or loss per cent is calculated on cost price.

$$\text{Profit \%} = \frac{\text{Profit}}{\text{CP}} \times 100$$

$$\text{Loss \%} = \frac{\text{Loss}}{\text{CP}} \times 100$$

$$\text{SP} = \frac{\text{CP} \times (100 + \text{Profit\%})}{100}, \text{ if there is gain}$$

$$\text{SP} = \frac{\text{CP} \times (100 - \text{Loss\%})}{100}, \text{ if there is loss}$$

$$\text{CP} = \text{SP} \times \left(\frac{100}{100 + \text{Profit\%}}\right), \text{ if there is gain}$$

$$\text{CP} = \text{SP} \times \left(\frac{100}{100 - \text{Loss\%}}\right), \text{ if there is loss}$$

If an article is sold at a gain of 20%,

then, SP = (120% of CP)

If an article is sold at a loss of 20%,

then, SP = (80% of CP)

Overheads

The expenses incurred on transportation, rent, personnel salary, maintenance, packaging, advertisements and the like are included under the general heading of overheads. These overhead and the profit when added to the cost price determine the selling price. If the overheads are not separately mentioned in the problem, we assume it to be zero or else these have been included in the cost price itself.

Discount

It is an offer made by the seller to the buyer for reduction in price to be paid. There are several cases where discounts are allowed. For instance, to dispose off old goods, to increase its market share when the customer is ready to pay the whole amount in cash instead of instalment and so on. It is subtracted from the original price and is usually expressed as per cent or a fraction of the marked price. The price obtained after deducting the discount from the original price is the selling price which the customer has to pay.

EXAMPLE: If an article is purchased for ₹ 570 and sold for ₹ 518.70, find the lost per cent.

SOLUTION: CP = ₹ 570

SP = ₹ 518.70

∴ Loss = CP – SP

= 570 – 518.70 = ₹ 51.30

$$\text{Loss \%} = \frac{\text{Loss}}{\text{CP}} \times 100 = \frac{51.30}{570} \times 100$$

$$= \frac{5130}{570} = \frac{513}{57} = 9\%$$

EXAMPLE: A man buys a TV for ₹ 16,000. After two years he sells it for ₹ 12800. Find his loss per cent.

SOLUTION:

$$\text{Loss \%} = \frac{\text{Loss}}{\text{CP}} \times 100 = \frac{16000 - 12800}{16000} \times 100$$

$$= \frac{3200}{16000} \times 100 = 20\%$$

EXAMPLE: Mohan sells his watch at a loss of ₹ 500 for ₹ 1000. Find the cost price and loss per cent.

SOLUTION: CP = SP + Loss

= 1000 + 500 = ₹ 1500

$$\text{Loss \%} = \frac{\text{Loss}}{\text{CP}} \times 100 = \frac{500}{1500} \times 100$$

$$= \frac{100}{3} = 33\frac{1}{3}\%$$

EXAMPLE: Ravi buys an article for ₹ 5000 and sells it at 20% gain. Find it selling price.

SOLUTION: $\text{Profit} = 20\% \text{ of CP} = \frac{20}{100} \times 5000$

⇒ Profit = ₹ 1000

SP = CP + Profit

= 5000 + 1000 = ₹ 6000

EXAMPLE: A man sells an article at 20% gain for ₹ 3600. Find its cost price.

SOLUTION: Let CP = ₹ 100

then SP = 100 + 20 = ₹ 120

When SP ₹ 120 then CP = ₹ 100

When SP ₹ 3600 then CP = $\frac{100}{120} \times 3600$

Hence CP = ₹ 3000

EXAMPLE: The cost price of 6 pens is equal to the selling price of 4 pens. Find the profit per cent.

SOLUTION: SP of 4 pens = CP of 6 pens

SP of 2 pens = CP of $\frac{6}{4} \times 2 = 3$ pens

Profit = CP of 3 pens

investment = CP of 6 pens

Profit % = $\frac{3}{6} \times 100 = 50\%$

Alternatively:

Let the CP of 1 pen be ₹ x.

∴ CP of 6 pens = ₹ $6x$

Also, SP of 4 pens = ₹ $6x$

∴ SP of 6 pens = $\frac{6x}{4} \times 6 =$ ₹ $9x$

Profit = SP – CP = $9x - 6x = 3x$

Profit % = $\frac{3x}{6x} \times 100 = 50\%$

EXAMPLE: If CP of 20 tables is equal to the SP of 25 tables. Find the loss percent.

SOLUTION: Let the CP of 1 table be ₹ x.

∴ CP of 20 tables = ₹ $20x$

Also, SP of 25 tables = ₹ $20x$

∴ SP of 20 tables = ₹ $\frac{20x}{25} \times 20 =$ ₹ $16x$

Loss = $20x - 16x = 4x$

Loss % = $\frac{\text{Loss}}{\text{CP}} \times 100$

= $\frac{4x}{20x} \times 100 = 20\%$

EXAMPLE: Ram sold a book at a profit of 6%. Had he sold it for ₹ 2 more he would have gained 10%. Find the cost price of the book.

SOLUTION: (10% – 6%) of CP = 4% of CP = ₹ 2

⇒ $\frac{4}{100} \times \text{CP} = 2$

⇒ CP = $\frac{200}{4} =$ ₹ 50

EXAMPLE: An article is sold for ₹ 4600 at a gain of 15%. What would be the profit or loss per cent if it is sold for ₹ 3600?

SOLUTION: CP = $4600 \times \frac{100}{115} =$ ₹ 4000

Loss % = $\frac{4000 - 3600}{4000} \times 100 = 10\%$

MULTIPLE CHOICE QUESTIONS

1. A loss of 5% was suffered by selling a plot for ₹ 4085. The cost price of the plot was:
A. ₹ 4350 B. ₹ 4259.25
C. ₹ 4200 D. ₹ 4300

2. On selling an article for ₹ 240, a trader loses 4%. In order to gain 10%, he must sell that article for:
A. ₹ 264.00 B. ₹ 273.20
C. ₹ 275.00 D. ₹ 280.00

3. A man purchased a watch for ₹ 400 and sold it at a gain of 20% of the selling price. The selling price of the watch is:
A. ₹ 300 B. ₹ 320
C. ₹ 440 D. ₹ 500

4. If 5% more is gained by selling an article for ₹ 350 than by selling it for ₹ 340, the cost of the article is:
A. ₹ 50 B. ₹ 160
C. ₹ 200 D. ₹ 225

5. Profit after selling a commodity for ₹ 425 is same as loss after selling it for ₹ 355. The cost of the commodity is:
A. ₹ 385 B. ₹ 390
C. ₹ 395 D. ₹ 400

6. The cost price of an article, which on being sold at a gain of 12% yields ₹ 6 more than when it is sold at a loss of 12%, is:
A. ₹ 30 B. ₹ 25
C. ₹ 20 D. ₹ 24

7. The CP of an article which is sold at a loss of 25% for ₹150, is:
A. ₹ 125 B. ₹ 175
C. ₹ 200 D. ₹ 225

8. When the price of pressure cooker was increased by 15%, its sale fell down by 15%. The effect on the money receipt was:
A. no effect B. 15% decrease
C. 7.5% increase D. 2.25% decrease

9. A man sells 320 mangoes at the cost price of 400 mangoes. His gain per cent is:
A. 10% B. 25%
C. 15% D. 20%

10. By selling 12 oranges for one rupee a man loses 20%. How many for a rupee should he sell to get a gain of 20%?

A. 5 B. 8
C. 10 D. 15

11. A man sells a car to his friend at 10% loss. If the friend sells it for ₹ 54000 and gains 20%, the original CP of the car was:

A. ₹ 25000 B. ₹ 37500
C. ₹ 50000 D. ₹ 60000

12. The loss incurred on selling an article for ₹ 270 is as much as the profit made after selling it at 10% profit. The CP of the article is:

A. ₹ 90 B. ₹ 110
C. ₹ 363 D. ₹ 300

13. An item costing ₹ 200 is being sold at 10% loss. If the price is further reduced by 5%, the selling price will be:

A. ₹ 179 B. ₹ 175
C. ₹ 171 D. ₹ 170

14. A trader lists his articles 20% above CP and allows a discount of 10% on cash payment. His gain per cent is:

A. 10% B. 6%
C. 8% D. 5%

15. A discount series of 10%, 20% and 40% is equal to a single discount of:

A. 50% B. 56.80%
C. 70% D. 70.28%

16. An umbrella marked at ₹ 80 is sold for ₹ 68, the rate of discount is:

A. 12% B. 15%
C. $17\frac{11}{17}\%$ D. 20%

17. A reduction of 20% in the price of mangoes enables a person to purchase 12 more for ₹ 15. The price of 16 mangoes before reduction was:

A. ₹ 5 B. ₹ 6
C. ₹ 7 D. ₹ 9

18. Tarun bought a TV with 20% discount on the labelled price. Had he bought it with 25% discount, he would have saved ₹ 500. At what price did he buy the TV?

A. ₹ 5,000 B. ₹ 10,000
C. ₹ 12,000 D. None of these

19. If a commission of 10% is given on the marked price of a book, the publisher gains 20%. If the commission is increased to 15%, the gain is:

A. $16\frac{2}{3}\%$ B. $13\frac{1}{3}\%$
C. $15\frac{1}{6}\%$ D. None of these

20. There would be 10% loss if rice is sold at ₹ 5.40 per kg. At what price per kg should it be sold to earn a profit of 20%?

A. ₹ 7.20 B. ₹ 7.02
C. ₹ 6.48 D. ₹ 6

21. A merchant sold two cows for ₹ 8400 and ₹ 8800 respectively. If he earns profit of 20% on the first and 10% on the second, his total profit is:

A. ₹ 4200 B. ₹ 2100
C. ₹ 2400 D. ₹ 2200

22. By selling an article for ₹ 4080 a man loes 15%. Cost price of article is:

A. ₹ 4800 B. ₹ 4500
C. ₹ 5000 D. ₹ 5180

ANSWERS

1	2	3	4	5	6	7	8	9	10
D	C	D	C	B	B	C	D	B	B
11	**12**	**13**	**14**	**15**	**16**	**17**	**18**	**19**	**20**
C	D	C	C	B	B	A	D	B	A
21	**22**								
D	A								

EXPLANATORY ANSWERS

1. Loss = 5%, SP = ₹ 4085

Let CP = ₹ 100

∴ SP = ₹ 100 − 5 = ₹ 95

When SP ₹ 95 then CP = ₹ 100

When SP ₹ 4085 then CP = $\frac{100}{95}\times 4085$

= 4300

Hence, the cost price of the plot was ₹ 4300.

2. Loss = 4%, SP = ₹ 240

Let CP = ₹ 100 ∴ SP = 100 − 4 = 96

When SP ₹ 96 then CP = ₹ 100

When SP ₹ 240 then CP = $\frac{100}{96}\times 240$ = ₹ 250

Again 100 + 10 = 110

When CP 100 then SP = ₹ 110

When CP 250 then SP = $\frac{110}{100}\times 250$ = ₹ 275

3. Let SP = ₹ x

then, profit = $\frac{20}{100}\times x$ = ₹ $\frac{x}{5}$

$CP = SP - \text{profit} = x - \frac{x}{5} = ₹\frac{4x}{5}$

According to the question,

$$\frac{4x}{5} = 400 \quad \Rightarrow \quad 4x = 2000$$

$$\Rightarrow \quad x = 500$$

Hence, selling price of the watch = ₹ 500.

4. Let CP = ₹ x

Then, if SP = ₹350

Profit = SP − CP = ₹ $(350 - x)$

if SP = ₹ 340 then, profit = ₹ $(340 - x)$

$$\therefore (350 - x) - (340 - x) = \frac{5}{100}x$$

$$\Rightarrow 10 = \frac{5}{100}x \quad \Rightarrow x = 200$$

Hence, the cost of the article = ₹ 200.

5. Let CP = ₹ x,

then, $425 - x = x - 355 \Rightarrow 2x = 780$

$\Rightarrow x = 390$

Hence, the cost of commodity is ₹ 390.

6. Let CP of the article = ₹ x

$$\text{Then, SP when profit is 12\%} = \left(\frac{12x}{100} + x\right) = \frac{112x}{100}$$

$$\therefore \quad \frac{112x}{100} - \frac{88x}{100} = 6$$

$$\Rightarrow \quad 24x = 600$$

$$\Rightarrow \quad x = \frac{600}{24} = 25$$

∴ CP of the article is ₹ 25.

7. $100 - 25 = 75$

When SP 75 then CP = ₹ 100

$$\text{When SP 150 then CP} = ₹\frac{100}{75} \times 150 = ₹\ 200$$

8. Let the original cost of each cooker be ₹ 1 and let the number sold originally be 100. Total sale proceed = ₹ (100 × 1) = ₹ 100

New rate = (115% of ₹ 1) = ₹ 1.15

Number sold now = 85

∴ Sale proceed now = ₹(1.15 × 85) = ₹ 97.75

So, there is a decrease of 2.25% in the money receipt.

9. Let CP of each mango be ₹ 1.

Then, CP of 400 mangoes = ₹ 400

∴ CP of 320 mangoes = ₹ 320

SP of 320 mangoes = ₹ 400

Profit = 400 − 320 = ₹ 80

$$\text{Profit\%} = \frac{80}{320} \times 100 = 25\%$$

10. SP = ₹ 1, Loss = 20%

$$\Rightarrow CP = \left(\frac{100}{80} \times 1\right) \Rightarrow CP = ₹\frac{5}{4}$$

Now, CP = ₹$\frac{5}{4}$, gain, 20%

$$\Rightarrow SP = \frac{120}{100} \times \frac{5}{4} = ₹\frac{3}{2}$$

For ₹$\frac{3}{2}$, he must sell 12 oranges

For ₹ 1, he must sell $\left(12 \times \frac{2}{3}\right) = 8$ oranges.

11. SP = ₹ 54000 and gain earned = 20%

$$CP = ₹\left(\frac{100}{120} \times 54000\right) = ₹\ 45000$$

Now, SP = ₹ 45000 and Loss = 10%

$$\therefore CP = ₹\left(\frac{100}{90} \times 45000\right) = ₹\ 50000$$

12. Let CP be ₹ x. Then,

$$x - 270 = 10\% \text{ of } x = \frac{x}{10}$$

$$\Rightarrow \quad x - \frac{x}{10} = 270$$

$$\Rightarrow \quad 9x = 10 \times 270$$

$$\Rightarrow \quad x = \frac{10 \times 270}{9}$$

$$\Rightarrow \quad x = 300$$

∴ CP of the article is ₹ 300.

13. SP = 90% of ₹ 200 = ₹ 180

Further, SP = (95% of ₹180) = ₹ 171

14. Let CP = ₹ 100. Then, MP = ₹ 120.

$$SP = 90\% \text{ of ₹ } 120 = \frac{90}{100} \times 120 = ₹\ 108$$

Profit = SP − CP = 108 − 100 = ₹ 8

$$\text{Profit \%} = \frac{\text{Profit}}{\text{CP}} \times 100 = \frac{8}{100} \times 100 = 8\%$$

15. Let original price = ₹ 100

Price after 1st discount = ₹ 90

$$\text{Price after 2nd discount} = ₹\left(\frac{80}{100} \times 90\right) = ₹\ 72$$

$$\text{Price after 3rd discount} = ₹\left(\frac{60}{100} \times 72\right) = ₹\ 43.20$$

∴ Single discount = 100 − 43.20 = 56.8%.

16. Marked price = ₹ 80

SP = ₹ 68

Discount = MP − SP = 80 − 68 = ₹ 12

$$\text{Discount \%} = \frac{\text{discount}}{\text{MP}} \times 100$$

$$= \frac{12}{80} \times 100 = 15\%$$

17. Suppose the price of 1 mango be x paise.

Number of mangoes for ₹ 15 = $\frac{1500}{x}$

New price of one mango = (80% of x) = $\frac{4x}{5}$ paise

Number of mangoes for ₹ 15 = $\left(\frac{1500 \times 5}{4x}\right)$

$\therefore \quad \frac{7500}{4x} - \frac{1500}{x} = 12 \Rightarrow x = 31.25$

∴ Cost of 16 mangoes before reduction

$= ₹\left(\frac{31.25 \times 16}{100}\right) = ₹\ 5$

18. Let SP of TV (by trader) = ₹ 100

If SP is ₹ 80, MP = ₹ 100

If SP is ₹ 100, MP = ₹$\left(\frac{100}{80} \times 100\right)$ = ₹ 125

Now, if discount is 25%

then SP = (75% of ₹ 125)

$= \frac{75}{100} \times 125 = ₹\frac{375}{4}$

Difference between two SP

$= \left(100 - \frac{375}{4}\right) = ₹\frac{25}{4}$

When difference is ₹$\frac{25}{4}$ then SP = ₹ 100

When difference is ₹ 500 then SP = $\frac{100}{\frac{25}{4}} \times 500$

$= \frac{100 \times 4 \times 500}{25} = ₹\ 8000$

19. Let marked price be ₹ 100.

SP with 10% discount = ₹ 90

∴ 120% of CP = ₹ 90

$\Rightarrow \quad \frac{120}{100} \times CP = 90$

$\Rightarrow \quad CP = \frac{90 \times 100}{120} = ₹\ 75$

SP with 15% commission = ₹ 85

Profit = ₹ 85 – ₹ 75 = ₹ 10

Profit% = $\frac{10}{75} \times 100 = \frac{40}{3} = 13\frac{1}{3}\%$

20. Let CP per kg be ₹ x. Then,

x – 10% of x = 5.40

$\Rightarrow \quad x - \frac{10}{100} \times x = 5.40$

$\Rightarrow \quad 9x = 54$

$\Rightarrow \quad x = 6$

∴ SP = ₹ [6 + 20% of 6]

$= ₹\left[6 + \frac{20}{100} \times 6\right]$

$= ₹\left[6 + \frac{120}{100}\right]$

= ₹ (6 + 1.20) = ₹ (7.20)

Hence, SP is ₹ 7.20.

21. For the First Cow:

SP = ₹ 8400

$CP = 8400 \times \frac{100}{120} = ₹\ 7000$

∴ Profit = 8400 – 7000 = ₹ 1400

For the second cow:

SP = ₹ 8800

Profit = 10%

$\therefore \quad CP = 8800 \times \frac{100}{110} = ₹\ 8000$

Profit = 8800 – 8000 = ₹ 800

Hence, total profit = 1400 + 800 = ₹ 2200

22. S.P. of the article = ₹ 4080

Loss = 15%

$\therefore \quad CP = \frac{SP}{\left(1 - \frac{Loss\%}{100}\right)} = \frac{SP \times 100}{100 - loss\%}$

Hence, CP = $\frac{4080 \times 100}{(100 - 15)}$

$= \frac{4080 \times 100}{85} = ₹\ 4800$

9. DISCOUNT

Market Price (M.P.)—The attached price is called the market price (M.P.) or list price (L.P.) of the article and the reduction allowed in the price is called the **discount**.

(*i*) Discount = M.P. – S.P.

(*ii*) Discount % = $\dfrac{\text{Discount} \times 100}{\text{M.P.}}$

(*iii*) S.P. = M.P. – $\dfrac{\text{Discount\%} \times \text{M.P.}}{100}$

(*iv*) S.P. = M.P. × $\left(1 - \dfrac{\text{Discount\%}}{100}\right)$

(*v*) M.P. = $\dfrac{100 \times \text{S.P.}}{100 - \text{Discount\%}}$

S.P. = M.P. $\left(\dfrac{100 - \text{Discount\%}}{100}\right)$

M.P. – S.P. = $\dfrac{\text{M.P.} \times \text{Discount\%}}{100}$

Discount% = $\left(\dfrac{\text{M.P.} - \text{S.P.}}{\text{M.P.}}\right) \times 100$

MULTIPLE CHOICE QUESTIONS

1. A cloth merchant offers 15% festival discount on every saree sold. If a certain saree is sold for ₹ 680, what is its marked price?

A. ₹ 800 B. ₹ 900
C. ₹ 1250 D. ₹ 1300

2. A shopkeeper offers 10% discount on an article and still makes a profit of 20%. What is the C.P. of the article if the marked price is ₹ 350?

A. ₹ 259.20 B. ₹ 262.50
C. ₹ 265.75 D. ₹ 272.5

3. A manufactures marks his goods in such a way that after allowing 20% discount, he makes a profit of 18%. What is the marked price of an item which costs him ₹ 200?

A. ₹ 295 B. ₹ 310
C. ₹ 315 D. ₹ 375

4. The marked price of a brand of coffee is ₹ 35 for 100g. But the shopkeeper gives a cup costing ₹ 7.50 free with it. Even then he gets a gain of 10%. What is the cost price of 100g of coffee?

A. ₹ 15 B. ₹ 25
C. ₹ 35 D. ₹ 65

5. A car is marked at ₹ 2,25,000. The manufacturer gives a discount of 10%. The dealer also gives a discount of 5%. What is the S.P. of the car?

A. ₹ 1,72,369
B. ₹ 1,64,370
C. ₹ 1,52,39
D. ₹ 1,92,375

6. A cycle merchant allows 25% commission on his advertised price and still makes a profit of 20%. If he gains ₹ 60 over the sale of one cycle. What is his advertised price?

A. ₹ 290 B. ₹ 310
C. ₹ 480 D. ₹ 520

7. The marked price of a shirt was ₹ 165 and it was at a discount of 12%. What the selling price of the shirt?

A. ₹ 145.20
B. ₹ 155.30
C. ₹ 165.20
D. ₹ 175.25

8. A trader marks his goods 40% above the cost price and gives a discount of 20% on the marked price. What is his gain per cent?

A. 8% B. 9%
C. 12% D. 15%

9. How much per cent more than the C.P. should a manufacturer mark his goods so that after allowing a discount of 20% on the marked price, he gains 10%.

A. 34.5%
B. 27.5%
C. 37.5%
D. 38.5%

10. A shopkeeper allows a discount of 10% to his customers and still gains 20%. What is the marked price of an article which costs ₹ 450 to the shopkeeper?

A. ₹ 600 B. ₹ 700
C. ₹ 800 D. ₹ 900

ANSWERS

1	2	3	4	5	6	7	8	9	10
A	B	A	B	D	C	A	C	C	A

EXPLANATORY ANSWERS

1. S.P. = ₹ 680, Discount = 15%

$$\text{M.P.} = \frac{100 \times \text{S.P.}}{100 - \text{Discount}\%}$$

$$= \frac{100 \times 680}{100 - 15} = \frac{100 \times 680}{85} = ₹\ 800$$

2. C.P. = ₹ x, 120% of x = 350 − 350 × 10%

$$\frac{120}{100} \times x = 350 - 35 = 315.$$

$$x = \frac{315 \times 5}{6} = \frac{525}{2},$$

C.P. = ₹ 262.50.

3. Let M.P. = ₹ x

80% x = 118% of 200

$$\frac{80}{100} \times x = \frac{118}{100} \times 200$$

$$\Rightarrow \quad x = \frac{236 \times 5}{4} = ₹\ 295.$$

4. Let C.P. of 100 gm coffee = ₹ x

110% of x = 35 − 7.50 = 27.50

$$\frac{110}{100} \times x = 27.50$$

$$x = \frac{27.50 \times 100}{110 \times 100}$$

C.P. = ₹ 25.

5. M.P. = ₹ 225000

$$\text{1st S.P.} = 225000 - 225000 \times \frac{10}{100}$$

= 225000 − 22500 = 202500

$$\text{2nd S.P.} = 202500 - 202500 \times \frac{5}{100}$$

= 202500 − 10125 = ₹ 192375

6. Let M.P. = 100

Commission = 25%

S.P. = 100 − 25 = 75

Profit = 20%

$$\text{C.P.} = \frac{100}{120} \times 75 = \frac{375}{6} = 62.50$$

Gain = 75 − 62.50 = ₹ 12.50

$$\text{M.P.} = \frac{100}{12.50} \times 60 = ₹\ 480$$

7.

$$\text{S.P.} = \frac{\text{M.P.}(100 - \text{Discount})}{100}$$

$$= \frac{165 \times (100 - 12)}{100} = \frac{165 \times 88}{100}$$

= 33 × 4.4 = ₹ 145.20

8. Let C.P. = 100, M.P. = 140, Discount = 20%

$$\text{S.P.} = 140 - 140 \times \frac{20}{100} = 140 - 28 = 112$$

Profit = 112 − 100 = 12

$$\text{Profit } \% = \frac{12 \times 100}{100} = 12\%$$

9. Let, C.P. = ₹ x, S.P. = 110% of $x = \frac{110}{100} \times x = \frac{11}{10}x.$

Discount = 20%

$$\text{M.P.} = \frac{100 \times \frac{11}{10}x}{100 - 20} = \frac{100 \times \frac{11}{10}x}{80} = \frac{11}{8}x.$$

$$\text{Required } \% = \frac{\frac{11x}{8} - x}{x} \times 100$$

$$= \frac{3x \times 100}{8x} = 37.5\%$$

10. C.P. = 450, Gain = 20%

$$\text{S.P.} = 450 + 450 \times \frac{20}{100}$$

= 450 + 90 = 540

Discount = 10%

$$\text{M.P.} = \frac{100 \times \text{S.P.}}{100 - \text{Discount}}$$

$$= \frac{100 \times 540}{100 - 10}$$

$$= \frac{100 \times 540}{90} = ₹\ 600$$

10. SIMPLE AND COMPOUND INTEREST

In any money transaction there is a **lender** who gives money, and a **borrower** who receives money. The amount of loan borrowed, is called the principal (P). The borrower pays a certain amount for the use of this money. This is called **Interest (I)**. Interest is always calculated on the principal borrowed. The borrowing is for a specified **Time (t)** and on specified terms. The specified term is expressed as per cent of the principal and is called rate of interest.

The sum of the principal and the interest is called the **Amount A**. In general, the rate of interest may be yearly, half yearly, quarterly or monthly as mutually agreed upon by both parties at the time of transaction. Depending upon the period of rate of interest, time is expressed in multiples of this period.

Interest is of two kinds—**Simple Interest and compound Interest**. If the interest is calculated only, on a certain sum borrowed it is called Simple Interest.

The simple interest (SI) on a principal P at R% per annum for T years is given by:

$$SI = \frac{P \times R \times T}{100}$$

$$\therefore \quad P = \frac{SI \times 100}{R \times T}$$

$$\therefore \quad R = \frac{SI \times 100}{P \times T}$$

$$\therefore \quad T = \frac{SI \times 100}{P \times R}$$

Compound Interest differs from Simple Interest that in CI the interest for the future period is calculated not only on the principal but also on the interest earned until the previous period. Thus, the total interest earned in case of CI is not uniformly distributed over time units whereas in Simple Interest it is uniformly distributed. The interest due at the end of the first unit of time is added to the principal and the amount so obtained becomes the principal for the second unit. Similarly, the amount after the 2nd unit of time becomes the principal for the third unit of time and continues till the last unit of time.

The difference between the final amount A. obtained at the last unit of time and the original principal is called the **Compound Interest**.

Important Relations

Principal = ₹ P (in rupees)

Rate = R % (in per cent per annum)

Time period = T years (in years)

Amount = ₹ A (in rupees)

I. When interest is compounded annually,

$$A = P\left[1 + \frac{R}{100}\right]^T$$

II. When interest is compounded half-yearly,

$$A = P\left[1 + \frac{R/2}{100}\right]^{2T} = P\left[1 + \frac{R}{200}\right]^{2T}$$

[R is divided by 2 and T is multiplied by 2.]

III. When interest is compounded quarterly,

$$A = P\left[1 + \frac{R/4}{100}\right]^{4T} = P\left[1 + \frac{R}{400}\right]^{4T}$$

[R is divided by 4 and T is multiplied by 4.]

IV. When interest is R_1% for first year, R_2% for 2nd year and R_3% for third year;

$$A = P\left[1 + \frac{R_1}{100}\right]\left[1 + \frac{R_2}{100}\right]\left[1 + \frac{R_3}{100}\right]$$

V. CI = A – P

EXAMPLE: Find the simple interest on ₹ 1000 for 3 years at 10% p.a.

SOLUTION: $SI = \frac{P \times R \times T}{100} = \frac{1000 \times 10 \times 3}{100} = ₹\,300$

EXAMPLE: Find the amount of ₹ 600 in 4 years at 3% p.a.

SOLUTION: $SI = \frac{P \times R \times T}{100} = \frac{600 \times 3 \times 4}{100} = ₹\,72$

$\therefore$ Amount = P + SI = 600 + 72 = ₹ 672

EXAMPLE: In what time will ₹ 7000 give ₹ 3675 as interest at the rate of 7% p.a. simple interest?

SOLUTION: $T = \frac{SI \times 100}{P \times R} = \frac{3675 \times 100}{7000 \times 7}$

$= \frac{15}{2} = 7\frac{1}{2}$ years.

EXAMPLE: At what rate per annum will a sum of ₹ 5000 amount to ₹ 6000 in 4 years?

SOLUTION: SI = A – P = 6000 – 5000 = ₹ 1000

$R = \frac{SI \times 100}{P \times T} = \frac{1000 \times 100}{5000 \times 4} = 5\%$

EXAMPLE: In how many years will a sum of money double itself at 5% rate of interest?

SOLUTION: A sum doubles itself when amount of interest becomes equal to the principal

$$SI = P, R = 5\%$$

$$\therefore \quad T = \frac{100 \times P}{P \times 5} = 20 \text{ years}$$

EXAMPLE: A certain sum amounts to ₹ 115200 in 2 years and to ₹ 165888 in 4 years. Find the sum and rate per cent.

SOLUTION: Here, amount on ₹ 115200 for 2 years at CI is ₹ 165888

$$\therefore \quad 115200\left(1+\frac{R}{100}\right)^2 = 165888$$

$$\left(1+\frac{R}{100}\right)^2 = \frac{165888}{115200} = 1.44$$

$$\therefore \quad 1+\frac{R}{100} = 1.2$$

$$\frac{R}{100} = 1.2 - 1 = 0.2$$

$$\Rightarrow \quad R = 0.2 \times 100 = 20\%$$

Amount after 2 years is ₹ 115200

$$\therefore \quad P\left(1+\frac{20}{100}\right)^2 = 115200$$

$$\Rightarrow \quad P = \frac{115200}{\left(1+\frac{20}{100}\right)^2} = \frac{115200}{1.44} = 80000$$

$$\therefore \quad \text{Principal} = ₹\ 80000$$

EXAMPLE: A sum of money doubles itself at CI in 15 years. In how many years will it become eight times?

SOLUTION: $P\left(1+\frac{R}{100}\right)^{15} = 2P$

$$\Rightarrow \quad \left(1+\frac{R}{100}\right)^{15} = 2$$

Let T be the required number of years that makes the principal 8 times of it.

$$\therefore \quad P\left(1+\frac{R}{100}\right)^T = 8P$$

$$\Rightarrow \quad \left(1+\frac{R}{100}\right)^T = 8 = (2)^3$$

$$\Rightarrow \quad \left(1+\frac{R}{100}\right)^T = \left[\left(1+\frac{R}{100}\right)^{15}\right]^3$$

$$\Rightarrow \quad \left(1+\frac{R}{100}\right)^T = \left(1+\frac{R}{100}\right)^{45}$$

$$\Rightarrow \quad T = 45 \text{ years}$$

Hence, required number of years is 45 years.

EXAMPLE: The difference between simple and compound interest on a sum of money at 5% p.a. for 2 years is ₹ 25. Find the sum.

SOLUTION: Let P = ₹ 100

$$SI = \frac{P \times R \times T}{100} = \frac{100 \times 5 \times 2}{100} = ₹\ 10$$

$$A = P\left(1+\frac{R}{100}\right)^T = 100\left(1+\frac{5}{100}\right)^2$$

$$= \frac{100 \times 21 \times 21}{400} = ₹\ \frac{441}{4}$$

$$CI = A - P = \frac{441}{4} - 100 = ₹\ \frac{41}{4}$$

$$CI - SI = \frac{41}{4} - 10 = \frac{41-40}{4} = ₹\ \frac{1}{4}$$

When difference ₹ $\frac{1}{4}$ then P = ₹ 100

When difference ₹ 25 then P = 100 × 4 × 25 = ₹ 10000

Hence, sum = ₹ 10000.

MULTIPLE CHOICE QUESTIONS

1. The simple interest on ₹ 500 for 6 years at 5% p.a. is:

A. ₹ 250 B. ₹ 150
C. ₹ 140 D. ₹ 120

2. A certain sum of money at SI amounts to ₹ 1012 in $2\frac{1}{2}$ years and to ₹ 1067.20 in 4 years. The rate of interest per annum is:

A. 2.5% B. 3%
C. 4% D. 5%

3. ₹ 1200 amounts to ₹ 1632 in 4 years at a certain rate of simple interest. If the rate of interest is increased by 1%, it would amount to how much?

A. ₹ 1635 B. ₹ 1644
C. ₹ 1670 D. ₹ 1680

4. A man will get ₹ 87 as simple interest on ₹ 725 at 4% per annum in:

A. 3 years
B. 3½ years
C. 4 years
D. 5 years

5. At simple interest, a sum doubles after 20 years. The rate of interest per annum is:
A. 5% B. 10%
C. 20% D. Data inadequate

6. A lent ₹ 600 to B for 2 years and ₹ 150 to C for 4 years and received altogether from both ₹ 90 as simple interest. The rate of interest is:
A. 12% B. 10%
C. 5% D. 4%

7. Interest on a certain sum of money for $2\frac{1}{3}$ years at $3\frac{3}{4}\%$ per annum is ₹ 210. The sum is:
A. ₹ 2800 B. ₹ 1580
C. ₹ 2400 D. None of these

8. A certain sum of money at simple interest amounts to ₹ 1260 in 2 years and to ₹ 1350 in 5 years. The rate per cent per annum is:
A. 2.5% B. 3.75%
C. 5% D. 7.5%

9. A sum of money doubles itself in 5 years. It will become 4 times itself in:
A. 10 years B. 12 years
C. 15 years D. 20 years

10. The simple interest on a sum of money will be ₹ 600 after 10 years. If the principal is trebled after 5 years, the total interest at the end of 10 years will be:
A. ₹ 600 B. ₹ 900
C. ₹ 1200 D. Data inadequate

11. ₹ 800 amounts to ₹ 920 in 3 years at simple interest. If the interest rate is increased by 3%, it would amount to how much?
A. ₹ 1056 B. ₹ 1112
C. ₹ 1182 D. ₹ 992

12. A sum of money at simple interest amounts to ₹ 2240 in 2 years and ₹ 2600 in 5 years. The sum is:
A. ₹ 1880 B. ₹ 2000
C. ₹ 2120 D. Data inadequate

13. If ₹ 7500 are borrowed at CI at the rate of 4% per annum, then after 2 years the amount to be paid is:
A. ₹ 8082 B. ₹ 7800
C. ₹ 8100 D. ₹ 8112

14. Simple interest on a sum at 4% per annum is ₹ 80 in 2 years. The compound interest on the same sum for the same period is:
A. ₹ 81.60 B. ₹ 160
C. ₹ 1081.60 D. None of these

15. ₹ 800 at 5% per annum compound interest will amount to ₹ 882 in:
A. 1 year B. 2 years
C. 3 years D. 4 years

16. What is the principal amount which earns ₹ 132 as compound interest for the second year at 10% per annum?
A. ₹ 1000 B. ₹ 1200
C. ₹ 1320 D. None of these

17. The difference between the compound interest and the simple interest on a certain sum at 5% per annum for 2 years is ₹ 1.50. The sum is:
A. ₹ 600 B. ₹ 500
C. ₹ 400 D. ₹ 300

18. The compound interest on a certain sum of money for 2 years at 10% per annum is ₹ 420. The simple interest on the same sum at the same rate and for the same time will be:
A. ₹ 350 B. ₹ 375
C. ₹ 380 D. ₹ 400

19. A sum amounts to ₹ 2916 in 2 years and to ₹ 3149.28 in 3 years at compound interest. The sum is :
A. ₹ 1500 B. ₹ 2000
C. ₹ 2500 D. ₹ 3000

20. A sum of money amounts to ₹ 10648 in 3 years and ₹ 9680 in 2 years. The rate of interest is:
A. 5% B. 10%
C. 15% D. 20%

ANSWERS

1	2	3	4	5	6	7	8	9	10
B	C	D	A	A	C	C	A	C	C
11	**12**	**13**	**14**	**15**	**16**	**17**	**18**	**19**	**20**
D	B	D	A	B	B	A	D	C	B

EXPLANATORY ANSWERS

1. $SI = \frac{P \times R \times T}{100} = \frac{500 \times 5 \times 6}{100} = ₹\,150$

2. SI for $1\frac{1}{2}$ years $= 1067.20 - 1012 = ₹\,55.20$

SI for $2\frac{1}{2}$ years $= 55.20 \times \frac{2}{3} \times \frac{5}{2} = ₹\,92$

$\therefore$ Principal = ₹ (1012 – 92) = ₹ 920

$$R = \frac{SI \times 100}{P \times T} = \frac{92 \times 100 \times 2}{920 \times 5} = 4\%$$

3. $R = \frac{SI \times 100}{P \times T} = \frac{432 \times 100}{1200 \times 4} = 9\%$

New rate = (9 + 1)% = 10%

$$SI = \frac{P \times R \times T}{100} = \frac{1200 \times 10 \times 4}{100} = ₹\,480$$

Amount = P + SI = 1200 + 480 = ₹ 1680

4. $T = \frac{SI \times 100}{P \times R} = \frac{87 \times 100}{725 \times 4} = 3$ years

5. Let P be ₹ x then A = ₹ $2x$

SI = A – P = $2x - x$ = ₹ x

$$R = \frac{SI \times 100}{P \times T} = \frac{x \times 100}{x \times 20} = 5\%$$

6. $SI = \frac{P \times R \times T}{100} = \frac{600 \times R \times 2}{100} = 12R$

Again $SI = \frac{P \times R \times T}{100} = \frac{150 \times R \times 4}{100} = 6R$

Total SI = 12R + 6R = 18R

According to the question,

$$18R = 90 \Rightarrow R = \frac{90}{18} = 5\%$$

7. $T = 2\frac{1}{3} = \frac{7}{3}$ years,

$$R = 3\frac{3}{4}\% = \frac{15}{4}\%$$

$$P = \frac{SI \times 100}{P \times T} = \frac{210 \times 100}{\frac{15}{4} \times \frac{7}{3}}$$

$$= \frac{210 \times 100 \times 4 \times 3}{15 \times 7} = ₹\,2400$$

8. SI for 3 years = ₹ 1350 – ₹ 1260 = ₹ 90

SI for 1 year = $\frac{90}{3}$ = ₹ 30

SI for 2 years = ₹ 30 × 2 = ₹ 60

P = A – SI = 1260 – 60 = ₹ 1200

$$R = \frac{SI \times 100}{P \times T} = \frac{60 \times 100}{1200 \times 2} = \frac{5}{2} = 2.5\%$$

9. Let P be ₹ x, A = ₹ $2x$,

SI = $2x - x$ = ₹ x

$$R = \frac{SI \times 100}{P \times T} = \frac{x \times 100}{x \times 5} = 20\%$$

Again, P = ₹ x, A = $4x$,

SI = $4x - x = 3x$

$$T = \frac{SI \times 100}{P \times R} = \frac{3x \times 100}{x \times 20} = 15 \text{ years}$$

10. Let P be ₹ x

SI = ₹ 600, T = 10 years.

$$R = \frac{SI \times 100}{P \times T} = \frac{600 \times 100}{x \times 10} = \frac{6000}{x}\%$$

SI for first 5 years = $\frac{x \times 5 \times 6000}{100 \times x}$ = ₹ 300

SI for last 5 years = $\frac{3x \times 5 \times 6000}{100 \times x}$ = ₹ 900

Total interest at the end of 10 years

= 900 + 300 = ₹ 1200.

11. P = ₹ 800, SI = 920 – 800 = ₹ 120

T = 3 years

$$R = \frac{SI \times 100}{P \times T} = \frac{120 \times 100}{800 \times 3} = 5\%$$

New rate = 8% (increase 3%)

$$SI = \frac{P \times R \times T}{100} = \frac{800 \times 8 \times 3}{100} = ₹\,192$$

∴ A = P + SI = 800 + 192 = ₹ 992.

12. SI for 3 years = 2600 – 2240 = ₹ 360

SI for 2 years = $\frac{360}{3} \times 2$ = ₹ 240

∴ Sum = 2240 – 240 = ₹ 2000

13. $A = P\left(1 + \frac{R}{100}\right)^T = 7500\left(1 + \frac{4}{100}\right)^2$

$$= 7500 \times \frac{26}{25} \times \frac{26}{25} = ₹\,8112$$

14. $P = \frac{SI \times 100}{T \times R} = \frac{80 \times 100}{4 \times 2} = ₹\,1000$

$$A = P\left(1 + \frac{R}{100}\right)^T = 1000\left(1 + \frac{4}{100}\right)^2$$

$$= 1000 \times \frac{26}{25} \times \frac{26}{25} = 1081.60$$

CI = A – P = 1081.60 – 1000 = ₹ 81.60

15. Let time = x years

$$A = P\left(1 + \frac{R}{100}\right)^T$$

$$882 = 800\left(1 + \frac{5}{100}\right)^x$$

$$\Rightarrow \frac{882}{800} = \left(\frac{21}{20}\right)^x$$

$$\Rightarrow \left(\frac{21}{20}\right)^2 = \left(\frac{21}{20}\right)^x \Rightarrow x = 2$$

∴ Time = 2 years

16. Let x be the principal at the end of first year

Then, $\frac{x \times 10 \times 1}{100} = 132 \Rightarrow x = 1320$

Let y be the original principal

Then, $y + \frac{y \times 10 \times 1}{100} = 1320$

$\Rightarrow \quad y = 1200$

17. Let P = ₹ 100

$$SI = \frac{P \times R \times T}{100} = \frac{100 \times 5 \times 2}{100} = ₹\,10$$

$$A = P\left(1+\frac{R}{100}\right)^T = 100\left(1+\frac{5}{100}\right)^2$$

$$= 100 \times \frac{21}{20} \times \frac{21}{20} = \frac{441}{4}$$

$$CI = A - P = \frac{441}{4} - 100 = \frac{41}{4}$$

$$CI - SI = \frac{41}{4} - 10 = ₹\,\frac{1}{4}$$

When difference ₹ $\frac{1}{4}$ then P = ₹ 100

When difference ₹ 1.5 then $P = \frac{100}{1/4} \times 1.5$

$$\Rightarrow P = \frac{100 \times 4 \times 15}{10} = ₹\,600$$

18. Let P = ₹ 100

$$A = P\left(1+\frac{R}{100}\right)^T = 100\left(1+\frac{10}{100}\right)^2$$

$$= 100 \times \frac{11}{10} \times \frac{11}{10} = ₹\,121$$

CI = A – P = 121 – 100 = ₹ 21

When CI ₹ 21 then P = ₹ 100

When CI ₹ 420 then $P = \frac{100}{21} \times 420 = ₹\,2000$

$$SI = \frac{P \times R \times T}{100} = \frac{2000 \times 10 \times 2}{100} = ₹\,400$$

19. $A = P\left(1+\frac{R}{100}\right)^T$

$$P\left(1+\frac{R}{100}\right)^3 = 3149.28 \quad ...(i)$$

and $P\left(1+\frac{R}{100}\right)^2 = 2916 \quad ...(ii)$

Dividing (*i*) by (*ii*) we get

$$1 + \frac{R}{100} = \frac{3149.28}{2916}$$

$$\Rightarrow \quad \frac{R}{100} = \frac{3149.28}{2916} - 1$$

$$= \frac{3149.28 - 2916}{2916} = \frac{233.28}{2916}$$

$$R = \frac{233.28 \times 100}{2916} = 8\%$$

Now, $P\left(1+\frac{R}{100}\right)^2 = 2916$

$$\Rightarrow \quad P\left(1+\frac{8}{100}\right)^2 = 2916$$

$$\Rightarrow \quad P\left(\frac{27}{25} \times \frac{27}{25}\right) = 2916$$

$$P = \frac{25 \times 25 \times 2916}{27 \times 27} = ₹\,2500$$

20. $10648 = P\left(1+\frac{R}{100}\right)^3 \quad ...(i)$

and $9680 = P\left(1+\frac{R}{100}\right)^2 \quad ...(ii)$

Dividing (*i*) by (*ii*), we get

$$\frac{10648}{9680} = 1 + \frac{R}{100}$$

$$\Rightarrow \quad \frac{R}{100} = \frac{1}{10} \quad \Rightarrow R = 10\%$$

11. MENSURATION

1. AREA AND PERIMETER

The area of any figure is the amount of surface enclosed within its boundary lines. It is measured by the number of square metres or square centimetres or square inches (or some other units of square measure) it contains.

☛ Perimeter

Perimeter of a geometrical figure is the total length of the sides enclosing the figure.

☛ Triangle

A triangle is a plane figure bounded by three sides. It includes three angles. It is denoted by the symbol Δ. The sum of angles of a triangle is 180°.

(i) **Equilateral Triangle:** A triangle in which all sides are equal is called an equilateral triangle.

(ii) **Isosceles Triangle:** A triangle in which two sides are equal is called an isosceles triangle.

(iii) **Scalene Triangle:** A triangle in which all sides are different or unequal is called scalene triangle.

(iv) **Right Angled Triangle:** A triangle having one of the angles equal to 90° is called a right angled triangle. The side opposite to the right angle of a triangle is called its hypotenuse.

☛ Quadrilateral

A plane figure bounded by four straight lines is called a quadrilateral.

Various Types of Quadrilaterals:

(i) **Rectangle:** A quadrilateral whose opposite sides are equal and all angles are at right angles. The diagonals of a rectangle are equal.

(ii) **Square:** A rectangle having all sides are equal is called a square.

(iii) **Parallelogram:** A quadrilateral whose opposite sides are equal and parallel is called parallelogram.

(iv) **Rhombus:** A parallelogram having all the sides equal is called a rhombus. Diagonals of a rhombus are not equal and they bisect each other at right angles.

(v) **Trapezium:** A quadrilateral having one pair of opposite sides parallel, is called a trapezium.

☛ Circle

The path traced by a point which moves in such a way that its distance from a fixed point is always same, is called a circle. The fixed point is called its centre and fixed distance is called its radius. The length of the whole path of a circle is called its circumference.

(i) **Arc:** Any part of the circumference of a circle is called an arc.

(ii) **Chord:** The straight line joining the ends of an arc of a circle is called a chord.

(iii) **Diameter:** The chord passing through the centre of a circle is called its diameter.

The diameter of a circle divides the circle into two equal parts, each one of which is called a semi-circle.

(iv) **Segment:** The area enclosed by an arc and a chord is called a segment.

(v) **Sector:** The area bounded by an arc and two radii is called a sector.

Formulae for Area of Various Figures:

(i) **Rectangle:**

Area of rectangle = $l \times b$

Perimeter of rectangle = $2(l + b)$.

(ii) **Square:**

Area of square = $(\text{side})^2$

Perimeter of square = $4 \times$ side

Area of room = $l \times b$

Area of 4 walls of a room = $2(l + b) \times h$

(iii) **Parallelogram:**

Area of 11^{gm} = $b \times h$

Area of rhombus = $\frac{1}{2} \times d_1 \times d_2$.

(iv) **Trapezium:**

Area of trapezium = $\frac{1}{2}$(sum of parallel sides) × (distance between them)

(v) **Triangle:**

A. Area of right triangle = $\frac{1}{2} \times b \times h$

B. Area of equilateral triangle = $\frac{\sqrt{3}}{4} \times (\text{side})^2$

C. Area of scalene triangle

$$= \sqrt{s(s-a)(s-b)(s-c)}$$

where, $s = \frac{a+b+c}{2}$

(*vi*) **Circle:**

A. Area of circle = πr^2

B. Circumference of a circle = $2\pi r$

C. Length of arc = $\frac{\theta}{360} \times 2\pi r$

D. Area of sector = $\frac{\theta}{360} \times 2\pi r$

(*e*) Area of segment = $\frac{\pi r^2\theta}{360} - \frac{1}{2} r^2 \sin\theta$

☛ Polygon

A polygon is plane figure bounded by multiple number of sides. Normally, it is used for figures enclosed by more than four sides: *e.g.*, pentagon, hexagon, octagon etc.

☛ Regular Polygon

It is a polygon whose all sides are equal.

For a regular polygon of n equal sides, its vertex angle θ is given by

$$\theta = \left(\frac{n-2}{n}\right) \times 180°.$$

MULTIPLE CHOICE QUESTIONS

1. The length of a plot is four times its breadth. A playground measuring 1200 square metres occupies a third of the total area of the plot. What is the length of the plot, in metres?

A. 20 B. 30
C. 60 D. None of these

2. The width of a rectangular hall is $\frac{3}{4}$ of its length. If the area of the hall is 300 m^2, then the difference between its length and width is:

A. 3 m B. 4 m
C. 5 m D. 15 m

3. The length and breadth of a rectangular piece of land are in ratio of 5 : 3. The owner spent ₹ 3000 for surrounding it from all the sides at ₹ 7.50 per metre. The difference between its length and breadth is:

A. 50 m B. 100 m
C. 150 m D. 200 m

4. A room 8 m × 6 m is to be carpeted by a carpet 2 m wide. The length of carpet required is:

A. 12 m B. 36 m
C. 24 m D. 48 m

5. The length of a rectangle is increased by 60%. By what per cent would the width have to be decreased to maintain the same area?

A. $37\frac{1}{2}\%$ B. 60%
C. 75% D. 120%

6. A man walked 20 m to cross a rectangular field diagonally. If the length of the field is 16 m, the breadth of the rectangle is:

A. 4 m B. 16 m
C. 12 m D. cannot be determined

7. If the ratio of the areas of two squares is 9 : 1, the ratio of their perimeters is:

A. 9 : 1 B. 3 : 1
C. 3 : 4 D. 1 : 3

8. The perimeter of both, a square and a rectangle are each equal to 48 m and the difference between their areas is 4 m^2. The breadth of the rectangle is:

A. 10 m
B. 12 m
C. 14 m
D. None of these

9. Area of a square with side x is equal to the area of a triangle with base x. The altitude of the triangle is:

A. $\frac{x}{2}$ B. x
C. $2x$ D. $4x$

10. If only the length of the rectangular plot is reduced to $\frac{2}{3}$rd of its original length, the ratio of original area to reduced area is:

A. 2 : 3 B. 3 : 2
C. 1 : 2 D. None of these

EXPLANATORY ANSWERS

1. (D): Area of the plot = 3 × 1200 = 3600 m^2

Let breadth be x m. Then length = $4x$ m

According to the question,

$4x \times x = 3600 \Rightarrow x^2 = 900 \Rightarrow x = 30$

Hence, length of the plot = 4 × 30 = 120 m.

2. (C): Let length be x m, then breadth = $\frac{3x}{4}$ m

Area of the hall = $x \times \frac{3x}{4} = \frac{3x^2}{4}$

According to the question,

$\frac{3x^2}{4} = 300 \Rightarrow x^2 = 400 \Rightarrow x = 20$

Length = 20 m and breadth = $\frac{3}{4} \times 20 = 15$ m

Difference = 20 – 15 = 5 m.

3. (A): Let length = $5x$ m and breadth = $3x$ m

Perimeter of rectangle = $2(5x + 3x) = 16x$ m

But perimeter = $\frac{\text{Total cost}}{\text{Rate}} = \frac{3000}{7.50} = 400$ m

Now, $16x = 400 \Rightarrow x = 25$

Length = $5x = 5 \times 25 = 125$ m

Breadth = $3x = 25 \times 3 = 75$ m

Difference = $125 - 75 = 50$ m.

4. (C): Length of the carpet = $\frac{8 \times 6}{2} = 24$ m.

5. (A)

6. (C): Breadth = $\sqrt{(20)^2 - (16)^2}$

$= \sqrt{400 - 256} = \sqrt{144} = 12$ m.

7. (B): Let the areas of the squares be $(9x^2)$ m^2 and (x^2) m^2

Then, their sides are $3x$ m and x m respectively

Ratio of their perimeters = $\frac{12x}{4x} = 3 : 1$.

8. (A): Let length of rectangle = x m

and breadth of rectangle = y m

Also, let the side of the square be z m

According to the question,

$2(x + y) = 4z = 48$

$x + y = 24$ and $z = 12$

Also, $z^2 - xy = 4$

$\Rightarrow (12)^2 - 4 = xy \Rightarrow xy = 140$

$\because x + y = 24$ and $xy = 140$

$(x - y)^2 = (x + y)^2 - 4xy$

$\Rightarrow (x - y)^2 = (24)^2 - 4(140)$

$\Rightarrow (x - y)^2 = 576 - 560 = 16$

$\Rightarrow x - y = 4$ Now, $x + y = 24 \Rightarrow x - y = 4$

Solving and get $x = 14$, $y = 10$

Hence, breadth of rectangle = 10 m.

9. (C): According to the question,

$$x^2 = \frac{1}{2} \times x \times h \Rightarrow h = \frac{2x^2}{x} = 2x.$$

10. (B): Let length = x and breadth = y

New length = $\frac{2}{3}x$

$$\therefore \frac{\text{Original area}}{\text{Reduced area}} = \frac{xy}{\frac{2}{3}xy} = \frac{3}{2} = 3 : 2.$$

2. VOLUME AND SURFACE AREA

We know that every real object occupies some space. It is usually specified by its three dimensions—length, breadth and depth (or height or thickness). It may be a solid or a hollow object. In case of circular, cylindrical and spherical object the specifying dimensions may change to radius, angle etc. The amount of space occupied by the object is called its volume. Its unit of measurement is m^3, cm^3, (inches)^3 etc. The area of the surfaces (plane/curved) of the object is called its surface area.

☛ A Cuboid and A Cube

The solid like wooden boxes, tea containers, match box etc. which have six faces, each of which is a rectangle, are called cuboids. It has 12 edges.

A cuboid in which every face is a square is called a cube. Length of each face of a cube is called its edge.

☛ Prism

A right prism is a solid in which the two ends are congruent parallel figures and the side faces are rectangles. The total area of side faces of a prism is called the lateral surface of the prism.

☛ Cylinder

The solid generated by the revolution of a rectangle about one of its sides as axis is called a cylinder.

☛ Pyramid

A solid whose base is a plane rectilinear figure having the side faces as triangles meeting at a common vertex is called a pyramid. When the base of a pyramid is a triangle, the pyramid is called a tetrahedron.

☛ Cone

The solid generated by the revolution of a right angled triangle about one of the sides containing the right angle as the axis is called a right circular cone.

The perpendicular distance from the vertex to the base is called the height of the cone and the length of slant face from vertex to the base is called the slant height of the cone.

☛ Frustum

If a cone is cut by a plane parallel to the base so as to divide the cone into two parts, then the lower part is called the frustum of the cone.

☛ Sphere

When a semicircle moves about its diameter, the solid generated is called a sphere.

Formulae

Cuboid:

Volume of cuboid = $l \times b \times h$ cubic units

Whole surface area = $2(lb + bh + hl)$ square units

Diagonal of cuboid = $\sqrt{l^2 + b^2 + h^2}$ units

Area of 4 walls of a room = $2(l + b) \times h$ square units

Cube:

Volume of cube = a^3 cubic units

Side of cube = $\sqrt[3]{\text{Volume}}$

Lateral surface area = $4a^2$ square units

Total surface area = $6a^2$ square units

Diagonal of the cube = $\left(\sqrt{3}\,a\right)$ units

Cylinder:

Volume of cylinder = $\pi r^2 h$ cubic units

Lateral surface area = $2\pi rh$ square units

Total surface area = $2\pi r(h + r)$ square units

Cone:

Volume of cone = $\frac{1}{3}\pi r^2 h$ cubic units

Lateral surface area = πrl square units

Total surface area = $\pi r(l + r)$ square units

Slant height (l) = $\sqrt{r^2 + h^2}$

Sphere:

Volume of sphere = $\frac{4}{3}\pi r^3$ cubic units

Surface area = $4\pi r^2$ square units

Hemisphere:

Volume = $\frac{2}{3}\pi r^3$ cubic units

Lateral surface area = $2\pi r^2$ square units

Total surface area = $3\pi r^2$ square units

Frustum:

Volume = $\frac{1}{3}\pi h(r_1^2 + r_1 r_2 + r_2^2)$ cubic units

Curved surface area = $\pi(r_1 + r_2) \times l$ square units

Total surface area = $\pi\left[r_1^2 + r_2^2 + (r_1 + r_2)l\right]$ square units

Pyramid: Volume = $\frac{1}{2} \times$ (area of base) $\times$ height cubic units

MULTIPLE CHOICE QUESTIONS

1. The surface area of a cube is 726 m^2. The volume of cube is:

A. 1300 m^3 B. 1331 m^3
C. 1452 m^3 D. 1542 m^3

2. Sum of the length, width and depth of a cuboid is s and its diagonal is d. Its surface area is:

A. s^2 B. d^2
C. $s^2 - d^2$ D. $s^2 + d^2$

3. A wooden box of dimensions 8 m × 7 m × 6 m is to carry rectangular boxes of dimensions 8 cm × 7 cm × 6 cm. The maximum number of boxes that can be carried in 1 wooden box is:

A. 1200000 B. 1000000
C. 9800000 D. 7500000

4. The length of the longest rod that can be placed in a room 30 m long, 24 m broad and 18 m high is:

A. 30 m B. $15\sqrt{2}$ m
C. 60 m D. $30\sqrt{2}$ m

5. If the volume of two cubes are in the ratio 8 : 1, the ratio of their edges is:

A. 8 : 1 B. $2\sqrt{2} : 1$
C. 2 : 1 D. None of these

6. A metal sheet 27 cm long 8 cm broad and 1 cm thick is melted into a cube. The difference between the surface areas of two solids will be:

A. 284 cm^2 B. 296 cm^2
C. 286 cm^2 D. 300 cm^2

7. If each edge of a cube is increased by 50%, the percentage increase in surface area is:

A. 50% B. 75%
C. 100% D. 125%

8. If a right circular cone of vertical height 24 cm has a volume of 1232 cm^3, then the area of its curved surface in cm^2 is:

A. 1254 B. 704
C. 550 D. 154

9. Two cubes have volumes in the ratio 1 : 27. The ratio of their surface areas is:

A. 1 : 3 B. 1 : 8
C. 1 : 9 D. 1 : 18

10. If the volumes of two cones are in the ratio 1 : 4 and their diameters are in the ratio 4 : 5, then the ratio of their heights is:

A. 1 : 5 B. 5 : 4
C. 5 : 16 D. 25 : 64

11. The radius of a wire is decreased to one-third. If volumes remains the same, length will increase:

A. 1 time B. 3 times
C. 6 times D. 9 times

12. A cylindrical piece of metal of radius 2 cm and height 6 cm is shaped into a cone of same radius. The height of cone is:

A. 18 cm B. 14 cm
C. 12 cm D. 8 cm

13. If 1 cubic cm of cast iron weight 21 g then the weight of a cast iron pipe of length 1 m with a bore of 3 cm and in which the thickness of the metal is 1 cm, is:

A. 21 kg B. 24.2 kg
C. 26.4 kg D. 18.6 kg

14. The number of solid spheres, each of diameter 6 cm, that could be moulded to form a solid metal cylinder of height 45 cm and diameter 4 cms, is:

A. 3 B. 4
C. 5 D. 6

15. A right cylinder and a right circular cone have the same radius and the same volume. The ratio of the height of the cylinder to that of the cone is:

A. 3 : 5 B. 2 : 5
C. 3 : 1 D. 1 : 3

EXPLANATORY ANSWERS

1. (B): Surface area of cube = $6a^2$

$6a^2 = 726 \Rightarrow a^2 = \frac{726}{6} = 121 \Rightarrow a = 11$ m

Volume of cube = $a^3 = 11 \times 11 \times 11 = 1331$ m³.

2. (C): $l + b + h = s$

and $\sqrt{l^2 + b^2 + h^2} = d$

$\Rightarrow l^2 + b^2 + h^2 = d^2$

$(l + b + h)^2 = s^2$

$\Rightarrow l^2 + b^2 + h^2 + 2(lb + bh + hl) = s^2$

$\Rightarrow d^2 + 2(lb + bh + hl) = s^2$

$\Rightarrow 2(lb + bh + hl) = s^2 - d^2$

$\therefore$ Surface area = $(s^2 - d^2)$.

3. (B): Number of boxes

$= \frac{800 \times 700 \times 600}{8 \times 7 \times 6} = 1000000.$

4. (D): Diagonal of cuboid = $\sqrt{l^2 + b^2 + h^2}$

$\therefore$ Length of longest rod = $\sqrt{30^2 + 24^2 + 18^2}$

$= \sqrt{900 + 576 + 324} = \sqrt{1800}$

$= \sqrt{30 \times 30 \times 2} = 30\sqrt{2}$ m.

5. (C): Let their volumes be $8x^3$ and x^3.

Then, their sides are $2x$ and x

$\therefore$ Ratio of their edges = 2 : 1.

6. (C): Volume of sheet = $27 \times 8 \times 1 = 216$ cm³

Volume of cube formed = 216 cm³

Side of cube = $\sqrt[3]{216} = 6$ cm

Surface area of cuboid = $2(lb + bh + hl)$

$= 2(27 \times 8 + 8 \times 1 + 1 \times 27) = 502$ cm²

Surface area of cube = $6(\text{side})^2 = 6 \times 36 = 216$ cm²

Difference in areas = $502 - 216 = 286$ cm².

7. (D): Let original length of cube = x

then, its surface area = $6x^2$

New edge = $\left(\frac{150}{100}x\right) = \frac{3}{2}x$

New surface area = $6 \times \left(\frac{3}{2}x\right)^2$

$= 6 \times \frac{9}{4}x^2 = \frac{27}{2}x^2$

Increase in surface area = $\left(\frac{27}{2} - 6\right)x^2 = \frac{15}{2}x^2$

$\therefore$ Increase % = $\frac{15x^2/2}{6x^2} \times 100$

$= \frac{15x^2}{12x^2} \times 100 = 125\%.$

8. (C): Volume of cone = 1232

$\Rightarrow \frac{1}{3}\pi r^2 h = 1232$

$\Rightarrow \frac{1}{3} \times \frac{22}{7} \times r^2 \times 24 = 1232$

$\Rightarrow r^2 = \frac{3 \times 7 \times 1232}{22 \times 24} = 49$

$\Rightarrow r = 7$ cm

$\Rightarrow l = \sqrt{r^2 + h^2}$

$= \sqrt{7^2 + 24^2}$

$= \sqrt{625} = 25$ cm

Lateral surface area of cone = πrl

$= \frac{22}{7} \times 7 \times 25$

$= 22 \times 25 = 550$ cm².

9. (C): Let their volumes are x^3 and $27x^3$.

Then, their sides are x and $3x$.

Ratio of their surface areas = $\frac{6x^2}{6(3x)^2} = \frac{x^2}{9x^2}$

$= 1 : 9.$

10. (D): Let the diameters of the bases of the cones be $4r$ and $5r$. Let their heights be h and H.

then, $\frac{\frac{1}{3}\pi \times \left(\frac{4r}{2}\right)^2 \times h}{\frac{1}{3}\pi\left(\frac{5r}{2}\right)^2 \times H} = \frac{1}{4}$

$\Rightarrow \quad \frac{16}{25} \times \frac{h}{H} = \frac{1}{4}$

$\Rightarrow \quad \frac{h}{H} = \frac{25}{64}.$

11. (D): Let original radius = r
and original length = h

New radius = $\frac{1}{3}r$

Let new length = H

then, $\pi r^2 h = \pi\left(\frac{1}{3}r\right)^2 \times H$

$= \frac{\pi r^2 H}{9}$

$\therefore$ H = $9h$

Thus length becomes 9 times.

12. (A): Volume of cone = Volume of cylinder

$\frac{1}{3}\pi r^2 h = \pi r^2 h$

$\Rightarrow \quad \frac{1}{3} \times \frac{22}{7} \times 2 \times 2 \times h = \frac{22}{7} \times 2 \times 2 \times 6$

$\Rightarrow \quad \frac{h}{3} = 6 \Rightarrow h = 18$ cm

$\therefore$ Height of cone = 18 cm.

13. (C): Diameter = 3 cm, h = 1 m = 100 cm

$\therefore$ Radius = $\frac{3}{2}$ cm = 1.5 cm

thickness = 1 cm

$\therefore$ R = 1.5 + 1 = 2.5 cm

r = 1.5 cm

Volume of metal = $\pi(R^2 - r^2) \times h$

$= \pi[(2.5)^2 - (1.5)^2] \times 100$

$= \pi[4] \times 100$

$= \pi \times 400 \text{ cm}^3$

$\because$ 1 cm^3 = 21 g

$\therefore$ $\pi \times 400$ cm^3 = 21 × π × 400 g

$= 21 \times \frac{22}{7} \times \frac{400}{1000}$ kg

= 26.4 kg.

14. (C): Number of spheres = $\frac{\text{Volume of cylinder}}{\text{Volume of sphere}}$

$= \frac{\pi \times 2 \times 2 \times 45}{\frac{4}{3}\pi \times (3)^3} = \frac{4 \times 45 \times 3}{4 \times 27} = 5.$

15. (D): Volume of cylinder = Volume of cone

$\pi r^2 h = \frac{1}{3}\pi r^2 H$

$\Rightarrow \quad 3h = H \Rightarrow \frac{h}{H} = \frac{1}{3}.$

12. PARTNERSHIP BUSINESS

Partnership is a form of association of two or more persons who contribute resources like money together in order to carry on a business. It may be of simple or compound type.

Simple partnership is one in which the capitals of the partners are invested for the same time. The profits or losses are divided among the partners in the ratio of their investments.

Compound partnership is one in which the capitals of the partners are invested for different periods. In such cases, equivalent capitals are calculated for each partner by multiplying their capital contributions with time. The profits or losses are then divided in the ratio of these equivalent capitals. Thus, the ratio of profits is directly proportional to both capital invested as well as time.

The partner who invests the money in the business as well as takes part in its management, is known as **Working partner**.

The partner who only invests the money in the business and does not work, is known as **Sleeping partner**.

A working partner gets either monthly payment or a share in the profit for his contribution in the management of the business. This payment is deducted from the total profit before its distribution.

EXAMPLE: A, B and C invest ₹ 15000, ₹ 20000 and ₹ 25000 respectively in a business. The profit earned is ₹ 1200. Find the share of each in the profit.

SOLUTION: This is a case of simple partnership

Ratio of investments, A : B : C

= 15000 : 20000 : 25000

= 3 : 4 : 5

Sum of the ratios = 3 + 4 + 5 = 12

Share in the profit

For A = $\frac{3}{12} \times 1200$ = ₹ 300

For B = $\frac{4}{12} \times 1200$ = ₹ 400

For C = $\frac{5}{12} \times 1200$ = ₹ 500

EXAMPLE: A and B are partners in a firm. A invests ₹ 15000 and B ₹ 25000. A is the working partner and gets 20% of the profit for his contribution in the management of the firm. B is the sleeping partner. If the profit is ₹ 475, find the share of each.

SOLUTION: First we have to deduct the payment to be made to A from the total profit for his contribution in the management of the firm.

20% of ₹ 475 = ₹ 95

Balance profit = 475 – 95 = ₹ 380

This has to be divided between A and B in the ratio of their investments *i.e.*, ₹ 15000 : ₹ 25000 = 3 : 5

A's share = ₹ 380 × $\frac{3}{8}$ = ₹ 142.5

B's share = ₹ 380 × $\frac{5}{8}$ = ₹ 237.5

Finally, A gets a total of (95 + 142.5) = ₹ 237.5 and B gets = ₹ 237.5

EXAMPLE: In a business A and B gained some amount in a certain ratio. B and C received the profit in the ratio as that of A and B. If B received ₹ 6400 and C received ₹ 10,000 then find the amount invested by B.

SOLUTION: Let the ratio of A's and B's profit be $\frac{a}{b}$.

Hence, the ratio of B's and C's profit = $\frac{a}{b}$

Thus, $A : B : C = a : b : \frac{b^2}{a}$

when A's profit, a = ₹ 6400

and C's profit, $\frac{b^2}{a}$ = ₹ 10,000

⇒ $b^2 = 10,000 \times 6400 = 100 \times 100 \times 80 \times 80$

⇒ $b = 100 \times 80 = 8000$

Hence, the amount invested by B = ₹ 8000.

MULTIPLE CHOICE QUESTIONS

1. A, B and C share the profit in the ratio of 3 : 5 : 7. If the gain is ₹ 2040, then C's share is:
   A. ₹ 360 B. ₹ 600
   C. ₹ 952 D. ₹ 120
2. A, B and C started a business with ₹ 47000. A puts in ₹ 5000 more than B and B ₹ 3000 more than C. The share of A out of the profit of ₹ 14100 will be:
   A. ₹ 3600 B. ₹ 4500
   C. ₹ 6000 D. ₹ 6300
3. A starts a business with ₹ 5000. After 4 months B joins him with a sum of ₹ 4000. In the end of the year there is a profit of ₹ 8970. The share of A in the profit will be:
   A. ₹ 3120 B. ₹ 4020
   C. ₹ 5850 D. ₹ 6360

4. A, B, C are three partners in a business. The profit share of A is $\frac{3}{16}$ of the profit and B's share is $\frac{1}{4}$ of the profit. If C receives ₹ 243, then the amount received by B will be:

A. ₹ 90 B. ₹ 96
C. ₹ 108 D. ₹ 120

5. A, B and C share the profit in the ratio 2 : 3 : 7. If the average gain is ₹ 8000, then B's share is:

A. ₹ 2000 B. ₹ 1000
C. ₹ 1500 D. ₹ 3000

6. Ashok started a business investing ₹ 90,000. After 3 months Shabir joined him with a capital of ₹ 1,20,000. If at the end of one year the total profit made by them was ₹ 96,000, what will be the difference between their shares?

A. ₹ 24000 B. ₹ 8000
C. ₹ 20000 D. None of these

7. Mahesh received ₹ 6000 as his share out of the total profit of ₹ 9000 which he and Ram entered at the end of one year. If Mahesh invested ₹ 20,000 for 6 months, whereas Ram invested his amount for the whole year, what was the amount invested by Ram?

A. ₹ 4000 B. ₹ 5000
C. ₹ 3000 D. ₹ 6000

8. A and B started a business jointly. A's investment was thrice the investment of B and the period of his investment was two times the period of investment of B. If B received ₹ 40,000 as profit, then their total profit is:

A. ₹ 2,40,000 B. ₹ 28000
C. ₹ 24000 D. ₹ 2,80,000

9. Anil started a business investing ₹ 70,000. After 8 months Vimal joined him with a capital of ₹ 1,80,000. In what ratio should Anil and Vimal share the profit after two years?

A. 8 : 7 B. 7 : 5
C. 7 : 6 D. None of these

10. A, B and C starts a business. A invests ₹ 3,20,000 for four months. B invests ₹ 5,10,000 for three months and C invests ₹ 2,70,000 for five months. If at the end of year there is a profit of ₹ 1,24,800, then share of B is:

A. ₹ 79000 B. ₹ 49200
C. ₹ 50000 D. ₹ 45900

11. A, B and C contract a work for ₹ 550. Together A and B are to do $\frac{7}{11}$ of the work. The share of C should be:

A. ₹ 400 B. ₹ 300
C. ₹ 200 D. ₹ $183\frac{1}{3}$

12. Jagmohan, Rooplal and Pankaj rented a video cassette for one week at a rent of ₹ 350. If they use it for 6 hrs, 10 hrs and 12 hrs respectively, the rent to be paid by Pankaj is:

A. ₹ 75 B. ₹ 125
C. ₹ 35 D. ₹ 150

13. Manoj got ₹ 6000 as his share out of the total profit of ₹ 9000 which he and Ramesh earned at the end of one year. If Manoj invested ₹ 20,000 for 6 months, whereas Ramesh invested his amount for the whole year, the amount invested by Ramesh was:

A. ₹ 60,000 B. ₹ 10,000
C. ₹ 4000 D. ₹ 5000

14. A, B and C invest ₹ 2000, ₹ 3000 and ₹ 4000 in a business. After one year A removed his money, B and C continued the business for one more year. If the net profit after 2 years be ₹ 3200, then A's share in the profit is:

A. ₹ 1000 B. ₹ 600
C. ₹ 800 D. ₹ 400

15. A and B enter into partnership investing ₹ 12000 and ₹ 16000 respectively. After 8 months, C also joins the business with a capital of ₹ 15000. The share of C in a profit of ₹ 46500 after 2 years will be:

A. ₹ 12000 B. ₹ 14400
C. ₹ 19200 D. ₹ 21200

16. A, B and C rent a pasture. A puts in 10 oxen for 7 months, B 12 oxen for 5 months and C 15 oxen for 3 months for grazing. If the rent of the pasture is ₹ 175, how much must C pay as his share of rent?

A. ₹ 45 B. ₹ 50
C. ₹ 55 D. ₹ 60

17. Sumit started software business with ₹ 50,000. After 6 months Nitin joined him with ₹ 80,000. After three years they earned ₹ 24500 as profit. What is the share of Sumit in the profit?

A. ₹ 11500 B. ₹ 9050
C. ₹ 10500 D. ₹ 9500

18. A starts a business with ₹ 3500 and after 5 months B joins A as his partner. After a year, the profit is divided in the ratio 2 : 3. What is B's contribution in the capital?

A. ₹ 8000 B. ₹ 8500
C. ₹ 9000 D. ₹ 750

19. M, P and Q together started a business. M invested ₹ 6500 for 6 months, P invested ₹ 8400 for 5 months and Q invested ₹ 10000 for 3 months. M is working member for which he gets 5% extra profit. If the total gain is ₹ 7400, then Q's share is:

A. ₹ 1500 B. ₹ 2100
C. ₹ 3200 D. None of the above

20. Sarita started a business by investing ₹ 50,000. After 6 months Abhishek joined her by investing ₹ 75000. After his 6 months Nisha joined with ₹ 125000. What is the ratio of profit share after 2 years among Sarita, Abhishek and Nisha?

A. 4 : 5 : 6 B. 8 : 9 : 10
C. 8 : 9 : 12 D. 4 : 5 : 8

21. A and B started a business with the investment of ₹ 80000 and ₹ 60000 respectively. At the end of the year total profit in the business will be divided between them in the ratio of:

A. 2 : 3 B. 3 : 4
C. 2 : 1 D. 4 : 3

22. A and B started a business in partnership with the investment of ₹ 4000 and ₹ 6000 respectively. If at the end of the year total profit is ₹ 2250, what will each of them get?

A. ₹ 900, ₹ 1350
B. ₹ 800, ₹ 1450
C. ₹ 1000, ₹ 1250
D. ₹ 1200, ₹ 1050

23. Sonu, Monu and Mohit together start a business with the investment of ₹ 1800, ₹ 1500 and ₹ 1600 respectively. If at the end of the year, Monu gains a profit of ₹ 900 the total profit in the business is:

A. ₹ 2880 B. ₹ 2940
C. ₹ 3200 D. ₹ 3240

ANSWERS

1	2	3	4	5	6	7	8	9	10
C	C	C	C	A	D	B	D	D	D
11	**12**	**13**	**14**	**15**	**16**	**17**	**18**	**19**	**20**
C	D	D	D	A	A	C	C	D	B
21	**22**	**23**							
D	A	B							

EXPLANATORY ANSWERS

1. C's share $= \frac{7}{15} \times 2040 =$ ₹ 952.

2. Let C's capital be ₹ x

Then B's capital = ₹ $(x + 3000)$

and A's capital = ₹ $(x + 3000 + 5000) = x + 8000$

$\Rightarrow \quad x + (x + 3000) + (x + 8000) = 47000$

$\Rightarrow \quad 3x + 11000 = 47000$

$\Rightarrow \quad 3x = 47000 - 11000 = 36000$

$\Rightarrow \quad x = 12000$

Thus, capital of A, B and C are ₹ 20000, ₹ 15000 and ₹ 12000 respectively.

$\therefore$ Profit sharing ratio = 20 : 15 : 12

$\therefore$ Profit of A $= \frac{20}{47} \times 14100 =$ ₹ 6000

3. ₹ 5000 × 12 = ₹ 60,000 for A

₹ 4000 × (12 – 4) = 4000 × 8 = ₹ 32000 for B

Ratio of profit sharing = 60000 : 32000

= 60 : 32 = 15 : 8

$\therefore$ Share of A in the profit $= \frac{15}{23} \times 8970$

= 15 × 390 = ₹ 5850

4. Let the profit be ₹ 1. Then,

$$A : B : C = \frac{3}{16} : \frac{1}{4} : \left[1 - \left(\frac{3}{16} + \frac{1}{4}\right)\right]$$

$$= \frac{3}{16} : \frac{1}{4} : \frac{9}{16} = \frac{3}{16} : \frac{4}{16} : \frac{9}{16} \text{ i.e., } 3 : 4 : 9$$

when C's share is ₹ 9, then B's share = ₹ 4

when C's share is ₹ 243, then B's share

$$= \frac{4 \times 243}{9} = ₹\ 108$$

5. B's share $= \frac{3}{2+3+7} \times 8000 = \frac{3 \times 8000}{12} =$ ₹ 2000

6. The ratio of their investment

= 12 × 90000 : (12 – 3) × 120000

= 12 × 9 : 9 × 12 = 1 : 1

Ashok's share $= \frac{1}{1+1} \times 96000 =$ ₹ 48000

Shabir's share $= \frac{1}{1+1} \times 96000 =$ ₹ 48000

Difference between their shares

= ₹ 48000 – ₹ 48000 = 0.

7. The ratio of their profit

= ₹ 6000 : ₹ (9000 – 6000)

= ₹ 6000 : ₹ 3000 = 2 : 1

Let ₹ x be the amount invested by Ram.

The ratio of their profit = The ratio of their investment

$\Rightarrow \quad 2 : 1 = 6 \times 20000 : 12 \times x$

$\Rightarrow \quad \frac{2}{1} = \frac{6 \times 20000}{12 \times x} \Rightarrow 2x = 10000$

$\Rightarrow \quad x = 5000$

$\therefore$ The investment of Ram is ₹ 5000.

8. Let ₹ x be the investment of B and n years be the period of investment of B.

Given : A's investment = 3 × ₹ x = ₹ $3x$

and period of investment of A = $2n$ years

$\therefore$ The ratio of investment of A and B

$= 2n \times 3x : n \times x = 6nx : nx = 6 : 1$

Let the total profit be ₹ y

Given B's share in profit = ₹ 40,000

$\Rightarrow \quad \frac{1}{6+1} \times y =$ ₹ 40,000 $\Rightarrow y =$ ₹ 2,80,000

$\therefore$ Total profit is ₹ 2,80,000.

9. The ratio of Anil's and Vimal's share in the profit
= Ratio of their investments
$= 24 \times 70000 : 16 \times 180000$
$= 24 \times 7 : 16 \times 18 = 7 : 12$

10. The ratio of investments of A, B and C
$= 4 \times 320000 : 3 \times 510000 : 5 \times 270000$
$= 4 \times 32 : 3 \times 51 : 5 \times 27$
$= 128 : 153 : 135$
Total profit after 1 year = ₹ 124800

$$\text{Share of B} = ₹\ \frac{153}{128+153+135} \times 124800$$

$$= ₹\ \frac{153}{416} \times 124800 = ₹\ 45900$$

11. $\text{C's share} = ₹\left(550 \times \frac{4}{11}\right) = ₹\ 200$

12. Ratio of rents $= 6 : 10 : 12 = 3 : 5 : 6$

$$\therefore \text{Pankaj's share of rent} = ₹\left(350 \times \frac{6}{14}\right) = ₹\ 150$$

13. Let amount invested by Ramesh be ₹ x
$\therefore 20000 \times 6 : 12x = 6000 : 3000$

$$i.e., \frac{12x}{120000} = \frac{3000}{6000} \text{ or } x = ₹\ 5000$$

14. Ratio of investments
$= (2000 \times 1) : (3000 \times 2) : (4000 \times 2)$
$= 1 : 3 : 4$

$$\therefore \text{A's share} = ₹\left(3200 \times \frac{1}{8}\right) = ₹\ 400.$$

15. Ratio of investments
$= (12000 \times 24) : (16000 \times 24) : (15000 \times 16)$
$= 6 : 8 : 5$

$$\text{C's share of profit} = ₹\left(45600 \times \frac{5}{19}\right) = ₹\ 12000$$

16. Ratio of A, B and C shares in the rent
$= 7 \times 10 : 5 \times 12 : 3 \times 15 = 14 : 12 : 9$

$$\therefore \quad \text{Rent paid by C} = \frac{9}{14+12+9} \times 175$$

$$= \frac{9}{35} \times 175 = ₹\ 45$$

17. Ratio of investments

$$= 50000 \times 3 : 80000 \times \frac{5}{2}$$

$$\left[2\frac{1}{2} \text{ years} = \frac{5}{2} \text{ years}\right]$$

$= 15 : 20 = 3 : 4$

$$\text{Sumit's share} = \frac{3}{3+4} \times 24500 = \frac{3}{7} \times 24500$$

$= 3 \times 3500 = ₹\ 10500$

18. Let B's contribution be x_2 for $(12 - 5) = 7$ months
Then, $\quad t_1x_1 : t_2x_2 = 2 : 3$
$\Rightarrow 12 \times 3500 : 7 \times x_2 = 2 : 3$
$\Rightarrow \quad 2 \times 7 \times x_2 = 3 \times 12 \times 3500$

$$\therefore \quad x_2 = \frac{3 \times 12 \times 3500}{2 \times 7} = ₹\ 9000$$

19. Total profit = ₹ 7400

$$\text{M's extra share} = 7400 \times \frac{5}{100} = ₹\ 370$$

Remaining profit $= 7400 - 370 =$ ₹ 7030
Profit share ratio = M : P : Q
$= 6 \times 6500 : 5 \times 8400 : 3 \times 10000$
$= 13 : 14 : 10$

$$\therefore \quad \text{Q's share} = \frac{10}{13+14+10} \times 7030$$

$$= \frac{10}{37} \times 7030 = ₹\ 1900$$

20. Required ratio $= t_1x_1 : t_2x_2 : t_3x_3$
$= 24 \times 50000 : (24 - 6) \times 75000 : (24 - 12) \times 125000$
$= 24 \times 50 : 18 \times 75 : 12 \times 125$
$= 24 \times 2 : 18 \times 3 : 12 \times 5$ [dividing by 25]
$= 4 \times 2 : 3 \times 3 : 2 \times 5$ [dividing by 6]
$= 8 : 9 : 10$

21. The two partners invest their capitals for the same period
$\therefore$ Profit will be divided between them in the ratio of their capitals
$\therefore$ Ratio between their profits $= 80000 : 60000$
$= 4 : 3$

22. A and B ivest their capitals for the same period.
Ratio between the profits of A and B
$= 4000 : 6000 = 2 : 3$

Sum of proportionals $= 2 + 3 = 5$
Total profit = ₹ 2250

$$\therefore \text{A's share} = \frac{2}{5} \times 2250 = ₹\ 900$$

$$\text{B's share} = \frac{3}{5} \times 2250 = ₹\ 1350$$

23. Sonu, Monu and Mohit invest their capitals for the same period
Ratio of their profits $= 1800 : 1500 : 1600$
$= 18 : 15 : 16$

Sum of proportionals $= 18 + 15 + 16 = 49$
Mohit's profit = ₹ 900

$$\therefore \text{Total profit in the business} = \frac{900}{15} \times 49$$

$= ₹\ 2940$

13. MIXTURE AND ALLEGATION

Alligation Rule : When two or more quantities of different values are mixed together to produce a mixture of a mean value, the ratios of their amounts are inversely proportional to the differences of their values from the mean value. Thus,

$$\frac{\text{Amount of Quantity of Smaller value}}{\text{Amount of Quantity of Larger value}} = \frac{\text{Larger value} - \text{Mean value}}{\text{Mean value} - \text{Smaller value}}$$

Similarly, if two ingredients (one cheeper and the other dearer) are mixed in a ratio, then

$$\frac{\text{Quantity of Cheaper Article}}{\text{Quantity of Dearer Article}} = \frac{\text{CP of Dearer Article} - \text{Mean price}}{\text{Mean price} - \text{CP of Cheaper Article}}$$

or

Cost Price of a unit quantity of cheaper article C. Cost Price of a unit quantity of dearer article D.

Mean Price (m)

(d – m) (m – c)

(Cheaper quantity) : (Dearer quantity)

= (d – m) : (m – c)

The Alligation Rule has its application in the following situations :

1. When we have to find the proportion in which different ingredients of known values are to be mixed to produce a mixture of a given mean value.
2. When we have to find the mean value of a mixture when the proportion and value of its ingredients are known.
3. When we have to find the mean or average price of a mixture when the proportion and value of its ingredients are known.

MULTIPLE CHOICE QUESTIONS

1. If goods be purchased for ₹ 450 and one - third be sold at loss of 10%, what per cent of profit should be taken on the remainder so as to gain 20% on the whole transaction?

A. 35% B. 30%
C. 40% D. 45%

2. Kamal mixes 80 kg sugar worth ₹ 6.75 per kg with 120 kg sugar worth of ₹ 8 per kg. At what rate should he sell the mixture to gain 20%?

A. ₹ 7.50 B. ₹ 9
C. ₹ 8.20 D. ₹ 8.85

3. A merchant has 50 kg of sugar, part of which he sells at 8% profit and the rest at 18% profit. He gains 14% on the whole. The quantity sold at 18% profit is :

A. 20 kg B. 30 kg
C. 15 kg D. 35 kg

4. A man travelled a distance of 60 km in 7 hours partly on foot at the rate of 8 km per hour and partly on bicycle at 16 km per hour. Distance travelled by foot is :

A. 52 km B. 48 km
C. 36 km D. 44 km

5. In what ratio should water and wine be mixed so that after selling the mixture at the cost price a profit of 20% is made?

A. 1 : 5 B. 1 : 6
C. 1 : 7 D. 1 : 9

6. Find the quantity of rice @ ₹ 10 per kg which should be mixed with 25 kg of rice @ ₹ 8 per kg, so that on selling the mixture @ ₹ 15 per kg there is 80% profit.

A. 6 kg B. 7 kg
C. 3 kg D. 5 kg

7. A trader has 50 kg of rice, a part of which he sells at 14% profit and the rest at 6% loss. On the whole his loss is 4 %. What are the quantities sold at 14% profit and that at 6% loss?

A. 5 kg and 45 kg B. 5 kg and 55 kg
C. 5 kg and 50 kg D. 5 kg and 40 kg

8. A sum of rupees 210 made up of coins consisting of rupee, 50 *P* and 25 *P*, of which the numbers are proportional to 5, 6 and 8. How many of rupee coins are there?

A. 63 B. 168
C. 105 D. 100

9. A vessel of 80 litre is filled with milk and water. 70% of milk and 30 % of water is taken out of the vessel. It is found that the vessel is vacated by 55% . The initial quantity of milk and water was :

A. 50 litres and 35 litres
B. 50 litres and 30 litres
C. 50 litres and 40 litres
D. 50 litres and 45 litres

10. Two equal glasses are respectively 1/4 and 1/3 full of milk. They are then filled up with water and contents mixed in a tumbler. The ratio of milk and water in the tumbler is :

A. 3 : 11
B. 7 : 17
C. 9 : 23
D. 11 : 23

EXPLANATORY ANSWERS

1. (A) : 1st Part   2nd Part

– 10% x%

20%

1/3   2/3   Ratio = 1 : 2

We see that 20 – (–10) = 20 + 10 = 30.

As 2 is written in place of 30, there should be 15 in place of 1.

Therefore, x = 20 + 15 = 35%.

2. (B) : Total CP = 80 × 6.75 + 120 × 8 = ₹ 1500

$$\text{SP per kg} = \frac{120 \times 1500}{100 \times 200} = ₹9.$$

3. (B) : 8   18

14

4   6   Ratio = 4 : 6 = 2 : 3

$$\text{Quantity sold on 18\% profit} = \frac{50}{5} \times 3 = 30 \text{ kg.}$$

4. (A) : Let the distance travelled by bicycle be x km.

∴ The distance travelled on foot will be $(60 - x)$ km.

According to question,

$$\frac{60 - x}{8} + \frac{x}{16} = 7$$

$$\Rightarrow \frac{120 - 2x + x}{16} = 7$$

$$\Rightarrow x = 8$$

Distance travelled on foot = 60 – 8 = 52 km

5. (A) : Water : Wine = 20 : 100 = 1 : 5.

6. (D) : 8   10

$\frac{25}{3}$

$\frac{1}{5}$ $\frac{1}{3}$

$$\text{CP of the mixture} = 15 \times \frac{100}{180} = ₹\frac{25}{3} \text{ per kg}$$

$$\frac{\text{Quantity of rice @ ₹ 8 per kg}}{\text{Quantity of rice @ ₹ 10 per kg}} = \frac{5/3}{1/3} = \frac{5}{1}$$

$$\text{Quantity of rice @ ₹ 10 per kg} = 25 \times \frac{1}{5} = 5 \text{ kg}$$

7. (A) : I Part   II Part

14   (–) 6

(–) 4 (as there is loss on whole)

2   18

So, ratio of quantities sold at 14% profit and 6% loss = 2 : 18 = 1 : 9

So, quantity sold at 14% profit = $\frac{50}{10} \times 1 = 5$ kg and sold at 6% loss = 50 – 5 = 45 kg

8. (C) : Ratio = 5 : 6 : 8, Value = 5 : 3 : 2

$$\text{Number of rupee coins} = \frac{210}{10} \times 5 = 105.$$

9. (B) : Here, the % values of milk and water that is taken from the vessel should be taken into consideration.

(Milk) 70%   (Water) 30%

55%

25%   15% ⇒ 5 : 3

Ratio of milk to water = 5 : 3

$$\text{So, quantity of milk} = \frac{80}{8} \times 5 = 50 \text{ litres}$$

$$\text{and quantity of water} = \frac{80}{8} \times 3 = 30 \text{ litres}$$

10. (B) : Quantity of milk in tumbler = 1/4 + 1/3 = 7/12

Quantity of water in tumbler

= (1 – 1/4) + (1 – 1/3) = 3/4 + 2/3 = 17/12

So, ratio of milk and water = 7/12 : 17/12

= 7 : 17.

14. TIME AND WORK

The problem on Time and Work are based on the calculation of time required by a given number of workforce (which may include men, women and children) to complete the given period of time. Thus, it can be said that the problems on time and work fall in two categories:

(i) To find the time required to complete a given job.

(ii) To find the work done in given period of time.

- It is important to consider the capacity of a man doing work in terms of the part of the work he can do in one day. For instance, if a man can do a piece of work in 6 days, then 1/6th of work is done in one day. The whole work can be finished in 6 days.
- Again, if *A* can do a work in 4 days and *B* in 7 days, the ratio of the work done by *A* and *B* in the same time is 7 : 4.
- If *A* is twice as good a workman as *B*. *A* will take half of the time taken by *B* to do certain piece of work. It means the ratio of the work done by *A* and *B* is 2 : 1.

Wages are paid in proportion to units of job done by each in the same time.

All the above points can be summarized as given below :

If '*M*' number of people take' *D*' days to complete the given job, the total number of 'Man-Days' required to complete the given job are given by the product of '*M*' and '*D*'. This product '*MD*' now remains unchanged. Thus, if '*M*' changes into 'M_1', '*D*' will change into 'D_1' in such a way that $MD = M_1D_1$. Similarly, if '*D*' changes to 'D_2' '*M*' will change to 'M_2' in such a way that $MD = M_2D_2$.

1. This is the basic relationship and all-in one formula. We can also derive :
2. More men-less days and conversely, more days-less men.
3. More men-more work and conversely, more work-more men.
4. More days-more work and conversely, more work-more days.
5. Number of days required to complete the given work $= \dfrac{\text{Total work}}{\text{One day's work}}$

Note : Since the total work is assumed to be One (unit), the number of days required to complete the given work would be the reciprocal of the one day's work.

Sometimes the problems on Time and Work can be solved using proportional rule :

(Man × Day × Hour × 1/work) in one situation
= (Man × Day × Hour × 1/work) in another situation.

MULTIPLE CHOICE QUESTIONS

1. *A* can do a piece of work in 25 days and *B* can finish it in 20 days. They work together for 5 days and then *A* goes away. In how many days will *B* finish the work?

A. 10 days B. 11 days
C. 20 days D. $33\frac{1}{11}$ days

2. *A* can do a piece of work in 25 days which *B* alone can do in 20 days. *A* started the work and was joined by *B* after 10 days. The work lasted for:

A. 15 days B. $12\frac{1}{2}$ days
C. $16\frac{1}{2}$ days D. None of these

3. *A* can do a piece of work in 40 days. He worked at it for 5 days and *B* finished the remaining work in 21 days. In how many days can *A* and *B* together finish the work?

A. 13 days B. 15 days
C. $6\frac{2}{3}$ days D. $18\frac{1}{7}$ days

4. *A* is thrice as good a workman as *B*. Together they can do a job in 15 days. In how many days *B* will finish it alone?

A. 60 days
B. 45 days
C. 20 days
D. 40 days

5. *A* can do a work in 8 days and *B* in 6 days. *A* and *B* can do the work on alternate days. If *A* begins the work, then the work can be finished in how many days?

A. 5 days B. 7 days
C. $6\frac{3}{4}$ days D. $7\frac{1}{2}$ days

6. *A* can do a piece of work in 6 days and *B* alone can do it in 8 days. *A* and *B* undertook to do it for ₹ 320 and with the help of *C* they finished it in 3 days. How much is paid to *C*?

A. ₹ 80 B. ₹ 60
C. ₹ 37.50 D. ₹ 40

7. *A, B, C* are employed to do a piece of work for ₹ 529. *A* and *B* together are supposed to do 19/23 of the work, what should *C* be paid?

A. ₹ 82 B. ₹ 92
C. ₹ 437 D. ₹ 300

8. Eight children and 12 men complete a certain piece of work in 9 days. Each child takes twice the time taken by a man to finish the work. In how many days will 12 men finish the same work?

A. 8 days B. 15 days
C. 9 days D. 12 days

9. A cistern can be filled by pipes *A* and *B* in 12 minutes and 16 minutes respectively. When full, the tank can be emptied by a third pipe *C* in 8 minutes only. If all the taps be turned on at the same time, the cistern will be full in :

A. 20 min
B. 24 min
C. 36 min
D. 48 min

10. If 30 men working 7 hours a day can do a piece of work in 18 days, in how many days will 21 men working 8 hours a day do the same piece of work?

A. 25 days B. 20 days
C. $22\frac{1}{2}$ days D. 30 days

EXPLANATORY ANSWERS

1. (B) : $(A + B)$'s 5 days' work = $(1/25 + 1/20) \times 5 = 9/20$
Remaining work = $1 - 9/20 = 11/20$

B will finish it in = $\frac{11}{20} \times 20 = 11$ days.

2. (D) : *A*'s 10 days' work = $10/25 = 2/5$
Remaining work = $1 - 2/5 = 3/5$
$(A + B)$'s 1 day's work = $1/25 + 1/20 = 9/100$
So, $(A + B)$ complete 3/5 of the work in

$$= \frac{100}{9} \times \frac{3}{5} = 6\frac{2}{3} \text{ days}$$

So, work lasted for $= 10 + 6\frac{2}{3} = 16\frac{2}{3}$ days.

3. (B) : *A*'s 5 days' work = $5/40 = 1/8$
Remaining work = $1 - 1/8 = 7/8$

B can do a piece of work in = $\frac{8}{7} \times 21 = 24$ days

i.e., $A = 1/40$, $B = 1/24$
So, $(A + B)$ can complete the work in

$$= \frac{40 \times 24}{40 + 24} = 15 \text{ days.}$$

4. (A) : $A = 3B$
So $(A + B)$'s 1 day's work = $1/15$
$4B$'s 1 day's work = $1/15$
B's 1 day work = $1/15 \times 4 = 1/60$
So, *B* alone will complete the work in 60 days.

5. (B) : Trick : Numbers of days = $\frac{8+6}{2} = 7$ days.

6. (D) : C's share of work = $1 - \left(\frac{3}{6} + \frac{3}{8}\right) = \frac{1}{8}$

So, *C*'s share = $\frac{1}{8} \times 320$ = ₹ 40.

7. (B) : Trick : *C*'s share = $529 \times (1 - 19/23)$
= $529 \times 4/23$ = ₹ 92

8. (D) : Trick : 2 children = 1 man
So, (8 children + 12 men) = 16 men

So, 12 men will complete the same work in $\frac{16 \times 9}{12}$

= 12 days.

9. (D) : $(A + B + C)$'s 1 min work

$$= \frac{1}{12} + \frac{1}{16} - \frac{1}{8}$$

$$= \frac{4+3-6}{48} = \frac{1}{48}$$

Hence, cistern will full in 48 min.

10. (C) : Trick : Man × Day × hours

Number of days = $\frac{30 \times 18 \times 7}{21 \times 8}$

$$= 22\frac{1}{2} \text{ days.}$$

15. TIME AND DISTANCE

The following rules/tricks should be remembered for solving problems on the Time and Distance :

A. Basic Formulae :

(*i*) Distance Travelled = Average speed × Time Taken

(*ii*) $\text{Average Speed} = \dfrac{\text{Distance Travelled}}{\text{Time Taken}}$

(*iii*) $\text{Time Taken} = \dfrac{\text{Distance Travelled}}{\text{Average Speed}}$

Trains passing a telegraph post or a stationary man

Example 1 : How many seconds will a train 100 metres long running at the rate of 36 km per hour take to pass a certain telegraph post?

Solution : In passing the post the train must travel its own length.

Now, 36 km/hr = 36 × 5/18 = 10 m/sec

So, required time = 100/10 = 10 seconds

Trains crossing a bridge or passing a railway station

Example 2 : How long does a train 110 metres long running at the rate of 36 km/hr take to cross a bridge 132 metres in length?

Solution : In crossing the bridge the train must travel its own length plus the length of the bridge. Now, 36 km/hr = 36 × 5/18 = 10 m/sec.

So, required time = 242/10 = 24.2 seconds

Trains running in opposite directions

Example 3 : Two trains 121 metres and 99 metres in length respectively are running in opposite directions, one at the rate of 40 km/hr and the other at the rate of 32 km/hr. In what time will they be completely clear of each other from the moment they meet?

Solution : As the two trains are moving in opposite directions their relative speed = 40 + 32 = 72 km/hr, or 20 m/sec.

$$\text{So, the required time} = \frac{\text{Total length}}{\text{Relative speed}}$$

$$= \frac{121+99}{20} = 11 \text{ sec}$$

Trains running in the same direction

Example 4 : In Example 3 if the trains were running in the same direction, in what time will they be clear of each other?

Solution: Relative speed = 40 – 32

$$= 8 \text{ km/hr} = \frac{20}{9} \text{ m/sec}$$

Total length = 121 + 99 = 220 m

$$\text{So, required time} = \frac{\text{Total length}}{\text{Relative speed}} = \frac{220}{20} \times 9 = 99 \text{ sec}$$

Train passing a man who is walking

Example 5 : A train 110 metres in length travels at 60 km/hr. In what time will it pass a man who is walking at 6 km/hr (*i*) against it (*ii*) in the same direction?

Solution : This question is to be solved like the above examples 3 and 4, the only difference being that the length of the man is zero.

(*i*) Relative speed = 60 + 6 = 66 km/hr = $\dfrac{55}{3}$ m/sec.

$$\text{So, required time} = \frac{110}{55} \times 3 \times 3 = 6 \text{ seconds}$$

(*ii*) Relative speed = 60 – 6 = 54 km/hr = 15 m/sec.

So, required time = 110/15 = $7\frac{1}{3}$ seconds.

MULTIPLE CHOICE QUESTIONS

1. The speed of a 100 m long running train *A* is 40 % more than the speed of another 180 m long train *B* running in the opposite directions. To find out the speed of train *B*, which of the information given in statements *P* and *Q* is/are sufficient?

   P : The two trains cross each other in 6 seconds

   Q : The difference between the speeds of the two trains was 26 kmph.

   A. Only P is sufficient
   B. Only Q is sufficient
   C. Both P and Q are needed
   D. Both P & Q are not sufficient

2. Two stations *A* and *B* are 110 km apart on a straight line. One train starts from *A* at 7 a.m. and travels towards *B* at 20 kmph. Another train starts from *B* at 8 a.m. and travels towards *A* at a speed of 25 kmph. At what time will they meet?

   A. 9 am B. 10 am
   C. 11 am D. 10:30 am

3. The length of the train that takes 8 seconds to pass a pole when it runs at a speed of 36 km/hr is :

A. 70 m B. 80 m
C. 85 m D. 90 m

4. A train running at certain speed crosses a stationary engine in 20 seconds. To find out the speed of the train, which of the following information is necessary :

A. Only the length of the train
B. Only the length of the engine
C. Either the length of the train or the length of the engine
D. Both the length of the train and the length of the engine

5. How long will a train 60 m long travelling at 40 km/hr take to pass through a station whose platform is 90 m long?

A. 12.5 seconds B. 13.5 seconds
C. 14.5 seconds D. 15.5 seconds

6. A train overtakes two persons who are walking in the same direction in which the train is going, at the rate of 2 kmph and 4 kmph and passes them completely in 9 and 10 seconds respectively. The length of the train is :

A. 72 m B. 54 m
C. 50 m D. 45 m

7. Two trains of equal lengths take 10 seconds and 15 seconds respectively to cross a milestone. If the length of each train be 120 metres, in what time (in seconds) will they cross each other travelling in opposite direction?

A. 20 sec B. 15 sec
C. 12 sec D. 10 sec

8. A train is running at the rate of 40 kmph. A man is also going in the same direction parallel to the train at the speed of 25 kmph. If the train crosses the man in 48 seconds, the length of the train is :

A. 100 m B. 200 m
C. 300 m D. 400 m

9. A train 700 m long is running at 72 kmph. If it crosses a tunnel in 1 minute, the length of the tunnel is :

A. 700 m B. 600 m
C. 550 m D. 500 m

EXPLANATORY ANSWERS

1. (A) : Let speed of B be x kmph.

Then, speed of $A = \frac{140x}{100} = \frac{7x}{5}$ kmph

Relative speed $= \left(x + \frac{7x}{5}\right)$ kmph

$= \frac{12x}{5} \times \frac{5}{18}$ m/sec $= \frac{2x}{3}$ m/sec

Time taken to cross each other

$= \left[(100 + 180) \times \frac{3}{2x}\right]$ sec. $= \frac{420}{x}$ sec

Now, $420/x = 6 \Rightarrow x = 70$ kmph.

Thus, only P is sufficient.

2. (B) : Suppose they meet in x hours after 7 a.m. Distance covered by A in x hours $= 20x$ km

Distance covered by B in $(x-1)$ hours $= 25(x-1)$ km

$\because 20x + 25(x-1) = 110 \Rightarrow 45x = 135 \Rightarrow x = 3$

So, they meet at 10 a.m.

Quicker Maths (Direct formula) :

They will meet at

$$8 \text{ a.m.} + \frac{110 - (8 \text{ a.m.} - 7 \text{ a.m.})\,20}{20 + 25}$$

$= 8$ a.m. $+ 2$ hr $= 10$ a.m.

3. (B) : 36 km/hr $= 36 \times 5/18 = 10$ m/s

Distance covered by train in 8 seconds = length of train $= 8 \times 10 = 80$ m

4. (D) : Since the sum of the lengths of the train and the engine is needed, both the lengths must be known.

5. (B) : Speed $= 40$ km/hr $= 40 \times \frac{5}{18}$ m/s

So, Time $= \frac{(60 + 90)}{40 \times 5} \times 18 = \frac{150 \times 18}{40 \times 5}$

$= 13.5$ seconds.

6. (C) : 2 kmph $= (2 \times 5/18)$ m/sec $= 5/9$ m/sec

and 4 kmph $= \left(4 \times \frac{5}{18}\right)$ m/sec $= 10/9$ m/sec

Let the length of the train be x metres and its speed be y m/sec

Then $\frac{x}{(y - 5/9)} = 9$ and $\frac{x}{(y - 10/9)} = 10$

So, $9y - 5 = x$ and $10(9y - 10) = 9x$

So, $9y - x = 5$ and $90y - 9x = 100$

On solving we get : $x = 50$

So, length of the train is 50 m.

7. (C) : Speed of first train $= \frac{120}{10} = 12$ m/s

Speed of second train $= \frac{120}{15} = 8$ m/s

Their relative speed $= 12 + 8 = 20$ m/s

Hence, required time $= \frac{120 + 120}{20} = \frac{240}{20} = 12$ sec

8. (B) : Length of train = Relative speed × time

$= (40 - 25)\left(\frac{5}{18}\right) \times 48 = \frac{15 \times 5 \times 48}{18} = 200$ m

9. (D) : Let length of the tunnel be x m;

speed $= (72 \times 5/18)$ m/ sec $= 20$ m/sec

Time $= 60$ sec

$\because \quad 60 = \frac{700 + x}{20} \Rightarrow 700 + x = 1200 \Rightarrow x = 500$ m

16. TABLES AND GRAPHS

TABLES

Tables are often used in reports, magazines and newspaper to present as set of numerical data. It is one of the easiest and most accurate ways of presenting data. One of the main purposes of tables is to make complicated information easier to understand. Hence, the advantage of presenting data in a table is that one can see the information at a glance. We present below an example of tabular presentation of annual expenditure of 5 families for last 4 years.

Annual Expenditure of 5 families (in ₹ Thousands)

Years → Families ↓	2005	2006	2007	2008
A	35	50	55	60
B	40	60	65	75
C	45	50	70	80
D	30	40	45	50
E	50	55	60	70

Essentials of a Tables:

(i) **Title:** Heading of the table

(ii) **Stub:** The section of the table containing row headings in called Stub.

(iii) **Column Captions :** The heading of each column is designated as column caption.

(iv) **Body**

(v) **Footnotes**

(vi) **Source**

BAR GRAPHS

Given quantity of a bar graph can be compared by the height or length. A bar graph can have either vertical or horizontal bars. You can compare different quantities or the same quantity at the different times. The bars may be placed adjacent to each other or may be separated from each other by spaces depending upon the problem.

For Example:

Registration of New Vehicles in Delhi (in thousands)

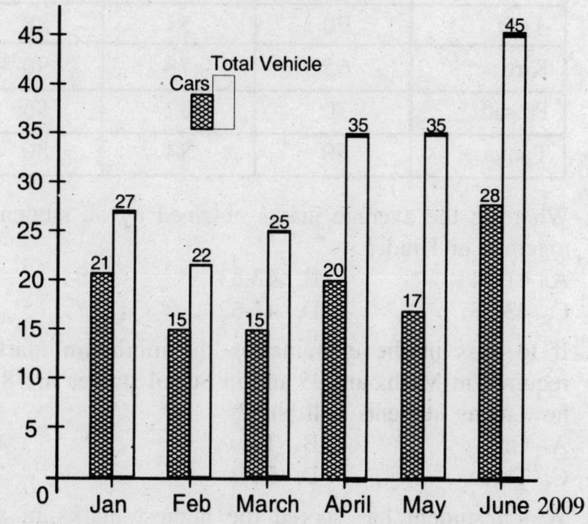

PIE CHARTS

These are used to show the share of various sectors in the total. They usually show the percentage share of each sector in the whole (taken as 100%). In such representation the total quantity in question is distributed over a total angle of 360°. The area of each sector is proportional to the relative frequency of the class represented by the sector.

$$\text{Sector angle} = \frac{\text{Class frequency}}{\text{Total frequency}} \times 360°$$

For Example:

Distribution of Expenditure of a family

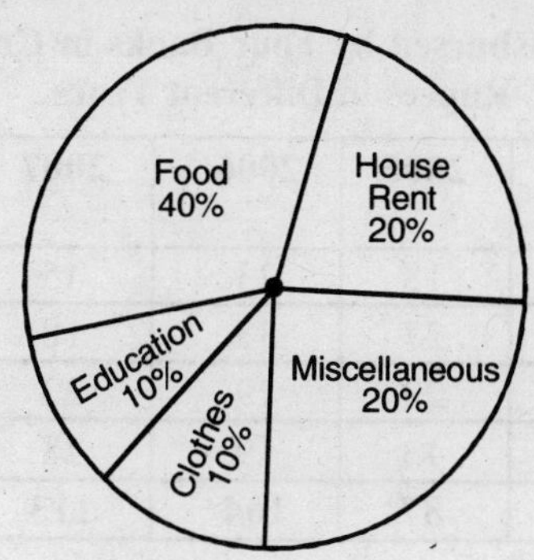

MULTIPLE CHOICE QUESTIONS

Directions (Qs. 1-5): *Study the table carefully to answer the questions that follow:*

PERCENTAGE OF MARKS OBTAINED BY SIX STUDENTS IN SIX DIFFERENT SUBJECTS

Subject → Student ↓	Science (Out of 150)	English (Out of 100)	Hindi (Out of 50)	Maths (Out of 150)	Social Studies (Out of 125)	Maithili (Out of 50)
Ravi	85	67	84	70	70	78
Riya	80	53	86	60	80	78
Amit	90	51	88	65	50	66
Kirti	65	78	90	85	70	68
Prasad	70	82	86	80	60	72
Tanya	60	84	80	65	50	76

1. What are the average marks obtained by all students together in Hindi?
A. 41.54 B. 42.83
C. 43.28 D. 44.62

2. If to pass in the examination the minimum marks required in Maths are 95 and in Social studies are 85, how many students will pass?
A. One B. Two
C. Three D. Four

3. Which student has scored the highest marks in all subjects together?
A. Amit B. Kirti
C. Prasad D. Ravi

4. What are the total marks obtained by Tanya in all the subjects together?
A. 402 B. 408
C. 412 D. 418

5. What is the Riya's overall percentage of marks in all subjects together?
A. 68.3 B. 71.2
C. 72.8 D. 75.6

Directions (Qs. 6-9): *Study the table given below and answer the following questions:*

Loans Disbursed by Four Banks in Crores of Rupees in Different Years

Years → Banks ↓	2005	2006	2007	2008
A	18	23	45	30
B	27	33	18	41
C	29	29	22	17
D	13	19	28	32
Total	**87**	**104**	**113**	**120**

6. In which year the disbursement of loans by all the banks combined together was nearest to the average disbursement of loans over the years?
A. 2005 B. 2006
C. 2007 D. 2008

7. In which year was the total disbursement of loans of banks A and B exactly equal to the total disbursement of loans of banks C and D?
A. 2005 B. 2006
C. 2008 D. None of these

8. What was the percentage increase of disbursement of loans of all the banks together from 2007 to 2008?
A. 6% B. $6\frac{11}{113}\%$
C. $6\frac{22}{113}\%$ D. $7\frac{11}{113}\%$

9. In which bank was the loan disbursement more than 30% of the disbursement of all banks combined together in 2008?
A. A B. B
C. C D. D

Directions (Qs. 10-13): *The bar graph given here represents the number of persons killed in road accidents during rainy season in the year 2009. Study the graph carefully and answer the questions that follow:*

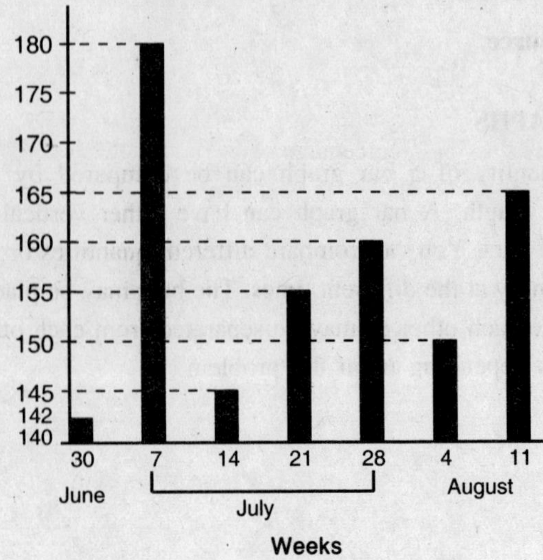

10. During which of the following successive weeks number of persons killed was the highest?
A. 4 August – 11 August
B. 14 July – 21 July
C. 30 June – 7 July
D. 21 July – 28 July

11. In how many weeks number of persons killed was more than 150?
A. 3 B. 2
C. 4 D. 1

12. In how many weeks number of persons killed was less than 150?
A. 2 B. 0
C. 1 D. 3

13. During which of the following successive weeks number of persons killed came down to a minimum level?
A. 28 July – 4 August
B. 7 July – 14 July
C. 30 June – 7 July
D. 21 July – 28 July

Directions (Qs. 14-18): *The bar graph given below shows annual result of different classes of a school. Study the graph carefully and attempt the questions that follow:*

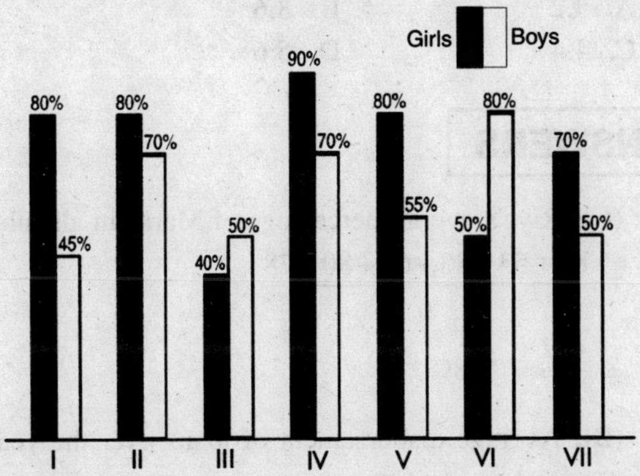

14. Result of which class shows maximum difference between pass percentage of the girls and the boys?
A. I B. IV
C. III D. VI

15. In which class pass percentage of boys is more than the average pass percentage of girls of the school?
A. VI B. VII
C. III D. V

16. In which of the following classes pass percentage of girls is less than the average pass percentage of the school?
A. III-VI B. V-VI
C. VI-VII D. III-IV

17. In which class number of failed girls is minimum?
A. I B. III
C. IV D. VII

18. Average pass percentage of boys in classes II and III is equal to average pass percentage of girls in which of the following classes?
A. II-VI B. I-V
C. VI-VII D. V-VI

Directions (Qs. 19-23): *Study the following Graph carefully and answer the questions given below:*

Percentage of students in various courses (A, B, C, D, E, F) and Percentage of girls out of these. Total students = 1200 (800 girls + 400 boys)

Percentage in Various Courses

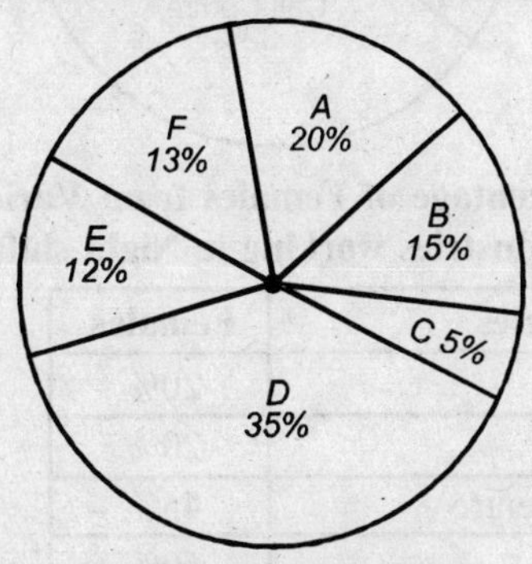

(Total girls = 800)

Percentage of Girls in Various courses

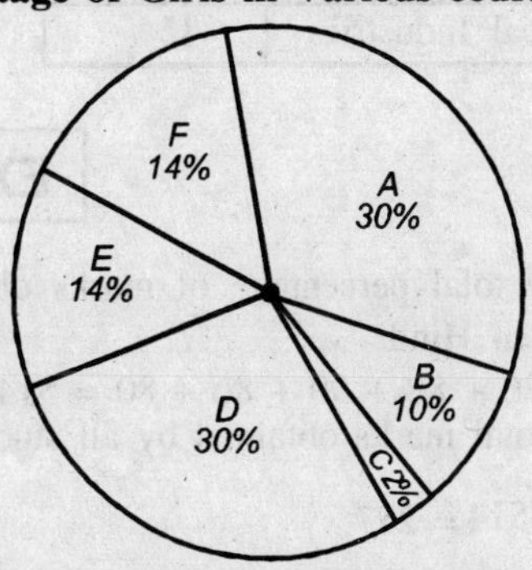

19. For which course is the number of boys the minimum?
A. A B. C
C. E D. F

20. For course D what is the respective ratio of boys and girls?
A. 3 : 4 B. 3 : 5
C. 4 : 5 D. 5 : 6

21. For course E, the number of girls is how much per cent more than the boys for course E?
A. 80 B. 150
C. 250 D. 350

22. How many girls are there in course C?
A. 16 B. 40
C. 44 D. 160

23. For which pair of courses is the number of boys the same?
A. A and D B. B and D
C. C and F D. E and F

Directions (Qs. 24-28): *Study the following Pie-chart carefully and answer the questions given below:*

Percentage of People in a City working in Night shifts from various Industries (Total number of people = 40250)

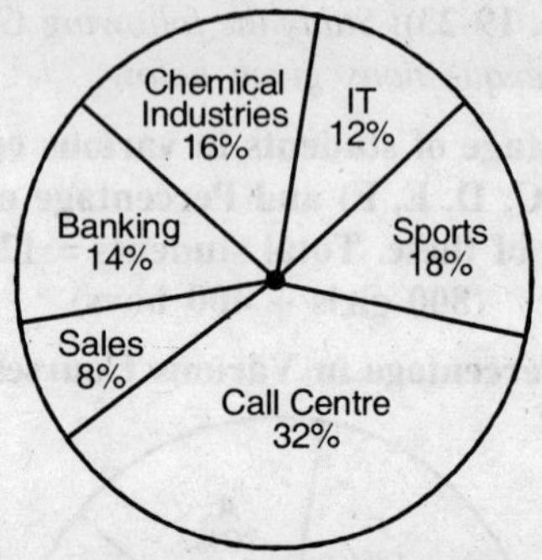

Percentage of Females from Various Industries working in Night shifts

Industries	Females
IT	20%
Sports	20%
Call Centre	45%
Sales	60%
Banking	40%
Chemical Industries	15%

24. What is the respective ratio of men to women working in night shifts from the Call centre Industry?
A. 9 : 11 B. 11 : 9
C. 8 : 13 D. 13 : 8

25. What is the total number of men working in night shifts from all the industries together?
A. 25788
B. 26887
C. 28297
D. 28678

26. What is the difference between the total number of men and the total number of women working in night shifts from all the industries together?
A. 13254 B. 13363
C. 13524 D. 13542

27. What is the approximate average number of females working in night shifts from all the industries together?
A. 2227 B. 2823
C. 3326 D. 4107

28. The number of women from the sports industry are what per cent of the total number of people working in the night shifts from all the industries together?
A. 3.2 B. 3.6
C. 4.4 D. 5.6

EXPLANATORY ANSWERS

1. (B): The total percentage of marks obtained by all students in Hindi

= 84 + 86 + 88 + 90 + 86 + 80 = 514

Hence, total marks obtained by all students in Hindi

$= \frac{50}{100} \times 514 = 257$

Since, their average $= \frac{257}{6} = 42.83\%$

2. (B): Pass percentage in Maths $= 95 \times \frac{100}{150} = 63.3\%$

Pass percentage in Social studies $= 85 \times \frac{100}{125} = 68\%$

It is clear from the table that Ravi and Kirti will pass in the examination.

3. (B): It is clear from the table that Kirti has scored the highest marks in all the subjects.

4. (C): Total marks obtained by Tanya in all the subjects

$= \frac{150}{100} \times 60 + 84 + \frac{50}{100} \times 80 + \frac{150}{100} \times 65 + \frac{125}{100} \times 50 + \frac{50}{100} \times 76$

= 90 + 84 + 40 + 97.5 + 62.5 + 38 = 412

5. (C): Riya's overall percentage of Marks in all subjects

$= \frac{80+53+86+60+80+78}{6}$

$= \frac{437}{6} \approx 72.8\%$

6. (B): Average disbursement of loans over the years $= \frac{87+104+113+120}{4}$

$= \frac{424}{4} = 106 \approx 104$

which is nearly equal to the disbursement of loans in year 2006.

7. (D): In 2005,

Total disbursement of loans of banks A and B = 18 + 27 = 45

Total disbursement of loans of banks C and D = 19 + 13 = 32

In 2006,

Total disbursement of loans of banks A and B = 23 + 33 = 56

Total disbursement of loans of banks C and D = 29 + 19 = 48

In 2007,

Total disbursement of loans of banks A and B = 45 + 18 = 63

Total disbursement of loans of banks C and D = 22 + 28 = 50

In 2008,

Total disbursement of loans of banks A and B = 30 + 41 = 71

Total disbursement of loans of banks C and D = 17 + 32 = 49

Since, it is clear that total disbursement of loans of banks A and B is not equal to the total disbursement of loans of banks C and D in any year.

8. **(C):** Required percentage

$= \frac{120-113}{113} \times 100 = \frac{700}{113} = 6\frac{22}{113}\%$

9. **(B):** In 2008, the percentage of loan disbursement of bank B to the disbursement of loans of all the banks

$= \frac{41}{120} \times 100 = 34.17\% > 30\%$

10. **(C):** According to the graph, the two successive weeks *vis*., 30 June – 7 July shows highest increase of 180 – 142 = 38 in the number of persons killed.

11. **(C):** According to the bar graph, number of person killed was more than 150 during the weeks beginning from 7 July, 21 July, 28 July and 11 August. Therefore number of such weeks = 4.

12. **(D):** It is obvious from the bar graph that during the weeks beginning from 30 June, 14 July and 4 August, number of persons killed remained less than 150.

13. **(B):** According to the bar graph, two successive weeks, *i.e.* 7 July – 14 July shows maximum decline in the number of persons killed in road accidents.

14. **(A):** Difference between pass percentage of girls and boys in class I = 80 – 45 = 35%

Difference between pass percentage of girls and boys in class II = 80 – 70 = 10%

Difference between pass percentage of girls and boys in class III = 50 – 40 = 10%

Difference between pass percentage of girls and boys in class IV = 90 – 70 = 20%

Difference between pass percentage of girls and boys in class V = 80 – 55 = 25%

Difference between pass percentage of girls and boys in class VI = 80 – 50 = 30%

Difference between pass percentage of girls and boys in class VII = 70 – 50 = 20%

Hence, it is clear that result of class I shows maximum difference between pass percentage of the girls and the boys.

15. **(A):** Average pass percentage of girls

$= \frac{80+80+40+90+80+50+70}{7} = \frac{490}{7} = 70\%$

Therefore, in class VI pass percentage of boys is more than the average pass percentage of girls.

16. **(A):** Average pass percentage of the school

$= \frac{80+45+80+70+40+50+90+70+80+55+50+80+70+50}{14}$

$= \frac{910}{14} = 65\%$

Therefore, it is clear that pass percentage of the girls in III and VI classes is less than the average pass percentage of the school.

17. **(C):** In class IV pass percentage of girls is the highest. Thereore in this class only number of failed girls is the minimum.

18. **C.:** Average pass percentage of the boys in classes II and III $= \frac{70+50}{2} = \frac{120}{2} = 60\%$

Average pass percentage of the girls in class VI and VII $= \frac{50+70}{2} = 60\%$

Therefore, average pass percentage of boys in classes II and III is equal to the average pass percentage of girls in classes VI and VII.

19. **(A):** Number of boys in course 'A'

$= \frac{20}{100} \times 1200 - \frac{30}{100} \times 800 = 240 - 240 = 0$

Number of boys in course 'C'

$= \frac{5}{100} \times 1200 - \frac{2}{100} \times 800 = 60 - 16 = 44$

Number of boys in course 'E'

$= \frac{12}{100} \times 1200 - \frac{14}{100} \times 800 = 144 - 112 = 32$

Number of boys in course 'F'

$= \frac{13}{100} \times 1200 - \frac{14}{100} \times 800 = 156 - 112 = 44$

Hence, in course 'A' number of boys is minimum *i.e.*, zero.

20. **(A):** For course D,

Number of boys $= \frac{35}{100} \times 1200 - \frac{30}{100} \times 800$

$= 420 - 240 = 180$

Number of girls $= \frac{30}{100} \times 800 = 240$

Since, required ratio = 180 : 240 = 3 : 4

21. **(C):** For course E,

Number of boys = $\frac{12}{100}\times 1200-\frac{14}{100}\times 800$

= 144 − 112 = 32

Number of girls = $\frac{14}{100}\times 800=112$

Required percentage = $\frac{112-32}{32}\times 100$

= $\frac{80}{32}\times 100$ = 250%

22. **(A):** Number of girls in course 'C'

= $\frac{2}{100}\times 800$ = 16

23. **(C):** Number of boys in course A

= $\frac{20}{100}\times 1200-\frac{30}{100}\times 800$ = 240 − 240 = 0

Number of boys in course B

= $\frac{15}{100}\times 1200-\frac{10}{100}\times 800$ = 180 − 80 = 100

Number of boys in course C

= $\frac{5}{100}\times 1200-\frac{2}{100}\times 800$ = 60 − 16 = 44

Number of boys in course D

= $\frac{35}{100}\times 1200-\frac{30}{100}\times 800$ = 420 − 240 = 180

Number of boys in course E

= $\frac{12}{100}\times 1200-\frac{14}{100}\times 800$ = 144 − 112 = 32

Number of boys in course F

= $\frac{13}{100}\times 1200-\frac{14}{100}\times 800$ = 156 − 112 = 44

Hence, number of boys in course 'C' and 'F' are same.

24. **(B):** Number of people working in night shifts from Call Centre Industry = $\frac{32}{100}\times 40250$ = 12880

Number of women working in night shifts from Call Centre Industry = $\frac{45}{100}\times 12880$ = 5796

So, the number of men working from same Industry = 12880 − 5796 = 7084

Hence, Required ratio = 7084 : 5796

= 11 : 9

25. **(B):** Number of men working in night shifts in different industries:

IT ⇒ $\frac{80}{100}\times\frac{12}{100}\times 40250$ = 3864

Sports ⇒ $\frac{80}{100}\times\frac{18}{100}\times 40250$ = 5796

Call Centre ⇒ $\frac{55}{100}\times\frac{32}{100}\times 40250$ = 7084

Sales ⇒ $\frac{40}{100}\times\frac{8}{100}\times 40250$ = 1288

Banking ⇒ $\frac{60}{100}\times\frac{14}{100}\times 40250$ = 3381

Chemical Industries

⇒ $\frac{85}{100}\times\frac{16}{100}\times 40250$ = 5474

Hence, total number of men working in night shifts in different industries

= 3864 + 5796 + 7084 + 1288 + 3381 + 5474

= 26887

26. **(C):** Total number of men = 26887

Total number of women = 40250 − 26887

= 13363

Their difference = 26887 − 13363 = 13524

27. **(A):** Required average number of females

= $\frac{13363}{6}$ = 2227.16 ≈ 2227

28. **(B):** Number of women from Sports Industry

= $\frac{20}{100}\times\frac{18}{100}\times 40250$ = 1449

Required percentage = $\frac{1449}{40250}\times 100$ = 3.6%

17. TRIGONOMETRY

Measurement of Angles: In general, the angles are measured in degrees or in radians which are defined as follows:

(*a*) ***Degrees***: A right angle is divided into 90 equal parts and each part is called a degree. Thus a right angle is equal to 90 degrees. One degree is denoted by 1°.

A degree is divided into sixty equal parts and each part is called a minute and is denoted by 1'.

A minute is divided into sixty equal parts and each part is called a second and is denoted by 1″.

Thus, we have

1 right angle = 90° (read as 90 degrees)

1° = 60′ (read as 60 minutes)

1′ = 60″ (read as 60 seconds)

(*b*) ***Radians***: A radian is the angle subtended at the centre of a circle by an arc equal in length to the radius of the circle.

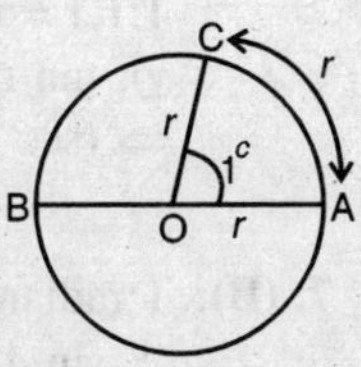

In the adjacent figure OA = OC = arc AC = r = radius of the circle, then measurement of ∠ AOC is one radian and is denoted by 1^c. Thus ∠ AOC = 1^c.

Trigonometrical Ratios: In a right angled triangle ABC, if ∠ CAB = θ, then BC = side opposite to the angle θ = Perpendicular = p (say), AC = side opposite to the right angle = Hypotenuse = h (say) and AB = b (say).

The six trigonometrical ratios are given as follows:

$\sin\theta = p/h$, $\cos\theta = b/h$,

$\tan\theta = p/b$.

(Also $\tan\theta = \sin\theta/\cos\theta$,

$\text{cosec}\,\theta = 1/\sin\theta$,

$\sec\theta = 1/\cos\theta$,

$\cot\theta = 1/\tan\theta$,)

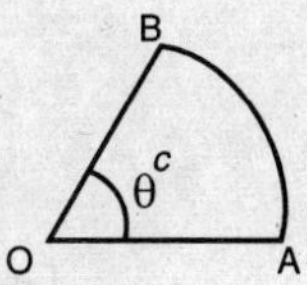

Basic Formulae Connecting Six Trigonometrical Ratios: The formulae connecting the six trigonometrical ratios are:

(*i*) $\sin^2\theta + \cos^2\theta = 1$ *or* $\cos^2\theta = 1 - \sin^2\theta$ *or* $\sin^2\theta = 1 - \cos^2\theta$.

(*ii*) $1 + \tan^2\theta = \sec^2\theta$ *or* $\sec^2\theta - \tan^2\theta = 1$

(*iii*) $1 + \cot^2\theta = \text{cosec}^2\theta$ *or* $\text{cosec}^2\theta - \cot^2\theta = 1$.

MULTIPLE CHOICE QUESTIONS

1. The angles of a triangle are in A.P. and the radian measure of the smallest to the degree measure of the mean is π : 200. The greatest angle in radians is:

A. (11/30)π B. π/3
C. π/2 D. None of these

2. The moon's distance from the earth is 3,50,000 kilometres and its diameter subtends an angle of 31' at the eye of the observer. The diameter of the moon is:

A. 3157 (11/27) km B. 315 (11/27) km
C. 3050 (11/27) km D. None of these

3. If sin θ = – 3/5 and θ lies in the third quadrant, then the value of cos (θ/2) is:

A. 1/5 B. –1/√(10)
C. –1/5 D. 1/√(10)

4. If tan θ = – 4/3, then sin θ is:

A. –4/5 but not 4/5
B. –4/5 or 4/5
C. 4/5 but not –4/5
D. None of these

5. If the angle θ is in the third quadrant and tan θ = 3, then the value of sin θ is:

A. 1/√(10) B. –1/√(10)
C. –3/√(10) D. 3/√(10)

6. If (sec α + tan α) (sec β + tan β) (sec γ + tan γ) = tan α tan β tan γ, then (sec α – tan α) (sec β – tan β) (sec γ – tan γ) = ?

A. cot α cot β cot γ
B. tan α tan β tan γ
C. cot α + cot β + cot γ
D. tan α + tan β + tan γ

7. Which of the following is correct?

A. sin 1° > sin 1
B. sin 1° < sin 1
C. sin 1° = sin 1
D. sin 1° = (π/180) sin 1

8. Which of the following is correct?

A. tan 1 > tan 2 B. tan 1 = tan 2
C. tan 1 < tan 2 D. tan 1 = 1

9. The value of log tan1° + log tan2° + ... + log tan89° is:

A. 0 B. 1

C. ∞ D. None of these

10. The value of cos105° + sin105° is:

A. 0 B. $\sqrt{(3/2)}$

C. $1/\sqrt{2}$ D. $(\sqrt{3}+1)/2$

EXPLANATORY ANSWERS

1. (A): Let the angles in degrees in A.P. be taken as

$A = \theta - \phi, B = \theta, C = \theta + \phi$

$\therefore A + B + C = 180° = 3\theta \Rightarrow B = \theta = 60°$

Now $\frac{\pi}{200} = \frac{\text{A in radian}}{\text{B in degrees}}$

$= \frac{(60-\phi)(\pi/180)}{60}$

$\Rightarrow \phi = 6°$

$\therefore$ Greatest angle $C = \theta + \phi = 66°$

$= 66 \times (\pi/180) = (11/30)\ \pi$ radians.

2. (A): Let l be the diameter of moon and a its distance from the earth. If the moon subtends an angle θ at the eye of the observer, then

$l = a\theta = 350000 \times \left(\frac{31}{60} \times \frac{\pi}{180}\right)$

$= \frac{3500 \times 31}{6 \times 18} \times \frac{22}{7} = 3157\ \frac{11}{27}$ km.

3. (B): $\because$ θ lies in the third quadrant

$\because$ cos θ is –ve

$\because$ sin θ = – 3/5

$\Rightarrow \cos\theta = -\sqrt{(1 - \sin^2\theta)} = -4/5$

Now, $\cos^2 \frac{1}{2}\theta = \frac{1}{2}(1 + \cos\theta)$

$= \frac{1}{2}(1 - 4/5) = 1/10$

$\Rightarrow \cos\frac{1}{2}\theta = \pm 1/\sqrt{(10)}$

But given that, $180° < \theta < 270°$

$\Rightarrow 90° < \theta/2 < 135°$

i.e., θ/2 lies in the second quadrant

$\Rightarrow \cos\frac{1}{2}\theta$ is –ve

Hence, $\cos\frac{1}{2}\theta = -1/\sqrt{10}$.

4. (B): tan θ = – 4/3

$\Rightarrow$ θ lies in 2nd or 4th quadrant.

$\therefore$ sin θ is positive or negative according as θ lie in 2nd or 4th quadrant respectively, *i.e.*, sin θ may be positive or negative.

Now $\sin\theta = \tan\theta/\sqrt{(1 + \tan^2\theta)} = 4/5$

Hence, sin θ = – 4/5 or 4/5.

5. (C): $\because$ θ is in the third quadrant,

$\because \sin\theta < 0$.

Thus, $\sin\theta = -\tan\theta/\sqrt{(1 + \tan^2\theta)} = -3/\sqrt{(10)}$.

6. (A): Multiplying both sides of the given expression by (secα – tanα). (secβ – tanβ). (secγ – tanγ), we get,

1.1.1 = (secα – tanα) . (sec β – tan β). (sec γ – tan γ). tan α tan β tan γ

$\Rightarrow$ (sec α – tan α).(sec β – tan β).(sec γ – tan γ) = cot α.cot β.cot γ.

7. (B): 1 radian = (180/π) Degrees = 57° (appr.)

$\therefore \sin 1° < \sin 57° \Rightarrow \sin 1° < \sin 1$.

8. (A): 1 radian = 57° (appr.)

which lie in first quadrant. $\therefore$ tan 1 > 0,

and 2 radians = 114° (appr.), which lie in second quadrant $\therefore$ tan 2 < 0

Hence, tan 1 > tan 2.

9. (A): $\log\tan 1° + \log\tan 2° + ... + \log\tan 89°$

$= \log[\tan 1°.\tan 2°...\tan 45°...\tan 88°.\tan 89°]$

$= \log[\tan 1°.\tan 2°...\tan 45°...$

$\tan(90° - 2°)\tan(90° - 1°)]$

$= \tan[\tan 1°.\cot 1°.\tan 2°.\cot 2°...1]$

$= \log 1 = 0$

10. (C): $\cos 105° + \sin 105°$

= cos(60° + 45°) + sin(60° + 45°)

= cos60° cos45° – sin60° sin45° + sin60° cos45° + cos60° sin45°

$= \frac{1}{2}.\frac{1}{\sqrt{2}} - \frac{\sqrt{3}}{2}.\frac{1}{\sqrt{2}} + \frac{\sqrt{3}}{2}.\frac{1}{\sqrt{2}} + \frac{1}{2}.\frac{1}{\sqrt{2}}$

$= \frac{2}{2\sqrt{2}} = \frac{1}{\sqrt{2}}$

18. ALGEBRA

Algebric Identies

Some Important Formula

(i) $(a + b)^2 = a^2 + 2ab + b^2$

(ii) $(a - b)^2 = a^2 - 2ab + b^2$

(iii) $a^2 - b^2 = (a - b)(a + b)$

(iv) $(a + b + c)^2 = a^2 + b^2 + c^2 + 2ab + 2bc + 2ca$

(v) $(a + b - c)^2 = a^2 + b^2 + c^2 + 2ab - 2bc - 2ca$

(vi) $(a - b + c)^2 = a^2 + b^2 + c^2 - 2ab - 2bc + 2ca$

(vii) $(-a + b + c)^2 = a^2 + b^2 + c^2 - 2ab + 2bc - 2ca$

(viii) $(a + b)^3 = a^3 + b^3 + 3ab(a + b)$ or

$= a^3 + b^3 + 3a^2b + 3ab^2$

(ix) $(a - b)^3 = a^3 - b^3 - 3ab\ (a - b)$ or

$= a^3 - b^3 - 3a^2b + 3ab^2$

(x) $a^3 + b^3 = (a + b)\ (a^2 + b^2 - ab)$ or

$= (a + b)^3 - 3ab(a + b)$

(xi) $a^3 - b^3 = (a - b)\ (a^2 + b^2 + ab)$ or

$= (a - b)^3 + 3ab\ (a - b)$

(xii) $a^3 + b^3 + c^3 - 3abc$

$= (a + b + c)(a^2 + b^2 + c^2 - ab - bc - ca)$

If $a + b + c = 0$

$a^3 + b^3 + c^3 = 3abc$

(xiii) $(x + a)\ (x + b) = x^2 + (a + b)x + ab$

(xiv) $(a + b)^2 + (a - b)^2 = 2(a^2 + b^2)$

(xv) $(a + b)^2 - (a - b)^2 = 4ab$

(xvi) $(a + b)^3 + (a - b)^3 = 2(a^3 + 3ab^2)$

(xvii) $(a + b)^3 - (a - b)^3 = (2(b^3 + 3a^2b)$

(xviii) If $x+\frac{1}{x}=t$ Then, $x^2+\frac{1}{x^2}=t^2-2$

(xix) If $x-\frac{1}{x}=t$ Then, $x^2+\frac{1}{x^2}=t^2+2$

(xx) $x^3+\frac{1}{x^3}=\left(x+\frac{1}{x}\right)^3-3\left(x+\frac{1}{x}\right)$

(xxi) $x^2-\frac{1}{x^3}=\left(x-\frac{1}{x}\right)^3+3\left(x-\frac{1}{x}\right)$

(xxii) $x+\frac{1}{x}=\sqrt{x^2+\frac{1}{x^2}+2}$

(xxiii) $x-\frac{1}{x}=\sqrt{x^2+\frac{1}{x^2}-2}$

Factorization of Algebraic Expressions

Factorization : The process of writing an algebraic expression as the product of two or more algebraic expressions is called factorization.

Factors : The algebraic expressions that may be multiplied to obtain the given algebraic expressions are called factors of the given expression.

Factor Theorem : If $f(x)$ is completely divisible by $(x - a)$ then $fA. = 0$, $(x - a)$ is called factor of $f(x)$, if and only if $fA. = 0$

Remainder Theorem : If an expression $f(x)$ is divided by $(x - a)$ then the remainder is fA.

e.g., $f(x) = ax^3 + bx + cx + d$

$fA. = a\ .\ a^3 + b\ .\ a + c\ .\ a + d$ is known as remainder of the given polynomials.

Surds

Given a number, it is not always possible to find some whole number which when multiplied by itself will give the given number. In other words all given numbers are not perfect square numbers. For example, square root of 9, *i.e.*, $\sqrt{9}$ is 3, which is a whole number. But square root of 15, *i.e.*, $\sqrt{15} = 3.873$, which is not a whole number.

Hence square roots of natural numbers which are not perfect squares are not rational numbers. These are irrational numbers and are called **Surds**.

For example, $\sqrt{3}$, $\sqrt{7}$, $2+\sqrt{11}$, $4+\sqrt{13}$ ..... etc. are Surds.

Given below are a few formulas which are quite helpful in solving the problems related to surds:

1. $\sqrt{a}\times\sqrt{a}=a$

2. $\sqrt{a}\times\sqrt{b}=\sqrt{ab}$

3. $\left(\sqrt{a}+\sqrt{b}\right)^2 = a + b + 2\sqrt{ab}$

4. $\left(\sqrt{a}-\sqrt{b}\right)^2 = a + b - 2\sqrt{ab}$

5. $x\sqrt{a}+x\sqrt{b}=x\left(\sqrt{a}+\sqrt{b}\right)$

6. $\dfrac{1}{\sqrt{a}+\sqrt{b}}=\dfrac{1}{\sqrt{a}+\sqrt{b}}\times\dfrac{\sqrt{a}-\sqrt{b}}{\sqrt{a}-\sqrt{b}}=\dfrac{\sqrt{a}-\sqrt{b}}{a-b}$

7. $\dfrac{1}{\sqrt{a}-\sqrt{b}}=\dfrac{1}{\sqrt{a}-\sqrt{b}}\times\dfrac{\sqrt{a}+\sqrt{b}}{\sqrt{a}+\sqrt{b}}=\dfrac{\sqrt{a}+\sqrt{b}}{a-b}$

8. $a+\sqrt{b}=c+\sqrt{d} \Rightarrow a=c$ and $b=d$

9. $\sqrt{2}=1.41421$, $\sqrt{3}=1.73205$, $\sqrt{5}=2.23607$,

$\sqrt{6}=2.4494$ $\sqrt{7}=2.64575$, $\sqrt{8}=2.82842$,

$\sqrt{10}=3.16227$, $\sqrt{11}=3.31662$

MULTIPLE CHOICE QUESTIONS

1. $(28)^3+(-15)^3+(-13)^3=$?
A. 16380 B. 16250
C. 16420 D. 16280

2. If $x+\dfrac{1}{x}=5$, What is the value of $x^3+\dfrac{1}{x^3}$:
A. 120 B. 210
C. 110 D. 105

3. If $x^2+\dfrac{1}{x^2}=83$, what is the value of $x^3-\dfrac{1}{x^3}=$?
A. 756 B. 754
C. 856 D. 932

4. $23^3-17^3=$?
A. 7254 B. 7153
C. 7271 D. 7154

5. If $x+\dfrac{1}{x}=15$, then the value of $x^2+\dfrac{1}{x^2}$ will be:
A. 228 B. 230
C. 323 D. 223

6. If $x=12$ and $y=4$, the value of $(x+y)^{x/y}$ will be:
A. 4096 B. 3896
C. 4196 D. 5086

7. If $x+y=2z$, then the value of $\left(\dfrac{x}{x-z}+\dfrac{z}{y-z}\right)$ will be:
A. 1 B. 4
C. 3/2 D. 2

8. If $x+y+z=0$, then the value of $\dfrac{(x+y)(y+z)(z+x)}{xyz}$ will be:
A. –3 B. –2
C. 0 D. –1

9. If $x+\dfrac{1}{x}=3$, the value of $x^4+\dfrac{1}{x^4}$ will be:
A. 49 B. 47
C. 37 D. 42

10. If $\left(x+\dfrac{1}{x}\right)^2=0$, then the value of $\left(x^2+\dfrac{1}{x^2}\right)$ will be:
A. 1 B. –1
C. 2 D. –2

11. If $\left(a+\dfrac{2}{a}\right)=3$, then the value of $\left(a-\dfrac{2}{a}\right)$ will be:
A. ± 4 B. ± 5
C. ± 2 D. ± 1

12. If $\sqrt{a}+\dfrac{1}{\sqrt{a}}=4$, then the value of $a^2+\dfrac{1}{a^2}$ will be:
A. 194 B. 199
C. 178 D. 192

13. Factors of x^2-25 are:
A. $(x-1)(x-25)$
B. $(x+25)(x-1)$
C. $(x+5)(x-5)$
D. $(x-5)(x-5)$

14. Square of $\left(x-\dfrac{1}{x}\right)$ will be
A. $x^2-2-\dfrac{1}{x^2}$ B. $x^2-2+\dfrac{1}{x^2}$
C. $x^2-4-\dfrac{1}{x^2}$ D. $x^2-2+\dfrac{1}{x}$

15. Factors of $36-9x^2$ will be:
A. $(6+3x)(6-3x)$
B. $(3x-6)(6-3x)$
C. $(3x+6)(3x-6)$
D. $(12x-3x)(3+3x)$

EXPLANATORY ANSWERS

1. (A): Let $a=28$, $b=-15$ and $c=-13$. Then

$$a+b+c=28-15-13=0$$
$$a^3+b^3+c^3=3abc$$
$$(28)^3+(-15)^3+(-13)^3=3\times28\times(-15)\times(-13)=16380$$

2. (C): $x^3+\dfrac{1}{x^3}=\left(x+\dfrac{1}{x}\right)^3-3\left(x+\dfrac{1}{x}\right)$

$=(5)^3-3\times5=125-15=110.$

3. (A): If $x^2+\frac{1}{x^2}=83$, what is the value of $x^3-\frac{1}{x^3}=?$

$$\left(x-\frac{1}{x}\right)^2 = x^2+\frac{1}{x^2}-2$$

$$x-\frac{1}{x} = \sqrt{83-2}=\sqrt{81}$$

$$x-\frac{1}{x} = 9$$

$$\therefore \quad \left(x^3-\frac{1}{x^3}\right) = \left(x-\frac{1}{x}\right)^3+3\left(x-\frac{1}{x}\right)$$

$$= (9)^3 + 3 \times 9 = 729 + 27 = 756$$

4. (A): $23^3 - 17^3 = (20 + 3)^3 - (20 - 3)^3$

$$= 2(3^3 + 3 \times 20^2 \times 3)$$

$$[\because (a + b)^3 - (a - b)^3 = 2(b^3 + 3a^2b)]$$

$$= 2\ (27 + 3600) = 54 + 7200 = 7254$$

5. (D): $\because x+\frac{1}{x}=15 \Rightarrow \left(x+\frac{1}{x}\right)^2=(15)^2$

$$\Rightarrow x^2+\frac{1}{x^2}+2.x\frac{1}{x}=225$$

$$\therefore \quad x^2+\frac{1}{x^2}=225-2=223.$$

6. (A): $(x+y)^{x/y}=(12+4)^{12/4}=(16)^3=4096.$

$[\because x=12, y=4]$

7. (A): $\because x+y=2z \Rightarrow x-z=z-y=-(y-z)$

$$\therefore \frac{x}{x-z}+\frac{z}{y-z}=\frac{x}{-(y-z)}+\frac{z}{y-z}=\frac{z-x}{y-z}=1.$$

$$[\because x-z=z-y]$$

8. (D): $\because \quad x+y+z=0 \Rightarrow x+y=-z$

$x+y+z=0 \Rightarrow y+z=-x$

and $\quad x+y+z=0 \Rightarrow z+x=-y$

$$\therefore \quad \frac{(x+y)(y+z)(z+x)}{xyz}=\frac{(-z)(-x)(-y)}{xyz}$$

$$=-1.$$

9. (B): $\because x+\frac{1}{x}=3 \Rightarrow \left(x+\frac{1}{x}\right)^2=(3)^2$

$$\Rightarrow \quad x^2+\frac{1}{x^2}+2.x.\frac{1}{x}=9$$

$$\Rightarrow \quad x^2+\frac{1}{x^2}=9-2=7$$

$$\because \quad x^2+\frac{1}{x^2}=7$$

$$\Rightarrow \quad \left(x^2+\frac{1}{x^2}\right)^2=(7)^2$$

$$\Rightarrow \quad x^4+\frac{1}{x^4}+2.x^2.\frac{1}{x^2}=49$$

$$\therefore \quad x^4+\frac{1}{x^4}=49-2=47.$$

10. (D): $\left(x+\frac{1}{x}\right)^2=0 \Rightarrow x^2+\frac{1}{x^2}+2x.\frac{1}{x}=0$

$$\Rightarrow \quad x^2+\frac{1}{x^2}=-2.$$

11. (D): $\because \left(a-\frac{2}{a}\right)^2=\left(a+\frac{2}{a}\right)^2-4.a.\frac{2}{a}$

$$=(3)^2-8=9-8=1$$

$$\therefore \quad \left(a-\frac{2}{a}\right)=\pm\sqrt{1}=\pm 1.$$

12. (A): $\because \sqrt{a}+\frac{1}{\sqrt{a}}=4 \Rightarrow \left(\sqrt{a}+\frac{1}{\sqrt{a}}\right)^2=(4)^2$

$$\Rightarrow a+\frac{1}{a}+2.\sqrt{a}.\frac{1}{\sqrt{a}}=16 \because \left(a+\frac{1}{a}\right)=14$$

$$\Rightarrow \left(a+\frac{1}{a}\right)^2=(14)^2 \Rightarrow a^2+\frac{1}{a^2}+2.a.\frac{1}{a}=196$$

$$\therefore \quad a^2+\frac{1}{a^2}=196-2=194.$$

13. (C): $x^2-25=(x)^2-(5)^2$, [which is of the form a^2-b^2]

$$=(x+5)(x-5).$$

14. (B): According to question:

$$\text{Square of } \left(x-\frac{1}{x}\right)=\left(x-\frac{1}{x}\right)^2$$

$$=x^2-2.x.\frac{1}{x}+\left(\frac{1}{x}\right)^2$$

$$=x^2-2+\frac{1}{x^2}.$$

15. (A): $36-9x^2=(6)^2-(3x)^2$ [which is of the form a^2-b^2]

$$=(6+3x)(6-3x).$$

19. GEOMETRY

Familiarity with Elementary Geometric Figures and Facts

ANGLE

An angle is the union of two non-collinear rays with a common initial point.

The two rays forming an angle are called the "arms" of the angle and the common initial point is called the "vertex" of the angle.

The angle formed by the rays AB and AC denoted by the ∠BAC or ∠CAB.

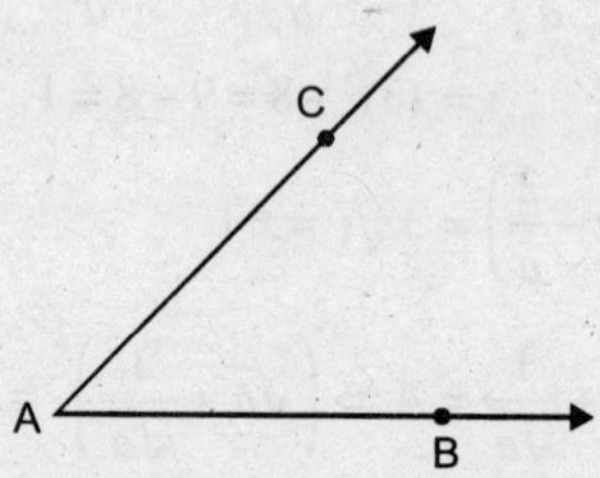

For the sake of convenience the angle ∠BAC or ∠CAB can also be referred simply as ∠A. However, this cannot be done if there are more than one angle with the same vertex A. In such cases we can denote the angles by the symbols such as ∠1, ∠2, ∠3, etc.,

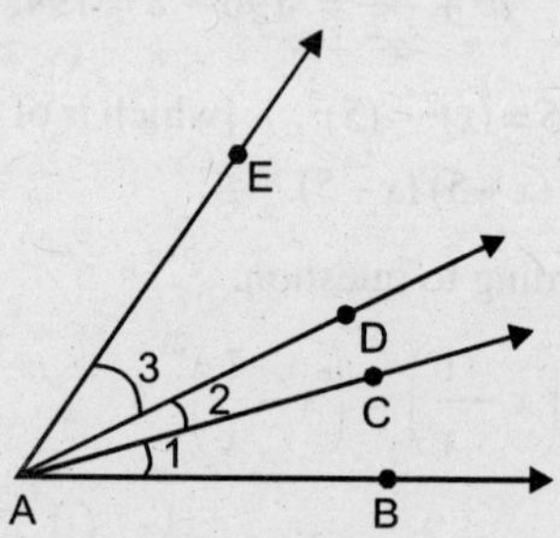

∠BAC divided the plan containing it into two parts: (*i*) the part of the plane which lies between the rays AB and AC and (*ii*) the part of the plane which does not lie between the rays AB and AC. The first part is known as the interior of ∠BAC and the second part is the exterior of ∠BAC as defined below.

- **Interior of an Angle:** The interior of an angle BAC is the set of all points in its plane, which lie on the same side of AB as C and also on the same side of AC as B.

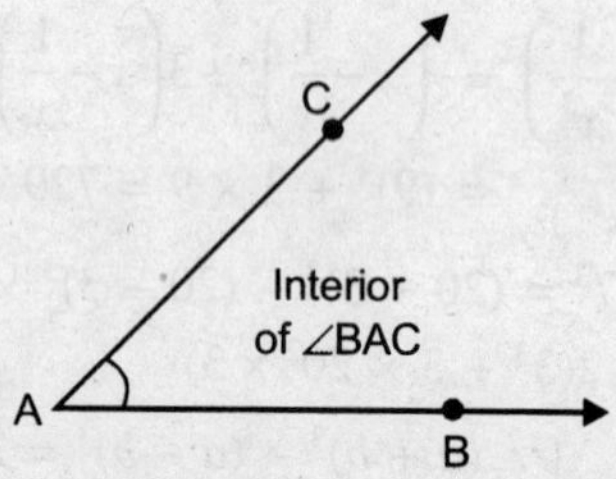

- **Exterior of an Angle:** The exterior of an angle BAC is the set of all points in its plane, which do not lie on the angle or in its interior.

Types of Angle

In this section, we shall define various types of angles on the basis of their measure and the relation of their measures with the measure of some given angle.

- **Right Angle:** An angle whose measure is 90° is called a right angle.

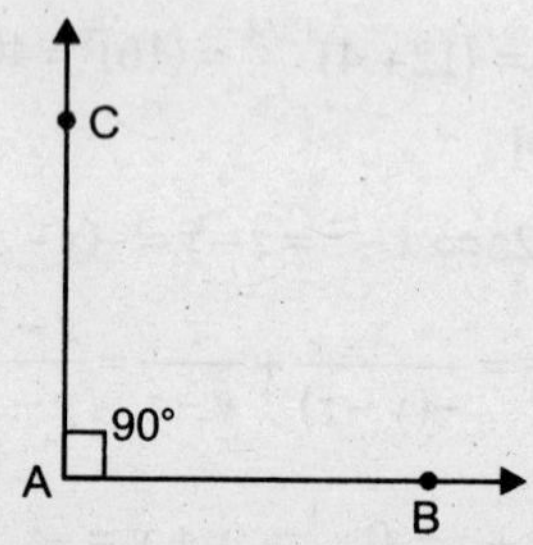

- **Acute Angle:** An angle whose measure is less than 90° is called an acute angle.

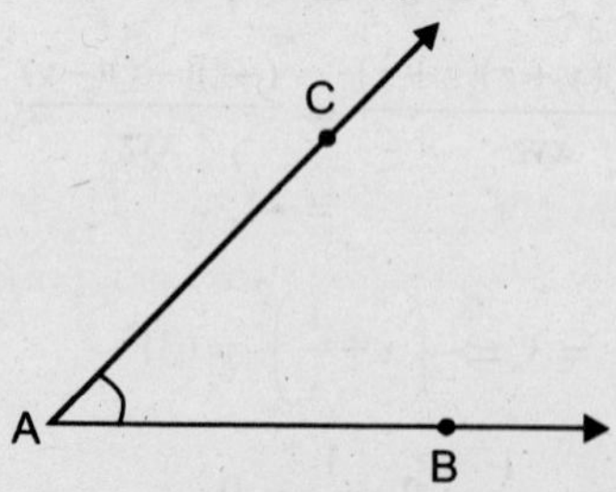

Thus, an angle whose measure is less than the measure of a right angle is an acute angle.

∴ ∠BAC is an acute angle if $0 < \angle BAC < 90°$

- **Obtuse Angle:** An angle whose measure is more than 90° but less than 180° is called an obtuse angle.

Thus, an angle whose measure is more than the measure of a right angle is an obtuse angle.

$\therefore$ ∠BAC is an obtuse angle, if $90° < \angle BAC < 180°$

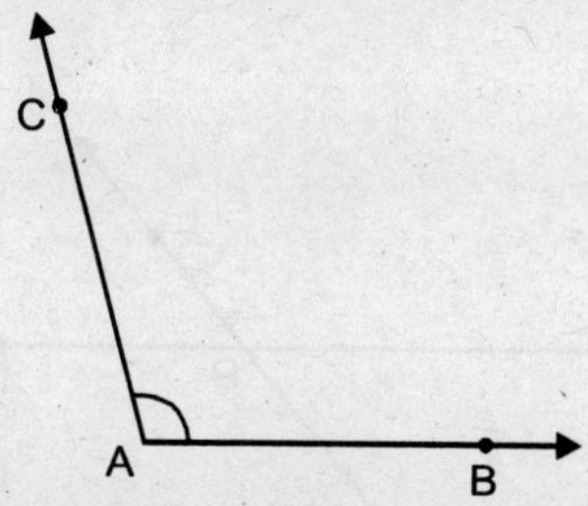

- **Straight Angle:** An angle whose measure is 180° is called a straight angle.

  Thus, if two rays forming an angle are opposite, they form a straight angle.

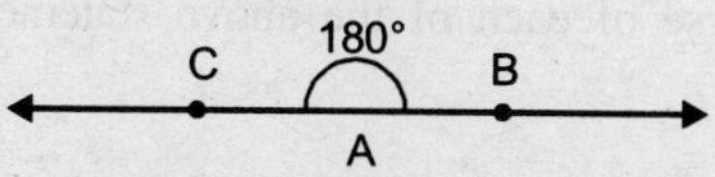

- **Reflex Angle:** An angle whose measure is more than 180° is called a reflex angle.

  The measure of a reflex angle is more than 180° and less than 360°.

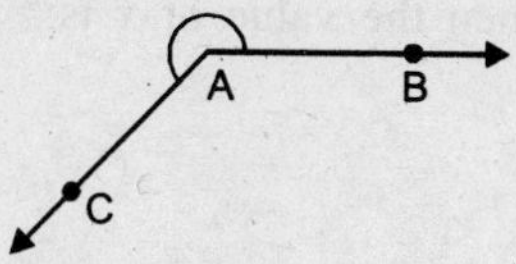

- **Complementary Angle:** Two angles, the sum of whose measures is 90°, are called complementary angles.

  Thus, ∠BAC and ∠XAC are complementary angles, if $x + y = 90°$

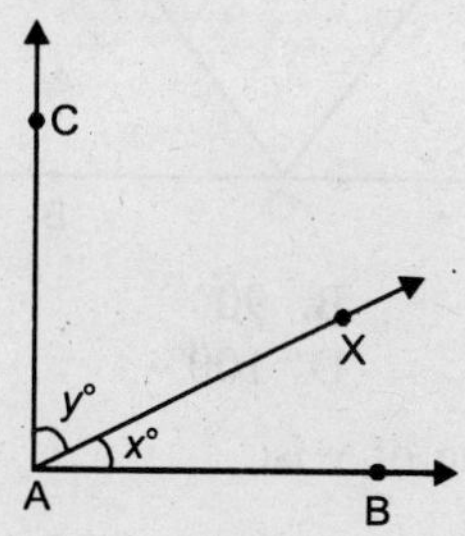

- **Supplementary Angle:** Two angles, the sum of whose measures is 180°, are called the supplementary angles.

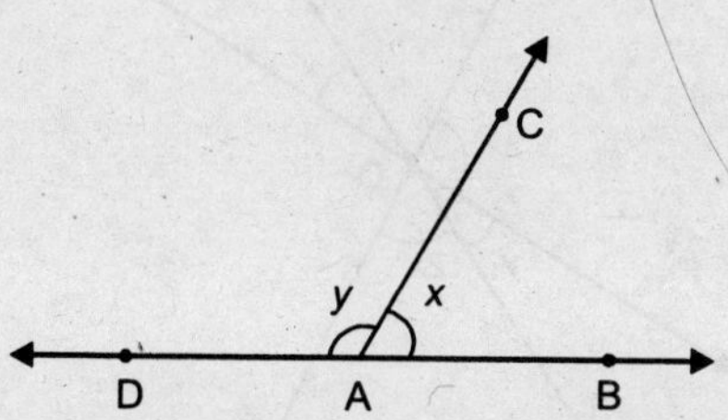

- **Angle Bisector:** A ray AX is said to be the bisector of ∠BAC, if X is a point in the interior of ∠BAC and ∠BAX = ∠XAC.

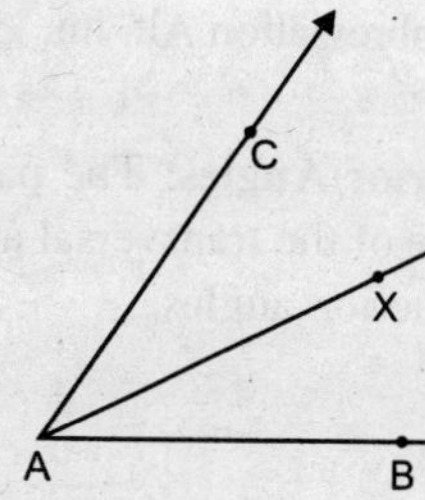

Thus, if ray AX is the bisector of ∠BAC, then

$$\angle BAC = \angle CAX = \frac{1}{2}\angle BAC$$

ANGLES MADE BY A TRANSVERSAL WITH TWO LINES

Transversal

A line which intersects two or more given lines at distinct points, is called a transversal of the given lines.

In the given figure, LM line is transversal of the lines AB and CD respectively.

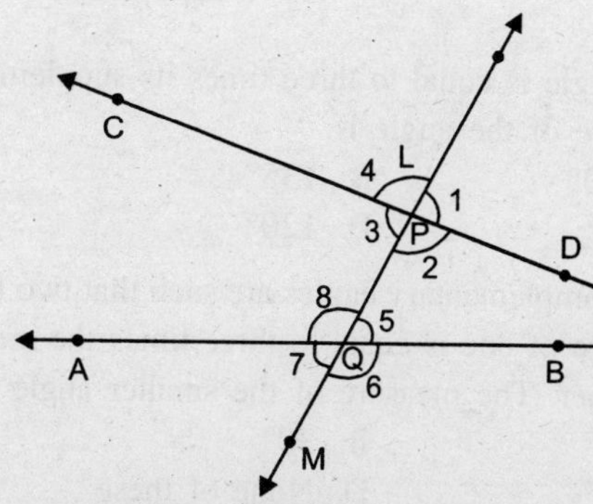

It is evident from the figure that the lines AB, CD and LM determine eight angles, four angles at P and the remaining four angles at Q. We classify these eight angles in the following groups:

- **Corresponding Angles:** Two angles on the same side of transversal are known as the corresponding angles if both lie either above the two lines or below the two lines.

  In the following pairs of angles are the pairs of corresponding angles:

  (*i*) ∠1 and ∠5
  (*ii*) ∠4 and ∠8
  (*iii*) ∠2 and ∠6
  (*iv*) ∠3 and ∠7

  We shall use the abbreviation corres. ∠*s* for corresponding angles.

- **Alternate Interior Angles:** The following pairs of angles are called the pairs of alternate interior angles:

  (*i*) ∠3 and ∠5
  (*ii*) ∠2 and ∠8

We shall use the abbreviation Alt. int. ∠s for alternate interior angles.

- **Consecutive Interior Angles:** The pairs of interior angles on the same of the transversal are called pairs of consecutive interior angles.
  (*i*) ∠2 and ∠5
  (*ii*) ∠3 and ∠8

When a transversal intersects two lines, we recognize certain pairs of angles and know them by their special names assigned earlier. In general, there is no relation between the angles of any of the pairs introduced above. However, when the lines are parallel, we have a number of interesting and useful relations between the angles of each of the earlier mentioned pairs.

Consider the parallel lines AB and CD and transversal LM intersecting AB and CD at P and Q respectively. By having a careful look at these three lines it seems that:

(*i*) each pair of corresponding angles are equal
(*ii*) each pair of alternate interior angles are equal and,
(*iii*) each pair of consecutive interior angles are supplementary.

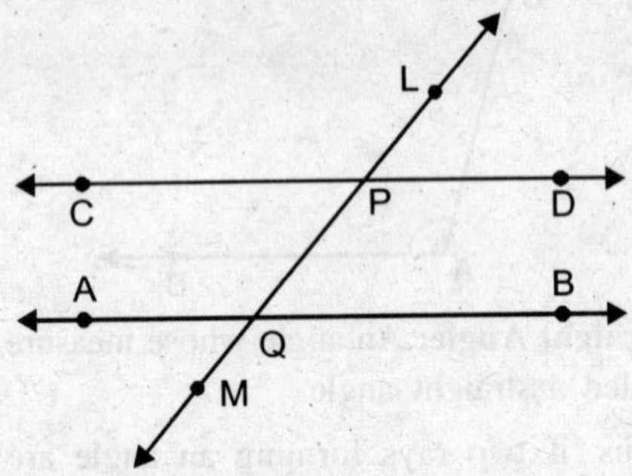

The converse of each of the above statements is also true.

MULTIPLE CHOICE QUESTIONS

1. One angle is equal to three times its supplement. The measure of the angle is:
A. 130° B. 135°
C. 90° D. 120°

2. Two complementary angles are such that two times the measure of one is equal to three times the measure of the other. The measure of the smaller angle is:
A. 45° B. 30°
C. 36° D. None of these

3. Two straight lines AB and CD intersect one another at the point O. If ∠AOC + ∠COB + ∠BOD = 274°, then ∠AOD =
A. 86° B. 90°
C. 94° D. 137°

4. Two straight lines AB and CD cut each other at O. If ∠BOD = 63°, then ∠BOC =
A. 63° B. 117°
C. 17° D. 153°

5. Consider the following statements:
When two straight lines intersect:
(*i*) adjacent angles are complementary
(*ii*) adjacent angles are supplementary
(*iii*) opposite angles are equal
(*iv*) opposite angles are supplementary

Of these statements
A. (*i*) and (*iii*) are correct
B. (*ii*) and (*iii*) are correct
C. (*i*) and (*iv*) are correct
D. (*ii*) and (*iv*) are correct

6. Given ∠POR = $3x$ and ∠QOR = $2x + 10°$. If POQ is a straight line, then the value of x is:
A. 30°
B. 34°
C. 36°
D. None of these

7. In the given figure AOB is a straight line. If ∠AOC = ∠BOD = 85°, then ∠COD =

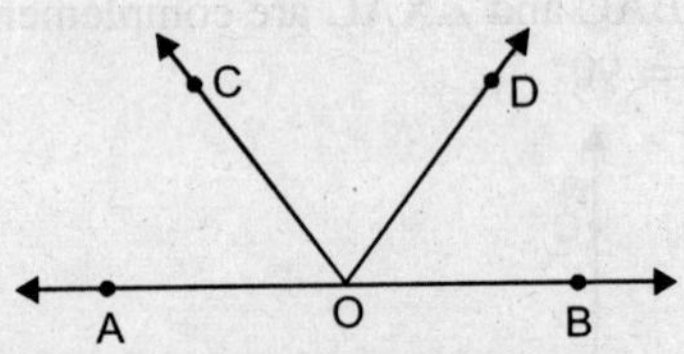

A. 85° B. 90°
C. 95° D. 100°

8. In Fig. the value of y is:

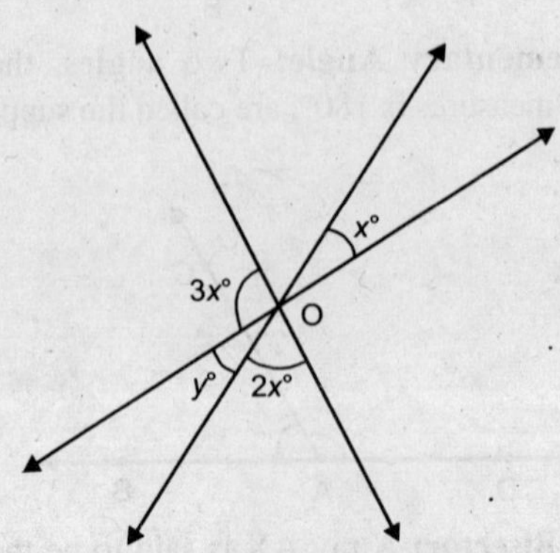

A. 20° B. 30°
C. 45° D. 60°

9. In Fig. if $\frac{y}{x} = 5$ and $\frac{z}{x} = 4$, then the value of x is:

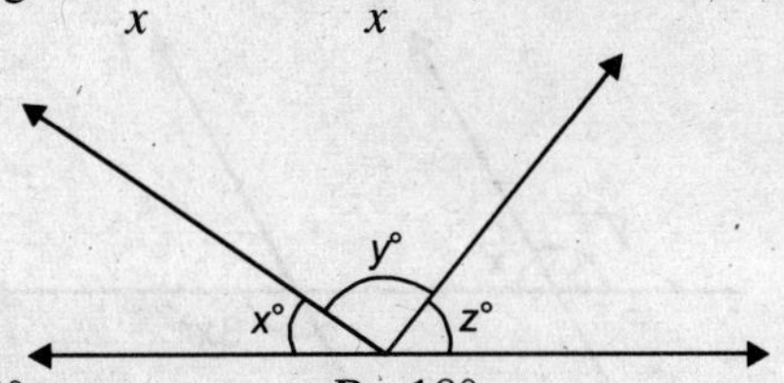

A. 8° B. 18°
C. 12° D. 15°

10. In Fig. the value of x is:

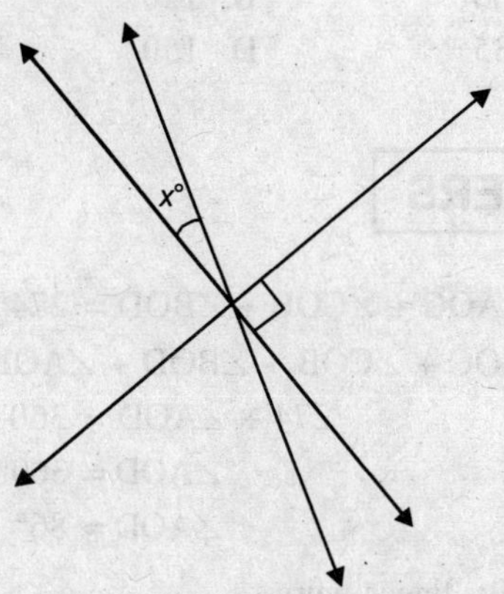

A. 12 B. 15
C. 20 D. 30

11. In Fig. which of the following statements must be true?

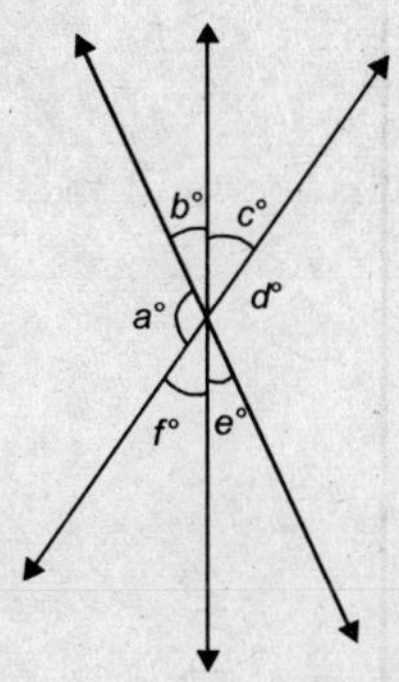

(*i*) $a + b = d + c$
(*ii*) $a + c + e = 180°$
(*iii*) $b + f = c + e$

A. (*i*) only
B. (*ii*) only
C. (*iii*) only
D. (*ii*) and (*iii*) only

12. If two interior angles on the same side of a transversal intersecting two parallel lines are in the ratio 2 : 3, then the measured of the larger angle is:

A. 54° B. 120°
C. 108° D. 136°

13. In Fig. AB || CD || EF and GH || KL. The measure of ∠HKL is:

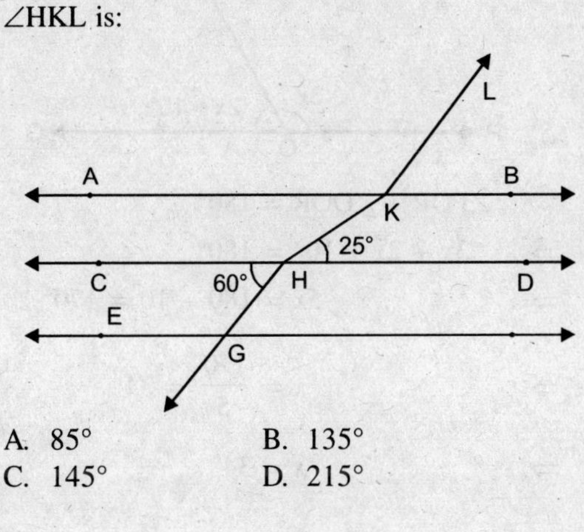

A. 85° B. 135°
C. 145° D. 215°

14. In Fig. if AB || CD, then the value of x is:

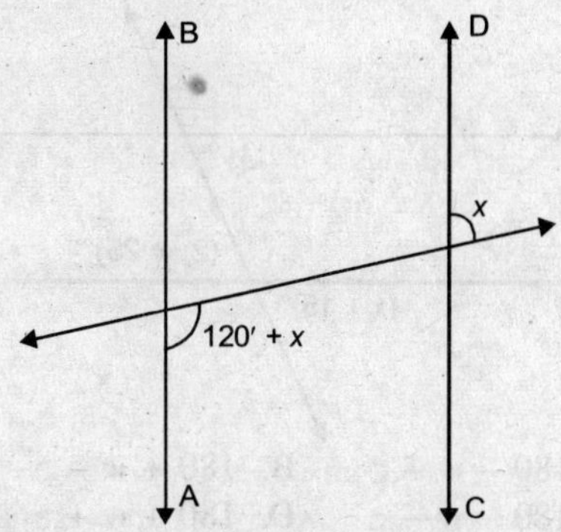

A. 20° B. 30°
C. 45° D. 60°

15. AB and CD are two parallel lines. PQ cuts AB and CD at E and F respectively. EL is the bisector of ∠FEB. If ∠LEB = 35°, then ∠CEQ will be:

A. 55° B. 70°
C. 110° D. 130°

16. Two lines AB and CD intersect at O. If ∠AOC + ∠COB + ∠BOD = 270°, then ∠AOC =

A. 70° B. 80°
C. 90° D. 180°

17. In Fig. PQ || RS, ∠AEF = 95°, ∠BHS = 110° and ∠ABC = x°. Then the value of x is:

A. 15° B. 25°
C. 70° D. 35°

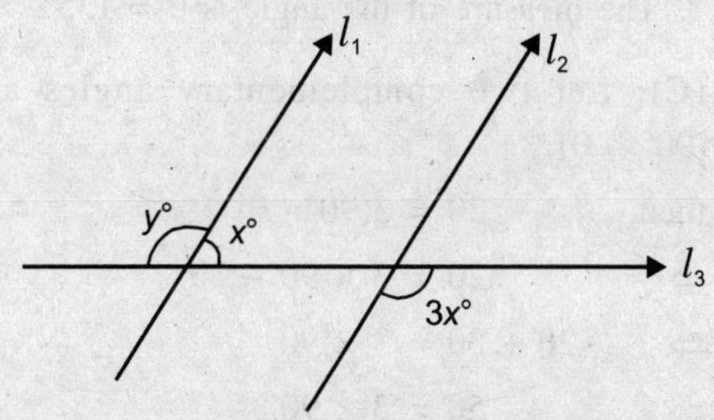

18. In Fig. if $l_1 \parallel l_2$, what is the value of x?

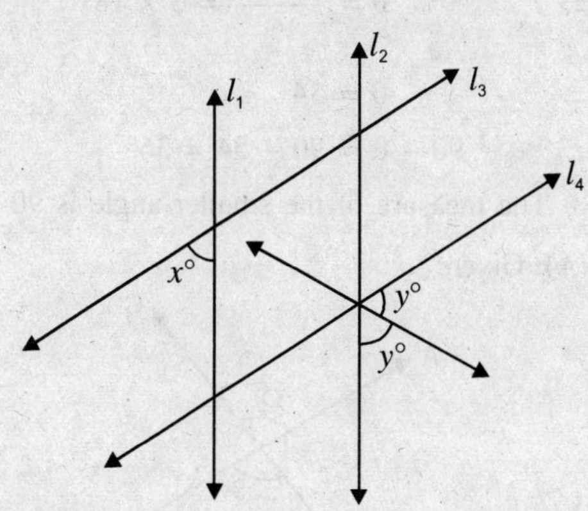

A. 90° B. 85°
C. 75° D. 70°

19. In Fig. if $l_1 \parallel l_2$, what is $x + y$ in terms of w and z?

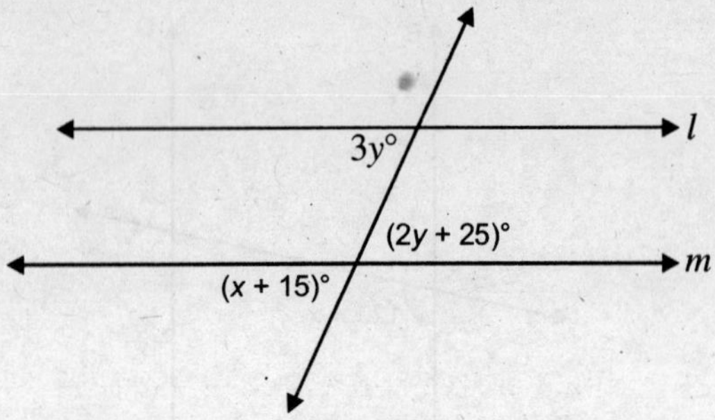

A. $180 - w + z$ B. $180 + w - z$
C. $180 - w - z$ D. $180 + w + z$

20. In Fig. if $l_1 \parallel l_2$, what is the value of y?

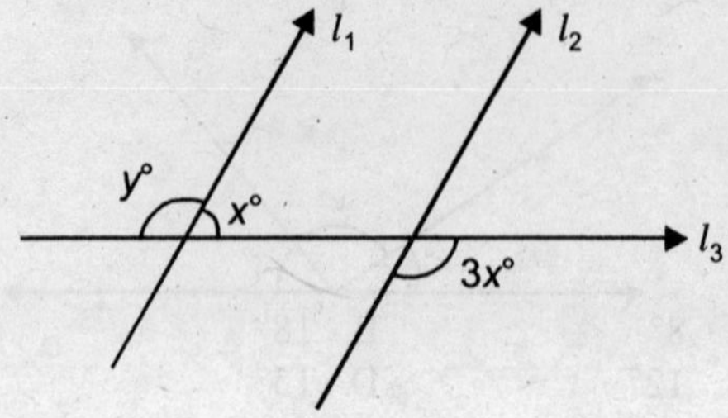

A. 100 B. 120
C. 135 D. 150

EXPLANATORY ANSWERS

1. (B): Let the angle = θ

then its supplementary angle = 180 – θ

$\therefore \quad \theta = 3(180 - \theta)$

$\Rightarrow \quad \theta = 3 \times 180 - 3\theta$

$\Rightarrow \quad \theta + 3\theta = 3 \times 180°$

$\Rightarrow \quad 4\theta = 3 \times 180°$

$\Rightarrow \quad \theta = \dfrac{3 \times 180°}{4} = 3 \times 45°$

$\Rightarrow \quad \theta = 135°$

$\therefore$ The measure of the angle is θ = 135°.

2. (C): Let two complementary angles are θ and (90° – θ)

then, $2\theta = 3(90 - \theta)$

$\Rightarrow \quad 2\theta = 3 \times 90 - 3\theta$

$\Rightarrow \quad 2\theta + 3\theta = 3 \times 90$

$\Rightarrow \quad 5\theta = 3 \times 90°$

$\Rightarrow \quad \theta = \dfrac{3 \times 90}{5} = 3 \times 18$

$\Rightarrow \quad \theta = 54$

$\therefore \quad 90 - \theta = 90 - 54 = 36°$

$\therefore$ The measure of the smaller angle is 90 – θ = 36°

3. (A): Given,

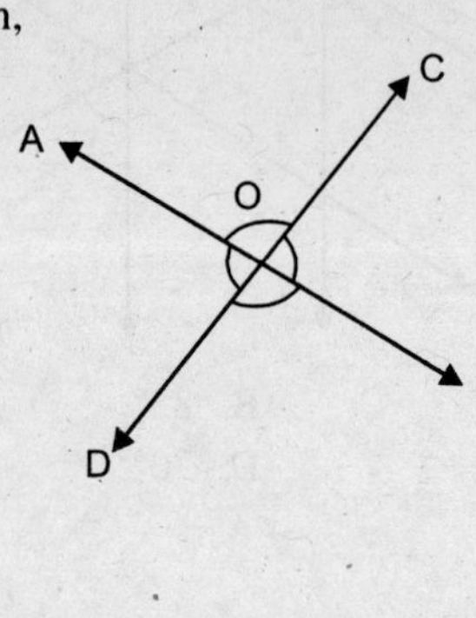

$\angle AOC + \angle COB + \angle BOD = 274°$

$\because \angle AOC + \angle COB + \angle BOD + \angle AOD = 360°$

$\therefore \quad 274 + \angle AOD = 360°$

$\Rightarrow \quad \angle AOD = 360° - 274°$

$\Rightarrow \quad \angle AOD = 86°$

4. (B): By linear pairs

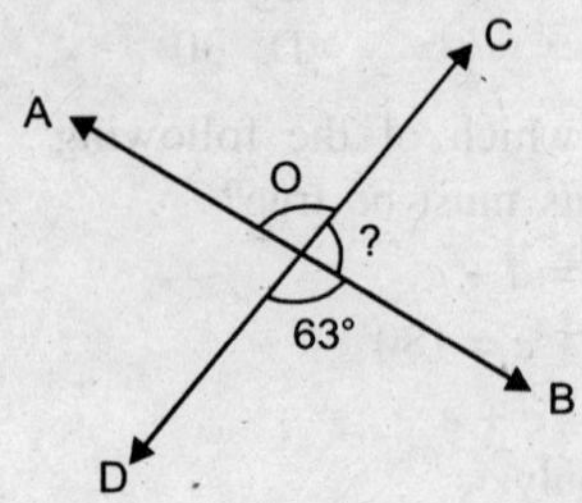

$\angle BOC + \angle BOD = 180°$

$\Rightarrow \quad \angle BOC + 63° = 180°$

$\Rightarrow \quad \angle BOC = 180° - 63°$

$\Rightarrow \quad \angle BOC = 117°$

5. (B)

6. (B): By linear pairs

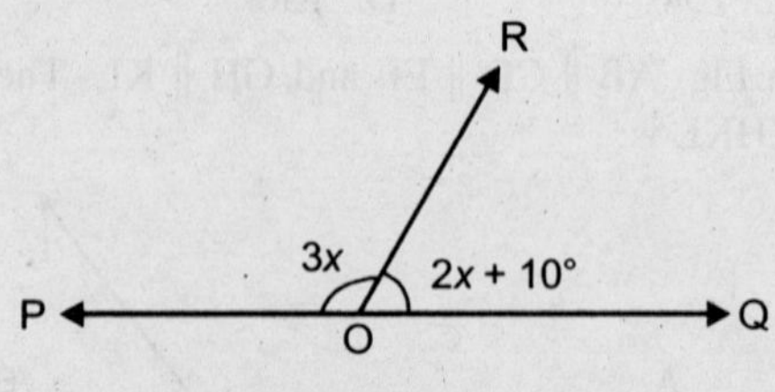

$\angle POR + \angle QOR = 180°$

$\Rightarrow \quad 3x + 2x + 10° = 180°$

$\Rightarrow \quad 5x = 180 - 10 = 170°$

$\Rightarrow \quad x = \dfrac{170}{5} = 34$

$\Rightarrow \quad x = 34°$

7. (C): $\angle AOC + \angle COD + \angle BOC = 180^\circ$

$\Rightarrow \quad \angle AOC + \angle COB = 180^\circ$

$\Rightarrow \quad 85^\circ + \angle COB = 180^\circ$

$\Rightarrow \quad \angle COB = 180^\circ - 85^\circ = 95^\circ$

$\Rightarrow \quad \angle COB = 95^\circ$

8. (B): From figure,

$x^\circ = y^\circ$ (vertically opposite angles)

$\because \quad 3x + y + 2x = 180^\circ$

$\therefore \quad 3x + x + 2x = 180^\circ$

$\Rightarrow \quad 6x = 180^\circ$

$\Rightarrow \quad x = 30^\circ$

$\Rightarrow \quad y = 30^\circ$

9. (B): Given, $\quad \frac{y}{x} = 5 \Rightarrow y = 5x$

and $\quad \frac{z}{x} = 4 \Rightarrow z = 4x$

$\because \quad x^\circ + 5x^\circ + 4x = 180^\circ$

$\Rightarrow \quad 10x^\circ = 180^\circ \Rightarrow x = 18^\circ$

10. (C): Here, $x^\circ + 90^\circ + 3x + 10^\circ = 180^\circ$

$\Rightarrow \quad 4x + 100 = 180^\circ$

$\Rightarrow \quad 4x = 180 - 100^\circ$

$\Rightarrow \quad 4x = 80^\circ$

$\Rightarrow \quad x = 20^\circ$

11. (D) **12. (C)**

13. (C): $\angle CHG = \angle HGF = 60^\circ$ (Alternate angles)

$\therefore \quad \angle HGE = 180^\circ - 60^\circ = 120^\circ$

$\because \quad GH \parallel LK$

$\therefore \quad \angle HGE = \angle LKA = 120^\circ$ (Corresponding angles)

and $\angle KHB = \angle HKA = 25^\circ$ (Alternate angle)

$\therefore \quad \angle HKL = \angle HKA + \angle LKA$

$= 25^\circ + 120^\circ$

$= 145^\circ$

$\Rightarrow \quad \angle HKL = 145^\circ$

14. (B): $\because$ $180 - (120 + x) = x$ (Corresponding angle)

$\therefore \quad 60 - x = x$

$\Rightarrow \quad x + x = 60^\circ$

$\Rightarrow \quad 2x = 60^\circ \Rightarrow x = 30^\circ$

15. (C)

16. (C): Given,

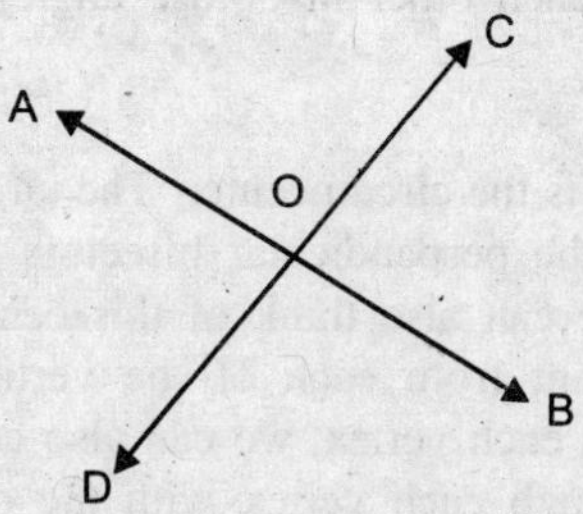

$\angle AOC + \angle COB + \angle BOD = 270^\circ$

$\because \angle AOC + \angle COB + \angle BOD + \angle AOD = 360^\circ$

$\therefore \quad 270^\circ + \angle AOD = 360^\circ$

$\Rightarrow \quad \angle AOD = 360^\circ - 270^\circ$

$\Rightarrow \quad \angle AOD = 90^\circ$

$\Rightarrow$

17. (B) **18. (B)** **19. (A)** **20. (C)**

Triangle and its Various Kinds of Centres

There are 4 very important ways of viewing the center of a triangle. We can look at its CENTROID, ORTHOCENTER, CIRCUMCENTER, and the INCENTER.

Centroid

The centroid is the first center and is obtained by locating the intersection of the three medians of the triangle. The median of a triangle is obtained by joining each vertex with the midpoint of the opposite side.

- It is the point of the intersection of the three median of the triangle. It is denoted by G.
- A centroid divides the area of the triangle in exactly three parts.

Medians:

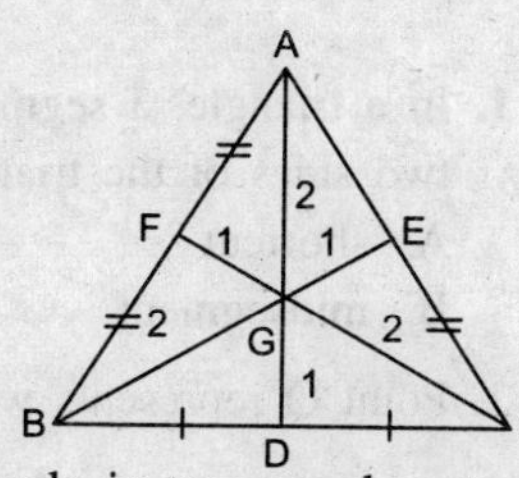

- A line segment joining the midpoint of the side with the opposite vertex is called median.
- Median bisects the opposite side as well as divide the area of the triangle in two equal parts.

Orthocenter

The second center of a triangle is the orthocenter. It is obtained by finding the intersection of the 3 altitudes of the triangle. An altitude is found by joining each vertex with the point on the opposite side that creates a perpendicular line with the opposite side.

It is the point of intersection of all the three altitudes of the triangle.

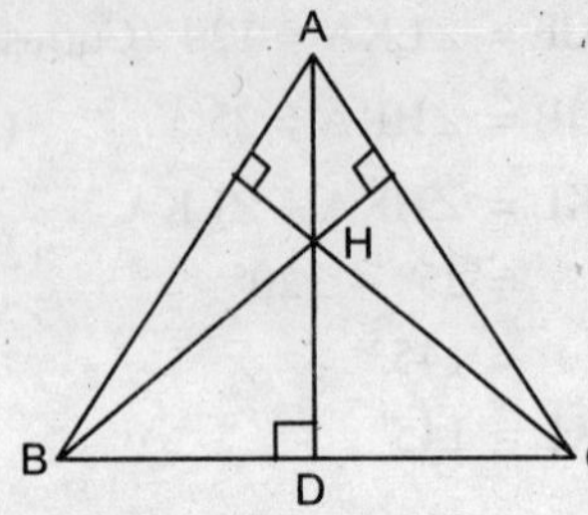

$\angle BHC = 180 - \angle A$
$\angle AHB = 180 - \angle C$
$\angle AHC = 180 - \angle B$

Position of orthocentre inside the triangle:

Acute angled triangle: lies inside the triangle.

Obtuse angle triangle: lies outside the triangle on the backside of the obtuse angle. Orthocentre and circumcentre lie opposite to each other in obtuse angle triangle.

Circumcenter

The third center is the circumcenter. The circumcenter is the intersection of the perpendicular bisectors of each side of the triangle. We can also think of this center as the point that is equidistant from each of the vertices. Since it is equidistant from each vertex, we can also construct a circle that passes through each vertex with the center being the circumcenter.

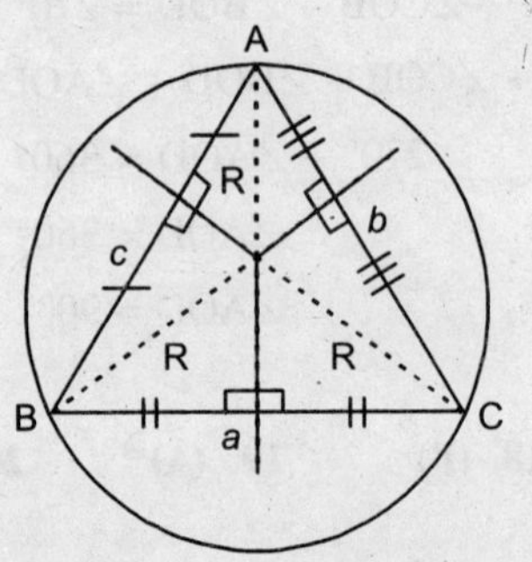

The distance between the circumcentre and the three vertices of a triangle is always equal.

OA = OB = OC = R (circumradius) = $abc/4A$

$\angle BOC = 2\angle A$, $\angle AOC = 2\angle B$, $\angle AOB = 2\angle C$

Location of circumcentre in various types of triangle:

Acute angle triangle: Lies inside the triangle

Obtuse angle triangle: Lies outside the triangle

Right angle triangle: Lies at the midpoint of the hypotenuse.

Incenter

The last center is the incenter. The incenter is found by first constructing the angle bisectors of each of the three angles. The incenter is the intersection of these 3 segments.

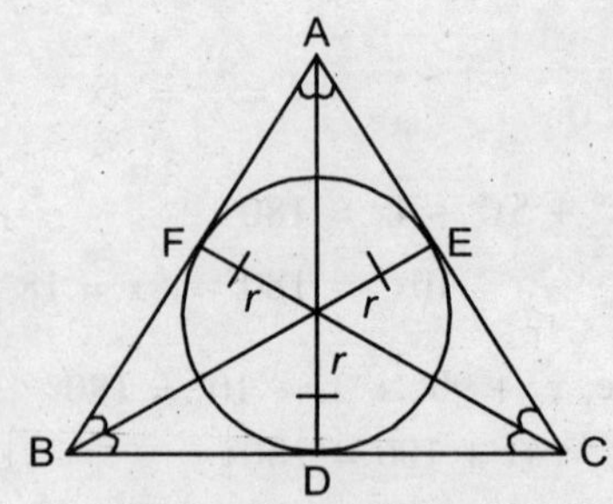

The distance of the in-centre from the all the three sides is equal (ID = IE = IF = inradius "r")

Inradius (r) = Area of triangle/Semiperimetre = A/S

$\angle BIC = 90 + \angle A/2$
$\angle AIC = 90 + \angle B/2$
$\angle AIB = 90 + \angle C/2$

MULTIPLE CHOICE QUESTIONS

1. In a triangle, a segment connecting the midpoints of two sides of the triangle is called a ______.

A. shortcut C. centroid
B. midsegment D. vertex

2. Point Q represents which point of concurrency?

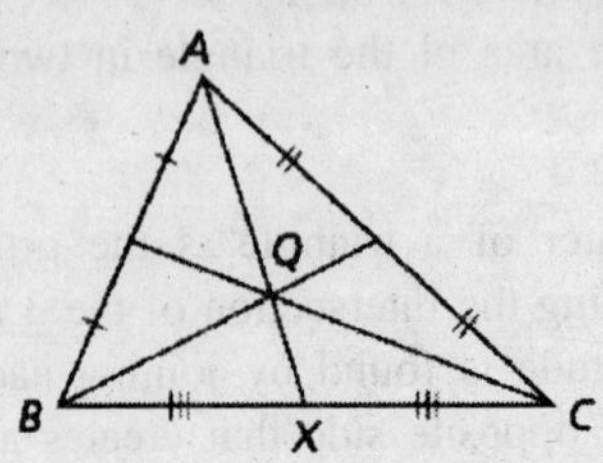

A. centroid
C. orthocenter
B. incenter
D. circumcenter

3. Point P represents which point of concurrency?

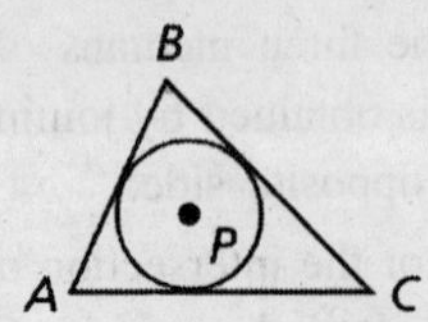

A. centroid C. orthocenter
B. incenter D. circumcenter

4. Point P represents which point of concurrency?

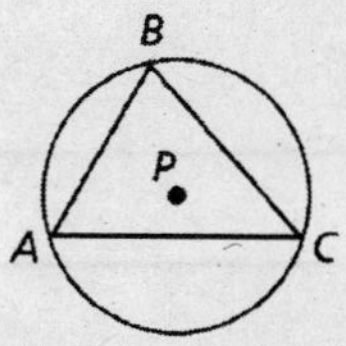

A. centroid B. incenter
C. orthocenter D. circumcenter

5. Point T represents which point of concurrency?

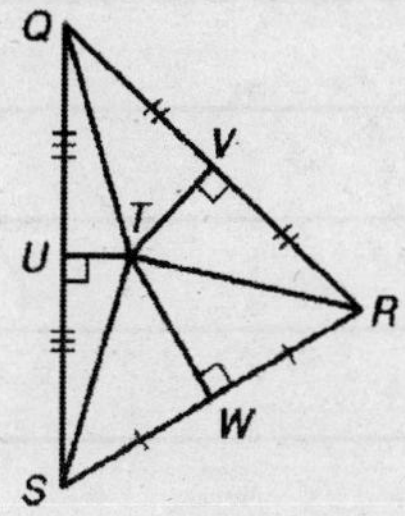

A. centroid B. incenter
C. orthocenter D. circumcenter

6. Point M represents which point of concurrency?

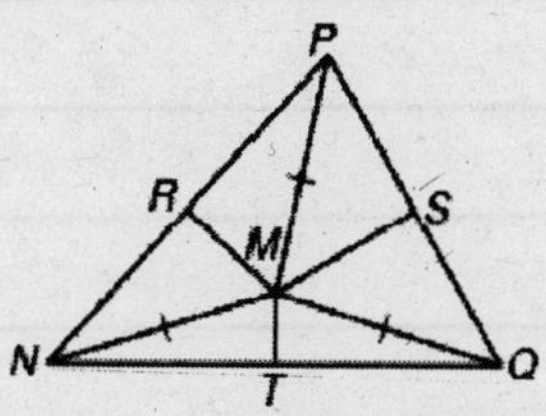

A. centroid B. incenter
C. orthocenter D. circumcenter

7. Point M represents which point of concurrency?

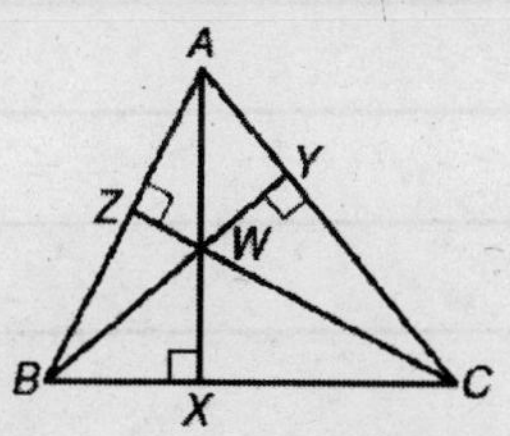

A. centroid B. incenter
C. orthocente D. circumcenter

8. Point L represents which point of concurrency?

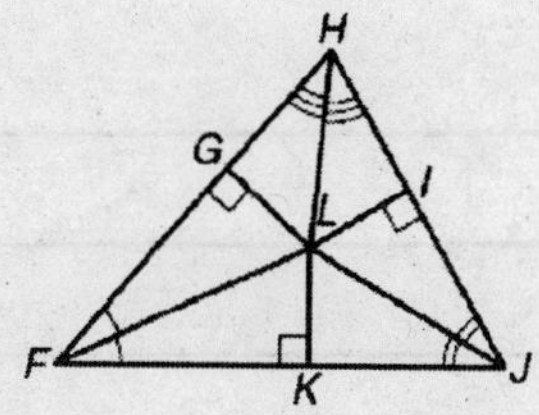

A. centroid B. incenter
C. orthocenter D. circumcenter

9. Which point of concurrency is the intersection of the medians of the triangle?
A. centroid B. incenter
C. orthocenter D. circumcenter

10. Which point of concurrency is the intersection of the altitudes of the triangle?
A. centroid B. incenter
C. orthocenter D. circumcenter

11. Which point of concurrency is the intersection of the angle bisectors of the triangle?
A. centroid B. incenter
C. orthocenter D. circumcenter

12. Which point of concurrency is the intersection of the perpendicular bisectors of the triangle?
A. centroid B. incenter
C. orthocenter D. circumcenter

13. Which point of concurrency is equidistant from the three sides of a triangle?
A. centroid B. incenter
C. orthocenter D. circumcenter

14. Which point of concurrency is equidistant from the three verticles of a triangle?
A. centroid B. incenter
C. orthocenter D. circumcenter

15. Which point of concurrency is the center of gravity of a triangle?
A. centroid B. incenter
C. orthocenter D. circumcenter

ANSWERS

1	2	3	4	5	6	7	8	9	10
B	A	B	D	D	D	C	B	A	C
11	**12**	**13**	**14**	**15**					
B	D	B	D	A					

YOUR SPACE

GENERAL SCIENCE

PHYSICS

Units and Measurement

Unit is that physical quantity which expresses the length, mass and time.

Types of Units: There are three systems of the fundamental units which are commonly used and internationally recognized these are:

(i) ***Metric System Unit (M.K.S.):*** In this system of unit 'M' stands for metre, 'K' for kilogram and S for second (time). Metre as unit of length, Kilogram as unit of mass and Second as unit of time.

(ii) ***C.G.S. System of unit:*** In this system 'C' stands for centimetre 'G' stands for gram and 'S' for Second. Centimetre is the unit of length, Gram is the unit of mass and Second is the unit of time.

(iii) ***F.P.S. System of Unit:*** In this system of unit 'F' stands for foot, 'P' stands for pound and 'S' for second. Foot is the unit of length, Pound is unit of mass, second is unit of time.

Scientific Instruments

1. **Altimeter:** It is used for measuring altitudes specially used in aircraft.
2. **Ammeter:** It is used for measuring the strength of the current in amperes.
3. **Barometer:** It is used for measuring the atmospheric pressure.
4. **Dynamo:** It is used to convert mechanical energy into electrical energy.
5. **Galvanometer:** It is used for detecting the presence of current.
6. **Hygrometer:** It is used for measuring humidity in air.
7. **Periscope:** A device to see the objects which are above the eye level of the observer.
8. **Potentiometer:** It is used for measuring or adjusting electrical potential.
9. **Sextant:** It is used for measuring angular elevation.
10. **Transformer:** It is used to decrease or increase the voltage of an alternating current.
11. **Thermocouple:** It is based on thermoelectricity used for measuring temperature.
12. **Thermometer:** It is used measuring temperature.
13. **Viscometer:** It is used for measuring viscosity of liquids.
14. **Voltmeter:** It measures the potential difference.

Mechanics

Branch of science dealing with the study of motion of object in called mechanics.

Distance: The length of path traversed by a particle in a given time is known as distance.

Displacement: The distance covered by a particle in a particular direction with respect to the point of reference is known as displacement.

Speed: The distance travelled by a particle in unit time is defined as its speed.

Average or Mean Speed: The ratio of the total distance travelled by a particle to the time taken to cover that distance is defined as its average speed.

Velocity: The ratio of the total displacement of a particle to the time taken to cover that displacement is defined as average velocity.

Acceleration: The change in velocity of a particle in unit time is defined as its average acceleration.

Retardation: The rate of decrease of velocity of a particle is defined as retardation. It is a negative acceleration.

Inertia: The property of a body by virtue of which it opposes any change in its state is defined as its inertia.

Mass: The quantity of matter contained in a body is defined as its mass.

(a) The mass of a body can never be zero.

(b) The mass of a body remains constant at all places of earth.

(c) It can be determined by a physical balance.

(d) There are two types of mass, *i.e.*, (i) gravitational mass, and (ii) inertial mass.

Gravitational Mass: The ratio of the weight of a body and acceleration due to gravity at that place is defined as gravitational mass. The mass determined by a chemical or physical balance is the gravitational mass.

Inertial Mass: The ratio of the force applied and the acceleration produced in a body at a place with zero gravity is defined as the inertial mass.

Force: The push or pull which one system exerts on another is defined as force.

Momentum: The product of mass and velocity of a moving body is known as its linear momentum.

Impulse: The product of applied force on a body and the time internal for which the force acts is defined as impulse.

Energy: The capacity of doing work is known as energy. Energy can be converted from one form to another form.

Mechanical Energy: The energy present in a body on account of its position or motion is defined as mechanical energy. This is of two type viz., (*i*) Potential energy and (*ii*) Kinetic energy.

Newton's Laws of Motion

(*i*) *First Law or Law of Inertia:* A body to be in its state of rest or of uniform motion until and unless it is acted upon by some external forces. This law defines forces.

(*ii*) *Second Law:* The force applied to a body is equal to the rate of change of its momentum.

(*iii*) *Third Law or Law of Action and Reaction:* To every action force there is an equal and opposite reaction force.

Gravitational Field: The region of space around a body in which gravitational force is experienced by other bodies is defined as the gravitational field of that body.

Newton's Law of Gravitation: Every particle in the universe attracts energy other particle with a force which is directly proportional to the product of their masses and inversely proportional to the square of distance between them.

Force of Gravity: The force with which earth attracts anybody towards its centre is defined as the force of gravity. The force exerted by earth on the body is known as the weight of the body.

Acceleration due to Gravity: The rate of change of velocity of a body falling freely due to earth's force of gravity is defined as acceleration due to gravity

Satellites: The bodies revolving around a planet in its gravitational field are defined as satellites.

Natural Satellites: The natural heavenly bodies which revolve around a planet are known as natural satellites, *e.g.*, moon is the natural satellite of earth.

Artificial Satellites: The man made bodies which are established in a particular orbit and are made to revolve around the earth are known as artificial satellites, *e.g.*, Aryabhatta, Rohini, Bhaskar.

Orbital Satellite: The satellites which always revolve in different orbits around earth are known as orbital satellites.

Communication Satellites: The satellite which remain stationary with respect to earth are known as communication satellites, *e.g.*, INSAT, 1B, 2A, 2E etc.

Power: The rate of doing work by a machine or a person is defined as power.

Law of Conservation of Momentum: In the absence of an external force, the total momentum of a system remains constant.

Deforming Force: The external force acting on a body on account of which is size or shape or both change is defined as the deforming force.

Elasticity: The property of a body, by virtue of which it regains its original form (size and shape) after the removal of external deforming force, is defined as elasticity.

Perfectly Elastic Body: The body which perfectly regains its original form on removing the external deforming force, is defined as a perfectly elastic body, *e.g.*, quartz.

Plastic Body: The body which does not have the property of opposing the external deforming force is known as a plastic body.

Elastic Limit: The maximum deforming force after which a body loses its property of elasticity and it gets permanently deformed, is defined as the elastic limit.

Stress: The internal reactional force per unit area developed as a result of applied external force is defined as stress.

Strain: The change in dimensions per unit original dimensions due to applied deforming force is defined as strain.

Hooke's Law: Within elastic limit, stress is directly proportional to strain.

Cohesive Force: The force of attraction acting between the molecules of same material is defined as cohesive force, *e.g.*, the force acting between water molecule.

Adhesive Force: The force of attraction acting between the molecules of two different materials is defined as adhesive force, *e.g.*, the force acting between the molecules of paper and ink.

Surface Tension: The property of a liquid, on account of which it lends to keep surface area in its free surface, is defined as surface tension.

Viscosity: The property of fluids, by virtue of which they oppose the relative motion between their different layers, is known as viscosity.

Heat

Temperature: Temperature of a body is that property which tells us that how much hot or cold a particular body is.

Scales of Temperature:

(*i*) Temperature in Kelvin = Temperature in Celsius + 273

(*ii*) 1°C temperature difference = 1° K

(*iii*) The temperature of –40°C is same in °C and °F

(*iv*) The temperature of a normal person is 37°C or 98.6°F.

Heat: Heat is a form of energy which is exchanged among various bodies or systems on account of temperature difference.

Latent Heat: The amount of heat used to change the state of matter, without changing its temperature is defined as latent heat.

Specific Heat: The amount of heat required to increase the temperature of 1 gm of material by 1°C is defined as its specific heat.

Boyles Law: At a constant temperature the volume of the given mass of gas is inversely proportional to its pressure.

Charle's Law: At constant pressure the volume of a given mass of gas is directly proportional to its absolute temperature. At constant pressure the volume of a given mass of gas increases by $\frac{1}{273}$ of its volume at 0°C for 1°C size in its temperature.

Gay Lussac's Law: At constant volume, the pressure of given mass of gas is directly proportional to its absolute temperature.

Graham's Law of Diffusion: At constant temperature and pressure, the rate of diffusion of a gas is inversely proportional to the square root of its density.

Dalton's Law of Partial Pressure: The total pressure exerted by the mixture of inactive gases in a vessel is equal to the sum of the partial pressures due to individual gas.

Avogadro's Law: If the temperature, pressure and volume of two gases are same then the number of molecules in them will also be equal.

Sound

Wave: A disturbance created in the medium which propagates in the forward direction with constant velocity without changing its shape, is defined as a wave.

Wave Motion: The mode of energy transfer in which a disturbance advances in the forward direction by affecting the medium without mass transfer, is defined as wave motion.

Characteristics of Wave Motion:

(*i*) The particle of the medium do not leave their mean positions rather they keep on vibrating about their mean positions.
(*ii*) The medium itself does not move.
(*iii*) The energy and momentum are transferred in the medium.
(*iv*) The phase of various particle of the medium keep on changing constantly.

Properties of Medium Necessary for Wave Propagation

(*i*) The medium should have the property of inertia.
(*ii*) The medium should posses the property of elasticity.
(*iii*) The medium should have low resistance.

Longitudinal Waves: In these waves the particles of the medium vibrate in the direction of propagation of waves.

Transverse Waves: In these waves the particles of the medium vibrate at right angles to the direction.

Ultrasonic Waves: The waves with frequency greater than that of sound, *i.e.*, 20×10^3 Hz are defined as Ultrasonic waves.

Shock Waves: When a sound source move with a velocity greater than that of sound then it leave behind it waves whose wave front is conical. These waves are defined as shock wave.

Terms Related to Wave Motion

(*i*) ***Displacement:*** The distance covered by a particle from mean position in a particular direction in SHM is known as displacement.
(*ii*) ***Amplitude:*** The maximum displacement of a particle executing SHM from its mean position, is defined as amplitude.
(*iii*) ***Time Period:*** The time taken by a particle in completing one vibration is defined as time period.
(*iv*) ***Frequency:*** The number of vibrations per second made by any particle of the medium is defined as its frequency.
(*v*) ***Wavelength:*** The distance between two nearest particles in one complete vibration is defined as the wavelength.
(*vi*) ***Wave Number:*** The number of wave present in unit length is defined as the wave number.
(*vii*) ***Wave Velocity:*** The velocity with which the crests and troughs or compression and rarefactions travel in medium, is defined as wave velocity.
(*viii*) ***Beats:*** When two waves of nearly same frequency, travelling in the same direction of the medium, superimpose over each other then the intensity at any point of the medium changes periodically with time. This phenomenon is defined as beats.
(*ix*) ***Beat Frequency:*** The number of beats heard per second is defined as beat frequency.
(*x*) ***Note:*** Any musical sound which is produced by the SHM of sound source is known as note.
(*xi*) ***Tone:*** Every component of musical sound is known as a tone. Every musical sound consists of a number of components of different frequencies. Every component is known as a tone.
(*xii*) ***Organ Pipe:*** The pipe filled with air and which when vibrated produces sound waves is known as organ pipe.
(*xiii*) ***Loudness:*** It is that characteristic of sound, on account of which the sound appears to be intense or slow is defined as loudness of sound or the power crossing per unit area at any point of the medium is defined as loudness.
(*xiv*) ***Pitch:*** It is that characteristic of sound on account of which it appears to be shrill or grave, is known as pitch.

Light

Light: The light is an electromagnetic radiation with the help of which our eyes experience the sensation of vision is known as light.

Ray of Light: The path of light energy from one point to another is known as a ray of light.

Properties of Light

(*i*) It propagates in straight line.

(*ii*) It exhibits the phenomenon of reflection, refraction, interference, diffraction, polarisation and double refraction.

(*iii*) The properties of the medium through which light passes remain unchanged.

(*iv*) Its velocity is different in different media. In rarer medium it is more and in denser medium it is less.

(*v*) Its velocity in vacuum is maximum whose value is 3×10^8 m/s.

Reflection of Light: The phenomenon of returning of incident light in the same medium is known as reflection.

Laws of Reflection:

(*i*) The incident ray, the reflected ray and the normal all lie in the same plane.

(*ii*) In regular reflection the angle of incidence is equal to the angle of reflection.

(*iii*) When light is reflected by a rarer medium then its phase remains unchanged whereas phase difference of a path difference of $\lambda/2$ or time difference T/2 is created when it is reflected by a denser medium. This is also known as Stoke's Law.

Refraction of Light: When a ray of light enters from one medium to another then at the boundary of separation it deviates from its initial path. This phenomenon is known as refraction.

Law of Refraction:

(*i*) The incident ray, the refracted ray and the normal all three lie in the same plane.

(*ii*) For given two media and for a given wavelength, the ratio of the sine of angle of incidence to the sine of angle of refraction always remain constant.

(*iii*) Light bends towards the normal if passes through rarer medium to denser medium.

(*iv*) Light bends away from the normal if passes through denser medium to rarer medium.

Critical Angle: When a ray of light enters from denser to rarer medium, then the angle of incidence corresponding to which the angle of refraction is 90º, is defined as the critical angle.

Total Internal Reflection: When a ray of light passes from a denser to rarer medium at an angle greater than the critical angle, then it gets totally reflected. This phenomenon is known as total internal reflection.

Refractive Index: The ratio of velocities of light in two media is defined as refractive index.

Dispersion of Light: The phenomenon of splitting of a ray of light into difference colours by a prism is defined as dispersion.

Spectrum: The whole band of colours from violet to red colour is known as spectrum. There are seven colours in the spectrum in the following order Violet, Indigo, Blue, Green, Yellow, Orange and Red or VIBGYOR.

Rainbow: The seven coloured curved strip formed as a result of dispersion of light through water droplets which keep suspended in the atmosphere after rains, is known as rainbow.

LASER (Light Amplification by Stimulated Emission of Radiation)

(*i*) The light amplification by induced emission of radiation is known as laser.

(*ii*) It is highly coherent and highly monochromatic light.

(*iii*) It is perfectly unidirectional and highly intense and powerful.

Polaroids: Microcrystals of iodo-sulphate of quinine are deposited on thin sheet of nitro-cellulose and then squeezed them out through a fine slit. In this process only the crystals having axes parallel to the slit pass through it and form a sheet. These sheets are kept between ordinary glass plates and called polaroids.

Uses of Polaroids: In winds screen; Window panes of aeroplanes; Camera filters and sun glasses in 3-D movies.

Luminous Flux: The luminous flux through a given surface is the amount of luminous energy that passes through the surface in one second in a direction normal to surface.

Lumen: One lumen is the amount of luminous flux emitted per unit solid angle by a source of light of luminous intensity one candela.

Luminous Intensity: The luminous intensity of a source is defined as the luminous flux emitted per unit solid angle by the source. It is also known as illuminating power.

Candela: One candela is the luminous intensity in a given direction due to a source, which emits monochromatic radiation of frequency 5.4×10^{14} Hz and whose radiant intensity in that direction is 1/683 watt per steradian.

Mirror: The highly polished reflecting surface is known as mirror. Mirror are of three types: Plane mirror; Concave mirror and Convex mirror.

Properties of Image Formed by Plane Mirror

(*i*) The image formed by a plane mirror is erect, virtual laterally reversed.

(*ii*) The size of image formed by it is equal to that of the object.

(*iii*) The image is formed behind the mirror at a distance equal to the distance of the object in front of mirror.

(*iv*) When the mirror is rotated through an angle θ, then the reflected ray rotates through an angle 2θ.

(*v*) When two mirrors are kept parallel to each other, then the number of images will be infinity as

Spherical Mirror: The smooth, polished spherical surface is known as spherical mirror, or the reflecting surface which is a part of a sphere is known as spherical mirror. It is of two types: (*i*) Concave mirror and (*ii*) Convex mirror

Magnification (m): The ratio of the size of image to size of object is defined as the magnification of spherical mirror, or *magnification* = $\frac{v}{u}$ = $\frac{\text{Size of image}}{\text{Size of object}}$

or *magnification* = $\frac{\text{Length of image}}{\text{Length of object}}$

Use of Plane Mirrors:

(*a*) In dressing tables

(*b*) In looking-glass

(*c*) In scientific apparatus. Plane mirrors are used to bend the paths of rays of light in scientific apparatus.

Uses of Concave Mirror:

(*a*) As shaving and hair dressing mirrors.

(*b*) As reflectors—concave mirrors are used as reflectors in search lights and head light.

(*c*) The ENT specialists use concave mirror for viewing the inner parts of ear, nose and throat.

(*d*) In lighthouses in seas.

(*e*) In a torch for hunting purpose.

Use of Convex Mirror:

(*a*) To spread light on roads.

(*b*) As side mirrors on cars in order to view the vehicle following the cars.

(*c*) For decoration purpose as these form the very small images which look beautiful.

Lens: The part of an isotropic transparent medium by two spherical, cylindrical, parabolic or one plane and another spherical surfaces is defined as lens.

Lenses are of Two types:

(*i*) Concave lens or diverging lens.

(*ii*) Convex lens or converging lens.

Concave lenses are of three types:

(*i*) *Concave-concave lens:* Both of its surfaces are concave. The radii of curvature of its two concave surfaces may be same or different.

(*ii*) *Plano-concave lens:* Its one surface is plane and second surface is concave.

(*iii*) *Convexo-concave:* One of its surfaces is convex and another surface is concave. The radii of curvature of convex and concave surfaces are different.

Convex Lenses are of Three Types:

(*i*) *Convexo-convex:* Both of its surface are convex. The radii of curvature of its convex surfaces may be same or different.

(*ii*) *Plano-convex:* One of its surfaces is convex and another one is plane.

(*iii*) *Concavo-convex:* One of its surfaces is concave and another one is convex. The radii of its concave and convex surfaces are different.

Power of Lens:

(*i*) The power of a thin lens is equal to the reciprocal of its focal length measured in meter, *i.e.*, $P = \frac{1}{f}$.

The unit of power of lens is dioptre.

(*ii*) When two lenses are kept in contact then the power of compound lens is equal to the sum of power of two lenses, *i.e.*, $P = P_1 + P_2$.

(*iii*) When a concave lens and a convex lens of equal focal lengths are kept in contact then the power of the compound lens becomes zero, *i.e.*, it behaves like a plane glass plate.

(*iv*) Magnification: The ratio of the size of image formed by lens to the size of object is defined as its linear magnification.

Prism: An isotropic transparent medium closed by surfaces inclined at an angle is define as a prism.

Dispersion: The phenomen of splitting of a white ray of light into seven colours is defined as dispersion.

Visible Spectrum: The spectrum which can be viewed with the help of eye is known as visible spectrum. The spectrum spreads from violet and (wavelength 3500Å).

Magnetism

Magnet: A piece of matter, which when suspended freely rests in a particular direction (North-South) and which possesses a net magnetic moment and which attracts ferrous bodies towards it, is called a magnet.

Natural Magnet: The magnet which is found naturally in mines is called a natural magnet, *e.g.*, magnetite. Its shape and size are indefinite, hence it cannot be used for scientific purpose. Its magnetism is quite weak.

Artificial Magnet: The magnet which are artificially prepared are known as artificial magnets. There are generally made of iron, steel and nickel. Its shape and size are definite.

Bar Magnet: A system composed of two poles, equal in magnitude but opposite in polarity, plane, at a small displacement apart is known as a bar magnet. It is also known as a magnetic dipole.

Properties of a Magnet: Like pole repel and unlike pole attract each other; it can be magnetically saturated; it can be demagnetized by beating, mechanical jerks, heating and with lapse of time; it produces magnetism in other materials by induction.

Magnetism: It is the property of a magnet, by virtue of which it attracts ferromagnetic materials towards it and rests itself in North-South direction, is known as magnetism. The magnetism of materials is mainly due to the spin motion of its electrons.

Magnetic Poles: The two points at the ends of a magnet at which magnetism is maximum are defined as magnetic poles. The magnetic poles are of two types—(*i*) North pole, (*ii*) South pole.

Magnetic Axis: The imaginary line joining the two poles of a magnet is defined as magnetic axis.

Magnetic Meridian: An imaginary plane passing through the axis of a freely suspended stationary magnet is defined as magnetic meridian. It is not a particular plane rather it is the direction of earth's magnetic field.

Pole Strength: The strength of a magnetic pole to attract magnetic materials towards it is known as pole strength.

Magnetic Field: The space around a magnet in which a torque acts on a magnetic needle is known as magnetic field.

Magnetic Dipole: The structure, which tend to align along the direction of magnetic field, are known as magnetic dipoles.

Magnetic Flux: The number of lines of forces passing through a given area is defined as magnetic flux.

Magnetic Moment: The product of the pole strength of a magnet and its length is defined as its magnetic moment.

Electromagnetic Induction: The phenomenon of production of electromotive force on account of change in magnetic flux linked with a circuit, is defined as electromagnetic induction.

Induced emf: The emf generated on account of change in magnetic flux linked with a plane or a circuit, is defined as induced emf.

Induced Charge: The electric charge flowing in a closed circuit on account of induced current is defined as induced charge.

Transformer: The device based on the principle of mutual induction used to change the value of alternating voltage is defined as transformer. There are two types of transformer: (*a*) Step-up transformer, (*b*) Step-down transformer

Dynamo: The device used to convert mechanical energy into electrical energy is known as dynamo.

Electrostatics and Current Electricity

Electrostatics: The branch of physics in which we study charges at rest, is known as electrostatics.

Electric Charge: It is a fundamental property of matter which can never be isolated from matter.

Charges are of two types: (*a*) Positive charges; (*b*) Negative charges

Positive Charges: The deficiency of electron on a body or particle is known as positive charge.

Negative Charge: The excess of electrons on a body or a particle is known as negative charge. When a negative charge is given to a body then its mass some what increases.

Properties of Charges:

(*i*) Like charges repel and unlike charges attract each other.

(*ii*) A charged body attracts other uncharged light particles.

(*iii*) Total charge of an isolated physical system is always conserved.

Law of Conservation of Charge: Charges can neither be created nor be destroyed, rather these can be transferred from one body to another.

Coulomb's Law: The force of attraction or repulsion acting between two stationary point charges is directly proportional to the product of strengths of charges and inversely proportional to the square of distance between two charges. Its direction is along the line joining the two charges.

Electric Field: The region of space around a charge in which any other charge experiences coloumb forces is known as electric field.

Electric Intensity: The resultant coulomb force per unit test charge at any point in an electric field is defined as the intensity of electric field at that point.

Electromotive Force: The total work done in carrying a unit positive test charge around a closed path in an electric field, is defined as electromotive force.

Electric Potential: The work done against electric field in carrying a unit positive test charge from infinity to any point in electric field is defined as electric potential at that point.

Potential Difference: The negative of work done in carrying a unit positive test charge from one point to another point in an electric field is defined as electric potential difference between those two points.

Capacitance: It is numerically equal to that electric charge which raises its potential by unity. Unit of capacitance is farad.

Condenser: The pair of conductors of opposite charges, on which sufficient quantity of charge may be accommodated is defined as condenser.

Current: The rate of flow of charge in a circuit is defined as current. Electric current is equal to the charge that flow in one second.

Conductor: The materials, in which the number of free electron is very large are defined as conductors, *e.g.*, silver, copper, aluminium, etc.

Insulator: The materials, in which the number of free electrons at ordinary temperatures is negligible, are defined as insulators.

Resistance: The property of a conductor by virtue of which it opposes the flow of current in it is defined as resistance.

Ohm's Law: If the physical circumstances of the conductor (temperature, etc.) remains constant, then the applied potential difference is directly proportional to the current flowing in it.

Resistivity: The resistivity of a material is equal to the resistance of the wine of that material with unit cross-sectional area and unit length.

Conductivity : The reciprocal of specific resistance is defined as specific conductance.

Nuclear Physics

Isotopes: The elements which have same atomic number, same chemical properties, same electron number and same structure, but different mass is called isotopes.

Isobars: The elements which have same atomic mass, but different atomic number, physical and chemical properties is called isobars.

Photo-electric Cell: The device, by which light energy is directly converted into electrical energy, is known as the photo-electric cell.

X-rays: There are electromagnetic waves whose wavelength is more than that of γ-rays but less than that of ultraviolet rays, *i.e.*, these rays lie in between the ultraviolet region and γ-rays region of electromagnetic spectrum.

Mass Defect: When neutrons and protons combine to form a nucleus, then the mass of the nucleus is some what less than the sum of masses of its constituent particles.

Mass defect (Δm) = total mass of all the neutrons present inside nucleus + total mass of protons – mass of the nucleus.

Binding Energy: The minimum energy required to keep the neutrons and protons bound inside the nucleus, is defined as binding energy.

Nuclear Fission: The phenomenon in which a heavy unstable nuclear breaks into two parts of nearly same mass, is defined as nuclear fission.

Chain Reaction: The process of nuclear fission, which when once started, continues spontaneously is defined as chain reaction.

Nuclear Reactor: The device in which energy is generated by chain reaction of nuclear fission is known as nuclear reactor.

Nuclear Fusion: The process in which two or more than two lighter nuclei combine to form a heavier nucleus, is known as nuclear fusion.

Radioactivity: The phenomenon of spontaneous disintegration of nuclei of unstable atoms is defined as radioactivity.

Decay Constant: It is equal to the reciprocal of that time in which the number of radioactive atoms remains its initial value.

Half-life: The time, in which the number of atoms (N) reduces to half of its initial value is defined as the half-life of the element.

Mean-life: The time, for which a radioactive remains active, is defined as mean life of that material.

CHEMISTRY

Atoms and its Structure

***Nucleus**:* The nucleus (atomic nucleus) is the center of an atom. It is composed of one or more protons and usually some neutrons as well. The simplest atom of all, hydrogen, has one proton in its nucleus.

Proton is a subatomic particle with a positive electric charge of 1.6×10^{-19} coulomb and a mass of 938 MeV ($1.6726231 - 10^{-27}$ kg, or about 1800 times the mass of an electron).

Neutron is a subatomic particle with no net electric charge and a mass of 940 MeV (very slightly more than a proton). The nucleus of most atoms consists of protons and neutrons.

Electron is a subatomic particle with a negative charge. In an atom the electrons surround the nucleus of protons and neutrons. The electron has a negative electric charge of -1.6×10^{-19} coulombs, and a mass of about 9.10×10^{-31} kg, which is 1/1800 of the proton mass.

Famous Inventions

Atomic Theory	**John Dalton**
Electron	**J.J. Thomson**
Proton	**Rutherford**
Neutron	**Masley**
Dynamite	**Alfred Nobel**
Atomic Number	**Chadwick**
Periodic Table	**Dmitry Mendeleyev**
Radioactivity	**Henri Becquerel**
Oxygen	**J. Priestly**
Hydrogen	**Cavendish**

Atomic Number: The number of protons in an atoms nucleus is called the atomic number (Z), and determines the element (for example, hydrogen, carbon, oxygen, etc.).

Atomic Weight (A): The atomic weight is the sum of neutrons and protons in the nucleus of the atom also called Mass Number.

Molecular Weight: The molecular weight of a molecule is the sum of the atomic weights of the atoms making up that molecule.

Isotopes: Isotopes are atoms of a chemical element whose nuclei have the same atomic number, Z, but different atomic weights, A.

Isobars: Isobars have the same isotopic mass but different atomic number, *e.g.*, Argon, Potassium and Calcium $^{18}Ar_{40}$, $^{19}K_{40}$, $^{20}Ca_{40}$.

Isotone : Isotone contains the same number of neutrons but different numbers of protons.

Elements

Elements are substances compose of same type of atom. Hydrogen, oxygen, chlorine, sodium, and iron are examples of elements. Ninety-two elements are known to occur in nature, and 22 more have been made artificially.

Some Common Elements and their Applications

Nitrogen: Nitrogen is the most abundant constituent in the atmosphere composes about four-fifths (78.03 per cent) by volume of the atmosphere. Nitrous oxide is known as laughing gas. Nitrous oxide is used as an anesthesia. Liquid nitrogen is used as coolant in cryogenics.

Oxygen: It was discovered by Joseph priestly. Oxygen composes 21 percent by volume of atmosphere. It is used in high-temperature welding torches, administered to patients whose breathing is impaired and oxygen-enriched air is used in open-hearth furnaces for steel manufacture. High-purity oxygen is used also in the metal-fabrication industries; in liquid form it is used in a propellant for guided missiles and rockets.

Argon: Argon is the third most prevalent gas in the earth atmosphere. Argon is also used in one type of neon lamp giving blue light whereas pure neon gives a red light. It is preferred because it requires a lower voltage than neon.

Hydrogen: Hydrogen exits as a gas at room temperature and is highly flammable. In stars, hydrogen nuclei combine with each other in nuclear reactions to form helium atoms. The isotopes of Hydrogen are Deuterium and Tritium. Spacecrafts use hydrogen as fuel that reacts with fluorine or oxygen. Nuclear plants use D_2O as a moderator.

Carbon dioxide: Carbon dioxide does not burn and support ordinary combustion; it is used in fire extinguishers. Solid carbon dioxide is known as Dry ice widely used as refrigerant. The presence of carbon dioxide in the blood stimulates breathing. For this reason, CO_2 is added to the oxygen in artificial respiration.

Methane: Methane also know as marsh gas, gas composed of carbon and hydrogen with formula CH_4, the first member of the paraffin or alkane series of hydrocarbons. It is lighter than air, colourless, odourless, and flammable. It occurs in natural gas, in coal mines, as a by-product of petroleum refining, and as a product of decomposition of matter in swamps.

Iron: Iron is a metal extracted from iron ore, and is hardly ever found in the free (elemental) state. Depending upon the carbon content Iron can be classified into: Pig Iron (4%–5%), Cast iron (2–3.5%), carbon steel (0.5–1.5%) and Wrought Iron (< 0.5%).

Sodium: Sodium is a constituent of table salt and baking soda. Sulfur, however, is a common impurity in fossil fuels used for home heating and the production of electricity. Large amounts of SO_2 are causing both local air pollution as well as acid rain.

The halogens: The halogens are: fluorine, chlorine, bromine, iodine, and astatine.

- Chlorine gas is greenish yellow. It is a powerful bleaching, and disinfecting agent. Chlorine is an important chemical in water purification.
- Bromine is a red volatile liquid at room temperature.
- Astatine is radioactive and heaviest of Halogens.
- Iodine is a bluish-black, lustrous solid. Potassium Iodide is used in Photography. Iodine 131 is used as a tracer in medicine.

Compound

Compound is a substance formed from two or more elements, *e.g.*, Water. **Mixture** is the product of a mechanical blending or mixing of chemical substances without other chemical change, so that each ingredient substance retains its own chemical properties. While there are no chemical changes in a mixture, physical properties of a mixture, such as its melting point, may differ from those of its components. Mixtures can usually be separated by mechanical means. There are different types of Compounds are Acids, Bases, Salts, Oxides and organic compounds.

Acids: An acid is a water-soluble, sour-tasting chemical compound. An acid always has a pH of less than 7 and turns litmus red. An acid reacts with a base in a neutralization reaction to form a salt.

Acid	Used as
Ascetic Acid	Vinegar
Amino Acid	Basis of protein
Ascorbic Acid	Vitamin C
Carbolic Acid/Phenol	Disinfectant
Citric Acid	Citrus fruits
Nitrohydrochloric Acid (Aqua Regia)	Dissolving gold and platinum
Tartaric Acid	Used in baking powder
Carbonic Acid	Carbonated beverages
Formic Acid	Ants
Lactic Acid	Sour milk
Malic Acid	Unripe apples
Nitric Acid/Aqua Fortis	Used in explosives and rocket fuels
Prussic Acid/ Hydrocynic Acid	Poison
Salicylic Acid	Basis of aspirin
Tannic Acid/Tannin	Found in tea
Uric Acid	In the urine of birds and reptiles
Oxalic Acid	Spinach

Bases : A base is a chemical compound that will neutralize an acid and form a salt and water. Bases are typically water-soluble, bitter tasting, turns litmus blue and always have a pH greater than 7 in solution, *e.g.,* baking soda , sodium carbonate etc.

Litmus: A mixture of pigments extracted from certain lichens that turns blue in basic solution and red in acidic solution.

Salt: A salt is a neutral compound composed of cations bound to anions. A cation is a positively charged ion. Metals typically form cations where as anions are negatively charged ion.

Organic compound: These contain carbon chemically bound to hydrogen. They often contain other elements (particularly O, N, halogens, or S).

Metals and Non-metals

Metals: Metals are shiny (lustre), high density, ductile and malleable, high melting point, hard, and conduct electricity and heat.

Ores: An ore is a mineral containing a metal as a proportion of its content, which is economical to extract its metallic component.

Substance	Important Ores
Aluminium	Bauxite
Antimony	Stibnite
Beryllium	Beryl, Crysoberyl
Calcium	Lime stone, Marble, Chalk, Gypsum, Flurosper
Chromium	Chromite
Cobalt	Smaltite
Copper	Cuprite, Bornite
Iron	Hematite, Magnatite
Lead	Galena, Masicot, Serusite
Magnicium	Magnesite, Dolomite, Carnallite
Manganese	Pyrolusite, Hausmannite
Mercury	Cinnabar
Molybdenum	Molybdenite and wulfenite
Nickel	Pantilandite and Gargnierite
Phosphorous	Phosphorite Apatite, Chlorapatite
Potassium	Carnelite, Saltpetre
Silver	Argentite
Sodium	Rock Salt, Chile Saltpetre
Sulphur	Galena, Copper Pyrites and Iron Pyrites
Tin	Cassiterite, Tin stone
Titanium	Rutile, Ilmenite
Uranium	Pitchblende
Zinc	Zinc Blends,Calamine

Some Important Processes

(*a*) ***Gravity separation:*** The heavier metal or metallic mineral particles separated from the lighter gangue. Gold and magnetite are separated in this way.

(*b*) ***Flotation:*** In this method, finely ground ore is mixed with a liquid. The metal or metallic mineral floats while the gangue sinks.

(*c*) ***Magnetic separation:*** Metals that have magnetic properties are separated from the gangue, *e.g.*, magnetite.

(*d*) ***Smelting:*** The ore is heated with a reducing agent and a flux to a high temperature. The reducing agent combines with the oxygen in a metallic oxide, leaving pure metal; and the flux combines with the gangue to form a slag that is liquid poured away from the metal. The production of pig iron extract copper, lead, nickel use this process.

(*e*) ***Amalgamation*** is a metallurgical process that utilizes mercury to dissolve silver or gold to form an amalgam.

(*f*) ***Electrolysis:*** In this process, the metal is deposited at the cathode from aqueous solutions or in an electrolytic furnace. Copper, nickel, zinc, silver, and gold are several examples of metals that are refined by deposition from aqueous solutions. Aluminium, barium, calcium, magnesium, beryllium, potassium, and sodium are metals that are processed in electrolytic furnaces.

Some Interesting Points

Osmium and iridium are the most dense metals, and lithium is the least dense. Bismuth has the lowest electrical conductivity of the metallic elements, and silver the highest at ordinary temperatures. Gallium, mercury, cesium, and rubidium are the only metal elements that melt near room temperature.

Metalloids have intermediate in properties between the metals and the non-metals. Most common is that metalloids are usually semiconductors rather than conductors. They are boron, silicon, germanium, arsenic, antimony, tellurium, polonium.

Non-metal: A non-metal is a substance that conducts heat and electricity poorly, is brittle or waxy or gaseous, and cannot be hammered into sheets or drawn into wire. The non-metals are: nitrogen, oxygen, fluorine, phosphorus, sulfur, chlorine, selenium.

Alkali metals: They are soft compared to other metals, have low melting points, and are so reactive that they are never found freely in nature, *e.g.*, lithium, sodium, potassium, rubidium, cesium, and francium. Francium exists only in a radioactive form.

Alkaline Earth Metals: They are brittle, the alkaline earth metals are malleable, conduct electricity and when heated, burn readily in air, *e.g.*, beryllium, magnesium, calcium, strontium, barium, and radium.

Alloys

An alloy is a compound, of two or more elements, at least one of which is a metal.

Alloy	Composition
Duraluminium	Aluminium, copper, magnesium, and manganese
Gun Metal	Copper, Tin
Steel	Iron, Carbon
Stainless Steel	Iron, carbon, chromium, tungsten
Petwar	Tin, Antimony and Copper
Bronze	Copper, Tin and Zinc
German Silver	Copper, Zinc and Nickel
Electrum	Gold and Silver
18 carat Gold	Gold, Silver and Copper
Dentist Amalgam	Mercury Copper
Yellow Brass	Copper Zinc
Brass	Copper and Zinc
Nichrome	Nickel and Chromium
Plumbers Solder	Lead and tin

Common Chemicals and their Chemical Names

Common Name	Chemical Name
grain alcohol	ethyl alcohol
wood Alcohol	methyl alcohol
alum	aluminum potassium sulfate
alumina	aluminum oxide
baking soda	sodium bicarbonate
bleaching powder	chlorinated lime
blue vitriol	copper sulfate
brimstone	sulfur
carbolic acid	phenol
carbonic acid gas	carbon dioxide
epsom salts	gypsum
hypo (photography)	sodium thiosulfate solution
gypsum	natural calcium sulfate
lime	calcium oxide
lime, slaked	calcium hydroxide
limewater	calcium hydroxide
lunar caustic	silver nitrate
magnesia	magnesium oxide
mercury oxide, black	mercurous oxide
methanol	methyl alcohol
methylated spirits	methyl alcohol
pearl ash	potassium carbonate

Important Points to Remember

- Temporary hardness of water is due to the presence of bicarbonates of calcium and magnesium in water. Whereas the permanent hardness is due to the presence of Calcium Sulphate, which can be eliminated by the use of Zeolites.
- The gas used in balloons is helium.
- Gobar gas is obtained by decomposition of vegetable matter and animal dung.
- L.P.G. (liquefied petroleum gas) consists of mainly propane and butane.
- Natural gas is composed primarily of methane and other light hydrocarbons.
- Ethylene gas is used for artificial fruit ripening.
- Sodium and potassium react vigorously with cold water so it is preserved under kerosene while phosphorus is spontaneously inflammable in air so preserved under water.
- Nitrous oxide is called laughing gas, in mild doses it is used as anesthetic.
- Nitric acid is used as fertilizers and explosives.
- Tri-nitro toluene and nitro glycerene are common explosives.
- Smelling salt is ammonium carbonate.
- Potassium nitrate or Nitre or Indian salt petre is used as Gun powder.
- The paste applied to the side of a match box is a mixture of Phosphorous Trisulphide, glass powder and sand to cause frictions and glue. The match head contains a readily combustible substance like atimony trisulphide, potassium chlorate which maintain the combustion and a binding material like glue.
- Marble is calcium carbonate.
- Methylated spirit is a mixture of methyl alcohol and ethyl alcohol.
- Urea is the first organic compound prepared in the laboratory.
- Carbonic acid is soda water.
- Mercaptans leakage in L.P.G. cylinders is easily detected.
- Hydrazine is used to propel rockets.
- Coke is obtained by healthy wood out of contact with air.
- Terylene and nylon are synthetic fibres produced by a process of polymerization. Terylene is a polyester and Nylon a polymide.
- Pyrene is carbon tetrachloride specially used to extinguish electrical fires.
- Tincture iodine is a solution of iodine in alcohol.
- Nickel is used in conversion of oil into solid fat.
- Coal gas is the product of destructive distillation of coal *i.e.*, heating coal out of contact of air.
- Rust is hydrated ferric oxide.
- The chief component of pearl is ferric component.

BIOLOGY

The term *biology* derived from the Greek work, bios, "life" and the suffix-*logia*, "study of." **Biology** is a natural science concerned with the study of life and living organisms.

Branches of Biology

Apiculture	Culture of Bee
Cytology	Study of Cells
Dermatology	Study of Skin
Entomology	Study of Insects
Evolution	Study of Origin of new from old
Floriculture	Study of Flower Yielding Plants
Genetics	Study of Heredity and Variations
Gynaecology	Study of Female Reproductive Organ
Horticulture	Study of Garden Cultivation
Haematology	Study of Blood
Mycology	Study of Fungi
Nephrology	Study of Kidneys
Neurology	Study of Nervous System

Obstetrics	Branch of Medicine Dealing with Pregnancy
Ophthalmology	Study of Eyes
Ornithology	Study of Birds
Osteology	Study of Bones
Palaeontology	Study of Fossils
Phycology	Study of Algae
Pisciculture	Study of Fish
Pomology	Study of Fruits
Sericulture	Culture of Silk Moth and Pupa
Serpentology	Study of Snakes
Virology	Study of Virus

Cell

1. **Cell Membrane:** Cells are enclosed by a thin film like membrane called plasma membrane, cytoplasmic membrane or plasma lemma.
   Endocytosis: Taking substance inside the cell by the plasma membrane. It is of two types : *Phagocytosis :* Cell Eating. *Pinocytosis :* Cell drinking. *Exocytosis:* Reverse of Endocytosis.
2. **Cytoplasm:** It is a part of protoplasm lying between plasma membrane and nucleus.
3. **Cell Wall :** Cells of most fungi, prokaryotes (bacteria and blue-green algae) and plants (except gametes) are surrounded by the cell wall. It is absent in animals.
4. **Nucleus:** Discovered by Robert Brown. Nucleus controls the metabolic activities of the cell by controlling the synthesis of enzymes.
   - Contains nucleoplasm (nuclear sap) which contains chromatin.
   - Chromatin organizes itself into thread like structures called Chromosomes.
   - The function of chromosomes is to carry genetic information from one cell generation to another.
   - Nucleolus is also present which helps in the production of ribosomes.
5. **Chromosomes :** Waldeyer coined the term chromosome. Each chromosome is made up of DNA.
   - Chromosome number is constant for a particular species. Diploid number (2n) of chromosomes are present in somatic cells and haploid number (n) of chromosomes are there in gametes.
   - In humans, the diploid number is 46.
6. **Mitochondria :** Powerhouse of the cell and energy is stored as ATP
   - They are semi-autonomous organelles. They contain DNA.
   - Mitochondria is enclosed by a double-membraned envelope.
7. **Endoplasmic Reticulum :** Provides an increased surface area for various metabolic activities within the cell. Types: Rough ER and smooth ER.
8. **Golgi Complex :** Main function is secretion. Secretions are in the form of granules in cytoplasm.
9. **Lysosomes :** Also called Suicidal bags. Contain enzymes acid hydrolases which digest worn - out or unnecessary parts of the cell, or even whole cells by process called 'Autophagy'.
10. **Ribosomes :** Made of RNA and proteins in equal amounts. Sites of protein synthesis.
11. **Vacuoles :** Large vacuole found in plant cells. Membrane surrounding the vacuole is tonoplast. Regulation of water, in osmoregulation, in storage and in digestion.
12. **Plastids :** Found only in plant cells.
    - ***Chloroplast :*** Green contains the pigment chlorophyll.
    - ***Leucoplasts :*** Colourless, occur in large number in cells of fruits, seeds, etc. They store nutrients (*e.g.*, amyloplasts of potato store starch).
    - ***Chromoplasts :*** Coloured, containing fat soluble yellow, orange and red pigments. Found in flowers and fruits.
13. **Centrosome :** Found in animal cells and cells of lower plants (*e.g.*, Algae) only. The first indication that the cell is about to divide is generally given by the centrosome.

Balanced Diet

A Balanced Diet comprising of healthy and diverse foods is key to promoting good health. The components of food are:

1. **Carbohydrates:** Constitutes 3 elements: Carbon, Hydrogen and Oxygen. 1 gm gives 17 kJ of energy (or 4.1 kcal of energy). Carbohydrates form a better fuel than proteins and fats because their molecules have relatively more oxygen.
   - Cellulose is present in the cell-wall of plants.
   - D-fructose is the sweetest of sugars. It is found in Fruit Juices, Honey, etc.
   - Excess Sugar is stored as Glycogen in liver.
   - ***Sources of Carbohydrates are:*** Cereals (Wheat, Rice and Maize), Sugarcane, Milk (contains Lactose — a type of Sugar), Fruits, Honey, Beet, etc.
   - ***Types of Carbohydrates:*** ***(i)*** **Monosaccharides :** They are the simplest carbohydrates consist of one unit (*e.g.*, glucose, fructose, galactose). ***(ii)*** **Disaccharides :** Consist of 2 units of monosaccharides (*e.g.*, sucrose, lactose and 1 maltose). ***(iii)*** **Polysaccharides :** Consist of more than three monosaccharide units (*e.g.*, starch in plants and glycogen in animals).
2. **Fats:** Provides twice the energy of carbohydrates (1 gm provides 37 kJ or 9 kcal of energy). Acts as the reserve food material, excess fat is stored in the liver and adipose tissue.
   - ***Types of fatty acids :*** Saturated and Unsaturated. (*i*) **Saturated Fatty Acids :** Solids at room temperature. (*ii*) **Unsaturated Fatty Acids :** Liquids at room temperature.

- Excess of saturated fats increases the blood — cholesterol level and may cause arteriosclerosis (hardening of arteries). This may lead to heart attack.
- Essential Fatty Acids include Linoleic, Linolenic and Arachidonic Acids are present in Groundnut Oil, Sunflower Oil.
- ***Hydrogenation :*** Process by which unsaturated fatty acids are converted into saturated fatty acids by the addition of Hydrogen.

3. Proteins : Made up of Carbon, Hydrogen, Oxygen, Nitrogen and Sulphur. Important for growth and repair of the body (75% of our body is proteins only).

- ***Types of Amino acids are:*** **(*i*) Essential Amino Acids :** They cannot be synthesised in the body, *e.g.*, isoleucine, leucine, lysine, methionine, phenylalanine, threonine, tryptophan and valine. **(*ii*) Non - Essential Amino Acids :** They are synthesized in the body, *e.g.*, Alanine, Arginine, Asparagine, Aspartic Acid, Cysteine, Glutamine, Glutamic Acid, Glycine, Histidine, Proline, Serine and Tyrosine.
- ***Some Important Proteins are: Enzymes:*** *e.g.*, Pepsin, Trypsin. **Hormone:** *e.g.*, Insulin, Glucogon, **Carrier:** *e.g.*, Haemoglobin — Transports O_2 in blood, Myoglobin — Stores O_2 in muscles. **Contractile Proteins:** *e.g.*, Actin and Myosin. **Structural Proteins:** *e.g.*, Collagen — Component of Bones, Tendons, Cartilage. Keratin — Component of Skin, Feathers, Nails, Hair, Horn. **Protective Proteins:** *e.g.*, Gamma globulins. **Visual Proteins :** Rhodopsin and Iodopsin of rods and cones. (present in Retina of the eye).
- ***Protein Energy Malnutrition:*** **(*i*) Kwashiorkar :** Due to deficiency of protein. Abdomen and feet swells, Skin becomes Dark and Scaly, Enlarged Liver, Anaemia. **(*ii*) Marasmus :** Deficiency of Proteins. Losing of body weight, wasting of muscles, ribs look prominent. (Oedema and skin pigmentation absent).

4. Minerals: Minerals maintain water balance and nutrition in the body

- Although needed in very small quantities, mineral salts of various kinds are essential for the proper functioning of the body.
- They yield no energy but are important constituents of certain tissues, besides playing a major role in the regulation of metabolic activities.
- Calcium is the principal component of the skeleton.
- Meat, eggs, milk, cheese and vegetables are important sources of minerals, and usually, the body gets adequate amounts of them from a normal diet.

Minerals Required in Human beings

Minerals	Sources	Functions	Deficiency
Macro Elements			
Calcium	Milk, Cheese	Formation of Teeth and Bones	Weak Teeth and Bones
Phosphorus	Milk, Meat	Component of ATP, DNA, RNA	Weak Teeth and Bones; Retarded Growth
Sulphur	Proteins of Food	Component of Amino Acids	Disturbed Protein Metabolism.
Potassium	Meat, Milk, Cereals, Fruits	Water Regulation	Weak Muscles; Risk of Paralysis
Chlorine	Table salt	Acid-Base Balance	Loss of Appetite; Muscle Cramps.
Sodium	Table salt	Acid - Base and Water Balances	Low Blood Pressure, Loss of Appetite;
Magnesium	Cereals, Green Vegetables	Cofactor of Enzymes	Affects Nervous Functions.
Iron	Meat, Eggs, Cereals	Component of haemoglobin	Anaemia, Weakness
Iodine	Sea Food, Iodized Salt	Component of Thyroxine	Goitre, Cretinism
Micro Elements			
Flourine	Drinking Water, Tea, Sea Food	Maintenance of Bones and Teeth	Weak Teeth,
Manganese	Dry Fruits, Cereals,	Cofactor of some Enzymes	Irregular Growth of Bones, Cartilages

Vitamins Required in Human beings

Vitamins : Discovered by Funk. It do not provide energy but help in different physiological processes.

Vitamin	Sources	Effect of Deficiency
Water - Soluble Vitamins		
B_1 (Thiamine)	Rice Bran, Whole Wheat Flour	Beri - beri
B_2 (Riboflavin)	Cheese, Eggs, Yeast,	Cheilosis Keratitis of Cornea
B_3 (Nicotinic Acid)	Fresh Meat, Liver, Fish,	Pellagra, Muscle Atrophy,
B_6 (Pyridoxine)	Milk, Cereals, Fish, Meat, Liver	Dermatitis, Convulsions, Nausea, Mental Disorders
B_5 (Pantothenic Acid)	Yeast, Liver, Kidneys, Eggs, Meat,	Dermatitis, Anaemia, Fatigue, Nausea.
H (Biotin)	Yeast, Vegetables, Fruits, Eggs,	Skin Lesions, Loss of Appetite, Hair Fall.
Folic Acid Group	Green Vegetables, Soyabean,	Retarded Growth.
B_{12} (Cyanocobabmine)	Meat, Fish, Liver, Eggs,	Pernicious Anaemia
C (Ascorbic acid)	Lemon, Orange	Scurvy
Fat - Soluble Vitamins		
A (Retinol)	Milk, Butter, Egg Yolk, Liver,	Xerophthalmia
D (Cholecalciferol)	Synthesized in skin cells	Rickets, Osteomalacia.
E (Tocopherol)	Green Vegetables	Causes sterility, Muscular dystrophy,
K (Phylloauinone)	Carrots, Lettuce	Haemorrhages, delayed blood clotting

Digestive System of Humans

The process of converting food into energy giving substances is carried out by this system.

1. **Buccal Cavity :** In the mouth salivary glands secrete saliva which contains the enzyme Ptyalin
   - ***Teeth :*** They are produced in two sets — Temporary and Permanent. The teeth are of four types : Incisors, Canines, Premolars and Molars.
   - ***Structure of a Tooth :*** A tooth consists of 3 Regions: Crown, Neck and Root. Enamel is the hardest substance in the human body.
   - ***Dental Formula :*** 2123 / 2123, means that there are 2 incisors, 1 canine, 2 Premolars and 3 molars in half of the upper jaw and exactly the same arrangement in half of the lower jaw.
   - In elephants, incisors of the upper jaw grow into huge tusks.
   - Canines are very large in predators such as cat, dog and lion.
   - Rabbit and squirrel lack canines. In walrus, the upper canines are enlarged into projecting tusks.
   - The last molars are called the wisdom teeth.
2. **Pharynx:** Links Buccal Cavity to Oesophagus. Food is carried by peristaltic movement. Trachea opens into Pharynx through an aperture called Glottis.
3. **Oesophagus:** 25 cm long tube. Longitudinal folds keep its cavity almost closed, except during swallowing of food.
4. **Stomach:** Oesophagus opens into it. In stomach, the food is called chyme. Has 3 Parts: Fundus, Cardiac and Pyloric. Gastric juices produced in the stomach help in digestion of food. Also contains HCl which provides acidic medium. Besides it activates pepsinogen to pepsin and prorennin to rennin.
   - Ruminents (Cattle, Buffaloes, Goats, Sheep, Deer, Camel) have their stomach consisting of 4 Chambers: Rumen, Reticulum, Omasum and Abomasum.
5. **Small Intestine:** Here the food from the stomach is mixed with bile and pancreatic juice.
   - Duodenum receives the bile — pancreatic duct formed by the union of bile duct and pancreatic duct.
   - Both jejunum and ileum have numerous figure like projections called the villi. The villi contain blood vessels to absorb digested food.
6. **Large Intestine:** It receives undigested material from the small intestine and absorbs water.
   - Caecum is the diverted part of intestine. Cellulose digestion takes place in it. It is very large in herbivores.
   - Vermiform appendix is a part of caecum. Both caecum and appendix are vestigial in humans.

Blood in Human Body

Blood is a fluid connective tissue. It is 6.8 litres in man and 500 ml less in woman. 6-8% of body weight (pH 7.4).

1. **Red Blood Corpuscles:** Also called Erythrocytes, disc - shaped (for increased Surface Area), no nucleus contains a pigment called Haemoglobin, which gives blood its Red Colour.
   - ***Amount of Haemoglobin*** is 14-15.6 gm/ 100 cc of blood (11-14 in woman).
   - Life of RBC is 120 days after which they are broken down in spleen or liver.

- Product of breakdown of haemoglobin is a pigment (yellow colour), called bilirubin. Retention of bilirubin leads to jaundice.

2. **White Blood Corpuscles:** Also called Leucocytes, rounded, with a nucleus, far less numerous than RBCs, life 3-4 days.
   - ***Types:*** Granulocytes (Basophils, Eosinophils, Neutrophils) and Agranulocytes (Monocytes, Lymphocytes).
   - ***Basophils :*** Take up basic stains. Have an S-shaped nucleus. Secrete an anti-coagulant Heparin, which prevents clots within the blood vessels.
   - ***Eosinophils or Acidophils :*** Take up acidic stains. Assists in defence mechanism.
   - ***Neutrophils :*** Most numerous of the WBCs (65-70%). Defence.
   - ***Monocytes :*** Largest of all. Very motile. Defence.
   - ***Lymphocytes :*** 25% of the WBC. Takes part in antigen and antibody formation.
3. **Platelets :** Also called Thrombocytes, formed in bone marrow, life 3-7 days, sets off blood clotting.

   Plasma (65%) : Watery part of blood, clear, yellow fluid. Contains about 90% water, proteins and organic salts.
   - ***Lymph :*** Lymph = Blood - RBC, *i.e.*, Plasma + WBC. All interchanges of nutrients and waste products between blood and tissue takes place through lymph only.
   - Spleen produces lymph. At the same time it also acts as the graveyard of lymph.

   Blood Groupings
   - ***Father of Blood Grouping:*** Karl Landsteiner. He discovered A, B and O blood groups in 1900.
   - Decastello and Sturle in 1902 discovered AB blood group.
   - ABO system of blood groups is based on antigens and antibodies.
   - AB: Universal recipient.
   - O: Universal donor.

RH Factor: It is based on Rh antigen. Discovered in 1940 by Landsteiner and A.S. Veiner. It discovered in Rhesus monkey. A person can be Rh^+ or Rh^-.

- In world population Rh^+ are 85% and Rh^- are 15% only.
- Blood transfusion technique was first developed by James Blundell in 1825.

Excretory System of Humans

Waste materials excreted in animals are of many kinds : Nitrogenous Substances, Carbon dioxide, Pigments, Excess Water, etc.

The Nitrogenous Waste can be excreted in the following forms :

- **Ammonia :** Highly Toxic. In aquatic animals (called Ammoniotelic).
- **Urea :** Far less toxic than ammonia In Mammals, Alligators, Turtles (called Ureotelic).
- **Uric Acid :** In animals where conservation of water is needed. In Birds, Insects, Land Reptiles (called Uricotelic).

Excretory System of Mammals

1. **Kidneys :**A kidney is composed of 1.2 million microscopic structural and functional units called nephrons or uriniferous tubules.
2. **Ureters :** Open into Urinary Bladder.
3. **Urinary Bladder :** Size depends upon the amount of mine in it (up to 700-800 ml).

   The lower part is guarded by 2 Sphinctors : inner involuntary and outer voluntary.
4. **Urethra :** Leads to the exterior. In females, it carries only urine. In males it carries urine as well as spermatic fluid.

   Nephron : Functional unit of kidney. It is a long tube differentiated into 4 regions.

1. **Bowman's Capsule :** Contains a globular bunch of capillaries, the glomerulus. In glomerular filtrate: water (99%), inorganic salts, amino acids, fatty acids, glucose, urea, uric acid, hormones, vitamins are present.
2. **Proximal Convoluted Tubule :** Starts from the neck of Bowman's capsule and is highly twisted. Almost whole of the glucose and vitamins, amino acids, Na and K, Ca and Mg and water is absorbed.
3. **Loop of Henle:** U-shaped. Consist of 2 straight limbs: descending and ascending. No water is absorbed in ascending limb.
4. **Distal Convoluted Tubule :** Greatly twisted. Reabsorbs some Na and Cl. Leads to Collecting Tubules which lead to ureters.
   - The yellow colour of urine is caused by the pigment urochrome, which is a breakdown product of haemoglobin from worn out RBCs.
   - The urine gives a pungent smell due to conversion of urea into ammonia by bacteria.
   - Kidney stones: Calcium Oxalate.

Respiratory System of Humans

I. **Anaerobic Respiration :** When nutrients are oxidized without using O_2 (also called fermentation). *e.g.*, Ascaris, Fasciola, Taenia also respire anaerobically. It is a low energy yielding process.

II. **Aerobic Respiration :** Cells utilize O_2 for oxidizing nutrients. It is found in most plants and animals. It involves:

1. **External Respiration:** Gaseous exchange of O_2 and CO_2 between blood and air (or water).
2. **Internal Respiration:** Gaseous exchange between blood and tissues.
3. **Cellular Respiration:** Oxidation of nutrients in the cells and liberation of energy.

Endocrine System of Humans

Formed by endocrine glands (or Ductless Glands). They secrete hormones directly into the blood stream.

Hypothalamus : Forms a part of fore-brain, secretes neurohormones, which effect the release of hormones from pituitary.

Pituitary Gland: Also called Master Gland. It is the smallest endocrine gland. It secretes:

1. ***Somatotrophic Hormone :*** Controls the general growth of the body. Hyper-secretion leads to acromegaly and gigantism and hyposecretion leads to dwarfness.
2. ***Gonadotrophic Hormone :*** Stimulates the primary sex hormones, *i.e.*, ovaries and testes.
3. ***Lactogenic Hormone :*** Initiates milk production in the pregnant females.
4. ***Thyrotrophic Hormone :*** Aids in the regulation of thyroid secretion.
5. ***Adrenocorticotrophic Hormone :*** Influences the secretion from the cortex of adrenal glands.
6. ***Oxytocin or Pitocin :*** Stimulates smooth muscle contractions during child birth. Also helps in the secretion of milk in females.
8. ***Vasopressin (Anti-Diuretic Hormone) :*** Regulates reabsorption of water from the kidney tubules, causing increase in Blood Pressure.

Thyroid Gland : It is the largest endocrine gland located in the neck between the trachea and larynx.

1. ***Thyroxine :*** Regulates physical, mental and sexual development.
   - Poor in iodine is insufficient for the synthesis of thyroxin, leads to simple goitre.
2. ***Thyrocalcitonin :*** It controls the amount of calcium in the body.
   - *Hashimoto Disease :* Due to age factor or injury in thyroid gland secretion of thyroid reduces.

Parathyroid Gland : Secretes Parathormone. It influences calcium and phosphorus metabolism.

Thymus Gland : Situated near the heart. Produces Thymine. Preventing development of gonads.

Pancreas : It is an exocrine as well as an endocrine gland. Its endocrine part is known as Islets of Langerhans. Beta cells secrete Insulin which controls the amount of sugar in the blood.

Adrenal Glands : Consists of 2 Distinct Parts: Outer cortex and Inner medulla.

1. Adrenal Medulla secretes Adrenaline or epinephrine which effects liberation of glucose from glycogen stored in liver.
2. Adrenal Cortex secretes two types of Hormones:
   (*a*) *Mineralo Corticoids :* Maintain electrolyte balance. Its hyposecretion results in Addison's disease.
   (*b*) *Gluco Corticoids :* It influences carbohydrate metabolism. Its hypersecretion leads to Cushing Disease.

Reproductive System of Humans

It is the process by which an individual multiplies in number by producing more individuals of its own type.

I. Asexual Reproduction: Asexual Reproduction is the process of multiplication of individuals without the formation or fusion of gametes.

Binary Fission : It involves the division of the nucleus followed by that of the cytoplasm, breaking the body into two young ones. *e.g.*, Amoeba, Euglena, Paramecium, etc.

II. Sexual Reproduction : The process of sexual reproduction involves the formation and fusion of gametes (Syngamy) and results in the formation of a new organism genetically different from parent.

Mammalian Reproductive System : The reproductive system of sexually reproducing animals consists of:

Sex	Primary Sex Organs	Secondary Sex Organs
Male	Testes	Epididymis, Vas deferens, Ejaculatory duct, Urethra Seminal vesicle, Prostate Gland Cowper's gland, Penis
Female	Ovary	Fallopian tubes, Uterus, Vagina, External Genitalia/ Vulva Bartholian's Gland, Mammary glands

Sensory Organs of Humans

Eye: Eye is made up of 3 Layers : Upper Sclerotic, Middle Choroids, Inner Retina.

1. ***Sclerotic Layer :*** The Transparent bulging, circular part of sclerotic layer which lies in the front is called cornea. Cornea is covered by the thin Conjunctiva.
2. ***Choroid Layer :*** Choroid layer starts from iris which is next to cornea. The circular aperture of iris is called pupil.
   - Lens is a proteinous. It is biconvex in nature.
3. ***Retina :*** Image of the object is formed on retina. Retina is composed of 2 types of Cells:
   - *Rod Cells :* Sensitive to dim light and contain the pigment Rhodopsin (in nocturnal animals more).
   - *Cone Cells :* Colour sensitive for 3 primary colours (Red, Blue and Green). They are found more in diurnal animals.

Yellow Spot (Macula Lutea) : On retina, finest image is formed here. Favea centralis is the depression in the middle of yellow spot.

Blind Spot : No image formation takes place here as the optic nerves innervate the eyeball here.

- Cornea is donated in Eye Donation.
- Eyes glow in animals due to tapetum.

Defects of Eye

1. ***Myopia:*** Cannot see distant objects, image formed before retina, concave lens is used.
2. ***Hypermetropia :*** Cannot see near objects, image formed behind retina, convex lens is used.
3. ***Astigmatism :*** Curvature of cornea becomes irregular and image is not clear cylindrical lens is used.
4. ***Cataract :*** Due to defective protein metabolism the lens becomes opaque Operation is needed.
5. ***Gloucoma :*** Due to defect in aqueous humour.
6. ***Presbiopia :*** In this, power of accommodation of lens decreases due to age factor and defected metabolism. Can be removed by bifocal lens.

Ear : Divided into 3 Parts :

1. ***External Ear:*** Pinna + External Auditary Meatus
   - Has wax glands which produce cerumen to trap dust particles.
2. ***Middle Ear:*** It encloses 3 Ear Ossicles : Malleus (Hammer-Shaped), Incus (Anvil- Shaped), Stapes (Stirrup-Shaped)

Fanastra Ovalis : Connects middle ear to internal ear. Middle ear is connected to the pharynx by Eustachian tube.

3. ***Internal Ear (Membranous Labyrinth) :*** Most delicate part. Enclosed by parotic bone. It perform two functions : Maintenance of balance and hearing.
   - In the internal ear are 3 semi-circular canals and utriculus which are filled with a fluid, endolymph.

Diseases in Human

Human Viral Diseases	Human Bacterial Diseases
Chickenpox	Cholera
Measles	Diphtheria
Polio	Tuberculosis
Rabies	Leprosy
Mumps	Tetanus
Influenza	Typhoid
Hepatitis	Plague
Herpes	Whooping Cough
AIDS	Sore Throat
Trachoma (of Cornea)	Pneumonia
Human Protozoans Diseases	Gonorrhoea
Amoebiasis	Syphilis
Malaria	Botulism
Sleeping Sickness	**Human Fungal Diseases**
Kalazar	Ringworm
Diarrhoea	Athlete's foot
Piarrhoea	Dhobie itch

Some Important Facts of Human Body

Length of Alimentary Canal	Approximately 8 metres
Number of Cells in Body	75 trillion
Longest Bone	Femur (Thigh bone)
Smallest Bone	Ear ossicle, stapes
Weight of Brain	1400 gms
Blood Volume	6.8 litres (in 70 kg body)
Normal B.P.	120/80 mm Hg
Number of R.B.C.	(*a*) In Male : 4.5-5.0 million/cubic mm. (*b*) In Female : 4.0-4.5 million/cubic mm
Life Span of R.B.C.	120 days
Normal W.B.C. Count	5000-1000/cubic mm
Life Span of W.B.C.	3-4 days
D.L.C. (Differential Leucocyte Count)	(*a*) Basophils : 0.5-1% (*b*) Eosinophils : 1-3% (*c*) Monocytes : 3-8% (*d*) Neutrophils : 40-70% (*e*) Lymphocytes : 2-25%
Blood Platelets Count	2,00,000-4,00,000/cubic mm
Haemoglobin	(*a*) In Male : 14-15.6 gm/100 c.c. of blood (*b*) In Female : 11-14 gm/100 c.c. of blood
Hb Content in Body	500-700 gm
Universal Blood Donor	O Rh–ve
Universal Blood Recipient	AB
Blood Clotting Time	2-5 minutes
Average Body Weight	70 kg
Normal Body Temperature	98.4°F or 37°C
Breathing Rate	16-20/minute

Dental Formula	Adult : 2123/2123 = 32; Child : 2120/2120 = 22 Milk Teeth
Number of Cranial Nerves	12 pairs
Number of Spinal Nerves	31 pairs
Largest Endocrine Gland	Thyroid
Gestation Period	9 months (253-266 days)
Normal Heart Beat	72-75/minute
Largest Gland	Liver
Largest Muscle in the Body	Gluteus maximus (Buttock Muscle)
Smallest Muscle in the Body	Stapedius
Largest Artery	Abdominal Aorta
Largest Vein	Inferior Venacava
Greatest Regeneration Power	In liver
Longest Nerve	Sciatic
Longest Cell	Neuron (Nerve Cell)
Minimum Regeneration Power	In Brain Cells
pH of Gastric Juice	1.4
pH of Urine	6.0
pH of Blood	7.35-7.45
Total Number of Muscles in the Body	639
Total Number of Bones in the Body	206

MULTIPLE CHOICE QUESTIONS

1. Which of the following is an antibiotic?
A. Aspirin B. Paracetamol
C. Penicillin D. Sulphadizine

2. Digestion of food starts in:
A. mouth B. liver
C. stomach D. intestines

3. By taking the pulse rate of the human body, a doctor determines:
A. heartbeat
B. functioning of heart valves
C. the amount of blood in body
D. the condition of liver

4. A thermostat is used to:
A. purify air
B. regulate humidity
C. regulate temperature
D. regulate air pressure

5. Heat from the sun reaches the earth by:
A. reflection B. conduction
C. convection D. radiations

6. Dew forms most readily on nights that are:
A. calm and clear B. stormy
C. windy D. cloudy

7. The full moon rises in the:
A. South B. North
C. East D. West

8. An aeroplane is able to fly because;
A. it is lighter than air
B. it is heavier than air
C. it is made of very light materials
D. moving air can lift objects

9. The souring of milk is caused by the action of:
A. a protozoa B. bacteria
C. viruses D. None of these

10. The smallest living thing that can cause disease in the human body is:
A. flea B. bacteria
C. a protozoa D. viruses

11. The most abundant gas in the air is:
A. oxygen B. carbon dioxide
C. nitrogen D. hydrogen

12. Which is the element common to brass and bronze?
A. Copper B. Iron
C. Zinc D. Aluminium

13. The densest element known so far is:
A. iron B. mercury
C. osmium D. tungsten

14. The most ductile element is:
A. gold B. silver
C. iron D. aluminium

15. The metal having highest melting point is:
A. chromium B. tungsten
C. diamond D. silver

16. The gas which constitutes most of Venus's atmosphere is:

A. oxygen B. nitrogen
C. hydrogen D. carbon dioxide

17. The most common acid found in the nature is:

A. acetic acid B. citric acid
C. lactic acid D. hydrochloric acid

18. The bomb that cannot destroy the property but can damage the life only is:

A. atom bomb B. hydrogen bomb
C. fission bomb D. neutron bomb

19. The waves received by our Television sets are:

A. light waves B. radio waves
C. cosmic waves D. micro waves

20. Which of the following machines will fail to give satisfactory result in vacuum?

A. Bicycle B. Sewing machine
C. Fan D. Washing machine

21. Which of the following is the best conductor of electric current?

A. Aluminium B. Copper
C. Silver D. Gold

22. Tungsten is mainly used for making filament of electric bulbs because of its:

A. low cost
B. high melting point
C. high electrical conductivity
D. low thermal conductivity

23. The element common to bone and cement is:

A. silicon B. calcium
C. nitrogen D. phosphorus

24. The raw material common to cement and glass is:

A. soda B. rock
C. gypsum D. sand

25. What is essentially required to digest the food in stomach?

A. Air B. Water
C. Enzymes D. Minerals

26. Domestic electric meters record the consumption of electricity in:

A. Volts B. Amperes
C. Watts D. Ohms

27. Which of the following gases does not pollute air?

A. Carbon dioxide B. Carbon monoxide
C. Nitrogen dioxide D. Sulphur dioxide

28. Polio is a disease caused due to:

A. bacterial infection B. virus infection
C. protozoal infection D. food poisoning

29. Which form of gold is the softest?

A. 16 Carat B. 18 Carat
C. 20 Carat D. 22 Carat

30. Filtration of wastes from the blood in human body is done by:

A. heart B. lungs
C. kidney D. intestines

31. Speed of sound waves is maximum in:

A. vacuum B. gases
C. liquids D. solids

32. How many colours are there in the rainbow?

A. 7 B. 10
C. 12 D. 5

33. Barometer measures:

A. wind velocity B. atmospheric pressure
C. amount of rainfall D. atmospheric moisture

34. Anemometer measures:

A. amount of rainfall
B. atmospheric pressure
C. wind velocity
D. amperage of an electrical current

35. Sphygmomanometer measures:

A. specific heat, latent heat, heat of chemical combination and other thermal properties
B. intensity of light
C. distance covered, or steps taken, by a person walking
D. blood pressure

36. Meteorology is the study of:

A. meteors and meteorites
B. the climate
C. the weather
D. the measurement of length

37. Oil, water and gas can be present in a well in the ascending order of:

A. water, oil, gas B. gas, water, oil
C. water, gas, oil D. oil, water, gas

38. Vegetables can be cooked quickly in a pressure cooker because:

A. steam can boil vegetables faster than water
B. boiling point increases with the increase in pressure
C. high pressure lowers the boiling point
D. All the above

39. A person suffering from which of the following cannot see with clarity the horizontal and vertical lines simultaneously?

A. Myopia B. Hypermitropia
C. Astigmatism D. Squint

40. When a flake of ice melts in a water bowl, the level of water inside the bowl:

A. remains unchanged
B. goes down
C. increases
D. nothing can be said definitely

41. To an astronaut in a satellite the colour of the sky would appear to be:

A. black B. blue
C. grey D. white

42. A fuse wire is used for:

A. allowing high currents to flow harmlessly
B. breaking the electrical circuit
C. saving a man from receiving electric shocks
D. All the above

43. Excessive intake of alcohol damages a person's:
A. kidneys
B. liver
C. stomach
D. All the above to a certain degree

44. Which of the following is common in all acids?
A. Hydrogen B. Oxygen
C. Nitrogen D. None of the above

45. After boiling, rice grains grow in volume and weight because:
A. starch swells in water and heat
B. heat enlarges solid
C. rice is a fatty grain
D. All the above

46. Hygrometer is used for measuring:
A. temperature B. relative humidity
C. rainfall D. density of water

47. Phobos and Deimos are the satellites of:
A. Uranus B. Mars
C. Venus D. Saturn

48. Plants are grown along river banks in order to check:
A. siltage and floods B. pollution
C. rainfall D. All the above

49. Which one of the following signifies the optical technique of recording waves and amplitude?
A. Holography B. Bibliography
C. Audiography D. None of the above

50. People use iron ploughs now, instead of the old wooden ploughs. This change signifies:
A. advance technology
B. appropriate technology
C. obsolete technology
D. ultimate technology

51. Acetyl salicylic acid is used commonly as:
A. pain-reliever B. tear gas
C. chemical fertilizer D. preservative

52. In a village where fuel is not available and people are poor, which of the following measures is the most suitable to prevent disease through contaminated water from the wells?
A. Using chemicals to purify water
B. Boiling the water
C. Use of micro-organisms to purify water
D. None of the above

53. One of the main constituents of Gobar gas is:
A. thyamine B. methane
C. phosphate D. carbon monoxide

54. Quartz is softer than:
A. Diamond B. Corundum
C. Topaz D. All the above

55. Emerald and diamond are made of:
A. Beryllium and Carbon
B. Carbon
C. Silica
D. Silica and Beryllium

56. Human brain receives and sends signals as:
A. chemical impulses
B. physical impulses
C. electrical impulses
D. mechanical impulses

57. The ductless glands secreting hormones directly into human blood are known as:
A. exocrine glands B. endocrine glands
C. metabolic glands D. ductlands

58. Arrange the three forms of iron in descending order of carbon contents and other impurities in them:
I. wrought iron
II. cast iron
III. pig iron
A. III, II, I B. III, I, II
C. I, II, III D. II, I, III

59. Foot and mouth diseases attack:
A. cattle, sheep and pigs
B. cattle only
C. cattle and pigs only
D. cattle and sheep only

60. Which one of the following has maximum nitrogen content?
A. Sodium nitrate
B. Urea
C. Ammoniam sulphate
D. None of the above has enough nitrogen

61. Radio carbon dating is used for determining the age of:
A. fossils B. buildings
C. babies D. rocks

62. Pasteurization of milk means:
A. heating of milk upto 100°C
B. heating of milk at 65°C
C. cooling of milk at 100°C
D. cooling of milk upto 0°C

63. Ranikhet disease affects:
A. dogs B. cows
C. poultry D. sheep

64. Wisdom teeth appear in a human being between:
A. 17 and 20 years of age
B. 30 and 40 years of age
C. 10 and 17 years of age
D. 4 and 8 years of age

65. Decomposition of matter takes place due to the effect of:
A. bacteria B. virus
C. fungi D. algae

66. Bile is secreted by:
A. pancreas B. small intestine
C. stomach D. liver

67. Polio myelitis which causes polio is spread by:
A. mosquito B. virus
C. water D. adulterated food

68. Which of the following is a genetically transmitted disease?

A. Myopia B. Long sightedness
C. Colour blindness D. Night blindness

69. Which of the following is a metal?
A. Arsenic B. Sulphur
C. Potassium D. Carbon

70. How does weedicide remove weeds?
A. It removes the water required for growth
B. It destroys the roots of the weeds
C. It destroys the nutrients required for the growth of weeds
D. All of the above

71. A diamond is a:
A. form of fossilised mammal of ancient times
B. crystalline form of pure carbon
C. hard rolled under sea stone made into a diamond by the saliva of huge sea monsters and thereafter dug out from the mines
D. natural crystallized glass

72. High heel and/or pointed shoes are harmful because:
A. they injure the feet
B. they weaken the eyesight
C. they cause polio
D. they cause backache and sleeplessness

73. When returning to the earth, spacecrafts have a communication blackout, the reason is:
A. the returning spacecraft is doing so against the force of gravity which interferes with the radio waves
B. during the re-entry period the density of the plasma generated by the intense frictional heat is so high that the operational frequencies used for communication becomes very much less than the plasma cut-off frequency resulting in a total blackout
C. stellar X-rays attract and absorb the sound waves
D. the sounds created by the whirring of the mechanism of the spacecraft renders the sounds inaudible

74. Respiration is:
A. to change the food into energy
B. the process during which food is oxidized and its chemical energy is transformed into useful form
C. a sort of exercise
D. interconversion of food and energy

75. Dialysis is:
A. the same process as osmosis
B. the diffusion of sugar molecules through water
C. the process involved in the diffusion of toxic substance through a membrane
D. the evaporation of surplus sugar

76. Mycology is the study of:
A. Mica
B. Ants
C. Changes of a structure as a result of environment
D. Fungi

77. In human body, quantity of water is about:
A. 10% B. 20%
C. 65% D. 80%

78. What does the urine of a man contain mainly?
A. Urea B. Sugar
C. Salt D. None of the above

79. The filament of electric bulb is made of:
A. iron B. tungsten
C. nichrome D. silver

80. The lightning rod used for protecting building from lightning is made of:
A. glass B. cement
C. wood D. copper

81. When a body becomes positively charged, it:
A. loses electrons
B. gains electrons
C. loses protons
D. None of the above is correct

82. During which season our body needs more fats?
A. Summer season B. Rainy season
C. Winter season D. Spring season

83. Deficiency of insulin causes:
A. Beri-Beri B. Fever
C. Cancer D. Diabetes

84. Iron is heavier than water, still the ship floats on the sea because:
A. weight of the ship is less than the weight of water in the sea
B. weight of the ship is more than sea water
C. weight of the ship is less than the weight of water that the ship displaces
D. weight of ship is equal to the weight of water that ship displaces

85. Photosynthesis results in:
1. release of oxygen
2. release of carbon dioxide
3. formation of carbohydrates
4. intake of carbon dioxide

A. 1, 2, 3 are correct B. 1,3,4 are correct
C. 2,3,4 are correct D. only 1 is correct

86. The Pythagorean Theorem states that:
A. in any triangle the square of the longest side equals the sum of the squares of the other sides
B. in any triangle the square of the longest side equals the square of the sum of the other sides
C. in a right-angled triangle the square of the hypotenuse equals the sum of the squares of the other two sides
D. in an isosceles triangle the third side equals the sum of the two equal sides

87. The formula for inter conversion of Centigrade, Fahrenheit and Reaumur scales is:
A. $\frac{F-32}{9}=\frac{C}{5}=\frac{R}{4}$ B. $\frac{F+32}{9}=\frac{C}{5}=\frac{R}{4}$
C. $\frac{F-32}{9}=\frac{C}{9}=\frac{R}{4}$ D. $\frac{F-32}{4}=\frac{C}{9}=\frac{R}{5}$

88. Which one of the following statements is incorrect?
A. The length of the days and nights is not the same all the year round
B. The axis of the earth is inclined at an angle of 66-1/2 to the plane of its orbit
C. Water pipes are apt to burst in very cold weather
D. Evaporation produces heat

89. Which of the following statements is correct?
A. Boiling of an egg is a chemical change
B. Freezing of ice cream is a chemical change
C. Burning of a candle is a physical change
D. Extracting the juice from an orange is a chemical change

90. When a bullet is fired why does the gun kick back?
A. Because the man firing the gun is light in weight
B. Because the gun is heavier than the firing soldier
C. Because the bullet goes out very fast
D. Because to every action there is an equal and opposite reaction

91. Which one of the following definitions is wrong?
A. *Amino Acids:* Large chemical substances containing carbon and oxygen
B. *Proteins:* Giant molecules of carbon, nitrogen and oxygen which are broken into small molecules during digestion
C. *Carbohydrates:* Big molecules used for getting energy
D. *Lipids:* A group of organic compounds found in living cells

92. The depth to which a floating body sinks in pure water is a measure of its
A. Density B. Weight
C. Inertia D. Viscosity

93. Which one of the following is a contagious disease?
A. Malaria B. Small pox
C. Cholera D. Tuberculosis

94. A pure (sun) spectrum is that in which:
A. only ultra violet and infra red rays are not seen
B. all the seven colours which combine to make up the sun light are clearly, distinctly and separately visible
C. all the seven colours are found
D. where the rainbow is found

95. What do fertilisers contain?
A. Calcium B. Sodium
C. Phosphorus D. Nitrogen

96. In which the purest form of carbon is found?
A. Coke B. Diamond
C. Graphite D. Coal

97. What is Tritium?
A. Compound of hydrogen
B. Isobar of hydrogen
C. Isotope of hydrogen
D. Oxide of hydrogen

98. How do the centripetal forces pull a body?
A. Upward B. Downward
C. Inwards D. Outwards

99. What does Mycology study?
A. Minerals B. Sound
C. Insects D. Fungus

100. DNA is concentrated in the:
A. Microsome B. Nucleus
C. Chromatin D. Cell wall

101. Vinegar is obtained by the fermentation process; what does it contain?
A. Acetic acid B. Formic acid
C. Nitric acid D. Oxalic acid

102. When the leaves of a plant show chlorosis, the possible cause can be:
A. increase in nitrate content in the soil
B. increase in chloride content in the soil
C. decrease in phosphorus content in the soil
D. deficiency of trace elements in the soil

103. Which of the properties of elements is a whole number?
A. Atomic number B. Atomic weight
C. Molecular weight D. Equivalent weight

104. What does the process in which a heavy nucleus breaks to give two or more small nuclei and large amount of energy is called:
A. electrolysis B. fission
C. fusion D. ionization

105. What is the process in which two or more small nuclei join to form a large nucleus with evolution of energy is called:
A. electrolysis B. fission
C. ionization D. diffusion

106. The main endocrine gland present in the human body is:
A. Adrenal gland B. Pituitary gland
C. Thyroid gland D. Pancreas gland

107. Which one is wrongly matched?
A. Phosphorus – Match
B. Potassium Sulphate – Fertilizer
C. Methyl Isocynate – Tyre
D. Silicon – Glass

108. Which one of the following pairs is incorrect?
A. Malaria – Mosquitoes
B. Small Pox – Virus
C. Typhoid – Fungi
D. Cholera – Water

109. Which one group of the following belongs to 'lichens'?
A. Algae and bacteria B. Virus and bacteria
C. Algae and fungi D. All the above

110. Arrange the following elements, present in human body, in the descending order of their percentage:
1. Oxygen
2. Nitrogen
3. Carbon
A. 1 and 2 only B. 1 and 3 only
C. 1, 3, 2 D. 2 and 3 only

111. Which one of the following is given to a typhoid patient?

A. Chloroquin B. Vitamin A
C. Chloromycetin D. Sulphur

112. Which one of the following is called a growth gland?

A. Adrenal B. Thyroid
C. Pituitary D. None of the above

113. Which one of the following is a rich source of vitamin A?

A. Potato tuber B. Carrot root
C. Onion bulb D. Maize grains

114. Of the following the best way to put out a petrol fire is to use:

A. water
B. rugs
C. soda water fire extinguisher
D. carbon tetrachloride extinguisher

115. Which type of nerves carry impulses from the sense organs in response to stimulus?

A. Motor B. Sensory
C. Secretory D. All the above

116. The gas which helps in burning is:

A. Carbon Monoxide B. Hydrogen
C. Oxygen D. Nitrogen

117. Which one of the following best defines IQ?

A. $\frac{\text{Actual Age}}{\text{Mental Age}} \times 100$ B. $\frac{\text{Mental Age}}{\text{Actual Age}} \times 100^2$

C. $\frac{\text{Actual Age}}{\text{Mental Age}} \times 10$ D. $\frac{\text{Mental Age}}{\text{Actual Age}} \times 1000$

118. Which one of the following is called 'red planet'?

A. Mercury B. Jupiter
C. Venus D. Mars

119. The instrument used to measure radio activity is called:

A. Gyroscope B. Nephoscope
C. Machmeter D. Geiger Counter

120. Which one is the most popular fodder for poultry?

A. Barley B. Maize
C. Wheat D. Bajra

ANSWERS

1	2	3	4	5	6	7	8	9	10
C	A	A	C	D	A	C	D	B	D
11	**12**	**13**	**14**	**15**	**16**	**17**	**18**	**19**	**20**
C	A	C	A	B	D	A	D	D	C
21	**22**	**23**	**24**	**25**	**26**	**27**	**28**	**29**	**30**
C	B	B	C	C	C	A	B	D	C
31	**32**	**33**	**34**	**35**	**36**	**37**	**38**	**39**	**40**
D	A	B	C	D	C	A	B	C	A
41	**42**	**43**	**44**	**45**	**46**	**47**	**48**	**49**	**50**
A	B	D	A	A	B	B	A	A	A
51	**52**	**53**	**54**	**55**	**56**	**57**	**58**	**59**	**60**
A	A	B	D	A	A	B	A	A	B
61	**62**	**63**	**64**	**65**	**66**	**67**	**68**	**69**	**70**
A	B	C	A	A	D	B	C	C	D
71	**72**	**73**	**74**	**75**	**76**	**77**	**78**	**79**	**80**
B	D	B	B	C	D	C	A	B	D
81	**82**	**83**	**84**	**85**	**86**	**87**	**88**	**89**	**90**
A	C	D	C	B	C	A	D	A	D
91	**92**	**93**	**94**	**95**	**96**	**97**	**98**	**99**	**100**
A	A	B	B	D	B	C	C	D	C
101	**102**	**103**	**104**	**105**	**106**	**107**	**108**	**109**	**110**
A	D	A	B	D	B	C	C	C	C
111	**112**	**113**	**114**	**115**	**116**	**117**	**118**	**119**	**120**
C	B	B	C	B	C	A	D	D	B

COMPUTER KNOWLEDGE

1. COMPUTER TERMINOLOGY

Below are definitions for some of most of the common words and terms in today's technology vocabulary.

Accumulator: A Storage area in memory used to develop totals of units or of amounts being computed.

ActiveX: A Microsoft programming architecture that allows programs to interact with other programs over a network, such as the Internet. The controls created with ActiveX enable developers to add extra capabilities to Web sites, such as animation.

ADSL: Asymmetric Digital Subscriber Line, a modem arrangement, connected to ends of a telephone line, that allows for high-speed transmissions of data—useful for interactive video and data communications. See also DSL, xDSL.

Alignment: Process of organising and fixing the position and order of words and lines in a document.

Applet: A small application program, made with the object-oriented programming language Java, which can be sent along the Web to a user. Applets can perform animations, calculations and other tasks without sending the user back to a server.

Application Program: A computer program used to perform a specific task, such as word processing, spreadsheet creation, or database management.

ASCII: Acronym for American Standard Code for Information Interchange. A standard set of characters used to enable compatibility between different computer devices.

Attachment: Content included in an e-mail, either as extra text or as a file.

Auxiliary Storage: Storage that supplements a computer's primary internal storage.

Back Up: The process of making duplicate copies of files, disks, or directories for safekeeping in case of data/file loss.

Bandwidth: How much data one can send through a connection. Usually measured in bits-per-second. A full page of English text is about 16,000 bits. A fast modem can move about 15,000 bits in one second. Full-motion, full-screen video would require roughly 10,000,000 bits per second, depending on compression.

BASIC (Beginner's All-purpose Symbolic Instruction Code): A programming language developed in the mid-1960's as an easy-to learn, easy-to-use language to teach students how to program. The language contains a limited set of powerful commands designed especially for use in a time sharing environment.

Batch File: A file that contains a series of DOS commands that execute automatically.

BBS: Bulletin Board System, a computer that creates a forum for sharing and exchanging messages and/or files. Most BBS's operate independent of the Internet, and must be reached with a modem or Telnet. But many BBS's have Web sites, as do service providers.

Binary: Pertaining to the number system with a radix of 2, or to a characteristic or property involving choice or condition in which there are two possibilities. For example, the binary numeral 1101 means:
$(1 \times 2^3) + (1 \times 2^2) + (0 \times 2^1) + (1 \times 2^0)$ which is equivalent to decimal 13.

BIOS (Basic Input Output System): Commands of function when a computer is switched on.

Bit: A binary digit; a digit (0 or 1) in the representation of a number in binary notation.

Booster Keys: Keys that do not perform actions by themselves but can be used with other keys to issue commands. The booster keys are Ctrl, Alt, and Shift.

Boot: To start a computer and load the operating system into RAM.

Bps—(Bits-per-Second): A measurement of how data is moved from one place to another. A 28,8 modem can move 28,800 bits per second.

Browser: A Client program (software) that is used to look at various kinds of Internet resources. Mosaic, Netscape Navigator and Internet Explorer are some of the commonly used browsers.

Bug: A mistake in the design of a program or a computer system, or an equipment fault.

BUS: Internal communication path in a computer.

Byte: A byte is eight bits.

Cell: The smallest unit of a spreadsheet filled with information.

Central Processor: The unit of a computer system that includes the circuits which controls the interpretation and execution of instructions. Synonymous with CPU (Central Processing Units) and main frame.

Chip: An integrated electronic circuit consisting of miniature transistors and other circuit elements contained on a silicon wafer.

Clip art: Small diagrams which can be pasted on a document.

Clipart: These are pre-prepared graphic images that one can incorporate into a document with a word processor or a desktop publishing program.

Cold Boot: To start a computer and load the operating system into RAM.

Compile: To prepare a machine language program (or a program expressed in symbolic coding) from a program written in another programming language (usually a procedure oriented language such as BASIC, COBOL or FORTRAN). The compilation process usually involves examining and making use of the overall structure of the program and/or generating more than one object program instruction for each source program statement. Contrast with assemble.

Compiler: A computer program that compiles. Compilers are an important part of the basic software for most computers permitting the use of procedure-oriented languages which can greatly reduce the human effort required to prepare computer programs.

Console: A portion of a computer that is used for communication between operators or maintenance engineers and the computer, usually by means of displays and manual control.

Cookie: A type of text file given to a browser by a server, used to record specific information about a user's preferences.

Current Directory: The directory that DOS is currently using.

Current Drive: The disk drive that DOS is currently using.

Data Base Administrator (DBA): The person in charge of defining and managing the content of a data base.

Data Base Management System (DBMS) : Software to manage and control data resources.

Data Bus: The internal pathway in a computer on which data moves.

DDR (Double Data Rate): A mechanism used to produce computer memory.

Debug: To trace and eliminate mistakes in a program or faults in equipment. The process is often assisted by a diagnostic routine.

Disk Drive: A mechanism that reads and writes data on a disk.

Disk Operating System (DOS): The name used for various operating systems. The primary function of a disk operating system is to control the flow of data to and from the CPU and peripherals.

Drag: To move something around the computer with the help of the mouse. This involves holding down one of the mouse buttons while user moves it.

DTP (Desk Top Publishing) : The process of making publication and taking printouts using specially designed computer software's.

Ethernet: A very common method of networking computers in a LAN. Ethernet will handle about 10,000,000 bits-per-second and can be used with almost any kind of computer.

File processing: The periodic updating of master files to reflect the effect of current data, often transaction data contained in detail files; e.g., a weekly payroll run updating the payroll master file.

Firewall: A system that protects a private network and its resources from unauthorized access.

GUI (Graphical User Interface): A computer mode of interaction using graphics.

Host: Any computer on a network that is a repository for services available to other computers on the network. It is quite common to have one host machine providing several services, such as WWW and USENET.

HTTP: Hypertext Transfer Protocol, the definitive manner in which messages are formatted, transmitted and received on the World Wide Web.

Hyper text: A text format with facilities like Link, Bold, Italics etc. like an HTML life.

Hyperlink: A pointer or reference to another document. Usually underlined text or a picture, it accesses another document when clicked on.

Integrated Circuit (IC): A device incorporating circuitry and semiconductor components within a single unit, usually a miniature chip. Circuit elements and components are created as part of the same manufacturing procedures.

Interface Card: Special utility cards like Sound card, Network card etc. connected to the mother board.

Interface Slot: Slot in mother board to connect interface cards.

IP: Internet Protocol, specifies and addresses the packets that the messages transmitted on the Internet are composed of. It usually works with another protocol called TCP, or Transfer Control Protocol, which establishes a connec-tion between a destination and a source.

IRC: Internet Relay Chat, a client/server-software chat system that allows people anywhere on the Internet to join in live discussions.

ISP (Internet Service Provider): An institution that provides access to the Internet in some form, usually for money. For example, in India, VSNL (Videsh Sanchar Nigam Limited) is the Internet Service Provider.

JPEG: A format to save and keep picture files.

Maximise Button: A button by which a software/window under use can be maximised.

Memory Slot: Part of a motherboard to connect memory cards.

MICR (Magnetic Ink Character Recognition): The automatic reading by machine of graphic characters printed with magnetic ink.

Monitor: The visual display unit of a computer system.

Motherboard: The main circuit board of a micro-computer.

OCR (Optical Character Recognition): The automatic reading by machine of graphic characters through the use of light-sensitive devices.

Parity Bit: A bit (binary digit) appended to an array of bits to make the sum of all the 1-bits in the array either always even ("even parity") or always odd ("odd parity").

PPP (Point to Point Protocol): Most well known as a protocol that allows a computer to use a regular telephone line and a modem to make TCP/IP connections and thus be really and truly on the Internet.

Programmable read-only memory (PROM): Computer memory chips that can be programmed permanently, by burning the circuits in patterns, to carry out predefined process.

PSET: Command in BASIC to show a point on the screen.

Reboot: To restart a computer by turning it off and then on again by pressing Ctrl, Alt, Del, or by pressing a reset button.

Resolution: It indicates the degree of details—that can be perceived. The higher the resolution, the finer the detail.

Router: A special purpose computer (or software package) that handles the connection between 2 or more networks. Routers spend all their time looking at the destination addresses of the packets passing through them and deciding which route to send them on.

Search Engine: A program, or a system of programs, which uses keywords to find Web pages containing matching words, returning the results to the user.

SMPS (Switched Mode Power Supply) : The part of a system unit which distributes power supply to all segments of a computer.

Source Program: A program written in a source language (e.g., written in COBOL, C, FORTRAN, or symbolic coding for input to a compiler or assembler).

Spam: Internet slang for unsolicited, and often commercial, e-mail or newsgroup postings.

Spider: A program that automatically culls Web pages. Spiders are often used in search engines.

Spooling: Computer processing technique under which input and output files originating on and destined for slow-speed devices are written to high-speed storage devices prior to and following processing. Thus, processing can take place at high speeds while input and output can be handled separately at relatively slow speeds.

SQL (Structured Query Language): A specialized programming language for sending queries to databases.

Streaming: Continuously playing audio (streaming audio) or video (streaming video). Users don't need to wait for large files to download before listening or viewing. Instead, the media plays as it arrives.

URL: Universal Resource Locator, the address of a document or file (resource) on the Internet. The first part of the URL describes which protocol to use, the second part specifies the domain name and IP address.

USB Port (Universal Serial Bus Port): A way by which external equipments can be attached to a computer.

Vector Image: Picture file madeup of geometric shapes like circuts, rectangles, ovals etc.

Webmaster: Individual who creates and or manages a Web site. May also be the individual who manages the technical aspects of a Web site.

Wildcard Characters: Special characters that can be used in most DOS commands as substitutes for other characters. The asterisk (*) and the question mark (?) symbols are wildcard characters.

Word Length: The number of bits or characters in a word.

WWW: World Wide Web, all the resources on the Internet that use HTTP, or hypertext transfer protocol, e.g. Web pages.

Zip Drive: Durable disk drive that uses 100 MB disks. Popular for backing up hard drives, or transporting large files.

Zip File: File made up of several other files compressed into one.

Zoom: The command to see a thing on the screen as enlarged or as reduced.

MULTIPLE CHOICE QUESTIONS

1. EDVAC is:

A. Electronic Detected Variable Automatic Computer
B. Electronic Discrete Variable Automatic Computer
C. Electronic Discrete Valuable Automatic Computer
D. Electronic Developed Valuable Automatic Computer

2. DRAM stands for:

A. Decimal Randam Access Memory
B. Direct Random Access Memory
C. Dynamic Random Access Memory
D. None of the above

3. DDR SDRAM stands for:

A. Double Data Rate Synchronous Dynamic Random Access Memory
B. Dynamic Data Rate Synchronous Dynamic Random Access Memory
C. Decimal Double Rate Synchronous Dynamic Random Access Memory
D. None of the above

4. EEPROM stands for:

A. Effective Erasable Programmable Read Only Memory
B. Electrically Erasable Programmable Read Only Memory
C. Entities Erasable Programmable Read only Memory
D. None of the above

5. DMA stands for ______.

A. Direct Memory Access
B. Distinct Memory Access
C. Direct Module Access
D. Direct Memory Allociation

6. MOS stands for ______.

A. Metal Oxide Semiconductor
B. Most Often Store
C. Method Organised Stack
D. None of the above

7. What is the meaning of DBMS?

A. Data-based Managements Systems
B. Data-based Management Systems
C. Database Management System
D. None of the above

8. What does DBA stands for?

A. Database Associate
B. Database Administrator
C. Database Actor
D. None of the above

9. WAN stands for:

A. Wide Area Network
B. Wireless Area Network
C. World Area Network
D. None of the above

10. The full form of TCP/IP is:

A. Transport control Protocol/Internet Protocol
B. Transmission Control Protocol/Internet Protocol
C. Both A & B
D. None of the above

11. What is the full-form of JPEG?

A. Joint Photographic Experts Group
B. Joint Philosophical Experts Group
C. Joint Philosophical Exports Group
D. Joint Photographic Exports Group

12. What is the full-form acronym of MPEG?

A. Motion Picture Experts Group
B. Multimedia Picture Experts Group
C. Moving Picture Experts Group
D. Motion Picture Experience Group

13. What is the full-form of DAT?

A. Digital Authoring Tape
B. Digital Audio Tracking
C. Digital Audio Tape
D. None of the above

14. What is the full-form of OLAP?

A. Online Analytical Processing
B. Offline Analytical Processing
C. Order Analytical Processing
D. Onshore Analytical Processing

15. What does ERP stands for?

A. Entreprivate Resource Planning
B. Enterprise Reform Planning
C. Enterprise Record Planning
D. Enterprise Resource Planning

16. Expand the acronym of 'SLC'.

A. Software Life Cycle approach.
B. Software Leasing Costs.
C. Systems Life Cycle approach.
D. System Loan Costs.

17. What does the acronym IDS stands for?

A. Intrusion Detection System
B. Internet Detection Standard
C. Internet Detection System
D. Intrusion Detection Standard

18. What does CSMA represent?

A. Carrier Sensing Minimal Access
B. Carrier Sensing Multiple Access
C. Carrier Sense Minimal Access
D. Carrier Sense Multiple Access

19. VIRUS stands for:

A. Very Important Resource Under Search
B. Vital Information Resource Under Siege
C. Verify Interchange Result Until Source
D. Very Important Record User Searched

20. MFT stands for ______.

A. Multiprogramming For Tasking
B. Multi Fix Tasking
C. Multiprogramming with Fixed Tasking
D. None of the above

21. MVT stands for ______.

A. Multi Variant Tasking
B. Multiple Variant Tasking
C. Multiprogramming Variable Tasking
D. None of the above

22. OLE stands for ______.

A. Object Linking Embedding
B. Object Link Environment
C. Object Link Enhancement
D. None of the above

23. EOF stands for ______.

A. End of File
B. Extend of File
C. Eliminate of File
D. None of the above

24. What is ODBC?

A. Open Database Connectivity
B. Open Dictionary Connectivity
C. Open Database Costing
D. Open Disk Data Connectivity

ANSWERS

1	2	3	4	5	6	7	8	9	10
D	C	A	B	A	A	C	B	A	B
11	**12**	**13**	**14**	**15**	**16**	**17**	**18**	**19**	**20**
A	C	C	A	D	A	A	D	B	C
21	**22**	**23**	**24**						
C	A	A	A						

✦✦✦✦✦

2. COMPUTER FUNDAMENTALS

DEFINITION OF A COMPUTER

A computer is an electronic device that has revolutionized the way society performs tasks and communicates with each other. It is a complex machine that integrates hardware and software components to process, store, retrieve, and communicate information efficiently and automatically.

The development of computers has greatly impacted many areas of life, from education and business to entertainment and communication.

FUNCTIONING OF A COMPUTER

Computers are electronic devices that are designed to process information and perform tasks quickly and efficiently. They consist of several key components that work together to make the computer function.

1. **Input devices:** Input devices are used to provide data and instructions to the computer. Some common input devices include keyboards, mouse, scanners, and microphones. The computer processes the data provided by these devices and converts it into a format that can be understood by the computer.
2. **Central processing unit (CPU):** The central processing unit, or CPU, is the brain of the computer. It performs most of the calculations and processing required to carry out instructions. The CPU is made up of two main components: the control unit and the arithmetic and logic unit (ALU). The control unit manages the flow of data between the CPU, memory, and input/output devices, while the ALU performs arithmetic and logical operations.
3. **Memory:** Memory is used to store data and instructions temporarily while they are being processed by the CPU. There are two types of memory in a computer: Random Access Memory (RAM) and Read Only Memory (ROM). RAM is volatile memory that is used to store data that is currently being processed, while ROM is non-volatile memory that stores permanent instructions.
4. **Storage devices:** Storage devices are used to store data and programs permanently. Examples of storage devices include hard disk drives, solid-state drives, and flash drives. These devices store data even when the computer is turned off.
5. **Output devices:** Output devices are used to display or print data that has been processed by the computer. Some common output devices include monitors, printers, and speakers.
6. **Software:** Software refers to the programs and instructions that tell the computer what to do. There are two types of software: system software and application software. System software is used to manage the computer's resources and includes the operating system, device drivers, and utility programs. Application software is used to perform specific tasks and includes programs like word processors, spreadsheets, and web browsers.

HISTORY OF COMPUTERS

ABACUS

Abacus is an ancient tool that was invented in China in 1602. It is considered to be the first mechanical calculating device, which was widely used for performing arithmetic calculations.

NAPIER'S BONES

Napier's Bones is a calculating device that was invented by John Napier in 1617.

PASCALINE

The Pascaline was the first mechanical adding machine, designed by the French mathematician Blaise Pascal in 1642. It was shaped like a rectangular box with eight discs, each representing a number of units.

JACQUARD'S LOOM

Jacquard's Loom is a device that revolutionized the weaving process, making it possible to produce intricate patterns on textiles. It was invented by Joseph Marie Jacquard in France in 1801.

ANALYTICAL ENGINE

The Analytical Engine was designed by Charles Babbage in 1837 and is widely considered the first general-purpose computer. The machine was designed to perform any calculation that could be carried out by a human being using a pencil and paper.

Tabulating Machine

The tabulating machine is an electromechanical device that was designed to process large amounts of data for the 1890 census in the United States. It was invented by Herman Hollerith and marked a major milestone in data processing technology.

MARK-1

MARK-1 or Harvard Mark I was an electro-mechanical computer consisting of interlocking panels of small glass, counters, switches, and control circuits. Howard Aiken, a Harvard University professor, led the development of the MARK-1 project, which was funded by IBM. The machine was completed in 1944 and demonstrated the ability to perform a variety of calculations with impressive speed and accuracy. Despite its limitations, it was a significant step forward in the development of computers and served as a prototype for many subsequent machines.

ENIAC

ENIAC (Electronic Numerical Integrator and Computer) was the first electronic digital computer, built between 1943 and 1945.

EDSAC – The First Stored-Program Computer

EDSAC, which stands for Electronic Delay Storage Automatic Calculator, was the first computer capable of running stored programs. It was designed and built by Maurice Wilkes and his team at the University of Cambridge in 1949.

UNIVAC

UNIVAC, short for Universal Automatic Computer, is considered the first commercially available general-purpose electronic computer.

IBM-650 Computer

The IBM-650 Computer was an early mainframe computer developed by IBM in the 1950s. It was an improved version of the earlier IBM 604 computer and was designed for scientific and engineering calculations. The IBM-650 was widely used by businesses, universities, and government agencies.

TYPES OF COMPUTERS

Computers have come a long way since their invention. The development of new technologies and advancements in hardware have led to the evolution of different types of computers. Each type of computer is designed to cater to specific needs and requirements, such as processing power, storage capacity, mobility, and more.

1. **Supercomputers:** Supercomputers are the most powerful computers available and are used for complex scientific calculations and simulations that require massive amounts of processing power. They are typically used by large organizations and government agencies. Supercomputers can handle complex data modeling and simulations in fields such as weather forecasting, molecular modeling, and financial analysis. Examples of supercomputers include the IBM Summit and Fujitsu Fugaku.
2. **Mainframes:** Mainframes are large, powerful computers used by large organizations and government agencies to manage large amounts of data and perform complex tasks. Mainframes are designed to handle thousands of users simultaneously and can process massive amounts of data at high speeds. Mainframes are used in industries such as banking, healthcare, and insurance to process transactions and store large amounts of data. Examples of mainframe computers include the IBM z15 and Fujitsu GS21.
3. **Workstations:** Workstations are specialized computers used for complex tasks like 3D modeling, graphic design, scientific simulations, and other tasks that require high processing power. Workstations are designed to handle heavy workloads and are equipped with advanced graphics cards, multiple CPUs, and large amounts of memory. Examples of popular workstation computers include the HP ZBook, Lenovo ThinkPad P Series, and Dell Precision Workstations.
4. **Personal computers (PCs):** Personal computers are the most common type of computer and are designed for individual use. They are available in two main types: desktop and laptop computers.

GENERATIONS OF COMPUTER

The generations of computers are often used to describe the evolution of computing devices from the earliest mechanical computers to the present-day computers that we use.

FIRST GENERATION (1940s-1950s)

The first generation of computers, which spanned from the 1940s to the early 1950s, was characterized by the use of vacuum tubes as the main component for logic circuitry and magnetic drums for data storage. These machines were massive and extremely expensive, with limited capabilities compared to modern computers.

SECOND GENERATION (1950s-1960s)

The second generation of computers, which spanned from the late 1950s to the early 1960s, was characterized by the use of transistors as the main component for logic circuitry and magnetic core memory for data storage. These machines were smaller, faster, and more reliable than their predecessors.

THIRD GENERATION (1960s-1970s)

The third generation of computers, which spanned from the 1960s to the mid-1970s, was characterized by the use of integrated circuits as the main component for logic circuitry and the introduction of high-level programming languages. These machines were smaller, faster, more reliable, and easier to program than their predecessors.

FOURTH GENERATION (1970s-1980s)

The fourth generation of computers, which spanned from the mid-1970s to the mid-1980s, was characterized by the use of microprocessors as the main component for logic circuitry and the introduction of personal computers.

These machines were smaller, cheaper, and more powerful than their predecessors, and paved the way for the widespread use of computers in homes and businesses.

FIFTH GENERATION (1980s-PRESENT)

The fifth generation of computers, which began in the 1980s, is characterized by the use of parallel processing and artificial intelligence technologies.

These machines were designed to be more intuitive and interactive, with the ability to understand natural language and learn from their experiences.

CENTRAL PROCESSING UNIT (CPU)

The Central Processing Unit (CPU), also known as the microprocessor or the brain of the computer, is the main component of a computer that performs arithmetic, logic, and control operations. It processes the instructions and data stored in the memory, and it provides the outputs that are displayed on the screen, stored in the memory, or sent to other devices.

The CPU is responsible for executing the instructions that make up a computer program. It performs these operations at a very high speed, performing millions of operations every second. The speed of the CPU is measured in hertz (Hz) or gigahertz (GHz), which represents the number of clock cycles that the CPU completes in one second. The clock speed, or the frequency of the CPU, determines the performance of the computer.

The CPU is also responsible for managing the other components of the computer. It communicates with the memory, input/output devices, and other components to coordinate their activities. This coordination ensures that the computer operates efficiently and that the programs run correctly.

TYPES OF CPUs

Types of CPUs include:

1. Complex Instruction Set Computing (CISC)
2. Reduced Instruction Set Computing (RISC)
3. Superscalar processors
4. Multi-core processors

Complex Instruction Set Computing (CISC)

Complex Instruction Set Computing (CISC) is a type of computer architecture for Central Processing Units (CPUs) that uses a large number of instructions to perform a wide range of tasks.

Reduced Instruction Set Computing (RISC)

Reduced Instruction Set Computing (RISC) is a type of computer architecture for Central Processing Units (CPUs) that uses a smaller instruction set and emphasizes speed and simplicity.

Superscalar Processors

Superscalar processors are a type of computer architecture for Central Processing Units (CPUs) that use multiple execution units to perform multiple operations in parallel.

Multi-Core Processors

Multi-core processors are a type of computer architecture for Central Processing Units (CPUs) that contain multiple processing cores on the same physical die.

The classification of CPUs based on the number of cores is a way to describe the processing capability of a CPU. The terms single-core, dual-core, quad-core, hexa-core, octa-core, and deca-core describe the number of processing units (cores) within a CPU.

Single-Core Processor: A single-core processor has one core that is responsible for executing all the instructions and performing all the calculations. This type of CPU is found in entry-level computers, older computers, and mobile devices.

Dual-Core Processor: A dual-core processor has two cores, each of which can perform cal-culations and execute instructions independently. This type of CPU is often used in mid-range computers and is a popular choice for users who want to balance performance and cost.

Quad-Core Processor: A quad-core processor has four cores and is capable of executing four instructions simultaneously. This type of CPU is found in high-performance computers and is ideal for demanding tasks such as video editing, gaming, and multi-tasking.

Hexa-Core Processor: A hexa-core processor has six cores and is capable of executing six instructions simultaneously. This type of CPU is typically used in high-end computers and is suitable for demanding applications such as 3D rendering and scientific simulations.

Octa-Core Processor: An octa-core processor has eight cores and is capable of executing eight instructions simultaneously. This type of CPU is used in high-performance computers and is ideal for demanding tasks such as video editing, gaming, and multi-tasking.

Deca-Core Processor: A deca-core processor has ten cores and is capable of executing ten instructions simultaneously. This type of CPU is used in high-end computers and is suitable for demanding applications such as 3D rendering and scientific simulations.

CPU COMPONENTS

CPU components include:

1. Control Unit (CU)

The Control Unit (CU) is a component of a Central Processing Unit (CPU) in a computer system that manages and coordinates the activities of the other components.

2. Arithmetic Logic Unit (ALU)

An Arithmetic Logic Unit (ALU) is a fundamental component of a Central Processing Unit (CPU) in a computer. It performs arithmetic and logic operations on data stored in the CPU's registers.

3. Registers

Registers are a small amount of very fast memory within a Central Processing Unit (CPU) in a computer. They are used to store data that the CPU is currently working on.

MOTHERBOARD

A motherboard, also known as a mainboard or system board, is the primary circuit board in a computer that connects and communicates with all the other components in the system. It provides the backbone for the computer, allowing the CPU, memory, storage, and other components to communicate with each other.

INPUT DEVICES

Input devices are hardware components used to interact with and provide data to a computer. Some common types of input devices include:

KEYBOARD

A keyboard is an input device that is used to input data into a computer. The following are the main features of a keyboard:

1. **Layout:** Keyboards come in various layouts, including the standard QWERTY layout, the AZERTY layout used in France, and the QWERTZ layout used in Germany.
2. **Keys:** Keyboards typically have around 100 keys that are used for typing text, entering numbers, and controlling the computer.
3. **Function Keys:** Keyboards often have function keys that perform specific tasks, such as adjusting the volume, controlling media playback, and opening applications.
4. **Special Keys:** Keyboards have special keys for specific purposes, such as the Enter key, which is used to start a new line, the Backspace key, which is used to delete text, and the Tab key, which is used to move the cursor.
5. **Modifiers:** Keyboards have modifier keys, such as the Shift key and the Ctrl key, that are used to modify the behavior of other keys.
6. **Connectivity:** Keyboards can be connected to a computer through a USB cable, a wireless connection, or via a Bluetooth connection.

MOUSE

A mouse is an input device that is used to control the movement of a cursor on a computer screen.

TOUCHPAD

A touchpad is a type of pointing device that is integrated into laptops and is used to control the movement of a cursor on a computer screen.

SCANNER

A scanner is an input device that is used to digitize images or text from physical documents.

MICROPHONE

A microphone is an input device that is used to capture audio and convert it into a digital signal that can be processed by a computer.

GAME CONTROLLER

A game controller is an input device that is used to control video games.

TRACKBALL

A trackball is a type of pointing device that consists of a ball that can be rotated with the fingers or palm of the hand. The rotation of the ball is translated into movement of the cursor on the screen.

JOYSTICK

A joystick is a type of pointing device that is typically used for controlling movement in video games or other applications. It consists of a handle or lever that can be moved in various directions, and sometimes includes buttons or other controls.

BARCODE READER

A barcode reader is a device used to read barcodes, which are printed patterns of lines and spaces used to store information. Barcode readers are widely used in retail, manufacturing, and other industries to quickly and accurately read product information or track inventory.

OPTICAL MARK READER

An optical mark reader (OMR) is a device that can read special marks or bubbles on paper forms, such as standardized tests, surveys, or ballots. The marks are typically made by a pencil or pen and represent different choices or answers. OMRs use light sensors to detect the marks and convert them into digital data.

OPTICAL CHARACTER RECOGNITION

Optical Character Recognition (OCR) is a technology that allows printed or written text to be converted into digital format that can be read by a computer. OCR software works by analyzing the shapes of individual characters and comparing them to a database of known character shapes.

BIOMETRIC SENSOR

A biometric sensor is a type of device that measures biological or physical characteristics of a person, such as their fingerprints, facial features, or iris patterns, and converts them into digital data that can be used for identification or authentication purposes.

OUTPUT DEVICES

Output devices are devices that are used to display the results of processing performed by a computer. Some common examples of output devices include:

MONITOR

A monitor is an output device that displays the images, videos, and text generated by a computer.

Examples

- **CRT Monitor:** A CRT (Cathode Ray Tube) monitor is an older technology that uses a vacuum tube to display images on the screen.
- **LCD Monitor:** An LCD (Liquid Crystal Display) monitor uses a backlight and liquid crystals to display images on the screen.
- **OLED Monitor:** An OLED (Organic Light-Emitting Diode) monitor uses organic materials to emit light and create images on the screen.
- **4K Monitor:** A 4K monitor is a high-resolution monitor with a resolution of 3840×2160 pixels.
- **Gaming Monitor:** A gaming monitor is a type of monitor that is specifically designed for gaming. It may have a higher refresh rate, lower input lag, and additional features to enhance the gaming experience.

PRINTER

A printer is an output device that is used to print text and images onto paper.

Types of Printers

Printers can be broadly classified into two types based on the technology used for printing: impact printers and non-impact printers.

1. **Impact Printers:** Impact printers work by physically striking an ink ribbon against the paper, leaving an impression on the page. These printers were popular in the early days of computing and are still used in some applications where multipart forms are required. Impact printers can be further classified into three types:

   (*a*) **Dot Matrix Printers:** Dot matrix printers work by striking a series of pins against an ink ribbon, creating a series of dots that form characters and images. They are relatively cheap and can print on multipart forms, making them useful for tasks such as printing invoices and receipts.

   (*b*) **Daisy Wheel Printers:** Daisy wheel printers use a wheel with spokes that each have a letter, number, or symbol attached to them. When a character needs to be printed, the wheel rotates to the appropriate spoke and strikes the ink ribbon against the paper. Daisy wheel printers produce high-quality prints, but are slow and relatively expensive.

(*c*) **Line Printers:** Line printers use a print head with several pins arranged in a line. The print head moves across the paper, striking the ink ribbon to produce a line of text or an image. Line printers are faster than dot matrix and daisy wheel printers, but produce lower quality prints.

2. Non-Impact Printers: Non-impact printers work by spraying ink or toner onto the paper to produce text and images. They are quieter, faster, and produce higher quality prints than impact printers. Non-impact printers can be further classified into four types:

(*a*) **Inkjet Printers:** Inkjet printers use small nozzles to spray ink onto the paper. They are popular for home use and can print high-quality images and text.

(*b*) **Laser Printers:** Laser printers use toner cartridges and a laser to create an image on a drum, which is then transferred to the paper. They are faster than inkjet printers and produce high-quality prints.

(*c*) **Thermal Printers:** Thermal printers use heat to create an image on heat-sensitive paper. They are commonly used in retail settings for printing receipts and other small documents.

(*d*) **Dye-Sublimation Printers:** Dye-sublimation printers use heat to transfer dye from a ribbon onto paper, creating high-quality prints. They are commonly used for printing photographs and other high-quality images.

PLOTTER

A plotter is a type of output device that is used to produce high-quality, large-format prints for engineering, architecture, and other design applications. Unlike traditional printers, which can only produce images on standard-sized paper, plotters can print on large sheets of paper or other materials such as vinyl, mylar, or even fabric.

Plotters work by moving a pen or other marking tool across the paper or other media, drawing the image line by line.

SPEAKER

A speaker is an output device that is used to produce sound.

PROJECTOR

A projector is an output device that projects an image or video onto a flat surface, such as a wall or screen.

HEADPHONES

Headphones are an output device that are used to produce sound directly into the user's ears.

In Terms of Output Device, Here are Some Important Points to Consider

Resolution

The resolution of an output device refers to the number of pixels it can display. The higher the resolution, the more detail can be shown. For monitors, the resolution is expressed in terms of the number of pixels across the width and height of the screen. For printers, the resolution is expressed in terms of dots per inch (dpi).

Color Depth

Color depth refers to the number of bits used to represent the color of each pixel on a screen or in a print. The more bits used to represent color, the more accurate the color representation will be.

Speed

The speed of an output device is an important factor to consider when choosing an output device. For printers, the speed is measured in pages per minute (ppm) and for monitors, the speed is measured in Hertz (Hz).

Quality

The quality of an output device refers to the sharpness and clarity of the output. For printers, quality is measured in terms of the resolution and the accuracy of the color representation. For monitors, quality is measured in terms of the resolution, color accuracy, and the viewing angle.

Connectivity

The connectivity options available for an output device are also important to consider. For example, some monitors may have HDMI, VGA, and DisplayPort inputs, while others may only have one or two options. For printers, connectivity options may include USB, Ethernet, and Wi-Fi.

Cost

The cost of an output device is an important consideration for many users. Higher-end output devices will generally have better performance and features, but they will also cost more.

COMPUTER MEMORY

Computer memory is an essential component of a computer system that enables the storage and retrieval of data and programs.

PRIMARY MEMORY AND SECONDARY MEMORY

Primary memory and secondary memory are two different types of computer memory that are used to store data and instructions in a computer system.

Primary memory, also known as main memory or random-access memory (RAM), is a type of volatile memory that is used to temporarily store data and instructions that the computer needs to access quickly. When a program is launched, the required data and instructions are loaded into the RAM from the storage devices, such as the hard disk drive or solid-state drive. The CPU then accesses the data and instructions stored in the RAM to perform the required calculations and operations. Primary memory is much faster than secondary memory, but it is also more expensive and has a smaller capacity.

Secondary memory, also known as auxiliary memory or non-volatile memory, is a type of non-volatile memory that is used to store data and instructions that are not immediately needed by the computer. Examples of secondary memory include hard disk drives, solid-state drives, optical disks, and USB drives. Data and instructions stored in secondary memory are not lost when the power to the computer is turned off, which makes it suitable for long-term storage. Secondary memory is slower than primary memory, but it is also much cheaper and has a larger capacity.

Primary memory and secondary memory work together to provide a complete storage solution for a computer system. Primary memory provides fast access to data and instructions that are needed immediately, while secondary memory provides larger and more permanent storage capacity for data and instructions that are not currently needed.

There are several types of primary memory and secondary memory. Here are some of the most common types:

Types of Primary Memory

1. **Random Access Memory (RAM):** Volatile memory that is used to temporarily store data and instructions that the CPU needs to access quickly. RAM is further classified into several subtypes such as SRAM (Static RAM), DRAM (Dynamic RAM), and SDRAM (Synchronous Dynamic RAM).
2. **Read-Only Memory (ROM):** Non-volatile memory that stores instructions that are required to boot the computer. The data stored in ROM cannot be modified or deleted, hence the name "read-only."
3. **Cache Memory:** A type of high-speed memory that is used to temporarily store frequently accessed data and instructions. Cache memory is typically smaller in size than RAM, but it is much faster.

Types of Secondary Memory:

1. **Hard Disk Drive (HDD):** A non-volatile storage device that is used to store large amounts of data permanently. It uses magnetic disks to store data, and it provides high capacity at a relatively low cost.
2. **Solid-State Drive (SSD):** A non-volatile storage device that is similar to an HDD but uses flash memory instead of magnetic disks. SSDs are faster, more reliable, and more power-efficient than HDDs, but they are also more expensive.
3. **Optical Discs:** Non-volatile storage devices that use lasers to read and write data. Examples include CD-ROMs, DVDs, and Blu-ray discs.
4. **USB Flash Drives:** Small and portable non-volatile storage devices that use flash memory to store data. They are popular because of their small size, durability, and ease of use.

RANDOM ACCESS MEMORY (RAM)

Random Access Memory (RAM) is a type of computer memory that is used to temporarily store data and instructions for the CPU to access and process.

Types of RAM

There are several types of RAM that are commonly used in modern computer systems, including:

1. **SDRAM (Synchronous Dynamic RAM):** This is a type of RAM that synchronizes its data transfer with the system clock, allowing for faster and more efficient data transfer. SDRAM is used in most modern computer systems, including desktops, laptops, and servers.
2. **DDR SDRAM (Double Data Rate Synchronous Dynamic RAM):** This is an improved version of SDRAM that can transfer data twice per clock cycle, providing even faster performance than standard SDRAM. DDR SDRAM is commonly used in high-performance desktops and gaming systems.
3. **DDR2 SDRAM (Double Data Rate 2 Synchronous Dynamic RAM):** This is a newer version of DDR SDRAM that provides even faster data transfer rates and improved power efficiency. DDR2 SDRAM is commonly used in mid-range and high-end desktop systems.
4. **DDR3 SDRAM (Double Data Rate 3 Synchronous Dynamic RAM):** This is the current standard for DDR SDRAM, providing even faster data transfer rates and lower power consumption than DDR2 SDRAM. DDR3 SDRAM is commonly used in modern desktops and laptops.
5. **DDR4 SDRAM (Double Data Rate 4 Synchronous Dynamic RAM):** This is the latest version of DDR SDRAM, providing even faster data transfer rates and lower power consumption than DDR3 SDRAM.

DDR4 SDRAM is commonly used in high-end desktops, gaming systems, and servers.

6. **LPDDR (Low Power Double Data Rate):** This is a type of RAM that is specifically designed for use in mobile devices, such as smartphones and tablets. LPDDR provides fast data transfer rates and low power consumption, allowing for longer battery life in mobile devices.

READ-ONLY MEMORY (ROM)

Read-Only Memory (ROM) is a type of computer memory that is used to store data and instructions that are essential for the basic operation of a computer.

The following are the main features of ROM:

1. **Non-volatile:** ROM retains its data even when the computer is turned off, unlike RAM, which loses its data when the power is turned off.
2. **Permanent:** The data stored in ROM is permanent and cannot be modified or deleted by the user.
3. **Built-in:** ROM is built into the computer and is not a removable component like RAM.
4. **Firmware:** ROM is often used to store the computer's firmware, which is the software that controls the basic functions of the computer.
5. **Types:** There are several types of ROM, including Programmable Read-Only Memory (PROM), Erasable Programmable Read-Only Memory (EPROM), and Electrically Erasable Programmable Read-Only Memory (EEPROM).
6. **Boot-up:** ROM is used to boot up the computer, and its contents are used to initiate the boot process and load the operating system into RAM.

Types of ROM

There are several types of ROM that are commonly used in modern computer systems, including:

1. **Mask ROM (MROM):** This is a type of ROM that is programmed at the factory during the manufacturing process. The data and instructions stored in MROM cannot be modified by the user, making it a secure storage option for sensitive data and critical system functions.
2. **PROM (Programmable Read-Only Memory):** This is a type of ROM that can be programmed by the user after it has been manufactured. PROM chips are programmed by applying electrical signals to specific memory cells, which permanently stores the data and instructions.
3. **EPROM (Erasable Programmable Read-Only Memory):** This is a type of ROM that can be programmed and erased by the user using ultraviolet light. The data and instructions stored in EPROM can be erased by exposing the chip to ultraviolet light, which resets the memory cells to their default state.
4. **EEPROM (Electrically Erasable Programmable Read-Only Memory):** This is a type of ROM that can be programmed and erased using electrical signals. EEPROM can be rewritten multiple times, allowing for updates and modifications to the data and instructions stored in the memory.
5. **Flash Memory:** This is a type of ROM that can be programmed and erased in blocks, rather than individual memory cells. Flash memory is commonly used in modern computer systems, including USB drives, memory cards, and solid-state drives (SSDs).

CACHE MEMORY

Cache memory is a type of computer memory that is used to temporarily store data and instructions that are frequently used by the processor.

MEMORY ORGANIZATION

Memory organization refers to the way that memory is structured, arranged, and managed within a computer system. Memory is a crucial component of a computer, as it is used to store data, programs, and other information that the computer needs to function.

Memory is usually organized into units called bytes, which are groups of eight bits (binary digits). The amount of memory in a computer is typically measured in kilobytes (KB), megabytes (MB), gigabytes (GB), or terabytes (TB). Bytes are organized into blocks of memory, each with a unique address that is used to locate and access the data stored in that block.

BACK-UP DEVICES

In the modern age of computing, the amount of data generated and stored by individuals and organizations has increased dramatically. To ensure that this data is protected against loss or damage, it is important to have a backup strategy in place.

Back-up devices refer to the various types of storage devices used to create a duplicate copy of important data and information, in case the original data is lost, damaged, or corrupted.

MULTIPLE CHOICE QUESTIONS

1. The least powerful computer is:
A. Minicomputer
B. Microcomputer
C. Mainframe computer
D. None of the above

2. The Central Processing Unit (CPU) consists of:
A. Registers and Arithmetic Logic Unit
B. Instruction Decoding Circuit
C. A control and timing section
D. All of the above

3. The main purpose of the supercomputer is:
A. High speed calculations
B. Weather forecasting
C. Data Retreieval operations
D. None of the above

4. What are the two essential parts of the Computer?
A. Keyboard and Mouse
B. Hardware and Software
C. Printer and Screen
D. Monitor and Keyboard

5. Future Generation computers will be based on:
A. Online processing B. Artificial intelligence
C. Time sharing D. None of the above

6. The basic operations performed by a computers are:
A. Arithmetic operation
B. Logical operation
C. Storage and relative
D. All of the above

7. The earliest calculating devices are:
A. Abacus B. Clock
C. Difference Engine D. None of the above

8. The Analytical Engine developed during First Generation of computers used .... as a memory unit.
A. RAM B. Floppies
C. Punch Cards D. Counter Wheels

9. The man who built the first Mechanical Calculator was:
A. Joseph Marie Jacquard
B. John Mauchly
C. Blaise Pascal
D. Harward Ailken

10. Punched cards were first introduced by:
A. Powers B. Pascal
C. Jacquard D. Herman Hollerith

11. Computers built in the First Generation of computers were:
A. Transistor B. Electro-mechanical
C. Electrical D. None of the above

12. Floppy Disk Drives were first introduced by which of the following computer manu-facturers?
A. IBM B. Sony
C. Panasonic D. Compaq

13. Supercomputer were primarily designed by:
A. Seymour Cray B. IBM
C. Hewlett-Packard D. C-DAC

14. The floppy drive have:
A. Magnetic coating B. Silver coating
C. Gold coating D. Lead coating

15. Which electronic component was use in second generation?
A. Vacuum tubes B. Transistors
C. IC chips D. All of the above

16. VLSI (Very-large scale integration) Integration Circuit technology was used in which generation?
A. first generation B. second generation
C. third generation D. fourth generation

17 IC chips was used in:
A. first generation B. second generation
C. third generation D. fourth generation

18. ENIAC was the computer of:
A. first generation B. second generation
C. third generation D. fourth generation

19. Manchester Mark I computer was based on:
A. stored program concept
B. processing concept
C. electronic change concept
D. All of the above

20. What was the size of chip used in third generation?
A. less then 8 mm B. less then 5 mm
C. less then 2 mm D. less then 5 mm

21. First Generation of computer have used the following Circuitry option:
A. Vacuum Tubes B. Transistor
C. IC D. VLSI

22. Second generation computer home used the following Circuitry options:
A. Vacuum Tubes B. Transistor
C. IC D. VLSI

23. Third Generation Computer have used the following Circuitry options:

A. Vacuum Tubes B. Transistor
C. IC D. VLSI

24. Fourth Generation computer have used the following Circuitry options:

A. Vacuum Tubes B. Transistor
C. IC D. VLSI

25. Which is the fastest storage device:

A. Floppy Disk B. Zip Disk
C. CD - ROM D. Hard Disk

26. Storage Device which uses light to store data:

A. Floppy Disk B. Hard Disk
C. CD-ROM D. Tape Drive

27. In CD 'X' Denotes:

A. Speed B. Storage Capacity
C. Time D. None

28. In CD - R user can write data.

A. Once B. More Than Once
C. Both A & B D. None of the above

29. Size of Floppy Disk is:

A. 3.5" B. 5.1/4"
C. Both A & B D. None of the above

30. The ability of an OS to run more than one application at a time is called ....

A. multi-tasking
B. object-oriented programming
C. multi-user computing
D. time-sharing

31. Which of the following statements is true?

A. Minicomputer works faster than Micro-computer
B. Microcomputer works faster than Minicomputer
C. Speed of both the computers is the same
D. The speeds of both these computers cannot be compared with the speed of advanced computer

32. Microcomputer hardware consists of three basic categories of physical equipment:

A. keyboard, monitor, hard drive
B. system unit, input/output, memory.
C. system unit, input/output, secondary storage
D. system unit, primary storage, secondary storage

33. A central computer that holds collections of data and programs for many PCs, work-stations, and other computers is a(n) ....

A. supercomputer B. minicomputer
C. laptop D. server

34. First Generation have used the following language:

A. Object oriented programmer
B. Artificial Intelligence
C. Assembly Language
D. Assembly & M/C Language

35. The first generation computers were general purpose computing machine in which ______ technology was used.

A. Vacuum Tube B. Transistors
C. Integrated circuits D. Registers

36. Computers have been classified under following classes, mark the wrong choice if any ______.

A. Micro Computers
B. Mini Computers
C. Mainframes
D. All of the above

37. What is the name of the series of Laptop computers manufactured by IBM called?

A. LapPad B. ThinkPad
C. Aptiva D. Notepaq

38. Which company did SCO sue for using code UNIX in its Operating System?

A. RedHat B. SuSE
C. IBM D. Microsoft

39. Who is the founder of BSD Unix?

A. Bill Gates B. Dennis Ritche
C. Bill Joy D. Linux Torvalds

40. Which computer periperal manufacturer quotes - Empowering your PC ....

A. Canon B. Epson
C. Mercury D. Samsung

41. The main objective of computer processing is to convert data into:

A. Information B. Files
C. Graphs D. Tables

42. Which type of computer is the fastest, largest, and most expensive?

A. Supercomputers B. Personal Computers
C. Laptops D. Notebooks

43. What is the name for a central computer that holds collections of data and programs for multiple PCs, workstations, and other computers?

A. Server B. Supercomputer
C. Minicomputer D. Laptop

44. How can personal computers be connected together?

A. Network B. Server
C. Supercomputer D. Enterprise

45. Which supercomputer was developed by Indian scientists?
A. Param B. Super30l
C. Compaq Presario D. Cray YMP

46. Which of the following is true of super-computers?
A. They are smaller in size and processing capability than mainframe computers.
B. They are common in the majority of households.
C. They contain thousands of micro-processors.
D. They are rarely used by researchers due to their lack of computing capacity.

47. What is the name of the computer's brain?
A. Monitor B. Hardware
C. CPU D. Byte

48. Which group consists only of input devices?
A. Mouse, Keyboard, Monitor
B. Mouse, Keyboard, Printer
C. Mouse, Keyboard, Plotter
D. Mouse, Keyboard, Scanner

49. What is a series of instructions that tells a computer what to do and how to do it called?
A. Program B. Command
C. User response D. Processor

50. Which of the following terms refers to any data or instruction entered into the memory of a computer?
A. storage B. output
C. input D. information

51. Which type of content can a scanner scan?
A. Pictures
B. Text
C. Both Pictures and Text
D. Neither Pictures nor Text

52. Which of the following is not an input device?
A. Keyboard B. Monitor
C. Joystick D. Microphone

53. Which part of a computer system can a user physically touch?
A. data B. operating system
C. hardware D. software

54. What are computer-readable codes consisting of lines of varying widths or lengths known as?
A. an ASCII code B. a magnetic tape
C. a bar code D. an OCR scanner

55. Which two components store and process images in a video processor?
A. CPU and VGA B. CPU and memory
C. VGA and memory D. VGI and DVI

56. What is the main circuit-board in the system unit called?
A. Computer program
B. Control unit
C. Motherboard
D. RAM

57. Which set of keys on a keyboard enable the input of numbers quickly?
A. Ctrl, Shift, and Alt
B. Function keys
C. Numeric keypad
D. Arrow keys

58. Why is the Caps Lock key referred to as a toggle key?
A. Its function goes back and forth every time it is pressed
B. It cannot be used for entering numbers
C. It cannot be used to delete
D. It cannot be used to insert

59. What term is used to describe any computer component required to perform work?
A. Bootstrap B. Kernel
C. Resource D. Source code

60. Which component of a computer is responsible for performing calculations and contains decision-making mechanisms?
A. Central Processing Unit
B. Memory Unit
C. Arithmetic and Logic Unit
D. Output Unit

61. What is the definition of output in computing?
A. What the processor takes from the user
B. What the user gives to the processor
C. What the processor gets from the user
D. What the processor gives to the user

62. Which process checks to ensure the components of a computer are operating and connected properly?
A. Booting B. Processing
C. Saving D. Editing

63. What type of data is processed by a computer into information?
A. Numbers B. Processor
C. Input D. Data

64. What is the primary function of a computer's Central Processing Unit (CPU)?
A. Creates invoices
B. Performs calculations and processing
C. Deletes data
D. Corrupts data

65. What is the term used for all the characters that a device can display or use?

A. Skill Set
B. Character Alphabet
C. Character Codes
D. Character Set

66. Which unit is responsible for controlling the movement of signals between CPU and I/O?

A. ALU
B. Control Unit
C. Memory Unit
D. Secondary Storage

67. What are the three main parts of the processor?

A. ALU, Control Unit, and Registers
B. ALU, Control Unit, and RAM
C. Cache, Control Unit, and Registers
D. Control Unit, Registers, and RAM

68. Which of the following does not relate to Input Unit?

A. If accepts data from the outside world.
B. It converts data into binary code that is understandable by the computer
C. It converts binary data into the human-readable form that is understandable to the users.
D. It sends data in binary form to the computer for further processing

69. Which type of printer cannot print more than one character at a time?

A. Line B. Daisy-wheel
C. Laser D. Dot-matrix

70. What does a Video Controller do?

A. Controls the resolution of images on screen
B. Controls the signals to be sent and received from the processor for display
C. Handles the entire electronic work behind the formation of images on the screen
D. Is responsible for allocating pixels for the formation of images

71. Which of these is a device used for pointing and drawing?

A. Mouse B. Scanner
C. Printer D. CD-ROM

72. Which of the following refers to a collection of related information sorted and dealt with as a unit?

A. Folder B. Database
C. Spreadsheet D. Text document

73. What do you call a disk's content that is recorded at the time of manufacture and cannot be changed or erased by the user?

A. Memory-only B. Write-only
C. Read-only D. Run-only

74. What type of storage device is most commonly used?

A. Persistent B. Optical
C. Magnetic D. Flash

75. Which term describes a computer's permanent memory?

A. RAM B. Floppy
C. CD-ROM D. ROM

ANSWERS

1	**2**	**3**	**4**	**5**	**6**	**7**	**8**	**9**	**10**
B	D	A	B	B	D	A	C	C	D
11	**12**	**13**	**14**	**15**	**16**	**17**	**18**	**19**	**20**
B	A	A	A	A	D	C	B	A	B
21	**22**	**23**	**24**	**25**	**26**	**27**	**28**	**29**	**30**
A	B	C	D	C	D	A	A	C	A
31	**32**	**33**	**34**	**35**	**36**	**37**	**38**	**39**	**40**
A	B	D	D	A	D	B	D	B	C
41	**42**	**43**	**44**	**45**	**46**	**47**	**48**	**49**	**50**
A	A	A	A	A	C	C	D	A	C
51	**52**	**53**	**54**	**55**	**56**	**57**	**58**	**59**	**60**
C	B	C	C	C	C	C	A	C	C
61	**62**	**63**	**64**	**65**	**66**	**67**	**68**	**69**	**70**
D	A	D	B	D	B	A	C	B	B
71	**72**	**73**	**74**	**75**					
A	B	C	C	D					

✤✤✤✤✤

3. WORD SOFTWARE, EXCEL SOFTWARE, POWERPOINT

Microsoft Office is a software which was developed by Microsoft in 1988. This Office suite comprises various applications which form the core of computer usage in today's world.

MS OFFICE APPLICATIONS & FUNCTIONS

Currently, MS Office 2016 version is being used across the world and all its applications are widely used for personal and professional purposes.

Discussed below are the applications of Microsoft Office along with each of their functions.

MS WORD

- First released on October 25, 1983
- Extension for Doc files is ".doc"
- It is useful in creating text documents
- Templates can be created for Professional use with the help of MS Word
- Work Art, colours, images, animations can be added along with the text in the same file which is downloadable in the form of a document
- Authors can use for writing/editing their work.

MS EXCEL

- Majorly used for making spreadsheets
- A spreadsheet consists of grids in the form of rows and columns which is easy to manage and can be used as a replacement for paper
- It is a data processing application
- Large data can easily be managed and saved in tabular format using MS Excel
- Calculations can be done based on the large amount of data entered into the cells of a spreadsheet within seconds
- File extension, when saved in the computer, is ".xls"

MS POWERPOINT

- It was released on April 20, 1987
- Used to create audiovisual presentations
- Each presentation is made up of various slides displaying data/ information
- Each slide may contain audio, video, graphics, text, bullet numbering, tables etc.
- The extension for PowerPoint presentations is ".ppt"
- Used majorly for professional usage
- Using PowerPoint, presentations can be made more interactive

MS ACCESS

- It was released on November 13, 1992
- It is Database Management Software (DBMS)
- Table, queries, forms and reports can be created on MS Access
- Import and export of data into other formats can be done
- The file extension is ".accdb"

MS OUTLOOK

- It was released on January 16, 1997
- It is a personal information management system
- It can be used both as a single-user application or multi-user software
- Its functions also include task managing, calendaring, contact managing, journal logging and web browsing
- It is the email client of the Office Suite
- The file extension for an Outlook file is ".pst"

MS ONENOTE

- It was released on November 19, 2003
- It is a note-taking application

- When introduced, it was a part of the Office suite only. Later, the developers made it free, standalone and easily available at play store for android devices
- The notes may include images, text, tables, etc.
- The extension for OneNote files is ".one"
- It can be used both online and offline and is a multi-user application

MICROSOFT OFFICE VERSIONS

When the Office suite was first released, it was entirely devoted for usage in computer systems but later with time the Office suite was modified for use in Laptops, Tablets and Mobile phones.

Given below are the various versions of Microsoft Office along with the years in which the version was released:

Microsoft office versions

Version name	*Release Date/Year*
Microsoft Office for Windows	October 1990
Microsoft Office 3.0	August 30, 1992
Microsoft Office 4.x	1994
Microsoft Office 1995	August 24, 1995
Microsoft Office 1997	1997
Microsoft Office 2000	June 7, 1997
Microsoft Office XP	May 31, 2001
Microsoft Office 2003	October 21, 2003
Microsoft Office 2007	January 30, 2007
Microsoft Office 2010	June 15, 2010
Microsoft Office 2013	January 30, 2012
Microsoft Office 2016	September 22, 2015

MULTIPLE CHOICE QUESTIONS

1. To create a new paragraph in MS Word document, which of the following keyboard keys can be used?
A. Tab B. Enter
C. Alt D. alt+@

2. Which of the following is not a version of MS Office?
A. Microsoft Office 3.0
B. Microsoft Office XP
C. Microsoft Office 2007
D. Microsoft Office 2009

3. What is the name of the file created on MS Excel to manage data in tabular form by managing them into various cells?
A. Document B. Docsheet
C. Workspace D. Spreadsheet

4. Which of these is the file extension for Microsoft PowerPoint presentation?
A. .ppp B. .ppt
C. .mpp D. .mp3

5. Which of the given type of software is similar to that of an Accountant's worksheet?
A. Spreadsheet B. Database
C. Graphics D. Document

6. Which keyboard keys can be used to align the text to the left side of the document in MS Word?
A. Alt+L B. Alt+Spacebar
C. Ctrl+L D. Ctrl+Spacebar

7. The block in an MS Excel spreadsheet where a column and row intersects each other is called ____. What shall come in place of the blank?
A. Key block B. Cell
C. Square D. Box

8. Which of the given combinations of key-board keys can be used as a shortcut to paste the text without removing its formatting?
A. Ctrl+C B. Ctrl+Alt+V
C. Alt+Shift+V D. Shift+Ctrl+V

9. Which of the given combinations of File type and its extension is incorrect?
A. MS Word – .doc
B. MS Excel – .xls
C. MS PowerPoint – .ppt
D. MS Outlook – .out

10. The cell reference for a range of cells that starts in cell D2 and goes over to column F and down to row 12 is:
A. D2:F12 B. D-2:F-12
C. F12:D2 D. F-12:D-2

ANSWERS

1	2	3	4	5	6	7	8	9	10
B	D	D	B	A	C	B	D	D	A

✤✤✤✤✤

4. INTERNET, WEB BROWSING

The history of the Internet is closely tied to the U.S. Department of Defense. The military was a leader in the use of computer technology in the 1960's and saw the need to create a network that could survive a single network computer's malfunction. In the 1970's, the Advanced Research Projects Agency (ARPA) developed a network that has evolved into today's Internet. The network was named ARPANET and had many objectives that are still relevant today.

The Internet is difficult to define. Essentially, the Internet is a network of computers that offers access to information and people. In some ways, it's like an information service, because it offers e-mail, bulletin boards, and information-retrieval services that can access file directories and databases around the world. However, the Internet is different from an information service, primarily because there's no central computer system – there is just a web of connections between thousands of independent systems connected to each other through telephone lines. It is estimated that there are more than 50 million such computers all over the world and they are growing at a rate of 10 per cent per month. Using the telephone network worldwide, these computers can communicate with each other. These connections can use the regular dial up telephone lines or dedicated higher capacity lines to connect a user to the nearest Internet Service Provider (ISP). ISP makes Internet access available on a local telephone call and helps user avoid direct long distance or international calls to connect to computers in other parts of the world.

However, since the Internet has grown to a phenomenal size, it has also become complex for users. To help the growing number of users, who are not computer professionals, various developments have occurred. First is the setting up of Online Services like Compu-Service, America Online, etc. These online services operate on one powerful computer, connected to the Internet. Users from any part of the world connect to this computer and avail various facilities there, which include access to information from database, software libraries, news, bulletin boards for various interest groups, online chat facilities, E-mail etc. A revolutionary development on the Internet is the World Wide Web (WWW).

WORLD WIDE WEB (WWW)

Tim Berners-Lee invented the World Wide Web (WWW) in 1989. The World Wide Web (WWW) is most often called the Web. The Web is a network of computers all over the world. All computers in the Web can communicate with each other. All the computers use a communication standard called Hypertext Transfer Protocol(HTTP). WWW is a component of the Internet that provides access to large amounts of information located on many different servers. It also provides access to many of the services available on the Internet.

The fundamental unit of the Web is the Web page. The Web page is a text document that contains links to other Web pages, graphic and audio files, and other Internet services such as file transfer protocol (FTP) and E-mail.

Web pages reside on servers that run special software that allow users to access Web pages and to activate links to other Web pages and to Internet services. Tens of thousands of Web servers are connected to the Internet. A user can directly access any Web page on one of these servers and then follow the links to other pages. This process creates a Web of links around the world and, thus, the name World Wide Web.

Computers reading the Web pages are called a Web Client. Web clients view the pages with a program called a Web Browser. The first such browser capable of displaying graphics within a Web page was Mosaic. Some of the popular browsers are Internet Explorer, Netscape Navigator, Mozilla Firefox, Opera. A browser fetches a Web page from a server by a request. This request is a standard HTTP request containing a page address. A page address looks like: http://www.name.com.

Web pages are created by using hypertext Markup Language (HTML). HTML lets the creator of a Web page specify how text will be displayed and how to link to other Web pages, files, and Internet services. These links are formally known as hypertext links, because they are activated when a user clicks on specific text or images within a Web page.

The World Wide Web (WWW) is "indexed" through the use of search engines. Each search engine works in a different way. Some engines scans for information in the title or header of the document whereas others look at the bold "heading" on the page for their information.

SEARCH ENGINE

Some popular search engines include:

1. Google
2. Microsoft Bing
3. DuckDuckGo
4. Yahoo
5. Internet Archive
6. Komo
7. Perplexity AI

SOFTWARE REQUIREMENTS FOR THE INTERNET

The Internet protocol (IP) is the method or protocol by which data is sent from one computer to another on the Internet. They can be of different types:

(*i*) *Hypertext Transfer Protocol (HTP):* It defines the format for communication between web browsers (web clients) and web servers.

(*ii*) *Internet Message Access Protocol (IMAP):* It defines the format for communication between e-mail servers and clients.

(*iii*) *Secure Sockets Layer (SSL):* A protocol developed by Netscape for transmitting private documents via the internet.

(*iv*) *Transfer Control Protocol/Internet Protocol (TCP/IP):* It is the main data transfer protocol used in the Internet. It manages all the information that moves across the Internet. It consists of multiple protocols, each of which transfers data across the network in a different format and with different options.

(*v*) *File Transfer Protocol (FTP):* A set of guidelines or standards that establish the format in which files can be transmitted from one computer to another.

(*vi*) *Trivial File Transfer Protocol (TFTP):* This protocol allows transferring of files between the network devices.

(*vii*) *Simple Mail Transfer Protocol (SMTP):* Network-based e-mail was initially exchanged on the ARPANET in extensions to the FTP, but it is now carried by the SMTP.

(*viii*) *Telnet:* A protocol that allows a computer to connect with a remote host computer on the Internet. The use of Telnet has diminished as the Web's HTTP has becomes the dominant protocol.

(*ix*) *Hypertext Markup Language (HTML):* It is a formatting language used to establish the appearance of a web page. It thus helps in creating pages on the World Wide Web. HTML also enables us to insert hypertext links within one web page or to other pages anywhere on the web.

(*x*) *Standardized General Markup Language (SGML):* A meta-language that can be applied to documents in order to maintain their structure and context is called SGML.

(*xi*) *Uniform Resource Locator (URL):* It is an address for a specific document found on the web. It can also be termed as the location of resource on the Internet. A URL specifies the address of the computer where the resource is lcoated, which may be the homepage of a website.

It is made up of several components like a domain name, the directories, and subdirectories of the site, and the extension. It is also known as the web address.

Internet Service Provider (ISP): A company that provides a subscription service to enable the user or organization to access the Internet is ISP. An ISP has a network of computers permanently linked to the Internet. Dedicated lines are also provided by some ISPs. ISPs also give you an e-mail address and space on the World Wide Web for setting up one's own website.

WEBSITE

A website is a collection of many web pages, and web pages are digital files that are written using HTML (HyperText Markup Language). To make your website available to every person in the world, it must be stored or hosted on a computer connected to the Internet round a clock. Such computers are known as a Web Server.

The website's web pages are linked with hyperlinks and hypertext and share a common interface and design. The website might also contain some additional documents and files such as images, videos, or other digital assets.

Components of a Website: We know that a website is a collection of a webpages hosted on a web-server. These are the components for making a website.

- **Webhost:** Hosting is the location where the website is physically located. Group of webpages (linked webpages) licensed to be called a website only when the webpage is hosted on the webserver. The webserver is a set of files transmitted to user computers when they specify the website's address.
- **Address:** Address of a website also known as the URL of a website. When a user wants to open a website then they need to put the address or URL of the website into the web browser, and the asked website is delivered by the webserver.
- **Homepage:** Home page is a very common and important part of a webpage. It is the first webpage that appears when a visitor visits the website.
- **Design:** It is the final and overall look and feel of the website that has a result of proper use and integration elements like navigation menus, graphics, layout, navigation menus etc.
- **Content:** Every web pages contained on the website together make up the content of the website. Good content on the webpages makes the website more effective and attractive.

- **The Navigation Structure:** The navigation structure of a website is the order of the pages, the collection of what links to what. Usually, it is held together by at least one navigation menu.

TYPES OF WEBSITE

Websites can be divided into two broad categories-static and interactive. Interactive sites are part of the Web 2.0 community of sites and allow for interactivity between the site owner and site visitors or users. Static sites serve or capture information but do not allow engagement with the audience or users directly. Some websites are informational or produced by enthusiasts or for personal use or entertainment. Many websites do aim to make money using one or more business models, including:

- Posting interesting content and selling contextual advertising either through direct sales or through an advertising network.
- E-commerce: products or services are purchased directly through the website.
- Advertising products or services available at a brick-and-mortar business.
- Freemium: basic content is available for free, but premium content requires a payment (e.g., WordPress website, it is an open-source platform to build a blog or website).
- Some websites require user registration or subscription to access the content. Examples of subscription websites include many business sites, news websites, academic journal websites, gaming websites, file-sharing websites, message boards, Web-based email, social networking websites, websites providing real-time stock market data, as well as sites providing various other services.

MULTIPLE CHOICE QUESTIONS

1. .... is a technology where the user opens a browser application and searches for information.

A. Pull Technology B. Push Technology
C. Cast Technology D. Pin Technology

2. An .... is a private network that uses Internet protocols, network connectivity, and possibly the public telecommunication system to securely share part of an organization's operations with suppliers, vendors, partners, customers or other businesses.

A. Extranet B. Intranet
C. Internet D. None of the above

3. .... handles lower-level transmissions from computer to computer as a message makes its way across the Internet, ... operates at a higher level, concerned only with the two end systems, for example your Web browser and a Web server.

A. TCP, IP B. IP, TCP
C. FTP, IP D. IP, HTTP

4. EBT stands for ....

A. Electronic Bank Transfer
B. Electronic Bank Transmission
C. Electronic Benefit Transmission
D. Electronic Benefit Transfer

5. .... is a form of electronic commerce in which products or services are sold from a firm to a consumer.

A. Business - to - Business
B. Business - to - Consumer
C. Consumer - to - Business
D. Consumer - to - Consumer

6. .... is a broker and a type of company that helps consumers uses online shops easier and potentially in a user customized interface, by providing currency conversion, language translation, and payment and delivery solutions.

A. Bounty B. Metamediary
C. Search Agent D. Shopping Facilitator

7. Upon receiving an order, the .... ships products directly to the consumer or to a wholesaler or manufacturer for delivery.

A. E-Traders B. E-Brokers
C. E-Trailers D. E-Providers

8. In .... model, companies allow users worldwide to interact with each other on the bases of similar areas of interest.

A. Electronic-Based
B. Advertising-Based
C. Community-Based
D. Fee-Based

9. EBPP stands for ....

A. Electrical Bill Presentment & Payment
B. Electronic Bill Payment & Presentment
C. Electronic Bill Presentment & Payment
D. Electrical Bill Payment & Presentment

10. These are high priced merchandise that is ordered rarely and usually requires customization.

A. Commodity-like Goods
B. Specialty Goods
C. Digital Goods
D. Convenience Goods

11. CRM stands for ....

A. Consumer Retail Manufacturing
B. Customer Relationship Manufacturing
C. Consumer Relationship Manufacturing
D. Customer Relationship Management

12. A good CRM program needs to ....

A. Identify customer success factors
B. Adopt customer based measures
C. Create a customer-based culture
D. All of the above

13. In this part of application architecture of CRM, support is given to analyze customer behaviour and implements business intelligence alike technology.

A. Collaborative B. Analytical
C. Design D. Operational

14. .... provides information about the business environment, including competitors, industry trends, and macro environmental variables.

A. Enterprise Marketing Automation
B. Customer Service and Support
C. Sales Force Automation
D. None of the above

15. .... is a functionality of CRM which has the ability to be used on a large scale, and to be reliably expanded to whatever scale is necessary.

A. Database B. Workflow
C. Assignment D. Scalability

16. The ...., also called the Web, contains billions of documents.

A. World Wide Web
B. HTTP
C. Web Portal
D. Domain

17. To make a notebook act as a desktop model, the notebook can be connected to a .... which is connected to a monitor and other devices.

A. bay B. docking station
C. port D. network

18. The software tools that enable a user to interact with a computer for specific purposes are known as ....

A. Hardware
B. Networked Software
C. Shareware
D. None of these

19. WWW means ....

A. World Wide Wonder
B. World Wide Wizard
C. World Wide Web
D. None of these

20. Documents converted to .... can be pusblished to the Web.

A. a doc file
B. http
C. machine language
D. HTML

21. The ...., also called the Web, contains billions of documents.

A. World Wide Web B. HTTP
C. Web Portal D. Domain

22. To make a notebook act as a desktop model, the notebook can be connected to a .... which is connected to a monitor and other devices.

A. bay B. docking station
C. port D. network

23. The software tools that enable a user to interact with a computer for specific purposes are known as ....

A. Hardware
B. Networked Software
C. Shareware
D. None of these

24. WWW means ....

A. World Wide Wonder
B. World Wide Wizard
C. World Wide Web
D. None of these

25. Documents converted to .... can be pusblished to the Web.

A. a doc file B. http
C. machine language D. HTML

26. The vast network of computers that connects millions of people all over the world is called ....

A. LAN B. Web
C. Hypertext D. Internet

27. Most World Wide Web pages contain commands in the language:

A. NIH B. URL
C. HTML D. IRC

28. A Website address is a unique name that identifies a specific .... on the web.

A. Web browser B. PDA
C. Web site D. link

29. What is Internet address known as ....?

A. Web address B. Web site
C. URL D. www

30. World Wide Web began from the year ....

A. 1987 B. 1988
C. 1989 D. 1990

31. You have added a new Web server to your network. Which of the following are sound practices when checking a Web server for security features?

A. Check with the vendor for the latest security patches for the Web software
B. Check the Web Server for any additional unused services
C. Check the Internet for any reports of software vulnerabilities
D. All of the above

32. What is the primary function of a DNS server?

A. Resolve 32-bit addresses in IPv4
B. Find other DNS servers
C. Resolve Fully Qualified Domain Names to IP addresses
D. Find MAC, 48-bit hardware addresses

33. During normal IP packet forwarding by a router, which of the following fields of the IP header is/are updated?

A. Source address B. Destination address
C. TTL D. Checksum

34. Which two methods can be used to submit data to a web server?

A. GET and POST B. GET and API
C. POST and API D. None of the above

35. In HTTP communications, what role does the web browser play?

A. As a client
B. As a server
C. Both A and B
D. None of the above

36. Which one of the following is an example of an 'internet search engine'?

A. LINUX B. Google
C. MS Word D. Windows

37. At which port number, Simple Network Management Protocol (SNMP) operates?

A. 160 B. 163
C. 164 D. 161

38. Which of the following is not an HTML tag?

A. < select > B. < input >
C. < textarea > D. < list >

39. Which among these is not a Web browser?

A. www B. Chrome
C. Opera D. NetSurf

40. World Wide Web was invented by:

A. Ted Nelson B. Tim Berners-Lee
C. Linus Torvalds D. Robert E. Kahn

ANSWERS

1	2	3	4	5	6	7	8	9	10
A	A	B	D	B	D	C	C	B	B
11	**12**	**13**	**14**	**15**	**16**	**17**	**18**	**19**	**20**
D	D	B	A	D	C	B	D	C	D
21	**22**	**23**	**24**	**25**	**26**	**27**	**28**	**29**	**30**
C	B	D	C	D	D	C	C	C	C
31	**32**	**33**	**34**	**35**	**36**	**37**	**38**	**39**	**40**
D	C	C	A	A	B	D	D	A	B

✤✤✤✤✤

5. COMMUNICATION

NETWORKS

A network is any collection of independent computers that communicate with one another over a shared network medium. A computer network is a collection of two or more connected computers. When these computers are joined in a network, people can share files and peripherals such as modems, printers, tape backup drives, or CD-ROM drives. When networks at multiple locations are connected using services available from phone companies, people can send e-mail, share links to the global Internet, or conduct video conferences in real time with other remote users. When a network becomes open sourced it can be managed properly with online collaboration software. As companies rely on applications like electronic mail and database management for core business operations, computer networking becomes increasingly more important.

Every network includes:

- At least two computers Server or Client workstation.
- Networking Interface Card's (NIC)
- A connection medium, usually a wire or cable, although wireless communication between networked computers and peripherals is also possible.
- Network Operating system software, such as Microsoft Windows NT or 2000, Novell NetWare, Unix and Linux.

TYPES OF NETWORKS

LANS (LOCAL AREA NETWORKS)

A network is any collection of independent computers that communicate with one another over a shared network medium. LANs are networks usually confined to a geographic area, such as a single building or a college campus. LANs can be small, linking as few as three computers, but often link hundreds of computers used by thousands of people. The development of standard networking protocols and media has resulted in worldwide proliferation of LANs throughout business and educational organizations.

WANS (WIDE AREA NETWORKS)

Wide area networking combines multiple LANs that are geographically separate. This is accomplished by connecting the different LANs using services such as dedicated leased phone lines, dial-up phone lines (both synchronous and asynchronous), satellite links, and data packet carrier services. Wide area networking can be as simple as a modem and remote access server for employees to dial into, or it can be as complex as hundreds of branch offices globally linked using special routing protocols and filters to minimize the expense of sending data sent over vast distances.

INTERNET

The Internet is a system of linked networks that are worldwide in scope and facilitate data communication services such as remote login, file transfer, electronic mail, the World Wide Web and newsgroups.

With the meteoric rise in demand for connectivity, the Internet has become a communications highway for millions of users. The Internet was initially restricted to military and academic institutions, but now it is a full-fledged conduit for any and all forms of information and commerce. Internet websites now provide personal, educational, political and economic resources to every corner of the planet.

INTRANET

With the advancements made in browser-based software for the Internet, many private organizations are implementing intranets. An intranet is a private network utilizing Internet-type tools, but available only within that organization. For large organizations, an intranet provides an easy access mode to corporate information for employees.

MANS (METROPOLITAN AREA NETWORKS)

It refers to a network of computers within a City.

VPN (VIRTUAL PRIVATE NETWORK)

VPN uses a technique known as tunneling to transfer data securely on the Internet to a remote access server on your workplace network. Using a VPN helps you save money by using the public Internet instead of making long–distance phone calls to connect securely with your private network. There are two ways to create a VPN connection, by dialing an Internet service provider (ISP), or connecting directly to Internet.

CATEGORIES OF NETWORK

Network can be divided into two main categories:

- Peer-to-peer.
- Server – based.

In peer-to-peer networking there are no dedicated servers or hierarchy among the computers. All of the computers are equal and therefore known as peers. Normally each computer serves as Client/Server and there is no one assigned to be an administrator responsible for the entire network.

Peer-to-peer networks are good choices for needs of small organizations where the users are allocated in the same general area, security is not an issue and the organization and the network will have limited growth within the foreseeable future.

The term Client/server refers to the concept of sharing the work involved in processing data between the client computer and the most powerful server computer.

The client/server network is the most efficient way to provide:

- Databases and management of applications such as Spreadsheets, Accounting, Communications and Document management.
- Network management.
- Centralized file storage.

The client/server model is basically an implementation of distributed or cooperative processing. At the heart of the model is the concept of splitting application functions between a client and a server processor. The division of labor between the different processors enables the application designer to place an application function on the processor that is most appropriate for that function. This lets the software designer optimize the use of processors—providing the greatest possible return on investment for the hardware.

Client/server application design also lets the application provider mask the actual location of application function. The user often does not know where a specific operation is executing. The entire function may execute in either the PC or server, or the function may be split between them. This masking of application function locations enables system implementers to upgrade portions of a system over time with a minimum disruption of application operations, while protecting the investment in existing hardware and software.

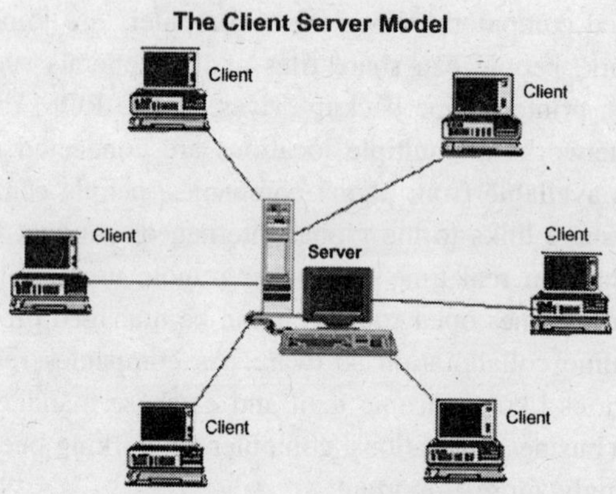

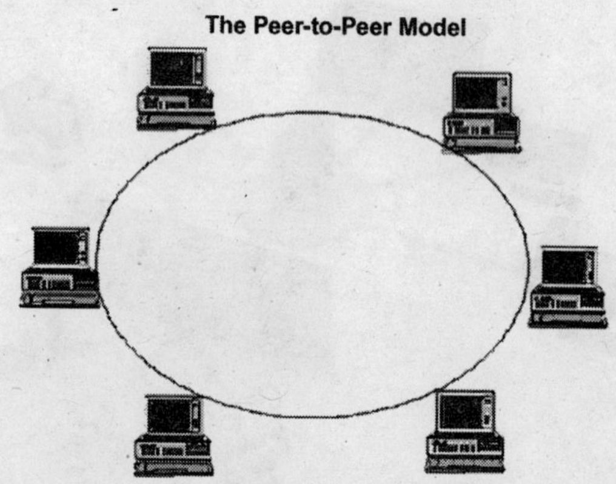

OSI MODEL

The **OSI Model** is composed of seven OSI layers that make up the model. Each layer is important to understand for proper understanding of network concepts of data packet creation and control. The layers start with Physical layer and end with the Application layer. The first, second, and third OSI layer are important to know concerning the network equipment implemented at these layers. For example a switch is a layer 2 device and a router is a layer 3 device, but some routers can be both a layer 2 and 3 device. See the YouTube video to learn more.

PHYSICAL LAYER

The Physical layer is where the data is either put onto the media or received off the media. The media could be the network cable or wireless.

The data is in the form of bits and is called Bits as the PDU (protocol data unit). These bits can be voltage levels that represent binary numbers of 1 or 0. They could also be light pulses traveling on a fiber optic cable or radio wave pulses for a wireless network.

DATA LINK LAYER

The Data Link layer is where framing of the data takes place. The Frame is the PDU name at this layer. The MAC (media access control) physical address is added or removed depending on which direction the data is traveling. The MAC address is used by switches to switch the data to the appropriate computer or node that it is intended for in a LAN (local area network).

NETWORK LAYER

The Network layer is where the IP (internet protocol) address is added or removed and the PDU at this layer is called a Packet. Routers operate at this level and use the IP (logical address) to route the data to the appropriate network. Network locations are found by the routers using routing tables to locate the appropriate networks.

TRANSPORT LAYER

The Transport layer is where the data is segmented (broken into pieces) and used by the TCP protocol to ensure accurate and reliable data is transferred. The data segments are numbers so that proper sequencing can be determined on the receiving side in order to rebuild accurate files. The PDU name at this layer is called Segment.

SESSION LAYER

The Session layer is where the session is created, maintained, and torn-down when finished.

PRESENTATION LAYER

The Presentation layer is where the data is formatted or decrypted into files that the user can understand.

APPLICATION LAYER

The Application layer is the user interface to the network where that data is either being generated or received.

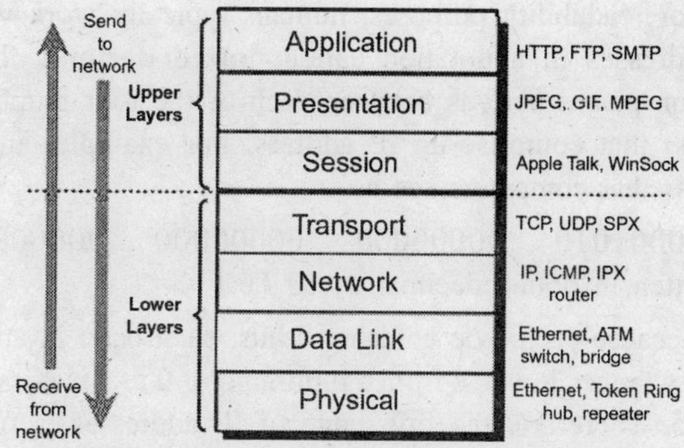

OSI Model with different protocols and devices

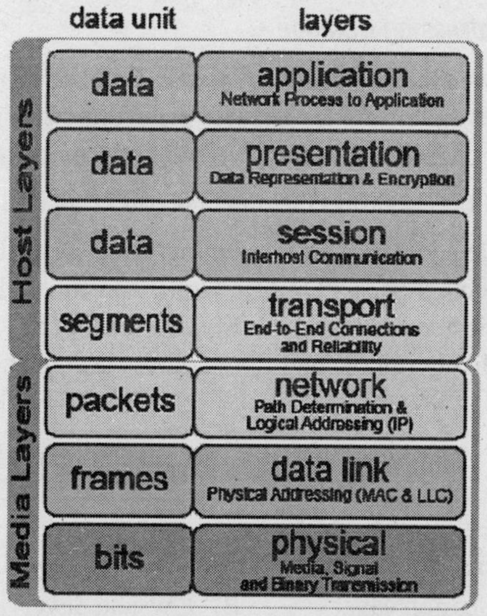

OSI Model with different form of data and bits

IP ADDRESS

Internet Protocol (IP) technology was developed in the 1970s to support some of the first research computer networks. Today, IP has become a worldwide standard for home and business networking as well. Our network routers, Web browsers, email programs, instant messaging software - all rely on IP or other network protocols layered on top of IP.

IP addresses are the fundamental method for computers to identify themselves on most computer networks. Every computer (or other network device) connected to the Internet has an IP address.

TYPES OF IP ADDRESS

Two versions of IP technology exist today. Essentially all home computer networks use IP version 4 (IPv4), but an increasing number of educational and research institutions have adopted the next generation IP version 6 (IPv6).

(a) IPv4 Addressing Notation

An IPv4 address consists of four bytes (32 bits). These bytes are also known as octets.

For readability purposes, humans typically work with IP addresses in a notation called **dotted decimal**. This notation places periods between each of the four numbers (octets) that comprise an IP address. For example, an IP address that computers see as

00001010 00000000 00000000 00000001

is written in dotted decimal as 10.0.0.1

Because each byte contains 8 bits, each octet in an IP address ranges in value from a minimum of 0 to a maximum of 255. Therefore, the full range of IP addresses is from **0.0.0.0** through **255.255.255.255**. That represents a total of 4,294,967,296 possible IP addreses.

(b) IPv6 Addressing Notation

IP addresses change significantly with IPv6. IPv6 addresses are 16 bytes (128 bits) long rather than four bytes (32 bits). This larger size means that IPv6 supports more than

300,000,000,000,000,000,000,000,000,000,000,000,000

possible addresses! In the coming years, as an increasing number of cell phones, PDAs, and other consumer electronics expand their networking capability, the smaller IPv4 address space will likely run out and IPv6 address become necessary.

IPv6 addresses are generally written in the following form:

hhhh:hhhh:hhhh:hhhh:hhhh:hhhh:hhhh:hhhh

In this **full notation**, pairs of IPv6 bytes are separated by a colon and each byte in turns is represented as a pair of hexadecimal numbers, like in the following example:

E3D7:0000:0000:0000:51F4:9BC8:C0A8:6420

As shown above, IPv6 addresses commonly contain many bytes with a zero value.**Shorthand notation** in IPv6 removes these values from the text representation (though the bytes are still present in the actual network address) as follows:

E3D7::51F4:9BC8:C0A8:6420

Finally, many IPv6 addresses are extensions of IPv4 addresses. In these cases, the rightmost four bytes of an IPv6 address (the rightmost two byte pairs) may be rewritten in the IPv4 notation. Converting the above example to **mixed notation** yields

E3D7::51F4:9BC8:192.168.100.32

IPv6 addresses may be written in any of the full, shorthand or mixed notation illustrated above.

MULTIPLE CHOICE QUESTIONS

1. Where is a hub specified in the OSI model?
A. Session layer B. Physical layer
C. Data Link layer D. Application layer

2. What flavor of Network Address Translation can be used to have one IP address allow many users to connect to the global Internet?
A. NAT B. Static
C. Dynamic D. PAT

3. What command is used to create a backup configuration?
A. copy running backup
B. copy running-config startup-config
C. config mem
D. wr mem

4. Which of the following is the valid host range for the subnet on which the IP address 192.168.168.188 255.255.255.192 resides?
A. 192.168.168.129-190
B. 192.168.168.129-191
C. 192.168.168.128-190
D. .192.168.168.128-192

5. What protocol does PPP use to identify the Network layer protocol?
A. NCP B. ISDN
C. HDLC D. LCP

6. Which of the following commands will allow you to set your Telnet password on a Cisco router?
A. line telnet 0 4
B. line aux 0 4
C. line vty 0 4
D. line con 0

7. Which protocol does DHCP use at the Transport layer?
A. IP B. TCP
C. UDP D. ARP

8. What does the passive command provide to dynamic routing protocols?
A. Stops an interface from sending or receiving periodic dynamic updates.
B. Stops an interface from sending periodic dynamic updates but not from receiving updates.
C. Stops the router from receiving any dynamic updates.
D. Stops the router from sending any dynamic updates.

9. Which protocol is used to send a destination network unknown message back to originating hosts?
A. TCP B. ARP
C. ICMP D. BootP

10. How many broadcast domains are created when you segment a network with a 12-port switch?

A. 1 B. 2
C. 5 D. 12

11. Which class of IP address has the most host addresses available by default?

A. A B. B
C. C D. A and B

12. In a network with dozens of switches, how many root bridges would you have?

A. 1 B. 2
C. 5 D. 12

13. What is a stub network?

A. A network with more than one exit point.
B. A network with more than one exit and entry point.
C. A network with only one entry and no exit point.
D. A network that has only one entry and exit point.

14. What PPP protocol provides dynamic addressing, authentication, and multilink?

A. NCP B. HDLC
C. LCP D. X.25

15. Which one of the following is true regarding VLANs?

A. Two VLANs are configured by default on all Cisco switches.
B. VLANs only work if you have a complete Cisco switched internetwork. No off-brand switches are allowed.
C. You should not have more than 10 switches in the same VTP domain.
D. VTP is used to send VLAN information to switches in a configured VTP domain.

16. How many collision domains are created when you segment a network with a 12-port switch?

A. 1 B. 2
C. 5 D. 12

17. Which protocol does Ping use?

A. TCP B. ARP
C. ICMP D. BootP

18. If you wanted to delete the configuration stored in NVRAM, what would you type?

A. erase startup B. erase nvram
C. delete nvram D. erase running

19. What protocols are used to configure trunking on a switch?

1. VLAN Trunking Protocol
2. VLAN
3. 802.1Q
4. ISL

A. 1 and 2 B. 3 and 4
C. 1 only D. 2 only

20. How many digits of the DNIC (Data Network Identification Code) identify the country?

A. first three B. first four
C. first five D. first six

21. A station in a network forwards incoming packets by placing them on its shortest output queue. What routing algorithm is being used?

A. hot potato routing B. flooding
C. static routing D. delta routing

22. You have a class A network address 10.0.0.0 with 40 subnets, but are required to add 60 new subnets very soon. You would like to still allow for the largest possible number of host IDs per subnet.
Which subnet mask should you assign?

A. 255.240.0.0 B. 255.248.0.0
C. 255.252.0.0 D. 255.254.0.0

23. Which of the following is used for modulation and demodulation?

A. modem B. protocols
C. gateway D. multiplexer

24. The Internet Control Message Protocol (ICMP)

A. allows gateways to send error a control messages to other gateways or hosts
B. provides communication between the Internet Protocol Software on one machine and the Internet Protocol Software on another
C. reports error conditions to the original source, the source must relate errors to individual application programs and take action to correct the problem
D. All of the above

25. Which of the following technique is used for fragment?

A. a technique used in best-effort delivery systems to avoid endlessly looping packets
B. a technique used by protocols in which a lower level protocol accepts a message from a higher level protocol and places it in the data portion of the low level frame
C. one of the pieces that results when an IP gateway divides an IP datagram into smaller pieces for transmission across a network that cannot handle the original datagram size
D. All of the above

26. Contention is

A. One or more conductors that serve as a common connection for a related group of devices
B. a continuous frequency capable of being modulated or impressed with a second signal

C. the condition when two or more stations attempt to use the same channel at the same time
D. a collection of interconnected functional units that provides a data communications service among stations attached to the network

27. When you ping the loopback address, a packet is sent where?
A. On the network
B. Down through the layers of the IP architecture and then up the layers again
C. Across the wire
D. Through the loopback dongle

28. Which of the following TCP/IP protocol is used for transferring electronic mail messages from one machine to another?
A. FTP B. SNMP
C. SMTP D. RPC

29. Which of the following device is used to connect two systems, especially if the systems use different protocols?
A. hub B. bridge
C. gateway D. repeater

30. Which of the following TCP/IP protocol allows an application program on one machine to send a datagram to an application program on another machine?
A. UDP B. VMTP
C. X.25 D. SMTP

31. If you get both local and remote echoes, every character you type will appear on the screen
A. once B. twice
C. three times D. never

32. What part of 192.168.10.51 is the Network ID, assuming a default subnet mask?
A. 192 B. 192.168.10
C. 0.0.0.5 D. 51

33. What can greatly reduce TCP/IP configuration problems?
A. WINS Server B. WINS Proxy
C. DHCP Server D. PDC

34. What is the port number for NNTP?
A. 119 B. 80
C. 79 D. 70

35. How many bits internet address is assigned to each host on a TCP/IP internet which is used in all communications with the host?
A. 16 - bits B. 32 – bits
C. 48 - bits D. 64 - bits

36. With an IP address of 100, you currently have 80 subnets. What subnet mask should you use to maximize the number of available hosts?
A. 192 B. 224
C. 240 D. 252

37. The geostationary satellite used for communication systems
A. rotates with the earth
B. remains stationary relative to the earth
C. is positioned over equator
D. All of the above

38. What device separates a single network into two segments but lets the two segments appear as one to higher protocols?
A. Switch B. Bridge
C. Gateway D. Router

39. Which of the following summation operations is performed on the bits to check an error-detecting code?
A. Codec B. Coder-decoder
C. Checksum D. Attenuation

40. Sending a file from your personal computer's primary memory or disk to another computer is called
A. Uploading B. downloading
C. logging on D. hang on

41. HMP (Host Monitoring Protocol) is:
A. a TCP/IP protocol used to dynamically bind a high level IP Address to a low-level physical hardware address
B. a TCP/IP high level protocol for trans-ferring files from one machine to another.
C. a protocol used to monitor computers
D. a protocol that handles error and control messages

42. Internet-like networks between a company and its business partners. Select the best fit for answer:
A. Bandwidth alternatives
B. Switching alternating
C. Inter organizational networks
D. Extranets

43. Which of the following layer protocols are responsible for user and the application programme support such as passwords, resource sharing, file transfer and network management?
A. Layer 7 protocols
B. Layer 6 protocols
C. Layer 5 protocols
D. Layer 4 protocols

44. FDDI is a

A. ring network B. star network
C. mesh network D. bus based network

45. Which of the following statement is incorrect?

A. The Addresses Resolution Protocol, ARP, allows a host to find the physical address of a target host on the same physical network, given only the target IP address.
B. The sender's IP - to- physical address binding is included in every ARP broadcast; receivers update the IP-to-Physical address binding information in their cache before processing an ARP packet.
C. ARP is a low-level protocol that hides the underlying network physical addressing, permitting us to assign IP-addresses of our choice to every machine.
D. All of the above

46. You are working with a network that has the network ID 192.168.10.0. What subnet should you use that supports up to 25 hosts and a maximum number of subnets?

A. 255.255.255.192 B. 255.255.255.224
C. 255.255.255.240 D. 255.255.255.248

47. On a class B network, how many hosts are available at each site with a subnet mask of 248?

A. 16,382 B. 8,190
C. 4,094 D. 2,046

48. You are working with three networks that have the network IDs 192.168.5.0, 192.168.6.0, and 192.168.7.0. What subnet mask can you use to combine these addresses into one?

A. 255.255.252.0
B. 225.255.254.0
C. 255.255.255.240
D. 255.255.255.252

49. With an IP address set starting with 150, you currently have six offices that you are treating as subnets. Plans are in place to open 10 more offices before the end of the year. What subnet mask should you use to satisfy the needed number of subnets and maximize the number of hosts available at each site?

A. 192 B. 224
C. 240 D. 248

50. Error detection at a data link level is achieved by

A. bit stuffing
B. cyclic redundancy codes
C. hamming codes
D. equalization

51. Computer Network is

A. Collection of hardware components and computers
B. Interconnected by communication channels
C. Sharing of resources and information
D. All of the Above

52. What is a Firewall in Computer Network?

A. The physical boundary of Network
B. An operating System of Computer Network
C. A system designed to prevent unauthorized access
D. A web browsing Software

53. How many layers does OSI Reference Model has?

A. 4 B. 5
C. 6 D. 7

54. DHCP is the abbreviation of

A. Dynamic Host Control Protocol
B. Dynamic Host Configuration Protocol
C. Dynamic Hyper Control Protocol
D. Dynamic Hyper Configuration Protocol

55. IPV4 Address is

A. 8 bit B. 16 bit
C. 32 bit D. 64 bit

56. DNS is the abbreviation of

A. Dynamic Name System
B. Dynamic Network System
C. Domain Name System
D. Domain Network Service

57. What is the meaning of Bandwidth in Network?

A. Transmission capacity of a communication channels
B. Connected Computers in the Network
C. Class of IP used in Network
D. None of the above

58. ADSL is the abbreviation of

A. Asymmetric Dual Subscriber Line
B. Asymmetric Digital System Line
C. Asymmetric Dual System Line
D. Asymmetric Digital Subscriber Line

59. What is the use of Bridge in Network?

A. to connect LANs
B. to separate LANs
C. to control Network Speed
D. All of the above

60. Router operates in which layer of OSI Reference Model?

A. Layer 1 (Physical Layer)
B. Layer 3 (Network Layer)
C. Layer 4 (Transport Layer)
D. Layer 7 (Application Layer)

61. Each IP packet must contain
A. Only Source address
B. Only Destination address
C. Source and Destination address
D. Source or Destination address

62. Bridge works in which layer of the OSI model?
A. Appliation layer B. Transport layer
C. Network layer D. Datalink layer

63. _______ provides a connection-oriented reliable service for sending messages
A. TCP B. IP
C. UDP D. All of the above

64. Which layers of the OSI model are host-to-host layers?
A. Transport, Session, Presentation, Application
B. Network, Transport, Session, Presentation
C. Datalink, Network, Transport, Session
D. Physical, Datalink, Network, Transport

65. Which of the following IP address class is Multicast
A. Class A B. Class B
C. Class C D. Class D

66. Which of the following is correct regarding Class B Address of IP address
A. Network bit – 14, Host bit – 16
B. Network bit – 16, Host bit – 14
C. Network bit – 18, Host bit – 16
D. Network bit – 12, Host bit – 14

67. The last address of IP address represents
A. Unicast address
B. Network address
C. Broadcast address
D. None of the above

68. How many bits are there in the Ethernet address?
A. 64 bits B. 48 bits
C. 32 bits D. 16 bits

69. How many layers are in the TCP/IP model?
A. 4 layers B. 5 layers
C. 6 layers D. 7 layers

70. Which of the following layer of OSI model also called end-to-end layer?
A. Presentation layer B. Network layer
C. Session layer D. Transport layer

ANSWERS

1	2	3	4	5	6	7	8	9	10
B	D	B	A	A	C	C	B	C	A
11	**12**	**13**	**14**	**15**	**16**	**17**	**18**	**19**	**20**
A	A	D	C	D	D	C	A	B	A
21	**22**	**23**	**24**	**25**	**26**	**27**	**28**	**29**	**30**
A	D	A	D	C	C	B	C	C	A
31	**32**	**33**	**34**	**35**	**36**	**37**	**38**	**39**	**40**
B	B	C	A	B	D	D	B	C	A
41	**42**	**43**	**44**	**45**	**46**	**47**	**48**	**49**	**50**
C	D	A	A	D	B	D	A	D	B
51	**52**	**53**	**54**	**55**	**56**	**57**	**58**	**59**	**60**
D	C	D	B	C	C	A	D	A	B
61	**62**	**63**	**64**	**65**	**66**	**67**	**68**	**69**	**70**
C	D	A	A	D	A	C	B	A	D

✤✤✤✤✤

6. E-MAIL

E-mail is an electronic message sent from one computer to another. We can send or receive personal and business-related messages with attachments, such as pictures or formatted documents. We can even send songs and computer programs.

The e-mail communication is incredibly simple. A person with a PC and a modem to connect to the network can communicate with the other(s) so connected to the network. The message can be prepared and sent instantly. The other person finds the e-mail when he checks his mailbox and may reply to the message in the same way. The message sent is private and no other person can read it.

Each user of e-mail service has a user ID or password serving as e-mail address. First thing to do is to get online using modem and communication software. The system requires userid and password. Now the user can prepare his message in the form of a document using a word processor. The e-mail address of the recipient has to be typed in before the message is sent.

With e-mail each person connected to the system is allotted a mailbox and the software required for sending and receiving e-mail. The mailbox is simply a file into which the e-mail system stores electronic documents. The user can check his mailbox for messages over the network. The sender specifies his identify and that of the recipient. The sender then prepares the document or retrieves the stored document and sends it.

E-mail is a document communication facility. To ensure that the recipient also understands the emotions as well, a set of special symbols is used to convey some non-verbal signals. A few of such symbols are given below.

E-mail is the transmission of information electronically from terminal to terminal. The document is prepared in a word processor and is mailed electronically. The basic facilities in e-mail include message creation, message transfer and post delivery service. The e-mail service may be traditional mainframe based or minicomputer based or LAN based system with PCS to access from.

HOW E-MAIL WORKS?

The first thing to be done is to type the message and the e-mail address of the recipient. Once the 'send' button is clicked, this e-mail is sent through the telephone line after its conversion into analog signal by the modem. The e-mail message arrives at our service provider's server. If the server recognizes the e-mail address as valid, the mail will be sent either through the network of the service provider or through internet gateway to the service provider of the recipient.

To send e-mail, we need a connection to the internet and access to a mail server that forwards the mail. The standard protocol used for sending internet e-mail is called SMTP, short for Simple Mail Transfer Protocol. It works in conjunction with POP servers. POP stands for Post Office Protocol.

When we send an e-mail message, our computer routes it to an SMTP server. The server looks at the e-mail address (similar to the address on an envelope), then forwards it to the recipient's mail server. Once the message arrives at the destination mail server, It's stored until the addressee retrieves it. We can send e-mail anywhere in the world to anyone who has an e-mail address.

With the advent of MIME, which stands for Multipurpose Internet Mail Extension, and other types of encoding schemes, we can not only send messages electronically, but we can also send formatted documents, photos, sound files, and video files.

INFRASTRUCTURE REQUIREMENT FOR E-MAIL

- Personal Computer
- Telephone Connection
- Modem
- Mailing software viz., Outlook Express or Netscape communicator or Internet Explorer etc.

ADVANTAGES OF E-MAIL

- Messages can be prepared and sent any time convenient for the sender.
- Message can be received at the convenience of the recipient.
- The transmission takes place instantly and the message gets stored in the mailbox of the recipient.
- The system can confirm delivery of message.
- Copies of message can be sent to multiple recipients.
- It reduces paper work.

DISADVANTAGES

- Recipients must be having e-mail connectivity. They must have computer terminals, modem and telephone.
- They must be subscribing to the same e-mail service provider.
- Poor telecommunication affects the quality of message transmitted.
- Despite all the disadvantages e -mail is a cheap form of information transmission.

INDONET, NICNET, DARTMAIL and ICNET provide this service in India. A user can be a subscriber to such e-mail service providing agencies and use their facility.

MULTIPLE CHOICE QUESTIONS

1. How can you tell the email that you have read from the email that you have not read?
A. The unread mail will be on top
B. The unread mail will be on botton
C. The unread mail will be bold
D. The unread mail will be blue

2. .... is the exchange of computer stored messages by telecommunication.
A. Download B. E-mail
C. Upload D. All of these

3. Which of the following is an advantage of an email?
A. Desired length B. Ease of communication
C. Lower cost D. All of these

4. Spam E-mail is also known as ....
A. Spoof B. Virus
C. Junk D. Draft

5. Which of this is not a medium for E-mail?
A. Intranet B. Paper
C. Extranet D. Internet

6. SMTP stands for:
A. Short Mail Transmission Protocol
B. Small Mail Transmission Protocol
C. Server Mail Transfer Protocol
D. Simple Mail Transfer Protocol

7. In MS Office, ... is the software for managing emails.
A. MS Access B. MS Publisher
C. MS Outlook D. MS Onenote

8. Transmission and delivery of information containing text, image, video, documents etc. to targeted recepient(s) over the Internet is called ....
A. email B. world wide web
C. e-commerce D. social media

9. The first part of email address identifies ....
A. name of individual user
B. name of the email server
C. name of the mobile phone operator
D. name of bank

10. The second part of email address identifies ....
A. name of individual user
B. name of the email server
C. name of the mobile phone operator
D. name of bank

11. The user name and email server parts of an email address are separated by .... symbol.
A. @ B. #
C. $ D. &

12. Gmail.com, yahoo.co.in, ymail .com, rediffmail.com, fastmail.lm, etc. are popular ....
A. FTP servers B. social media sites
C. email servers D. none of them

13. An email may contain non-text information which may be ....
A. uploaded B. downloaded
C. transmitted D. erased

14. An image displayed on web page can be .... to download the file.
A. right click and choose save image as
B. left click
C. double click
D. press delete button

ANSWERS

1	2	3	4	5	6	7	8	9	10
C	B	D	C	B	D	C	A	A	B
11	**12**	**13**	**14**						
A	C	B	A						

✤ ✤ ✤ ✤ ✤

7. DOWNLOADING AND UPLOADING DATA ON WEBSITES

DOWNLOADING AND UPLOADING

The terms downloading and uploading are generally used while browsing the Internet. Receiving data or a file from the Internet on your computer is referred to as "downloading". Uploading refers to the process of sending data or a file from your computer to a remote location on the Internet.

A remote site is one that is physically located in a different location than the user's site.

DOWNLOADING FILES FROM WEB

The process of copying a file (such as a game or utility) from one computer to another through the internet is known as downloading.

The transmission of a file from a server or remote computer system to a user's PC is known as downloading. Downloading a file, from the perspective of an Internet user, is making a request for a file from a server computer and receiving it.

When you download a game from our website, you are transferring it from the author's or publisher's web server to your own computer. This enables you to install and run the software on your own computer.

Using Download, Click Here, etc. types of links on Web pages, downloading photos, articles, and apps from the Internet has become a pleasure.

STEPS TO DOWNLOAD A FILE

To download a file (from a remote server), perform the following steps:

- **Step 1:** Select the software you wish to download by clicking on the download link. There are different websites that may provide download URLs for the same program, select one from them.

  Example: To download zoom on Windows: Go to the URL: "https://zoom.us/download" and then click on the download button.

- **Step 2:** You might be prompted whether you wish to save or run the file from its present location. Select "Save" (if asked).

  Note: Some browsers will choose "Save" for you automatically.

- **Step 3:** A regular "Save As" dialogue box will appear, prompting you to select the folder where you want to save the application or file. Before selecting the "Save" button, select the folder where you want to save the file. Generally, by default: "C:\Download", is chosen.
- **Step 4:** Your file's download will start. Your web browser will display a progress bar that fills up as you download to keep you informed about the download's progress.

In the example above, the file will be saved as "F:\ZoomInstaller.exe".

Depending on the sort of file you downloaded, what follows next is different. Most of the files you download will have one of two extensions.

EXE FILES

.exe files means executable files. It is an application that can be executed. From there, follow the on-screen directions to install the program on your computer and learn how to use it after it's installed.

ZIP FILES

ZIP is a popular file format for compressing and combining files to make them download faster. Some versions of Windows (such as XP and ME) can read ZIP files without the need for additional software. You'll need an unzipping application to read these ZIP files if you don't have one.

UPLOADING A FILE TO REMOTE SITE

The process of transferring data from one remote system to another is referred to as "remote uploading". Some internet file hosting services employ this.

Remote uploading is also utilized in circumstances when the computers that need to share data are on a different high-speed LAN and the remote control is done via a slower dial-up modem connection.

If a website accepts file uploads, it will feature an upload tool to assist with the process. This method is handled differently by each website, however, we'll provide some instances. The site's help sections will usually assist you through the upload process.

Many websites feature a button that opens a dialogue box when you click it.

Downloading is the process of sending a file from a server or remote computer system to a user's computer. From the standpoint of an Internet user, downloading a file entails requesting a file from a server computer and receiving it. The File Transfer Protocol (FTP) is an Internet service that allows you to download and upload data.

Example: Facebook has an upload option that uploads photos/videos on your wall.

STEPS TO UPLOAD A FILE

- **Step 1:** Choose the upload photo/video option.
- **Step 2:** After that, a dialogue box opens for choosing the file to be uploaded. Here we choose an image from the Pictures folder.
- **Step 3:** After choosing the desired image, it will be uploaded to your wall, once you click on the post.

SOME TIPS FOR SAFE DOWNLOADS

- To stay safe if something goes wrong while downloading, close all vital applications.
- Close all apps running on your computer while downloading any file, and only allow one set-up file to execute at a time.
- Scan all files after downloading them, whether from websites or links in e-mails.
- Set up firewalls and antivirus to scan all the things you download on a regular basis.
- Never download things such as music, video, games, or other types of media from untrustworthy websites, and don't rely on recommendations from friends or random online comments.
- To help detect and eliminate viruses and spyware from the application you want to download, keep your antivirus, spam filter, and spyware up to date.
- Before you download anything, make sure your browser settings are secure.
- Only download from websites that are worthy of your time. Don't click on any links on unauthorized websites to download anything.
- If any offensive phrases appear on the website, close the window immediately, regardless of how important it is, because spyware may be placed on your computer as a result of visiting such sites.
- Don't just click the link or file and wait for it to download; instead, download the file and save it where you want it to be saved before running it on the application.
- Read the instructions carefully before installing or running the application. That is to say, read the terms and conditions before proceeding.
- Before you download, check the file's size; it may appear to be extremely small at first, but once you click, the file's size rises.
- Never trust anything that claims that if you click on this link, your computer settings will be modified and your PC will be transformed into an XBOX and you will be able to play infinite games on it.
- Anything that offers you a free download may include dangerous software, so don't accept it.
- Don't download anything until you've read all the website's material and determined whether it's an original company's website.

MULTIPLE CHOICE QUESTIONS

1. What is a key risk associated with allowing unrestricted file uploads on a web application?

A. Enhanced user experience
B. Potential remote code execution
C. Improved server performance
D. Increased data availability

2. How can attackers exploit file upload vulnerabilities to compromise a web application?

A. By injecting SQL queries
B. By uploading files with malicious executable code
C. By encrypting data in transit
D. By enhancing user authentication

3. What is a common security measure to mitigate file upload vulnerabilities?

A. Implementing strong password policies
B. Enforcing network firewalls
C. Validating and restricting file types and sizes
D. Increasing server bandwidth

4. In the context of file uploads, what is the purpose of file type validation?

A. To improve server performance
B. To encrypt data during transmission
C. To ensure files are not corrupted
D. To prevent uploading of malicious files

5. What is a potential consequence of inadequate input validation in file uploads?

A. Improved data integrity
B. Remote code execution
C. Enhanced user experience
D. Increased server bandwidth

6. How can the use of random file names contribute to the security of file uploads?

A. It improves server performance
B. It prevents directory listing attacks
C. It enhances user authentication
D. It encrypts data in transit

7. What is the purpose of implementing a secure file storage location in the context of file uploads?

A. To increase server bandwidth
B. To improve data availability
C. To prevent unauthorized access to uploaded files
D. To enhance user authentication

8. How can content-disposition headers contribute to file download security?

A. By increasing server performance
B. By improving data integrity
C. By specifying how browsers should handle file downloads
D. By encrypting data during transmission

9. In the context of file downloads, what is a potential risk associated with directory traversal attacks?

A. Enhanced user experience
B. Unauthorized access to sensitive files
C. Improved server performance
D. Increased data availability

10. How can a secure file download process contribute to web application security?

A. By improving data availability
B. By encrypting data during transmission
C. By enhancing user authentication
D. By preventing the execution of malicious code

11. What is the purpose of implementing file upload rate limiting in web applications?

A. To improve server performance
B. To enhance user experience
C. To prevent denial-of-service attacks
D. To increase data availability

12. How can a lack of proper file extension validation contribute to file upload vulnerabilities?

A. By increasing server performance
B. By allowing the upload of files with malicious content
C. By enhancing user authentication
D. By improving data integrity

13. What is the primary risk associated with direct object reference in the context of file downloads?

A. Remote code execution
B. Unauthorized access to sensitive files
C. Increased data availability
D. Enhanced user experience

14. How can the use of a Content Delivery Network (CDN) enhance file download security?

A. By increasing server performance
B. By encrypting data during transmission
C. By distributing files across multiple servers
D. By improving user authentication

15. What is the purpose of implementing a secure file upload API in a web application?

A. To prevent directory traversal attacks
B. To improve data integrity
C. To enhance user authentication
D. To enable safe interaction with external services

16. In the context of file uploads, what is the role of client-side validation?

A. To prevent denial-of-service attacks
B. To enhance user experience
C. To improve server performance
D. To ensure the integrity of uploaded files

17. What is a potential consequence of insufficient file permission settings on uploaded files?

A. Improved user experience
B. Unauthorized access to sensitive data
C. Enhanced server performance
D. Increased data availability

18. How can the use of a Content Security Policy (CSP) header help mitigate file download vulnerabilities?

A. By encrypting data during transmission
B. By preventing the execution of malicious code in downloaded files
C. By improving user authentication
D. By increasing server bandwidth

19. What is the purpose of validating file content, not just file extension, during the file upload process?

A. To improve server performance
B. To enhance user experience
C. To prevent the upload of files with malicious content
D. To increase data availability

20. How can the use of secure hash algorithms contribute to file download security?

A. By preventing denial-of-service attacks
B. By improving server performance
C. By enhancing user experience
D. By ensuring the integrity of downloaded files

21. What is the purpose of "WebDAV" (Web-based Distributed Authoring and Versioning)?

A. File compression
B. Web content creation and editing
C. High-speed file transfers
D. Secure file storage

22. Which command is used to view the current working directory on the remote server in FTP?

A. PWD B. DIR
C. LS D. CD

23. In FTP, what is the purpose of "Active mode"?

A. A mode for high-speed data transfer
B. A mode for passive data transfer
C. A mode where the client initiates the data connection
D. A mode for secure file transfers

24. Which FTP command is used to create a new directory on the remote server?

A. MKDIR B. NEWDIR
C. CREATE D. ADDDIR

25. What is the primary purpose of FTP over SSL/TLS (FTPS)?

A. High-speed file transfers
B. Secure file transfers with encryption
C. Text-based file transfers
D. Simplified file management

ANSWERS

1	2	3	4	5	6	7	8	9	10
B	B	C	D	B	B	C	C	B	D
11	**12**	**13**	**14**	**15**	**16**	**17**	**18**	**19**	**20**
C	B	B	C	D	B	B	B	C	D
21	**22**	**23**	**24**	**25**					
B	A	C	A	B					

✤✤✤✤✤

GENERAL STUDIES

1

Indian History

ANCIENT INDIA

INDUS VALLEY CIVILISATION (2500-1750 BC)

- The earliest excavations in the Indus valley were done at Harappa in the West Punjab and Mohenjodaro in Sindh. Both places are now in Pakistan.

Important Sites

- The most important sites are Kot Diji in Sindh, Kalibangan in Rajasthan, Ropar in the Punjab, Banawali in Haryana, Lothal, Surkotada and Dhaulavira, all the three in Gujarat.
- Mohenjodaro is the largest of all the Indus cities and it is estimated to have spread over an area of 200 hectares.

Indus Valley Civilisation : An Objective Study

Major Sites	*Excavators*	*Year*	*River*	*Location*	*Important Findings*
1. Harappa	D.R. Sahni	1921	Ravi	West Punjab (Pakistan)	Granaries, Virgin Goddess, Cemetery, Stone symbol of Lingam and Yoni
2. Mohenjodaro	R.D. Banerjee	1922	Indus	Sindh (Pakistan)	Great Bath, Great Granary, Assembly Hall, Proto-Shiva, Brick Kilns, Mesopotamian seals
3. Chanhudaro	N.G. Mazumdar	1931	Indus	Sindh (Pakistan)	Bronze toy cart, Ink-pot, Lipstick, City without a citadel
4. Kalibangan	B.B. Lal & B.K. Thapar	1953	Ghaggar	Ganganagar (Rajasthan)	Decorated bricks, ploughed field surface, Firealtars
5. Lothal	S.R. Rao	1957	Bhogwa	Ahmedabad (Gujarat)	Dockyard, Rice husk, Fire altars, Double burial
6. Banawali	R.S. Bist	1973	Ghaggar	Hissar (Haryana)	Toy plough, Gridiron pattern of Town planning.
7. Dholavira	R.S. Bist	1990	Luni	Kutchh (Gujarat)	A Large well & a bath, A stadium
8. Surkotada	J. Joshi	1964	—	Gujarat	Bones of Horse, Pot burials

Salient Features of the Harappan Culture

- The Harappan Civilization was primarily Urban.
- Mohenjodaro and Harappa were the planned cities.
- The large-scale use of burnt bricks in almost all kinds of constructions are the important characteristics of the Harappan culture.
- Another remarkable feature was the underground drainage system connecting all houses to the street drains which were covered by stone slabs or bricks.
- The most important public place of Mohenjodaro is the Great Bath measuring 39 feet length, 23 feet breadth and 8 feet depth.
- Agriculture was the most important occupation. In the fertile soils, farmers cultivated two crops a year. They were the first who had grown paddy.
- Wheat and barley were the main crops grown besides sesame, mustard and cotton.
- Animals like sheep, goats and buffalo were domesticated. The use of horse is not yet firmly established.
- Bronze and copper vessels are the outstanding examples of the Harappan metal craft.
- A large number of seals numbering more than 2000 have been discovered.

Social Life

- Jewelleries such as bangles, bracelets, fillets, girdles, anklets, ear-rings and finger rings were worn by women. These ornaments were made of gold, silver, copper, bronze and semi precious stones.
- Fishing was a regular occupation while hunting and bull fighting were other pastimes.

- Manufacture of terracotta (burnt clay) was a major industry of the people.
- Figures of animals such as sacred bull and dove were discovered. The figures of Mother Goddesses were used for religious purposes.
- Most of the inscriptions were engraved on seals. It is interesting to note that the Indus script has not yet been deciphered.
- The Pipal tree was used as a religious symbol.
- The origin of the '*Swastika*' symbol can be traced to the Harrapan Civilization.
- The chief male deity was Pasupati, (proto-Siva) represented in seals as sitting in a yogic posture with three faces and two horns.

THE VEDIC PERIOD

RIG VEDIC AGE (1500 - 1000 B.C.)

- The Early Vedic period is known from the *Rig Veda*.
- The *Rig Veda* refers to Saptasindhu or the land of seven rivers. This includes the five rivers of the Punjab, namely, Jhelum, Chenab, Ravi, Beas and Sutlej along with the Indus and Saraswati.
- Historians view that the Aryans came from Central Asia. They entered India through the Khyber pass between 2000 B.C. and 1500 B.C. They first settled in seven places in the Punjab region which they called Sapta Sindhu. Slowly, they moved towards the Gangetic Valley.
- The Aryan Civilisation was a rural civilisation.

Vedic Literature

- The word 'Veda' is derived from the root 'vid', which means to know and signifies 'superior knowledge'.
- The Vedic literature consists of the four Vedas – Rig, Yajur, Sama and Atharva.
- The *Rig Veda* is the earliest of the four Vedas divided into 10 mandalas and it consists of 1028 hymns. The hymns were sung by *Hotri* in praise of various gods.
- The *Yajur Veda* consists of various details of rules to be observed at the time of sacrifice. Its hymns were recited by *Adharvayus*.
- The *Sama Veda* is set to tune for the purpose of chanting during sacrifice. It is called the book of chants and the origins of Indian music are traced in it. Its hymns were recited by *Udgatri*.
- The *Atharva Veda* contains details of rituals.
- Besides the Vedas, there are other sacred works like the Brahmanas, the Aranyakas, the Upanishads, and the epics Ramayana and Mahabharata.

Political Organisation

- During this period, the kingdom was tribal in character. Each tribe formed a separate kingdom.
- The basic unit of political organisation was *kula* or family.
- The highest political unit was called *jana* or tribe.
- There were several tribal kingdoms during the Rig Vedic period such as Bharatas, Matsyas, Yadus and Purus. The head of the kingdom was called as *rajan* or king.
- There were two popular bodies called the *Sabha* and *Samiti*. The former seems to have been a council of elders and the latter, a general assembly of the entire people.

Social Life

- Family was the basis of the society.
- The head of the family was known as *grihapathi*.

Economic Condition

- The Rig Vedic Aryans were pastoral people and their main occupation was cattle rearing. Their wealth was estimated in terms of their cattle.
- Carpentry was another important profession.

RELIGION

- The important Rig Vedic gods were Prithvi (Earth), Agni (Fire), Vayu (Wind), Varuna (Rain) and Indra (Thunder).
- Indra was the most popular among them during the early Vedic period.
- There were also female gods like Aditi and Ushas. There were no temples and no idol worship during the early Vedic period.

Rigvedic Rivers

River	Name in Rigveda
Indus	Sindhu
Jhelum	Vitasta
Chenab	Asikni
Ravi	Parushini
Beas	Vipasa
Sutlej	Sutudri
Gomati	Gomal
Saraswati	Sarasvati
Ghaggar	Prishadavati

LATER VEDIC PERIOD (1000–600 B.C.)

- This age is also called as the Epic Age because the two great epics the Ramayana and Mahabharata were written during this period.
- The Sama, Yajur, Atharva Vedas, Brahmanas, Aranyakas, Upanishads and the two epics are the sources of information for this period.

Political Organisation

- Larger kingdoms were formed during the later Vedic period.
- The king performed various rituals and sacrifices to strengthen his position.

- They include Rajasuya (consecration ceremony), Asvamedha (horse sacrifice) and Vajpeya (chariot race).
- Kingship became hereditary.
- Kings assumed titles like Ekrat, Samrat and Sarvabhauma.

Economic Condition

- Iron was used extensively in this period and this enabled the people to clear forests and to bring more land under cultivation. Agriculture became the chief occupation.
- Taxes like Bali, Sulk and Bhaga were collected from the people.
- Wealth was calculated in terms of cows.

Social Life

- The four divisions of society (Brahmins, Kshatriyas, Vaisyas and Sudras) or the Varna system was thoroughly established during the Later Vedic period.
- The Ashrama system was formed to attain 4 purusharthas. They were *Dharma*, *Artha*, *Kama* and *Moksha*.

Religion

- Gods of the Early Vedic period like Indra and Agni lost their importance. Prajapathi (the creator), Vishnu (the protector) and Rudra (the destroyer) became prominent during the Later Vedic period.

JAINISM AND BUDDHISM

JAINISM

- Jainism originated in the 6th century B.C. It rejected Vedic religion and avoided its rituals.
- Founded by Rishabha Deva. Rishabha Deva was succeeded by 23 Thirthankaras (prophets). Mahavira was the 24th Thirthankara.

Vardhamana Mahavira (540-468 B.C.)

- Vardhamana was born in a village called Kundagrama near Vaishali in Bihar.
- His father was *Siddhartha*. He was the head of a famous Kshatriya clan.
- His mother was *Trisala*. She was a princess of the Lichchhavi clan. She was the sister of the ruler of Vaishali.
- Vardhamana was married to *Yasoda,* a princess. They had a daughter.
- At the age of 30, he left his home and family. He became an ascetic (monk). He wandered from place-to-place in search of truth for 12 years.
- In the 13th year of his penance, he attained the highest spiritual knowledge called Kevalya or Jnana. Thereafter, he was called Mahavira and Jina. His followers were called Jains and his religion Jainism.
- He died at the age of 72 in 468 B.C. at a place called Pavapuri near modern Rajgir in Bihar.

Teachings of Jainism

- The three principles of Jainism, also known as Triratnas (three gems), are:
  1. right faith.
  2. right knowledge.
  3. right conduct.
- Mahavira preached his disciples to follow the five principles. They are:
  1. Ahimsa—not to injure any living beings
  2. Satya—to speak the truth
  3. Asteya—not to steal
  4. Tyag—not to own property
  5. Brahmacharia—to lead a virtuous life.

Spread of Jainism

- Mahavira preached his religion in Prakrit language which was the language of the masses.
- Chandragupta Maurya, Kharavela of Kalinga and the royal dynasties of south India such as the Gangas, the Kadambas, the Chalukyas and the Rashtrakutas patronised Jainism.
- Jainism was divided into two sects after Vallabhi Council, namely *Svetambaras* (wearing white dresses) under Sthulbhadra and *Digambaras* (naked) under Bhadrabahu.
- The first Jain Council was convened at Pataliputra by Sthulabahu, the leader of the *Digambaras*, in the beginning of the 3rd century B.C.
- The second Jain Council was held at Vallabhi in 5th century A.D. The final compilation of Jain literature called *Twelve Angas* was completed in this council.

BUDDHISM

Gautama Buddha (563-483 B.C.)

- Buddha's original name was *Siddhartha.*
- Siddhartha was born in the Lumbini Garden near Kapilavastu in Nepal. His father was Suddhodana. He was a Sakya chief of Kapilavastu. His mother, Mayadevi, died when Siddhartha was only seven days old. He was brought up by his step mother Mahaprajapati Gauthami.
- At the age of sixteen Siddhartha, married Yasodhara and gave birth to a son, Rahul.
- The sight of an old man, a diseased man, a corpse and an ascetic turned him away from worldly life. He left home at the age of twenty-nine in search of Truth.
- He wandered for seven years and at last, he sat under a bodhi tree at Bodh Gaya in Bihar and did intense penance, after which he got Enlightenment (Nirvana) at the age of thirty-five. Since then, he became known as the Buddha or 'the Enlightened One'.
- Buddha delivered his first sermon at Sarnath near Banaras (now Varanasi).
- He died at the age of 80 in 483 B.C. at Kushinagar in Uttar Pradesh.

Teachings of Buddha

- The Four Noble Truths of Buddha are:
  1. The world is full of suffering.
  2. The cause of suffering is desire.
  3. If desires are get rid off, suffering can be removed.
  4. This can be done by following the Eightfold Path.
- The Eightfold Path consists of:
  1. Right Thought.
  2. Right Belief.
  3. Right Speech.
  4. Right Action.
  5. Right Living.
  6. Right Efforts.
  7. Right Knowledge.
  8. Right Meditation.

Buddhist Literature

- In Pali language.
- Buddhist scriptures in Pali are commonly referred to as *Tripitakas, i.e.*, 'Three Baskets'.
- ***Vinaya Pitaka:*** Rules of discipline in Buddhist monasteries.
- ***Sutta Pitaka:*** Largest, contains collection of Buddha's sermons.
- ***Abidhamma Pitaka:*** Explanation of the philosophical principles of the Buddhist religion.

Main Buddhist Councils

Buddhist Council	Time	Place	Chairman	Patron
First	483 BC	Rajagriha	Mahakashyapa	Ajatasatru
Second	383 BC	Vaishali	Sabakamuni	Kalashoka
Third	250 BC	Patliputra	Moggaliputta Tissa	Ashoka
Fourth	AD 72	Kundalvana	Vasumitra, Ashwaghosa	Kanishka

The Mahajanapadas

Mahajanapadas	Capital
1. Kashi	Varanasi
2. Kosala	Shravasti
3. Anga	Champanagri
4. Magadh	Girivraj or Rajgriha
5. Vajji	Vaishali
6. Malla	Kushinagar and Pavapuri
7. Chedi	Shuktimati
8. Vatsa	Kaushambi
9. Kuru	Hastinapur, Indraprastha and Isukara
10. Panchal	Ahichhatra and Kampilya
11. Matsya	Viratnagar
12. Surasen	Mathura
13. Asmaka	Paudanya
14. Avanti	Ujjaini
15. Gandhara	Taxila
16. Kamboj	Rajpur (Hatak)

DYNASTIES OF ANCIENT INDIA

HARYANKA DYNASTY

- Bimbisara was the founder of Haryanka Dynasty.
- He was a contemporary of both Vardhamana Mahavira and Gautama Buddha.
- During his rule, Darius I, the Achaemenian emperor, conquered the Indus Valley area.
- Ajatasatru imprisoned his father Bimbisara.
- The first Buddhist Council was convened by Ajatasatru at Rajgir.
- The immediate successor of Ajatasatru was Udayin.
- Udayin laid the foundation of the new capital at Pataliputra situated at the confluence of the two rivers, the Ganges and the Sone.
- Shishunaga was the founder of Shishunaga dynasty.
- After Shishunaga, the mighty empire began to collapse. His successor was Kakavarman or Kalasoka. During his reign, the second Buddhist Council was held at Vaishali.
- Kalasoka was killed by the founder of the Nanda dynasty.

NANDAS

- The fame of Magadha scaled new heights under the Nanda dynasty.
- Mahapadmananda was the founder of Nanda rule in Magadha.
- The last Nanda ruler was Dhana Nanda. Alexander invaded India during his rule.

MAURYAN EMPIRE

CHANDRAGUPTA MAURYA (322–298 B.C.)

- Chandragupta Maurya was the founder of the Mauryan Empire. He overthrew Nanda dynasty with the help of Chanakya.
- Chandragupta defeated Seleukos Nikator, the Greek general of Alexander, in a battle in 305 B.C.
- Seleukos sent Megasthenes as Greek Ambassador to the Court of Chandragupta. Megasthenes wrote *Indica*.

- Chandragupta was a follower of Jainism.
- He came to Sravana Belgola, near Mysore with a Jain monk called Bhadrabahu. The hill in which he lived until his death is called Chandragiri.
- Chanakya served as prime minister during the reigns of Chandragupta and Bindusara.

BINDUSARA (298–273 B.C.)

- Chandragupta Maurya was succeeded by his son Bindusara.
- Bindusara was called by the Greeks as "*Amitraghatha*" meaning, slayer of enemies.

ASHOKA (273–232 B.C.)

- Ashoka was the most famous ruler of the Mauryan dynasty.
- The most important event of Ashoka's reign was his victorious war with Kalinga in 261 B.C.
- Ashoka convened the Third Buddhist Council at Pataliputra around 250 B.C. in order to strengthen the *Sangha*. It was presided over by Moggaliputta Tissa.
- Ashoka's edicts and inscriptions were deciphered by James Prinsep in 1837.
- The last Mauryan king, Brahadratha was killed by his minister Pushyamitra Sunga. It put an end to the Mauryan Empire.

SUNGAS

- The founder of the Sunga dynasty was *Pushyamitra Sunga*, who was the commander-in-chief under the Mauryas.
- He ascended the throne of Magadha in 185 B.C.
- Pushyamitra was a staunch follower of Brahmanism. He performed two asvamedha sacrifices.
- After the death of Pushyamitra, his son Agnimitra became the ruler.
- Agnimitra was a great conqueror. He was also the hero of the play *Malavikagnimitram* written by Kalidasa.

KANVA

- The last Sunga ruler was Devabhuti, who was murdered by his minister Vasudeva Kanva, the founder of the *Kanva dynasty*.
- The Kanva dynasty ruled for 45 years. After the fall of the Kanvas, the history of Magadha was a blank until the establishment of the Gupta dynasty.

SATAVAHANAS

- The founder of the Satavahana dynasty was Simuka.
- The greatest ruler of the Satavahana dynasty was *Gautamiputra Satakarni.*
- The greatest port of the Satavahanas was Kalyani on the west Deccan. Gandakasela and Ganjam on the east coast were the other important seaports.
- The fine painting at Amaravathi and Nagarjunakonda caves belong to this period.

SANGAM AGE (300 B.C. TO A.D. 300)

- The Sangam Age constitutes an important chapter in the history of South India.
- According to Tamil legends, there existed three Sangams (Academy of Tamil poets) in ancient Tamil Nadu popularly called Muchchangam. These Sangams flourished under the royal patronage of the Pandyas.
- *The first Sangam*, held at then Madurai, chaired by Agastya.
- *The second Sangam* was held at Kapadapuram, chaired by Tolkappiyar.
- *The third Sangam* at Madurai was founded by Mudathirumaran.

Political History

- The Tamil country was ruled by three dynasties namely the Chera, Chola and Pandyas during the Sangam Age.

CHERAS

- The Cheras ruled over parts of modern Kerala. Their capital was Vanji and their important seaports were Tondi and Musiris.
- The greatest Chera King was *Senguttuvan.*

CHOLAS

- The Chola kingdom of the Sangam period extended from modern Tiruchi district to southern Andhra Pradesh.
- Their capital was first located at Uraiyur and then shifted to Puhar. Kaveripattinam served as their port.

GUPTA PERIOD

- The Gupta period is considered as the *Golden Age* in the history of India because this period witnessed all round developments in Religion, Literature, Science, Art and Architecture.

CHANDRAGUPTA I (320-334 A.D.)

- In the beginning of the 4th Century A.D., Sri Gupta established a small Kingdom at Pataliputra. He is considered as the founder of the Gupta dynasty.
- The first notable ruler of the Gupta dynasty was Chandragupta I. He assumed the title *Maharajadhiraja.* The Meherauli Iron Pillar inscription mentions his extensive conquests.
- Chandragupta I is considered to be the founder of the Gupta era which starts with his accession in A.D. 320.

SAMUDRAGUPTA (335-380 A.D.)

- Samudragupta was the greatest of the rulers of the Gupta dynasty. The Allahabad Pillar inscription provides a detailed account of his reign.

- Because of his military achievements, Samudragupta was hailed as '*Indian Napoleon*'.

CHANDRAGUPTA II (380-414 A.D.)

- Samudragupta was succeeded by his son Chandragupta II Vikramaditya.
- The greatest of the military achievements of Chandragupta II was his war against the Saka *satraps* of western India.
- The famous Chinese pilgrim, Fahien visited India (A.D. 399 - A.D. 414) during the reign of Chandragupta II.

SUCCESSORS OF CHANDRAGUPTA II

- Kumaragupta (415-455) was the son and successor of Chandragupta II. His reign was marked by general peace and prosperity.
- Kumaragupta was the founder of the Nalanda University.
- Kumaragupta was followed by *Skandagupta* who ruled from A.D. 456 to A.D. 468.
- After Skandagupta's death, many of his successors like Purugupta, Narasimhagupta, Buddhagupta and Baladitya could not save the Gupta empire from the Huns. Ultimately, the Gupta power totally disappeared due to the Hun invasions and later by the rise of Yasodharman in Malwa.

PUSHYABHUTI DYNASTY (600 - 647 A.D.)

- The greatest king was *Harshavardhana*, son of Prabhakar Vardhana of Thaneshwar. He shifted the capital to *Kannauj*.
- *Hieun Tsang* visited during his reign.
- He established a large monastery at Nalanda. Banabhata adorned his court, wrote Harshacharita and Kadambari. Harsha himself wrote three plays–Priyadarshika, Ratnawali and Nagananda.

PALLAVAS

- The Pallavas established their kingdom in Tondaimandalam by Simhavishnu with its capital at Kanchipuram.
- Other great Pallava rulers were Mahendravarman I, Narasimhavarman I, and Narasimhavarman II.
- The *Kailasanatha temple* at Kanchipuram is the greatest architectural masterpiece of the Pallava art.

CHALUKYAS (543-755 A.D.)

- Pulakesin I was the founder of the Chalukya dynasty. He established a small kingdom with Vatapi or Badami as its capital.
- The structural temples of the Chalukyas exist at Aihole, Badami and Pattadakal (Virupaksha temple). Cave temple architecture was also famous under the Chalukyas. Their cave temples are found in Ajanta, Ellora and Nasik.

RASHTRAKUTAS (755-975 A.D.)

- The art and architecture of the Rashtrakutas were found at Ellora and Elephanta.

CHOLAS

- Cholas became prominent in the ninth century and established an empire comprising the major portion of South India. Their capital was Tanjore.
- The founder of the Chola kingdom was Vijayalaya.
- Rajaraja Chola built the famous Brihadeeswara temple at Tanjore.
- *Dancing Figure of Shiva* (Nataraja) belong to Chola period.

MEDIEVAL INDIA

ARAB CONQUEST OF SIND

- In 712 A.D., Muhammad bin Quasim invaded Sind. Quasim defeated Dahir, the ruler of Sind and killed him in a well-contested battle.

Mahmud of Ghazni

- In 1024, Mahmud marched from Multan across Rajaputana, defeated the Solanki King Bhimadeva I, plundered Anhilwada and sacked the famous temple of Somanatha. This was his last campaign in India. Mahmud died in 1030 A.D.
- Mahmud patronized art and literature. *Firdausi* was the poet-laureate in the court of Mahmud.

Muhammad Ghori

- Prithviraj Chauhan defeated Ghori in the first battle of Tarain near Delhi in 1191 A.D.
- In the Second Battle of Tarain in 1192, Muhammad Ghori thoroughly routed the army of Prithiviraj, who was captured and killed.
- After his brilliant victory over Prithviraj at Tarain, Muhammad Ghori returned to Ghazni leaving behind his favourite general Qutb-ud-din Aibak to make further conquests in India.

SULTANATE PERIOD

SLAVE DYNASTY (1206-1290)

- The Slave dynasty was also called Mamluk dynasty. Mamluk was the Quranic term for slave.

Qutb-ud-din Aibak

- Qutb-ud-din Aibak was a slave of Muhammad Ghori, who made him the Governor of his Indian possessions.

- After the death of Ghori in 1206, Aibak declared his independence. He assumed the title Sultan and made Lahore his capital.
- Muslim writers call Aibak Lakh Baksh or giver of lakhs because he gave liberal donations to them.
- He built the famous Quwat-Ul-Islam mosque at Delhi. He began the construction of the famous Qutb Minar at Delhi but did not live long to complete it. It was later completed by Iltutmish.

Iltutmish (1210-1236 A.D.)

- Iltutmish belonged to the Ilbari tribe and hence his dynasty was named as Ilbari dynasty.
- He shifted his capital from Lahore to Delhi.
- He organised the *Iqta system* and introduced reforms in civil administration and army.

Raziya (1236-1240 A.D.)

- She appointed an Abyssinian slave Yakuth as Master of the Royal Horses.
- In 1240, Altunia, the governor of Bhatinda revolted against her. She went in personally to suppress the revolt but Altunia killed Yakuth and took Raziya prisoner.
- Bahram Shah, son of Iltutmish killed her.

Balban (1266-1286 A.D.)

- Balban introduced rigorous court discipline and new customs such as prostration and kissing the Sultan's feet to prove his superiority over the nobles.
- He also introduced the Persian festival of *Nauroz* to impress the nobles and people with his wealth and power.
- He established a separate military department - *diwan-i-arz* – and reorganized the army.

KHILJI DYNASTY (1290-1320 A.D.)

- The founder of the Khilji dynasty was Jalaluddin Khilji.
- Ala-ud-din Khilji was the greatest ruler of the Khilji Dynasty.
- He was the first Muslim ruler to extend his empire right upto Rameshwaram in the South.
- The Sultan had built a new city called Siri near Delhi.
- Amir Khusrau the great Persian poet, patronised by Balban, continued to live in Ala-ud-din Khilji's court also.
- He introduced the system of *dagh* (branding of horses) and prepared *huliya* (descriptive list of soldiers).
- Ala-ud-din Khilji maintained a large permanent standing army and paid them in cash from the royal treasury.

TUGHLAQ DYNASTY

- Ghiyas-ud-din Tughlaq was the founder of the Tughlaq dynasty.
- To have the capital at the centre of the empire and safe from the Mongol raids, Tughlaq chose Devagiri as his new capital in A.D. 1327. The Sultan renamed the new capital Daulatabad.
- In 1329-30, Muhammad-bin-Tughlaq introduced a token currency.
- Firoz Shah Tughlaq became Sultan after the death of Muhammad-bin-Tughlaq in A.D. 1351.
- He was the first Sultan to impose irrigation tax.
- He had built new towns of Firozabad, Jaunpur, Hissar and Firozpur.
- Timur—Mongol leader of Central Asia, ordered general massacre in Delhi (AD 1398) at the time of Nasiruddin Mahmud (later Tughlaq king).

SAYYID DYNASTY

- Before his departure from India, Timur appointed Khizr Khan as governor of Multan. He captured Delhi and founded the Sayyid dynasty in 1414.
- Mubarak Shah, Mohammed Shah and Alam Shah were some of the other important noteworthy rulers of Sayyid Dynasty.

LODHI DYNASTY

- The Lodhis were Afghans.
- Bahlol Lodhi was the first Afghan ruler while his predecessors were all Turks. He died in 1489 and was succeeded by his son, Sikandar Lodhi.
- In 1504, Sikandar Lodhi founded the city of Agra and transferred his capital from Delhi to Agra.
- Babar marched against Delhi and defeated and killed Ibrahim Lodhi in the first battle of Panipat (1526).

BAHMANI AND VIJAYANAGAR KINGDOMS

- The break up of the Delhi Sultanate provided an opportunity for the rise of a number of kingdoms in the Deccan.
- After the decline of the Tughlaqs, there arose two important kingdoms in the Deccan. They were the Bahmani and Vijayanagar kingdoms.

VIJAYANAGAR EMPIRE

- The Vijayanagar Kingdom was set up in A.D. 1336. Its aim was to check the spread of Muslim power and protect Hindu Dharma in South India.
- Four dynasties – Sangama, Saluva, Tuluva and Aravidu – ruled Vijayanagar from A.D. 1336 to 1672.
- Vijayanagar was founded in 1336 by Harihara and Bukka of the Sangama dynasty.
- The Moroccan traveller, Ibn Batuta, Venetian traveller Nicolo de Conti, Persian traveller Abdur Razzak and the Portuguese traveller Domingo Paes were among them who left valuable accounts on the socio-economic conditions of the Vijayanagar Empire.

- The Hampi ruins and other monuments of Vijayanagar provide information on the cultural contributions of the Vijayanagar rulers.

KRISHNA DEVA RAYA (1509-1530)

- The Tuluva dynasty was founded by Vira Narasimha.
- The greatest of the Vijayanagar rulers, Krishna Deva Raya belonged to the Tuluva dynasty.
- Krishna Deva Raya himself authored a Telugu work, *Amukthamalyadha* and Sanskrit works, *Jambavati Kalyanam* and *Ushaparinayam*.
- He built the famous *Vittalaswamy* and *Hazara Ramaswamy* temples at Vijayanagar.
- Krishna Deva Raya renovated Virupaksha temple in A.D. 1510.
- After his death the enemies of Vijayanagar joined together and defeated the Vijayanagar ruler in the battle of Talaikota.

BAHMANI KINGDOM

- The founder of the Bahmani kingdom was Alauddin Bahman Shah also known as Hasan Gangu in 1347. Its capital was Gulbarga.
- Ahmad Wali Shah shifted the capital from Gulbarga to Bidar.
- *Gol Gumbaj* was built by *Muhammad Adil Shah*; it is famous for the so called '*Whispering Gallery*'.
- *Quli Qutub Shah* built the famous *Golcunda Fort*.

MUGHAL EMPIRE (1526-1707 AD)

BABAR (1526-1530 AD)

- Babar was the founder of the Mughal Empire in India.
- On 21st April, 1526 the first Battle of Panipat took place between Babar and Ibrahim Lodhi, who was killed in the battle.
- Babar was the first one to use guns or artillery in a battle on the Indian soil.
- Babar defeated Rana Sanga of Mewar in the battle of Kanwah in A.D. 1527.
- Babar was a soldier-scholar and wrote his own autobiography called Babar Nama in Turkish language.

HUMAYUN (1530-1556 AD)

- Sher Shah defeated Humayun at Chausa in A.D. 1539 and again at Kannauj in A.D. 1540.
- After losing his kingdom, Humayun became an exile for the next fifteen years.
- In 1555, Humayun defeated the Afghans and recovered the Mughal throne.
- After six months, he died in 1556 due to his fall from the staircase of his library.
- *Gulbadan Begum*, Humayun's half-sister wrote *Humayun-nama*.

SHER SHAH SURI

- The founder of the Sur dynasty was Sher Shah, whose original name was Farid.
- Sher Shah became the ruler of Delhi in 1540.
- Sher Shah organized a brilliant administrative system. The central government consisted of several departments.
- He built a new city on the banks of the river Yamuna near Delhi.
- Now the old fort called Purana Quila and its mosque is alone surviving.
- He built a Mausoleum at Sasaram, which is considered as one of the master pieces of Indian architecture.

AKBAR (1556-1605 AD)

- When Akbar ascended the throne in A.D. 1556 he was only 14 years old. His guardian Bairam Khan served him as a faithful minister and tutor.
- Bairam Khan, along with Akbar met Hemu in the second Battle of Panipat in 1556. Hemu was initially successful, but lost his consciousness after an arrow hit him. Akbar killed him.
- The Battle of Haldighati was fought between Rana Pratap of Mewar and Mughal army led by Man Singh and Asif Khan. Some historian say that this battle was indecisive but some say that Rana Pratap was defeated.
- Akbar abolished the pilgrim tax and in 1562, he abolished Jaziya.
- Akbar evolved a new faith called Din-i-Illahi or Divine Faith.

JAHANGIR (1605-1627 AD)

- When Akbar died, Prince Salim succeeded with the title Jahangir (Conqueror of World) in 1605.
- Jahangir's eldest son, Khusrau, rebelled against him. He was arrested and put into prison.
- *Guru Arjun Dev, the fifth Sikh Guru* was executed by Jahangir.
- In 1611, Jahangir married Mehrunnisa who was known as Nurjahan (Light of World).
- Jahangir died in A.D. 1627.

SHAHJAHAN (1628-1658 AD)

- The reign of Shahjahan is generally considered as the *Golden Age* of the Mughal period.
- Shahjahan is called as the *Prince of Builders*. He had built the Jama Masjid and Red Fort in Delhi and Taj Mahal in Agra.
- Fine arts like painting, music and literature reached high level of development during Shahjahan's time.

AURANGAZEB (1658-1707 AD)

- Aurangazeb was the last great Mughal ruler. He ascended the throne after killing his three brothers Dara, Shuja and Murad in a fratricidal war.
- Aurangazeb defeated Sikandar Shah of Bijapur and annexed his kingdom.
- Aurangazeb was against the Sikhs and he executed the ninth Sikh Guru Tegh Bahadur.
- He was called *Darvesh* or a *Zinda Pir*. He forbade *Sati*. Conquered Bijapur (AD 1686) and Golconda (AD 1687) and reimposed Jaziya and Pilgrim tax in AD 1679.
- He built *Biwi ka Makbara* on the tomb of his queen *Rabaud-Durani* at Aurangabad; *Moti Masjid* within Red Fort, Delhi; and the Jami or Badshahi Mosque at Lahore.
- Aurangazeb died in A.D. 1707.

LATER MUGHALS / FALL OF THE MUGHALS

Bahadur Shah (1707-1712)

- Assumed the title of *Shah Alam I*.

Jahandar Shah (1712-1713)

- First puppet Mughal emperor. He abolished *jaziya*.

Farrukhsiyar (1713-1719)

Mohammad Shah (1719-1748)

- Nadir Shah (*of Iran*) defeated him in the Battle of Karnal (1739) and took away *Peacock throne* and *Kohinoor diamond*.

Ahmad Shah (1748-1754)

Alamgir II (1754-1759),

Shah Alam II (1759-1806)

Akbar II (1806-1837)

- He gave Ram Mohan Roy the title '*Raja*'. He sent Raja Ram Mohan Roy to London to seek a raise in his allowance.

Bahadur Shah II (1837-1857)

- He was confined by the British to the Red Fort. During the revolt of 1857, he was proclaimed the Emperor by the rebels. He was deported to Rangoon after that.

Literature of Mughal Period

Author	Work
Babar	Tuzuk-i-Babari
Abul Fazal	Ain-i-Akbari, Akbarnamah
Jahangir	Tuzuk-i-Jahangiri
Hamid	Padshahnama
Darashikoh	Majm-ul-Bahrain
Mirza Md Qasim	Alamgirnama

THE MARATHAS

SHIVAJI (1627-1680 AD)

- Shivaji was born at Shivner in 1627. His father was Shahji Bhonsle and mother Jija Bai.
- His religious teacher was Samarth Ramdas and guardian was Dadaji Kondadev.
- In 1674, Shivaji crowned himself at Raigarh and assumed the title Chatrapathi.
- *Ashtapradhan* (eight ministers) helped in administration. These were Peshwas, Sar-i-Naubat (Military), Mazumdar or Amatya (Accounts); Waqenavis (Intelligence); Surnavis (Corres-pondence); *Dabir* or *Sumanta* (Ceremonies); *Nyayadhish* (Justice); and *Panditrao* (Charity).
- Successors of Shivaji were Shambhaji, Rajaram and *Shahu* (fought at Battle of Khed in AD 1708).

THE PESHWAS

- Balaji Vishwanath was the first Peshwa. He began his career as a small revenue official and became Peshwa in 1713. Baji Rao I was the eldest son of Balaji Vishwanath. He was considered as the "greatest exponent of guerilla tactics after Shivaji".
- It was during reign of Balaji Baji Rao (Nanasaheb) when the Marathas lost the Third Battle of Panipat.
- Baji Rao II (last Peshwa) was the first Maratha to have fled from the British attacks instead of fighting with them. Baji Rao II surrendered to Sir John Malcom.

THE SIKH

- Guru Nanak Dev was the founder of Sikhism, the religion that draws its elements from both Hinduism and Islam.
- Name of the ten Sikh Gurus and their works are given below:
  1. **Guru Nanak Dev (1469-1539AD):** The founder of Sikhism.
  2. **Guru Angad Dev (1504-1552AD):** Developed Gurmukhi.
  3. **Guru Amar Das (1479-1574AD):** Struggled against Sati system and Purdah system.
  4. **Guru Ram Das (1534-1581AD):** Founded Amritsar, the holy city of Sikhism.
  5. **Guru Arjun Dev (1563-1606AD):** He built the *Swarn Mandir* (Golden Temple).
  6. **Guru Hargobind (1595-1644 AD):** Established Akal Takht.
  7. **Guru Har Rai (1630-1661 AD)**
  8. **Guru Har Krishan (1656-1664 AD)**
  9. **Guru Tegh Bahadur (1621-1675 AD)**
  10. **Guru Gobind Singh (1666-1708 AD):** Founded the Khalsa and Sikh baptism, composed many poems, and nominated the Sikh sacred text as the final and enduring Guru.

MODERN INDIA

THE ADVENT OF THE EUROPEANS

THE PORTUGUESE

- Vasco-da-Gama, a Portuguese explorer, sailed through the route of Cape of Good Hope and reached near Calicut on 20th May 1498 A.D. during the reign of King Zamorin (Hindu King of Calicut).
- Vasco-da-Gama founded a factory at Cannanore on his second visit to India in 1501. In due course, Calicut, Cochin and Cannanore became the Portuguese trading centres.
- Francisco Almeida came to India in 1505. He was the first Governor of Portuguese possessions in India.
- The real founder of Portuguese power in India was *Alfonso de Albuquerque*. He captured Goa from the rulers of Bijapur in 1510. It was made their headquarters.

THE DUTCH

- The United East India Company of the Netherlands founded a factory at Masulipatnam in 1605.
- They built their first fort on the main land of India at Pulicut in 1609, near Madras (Chennai). They captured Nagapattinam from the Portuguese.
- They made Agra, Surat, Masulipatnam and Chinsura in Bengal as their trading centres.

THE DANES

- The Danish East India Company was established in 1616 in Denmark.
- They came to South India and founded a factory at Tranquebar (Tharangambadi) in 1620. They also made settlements at Serampore near Calcutta (Kolkata).

THE ENGLISH

- The English East India Company was formed in 1599 under a charter granted by Queen Elizabeth in 1600.
- The East India Company sent Sir William Hawkins to the court of the Mughal Emperor Jahangir in 1609 to obtain permission to erect a factory at Surat.
- In 1615, Sir Thomas Roe, another British merchant, came to Jahangir's court.
- He stayed for three years and succeeded in getting permission to set up their trading centres at Agra, Surat, Ahmedabad and Broach.
- In 1690, the British got permission from Aurangazeb to build a factory on the site of Calcutta. In 1696 a fort was built at that place. It was called Fort William.

THE FRENCH

- The French East India Company was established in 1664 under the inspiring and energetic leadership of Colbert, the economic adviser of the French King Louis XIV.
- In 1667, the first French factory was established at Surat by Francis Caron who was nominated as Director-General.
- French were defeated by English in the *Battle of Wandiwash* (1760).

EAST INDIA COMPANY

- After the Battle of Plassey in 1757 and the Battle of Buxar in 1764, the East India Company became a political power.
- India was under the East India Company's rule till 1858 when it came under the direct administration of the British Crown. Robert Clive was the first Governor of Fort William under the Company's rule.

GOVERNOR-GENERALS OF BENGAL

Warren Hastings (1772-85 AD)

- In 1772, the Company appointed Warren Hastings as the Governor of Fort William. The Dual System introduced by Robert Clive was abolished by Warren Hastings.
- Warren Hastings was known for his expansionist policy. His administration witnessed the Rohilla War, the First Anglo-Maratha War and the Second Anglo-Mysore War.
- Pitt's India Act (1784) was passed.

Lord Cornwallis (1786-93 AD)

- Cornwallis inaugurated the policy of making appointments mainly on the basis of merit thereby laying the foundation of the Indian Civil Service.
- Lord Cornwallis introduced Permanent Revenue Settlement.
- Tipu Sultan signed the Treaty of Srirangapatnam in 1792 with the British.

Sir John Shore (1793-98 AD)

- Played an important role in the introduction of Permanent Settlement.
- *Battle of Kharda* between the Nizams and the Marathas (1795).

Wellesley (1798-1805)

- Wellesley came to India with a determination to launch a forward policy that he adopted to achieve his object is known as the 'Subsidiary Alliance'.
- The Fourth Anglo-Mysore War started in 1799. The war was short and decisive. Tipu fought till his capital Srirangapatnam was captured and he himself was shot dead.
- Peshwa Baji Rao II signed the *Treaty* of *Bassein* with the British in 1802. It was a subsidiary treaty and the Peshwa was recognized as the head of the Maratha kingdom.
- The Treaty of Deogaon(1803) was signed between Bhonsle and Wellesley.

Lord Minto (1807-1813)

- Lord Minto concluded the Treaty of Amritsar with Ranjit Singh of Punjab in 1809.
- The Charter Act of 1813 was passed during this period.

Lord Hastings (1813-1823)

- Anglo Nepal War (1814-1816) and Treaty of Sugauli (1816).
- Third Maratha War (1817-18), dissolution of Maratha confederacy and creation of Bombay Presidency.
- He encouraged the freedom of the Press and abolished the censorship introduced in 1799.

GOVERNOR-GENERALS OF INDIA

Lord William Bentinck (1828-1835)

- Charter Act of 1833 was passed and he was made the first Governor-General of India. Before him, the designation was Governor-General of Bengal.
- The social reforms of William Bentinck made his name immortal in the history of British India. These include the abolition of *Sati*, the suppression of Thugs and the prevention of female infanticide.
- The Government Resolution in 1835 made English the official and literary language of India.

Lord Metcalfe (1835-36 AD)

- Known as liberator of press in India.

Lord Auckland (1836-42 AD)

- First Afghan War (1838-42), a disaster for the English.

Lord Ellenborough (1842-44 AD)

- Brought an end to Afghan war. War with Gwalior (1843), *Annexation of Sind* by Charles Napier (1843).

Lord Hardinge (1844-48 AD)

- First Anglo-Sikh War (1845-46) and Treaty of Lahore (1846). Gave preference to English educated persons in employment.

Lord Dalhousie (1848-1856)

- The Doctrine of Lapse was applied by Dalhousie.
- The first railway line connecting Bombay with Thane was opened in 1853.

VICEROYS OF INDIA

Lord Canning (1856-62 AD)

- Lord Canning became the first Viceroy of India in 1858.
- Revolt of 1857, Mutiny took place. Indian Penal Code 1860 was passed.

Lord Elgin (1862 AD)

- Wahabi Movement.

Lord John Lawrence (1864-69 AD)

- Established the *High Courts* at Calcutta, Bombay and Madras in 1865.
- Telegraphic communication was opened with Europe. Created the Indian Forest Department.

Lord Northbrooke (1872-76 AD)

- Kuka Rebellion in Punjab, Famine in Bihar.

Lord Lytton (1876-80)

- In 1878, the Vernacular Press Act was passed. This Act empowered a Magistrate to secure an undertaking from the editor, publisher and printer of a vernacular newspaper that nothing would be published against the English Government. This Act crushed the freedom of the Indian press. In 1878, the Arms Act was passed. This Act prevented the Indians to keep arms without appropriate license.
- Lord Lytton also held a Darbar at Delhi in 1877 in which Queen Victoria was declared as the Empress of India. This extravagant Darbar cost millions of ruppes.
- In 1878, the Statutory Civil Service was established exclusively for Indians.

Lord Ripon (1880-84 AD)

- Lord Ripon repealed the Vernacular Press Act and earned much popularity among Indians.
- Ripon appointed a Commission in 1882 under the chairmanship of Sir William Hunter.
- The Commission came to be known as the Hunter Commission. The Commission recommended for the expansion and improvement of the elementary education of the masses.
- Ripon was founder of local self-government in modern India.

Lord Dufferin (1884-88 AD)

- *Third Burmese War* (1885-86 AD). Establishment of the Indian National Congress in 1885.

Lord Lansdowne (1888-94 AD)

- Factory Act of 1891 granted weekly holiday and stipulated working hours for women and children.

Lord Elgin II (1894-99 AD)

- Southern uprisings of 1899. Great famine of 1896-1897 and Lyall Commission on famine was established.

Lord Curzon (1899-1905 AD)

- Curzon instituted in 1902, a Universities Commission to go into the entire question of university education in the country.
- On the basis of the findings and recommendations of the Commission, Curzon brought in the Indian Universities Act of 1904, which brought all the universities in India under the control of the government.

Lord Minto (1905-10 AD)

- Swadeshi Movement (1905-08); foundation of Muslim League (1906); Surat Session and split in the Congress (1907). Morley-Minto Reforms (1909).

Lord Hardinge (1910-16 AD)

- Capital shifted from Calcutta to Delhi (1911); Delhi Durbar; Partition of Bengal was cancelled.
- The Hindu Mahasabha was founded in 1915 by Pandit Madan Mohan Malaviya.

Lord Chelmsford (1916-21 AD)

- Gandhi returned to India (1915) and founded the Sabarmati Ashram (1916), Champaran Satyagraha, Satyagraha at Ahmedabad (1981), Kheda Satyagraha (1918).
- Rowlatt Act (March, 1919) and the Jallianwala Bagh Massacre (13th April, 1919).
- Khilafat Committee was formed and Khilafat Movement started (1919-20).
- Non-Cooperation Movement started (1920-22).

Lord Reading (1921-26)

- Moplah Rebellion (1921) took place. *Kakori Train* Robbery on 1st August, 1925.
- *Communal Riots* of 1923-25 in Multan, Amritsar, Delhi etc.

Lord Irwin (1926-31 AD)

- Lahore Session of Congress and *Poorna Swaraj* Declaration (1929).
- Simon Commission visited India in 1927.
- Dandi March (12th March, 1930). Civil Disobedience Movement (1930).
- First Round Table Conference was held in England in 1930. Gandhi-Irwin Pact.

Lord Willingdon (1931-36 AD)

- *Second Round Table Conference* in London in 1931 and *third* in 1932.

Lord Linlithgow (1936-43 AD)

- Congress Ministries resignation celebrated as '*Deliverance Day*' by the Muslim League (1939), the Lahore Resolution (23rd March, 1940) of the Muslim League demanding separate state for the Muslims. (It was at this session that Jinnah propounded his Two-Nation Theory). Outbreak of World War II in 1939. Cripps Mission in 1942. Quit India Movement (8th August, 1942).

Lord Wavell (1943-47 AD)

- Cabinet Mission Plan (16th May, 1946).
- First meeting of the Constituent Assembly was held on 9th December, 1946.
- Arranged the Shimla Conference on 25th June, 1945 with Indian National Congress and Muslim League but failed.

Lord Mountbatten (March to Aug, 1947)

- Last viceroy of British India and the first Governor-General of free India.
- Partition of India decided by the 3rd June Plan or Mountbatten Plan.

NATIONAL MOVEMENT (1885-1947)

INDIAN NATIONAL CONGRESS (1885)

- Allan Octavian Hume, a retired civil servant in the British Government took the initiative to form an all-India organization. Thus, the Indian National Congress was founded and its first session was held at Bombay in 1885. W.C. Banerjee was its first president. It was attended by 72 delegates from all over India.
- The second session was held in Calcutta in 1886 and the third in Madras in 1887. Between 1885 and 1905, the Congress leaders were moderates. The Moderates had faith in the British justice and goodwill. They were called moderates because they adopted peaceful and constitutional means to achieve their demands.
- In 1905, Gopal Krishna Gokhale founded the Servants of India Society to train Indians to dedicate their lives to the cause of the country.

Partition of Bengal (1905)

- By Lord Curzon on 16th October, 1905 through a royal proclamation, reducing the old province of Bengal in size by creating East Bengal and Assam out of the rest of Bengal.
- The partition of Bengal in 1905 provided a spark for the rise of extremism in the Indian National Movement.
- Curzon's real motives behind this partition were:
  - To break the growing strength of Bengali nationalism since Bengal was the base of Indian nationalism.
  - To divide the Hindus and Muslims in Bengal.
  - To show the enormous power of the British Government in doing whatever it liked.

Swadeshi Movement (1905)

- The Swadeshi Movement involved programmes like the boycott of government service, courts, schools and colleges and of foreign goods. It was both a political and economic movement.
- Lal, Bal, Pal and Aurobindo Ghosh played an important role.

Muslim League (1906)

- In December 1906, Muslim delegates from all over India met at Dacca for the Muslim Educational Conference.
- Taking advantage of this occasion, Nawab Salimullah of Dacca proposed the setting up of an organisation to look after the Muslim interests. The proposal was accepted.
- The All-India Muslim League was finally set up on December 30, 1906.

Minto Morley Reforms (1909)

- Minto, the Viceroy and Morley, the Secretary of State for India jointly proposed reforms to the Indian Councils. An Act, called the Indian Councils Act or the Minto-Morley Reforms Act was passed in 1909.
- A separate communal electorate was introduced for the Muslims.

The Lucknow Pact (1916)

- During the 1916 Congress session at Lucknow two major events occurred.
- The divided Congress became united. An understanding for joint action against the British was reached between the Congress and the Muslim League and it was called the Lucknow Pact.
- The signing of the Lucknow Pact by the Congress and the Muslim League in 1916 marked an important step in the Hindu-Muslim unity.

The Home Rule Movement (1916)

- Two Home Rule Leagues were established, one by B.G. Tilak at Poona in April 1916 and the other by Mrs. Annie Besant at Madras in September 1916.
- While Tilak's Movement concentrated on Maharashtra, Annie Besant's Movement covered the rest of the country.

August Declaration

- On 20 August, 1917, Montague, the Secretary of State in England, promised the gradual development of self-governing institutions in India.
- This August Declaration led to the end of the Home Rule Movement.

Rowlatt Act (1919)

- In 1917, a committee was set up under the presidentship of Sir Sydney Rowlatt to look into the militant Nationalist activities.
- On the basis of its report the Rowlatt Act was passed in March 1919 by the Central Legislative Council. As per this Act, any person could be arrested on the basis of suspicion. No appeal or petition could be filed against such arrests.
- This Act was called the Black Act and it was widely opposed. An all-India hartal was organized on 6 April, 1919.

Jallianwala Bagh Massacre (13 April, 1919)

- On 13th April, the Baisakhi day (harvest festival), a public meeting was organized at the Jallianwala Bagh (garden). Gen. Dyer marched in and without any warning opened fire on the crowd. The firing continued for about 10 to 15 minutes and it stopped only after the ammunition exhausted.
- According to official report 379 people were killed and 1137 wounded in the incident. There was a nationwide protest against this massacre and Rabindranath Tagore renounced his knighthood as a protest.

Khilafat Movement (1920)

- The chief cause of the Khilafat Movement was the defeat of Turkey in the First World War.
- The Muslims in India were upset over the British attitude against Turkey and launched the Khilafat Movement.
- Ali brothers, *Mohd Ali* and *Shaukat Ali* started this movement. It was jointly led by the Khilafat leaders and the Congress.

Non-Co-operation Movement (1920-22)

- Mahatma Gandhi announced his plan to begin Non-Cooperation with the government as a sequel to the Rowlatt Act, Jallianwala Bagh massacre and the Khilafat Movement.
- It was approved by the Indian National Congress at the Nagpur session in December, 1920.
- The Congress observed the Non-Co-operation movement in 1920. The main aim of this movement was to attain Swaraj through non-violent and peaceful means.
- The whole movement was abruptly called off on 11th February, 1922 by Gandhi following the Chauri-Chaura incident in the Gorakhpur district of U.P. Many top leaders of the country were stunned at this sudden suspension of the Non-Co-operation Movement.
- On 5th February an angry mob set fire to the police station at *Chauri-Chaura* and twenty two police men were burnt to death.

Swaraj Party

- Leaders like Motilal Nehru and Chittranjan Das formed a separate group within the Congress known as the Swaraj Party on 1 January, 1923.
- The Swarajists wanted to contest the council elections and wreck the government from within.

Simon Commission (1927)

- The Act of 1919 included a provision for its review after a lapse of ten years. However, the review commission under the chairmanship of Sir John Simon was appointed by the British Government two years earlier of its schedule in 1927.
- Indian leaders opposed the commission, as there were no Indians in it, they cried *Simon Go Back*.
- The government used brutal repression and at Lahore, *Lala Lajpat Rai* was severely beaten in lathi-charge.

Nehru Report (1928)

- The Secretary of State, Lord Birkenhead, challenged the Indians to produce a Constitution that would be acceptable to all. The challenge was accepted by the Congress, which convened an all party meeting on 28 February, 1928.
- A committee consisting of eight was constituted to draw up a blueprint for the future Constitution of India. It was headed by Motilal Nehru. The Report published by this Committee came to be known as the Nehru Report.

Lahore Session (1929)

- On Dec. 19, 1929, under the Presidentship of J.L. Nehru, the INC, as its Lahore session, declared Poorna Swaraj (Complete Independence) as its ultimate goal.
- On Dec. 31, 1929, the newly adopted tricolour flag was unfurled and Jan. 26, 1930 was fixed as the First Independence Day, which was to be celebrated every year.

Dandi March (1930)

- On 12th March, 1930, Gandhi began his famous March to Dandi with his chosen 79 followers to break the salt laws. He reached the coast of Dandi on 5 April, 1930 after marching a distance of 200 miles and on 6 April formally launched the Civil Disobedience Movement by breaking the salt laws.

Civil Disobedience Movement

- Countrywide mass participation by women.
- The Garhwal soldiers refused to fire on the people at Peshawar.

Round Table Conference

- The first Round Table Conference was held in November 1930 at London and it was boycotted by the Congress.
- On 8th March, 1931 the Gandhi-Irwin Pact was signed. As per this pact, Mahatma Gandhi agreed to suspend the Civil-Disobedience Movement and participate in the Second-Round Table Conference.
- In September 1931, the Second Round Table Conference was held at London. Mahatma Gandhi participated in the Conference but returned to India disappointed. In January 1932, the Civil-Disobedience Movement was resumed.

Poona Pact (1932)

- The idea of separate electorate for the depressed classes was abandoned, but seats reserved for them in the provincial legislature were increased.
- Thus, Poona Pact agreed upon a joint electorate for upper and lower castes.

Demand for Pakistan

- *Chaudhary Rehmat Ali* gave the term *Pakistan* in 1933.
- In March 1940, the Muslim League demanded the creation of Pakistan.

Cripps Mission (1942)

- The British Government in its effort to secure Indian co-operation in the Second World War sent Sir Stafford Cripps to India on 23 March, 1942. This is known as Cripps Mission. The main recommendations of Cripps was the promise of Dominion Status to India.
- Congress rejected it. Gandhi called Cripp's proposals as a "Post-dated Cheque".

Quit India Movement (1942-1944)

- The All India Congress Committee met at Bombay on 8th August, 1942 and passed the famous Quit India Resolution. On the same day, Gandhi gave his call of 'do or die'.
- On 8th and 9th August, 1942, the government arrested all the prominent leaders of the Congress. Mahatma Gandhi was kept in prison at Poona.
- Pandit Jawaharlal Nehru, Abul Kalam Azad, and other leaders were imprisoned in the Ahamednagar Fort. Quit India Movement was the final attempt for country's freedom.

Indian National Army (INA)

- On July 2, 1943, Subhash Chandra Bose reached Singapore and gave the rousing war cry of *'Dilli Chalo'*. He was made the President of Indian Independence League and soon became the supreme commander of the Indian National Army. He gave the country the slogan of *Jai Hind.*
- INA had three fighting brigades named after Gandhi, Azad and Nehru. Rani of Jhansi Brigade was an exclusive women force. INA headquarters were at Rangoon and Singapore.

Cabinet Mission (1946)

- The Cabinet Mission put forward a plan for solution of the constitutional problem. A proposal was envisaged for setting up an Interim Government, which would remain in office till a new government was elected on the basis of the new Constitution framed by the Constituent Assembly. Elections were held in July 1946 for the formation of a Constituent Assembly. Muslim league observed the *Direct Action Day* on 16 August, 1946.
- An Interim Government was formed under the leadership of Jawaharlal Nehru on 2 September, 1946.

Mountbatten Plan (1947)

- On 20 February 1947, Prime Minister Atlee announced in the House of Commons the definite intention of the British Government to transfer power to responsible Indian hands by a date not later than June 1948.
- Lord Mountbatten armed with vast powers became India's Viceroy on 24 March, 1947. The partition of India and the creation of Pakistan appeared inevitable to him.
- After extensive consultation Lord Mountbatten put forth the plan of partition of India on 3 June, 1947.
- The Congress and the Muslim League ultimately approved the Mountbatten Plan.

Indian Independence Act, 1947

- The salient features of this Act was the partition of the country into India and Pakistan would come into effect from 15 August, 1947.
- On 15th August, 1947 India, and on the 14th August Pakistan came into existence as two independent states.
- Lord Mountbatten was made the first Governor General of Independent India, whereas Mohammad Ali Jinnah became the first Governor General of Pakistan.
- C. Rajagopalachari became the first and last Indian Governor-General of India. When India became a Republic on 26 January, 1950 Dr. Rajendra Prasad became the first President of our country.

❒ ❒ ❒

2

Geography

WORLD GEOGRAPHY

THE UNIVERSE

- Existing matter and energy are together known as **Universe.**

GALAXY

- A galaxy is a huge system of billions of stars and clouds of dust and gases.
- Our solar system is a part of *Milky Way* galaxy.
- There are millions of galaxies that make the Universe.

STARS

- Stars account for 98 per cent of the matter in a galaxy. The stars nearest to the earth are *Proxima Centauri, Alpha Centauri, Barnard's Star, Sirius* and so on. Of these, *Sirius* is the brightest.

LIGHT YEAR

- Light year is the distance travelled by light in one year at a speed of 2,99,792.5 km. per second.

SOLAR SYSTEM

- The Sun, eight planets, satellites and some other celestial bodies known as asteroids and meteoroids form the solar system.

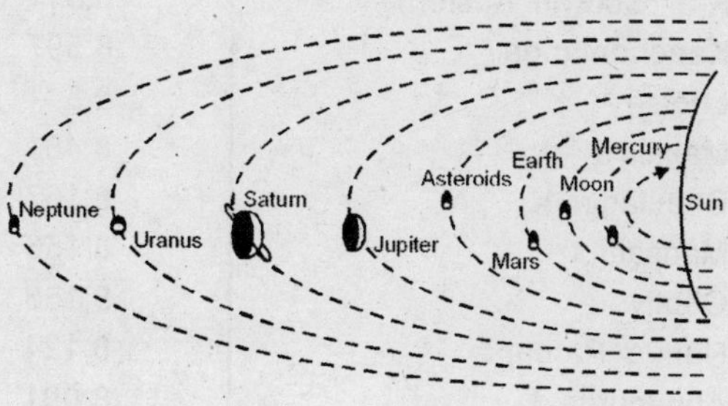

SUN

- The Sun is in the centre of the solar system.
- The Sun is a mixture of gases. It consists of 92% hydrogen, 7.8% helium and 0.2% other gases.
- The Sun is about 150 million km away from the earth.
- The sun is an ultimate source of energy for life on Earth.
- Sunlight takes 8 min 16.6 sec to reach earth.

Facts about Sun

Diameter	— 1.392×10^6 km
Volume	— 1.304 × 106 times the volume of earth
Temperature	— 6000°C at surface and 15 million degree C at the centre
Relative density	— 1.4
Gravitational Pull	— 28 times the gravitational pull of the earth

Facts about Planets

Closest to Sun	*Mercury*
Farthest from Sun	*Neptune*
Heaviest	*Jupiter*
Hottest	*Venus*
Inner	*Mercury, Venus, Earth, Mars*
Largest	*Jupiter*
Smallest	*Mercury*
Moons, None	*Mercury, Venus*
Moon; Largest	*Ganymede (Jupiter), larger than Mercury*
Nearest to Earth	*Venus*
Orbits; Order	*Mercury (closest to Sun), Venus, Earth, Mars, Jupiter, Saturn, Uranus, Neptune.*
Rings/largest number	*Saturn*
Spin; Backwards	*Venus (East to West)*

COMETS

- It has a head and a tail. Its tail originates only when it gets closer to the sun. The tail can be 20-30 million km long. It always point away from the sun because of the force exerted by solar wind and radiation on the cometory material.

THE EARTH

- The earth is the third nearest planet to the Sun.
- From the outer space, the earth appears blue because its two-thirds surface is covered by water. It is, therefore, called a blue planet. It is the densest of all planets.
- Rotation is the movement of the earth on its axis. Due to this rotation, day and night occur.
- The earth takes about 23 hours 56 minutes and 4 seconds to complete one rotation around its axis.
- Earth takes 365¼ days (one year) to revolve around the sun.

THE MOON

- Earth has only one satellite, that is, the moon.
- Its diameter is only one-quarter that of the earth. It is about 3,84,400 km away from us.
- The moon moves around the earth in about 27 days. It takes exactly the same time to complete one spin. As a result, only one side of the moon (only 59% of its surface) is visible to us on the earth.
- Moonlight takes 1.3 sec. to reach earth.

LATITUDE

- Imaginary lines drawn parallel to the equator. Measured as an angle whose apex is at the centre of the earth.
- The equator represents 0° latitude, while the North Pole is 90°N and the South Pole 90°S.
- 23½°N represents Tropic of Cancer while 23½°S represents Tropic of Capricorn.

LONGITUDE

- It is the angular distance measured from the centre of the earth. On the globe the lines of longitude are drawn as a series of semicircles that extend from the North Pole to the South Pole through the equator. They are also called meridians.
- The distance between any two meridians is not equal. At the equator, 1 degree = 111 km. At 30°N or S, it is 96.5 km. It goes on decreasing this way until it is zero at the poles.

INTERNATIONAL DATE LINE

- It is the 180° meridian running over the Pacific Ocean, deviating at Aleutian Islands, Fiji, Samoa and Gilbert Islands.
- Travellers crossing the Date Line from west to east repeat a day and travellers crossing it from east to west lose a day.

INDIAN STANDARD TIME (IST)

- Indian Standard Time is calculated on the basis of 82.5°E longitude which passes through Uttar Pradesh, Madhya Pradesh, Odisha, Chattisgarh and Andhra Pradesh.

EARTHQUAKES

- Earthquakes are a form of wave energy that is transferred through bedrock. It is transmitted from the point of the earthquake focus, as spherical seismic waves. They travel in all directions outward.
- The intensity of earthquake waves is recorded by *Seismograph*.

LANDFORMS

- There are three major landforms: mountains, plateaus and plains.

MOUNTAINS

- A mountain can be defined as an area of land that rises abruptly from the surrounding region.
- There are three types of mountains- *Fold Mountains, Block Mountains* and the ***Volcanic Mountains***.
- Himalayas, Alps, Andes, Rockies, Atlas, etc are examples of Fold Mountains. The Aravali range in India is one of the oldest **fold mountain** systems in the world.
- The Rhine valley and the Vosges mountain in Europe are examples of such mountain systems.
- Volcanic mountains are formed due to volcanic activity.
- Mt. Kilimanjaro in Africa and Mt. Fujiyama in Japan are examples of such mountains.

Major Mountain Ranges of the World

Range	Location	Highest Peak (m)	Length (km)
Andes	South America	6,960	7,200
Himalayas-Karakoram-Hindukush	South Central Asia	8,848	4,800
Rockies	North America	4,401	4,800
Great Dividing Range	East Australia	2,228	3,600
Western Ghat	Western India	2,637	1,610
Caucasus	Europe	5,642	1,200
Alaska	USA	6,194	1,130
Alps	Europe	4,808	1,050
Apennines	Europe	2,912	—
Ural	Asia	1,895	—
Atlas	North West Africa	—	1,930

PLATEAUS

- A plateau is an elevated flat land. It is a flat-topped table land standing above the surrounding area.

Principal Mountain Peaks of the World

Mountains	Height in Metres
1. Mount Everest	8,848
2. K-2 (Godwin Austen)	8,611
3. Kanchenjunga	8,597
4. Lhotse	8,511
5. Makalu I	8,481
6. Dhaulagiri I	8,167
7. Mansalu I	8,156
8. Chollyo	8,153
9. Nanga Parbat	8,124
10. Annapurna I	8,091
11. Gasherbrum I	8,068
12. Broad Peak I	8,047
13. Gasherbrum II	8,034
14. Shisha Pangma (Gosainthan)	8,014
15. Gasherbrum III	7,952

PLAINS

- A relatively low-lying and flat land surface with least difference between its highest and lowest points is called a Plain.

OCEANS

- Oceans of the world is classified into four groups: the Pacific, the Atlantic, the Arctic and the Indian.
- The Pacific is the largest ocean, being twice the size of the Atlantic. It covers about a third of the Earth's surface, and contains more than half the water on the planet.

Oceans of the World

Names	Area (Sq. Km.)	Greatest Depth
Pacific	166,240000	Mariana Trench
Atlantic	86,560000	Puerto Rico Trench
Indian	73430000	Java Trench
Arctic	13230000	—

Major Rivers of the World

River	Origin	Falls in	Length (Km.)
Nile	Victoria lake	Mediterranean Sea	6,650
Amazon	Andes (Peru)	Atlantic Ocean	6,428
Yangtze	Tibetan Kiang Plateau	China Sea	6,300
Mississippi Missouri	Itaska lake (USA)	Gulf of Mexico (USA)	6,275
Yenisei	Tannu-Ola Mts.	Arctic Ocean	5,539
Hoang Ho	Kunlun Mts.	Gulf of Chibli	5,464
Ob	Altai Mts., Russia	Gulf of Ob	5,410
Congo	Lualaba & Luapula rivers	Atlantic Ocean	4,700
Amur	Northeast China	Sea of Okhotsk	4,444
Lena	Baikal Mts	Laptev Sea	4,400
Mekong	Tibetan Highlands	South China Sea	4,350
Mackenzie	Great Slave Lake	Beaufort Sea	4,241
Niger	Guinea	Gulf of Guinea	4,200

Major Gulfs of the World

Names	Area (Sq. Km.)	Names	Areas (Sq. Km.)
Gulf of Mexico	15,44,000	Gulf of St. Lawrence	2,37,000
Gulf of Hudson	12,33,000	Gulf of California	1,62,000
Arabian Gulf	2,38,000	English Channel	89,900

Important Straits of the World

Straits	Water Bodies joined	Area
Bab-al-Mandeb	Red Sea & Arabian Sea	Arabia & Africa
Bering	Arctic Ocean & Bering Sea	Alaska & Asia
Bosphorus	Black Sea & Marmara Sea	Turkey
Dover	North Sea & Atlantic Ocean	England & Europe
Florida	Gulf of Mexico & Atlantic Ocean	Florida & Bahamas Islands
Gibralter	Mediterranean Sea & Atlantic Ocean	Spain & Africa
Malacca	Java Sea & Bay of Bengal	India & Indonesia
Palk	Bay of Bengal & Indian Ocean	India & Sri Lanka
Magellan	South Pacific & South Atlantic Ocean	Chile
Sunda	Java Sea & Indian Ocean	Indonesia

Important Lakes of the World

Lake	Location	Area (Sq. Km.)
Caspian	Russia and CIS	371000
Superior	Canada and USA	82414
Victoria	Tanzania (Africa)	69485
Huron	Canada and USA	59596
Michigan	USA	58016
Tanganyika	Africa	32892

Lake	Location	Area (Sq. Km.)
Baikal	Russia (CIS)	31502
Great Bear	Canada	31080
Malawi	Malawi (Tanzania)	30044
Great Slave	Canada	28438

Highest Waterfalls of the World

Name(s) (Foreign)	Location
Angel (Salto Angel)	Canaima Nat'l Park, Venezuela
Tugela	Natal Nat'l Park, South Africa
Utigord (Utigordsfoss)	Norway
Monge (Mongefoss)	Marstein, Norway
Gocta Cataracts	Chachapoyas, Peru
Mutarazi (Mtarazi)	Nyanga Nat'l Park, Zimbabwe
Yosemite	Yosemite Nat'l Park, California, U.S.
Espelands (Espelandsfoss)	Hardanger Fjord, Norway
Lower Mar Valley (Ostra Mardolafoss)	Eikesdal, Norway
Tyssestrengene	Odda, Norway

Continents: Some Facts

Continent	Biggest Counrty	Highest Peak	Longest River
Asia	China	Mt. Everest (8848 m)	Yangtze Kiang
Africa	Algeria	Mt. Kilimanjaro (5895 m)	Nile
North America	Canada	Mt. Mckinley (6194 m)	Mississippi Missouri
South America	Brazil	Mt. Acancagua (6960 m)	Amazon
Europe	Russia	Mt. Elbrus (5642 m)	Ob
Australia	Australia	Mt. Coscuisco (2228 m)	Darling
Antarctica	—	Vinson Massif (5140 m)	—

INDIAN GEOGRAPHY

AREA AND LOCATION

- India is in the southern parts of the Asian continent. In the west of India lies the Arabian Peninsula while in the east lies the Indo-China Peninsula.
- India extends between 8°4' N and 37°6' N latitudes and between 68°7' E and 97°2' E longitudes.
- India, has a total geographic area of 32,87,263 sq. km. This is only 2.42 % of the total geographic area of the world but holds 17.5 per cent of the world's population.
- The 23½°N, which is the Tropic of Cancer, runs across the country.
- India has a length of 3214 km from north to south and 2933 km from east to west. It has a land frontier of 15200 km.
- The total length of the coastline of the mainland, Lakshadweep Islands and Andaman and Nicobar Islands is 7,516.6 km.
- India ranks seventh among the countries of the world, in terms of the geographical extent.
- India is bordered on three sides by water and on one by land, it is also a peninsula.
- India shares its common border with Afghanistan and Pakistan in the north-west, China and Bhutan in the north, and Bangladesh in the east. In the south, Sri Lanka is separated from India by a strait, known as the Palk Strait.
- 82°30' E longitude is considered as the Indian Standard Meridian. The local time of this longitude is taken as the Indian Standard Time (IST). This is 5½ hours ahead of the Greenwich Mean Time.

THE INDIAN STATES/UT's ON INTERNATIONAL BOUNDARIES ARE:

- ***Bordering Pakistan:*** Jammu and Kashmir, Punjab, Rajasthan, Gujarat.

- ***Bordering China:*** Jammu and Kashmir, Ladakh, Himachal Pradesh, Uttarakhand, Sikkim, Arunachal Pradesh.
- ***Bordering Nepal:*** Bihar, Uttarakhand, UP, Sikkim, West Bengal.
- ***Bordering Bangladesh:*** West Bengal, Mizoram, Meghalaya, Tripura, Assam.
- ***Bordering Bhutan:*** West Bengal, Sikkim, Arunachal Pradesh, Assam.
- ***Bordering Myanmar:*** Arunachal Pradesh, Nagaland, Manipur, Mizoram.
- ***Bordering Afghanistan:*** Jammu and Kashmir (Pakistan-occupied area).

Important Passes

Jammu & Kashmir	Burzi-La
Himachal Pradesh	Bara La, Cha-La, Shipki-La
Uttarakhand	Niti-La, Lipu-Lekh-La
Sikkim	Jelep-La, Nathu-La
Arunachal Pradesh	Bomdi-La
Ladakh	Joji-La

Heighest Mountain Peaks of India

Peaks	Elevation• (in mts.)
Godwin Austin (K2)	8611*
Kanchenjunga	8598
Nanga Parvat	8126
Gasherbrum	8068*
Broad Peak	8047*
Dastegil	7885*
Masherbrum (East)	7821
Nanda Devi	7817
Masherbrum (West)	7806*
Rakoposhi	7788*
Kamet	7756
Saser Kangdi	7672

• *Above mean sea level in metres.*

* *Situated in Pak occupied Kashmir (PoK).*

Towns at River Banks

Town	River	Town	River
Agra	Yamuna	Varanasi	The Ganges
Ayodhya	Saryu	Kolkata	Hooghly
Cuttuck	Mahanadi	Delhi	Yamuna
Dibrugarh	Brahmaputra	Ferozepur	Satluj
Guwahati	Brahmaputra	Hardwar	The Ganges
Hyderabad	Musi	Jabalpur	Narmada
Kanpur	The Ganges	Kota	Chambal
Kurnool	Tungbhadra	Lucknow	Gomti
Ludhiana	Sutlej	Nasik	Godavari
Pandharpur	Bhima	Patna	The Ganges
Sambalpur	Mahanadi	Srinagar	Jhelum
Srirangapattam	Cauveri	Prayagraj	Confluence of the Ganges and the Yamuna
Surat	Tapti		
Vijaywada	Krishna		
Ahmedabad	Sabarmati		
Ferozpur	Sutlej	Raurkela	Brahmani
Jabaplpur	Narmada	Vadodara	Vishwamitri

Important Waterfalls of India

Waterfall	Hgt (Mt.)	River	State
Kunchikal	455	Varahi	Karnataka
Dudhsagar	310	Mandvi	Goa
Jog/Gersoppa	260	Sharavati	Karnataka
Rakim Kund	168	Gaighat	Bihar
Chachai	127	Bihad	Madhya Pradesh
Kevti	98	Mahanadi	Madhya Pradesh
Sivasamudram	90	Cauveri	Karnataka

Important Lakes of India

Name of lake	State/UT
Pulicat Lake	Tamil Nadu & Andhra Pradesh Border
Sambhar Lake	Rajasthan
Tso Moriri Lake	Jammu & Kashmir
Vembanad Lake	Kerala
Wular & Dal Lakes	Jammu and Kashmir
Chilka Lake	Odisha
Kolleru Lake	Andhra Pradesh
Loktak Lake	Manipur
Lonar Lake	Maharashtra
Pangong Lake	Ladakh

Rivers of India

Name	Originates From	Falls Into
Yamuna	Yamunotri	Ganga
Chambal	Singar Chouri Peak, Vindhyan escarpment	Yamuna
Ghaghara	Matsatung Glacier	Ganga
Kosi	Near Gosain Dham Peak	Ganga
Sabarmati	Aravalis	Gulf of Khambat
Krishna	Western Ghats	Bay of Bengal
Godavari	Nasik district in Maharashtra	Bay of Bengal
Caurey	Brahmagir Range of Western Ghats	Bay of Bengal

Name	Originates From	Falls Into
Tungabharda	Western Ghats	Krishna
Ganges	Combines Sources	Bay of Bengal
Sutlej	Mansarovar Rakas lakes	Chenab
Indus	Near Mansarovar Lake	Arabian Sea
Ravi	Kullu Hills near Rohtang Pass	Chenab
Beas	Near Rohtang Pass	Sutlej
Jhelum	Verinag in Kashmir	Chenab
Son	Amarkantak	Ganga
Brahmaputra	Near Mansarovar Lake	Bay of Bengal
Narmada	Amarkantak	Gulf of Khambat
Tapti	Betul District in Madhya Pradesh	Gulf of Khambat
Mahanadi	Raipur District in Chhattisgarh	Bay of Bengal
Luni	Aravallis	Rann of Kuchchh
Ghaggar	Himalayas	Near Fatehabad
Betwa	Vindhyanchal	Yamuna

Geographical Surnames

Bengal's Sorrow	Damodar River	City of Lakes	Srinagar
City of Palaces	Kolkata	Twin City	Hyderabad-Secunderabad
Gateway of India	Mumbai	City of Seven Islands	Mumbai
Pink City	Jaipur	Diamond Harbour	Kolkata
Paris of India	Jaipur	Switzerland of India	Kashmir
Manchester of India	Ahmedabad	Rice Bowl	Chhattisgarh
Kashmir of South	Kerala	Fruit Bowl	Himachal Pradesh
Son of Sea	Lakshadweep	Ganga of South	Cauvery
Queen of Mountains	Mussourie	Pitsburg of India	Jamshedpur
Iron City	Jamshedpur	City of Bridges	Srinagar
Hollywood of India	Mumbai	Residence of God	Allahabad
Scotland of East	Meghalaya	A Cross-road (Quadrivial) of National Highways	Kanpur
City of Nababs	Lucknow	Heart of India	Delhi
City of Temples & Ghats	Varanasi	Black River	Sharda
Land of Five Rivers	Punjab	City of Festivals	Madurai
City of Golden Temple	Amritsar	Queen of Deccan	Pune
Garden of India	Bangaluru	Sorrow of Bihar	Kosi River
Spice Garden of India	Kerala		

Major Indian Crops

Crops	Temp(°c)	Water(cm)	States where Produced
Wheat	15°-25°	60-90	Uttar Pradesh, Madhya Pradesh, Punjab
Rice	24°-26°	80-200	West Bengal, Telangana, Uttar Pradesh, Punjab
Maize	18°-21°	50-60	Karnataka, Bihar, Madhya Pradesh, Maharashtra
Jowar	20°-35°	40-60	Maharashtra, Madhya Pradesh, Karnataka
Soyabean	25°-27°	50-120	Maharashtra, Madhya Pradesh, Rajasthan
Cotton	20°-30°	80-150	Gujarat, Maharashtra, Telangana
Tobacco	20°-25°	75-80	Andhra Pradesh, Madhya Pradesh, Gujarat, Karnataka, Maharashtra, Uttar Pradesh
Tea	24°-30°	100-200	Assam, West Bengal, Kerala, Tamil Nadu, Uttar Pradesh
Ground Nut	15°-25°	60-130	Gujarat, Rajasthan, Madhya Pradesh, Tamil Nadu

❑❑❑

3

Indian Polity

INDIAN CONSTITUTION

- Demand for a Constituent Assembly composed of the people of India officially asserted by the Congress for the first time in 1935.
- The election for Indian Constitution Assembly held in 1946 according to the *Cabinet Mission Plan.*
- The first session of the Assembly was held in New Delhi on December 9, 1946. *Sachidanand Sinha* was elected provisional chairman of the session.
- On December 11, 1946, Dr. Rajendra Prasad was elected as the Permanent Chairman of the Constituent Assembly.
- The Constitution was framed by the Constituent Assembly of India, set-up in December 1946, in accordance with the Cabinet Mission Plan, under the Chairmanship of Sachidanand Sinha, initially.
- The total membership of Constituent Assembly after partition was 299, among them 70 were representatives from the Indian states and others from British India.
- The Chairman of the Drafting Committee was **Dr. BR Ambedkar**, also called the Father of the Constitution.
- The Constituent Assembly took 2 years, 11 months and 18 days to complete the Constitution.
- The Constitution, adopted on 8th November, 1949, contained 395 Articles and Schedules.
- The Constitution was delayed till 26th January because, in 1929, on this day Indian National Congress demanded Poorna Swaraj in Lahore Session under JL Nehru.
- Indian Constitution is a comprehensive document and it is the lengthiest written Constitution in the World.

THE PREAMBLE

- ***The Preamble of the Constitution:*** "We the people of India, having solemnly resolved to Constitute India into a Sovereign, Socialist, Secular Democratic Republic and to secure to all its citizen:

  Justice, Social, economic and political;

  Liberty of thought, expression, belief, faith and worship;

  Equality of status and of opportunity; and to promote among them all;

  Fraternity assuring the dignity of the individual and the unity and integrity of the nation;

  In our Constituent Assembly, this twenty-sixth day of November, 1949, do hereby adopt, enact and give to ourselves this constitution."

Foreign Sources of Indian Constitution

Foreign Sources	*Subject*
Britain	Parliamentary system, collective responsibilities of Cabinet
America	Fundamental right, Independent Judiciary, Judicial review
Canada	Division of powers
Ireland	Directive principles
Germany	Emergency provisions
Russia	Fundamental duties
Australia	Concurrent list

IMPORTANT ARTICLES

PART - I

UNION AND ITS TERRITORIES (ARTICLE 1 - 4)

- The Constitution says, "India, that is Bharat, shall be a Union of States".
- Parliament has the power to create any State, reduce it, change the name of boundaries of any State.

PART - II

CITIZENSHIP (ARTICLE 5 - 11)

- The Constitution provides for a single Citizenship.
- ***Indian Citizenship can be acquire:***
  1. by birth
  2. by descent
  3. by registration
  4. by naturalisation
  5. by incorporation of territory
- ***Indian Citizenship can be lost by:***
  1. renunciation;
  2. termination — it takes place if a citizen of India voluntary acquires the citizenship of another country; and
  3. deprivation — if the Government terminates the citizenship.

PART - III

FUNDAMENTAL RIGHTS (ARTICLE 12 - 35)

- Following fundamental rights are enjoyed by every Indian citizen, irrespective of caste, colour, creed and sex:
  1. ***Right to Equality:*** No special privileges, no distinction on grounds of religion, caste, creed and sex.
  2. ***Right to Freedom:*** The right to freedom of expression and speech, the right to choose one's own profession, the right to reside in any part of the Indian Union.
  3. ***Right to Freedom to Religion:*** Except when it is in the interest of public order, morality, health or other conditions, everybody has the right to profess, practice and propagate his religion freely.
  4. ***Cultural and Educational Rights:*** The Constitution provides that every community can run its own institutions to preserve its own culture and language.
  5. ***Right against Exploitation:*** Traffic in human beings and forced labour and the employment of children under 14 years in factories or mines, are punishable offences.
  6. ***Rights to Constitutional Remedies:*** When a citizen finds that any of his fundamental rights has been encroached upon, he can move the Supreme Court, which has been empowered to safeguard the fundamental rights of a citizen (Article 32).

PART - IV

DIRECTIVE PRINCIPLES OF STATE POLICY (ARTICLE 36 - 51)

- Directive principles are not enforceable through courts. Main aim of Directive principles is to provide social and economic base of a genuine democracy.

Some Important Directive Principles:

- Provisions for adequate means of livelihood for all citizens (Art. 39).
- Right to work (Art. 41).
- Right to human condition of work and maternity relief (Art. 42).
- Right to a living wage and condition of work ensuring decent standard of life of worker (Art. 43).
- Common Civil Code (Art. 44).
- Prohibit consumption of liquor (Art. 47).
- Prevent slaughter of useful cattle (Art. 48).
- Organise Panchayati Raj (Art. 40).
- Separate the judiciary from the executive (Art. 50).
- Protect and maintain places of historic monuments (Art. 49).
- International peace (Art. 51).

PART - IV A

FUNDAMENTAL DUTIES (ARTICLE 51A)

- The fundamental duties for the Indian citizens have been incorporated in the Constitution through the Constitution (42nd) Amendment Act, 1976. These duties are:
  1. to abide by the Constitution and respect its ideals and institutions, the National Flag and the National Anthem;
  2. to cherish and follow the noble deeds which inspired our national struggle for freedom;
  3. to uphold and protect the sovereignty, unity and integrity of India;
  4. to defend the country and render national service when called upon to do so;
  5. to promote harmony and the spirit of common brotherhood amongst all the people transcending religious, regional or sectional diversities and to renounce practices derogatory to the dignity of women;
  6. to value and preserve the rich heritage of our composite culture;
  7. to protect and improve natural environment including forests, lakes, rivers and wildlife, and to have compassion for living creatures;
  8. to develop the scientific temper, humanism and the spirit of inquiry and reform;
  9. to safeguard public property and to abjure violence;
  10. to strive towards excellence in all spheres of individual and collective activity so that the nation constantly rises to higher levels of endeavour and achievement.
  11. who is parent or guardian to provide opportunities for education to his child or, as the case may be, ward between age of six and fourteen years.

PART - V

UNION (ARTICLE 52 - 151)

The President

- The President is the Constitutional head of the Republic of India. He is more or less the titular head of the executive.
- He is the constitutional head but not the real executive. The real power is vested in the hands of the Council of Ministers.
- President is the first citizen of India.
- ***Qualifications:*** (i) Indian citizen, (ii) age not less than 35 years, (iii) should have qualification for election to Lok Sabha, (iv) should not hold any office of profit, (v) should not be a Member of Parliament or State Legislature.
- ***Election:*** Indirectly elected through Electoral College consisting of elected members of both the Houses of the

Parliament and elected members of the Legislative Assemblies of the States.

- According to the 70th Amendment Act, 1992, the expression 'States' include the National Capital Territory of Delhi and the Union Territory of Puducherry. Members of the Legislative Councils have no right to vote in the Presidential election.
- ***Powers:*** He makes appointments to all the constitutional posts.
- He can address either House of Parliament and dissolve Lok Sabha.
- All Bills passed by Parliament must receive his assent to become an Act.
- He issues ordinances when Parliament is not in session. No Money Bill can be introduced in Lok Sabha without his recommendation.
- He appoints 12 members of special repute in the Rajya Sabha.
- He has the power of *Pardon* to a criminal in special cases.
- The President holds the office for a period of five years. He is eligible for re-election.
- He is also entitled to rent free official residence called Rashtrapati Bhawan.

Vice-President

- ***Article 63*** of the Constitution stipulates a Vice-President for India.
- The Vice-President acts as the ex-officio Chairman of the Council of States (Rajya Sabha).
- He is elected by an electoral college consisting of the members of both Houses of Parliament in accordance with the system of proportional representation by means of the single transferable vote. He must be a citizen of India, not less than 35 years of age, and should be eligible for election as a member of the Council of States.
- Disputes in connection with election of a president or a vice-president are to be a dealt with in accordance with Article-71. Such disputes shall be decided by the Supreme Court.

Council of Ministers

- The Constitution of India provides for a parliament system of government under which the President is only Constitutional ruler and the real power is exercised by the Council of Ministers, headed by the Prime Minister.
- Council of Ministers is composed of all Union Ministers—the Prime Minister, Cabinet Ministers, Ministers of State and Deputy Ministers.
- The Council of Ministers is Collectively responsible to the Lok Sabha.
- The Prime Minister is a link between the President and the Council of Ministers.

Prime Minister

- The Prime Minister is the leader of the majority party in the Parliament.
- He is appointed by the President. Other Ministers are appointed by the president on his advice.
- The Prime Minister is the head of the Government and the head of the Council of Ministers.
- Jawaharlal Nehru was the first Prime Minister and the longest serving so far.

Union Legislature

- The Legislature of the Union, which is called 'Parliament' consists of the President and the two Houses of Parliament known as the Council of states (Rajya Sabha) and the House of the People (Lok Sabha).

RAJYA SABHA

- The Rajya Sabha is the Upper House of the Parliament and it is constituted of representatives from the States or the Constituent units of the Indian Union.
- It is a permanent body, one third of its members retiring after every two years.
- Its maximum strength is 250. Out of these, twelve members are nominated by the President from well-known personalities in the realm of Science, Art, Literature and Social Service. Rest of 238 representatives of the States and Union Territories are elected.
- Currently, the strength of the Rajya Sabha is 245.

LOK SABHA

- The Lok Sabha whose life is five years, is the Lower House of Parliament and comprises of members directly elected by the people.
- The House of the people (Lok Sabha) at present consists, 543 members directly elected from the states and Union Territories. By the 104th Constitutional amendment Act, 2019 the 2 Anglo-Indian reserved seats nominated by President in Lok Sabha are abolished.
- The House of the People shall continue for five years (unless sooner dissolved) from the date of its meeting and no longer and the expiry of the said period of 5 years shall operate as dissolution of the House.

Parliamentary Committees

- There are several Parliamentary Committees to assist the Parliament in its deliberations.
- These are appointed or elected by the respective Houses of Lok Sabha and Rajya Sabha on a motion made or are nominated by their presiding officers.
- Among the Standing Committees, three are financial Committees: (i) Public Account Committee; (ii) Estimate Committee; (iii) Public undertaking Committee.

Speaker of Lok Sabha

- Speaker is elected by the Lok Sabha from among its members.
- The Speaker will have the final power to maintain order within the House of the People and to interpret its rules of procedure.
- A Deputy-Speaker is also elected to officiate in absence of the Speaker.
- *G.V. Mavlankar* was the first Speaker of the Lok Sabha (1952-1956).

Supreme Court

- The Constitution provides for the Supreme Court, which consists of Chief Justice and 33 judges. They are appointed by the President of India.

QUALIFICATION AND TENURE

- Eligibility conditions for a judge of the Supreme Court are that he must be : (i) a citizen of India; (ii) a judge of a high court for a minimum period of 5 years; or (iii) an advocate of a high court for at least ten years or a distinguished jurist.
- Judges hold office till the age of 65.
- They can resign earlier or can be removed by the President on the recommendation of the two Houses of the Parliament by 2/3rd majority of the members present and voting.

Powers

- *Original jurisdiction:* Cases involving Government of India and the states or cases involving the enforcement of Fundamental Rights fall under original jurisdiction.
- *Appellate Jurisdiction:* In cases which are brought to it in the form of appeals against the judgement of the lower courts—It hears appeals in civil and criminal cases.
- *Advisory functions:* the Supreme Court advises the President on the constitutionality of a particular legal matter. However, its advice is not binding on the President.

Other Powers:

1. it is a court of record and can punish for contempt of itself;
2. it can make rules for regulating the practice and procedure of courts with the approval of the President; and
3. it can recommend to the President the removal of chairman and members of the UPSC. Supreme Court enjoys the power of judicial review (right of the court which declares as unconstitutional, the laws passed by the legislature and orders issued by executive) though it is not specifically mentioned in the Constitution.

- The first Chief Justice of India was H.J. Kania (1950-51).

COMPTROLLER AND AUDITOR GENERAL (CAG) (ARTICLE 148-151)

- The Comptroller and Auditor General of India is guardian of the public purse.
- It is his duty to see that not a *paisa* is spent out of consolidated fund of India or of a state without the authority of the appropriate legislature.
- He is appointed by President of India.
- A person with long administrative experience and knowledge of accounts is appointed.
- Holds office for 6 yrs or till 65 yrs of age.
- The President can remove him only on the recommendation of the 2 houses of Parliament (as in case of judge of Supreme Court).
- The CAG submits its reports to the President (in case of accounts relating to the Union Government) or to the State Governors (for State Government Accounts).
- The first CAG of India was *V Narahari Rao* (1948-1954).
- The CAG is not eligible for further office under the Union or State Governments. The expenses of the office of the CAG is charged to the Consolidated Fund of India.

ATTORNEY GENERAL OF INDIA

- The Attorney General of India is the first law officer of the Government of India.
- Though he is not a member of cabinet he has the right to speak in the House of Parliament, but he has no right to vote.
- The Attorney General of India shall be appointed by the President and shall hold office during his pleasure.
- His duty shall be to give advice on such legal matter from time-to-time as may be referred to him by the President.
- To be appointed as Attorney General, a candidate must be qualified to be appointed as a Judge of the Supreme Court.
- The Attorney General can participate in proceedings of the Parliament without the Right to Vote (Article 88).
- The first Attorney General of Independent India was MC Setalvad (1950-1963).

PART - VI

THE STATES (ARTICLE 152 - 237)

The Governor

- The Governor is appointed by the President and holds office during the pleasure of the President.
- Apart from the power to appoint the council of ministers, if the governor finds that the government of state cannot be carried on in accordance with the provisions of the

constitution (Art. 356), he may send his report to the President who may assume to himself the functions of the government of the state. (This is popularly known as 'President's Rule').

Article 161 gives the Governor the power to grant pardons, reprieves, remission of punishment to persons convicted under the state law.

- Article 171 states that the States where Legislative Councils exists, the Governor can nominate some members from amongst those distinguished in literature, science, arts, cooperative movement and social service.

STATES LEGISLATURE (ARTICLE 168 - 212)

- The state legislature consists of Governor and legislative assembly.
- In some state like *Bihar, Maharashtra, Andhra Pradesh, Karnataka, Uttar Pradesh and Telangana* have a legislative council.

The membership of the council should not be more than *one-third* of the legislative assembly but not less than 40.

The legislative assembly of each state shall be composed of members chosen by direct election on the basis of adult suffrage and the number of members shall not be more than 500 or less than 60.

The assembly of Sikkim, Goa, Puducherry and Mizoram have less than 60 members.

HIGH COURTS (ARTICLE 214-232)

- The High Court stands at the apex of the State Judiciary.
- As per the Constitution, there shall be a High Court in each State. But there may be a common High Court for two or more States and Union Territory, if it is provided by a law of the Parliament. For example, the Chennai High Court has its Jurisdiction over the State of Tamil Nadu and the Union Territory of Puducherry.
- The State Government has no control over it.
- There are 25 High Courts in India.
- The Calcutta High Court, established in 1862, is the oldest High Court in India.

THE PANCHAYATS (ARTICLE 243-243 O)

- Panchayati Raj was introduced in India with a view to associate the people with administration at grass-root level.
- It is a three-tier system as recommended by Balwant Rai Mehta Committee.
- Introduced by the 73rd Amendment Act, 1992 which envisaged a three tier system of local governance.

These are:

1. Gram Panchayat at the village level
2. Panchayat Samiti at the block level
3. Zila Parishad at the district level.

Jurisdiction and Seat of High Courts

Name	Year	Territorial Jurisdiction	Seat
Allahabad	1866	Uttar Pradesh	Prayagraj (Bench at Lucknow)
Andhra Pradesh	2019	Andhra Pradesh	Amaravati
Bombay	1862	Maharashtra, Goa, Dadar and Nagar Haveli and Daman and Diu	Mumbai (Benches at Nagpur, Panaji and Aurangabad)
Calcutta	1862	West Bengal and Andaman & Nicobar	Kolkata (Circuit Benches at Sri Vijaya Puram and Jalpaiguri)
Chhattisgarh	2000	Chhattisgarh	Bilaspur
Delhi	1966	Delhi	Delhi
Gauhati	1948	Assam, Nagaland, Mizoram and Arunachal Pradesh	Guwahati (Benches at Kohima, Aizawl and Itanagar)
Gujarat	1960	Gujarat	Ahmedabad
Himachal Pradesh	1971	Himachal Pradesh	Shimla
Jammu and Kashmir and Ladakh	1928	Jammu & Kashmir, Ladakh	Srinagar and Jammu
Jharkhand	2000	Jharkhand	Ranchi
Karnataka	1884	Karnataka	Bengaluru (Circuit Benches at Dharwar and Gulbarga)
Kochi	1958	Kerala & Lakshadweep	Ernakulam
Madhya Pradesh	1956	Madhya Pradesh	Jabalpur (Benches at Gwalior and Indore)
Madras	1862	Tamil Nadu & Puducherry	Chennai (Bench at Madurai)
Orissa	1948	Odisha	Cuttack
Patna	1916	Bihar	Patna
Punjab and Haryana	1966	Punjab, Haryana and Chandigarh	Chandigarh
Rajasthan	1949	Rajasthan	Jodhpur (Bench at Jaipur)
Sikkim	1975	Sikkim	Gangtok
Uttarakhand	2000	Uttarakhand	Nainital
Tripura	2013	Tripura	Agartala
Meghalaya	2013	Meghalaya	Shillong
Manipur	2013	Manipur	Imphal
Telangana	2019	Telangana	Hyderabad

THE MUNICIPALITIES (ARTICLE 243 P-243 ZG)

- Big cities have municipal corporations headed by the elected Mayor.
- For small towns there are elected boards or councils, in turn, elect their Presidents.
- Introduced by the 74th Amendment Act, 1993 which envisages three types of urban local bodies, namely, municipality (nagar palika), city council (nagar panchayat).
- Municipal governance in India was first introduced in Madras in 1688.

PART - XIII

(ARTICLE 301 - 307)

- In this part from Article 301-307 trade, commerce and intercourse within the territory of India are given.

PART - XIV

(ARTICLE 308 - 323)

- In this part services under the union and the states are given.
- ***Article 312:*** *All India Services* and ***Article 315:*** Public Service Commissions for the Union and for the States.
- The first Public Service Commission was set up in 1926, on the recommendations of the Lee Commission.

UNION PUBLIC SERVICE COMMISSION (UPSC)

- This Commission is responsible for:
  1. recruitment to all civil services and posts, under the Union Government by written examinations, interviews and promotions, and
  2. advising the Government on all matters relating to methods of recruitment, principles to be followed in making promotions and transfers. Its Chairman is appointed by the President.

STAFF SELECTION COMMISSION (SSC)

- The Union Government has constituted a Staff Selection Commission for recruitment to non-technical Class III posts in the central government and in subordinate offices.
- The Administrative Reforms Commission had recommended the setting up of such a Commission.
- The Commission has also been entrusted with the responsibility of making recruitment to Group 'B' services like Assistants' and Stenographers Grade 'C'.
- The Commission has a chairman and two members.

ELECTIONS (ARTICLE 324-329)

- The Constitution provides for an independent election commission to ensure free and fair election to the Parliament, the State legislature and the offices of President and Vice-President.
- Consists of Chief Election Commissioner +2 Election Commissioners. They all enjoy equal powers.
- The Chief Election Commissioner and other Election Commissioners are appointed by the President.
- Election Commissioners are appointed for a term of 5 yrs.
- They are not eligible for re-appointment. Also, they cannot hold any office of profit after their retirement.
- The Election Commission was established on 25th January, 1950 under Article 324 of the Constitution.
- The first Chief Election Commissioner was *Sukumar Sen.*

Functions

- Preparation of electoral rolls and keeping voters list updated.
- Recognition of various political parties and allotment of election symbols.

NITI AAYOG

- The Indian government has replaced Planing Commission with a new institution named **NITI Aayog (National Institution for Transforming India).**
- The Niti Aayog will comprise the following:
  1. Prime Minister of India as the Chairperson.
  2. Governing Council comprising the Chief Ministers of all the States and Lt. Governors of Territories.
  3. Regional Councils will be formed to address specific issues and contingencies impacting more than one state or a region. These will be formed for a specified tenure. The Regional Councils will be convened by the Prime Minister and will comprise of the Chief Ministers of States and Lt. Governors of Territories in the region. These will be chaired by the Chairperson of the NITI Aayog or his nominee.
  4. Experts, specialists and practitioners with relevant domain knowledge as special invitees nominated by the Prime Minister.
- The full-time organizational framework will comprise of, in addition to the Prime Minister as the Chairperson:
  1. Vice-Chairperson : To be appointed by the Prime Minister.
  2. Members : Full-time.
  3. Part-time members : Maximum of 2 from leading universities research organizations and other relevant institutions in an ex-officio capacity. Part time members will be on a rotational basis.
  4. Ex Officio members : Maximum of 4 members of the Council of Ministers to be nominated by the Prime Minister.
  5. Chief Executive Officer : To be appointed by the Prime Minister for a fixed tenure, in the rank of Secretary to the Government of India.
  6. Secretariat as deemed necessary.

FINANCE COMMISSION

- The constitution of the Finance Commission is laid down in Art. 280. The chairman must be a person having experience in public affairs; and the other four members also having wide experience in financial matters.
- It consists of Chairman and 4 other members.
- It shall be the duty of the Finance Commission to advice the President on matters such as the distribution between the Union and States of the net proceeds of taxes that is required to be shared.
- The Finance Commission is not a permanent body. It is dissolved after it has submitted its recommendations.

❑❑❑

4

Indian Economy

NATIONAL INCOME

- According to the National Income Committee (1949), "A national income estimate measures the volume of commodities and service turned out during a given period counted without duplication". Thus, national income measures the net value of goods and services produced in a country during a year and it also includes net earned foreign income. In other words, a total of national income measures the flow of goods and services in an economy.
- National income is a flow concept not a stock concept.
- In India, National income estimates are related with the financial year (April 1 to 31st March).
- The various concepts of national income are as follows:
  - *(i)* **GNP (Gross National Product):** GNP refers to the money value of total output or production of final goods and services produced by the nationals of a country during a given period of time, generally a year.
  - *(ii)* **NNP (Net National Product):** NNP is obtained by subtracting depreciation value from GNP. NNP can be calculated in two ways: *(a)* at market prices of goods and services and *(b)* at factor cost.
  - *(iii)* **National Income:** When NNP is obtained at factor cost, it is known as National Income. National Income is calculated by subtracting net indirect taxes from NNP at market prices. The obtained value is known as NNP at factor cost or National income.
  - *(iv)* **Personal Income:** Personal income is that income which is actually obtained by nationals. Personal income is obtained by subtracting corporate taxes and payments made for social securities provisions from national income and adding to it govern-ment transfer payments, business transfer payments and net interest paid by the government.

Methods of Measuring National Income

- According to Simon Kuznets, national income of a country is calculated by following mentioned three methods:
  - *(i)* **Product Method:** S. Kuznets gave a new name to this method, *i.e.*, product service method. In this method, net value of final goods and services produced in a country during a year is obtained and the total obtained value is called total final product.
  - *(ii)* **Income Method:** In this method, a total of net incomes earned by working people in different sectors and commercial enterprises is obtained.
  - *(iii)* **Consumption Method:** It is also called expenditure method. Income is either spent on consumption or saved. Hence, national income is the addition of total consumption and total savings.
- In India, a combination of production method and income method is used for measuring estimating national income.
- For measuring national income in India, in 1868, the first attempt was made by *Dada Bhai Nauroji.* He, in his book, *"Poverty and Un-British Rule in India"*, estimated Indian per capita annual income at a level of ₹ 20.
- After independence, the Government of India appointed the National Income Committee in August, 1949, under the Chairmanship of Prof. P.C. Mahalanobies, to compile authoritative estimates of national income.
- Estimation and publishing of National Income data by CSO (Central Statistical Organization) is done every year.
- National income includes the contribution of three sectors—primary sector, secondary sector, Tertiary sector.
- Under Primary Sector—Agriculture, Forest, Fisheries and allied sector are included.
- Under Secondary Sector—Manufacturing, Construction, Electricity, Gas and Water Supply are included.
- Under Teritiary Sector—Trade, Transport, Communication, Banking, Insurance, Real Estate, Community and Personal Services are included.
- The contribution of primary sector in GDP was 55.4% in 1950-1951. But now the share of primary sector in national income has come down. In 2023-24, the contribution of primary sector in GDP was 17.66%.
- The contribution of secondary sector has shown a steady increase from 15% in 1950-51 to 27.63% in 2023-24.
- The contribution of tertiary sector indicated a sharp improvement from 29.6% in 1950-51 to about 54.71% in 2023-24.
- At present estimation of national income is based on the base year of 2011-2012.

POPULATION

Census-2011: Population, Density, Decadal Growth Rate

S.N.	State/UTs	Population		Density		Decadal G. (%)
		2001	2011	2001	2011	2001–2011
1.	J&K	10,143,700	1,25,41,302	100	124	23.6
2.	Himachal Pradesh	6,077,900	68,64,602	109	123	12.9
3.	Punjab	24,358,999	2,77,43,338	484	551	13.9
4.	Chandigarh	900,635	10,55,450	7,900	9258	17.2
5.	Uttarakhand	8,489,349	1,00,86,292	159	189	18.8
6.	Haryana	21,144,564	2,53,51,462	478	573	19.9
7.	Delhi	13,850,507	1,67,87,941	9,340	11320	21.2
8.	Rajasthan	56,507,188	6,85,48,437	165	200	21.3
9.	Uttar Pradesh	166,197,921	19,98,12,341	690	829	20.2
10.	Bihar	82,998,509	10,40,99,452	881	1106	25.4
11.	Sikkim	540,851	6,10,577	76	86	12.9
12.	Arunachal Pradesh	1,097,968	13,83,727	13	17	26.0
13.	Nagaland	1,990,036	19,78,502	120	119	–0.6
14.	Manipur	2,293,896	28,55,794	103	128	31.79
15.	Mizoram	888,573	10,97,206	42	52	23.5
16.	Tripura	3,199,203	36,73,917	305	350	14.8
17.	Meghalaya	2,318,822	29,66,889	103	132	27.9
18.	Assam	26,655,528	3,12,05,576	340	398	17.1
19.	West Bengal	80,176,197	9,12,76,115	903	1028	13.8
20.	Jharkhand	26,945,829	3,29,88,134	338	414	22.4
21.	Odisha	36,804,660	4,19,74,218	236	270	14.0
22.	Chhattisgarh	20,833,803	2,55,45,198	154	189	22.6
23.	Madhya Pradesh	60,348,023	7,26,26,809	196	236	20.3
24.	Gujarat	50,671,017	6,04,39,692	258	308	19.3
25.	Daman & Diu	158,204	2,43,247	1,413	2191	53.8
26.	Dadra & N. Haveli	220,490	3,43,709	449	700	55.9
27.	Maharashtra	96,878,627	11,23,74,333	315	365	16.0
28.	Andhra Pradesh	76,210,007	4,93,86,799	277	308	11.0
29.	Karnataka	52,850,562	6,10,95,297	276	319	15.6
30.	Goa	1,347,668	14,58,545	364	394	8.2
31.	Lakshadweep	60,650	64,473	1,895	2149	6.3
32.	Kerala	31,841,374	3,34,06,061	819	860	4.9
33.	Tamil Nadu	62,405,679	7,21,47,030	480	555	15.6
34.	Puducherry	974,345	12,47,953	2,030	2546	28.1
35.	Andaman & Nicobar Islands	356,152	3,80,581	43	46	6.9
36.	Telangana	—	3,51,93,978	—	307	13.58
	India	**1,028,737,436**	**1,21,08,54,977**	**325**	**382**	**17.7**

AGRICULTURE

- Agriculture is an important sector of the economy. Though the share of agriculture in national income has come down since the inception of planning era in the economy but still it has substantial share in GDP.
- In terms of composition, out of the total share of 16 per cent that agriculture and allied sector had in GDP in 2022-23.
- Agriculture in our country provides livelihood to about 45.5% of the population.
- Gross Capital Formation (GCF) in Agriculture and Allied sector relative to GVA in this sector has been snowing a fluctuating trent from 18.3 per cent in 2011-12 to 19.9 per cent in 2022-23.
- Agriculture provides raw materials to various industries and other agro-based industries. Cotton and Jute textile industries, Sugar, Vanaspati industry etc. are directly dependent on agriculture.
- India's foreign trade is deeply associated with Agriculture Sector. Value of agriculture exports to total exports of the country was 13.8 per cent in 2013. But the share of agriculture has come down in foreign trade at present.

Various Crops and their producing states

Crops/Groups of Crops	Producing State (In Descending Order)
I. Foodgrains	
Rice	West Bengal, Telangana, Uttar Pradesh, Punjab
Wheat	Uttar Pradesh, Madhya Pradesh, Punjab
Maize	Karnataka, Bihar, Madhya Pradesh, Maharashtra
Total Nutri/ Coarse Cereals	Rajasthan, Karnataka, Madhya Pradesh, Maharashtra
Gram	Maharashtra, Madhya Pradesh, Rajasthan
Tur	Maharashtra, Karnataka, Uttar Pradesh
Total Pulses	Madhya Pradesh, Maharashtra, Rajasthan
Total Food-grains	Uttar Pradesh, Madhya Pradesh, Punjab
II. Oilseeds	
Groundnut	Gujarat, Rajasthan, Madhya Pradesh, Tamil Nadu
Rapeseed & Mustard	Rajasthan, Uttar Pradesh, Madhya Pradesh, Haryana
Soyabean	Maharashtra, Madhya Pradesh, Rajasthan
Sunflower	Karnataka, Telangana, Odisha, Haryana
Total Oilseeds	Rajasthan, Madhya Pradesh, Gujarat
III. Other Cash Crops	
Sugarcane	Uttar Pradesh, Maharashtra, Karnataka
Cotton	Gujarat, Maharashtra, Telangana
Jute & Mesta	West Bengal, Assam, Bihar

Source: Economic Survey 2023-24

ECONOMIC PLANNING

☞ **Five Year Plans in India**

Plans	Period	Investment (₹ Crore)	Objectives
First Plan	April 1, 1951-March 31, 1956	1,960	Priority to agriculture, electricity and irrigation.
Second Plan	April 1, 1956—March 31, 1961	4,672	Development of basic and heavy industries.
Third Plan	April 1, 1961—March 31, 1966	8,577	Long term development of India's economy.
Annual Plan	April 1, 1966—March 31, 1967	2,137	
Annual Plan	April 1, 1967—March 31, 1968	2,205	
Annual Plan	April 1, 1968—March 31, 1969	2,283	
Fourth Plan	April 1, 1969—March 31, 1974	15,779	Enlarge the income of rural population and supply of goods of mass consumption.
Fifth Plan	April 1, 1974—March 31, 1979	39,426	Attain increased self-reliance and employment avenues.
Annual Plan	April 1, 1979—March 31, 1980	12,176	
Sixth Plan	April 1, 1980—March 31, 1985	1,09,292	Removal of unemployment
Seventh Plan	April 1, 1985—March 31, 1990	2,18,730	Food work and productivity were the basic priorities.
Eighth Plan	April, 1992—March 31, 1997	4,95,670	Raising employment
Ninth Plan	April 1, 1997—March 31, 2002	9,41,041	Agriculture and rural development
Tenth Plan	April 1, 2002—March 31, 2007	14,91,610	Growth rate 7.8 percent per annum.
Eleventh Plan	April 1, 2007—March 31, 2012	36,44,718	Literacy, Employment, Rural development & Transport development.
Twelfth Plan	April 1, 2012–March 31, 2017	43,30,000	Longterm development of India's economy.

15-YEAR VISION PLANE

With the end of the Twelfth Plan in March 2017 the era of five year plans came to an end. NITI Aayog has come forward with a draft 15-year vision plan to catapult the country's economy to more than three times as compared to the present day. The new plan is set to replace the centralised five-year plans the country has been following for decades. The new plan is accompanied by shorter sub-plan—a seven-year strategy for 2017-24, and a three-year 'Action Agenda' from 2017-18 to 2019-20. No less than 300 specific action points covering a wide range of sectors points covering a wide range of sectors have been drawn up as part of the 15-year vision.

MONEY AND BANKING

RESERVE BANK OF INDIA

- Reserve Bank of India (RBI) is the central bank of the country.
- Reserve Bank of India was established on April 1, 1935 under Reserve Bank of India Act, 1934 with a authorised capital of ₹ 5 crore.
- The Reserve Bank of India was nationalised on January 1, 1949.
- The general administration and direction of RBI is managed by a Central Board of Directors consisting of 20 members which includes 1 Governor and 4 Deputy Governors.
- The head office of the Reserve Bank of India is in Mumbai.

☞ **Establishment Years of Major Financial Institutions in India**

Institution	Year
Imperial Bank of India	1921
Reserve Bank of India (Nationalisation of RBI took place on January 1, 1949)	April 1, 1935
Industrial Finance Corporation of India (IFCI)	1948
State Bank of India (SBI)	July 1, 1955
Unit Trust of India (UTI)	Feb. 1, 1964
IDBI	July 1964
NABARD	July 12, 1982
SIDBI	1990
EXIM Bank	January 1, 1982
National Housing Bank (NHB)	July 1988
Life Insurance Corporation (LIC)	Sept. 1956
General Insurance Corporation (GIC)	Nov. 1972
Regional Rural Banks (RRBs)	Oct. 2, 1975
Risk Capital and Technology Finance Corporation Ltd.	March 1975
Housing Development Finance Corporation Ltd. (HDFC)	1977

❒ ❒ ❒

5

General Science

IMPORTANT INVENTIONS

Name of Invention	Inventor	Nationality	Year
Aeroplane	Orville & Wilbur Wright	U.S.A.	1903
Ball-Point Pen	John J. Loud	U.S.A.	1888
Barometer	Evangelista Torricelli	Italy	1644
Bicycle	Kirkpatrick Macmillan	Britain	1839-40
Bifocal Lens	Benjamin Franklin	U.S.A.	1780
Car (Petrol)	Karl Benz	Germany	1888
Celluloid	Alexander Parkes	Britain	1861
Cinema	Nicolas & Jean Lumiere	France	1895
Clock (mechanical)	I-Hsing & Liang Ling-Tsan	China	1725
Diesel Engine	Rudolf Diesel	Germany	1895
Dynamo	Hypolite Pixii	France	1832
Electric Lamp	Thomas Alva Edison	U.S.A.	1879
Electric Motor (DC)	Zenobe Gramme	Belgium	1873
Electric Motor (AC)	Nikola Tesla	U.S.A.	1888
Electro-magnet	William Sturgeon	Britain	1824
Electronic Computer	Dr. Alan M. Turing	Britain	1943
Film (moving outlines)	Louis Prince	France	1885
Film (musical sound)	Dr. Le de Forest	U.S.A.	1923
Fountain Pen	Lewis E. Waterman	U.S.A.	1884
Gramophone	Thomas Alva Edison	U.S.A.	1878
Helicopter	Etienne Oehmichen	France	1924
Jet Engine	Sir Frank Whittle	Britain	1937
Laser	Charles H. Townes	U.S.A.	1960
Lift (Mechanical)	Elisha G. Otis	U.S.A.	1852
Locomotive	Richard Trevithick	Britain	1804
Machine Gun	James Puckle	Britain	1718
Microphone	Alexander Graham Bell	U.S.A.	1876
Microscope	Z. Janssen	Netherlands	1590
Motor Cycle	G. Daimler	Germany	1885
Photography (on film)	John Carbutt	U.S.A.	1888
Printing Press	Johann Gutenberg	Germany	c.1455
Razor (safety)	King C. Gillette	U.S.A.	1895
Refrigerator	James Harrison & Alexander Catlin	U.S.A.	1850
Safety Pin	Walter Hunt	U.S.A.	1849
Sewing machine	Barthelemy Thimmonnier	France	1829
Ship (steam)	J.C. Perier	France	1775
Ship (turbine)	Hon. Sir C. Parsons	Britain	1894
Skyscraper	W. Le Baron Jenny	U.S.A.	1882
Slide Rule	William Oughtred	Britain	1621
Steam Engine (condenser)	James Watt	Britain	1765
Steel Production	Henry Bessemer	Britain	1855
Steel (stainless)	Harry Brearley	Britain	1913
Submarine	David Bushnell	U.S.A.	1776

Name of Invention	Inventor	Nationality	Year
Tank	Sir Ernest Swinton	Britain	1914
Telegraph	M. Lammond	France	1787
Telegraph Code	Samuel F.B. Morse	U.S.A.	1837
Telephone (perfected)	Alexander Graham Bell	U.S.A.	1876
Television (mechanical)	John Logie Baird	Britain	1926
Television (electronic)	P.T. Farnsworth	U.S.A.	1927
Thermometer	Galileo Galilei	Italy	1593
Transformer	Michael Faraday	Britain	1831
Transistor	Bardeen, Shockley & Brattain	U.S.A.	1948
Washing Machine (elec.)	Hurley Machine Co.	U.S.A.	1907
Zip-Fastener	W.L. Judson	U.S.A.	1891

IMPORTANT DISCOVERIES

Discovery	Discoverer	Nationality	Year
Aluminium	Hans Christian Oerstedt	Denmark	1827
Atomic number	Henry Moseley	England	1913
Atomic structure of matter	John Dalton	England	1803
Chlorine	C.W. Scheele	Sweden	1774
Electromagnetic induction	Michael Faraday	England	1831
Electromagnetic waves	Heinrich Hertz	Germany	1886
Electromagnetism	Hans Christian Oersted	Denmark	1920
Electron	Sir Joseph Thomson	England	1897
General theory of relativity	Albert Einstein	Switzerland	1915
Hydrogen	Henry Cavendish	England	1766
Law of electric conduction	Georg Ohm	Germany	1827
Law of electromagnetism	Andre Ampere	France	1826
Law of falling bodies	Galileo	Italy	1590
Laws of gravitation & motion	Isaac Newton	England	1687
Laws of planetary motion	Johannes Kepler	Germany	1609-10
Magnesium	Sir Humphry Davy	England	1808
Neptune (Planet)	Johann Galle	Germany	1846
Neutron	James Chadwick	England	1932
Nickel	Axel Cronstedt	Sweden	1751
Nitrogen	Daniel Rutherford	England	1772
Oxygen	Joseph Priestly; C.W. Scheele	England; Sweden	1772
Ozone	Christian Schonbein	Germany	1839
Pluto (Planet)	Clyde Tombaugh	U.S.A	1930
Plutonium	G.T. Seaborg	U.S.A	1940
Proton	Ernest Rutherford	England	1919
Quantum Theory	Max Planck	Germany	1900
Radioactivity	Antoine Bacquerel	France	1896
Radium	Pierre & Marie Curie	France	1898
Silicon	Jons Berzelius	Sweden	1824
Special theory of relativity	Albert Einstein	Switzerland	1905
Sun as centre of solar system	Copernicus	Poland	1543
Uranium	Martin Klaproth	Germany	1789
Uranus (Planet)	William Herschel	England	1781
X-rays	Wilhelm Roentgen	Germany	1895

GEOGRAPHICAL EXPLORATIONS/DISCOVERIES

Place	Explorer/Discoverer	Nationality	Year
America	Christopher Columbus	Italy	1492
Hawaii Islands (Sandwich Islands)	Captain James Cook	England	1778
Newfoundland	John Cabot	England	1497
New Zealand	Abel Janszoon Tasman	Holland	1642
North Pole	Robert Peary	USA	1909
Sea Route to India (via Cape of Good Hope)	Vasco da Gama	Portugal	1498
South Pole	Roald Amundsen	Norway	1911

SCIENTIFIC INSTRUMENTS

Name of Instrument	Used for
Altimeter	measuring altitude
Ammeter	measuring strength of an electric current
Anemometer	measuring the velocity of wind
Audiometer	measuring level of hearing
Barometer	measuring atmospheric pressure
Callipers	measuring the internal and external diameters of tubes
Calorimeter	measuring quantity of heat
Compass	finding out direction
Dynamo	converting mechanical energy into electrical energy
Eudiometer	measuring volume changes during chemical reactions between gases
Galvanometer	detecting and determining the strength of small electric currents
Hydrometer	measuring specific gravity of a liquid
Hygrometer	measuring the humidity in the atmosphere
Lactometer	measuring the purity of milk
Manometer	measuring the gaseous pressure
Micrometer	measuring minute distances, angles, etc.
Microscope	seeing magnified view of very small objects
Photometer	measuring intensity of light from distant stars
Pyrometer	measuring high temperatures
Radar	detecting and finding the presence and location of moving objects like aircraft, missile, etc.
Radiometer	measuring the emission of radiant energy
Rain Gauge	measuring the amount of rainfall
Seismograph	measuring and recording the intensity and origin of earthquake shocks
Sextant	measuring altitude and angular distances between two objects or heavenly bodies
Spectrometer	measuring the refractive indices
Spherometer	measuring the curvature of spherical objects/surface
Sphygmomanometer	measuring blood pressure
Stethoscope	ascertaining the condition of heart and lungs by listening to their function
Stroboscope	viewing objects that are moving rapidly with a periodic motion as if they were at rest
Tachometer	measuring the rate of revolution or angular speed of a revolving shaft
Telescope	viewing magnified images of distant objects
Theodolite	measuring the horizontal and vertical angles
Thermocouple	measuring the temperature inside furnaces and jet engines
Thermometer	measuring human body temperature
Thermostat	regulating constant temperature
Ultrasonoscope	measuring utrasonic sounds
Viscometer	measuring the viscosity of a fluid
Voltmeter	measuring potential difference between two points.

DISEASES AND THE PARTS OF BODY THEY AFFECT

Disease	Part of body affected	Disease	Part of body affected
AIDS	Immune system of body	Jaundice	Liver
Arthritis	Inflammation of joints	Meningitis	Brain or spinal cord
Asthma	Lungs	Pleurisy	Pleura (inflammation of)
Cataract	Eyes	Polio	motor neurons
Conjunctivitis	Eyes	Pneumonia	Lungs
Diabetes	Pancreas	Pyorrhoea	Sockets of teeth
Diphtheria	Throat	Tuberculosis	Lungs
Glaucoma	Eyes	Typhoid	Intestine
Eczema	Skin	Malaria	Spleen
Goitre	Front of the neck (due to enlargement of thyroid gland)	Leukaemia	Blood
Gout	Joints of bone	Rickets	Bones

❒❒❒

6

Miscellaneous

CAPITAL & CURRENCIES

Country	Capital	Currency
✶ Afghanistan	Kabul	Afghani
✶ Algeria	Algiers	Dinar
✶ Angola	Luanda	New Kwanza
✶ Argentina	Buenos Aires	Peso
✶ Australia	Canberra	Dollar
✶ Austria	Vienna	Euro
✶ Azerbaijan	Baku	Manat
✶ Bahrain	Manama	Dinar
✶ Bangladesh	Dhaka	Taka
✶ Barbados	Bridgetown	Dollar
✶ Belarus	Minsk	Ruble
✶ Belgium	Brussels	Euro
✶ Bhutan	Thimphu	Ngultrum
✶ Bolivia	La paz	Boliviano
✶ Brazil	Brasilia	Real
✶ Bulgaria	Sofia	Euro
✶ Canada	Ottawa	Dollar
✶ Chile	Santiago	Peso
✶ China	Beijing	Yuan
✶ Colombia	Bogota	Peso
✶ Croatia	Zagreb	Kuna
✶ Cuba	Havana	Peso
✶ Cyprus	Nicosia	Euro
✶ Czech Republic	Prague	Koruna
✶ Denmark	Copenhagen	Krone
✶ Ecuador	Quito	Dollar
✶ Egypt	Cairo	Pound
✶ Ethiopia	Addis Ababa	Birr
✶ Fiji	Suva	Dollar
✶ Finland	Helsinki	Euro
✶ France	Paris	Euro
✶ Georgia	Tbilisi	Lari
✶ Germany	Berlin	Euro
✶ Ghana	Accra	Cedi
✶ Greece	Athens	Euro
✶ Guyana	George Town	Dollar
✶ Hungary	Budapest	Forint
✶ India	New Delhi	Rupee
✶ Indonesia	Jakarta	Rupiah

Country	Capital	Currency
✶ Iran	Teheran	Rial
✶ Iraq	Baghdad	Dinar
✶ Ireland	Dublin	Euro
✶ Israel	Jerusalem	Shekel
✶ Italy	Rome	Euro
✶ Japan	Tokyo	Yen
✶ Jordan	Amman	Dinar
✶ Kazakhstan	Astana	Tenge
✶ Kenya	Nairobi	Shilling
✶ Korea (S)	Seoul	Won
✶ Korea (N)	Pyongyang	Won
✶ Kyrgyzstan	Bishkek	Som
✶ Kuwait	Kuwait City	Dinar
✶ Laos	Vientiane	Kip
✶ Lebanon	Beirut	Pound
✶ Liberia	Monrovia	Dollar
✶ Libya	Tripoli	Dinar
✶ Malaysia	Kuala Lumpur	Ringgit
✶ Maldives	Male	Rufiyaa
✶ Mali	Bamako	Franc
✶ Mauritius	Port Louis	Rupee
✶ Mexico	Mexico City	Peso
✶ Mongolia	Ulan Bator	Tugrik
✶ Morocco	Rabat	Dirham
✶ Myanmar (Burma)	Nay Pyi Taw	Kyat
✶ Namibia	Winohoek	Dollar
✶ Nepal	Kathmandu	Rupee
✶ Netherlands	Amsterdam	Euro
✶ New Zealand	Wellington	Dollar
✶ Nigeria	Abuja	Naira
✶ Norway	Oslo	Krone
✶ Oman	Muscat	Rial
✶ Pakistan	Islamabad	Rupee
✶ Panama	Panama City	Balboa
✶ Peru	Lima	New Sole
✶ Philippines	Manila	Peso
✶ Poland	Warsaw	Zloty
✶ Portugal	Lisbon	Euro
✶ Qatar	Doha	Riyal
✶ Russia	Moscow	Ruble

Country	Capital	Currency
✶ Saudi Arabia	Riyadh	Rial
✶ Slovakia	Bratislava	Euro
✶ Spain	Madrid	Euro
✶ Sri Lanka	Colombo	Rupee
✶ Sudan	Khartoum	Dinar
✶ Sweden	Stockholm	Krona
✶ Switzerland	Berne	Swiss Francs
✶ Syria	Damascus	Pound
✶ South Africa	Capetown (Legislative) Pretoria *(Administrative)*	Rand
✶ Tajikistan	Dushanbe	Ruble
✶ Taiwan	Taipei	Dollar
✶ Tanzania	Dodoma	Shilling
✶ Thailand	Bangkok	Baht
✶ Tunisia	Tunis	Dinar
✶ Turkiye	Ankara	Lira
✶ Ukraine	Kiev	Hyrvnia
✶ United Arab Emirates	Abu Dhabi	Dirham
✶ U.K.	London	Pound Sterling
✶ U.S.A.	Washington	Dollar
✶ Uruguay	Montevideo	Peso
✶ Uzbekistan	Tashkent	Som
✶ Venezuela	Caracas	Bolivar
✶ Vietnam	Hanoi	Dong
✶ Yemen	Sana'a	Rial
✶ Zimbabwe	Harare	Dollar
✶ Congo (Democratic Republic)	Kinshasa	Franc (CDF)
✶ Zambia	Lusaka	Kwacha

GEOGRAPHICAL EXPLORATIONS/DISCOVERIES

Place	Explorer/Discoverer	Nationality	Year
America	Christopher Columbus	Italy	1492
Hawaii Islands (Sandwich Islands)	Captain James Cook	England	1778
Newfoundland	John Cabot	England	1497
New Zealand	Abel Janszoon Tasman	Netherlands	1642
North Pole	Robert Peary	USA	1909
Sea Route to India (via Cape of Good Hope)	Vasco da Gama	Portugal	1498
South Pole	Roald Amundsen	Norway	1911

NATIONAL MONUMENTS OF SOME FAMOUS COUNTRIES

Monument	Country	Monument	Country
Great Wall of China	China	Pyramid (Giza)	Egypt
Taj Mahal (Agra)	India	Kinder Disk	Denmark
Emperial Palace (Tokyo)	Japan	Leaning Tower of Pisa	Italy
Opera House (Sydney)	Australia	Statue of Liberty (New York)	USA
Eiffel Tower (Paris)	France	Kremlin (Moscow)	Russia

INTELLIGENCE AGENCIES OF SOME PROMINENT COUNTRIES

Country	Intelligence Agency
✶ India	*Research & Analysis Wing (RAW), Intelligence Bureau (I.B.), Central Bureau of Investigation (C.B.I.)*
✶ Pakistan	*Inter Service Intelligence (I.S.I.)*
✶ U.S.A.	*Central Intelligence Agency (CIA), Federal Bureau of Investigation (FBI)*
✶ Britain	*Military Intelligence (M.I.)-5 and 6, Special Branch, Ultra, Joint Intelligence Organisation*
✶ Israel	*Mosad*
✶ Egypt	*Mukhabarat*
✶ Japan	*Nicho*
✶ Russia	*K.G.B. (Komitel Gosudarstvennoy Bezopasnosty) (Committee for State Security)*
✶ Canada	*Security Intelligence Service (SIS)*
✶ S. Africa	*Bureau of State Security (BSS)*
✶ Iran	*Sabak*
✶ Iraq	*Al-Mukhabarat*
✶ Australia	*Australian Security and Intelligence Organisation (ASIO)*
✶ France	*S.D.E.C.E.*
✶ Spain	*C.E.S.I.D.*

MAJOR LANGUAGES OF THE WORLD AND THEIR SPEAKERS

Listing the languages spoken by approximately 1% of humankind (those spoken by more than 60,000,000 people), this table enumerates speakers of each tongue as a primary language.

Language	Speakers (millions)
∗ Chinese	1,322.8
∗ Spanish	471.4
∗ English	369.9
∗ Arabic	349.3
∗ Hindi	342.2
∗ Bengali	228.7
∗ Portuguese	232.4
∗ Russian	153.7
∗ Japanese	126.3
∗ Lahnda	99.6
∗ Marathi	83.1
∗ Telugu	82.6
∗ Turkish	82.2
∗ Malay	81.6
∗ Korean	81.5
∗ French	79.6
∗ Tamil	77.5
∗ Vietnamese	76.1
∗ German, Standard	76.5
∗ Urdu	69.0
∗ Javanese	68.3
∗ Persian	65.7
∗ Italian	64.8
∗ Gujarati	56.9
∗ Pushto	53.1
∗ Bhojpuri	52.3
∗ Hausa	48.6
∗ Kannada	43.6
∗ Yoruba	41.0
∗ Polish	40.0

*(**Source:** The World Almanac-2022)*

NAME OF PARLIAMENTS OF SOME COUNTRIES

Country	Name of Parliament
Afghanistan	Shora
Argentina	National Congress
Australia	Federal Parliament
Austria	National Assembly
Bangladesh	Jatiya Sansad
India	Lok Sabha and Rajya Sabha
Bhutan	Tshogdu (National Assembly)
Britain	House of Commons and House of Lords
Canada	House of Commons and Senate
China	National People Congress
Denmark	Folketing
Iran	Majlis (Islamic Consultative Assembly)
Israel	Knesset
Japan	Diet
Myanmar	Pyithu Hluttaw (People's Assembly)
Nepal	Rashtriya Panchayat
The Netherlands	States-General
Norway	Storting
Poland	Sejm
Russia	Federal Assembly (Council of the Federation and State Duma
South Africa	National Assembly and Senate
Spain	Cortes Generales
Sweden	Riksdag
Switzerland	Federal Assembly (Nationalrat and Standerat)
North Korea	Supreme People's Assembly
South Korea	National Assembly
U.S.A.	Congress (Senate and House of Representatives)
Ethiopia	Federal Council and House of Representatives
Iceland	Alpingi
Bulgaria	National Assembly
Cuba	National Assembly of People's Power

LARGEST AND SMALLEST COUNTRIES (Top 5)

Largest Country	Largest Country	Smallest Country	Smallest Country
(Area-wise)	(Population-wise, 2022)	(Area-wise)	(Population-wise, 2022)
Russia	China	Vatican City	Vatican City
Canada	India	Monaco	Tuvalu
China	USA	Nauru	Nauru
United States	Indonesia	Tuvalu	Palau
Brazil	Brazil	San Marino	San Marino

RELIGIONS OF THE WORLD

Religion	Member	Percentage	Religion	Member	Percentage
Christianity	2.5 billion	32.2%	Buddhism	545 million	6.9%
Islam	1.9 billion	24.7%	Sikhism	28 million	0.4%
Hinduism	1.07 billion	13.5%			

NATIONAL EMBLEMS OF IMPORTANT COUNTRIES

Country	National Emblem	Country	National Emblem
America	Golden Rod	Australia	Kangaroo
Ireland	Shamrock	Italy	White Lily
Israel	Candelabrum	Iran	Rose
Canada	White Lily	Great Britain	Rose
Chile	Candor and Huemul	Germany	Corn Flower
Japan	Chrysanthemum	Zimbabwe	Zimbabwe Bird
Denmark	Beach	Turkiye	Crescent and Star
The Netherlands	Lion	New Zealand	Kiwi, Fern Southern Cross
Norway	Lion	Nepal	Kukri
Pakistan	Crescent	Poland	Eagle
France	Lily	Belgium	Lion
Bangladesh	Water Lily	Mongolia	The Soyombo
Russia	Double headed eagle	Lebanon	Cedar Tree
Sudan	Secretary Bird	Syria	Eagle
India	Lioned Capital		

BOOKS AND AUTHORS

FOREIGN

Book	Author	Book	Author
∗ As You Like It	*William Shakespeare*	∗ Mother India	*Katherine Mayo*
∗ A Tale of Two Cities	*Charles Dickens*	∗ Nana	*Emile Zola*
∗ Ben Hur	*Lewis Wallace*	∗ Odyssey	*Homer*
∗ Das Kapital	*Karl Marx*	∗ Origin of Species	*Charles Darwin*
∗ David Copperfield	*Charles Dickens*	∗ Othello	*William Shakespeare*
∗ Hamlet	*William Shakespeare*	∗ Paradise Lost	*John Milton*
∗ Iliad	*Homer*	∗ Paradise Regained	*John Milton*
∗ Inferno	*A. Dante*	∗ Path to Power	*Margaret Thatcher*
∗ In Memoriam	*Lord Tennyson*	∗ Pickwick Papers	*Charles Dickens*
∗ Ivanhoe	*Walter Scott*	∗ Razor's Edge	*Somerset Maugham*
∗ Julius Caesar	*William Shakespeare*	∗ Republic	*Plato*
∗ Lady Chatterley's Lover	*D.H. Lawrence*	∗ The Tempest	*William Shakespeare*
∗ Lajja	*Taslima Nasreen*	∗ Time Machine	*H.G. Wells*
∗ Les Miserable	*Victor Hugo*	∗ Tom Sawyer	*Mark Twain*
∗ Leviathan	*Thomas Hobbes*	∗ Treasure Island	*R.L. Stevenson*
∗ Lolita	*V. Nobokov*	∗ Twelfth Night	*William Shakespeare*
∗ Lycidas	*John Milton*	∗ Unto This Last	*John Ruskin*
∗ Mein Kampf	*Adolf Hitler*	∗ Utopia	*Thomas More*
∗ Moor's Last Sigh	*Salman Rushdie*	∗ Wealth of Nations	*Adam Smith*
∗ Mother	*Maxim Gorky*	∗ Wonder that was India	*A.L. Basham*

INDIAN

Book	Author
✶ Ain-i-Akbari	*Abul Fazal*
✶ Anand Math	*Bankim Chandra Chatterjee*
✶ Arthashastra	*Kautilya*
✶ A Suitable Boy	*Vikram Seth*
✶ Bhagwat Gita	*Ved Vyas*
✶ Chidambara	*Sumitranandan Pant*
✶ Devdas	*Sarat Chandra Chatterjee*
✶ Discovery of India	*Jawaharlal Nehru*
✶ Ganadevata	*Tarashankar Bandopadhyaya*
✶ Geet Govind	*Jaya Dev*
✶ Geetanjali	*R. N. Tagore*
✶ Glimpses of World History	*Jawaharlal Nehru*
✶ Godaan	*Prem Chand*
✶ Gul-e-Nagma	*Firaq Gorakhpuri*
✶ Harsh Charita	*Bana Bhatta*
✶ India Divided	*Dr. Rajendra Prasad*
✶ Justice of Peace ke Aansu	Janardan Prasad Singh
✶ The Judgement	*Kuldip Nayyar*
✶ Kadambari	*Bana Bhatta*
✶ Kagaz Te Kanwas	*Amrita Pritam*
✶ Kamayani	*Jai Shankar Prasad*
✶ Kitni Nawon Mein Kitni Bar	*S. H. Vatsyayan*
✶ Kumar Sambhav	*Kalidas*
✶ Mahabharata	*Ved Vyas*
✶ Malgudi Days	*R.K. Narayan*
✶ Meghdoot	*Kalidas*
✶ Mritunjaya	*B.K. Bhattacharya*
✶ Mudrarakshasa	*Vishakhadatta*
✶ Prison Diary	*Jaya Prakash Narayan*
✶ Raghuvansha	*Kalidas*
✶ Rajtarangini	*Kalhana*
✶ Ramayana	*Balmiki*
✶ Ramcharit Manas	*Tulsidas*
✶ Rukh Te Rishi	*Harbhajan Singh*
✶ Satyarth Prakash	*Swami Dayanand*
✶ Sur Sagar	*Surdas*
✶ The Guide	*R.K. Narayan*

IMPORTANT DATES AND DAYS OF THE YEAR

✶ JANUARY

5-11 Road Safety Week
12 National Youth Day
15 Army Day
15-21 Pin Code Week
23 National Day of Patriotism
26 Republic Day
30 Martyr's Day

✶ FEBRUARY

1-14 Oil Conservation Fortnight
14 Valentine's Day

✶ MARCH

4 National Safety Day
8 International Women's Day
15 Consumers' Day
16 Immunisation Day
21 World Forest Day
22 World Day for Water
24 World Meteorological Day
1-7 Preservation of Blindness Week

✶ APRIL

7 World Health Day
7-13 Handloom Week
14-20 Fire Service Week
18 World Heritage Day
22 World Earth Day

✶ MAY

1 May Day
5 National Labour Day
8 World Red Cross Day
11 National Technology Day
15 International Day of the Family
17 World Telecommunication Day
24 Commonwealth Day
31 World No-Tobacco Day

✶ JUNE

5 World Environment Day
21 World Yoga Day
26 International Day against Drug Abuse and Illicit Trafficking

✶ JULY

11 World Population Day

✶ AUGUST

1-7 World Breast feeding Week
10 Sanskrit Divas
15 Independence Day
20 Sadbhavana Divas

✶ SEPTEMBER

1-7 National Nutrition Week
5 Teachers' Day
8 International Literary Day
14 Hindi Diwas

23 World Deaf Day
27 World Tourism Day

∗ OCTOBER

2 ∗ Gandhi Jayanti
∗ International Day of Non Violence
∗ Anti-Leprosy Day
4 World Animal Day
6 World Habitat Day *(Ist Monday)*
8 Indian Air Force Day
14 World Standard Day
15 International Day of Rural Women
16 World Food Day
24 United Nations Day
27 Infantry Day
28 World Thrift Day
31 Anti-Terrorism Day

∗ NOVEMBER

2 All Saints Day
14 Children's Day
15-21 National Cooperative Week
19-25 Quami Ekta Week
20 Child Rights Day
26 Constitution Day

∗ DECEMBER

1 World AIDS Day
3 World Day for the Disabled
4 Naval Day
7 Flag Day
8 SMRC Day
10 Human Rights Day
14 National Energy Conservation Day

INDIAN DEFENCE

- The Supreme Command of the Armed Forces is vested in the hands of the President of the Country.
- The responsibility for national defence, however, rests with the Cabinet. All important questions having a bearing on defence are decided by the Cabinet Committee on Political Affairs, which is presided over by the Prime Minister.
- The Defence Minister is responsible to Parliament for all matters concerning the Defence Services.
- All the administrative and operational control of Armed Forces are exercised by the Ministry of Defence. The three services—Army, Navy and Air Force function through their respective service head-quarters headed by the chief of Staff. The post of Chief of Defence Staff (CDS) was created in 2019.

Indian Army Commands

Command	*HQ Location*
Eastern Command	Kolkata
Western Command	Chandigarh
Northern Command	Udhampur
Southern Command	Pune
Central Command	Lucknow
Training Command	Shimla
South-Western Command	Jaipur

Indian Air Force Commands

Command	*HQ Location*
Western Air Command	New Delhi
Sout-Western Air Command	Gandhinagar
Central Air Command	Prayagraj
Eastern Air Command	Shillong
Southern Air Command	Thiruvananthapuram
Training Command	Bengaluru

Indian Navy Commands

Command	*HQ Location*
Eastern Naval Command	Vishakhapatnam
Western Naval Command	Mumbai
Southern Naval Command	Kochi

Commissioned Ranks in Defence Services

Army	*Navy*	*Air Force*
General	Admiral	Air Chief Marshal
Lieutenant-General	Vice-Admiral	Air Marshal
Major-General	Rear-Admiral	Air Vice-Marshal
Brigadier	Commodor	Air Commodor
Colonel	Captain	Group Captain
Lieutenant-Colonel	Commander	Wing Commander
Major	Lt.Commander	Squadron Leader
Captain	Lieutenant	Flight Lieutenant
Lieutenant	Sub-Lieutenant	Flying Officer

INDIAN CULTURE

☛ Dance

India has a very rich tradition of tribal, folk and classical dances.

☛ Classical Dance

Dance	State	Famous Artists
• Bharat Natyam	Tamil Nadu	Yamini Krishnamurthy, Rukmini Devi Arundale, Swapna Sundari, Sonal Mansingh, Vaijanti Mala, Mrinalini Sarabhai, Chandralekha, Indrani, Ram Gopal, Bal Saraswati
• Kathakali	Kerala	Gopinath, K.K. Nayar, Kunju-Kurup, T.K. Chandu
• Kuchipudi	Andhra Pradesh	Sapna Sundari, Raja Reddy, Radha Reddy, Vedantam Satyanarayan, Vimpanti Chinna Satyam.
• Kathak	North India	Birju Maharaj, Gopi Krishna, Shambhu Maharaj, Sitara Devi, Vishnu Sharma, Durga Lal, Shobhana Narayan
• Odissi	Odisha	Kelucharan Mahapatra, Indrani Rehman, Madhavi Mudgal, Pratima Bedi, Samyukta Panigrahi, Sonal Mansingh, Debudas
• Manipuri	Manipur	Uday Shankar, Bipin Singh, Suryamukhi, Darohra Jhaveri

☛ Famous Folk-Dance

- Andhra Pradesh: *Dandari, Banjara*
- Asom: *Bihu, Keli Gopal, Sataria*
- Bihar: *Chhau, Magahi, Durga dance*
- W. Bengal: *Kirtan, Kalatri, Asweabadh, Brita, Kalidance*
- Chhattisgarh: *Saila, Karama, Bhagoria*
- Gujarat: *Garba, Rasalila, Tippani, Dandia,*
- Haryana: *Damyal, Lahoor*
- Himachal Pradesh: *Dussehra dance, Hikat, Notio*
- Jammu & Kashmir: *Dumhal*
- Jharkhand: *Jhau, Ghumakudia, Jadur, Sarhul, Soharai, Karama, Vaima, Loojhari, Jat-Jatin, Vidayat*
- Karnataka: *Yakshagan, Dolu Kunitha*
- Kerala: *Mohini Attam, Padayuni*
- Madhya Pradesh: *Lota Nritya, Jawara*
- Maharashtra: *Tamasha, Dahi Handi, Gof, Deepak Dindi*
- Manipur: *Dhol Cholam*
- Meghalaya: *Nongakarem*
- Nagaland: *Bamboo dance*
- Odisha: *Chhau, Maya Shabari, Dalachai*
- Punjab: *Gidda, Bhangra, Panihari*
- Rajasthan: *Ghumar, Kathaputali, Tera Tali*
- Tamil Nadu: *Terukalathu, Kabalatam, Kargam, Pulivesham*
- Tripura: *Hazagiri*
- Uttar Pradesh: *Rasalila, Nautanki, Thali, Huraka, Dhurang, Jhumela, Bol.*
- Uttarakhand: *Kajari, Karan*
- Goa: *Dhode Modini*

☛ Musical Instruments and Artists

- **Flute:** Hari Prasad Chaurasia, Panna Lal Ghosh, T.R. Mahalingam, N. Ramani, Vijaya Raghava Rao
- **Tabla:** Allah Rakha, Gudai Maharaj, Latif Khan, Zakir Hussain
- **Violin:** Lalgudi Jayaraman, L. Subramaniam, M.S. Gopal Krishnan, S. Subrahmaniam, V.G. Jog, N. Rajan
- **Shehnai:** Bismilla Khan, Imrat Khan
- **Sarod:** Ali Akbar Khan, Amjad Ali Khan, Alauddin Khan, Saren Rani, Brij Narayan
- **Sitar:** Pandit Ravishankar, Vilayat Khan
- **Santur:** Shiv Kumar Sharma
- **Rudraveena:** Zia Mohiuddin Dagar
- **Pakhawaj:** Govind Rao, Anokhe Lal, Kanthi Maharaj
- **Mridanga:** Palghat R. Raghu, U.S. Burman
- **Harmonium:** Purushottam Walawakar, M. Dhaulpuri
- **Guitar:** Pt. Vishnu Mohan Bhatt, Brij Bhushan Kalra
- **Ghatam:** T.H. Vinayakaram
- **Janjira:** V. Nagarajan
- **Symphony:** Jubin Mehta

WORLD HERITAGE SITES IN INDIA

A World Heritage Site is a place that is listed by UNESCO for its special cultural or physical significance. The list of World Heritage Sites is maintained by the international 'World Heritage Programme', administered by the UNESCO World Heritage Committee. The United Nations Educational, Scientific and Cultural Organization (UNESCO) seeks to encourage the identification, protection and preservation of cultural and natural heritage around the world considered to be of outstanding value to humanity. This is embodied in an international treaty called the Convention concerning the Protection of the World Cultural and Natural Heritage, adopted by UNESCO in 1972. India has 44 world heritage sites that include 36 Cultural properties, 7 Natural properties and 1 mixed site.

Cultural Sites in India

- Agra Fort (1983)
- Ajanta Caves (1983)

- Archaeological Site of Nalanda Mahavihara at Nalanda, Bihar (2016)
- Buddhist Monuments at Sanchi (1989)
- Champaner-Pavagadh Archaeological Park (2004)
- Chhatrapati Shivaji Terminus (formerly Victoria Terminus) (2004)
- Churches and Convents of Goa (1986)
- Elephanta Caves (1987)
- Ellora Caves (1983)
- Fatehpur Sikri (1986)
- Great Living Chola Temples (1987, 2004)
- Group of Monuments at Hampi (1986)
- Group of Monuments at Mahabalipuram (1984)
- Group of Monuments at Pattadakal (1987)
- Hill Forts of Rajasthan (2013)
- Historic City of Ahmedabad (2017)
- Humayun's Tomb, Delhi (1993)
- Jaipur City, Rajasthan (2019)
- Khajuraho Group of Monuments (1986)
- Mountain Railways of India (1999, 2005, 2008)
- Mahabodhi Temple Complex at Bodh Gaya (2002)
- Qutub Minar and its Monuments, Delhi (1993)
- Rani-ki-Vav (the Queen's Stepwell) at Patan, Gujarat (2014)
- Red Fort Complex (2007)
- Rock Shelters of Bhimbetka (2003)
- Sun Temple, Konarak (1984)
- Taj Mahal (1983)
- The Architectural Work of Le Corbusier (2016)
- Victorian Gothic and Art Deco Ensembles of Mumbai (2018)
- The Jantar Mantar, Jaipur (2010)
- Dholavira : a Harappan City (2021)
- Kakatiya Rudreshwara (Ramappa) Temple, Telangana (2021)
- Santiniketan, West Bengal (2023)
- Hoyasala Temples, Karnataka (2023)
- Moidams—The Mound Burial System of the Ahom Dynasty, Assam (2024)
- Maratha Military Landscapes of India, Maharashtra and Tamil Nadu (2025)

Natural Sites in India

- Great Himalayan National Park Conservation Area (2014)
- Kaziranga National Park (1985)
- Keoladeo National Park (1985)
- Manas Wildlife Sanctuary (1985)
- Nanda Devi and Valley of Flowers National Parks (1988, 2005)
- Sundarban National Park (1987)
- Western Ghats (2012)

Mixed Site in India

- Khangchendzonga National Park (2016)

UNITED NATIONS (UN)

- The United Nations (UN) is an association of states which have pledged themselves to maintain international peace and security and cooperate in solving international political, economic, social cultural and humanitarian problems towards achieving this end.
- Trygve Lie of Norway (1946-52) was the first Secretary-General of the UN.
- ***Origin:*** UN Charter was signed by 50 members on June 26, 1945. Poland signed the charter later to become one of the original 51 member-states. It officially came into existence on October 24, 1945.
- ***UN Charter:*** The Charter is the Constitution of the UN and contains its aims and objectives and rules and regulations for its functioning.
- ***Aims and Objectives:*** They are security, welfare and human rights.
- ***Headquarters:*** New York.
- ***Flag:*** The flag is light blue in colour, and emblazoned in white, in its centre is the UN symbol—a polar map of world embraced by twin olive branches open at the top.
- ***Official Languages:*** The official languages of the UN are: English, French, Chinese, Russian, Arabic and Spanish. However, working languages are English and French only.
- ***Present Membership:*** At present 193 countries are members of the UN. South Sudan is the latest entrant to this world organisation.
- ***Main Organs of the UN:*** There are six main organs:
  1. General Assembly
  2. Security Council
  3. Economic and Social Council
  4. Trusteeship Council
  5. International Court of Justice, and
  6. Secretariat.

1. *General Assembly:* It consists of representative of all members of the UN. Each member country has only one vote. It meets once a year and passes UN Budget. It is the main place for discussions and policy making in the UN.

2. *Security Council:* It is the Executive body of the UN and is mainly responsible for maintaining international peace and security. It has 15 members, 5 of which (USA, UK, France, Russia and China) are permanent members. The 10 non-permanent members are elected by General Assembly for two-year term and are not eligible for immediate re-election.
3. *Economic and Social Council:* It has 54 members elected by General Assembly.
4. *Trusteeship Council:* It looks after interest of the people in areas not yet independent and leads them towards self-government.
5. *International Court of Justice:* It has 15 judges, no two of whom may be nationals of the same state. They are elected by General Assembly and Security Council for a term of 9 years. The Court elects its President and Vice-President for a 3-year term.
6. *Secretariat:* It is the Secretariat of the UN and is headed by the Secretary General.

AWARDS AND HONOURS

NATIONAL AWARDS

BHARAT RATANA

- Bharat Ratna is India's highest Civilian Award. It was first awarded in 1954.
- The actual award is designed in the shape of a *peepal* leaf with Bharat Ratna inscribed in Devanagri script in the Sun Figure.
- This is India's highest civilian award. It is given for exceptional work on art, literature, science and recognition of public service of the highest order.
- The emblem, the Sun and the rim are of platinum. The inscriptions are in burnished bronze.
- Government servants are not eligible for it.

REPUBLIC DAY AWARDS

Padma Awards

They fall in line after the Bharat Ratna. They are also discontinued in 1977 along with the Bharat Ratna and award was started again in 1980.

There are three Padma Awards:

- ***Padma Vibhushan:*** This award is given for exceptional and distinguished service in any field, including service rendered by Govt. servants.
- ***Padma Bhushan:*** This award is given for distinguished service of a high order in any field, including service rendered by Govt. servants.
- ***Padma Shri:*** This award is given for distinguished service in any field, including service rendered by Government servants.

Gallantry Awards

- ***Param Vir Chakra:*** The highest award for bravery or some daring and pre-eminent act of valour or self-sacrifice in the presence of the enemy, whether on land, at sea or in the air.
- ***Mahavir Chakra:*** It is the second highest decoration and is awarded for acts of conspicuous gallantry in the presence of the enemy, whether on land, at sea or in the air.
- ***Vir Chakra:*** It is the third in order of awards given for acts of gallantry in the presence of enemy, whether on land, at sea or in the air.
- ***Ashok Chakra:*** This medal is awarded for the most conspicuous bravery or some daring or pre-eminent act of valour or self-sacrifice on land, at sea or in the air but not in the presence of enemy.
- ***Vishishta Sewa Medal:*** It is awarded to personnel of all the three Services in class I, II and III in recognition of distinguished service of the "most exceptional" and "exceptional" and a "high" order respectively. Prefixes Parma and Ati are added before first two categories of medals respectively.
- ***Jeewan Raksha Padak:*** Awarded for meritorious acts or a series of acts of a human nature displayed in saving life from drowning, fire and rescue operations in mines etc.

OTHER NATIONAL AWARDS

NATIONAL SPORTS AWARDS

- **Major Dhyan Chand Khel Ratna Award:** The scheme was launched in the year 1991-92 with the objective of honouring sportspersons to enhance their general status and to give them greater dignity and place of honour in society.

  Under this scheme, an amount of ₹ 25 lakh is given as award for the most spectacular and outstanding performance by a sportsperson over a period of four years immediately preceding the year in which award is to be given.

- **Dronacharya Award:** Dronacharya Award is an award presented by ministry of youth Affairs and Sports, Government of India for excellence in sports coaching. The Dronacharya (Lifetime) awardees gets ₹ 15 lakh and Dronacharya (Regular) awardees gets ₹ 10 lakh a bronze statuette of Dronacharya and scroll of honour. The award was instituted in 1985.

- **Arjuna Award:** The Arjuna Awards are given by the ministry of youth Affairs and sports, government of India to recognize outstanding achievement in National sports. Instituted in 1961 the award carries a cash prize of 15,00,000 a bronze statue of Arjuna and a scroll.
- **Arujna Award (Lifetime):** Arjuna Award (Lifetime) is India's highest award for lifetime achievement in sports and games, given by the ministry of youth Affairs and sports, government of India. The award is initiated in 2002. The award carries a cash prize of ₹ 10,00,000 a plaque and a scroll of honour.
- **Maulana Abul Kalam Azad Trophy:** This trophy was instituted in 1956-57. The top overall performing university in the inter-university tournaments is given the Maulana Abul Kalam Azad (MAKA) Trophy, which is a rolling trophy. A small replica of the MAKA Trophy is also awarded for retention by the university. In addition, the university also gets a cash prize of ₹ 15 lakh. The second and third best universities also receive cash awards amounting to ₹ 5 lakh and ₹ 3 lakh respectively.

SAHITYA AKADEMI AWARDS

- These prizes are awarded annually to the authors of the most outstanding books of literary merit published in each of the 22 languages which are specified in the Eighth Schedule of the Constitution.
- There are also two awards for Rajasthani and English. The award, in form of a casket containing an inscribed copper plate and a cheque of ₹ 1 lakh is given to the author or his/her heir.

DADA SAHEB PHALKE AWARD

- The award carries a cash prize of ₹ 15 lakh, a Shawl and Swarna Kamal. Mrs Devika Rani Roerich was the first person to receive Dadasaheb Phalke Award in 1969.

BHARATIYA JNANPITH AWARD

- Instituted in 22nd May, 1961, carries a cash prize of ₹ 21 lakh, a citation and a bronze replica of Vagdevi (Saraswati).
- Instituted by a literary organisation in India.

SARASWATI SAMMAN

- Given for outstanding literary works, value ₹ 15 lakh.

KALINGA PRIZE

- This award is given each year by the UNESCO and founded by former Odisha Chief Minister late Shri Biju Patnaik for popularisation of science.

INTERNATIONAL AWARDS

NOBEL PRIZES

- These Prizes were instituted in 1901 by a Swedish scientist, Dr. Alfred Nobel; the discoverer of Dynamite.
- Six prizes are awarded annually for (*i*) Chemistry, (*ii*) Physics, (*iii*) Medicine, (*iv*) Literature, (*v*) Peace and (*vi*) Economics—started since 1969.
- Five Indians so far have been awarded these Prizes, (*i*) Rabindranath Tagore for literature in 1913 for his work 'Gitanjali', (*ii*) C.V. Raman for Physics in 1930, (*iii*) Mother Teresa for Peace in 1979, (*iv*) Prof. Amartya Sen for Economics in 1998, (*v*) Kailash Satyarthi for Peace in 2014.
- In addition, four non-resident Indians have also been awarded the Nobel Prize. They are: (*i*) Hargobind Khurana for Medicine in 1968, (*ii*) Subramanian Chandrasekhar for Physics in 1983, (*iii*) Venkatraman Ramkrishnan for Chemistry in 2009, (iv) Abhijit Vinayak Banerjee for Economics in 2019.

GANDHI PEACE PRIZE

- The government instituted this ₹ 1 crore prize on the lines of the Nobel Peace Prize in 1995.
- It is the highest Civilian International award by the Govt. of India.

MAN BOOKER INTERNATIONAL AWARD

- The Man Booker International Prize was established in 2005, biannually rewarding an author for a body of work originally written in any language as long as it was widely available in English.
- From 2016, the prize became a translation prize, awarded annually for a single work of fiction, translated into English and published in the UK. Underlining the importance of translation, the £ 50,000 prize is divided equally between the author and the translator.

Highest Honours of Some Countries

Country	Highest Honour
India	Bharat Ratna
Pakistan	Nishan-e-Pakistan
Kuwait	Mubarak-Al-kabir Medal
Saudi Arabia	Shah Abdul Aziz Medal
Argentina	The Order of Sona Martin
Nicaragua	Augusto-Caesar Sandino Order
Vietnam	The Order of the Golden Star
Hungary	The Order of Banner
Britain	Member of British Empire, Victoria Cross
Japan	Order of Moulovenice Sun
Denmark	Order of Diana Brog
France	Legend of Honour
America	Presidential Medal of Freedom
Germany	Pore Lee Merit Iron Cross
The Netherlands	Netherlands Lion

SPORTS

OLYMPICS

- First of all these games were held by the Greeks in 776 B.C. on Mount Olympus in honour of the Greek God Zeus. In this way, the history of Olympic Games is about twenty eight hundred years old. These games continued to be held every four years until 394 A.D. when these games were stopped by a royal order of the emperor of Rome.
- The modern Olympic Games which started in Athens in 1896, are the result of the devotion and dedication of a French educator Baron Pierre de Coubertin and the first Olympic meet in the modern series was held in 1896 in Athens, the Capital of Greece. Since then, they are being held every four years except for breaks during world wars.
- The Olympic flag is white in colour with five coloured rings, each ring symbolic of a continent. Summer as well as Winter Olympics are held in the same year.

COMMONWEALTH GAMES

- The Commonwealth Games are held every four years, in the year in which Asian Games are held. All the Commonwealth Countries (former colonies of Britain) can take part in it.
- The first Commonwealth Games were held in 1930 at Hamilton (Canada).
- There are currently 56 members of the Commonwealth of Nations, and 72 teams participated in the games.

ASIAN GAMES

- After the Second World War, most of the Asian Countries gained independence. On the lines of Olympic Games, Asian Games were planned every four years.
- India hosted the first Asian Games in 1951.

WORLD CUP CRICKET

- The first Cricket World Cup was organised in England in 1975. A separate women's Cricket World Cup has been held every 4 years since 1973.

HOCKEY WORLD CUP

- The first Hockey World Cup was organised in Barcelona (Spain) in 1971. Women's Hockey World Cup has been held since 1974.

FOOTBALL WORLD CUP

- The Football World Cup is organised by FIFA (Federation of International Football Association). The World Cup is called 'Jules Rimet Cup' named after the name of FIFA President Jules Rimet. The first Football World Cup was organised in Uruguay in 1930. In 1942 and 1946, the Football World Cup was not played due to World War II.
- Brazil is the only nation to have participated in every World Cup so far.

Number of Players in Some Games/Sports

Sports	No. of Players
Badminton	1 or 2
Baseball	9
Basketball	5
Billiards (Snooker)	1
Boxing	1
Bridge	2
Chess	1
Cricket	11
Croquest	13 or 15
Football (Soccer)	11
Hockey	11
Lacrosse	12
Netball	7
Polo Rugby	4
Football (Rugby)	15
Table Tennis	1 or 2
Lawn Tennis	1 or 2
Volleyball	6
Water Polo	7

IMPORTANT CUPS & TROPHIES

International

✶ *American Cup* : Yacht Racing
✶ *Ashes* : Cricket
✶ *Davis Cup* : Lawn Tennis
✶ *Derby* : Horse Race
✶ *Grand National* : Horse Streple Chase Race
✶ *Jules Rimet Trophy* : World Soccer Cup
✶ *King's Cup* : Air Races
✶ *Merdeka Cup* : Football
✶ *Swaythling Cup* : Table Tennis (Men)
✶ *Ryder Cup* : Golf
✶ *Thomas Cup* : Badminton
✶ *U. Thant Cup* : Tennis
✶ *Walker Cup* : Golf
✶ *Wightman Cup* : Lawn Tennis
✶ *Rothman's Trophy* : Cricket
✶ *European Champions Cup* : Football
✶ *Grand Prix* : Table Tennis
✶ *Edgbaston Cup* : Lawn Tennis
✶ *Grand Prix* : Lawn Tennis

National

- ∗ *Agha Khan Cup* : Hockey
- ∗ *Beighton Cup* : Hockey
- ∗ *Bombay Gold Cup* : Hockey
- ∗ *C.K. Naydu Trophy* : Cricket
- ∗ *Deodhar Trophy* : Cricket
- ∗ *Duleep Trophy* : Cricket
- ∗ *Durand Cup* : Football
- ∗ *Dhyan Chand Trophy* : Hockey
- ∗ *Dr. B.C. Roy Trophy* : Football (Junior)
- ∗ *Ezra Cup* : Polo
- ∗ *Guru Nanak Cup* : Hockey
- ∗ *Holkar Trophy* : Bridge
- ∗ *Irani Trophy* : Cricket
- ∗ *Indira Gold Cup* : Hockey
- ∗ *Murugappa Gold Cup* : Hockey
- ∗ *Nehru Trophy* : Hockey
- ∗ *Nixan Gold Cup* : Football
- ∗ *Rani Jhansi Trophy* : Cricket
- ∗ *Ranji Trophy* : Cricket
- ∗ *Rangaswami Cup* : Hockey
- ∗ *Ramanujan Trophy* : Table Tennis
- ∗ *Rene Frank Trophy* : Hockey
- ∗ *Rohinton Baria Trophy* : Cricket
- ∗ *Rovers Cup* : Football
- ∗ *Santosh Trophy* : Football
- ∗ *Subroto Cup* : Football

SPORTS TERMS

- ∗ ***Badminton:*** Mixed doubles; Deuce; Drop; Smash; Let; Foot work; Setting.
- ∗ ***Base Ball:*** Pitcher; Put out, Strike; Home; Bunt.
- ∗ ***Billiards:*** Cue; Jigger; Pot; Break; In Baulk; In Off; Cannons.
- ∗ ***Boxing:*** Upper cut; Round; Punch; Bout; Knock down; Hitting below the belt; Ring.
- ∗ ***Bridge:*** Finesse; Dummy; Revoke; Grand Slam; Little Slam; No Trump; Rubber.
- ∗ ***Chess:*** Bishop, Gambit; Checkmate; Stalemate.
- ∗ ***Cricket:*** L.B.W. (leg before wicket); Creases, Popping-creases; Stumped; Bye; Leg-Bye; Googly; Hattrick; Maiden over; Drive; Bowling; Duck; Follow-on; No ball; Leg Break; Silly point; Cover point; Hit-wicket; Late-cut; Slip; Off-spinner; In-swing.
- ∗ ***Football:*** Off Side; Block; Drop-kick; Penalty-kick (or goal kick); Corner-kick; Free-kick; Dribble; Thrown-in; Foul.
- ∗ ***Golf:*** Boggy; Foursome; Stymic; Tee; Put; Hole; Niblic; Caddie; Links; The green; Bunker.
- ∗ ***Hockey:*** Carried; Short Corner; Bully; Sticks; Off side; Roll in; Striking Circle; Under-cutting; Dribble.
- ∗ ***Horse racing:*** Jockey; Punter.
- ∗ ***Polo:*** Bunker; Chukker; Mallet.
- ∗ ***Tennis:*** Back hand drive; Volley; Smash; Half-volley; Deuce; Service; Let; Grand Slam.

Stadiums and Places Associated with Sports

Name of Stadium	*Sports*	*Place*
Narendra Modi Stadium	Cricket	Ahmedabad
Arun Jaitley Stadium	Cricket	Delhi
Jawaharlal Nehru Stadium	Athletics	Delhi
Shivajee Stadium	Hockey	Delhi
National Stadium	Hockey etc.	Delhi
Ambedkar Stadium	Football	Delhi
Brabourne Stadium	Cricket	Mumbai
Wankhede Stadium	Cricket	Mumbai
National Stadium	Hockey etc.	Mumbai
Eden Garden	Cricket	Kolkata
Green Park Stadium	Cricket	Kanpur
Keenan Stadium	Cricket	Jamshedpur
Nehru (Chepauk) Stadium	Cricket	Chennai
Barabati Stadium	Cricket	Cuttack
Lords, Oval, Leeds	Cricket	Britain
Hedingle Manchester	Cricket	Britain
Black Heath	Rugby Football	London
Henley	Boat race	England
Wimbledon	Lawn Tennis	London
Wembley Stadium	Football	London
White City	Dog-race	England
Aintree	Horse-race	England
Tentbridge	Cricket	England
Patnee Martlake	Boat-race	England
Tibankham	Rugby Football	England
Sandy Lodge	Golf	Scotland
Forest Hill	Tennis	New York
Brooklyn	Baseball	New York
Melbourne	Cricket	Australia

Name of Playing Compound of Different Games

Name of Compound	Related Sports
Court	Lawn Tennis, Badminton, Netball, Hand ball, Volleyball, Squash, Kho-Kho, Kabaddi
Diamond	Baseball
Ring	Boxing, Skating, Wrestling, Circus, Riding display
Course	Golf
Board	Table Tennis
Pool	Swimming
Alley	Bowling
Mat	Judo, Karate II
Arena	Horse Riding
Vellodrum	Cycling
Field	Polo, Football, Hockey
Track	Athletics
Pitch	Cricket, Rugby
Rink	Ice Hockey

❒❒❒

7

Multiple Choice Questions

1. Match List-I with List-II and select the correct answer from the codes given below the lists:

List-I	List-II
(*a*) Napoleon Bonaparte	1. 'A history is contemporary history'
(*b*) Jean Jacques Rousseau	2. 'Liberty what crimes are committed in thy name'
(*c*) Croce	3. 'Man is born free but every-where he is in chains.'
(*d*) Madame Roland	4. 'I am the Child of Revolution'

Codes :

	(*a*)	(*b*)	(*c*)	(*d*)
A.	1	2	3	4
B.	4	3	1	2
C.	3	4	2	1
D.	3	4	1	2

2. Abraham Lincon was elected the President of United States in:
A. 1862 B. 1860
C. 1875 D. 1855

3. Who was known as the 'Prince of Humanists'?
A. Francisco Petrarch B. Dante
C. Boccacio D. Erasmus

4. D-Day is the day when:
A. Germany declared war on Britain
B. US dropped the atom bomb on Hiroshima.
C. Allied Troops landed in Normandy
D. Germany surrendered to the allies

5. Whose teachings inspired the French Revolution?
A. Locke B. Rousseau
C. Hegel D. Plato

6. At a time when empires in Europe were crumbling before the might of Napoleon which one of the following Governor-Generals kept the British flag flying high in India?
A. Warren Hastings B. Lord Cornwallis
C. Lord Wellesley D. Lord Hastings

7. Which one of the following statements regarding Fascism in Italy is *not* true?
A. The Fascists came to power as a result of popular uprising
B. In 1926, all political parties except Mussolini's party were banned
C. The Fascists suppressed the Socialist movement
D. The Fascists were hostile to the Communists

8. The fall of Czar Nicholas-II is known as:
A. Bloody Sunday
B. Bolshevik Revolution
C. February Revolution
D. October Revolution

9. Industrial Revolution took place first in:
A. France B. Germany
C. United Kingdom D. Japan

10. The British Prime Minister at the outbreak of World War II was :
A. Churchill B. Baldwin
C. Attlee D. Chemberlain

11. The 'Great Depression' (1929) economic crisis was met by adopting the policy of
A. Stimulus B. Marshall Plan
C. New Deal D. Open Door

12. The slogan "No taxation without representation" was raised during the:
A. American War of Independence
B. Russian Revolution
C. French Revolution
D. Indian Freedom struggle

13. In the nineteenth century the people of Europe started moving from the villages to the cities due to the impact of :
A. Epidemics
B. War
C. Industrialisation
D. Population explosion in villages

14. The important cause of the Civil War in America was:
A. Abolition of slavery
B. Quest for freedom
C. Industrialisation
D. Rebellion by the native Americans

15. Industrial Revolution could not have come about without:
A. Merchant capitalism
B. The Enclosure Movement
C. The services of the proletariat class
D. An agricultural revolution

16. Consider the following statements :
The French Revolution came about mainly due to the:
1. Extreme poverty of the people
2. Impact of the works of great writers
3. Cruelty of the rulers
4. Impact of impulsive reaction
Which of the above statements are correct?
A. 1, 2 and 4 B. 2 and 3
C. 1, 3 and 4 D. 1, 2, 3 and 4

17. Asia's oldest and largest Buddhist monastery is situated in :
A. Tawang (Arunachal Pardesh)
B. Lhasa (Tibet)
C. Trincomallee (Sri Lanka)
D. Ulan Bator (Mongolia)

18. Who was the main architect of the Russian Revolution?
A. Karl Marx B. Lenin
C. Stalin D. Tolstoy

19. V.I. Lenin is associated with :
A. Russian Revolution of 1917
B. Chinese Revolution of 1949
C. German Revolution
D. French Revolution of 1789

20. Which one of the following statements is *not* correct?
A. Voltaire believed in Natural Religion
B. Rousseau wrote *Social Contract*
C. Montesquieu authored *The Spirit of Laws*
D. Necker believed in 'General Will'

21. 6th April, 1930 is well known in the history of India because this date is associated with..........
A. Dandi March by Mahatma Gandhi
B. Quit India Movement
C. Partition of Bengal
D. Partition of India

22. Which ruler enforced the system of 'Price Control' in India?
A. Mohammad Tughlak B. Razia Begum
C. Alauddin Khilji D. Sher Shah Suri

23. The concept of 'Din-e-Elahi' was founded by which king?
A. Dara Shikoh B. Akbar
C. Sher Shah Suri D. Shahjahan

24. Who are supposed to be the earliest inhabi-tants of India? Where did they come from?
A. Aryans from Central Asia
B. Dravidians from Mediterranean
C. Negroids from Africa
D. Bhils and the Santhals from West Asia

25. The one chief characteristic of temple architecture of the Gupta Age was :
A. Absence of dome
B. Huge size
C. Beautiful carvings
D. absence of a covered courtyard for the gathering of worshippers

26. The Rigveda consists of :
A. 1000 hymns B. 2028 hymns
C. 1028 hymns D. 1038 hymns

27. The central point in Ashoka's dharma was :
A. royalty to kings B. peace and non-violence
C. respect to elders D. religious tolerance

28. The social evil which was conspicuously absent during ancient India was :
A. *Sati*-System B. *Devadasi*-System
C. Polygamy D. *Purdah*-System

29. Which, among the following, can be accepted as a novelty introduced by Mughal emperors to their buildings?
A. Domes B. Minarets
C. Arches D. Attached gardens

30. The first ruler of India who defeated Muhammud of Ghur was :
A. Mularaja II of Gujarat
B. Prithviraja Chauhan of Delhi
C. Jayachand of Kannauj
D. Parmaldeva of Bundelkhand

31. What important event happened in India in 1911?
A. Bengal was partitioned
B. Non-Cooperation movement was launched
C. India's capital was shifted from Calcutta to Delhi
D. Mahatma Gandhi presided over the Congress session

32. The first phase of the Congress Party (1885-1905) was characterized by its efforts to secure:
A. limited independence
B. complete freedom
C. Indianization of services
D. constitutional reforms

33. The Muslim League demanded a separate homeland for the Indian Muslims openly for the first time at its annual session held in Lahore in the year :
A. 1931 A.D. B. 1936 A.D.
C. 1940 A.D. D. 1941 A.D.

34. Under whose governorship did the East India Company secure the Diwani Rights in Bengal, Bihar and Odisha from Emperor Shah Alam?
A. Lord Cornwallis B. Lord William Bentinck
C. Lord Clive D. Lord Wellesley

35. The Simon Commission was generally boycotted by the Indian political parties. What was the reason for this general non-cooperation?
A. the Commission aimed at dividing the people
B. it was an 'all white' Commission
C. it came after the Jallianwala Bagh carnage
D. it was an eye wash

36. Aligarh Muslim University was founded by :
A. Dr. Saifuddin Kitchlu
B. Mohammad Ali Jinnah
C. Sir Syed Ahmed Khan
D. Maulana Mohammad Ali

37. Ibn Batutah was an African traveller visiting India during the time of :
A. Alivardi Khan
B. Ala-ud-din Khalji
C. Iltutmish
D. Mohammad-bin-Tughlaq

38. The battle of Wandiawash was fought in :
A. 1726 B. 1760
C. 1818 D. 1857

39. The abolition of *Sati* by government regulation was at the time of :
A. Warren Hastings B. Lord Wellesley
C. Lord Bentinck D. Lord Ahmerst

40. Pick out the wrong combination :
A. Dilwara Temple : Mt. Abu
B. Pashupati Temple : Kathmandu
C. Padmanabh Temple : Bangalore
D. Minakshi Temple : Madurai

41. Match the following:
(*a*) Chanhudaro (*b*) Kalibangan
(*c*) Lothal (*d*) Surkotada
1. Alleged discovery of the skeleton of horse.
2. Bead making.
3. Traces of a dock and ship on seal.
4. Evidence of ploughing the fields.

The Correct code is :

	(*a*)	(*b*)	(*c*)	(*d*)
A.	2	4	3	1
B.	2	1	3	4
C.	1	2	3	4
D.	2	1	4	3

42. Match the Harappan settlements with the banks of rivers on which they were located :
(*a*) Harappa 1. Ravi
(*b*) Mohenjodaro 2. Indus
(*c*) Ropar 3. Sutlej
(*d*) Kalibangan 4. Ghaggar
(*e*) Lothal 5. Bhogava

Codes :

	(*a*)	(*b*)	(*c*)	(*d*)	(*e*)
A.	1	2	3	4	5
B.	1	2	3	5	4
C.	2	1	3	5	4
D.	2	1	4	3	5

43. The Goddess 'Kannagi' whose many temples were erected during the 'Sangam Age' was the goddess of:
A. Chastity B. Love
C. Prowess D. Wisdom

44. The Jain goal of life is to attain deliverance from the fetters of mudane existence, the way to which lies through three jewels. Which one of the following was not included among the 'three jewels' of Jainism?
A. Right faith B. Right action
C. Right knowledge D. Right conduct

45. The most striking feature of the Ashokan pillar is polish. Name the Ashokan pillar which is considered to be the most graceful of all Ashokan pillars.
A. Sarnath B. Rampurva
C. Laurya-Nandangarh D. Rummindei

46. Which are the correct statements?
1. The land grants, started in Satavahana period, paved the way for feudal developments in India.
2. Silk and spices were the Chief Indian export articles of Indo-Roman trade.
3. The Guptas issued the largest number of gold coins in ancient India.
4. The first memorial of a 'SATI' dated 510 A.D. is found at Eran in Madhya Pradesh.

A. 1 and 2 B. 1, 3, and 4
C. 1 and 4 D. 1, 2, 3 and 4

47. Who among the following patronised the 'Gandhara' (Indo-Greek style) School of Art?
A. Ashoka, the Great
B. Harsha Vardhana
C. Kanishka
D. Chandragupta Vikramaditya

48. The Sultanate of Delhi had five ruling dynasties. The dynasty having longest and shortest period were :
A. Ilbari and Khalji B. Tughlaq and Khalji
C. Tughlaq and Sayyid D. Ilbari and Lodis

49. Which one of the following events took place at the last during reign of Muhammad-bin-Tughlaq?
A. Introduction of token currency
B. Increase of land-revenue in Doab
C. Transfer of Capital from Delhi to Devagiri.
D. Conquest of Khurasan and Iraq

50. The most learned medieval Muslim ruler who was well versed in various branches of learning including astronomy, mathematics and medicine was :
A. Jalaluddin Khilji B. Sikander Lodi
C. Ghiyasuddin Tughlaq D. Muhammad-bin-Tughlaq

51. The 'Sufis' had 12 silsilas. They propounded the idea of Union with God through:
A. Love B. Rituals
C. Fasts D. Prayers

52. Match the following:
(*a*) Peshwa 1. Foreign affairs
(*b*) Panditrao 2. Audit and accounts
(*c*) Amatya 3. Providing grants to scholars
(*d*) Sumant 4. General supervision
5. Military affairs

Select the correct code :

	(a)	(b)	(c)	(d)
A.	2	3	4	5
B.	4	1	2	3
C.	4	3	2	1
D.	3	1	4	2

53. The Regulating Act of 1773 can be regarded as the first measure to :
A. assert the right of British Parliament to legislate for India
B. separate the legislature from the executive
C. separate the judiciary from the executive
D. centralise law-making

54. What was the exact constitutional status of the Indian Republic on 26th January, 1950?
A. A Democratic Republic
B. A Sovereign, Democratic Republic
C. A Sovereign, Secular, Democratic Republic
D. A Sovereign, Socialist, Secular, Democratic Republic

55. When the British obtained the grant of Diwani of Bengal, Bihar and Odisha they acquired the right to:
A. maintain law and order in these territories
B. administer civil justice and collect revenue in these territories
C. collect revenue and establish revenue administration in these territories
D. militarily defend these territories

56. Which of the following were responsible for the growth of nationalism in India during the British rule?
1. Economic exploitation of India.
2. Impact of western education.
3. Role of the Press.

Select the correct answer using the codes given below :
Codes:
A. 1, 2 and 3 B. 1 and 2
C. 2 and 3 D. 1 and 3

57. Which one of the following nationalist leaders has been described as being radical in politics but conservative on social issues?
A. G.K. Gokhale B. B.G. Tilak
C. Lala Lajpat Rai D. Madan Mohan Malviya

58. Provincial Autonomy in British India was envisaged by the :
A. Act of 1909 B. Act of 1919
C. Act of 1935 D. Act of 1947

59. Dyarchy means :
A. double government
B. a government in which the centre is very powerful
C. a government based on division of power between centre and provinces
D. None of the above

60. The Indian National Congress observed 'Independence Day' for the first time on 26th January in :
A. 1920 B. 1925
C. 1930 D. 1947

61. ....is situated near the banks of Sabarmati River
A. Bhavnagar B. Aurangabad
C. Ahmedabad D. Rajkot

62. Sericulture is:
A. science of the various kinds of serum
B. artificial rearing of fish
C. art of silkworm breeding
D. study of various cultures of a community

63. The most abundant constituents of earth's crust are:
A. Igneous rocks B. Sedimentary rocks
C. Metamorphic rocks D. Granite

64. Indian Standard Time is based on:
A. 80°E longitude B. 82½°E longitude
C. 110°E longitude D. 25°E longitude

65. Tides in the oceans are caused by :
A. Gravitational pull of the moon on the earth's surface including sea water
B. Gravitational pull of the sun on the earth's surface only and not on the sea water
C. Gravitational pull of the moon and the sun on the earth's surface including the sea water
D. None of these

66. Nagarjunasagar Project is situated on the river:
A. Tungabhadra B. Cauvery
C. Krishna D. Godavari

67. The difference between the Indian Standard Time and the Greenwich Mean Time is:
A. – 3½ hours B. + 3½ hours
C. – 5½ hours D. + 5½ hours

68. Which of the following dams is not on Narmada river?
A. Indira-Sagar Project
B. Maheshwar Hydel Power Project
C. Jobat Project
D. Koyna Power Project

69. Which of the following statements is **not true** about the availability of water on the earth, the crisis for which is going to increase in the years to come?
A. About 97.5 per cent of the total volume of water available on the earth is salty
B. 80 per cent of the water available to us for use comes in bursts as monsoons
C. About 2.5 per cent of the total water available on the earth is polluted water and cannot be used for human activities
D. Possibility is that some big glaciers will melt in the coming ten-fifteen years and sea level will rise by 3-4 metres all over the earth

70. Which of the following is **not** a cash crop?
A. Jute B. Paddy
C. Cashewnut D. Sugarcane

71. Through which States does Cauvery River flow?
A. Gujarat, M.P., Tamil Nadu
B. Karnataka, Kerala, Tamil Nadu
C. Karnataka, Kerala, Andhra Pradesh
D. M.P., Maharashtra, Tamil Nadu

72. Indian Standard Time is the local time of 82½°E which passes through :
A. Guntur B. Delhi
C. Allahabad D. Kolkata

73. The 17th parallel defines the boundary between:
A. North and South Korea
B. USA and Canada
C. North and South Vietnam
D. China and Russia

74. During the period of south-west monsoon, Tamil Nadu remains dry because:
A. the winds do not reach this area
B. there are no mountains in this area
C. it lies in the rain shadow area
D. the temperature is too high to let the winds cool down

75. Which country does top in producing cocoa?
A. Ivory Coast B. Brazil
C. Ghana D. Nigeria

76. The biggest reserves of thorium are in :
A. India B. China
C. Russia D. U.S.A.

77. The Girnar Hills are situated in which of the following states?
A. Gujarat B. Karnataka
C. Madhya Pradesh D. Maharashtra

78. During December 22nd the sun is vertically over:
A. Tropic of Cancer B. Tropic of Capricorn
C. The Equator D. None of the above

79. Photosphere is described as the :
A. Lower layer of atmosphere
B. Visible surface of the sun from which radiation emanates
C. Wavelength of solar spectrum
D. None of the above

80. Broadly, there are three layers of the earth of the crust, the mantle and the core. The crust forms what percentage of the volume of the earth?
A. 0.5% B. 2.5%
C. 7.5% D. 12.5%

81. The grassland of Argentina is known as :
A. Pampas B. Campos
C. Savanna D. None of the above

82. Different seasons are formed because :
A. Sun is moving around the earth
B. of revolution of the earth around the Sun on its orbit
C. of rotation of the earth around its axis
D. All of the above

83. Eskers and Drumlins are features formed by:
A. underground water B. running water
C. the action of wind D. glacial action

84. Match List-I and List-II and select the correct answer using the codes given below the Lists :

List-I *(Rivers)*	List-II *(Towns)*
(a) Ghaghara	1. Lucknow
(b) Brahmaputra	2. Hoshangabad
(c) Narmada	3. Ahmedabad
(d) Sabarmati	4. Guwahati
	5. Ayodhya

Codes :

	(a)	*(b)*	*(c)*	*(d)*
A.	4	5	1	2
B.	5	4	2	3
C.	5	4	3	1
D.	3	5	2	1

85. Which of the statements as regards the consequences of the movement of the earth is not correct?
A. Revolution of the earth is the cause of the change of seasons.
B. Rotation of the earth is the cause of days and nights.
C. Rotation of the earth causes variation in the duration of days and nights.
D. Rotation of the earth effects the movement of winds and ocean currents.

86. The world is divided into :
A. 12 time zones B. 20 time zones
C. 24 time zones D. 36 time zones

87. The 'Kiel' canal links the :
A. Pacific and Atlantic Oceans
B. Mediterranean Sea and Red Sea
C. Mediterranean Sea and Black Sea
D. North Sea and Baltic Sea

88. Match the following :

List-I	List-II
(a) Himadri	1. Outer Himalayas
(b) Shivalik	2. Inner Himalayas
(c) Himanchal	3. Middle Himalayas
(d) Sahyadri	4. Western Ghats

Codes :

	(a)	*(b)*	*(c)*	*(d)*
A.	1	2	3	4
B.	4	2	3	1
C.	2	1	3	4
D.	1	2	3	4

89. The term 'Regur' refers to:
A. Laterite soils
B. Black Cotton soils
C. Red Soils
D. Deltaic Alluvial Soils

90. Location of sugar industry in India is shifting from north to south because of:
A. cheap labour
B. expanding regional market
C. cheap and abundant supply of power
D. high yield and high sugar content in sugarcane

91. Consider the following statements :
1. Ozone is found mostly in the Stratosphere.
2. Ozone layer lies 55-75 km above the surface of the earth.
3. Ozone absorbs ultraviolet radiation from the Sun.
4. Ozone layer has no significance for life on the earth.

Which of the above statements are correct?
A. 1 and 3 B. 2 and 4
C. 2 and 3 D. 1 and 4

92. Match List-I with List-II and select the correct answer using the codes given below the Lists :

List-I (Crops)	***List-II (Producer)***
(*a*) Banana	1. Brazil
(*b*) Cocoa	2. Ivory Coast
(*c*) Coffee	3. India
(*d*) Tea	4. China

Codes :

	(*a*)	(*b*)	(*c*)	(*d*)
A.	2	3	1	4
B.	3	2	1	4
C.	3	2	4	1
D.	2	3	4	1

93. Darjeeling and Dharamsala would be the right places to visit if one wanted to get a clear view respectively of :
A. Kanchanjunga and Dhauladhar ranges
B. Nandadevi and Dhauladhar ranges
C. Kanchanjunga and Nandadevi ranges
D. Nandadevi and Nanga Parvat

94. Atmosphere exists because:
A. The Gravitational force of the Earth
B. Revolution of the Earth
C. Rotation of the Earth
D. Weight of the gases of atmosphere

95. Victoria lake is located in the continent:
A. Africa B. Asia
C. North America D. South America

96. The famous Lagoon Lake of India is :
A. Dal Lake B. Chilka Lake
C. Pulicat Lake D. Mansarover

97. Where are most of the earth's active volcanoes concentrated?
A. Indian Ocean B. Pacific Ocean
C. Aral Sea D. Atlantic Ocean

98. Through which of the following states does the river Chambal flow?
A. U.P., M.P., Rajasthan B. M.P., Gujarat, U.P.
C. Rajasthan, M.P., Bihar D. Gujarat, M.P., U.P.

99. Which country is called the sugar bowl of the world?
A. Cuba B. India
C. Argentina D. USA

100. The area covered by forest in India is:
A. 46% B. 33%
C. 21.76% D. 23%

101. A closed economy is the one which :
A. does not permit emigration or immigration
B. permits emigration but no immigration
C. engages in no foreign trade
D. engages in no foreign and domestic trade or transit

102. In a developed economy the major share of employment originates in the :
A. primary sector B. tertiary sector
C. secondary sector D. any of the above

103. The Economic and Social Commission for Asia and Pacific (ESCAP) is located at :
A. Bangkok B. Kuala Lumpur
C. Manila D. Singapore

104. Commercial vehicles are not produced by which of the following companies in India?
A. TELCO B. Ashok Leyland
C. DCM Daewoo D. Birla Yamaha

105. What is 'Stagflation'?
A. Inflation with growth
B. Deflation with growth
C. Inflation after deflations
D. Inflation with depression

106. The main argument advanced in favour of small scale and cottage industries in India is that:
A. cost of production is low
B. they require small capital investment
C. they advance the goal of equitable distribution of wealth
D. they generate a large volume of employment

107. The most serious economic problems of India are:
A. Poverty and unemployment
B. Stagnation, not poverty
C. Unemployment, not poverty
D. Underdevelopment, not poverty

108. Which of the following is not one of the three central problems of an economy?
A. What to produce B. How to produce
C. When to produce D. For whom to produce

109. If saving exceeds investment, the national income will:
A. fall B. rise
C. fluctuate D. remain constant

110. In which of the following industries in India are the maximum number of workers employed?
A. Sugar B. Jute
C. Textiles D. Iron and Steel

111. Terrace Cultivation is practiced mostly:
A. in urban areas B. on slopes of mountains
C. on tops of hills D. in undulating tracts

112. Which of the following is a Selective Credit Control method?
A. Bank Rate B. RBI directives
C. Cash Reserve Ratio D. Open market operations

113. Which of the following taxes is not shared by the Central Government with the States?
A. Union excise duties B. Customs duty
C. Income tax D. Estate duty

114. ICICI is the name of a:
A. Financial Institution
B. Chemical Industry
C. Cotton Industry
D. Chamber of Commerce and Industry

115. Structural Unemployment arises due to
A. Deflationary conditions
B. Heavy industry bias
C. Shortage of raw material
D. Inadequate productive capacity

116. ECOMARC is a symbol related to:
A. Export goods
B. Import goods
C. Goods safe for environment
D. Best quality

117. The largest public sector bank in India is:
A. Central Bank of India B. Punjab National Bank
C. State Bank of India D. Indian Overseas Bank

118. Which of the following statements best explains the term contraband goods?
A. Goods produced only for exports
B. Goods produced in joint sector only
C. Goods for the trading of which licence is not required
D. Goods that are forbidden, from export, import or even possession, by law

119. Price in the market is fixed by:
A. Stock exchange rates
B. The demand and supply ruling in the market at a particular time
C. The Finance Minister
D. None of the above

120. Devaluation of currency helps to promote:
A. National Income B. Savings
C. Imports at lower cost D. Exports

121. Balanced economic growth can be achieved only if:
A. All the sectors of economy grow at the same rate
B. Population growth is arrested
C. All the inter dependent sectors grow in harmony
D. Basic and heavy industries are assigned highest priority

122. First share market in India was established in:
A. Mumbai B. Delhi
C. Kolkata D. Chennai

123. 'MODVAT' stands for:
A. Ad Valorem tax on output
B. Deduction of cost of inputs from the value of output
C. Reduction in import duties
D. Imposition of tax on professions

124. The headquarters of ILO is at:
A. Washington B. Geneva
C. The Hague D. Manila

125. The term 'devaluation' means:
A. Reducing the value of a currency in terms of another currency
B. Increasing the value of a currency
C. Revising the value of a currency
D. None of the above

126. Per capita net availability of pulses has shown a tendency of:
A. Increase over time
B. Decrease over time
C. Constant over time
D. First increase then decrease

127. National Income is the same as:
A. Net national product at market price
B. Net domestic product at market price
C. Net national product at factor cost
D. Net domestic product at factor cost

128. Which one of the following is not an example of indirect tax?
A. Sales tax B. Excise duty
C. Customs duty D. Expenditure tax

129. The major aim of devaluation is to:
A. encourage imports
B. encourage exports
C. encourage both exports and imports
D. discourage both exports and imports

130. Structural unemployment arises due to:
A. deflationary conditions
B. heavy industry bias
C. shortage of raw materials
D. inadequate productive capacity

131. When was the Family Planning Programme officially started in India?
A. 1950 B. 1952
C. 1956 D. 1962

132. When was the Reserve Bank of India nationalised?
A. 1947 B. 1949
C. 1950 D. 1951

133. Which of the following is *not* a feature of the Indian economy?
A. High rate of population growth
B. Disguised unemployment
C. Lowest rate of adult literacy
D. High rate of exports

134. The 'Relative Deprivation' approach for measuring poverty has been adopted by:
A. developing countries
B. developed countries
C. under-developed countries
D. None of the above

135. One of the main factors that led to rapid expansion of Indian exports is:
A. Imposition of import duties
B. Liberalisation of the economy
C. Recession in other countries
D. Diversification of exports

136. Sustainable economic development means an increase in the rate of growth of real:
A. total and per capita product
B. total and per capita product and level of literacy rate
C. total and per capita product and life expectancy at birth
D. total and per capita product, taking into account the cost of degradation of the quality of environment in this process

137. Functional unemployment occurs when:
A. unemployed have no qualification for job
B. people frequently change their job
C. people were thrown out from job due to recession
D. None of these

138. Which among the following does **not** have a 'free trade zone'?
A. Kandla B. Mumbai
C. Visakhapatnam D. Thiruvanantpuram

139. Sun Belt of USA is important for which one of the following industries?
A. Cotton textile B. Petrochemicals
C. Hi-tech electronics D. Food Processing

140. Commercial banking system in India is
A. unit banking B. branch banking
C. mixed banking D. None of the above

141. Who gives recognition to political parties in India?
A. Parliament
B. President
C. Supreme Court
D. Election Commission

142. The Quorum of the Legislative Council is :
A. one-fourth of its total membership
B. one-third of its membership
C. one-tenth of its membership
D. 25

143. The Indian Constitution is:
A. federal
B. unitary
C. a happy mixture of the federal and unitary
D. federal in normal times and unitary in times of emergency

144. Universal adult franchise implies a right to vote to all:
A. adult residents of the State
B. adult male citizens of the State
C. residents of the State
D. adult citizens of the State

145. When a resolution prefering a charge against the President has been passed by a specified majority in the House, it is sent to the other House for investigation. If, as a result of such an investigation, a resolution is passed through a specified majority by the other House, declaring that the charge has been sustained, the President shall leave his office. The specified special majority must not be less than :
A. two-third of the members present and voting
B. one-third of the members present and voting
C. three-fourth of the members present and voting and two-third of the total membership
D. two-third of the total membership

146. Which one of the following judicial powers of the President of India has been *wrongly* listed?
A. he appoints the Chief Justice and other judges of the Supreme Court
B. he can remove the judges of the Supreme Court on grounds of misconduct
C. he can consult the Supreme Court on any question of law or fact which is of public importance
D. he can grant pardon, reprieves and respites to persons punished under Union Law

147. The Vice-president of India can be removed from his office before the expiry of his term if :
A. the Rajya Sabha passes a resolution by a majority of its members and the Lok Sabha agrees with the resolution
B. if the Supreme Court of India recommends his removal
C. the President so desires
D. None of the above

148. The Chief Justice of a High Court in India is appointed by the :
A. Governor of the State
B. Prime Minister of India
C. Chief Justice of the Supreme Court
D. President of India

149. Which of the following statements is constitu-tionally not true about the passing of the Union Budgets, and Finance Bill in India?

1. Under the law, Finance Bill should be adopted by both the Houses of the Parliament within 45 days of its introduction.
2. If the Finance Bill is not adopted within specified period, the government loses its authority to levy the taxes proposed in the budgets.
3. In the absence of full budget, a vote-on-account gives the power to the government to spend.
4. Government cannot raise revenues without a proper approval of the Finance Bill

A. Only 2 B. Only 3
C. Only 4 D. Only 1, 2 and 3

150. Normally, on whose advice the President's Rule is imposed in a State?
A. Chief Minister
B. Legislative Assembly
C. Governor
D. Chief Justice of High Court

151. Which Article of the Indian Constitution deals with Amendment procedure?
A. Article 368 B. Article 358
C. Article 367 D. All of these

152. Government is the agency through which the will of:
A. the state is expressed
B. the people is expressed
C. the head of the state is expressed
D. the majority is expressed

153. In a unitary system of government :
A. The centre is all powerful
B. The centre is weaker than the states
C. The centre and states stand at par
D. The states and centre are supreme in their respective spheres

154. In Cabinet System of Government the real executive authority rests with :
A. The Council of Ministers
B. The Prime Minister
C. The Constitution
D. The Parliament

155. The Head of the State under a parliamentary government:
A. is an elected representative
B. is a hereditary person
C. is a nominated person
D. may be any one of the above

156. In the event of a ministerial proposal being defeated on the floor of the legislature, under the parliamentary system :
A. the government waits for a general no-confidence motion
B. the minister concerned is taken to task by the Prime Minister
C. the minister is forced to resign
D. the whole Council of Ministers resign

157. The "due process of law" is an essential characteristic of the judicial system of:
A. UK B. France
C. USA D. India

158. Under the Constitution it is :
A. obligatory for the President to accept the advice of the Council of Ministers but is not obliged to follow it
B. obligatory for the President to accept the advice of the Council of Ministers
C. not obligatory for the President to seek or accept the advice of the Council of Ministers
D. obligatory for the President to seek the advice of the Council of Ministers if his own party is in power

159. Which one of the following statements is correct?
A. the Presiding Officer of Rajya Sabha is elected every year
B. the Presiding Officer of Rajya Sabha is elected for a term of two years at a time
C. the Presiding Officer of Rajya Sabha is elected for a term of six years
D. the Vice-President of India is the ex-officio Presiding Officer of Rajya Sabha

160. The introduction of "no confidence" motion in the Lok Sabha requires the support of at least:
A. 50 members B. 70 members
C. 60 members D. 80 members

161. The High Court comes under :
A. State List B. Union List
C. Concurrent List D. None of the above

162. Which one of the following has been wrongly listed as a Fundamental Duty of the Indian citizens?
A. to develop scientific temper, humanism and spirit of inquiry and reform
B. to work for raising the prestige of the country in the international sphere
C. to protect and improve the natural environment
D. to strive towards excellence in all spheres of individual and collective activity

163. Which one of the following is not a Fundamental Duty as outlined in Article 51A of the Constitution?
A. to abide by the Constitution and respect its ideals
B. to defend the country and render national service when called upon to do so
C. to work for the moral upliftment of the weaker sections of society
D. to preserve the rich heritage

164. The main characteristics of the Directive Principles of State Policy given in the Indian Constitution are :
A. not enforceable by any court
B. fundamental in the governance of the country
C. 'Like instruments, instructions, political manifesto and a code of moral precepts which have to guide governors of the country'
D. no law can be passed, which is opposed to these principles

165. Of the following which are true?
A. In a State, the Legislative Council is dominant with regard to non-financial bills and the Legislative Assembly with regard to financial (money) bills
B. Vidhan Parishad can virtually block legisla-tion even if the same is passed by the Vidhan Sabha
C. In case of a tie between the two Houses, the Governor is duty-bound to call a joint session of the two Houses to have the issue settled on a majority verdict
D. If a Bill is twice approved by the Vidhan Sabha, it becomes law even if rejected by the Vidhan Parishad

166. Which one of the following types of emergency can be declared by the President?
A. Emergency due to threat of war and external aggresion
B. Emergency due to break-down of constitu-tional machinery in a State
C. Financial emergency on account of threat to the financial credit of India
D. all the three emergencies

167. The chairman of which of the following parliamentary committees is invariably from the members of ruling party?
A. Committee on public undertakings
B. Public accounts committee
C. Estimates committee
D. Committee on delegated legislation

168. Which of the following is not a formally prescribed device available to the members of parliament?
A. Question hour
B. Zero hour
C. Half-an-hour discussion
D. Short duration discussion

169. Which of the following is not a tool of executive control over public administration?
A. Power of appointment and removal
B. Line agencies
C. Appeal to public opinion
D. Civil services code

170. If the Speaker of the State Legislative Assembly decides to resign, he should submit his resignation to the:
A. Judges of the High Court
B. Deputy Speaker
C. Chief Minister
D. Finance Minister

171. Provision for free legal aid is mentioned in:
A. Fundamental Rights
B. Fundamental Duties
C. No Where
D. Directive principles of State policy

172. India is a Federal State because of:
A. dual judiciary
B. dual citizenship prevalent here
C. share of power between the Centre and the States
D. rigid Constitution

173. Residuary Subjects are those subjects which are:
A. contained in the State list
B. contained in the Union list
C. contained in the Concurrent list
D. not covered by any of the three lists

174. Which of the following writs can be issued, by the Supreme Court, to enforce Fundamental Rights?
A. Writ of Habeas Corpus
B. Writ of Mandamus
C. Writ of Quo Warranto
D. All of these

175. When the offices of both the President and the Vice-President of India are vacant, who will discharge their functions?
A. Prime Minister B. Home Minister
C. Chief Justice of India D. The Speaker

176. The Supreme Court tenders advice to the President of India on a matter of law or fact:
A. on its own
B. only when such advice is sought
C. only if the matter relates to some basic issue
D. only if the issue poses a threat to the unity and integrity of the country

177. Six months shall **not** intervene between two sessions of the Indian Parliament because :
A. it is the customary practice
B. it is the British convention followed in India
C. it is an obligation under the Constitution of India
D. None of the above

178. The States of the Indian Union can be recognised or their boundaries altered by:
A. the Union Parliament by a simple majority in the ordinary process of legislation
B. two-thirds majority of both the Houses of Parliament
C. two-thirds majority of both the Houses of Parliament and the consent of the legisla-tures of concerned States
D. an executive order of the Union government with the consent of the concerned State governments

179. The Basic Feature theory of the Constitution of India was propounded by the Supreme Court in the case of:
A. Minerva Mills Vs. Union of India
B. Golaknath Vs. State of Punjab
C. Maneka Gandhi Vs. Union of India
D. Keshavananda Vs. State of Kerala

180. Which one of the following writs is issued by a court in case of illegal detention of a person?
A. Habeas corpus B. Mandamus
C. Certiorari D. Quo-warranto

181. Name the instrument with the help of which a sailor in a submarine can see the objects on the surface of the sea.
A. Telescope B. Periscope
C. Gycroscope D. Stereoscope

182. 'Hemophillia' is the disease of ....
A. liver B. blood
C. brain D. bones

183. Vitamin A is abundantly found in ....
A. Brinjal B. Tomato
C. Carrot D. Cabbage

184. .... is not soluble in water.
A. Vitamin A B. Vitamin B
C. Vitamin C D. None of these

185. The blood vessels with the smallest diameter are called ....
A. capillaries B. arterioles
C. venules D. lymphatics

186. Out of the following .... has the greatest elasticity.
A. steel B. rubber
C. aluminium D. annealed copper

187. Cooking gas is a mixture of which of the following two gases?
A. Carbon Dioxide and Oxygen
B. Butane and Propane
C. Carbon Monoxide and Carbon Dioxide
D. Methane and Ethylene

188. The substance most commonly used as a food preservative is:
A. sodium carbonate B. tartaric acid
C. acetic acid D. benzoic acid

189. Normally, the substances that fight against diseases in human systems are known as:
A. dioxyribonucleic acids B. carbohydrates
C. enzymes D. antibodies

190. The SI unit of temperature is ....
A. Kelvin B. Celsius
C. Fahrenheit D. None of the above

191. One of the common fungal diseases of man is :
A. plague B. ringworm
C. cholera D. typhoid

192. A clear sky is blue because:
A. red light is scattered more than blue
B. ultraviolet light has been absorbed
C. blue light is scattered more than red
D. blue light has been absorbed

193. Jenner introduced the method of making people immune to :
A. small pox B. rabies
C. cholera D. polio

194. The largest cell in the human body is :
A. Nerve cell B. Live cell
C. Muscle cell D. Kidney cell

195. What is the device that steps up or steps down the voltage?
A. Dynamo B. Conductor
C. Inductor D. Transformer

196. The protein deficiency disease is known as :
A. Kwashiorker B. Cirrhosis
C. Eczema D. Clycoses

197. Iron deficiency causes :
A. rickets B. anaemia
C. cirrhosis D. goitre

198. Blood group of an individual is controlled by :
A. Haemoglobin B. Shape of RBC
C. Shape of WBC D. Genes

199. In a normal man the amount of blood pumped out by the heart per minute is about :
A. 1 litre B. 3 litres
C. 4 litres D. 5 litres

200. Red/green colour blindness in man is known as :
A. Protanopia B. Deutetanopia
C. Both A and B above D. Marfan's syndrome

201. The blue colour of the water in the sea is due to :
A. Reflection of the blue light by the impurities in sea water
B. Reflection of the blue sky by sea water and scattering of blue light by water molecules
C. Absorption of other colours by water molecules
D. None of the above

202. The image formed on the retina of the eye is:
A. upright and real B. larger than the object
C. small and inverted D. enlarged and real

203. Unit of loudness of sound is:
A. bel B. decibel
C. phon D. none of these

204. Oil rises up the wick in a lamp :
A. because oil is volatile
B. due to the capillary action phenomenon
C. due to the surface tension phenomenon
D. because oil is very light

205. The 'stones' formed in human kidney consist mostly of :
A. calcium oxalate
B. sodium acetate
C. magnesium sulphate
D. calcium

206. We hear the sound later, while the light is seen earlier:
A. because light's speed is more than that of sound
B. because lights travel in a straight direction while sound in a zigzag direction
C. because sound's frequency is lower than light
D. All of the above

207. Which part of an eye is transplanted?
A. Cornea B. Retina
C. Iris D. Sciera

208. The Universal donor group of blood is:
A. O B. A
C. B D. AB

209. The green colour of the leaf is due to :
A. Presence of Chloroplast
B. Presence of Chromium
C. Presence of Nicoplast
D. Presence of excess of oxygen

210. Voice of a child is more shrill than that of an elderly person because:
A. the pitch of the child's voice is higher than that of the person
B. the pitch is lower
C. the child is more energetic
D. None of the above

211. Camel uses its hump for :
A. storing water
B. storing fat
C. for balancing the body
D. temperature regulation

212. A man standing in a free falling lift releases a ball from his hand. The ball would be :
A. moving down B. moving up
C. stationary D. moving up and down

213. To change the quality of sound produced by an instrument we need to vary the:
A. pitch B. loudness
C. amplitude D. number of overtonnes

214. The disease caused by Asbestos is:
A. Emphysema B. Paralysis
C. Diarrhoea D. Dysentery

215. Sweetness of a sound depends upon its
A. wavelength
B. frequency
C. amplitude
D. periodicity and regularity

216. Bats can fly in the dark because :
A. they have a better vision in the dark
B. the pupils of their eyes are very big
C. they are guided by ultrasonic waves produced by them
D. any bird can do so

217. Blood is formed in the human adult by the :
A. heart B. spleen
C. kidney D. bone marrow

218. Pencil 'lead' is made up of:
A. graphite B. charcoal
C. lead oxide D. lampblack

219. The deficiency of which one of the following vitamins leads to bleeding of gums and loosening of teeth?
A. Vitamin D B. Vitamin C
C. Vitamin B D. Vitamin A

220. How much blood does a normal person have in his body?
A. 8 litres B. 4 to 5 litres
C. 10 litres D. 2 litres

221. Match List-I with List-II and select the correct answer using the codes given below the Lists :

List-I	***List-II***
(*a*) Visakhadatta	1. Mrichhakatika
(*b*) Shudraka	2. Ritusamhara
(*c*) Kalidasa	3. Kamasutra
(*d*) Vatsyayana	4. Devichandraguptam

Codes :

	(*a*)	(*b*)	(*c*)	(*d*)
A.	1	4	2	3
B.	4	1	3	2
C.	1	4	3	2
D.	4	1	2	3

222. In which one of the following langauges is the *Dalit* writing more conspicuous?
A. Punjabi B. Assamese
C. Marathi D. Odiya

223. The first writer to use Urdu as the medium of poetic expression was:
A. Amir Khusrau B. Mirza Ghalib
C. Bahadur Shah Zafar D. Faiz

224. The religious text of the Zoroastrians is named as:
A. Torah B. The Analects
C. Tripatika D. Zend Avesta

225. Name the music duo which composed music for Raj Kapoor's film 'Bobby'?
A. Laxmikant Pyarelal B. Shankar Jaikishen
C. Kalyanji Anandji D. Nadeem Shravan

226. Raja Harishchandra, an early Indian film, was produced by :
A. D.G. Phalke B. Ashok Kumar
C. Ardeshir Irani D. None of the above

227. All films are certificed by .... before they are publicly exhibited.
A. Films Division
B. National Film Development Corporation (NFDC)
C. Directorate of Advertising and Visual Publicity (DAVP)
D. Central Board of Film Certificate (CBFC)

228. Who among the following was the director of the film 'Taal'?
A. Gulzar B. Shekhar Kapoor
C. Satish Shah D. Subhash Ghai

229. Who amongst the following actresses has played the leading role in the film Elizabeth?
A. Gwyneth Paltrow B. Cate Blanchett
C. Simi Garewal D. Kim Basinger

230. The film 'Train to Pakistan' is based on the novel of the same name, written by:
A. Bhishma Sahani B. Khushwant Singh
C. Amrita Pritam D. Khwaja Ahmed Abbas

231. Which of the following is a folk dance form of Jharkhand?
A. Pali B. Jhumar
C. Nati D. Chhau

232. The first feature film (talkie) to be produced in India was:
A. Hatimtai B. Alam Ara
C. Pundalik D. Raja Harishchandra

233. Who directed the film "Bombay"?
A. Shyam Benegal B. Meera Nair
C. Shekhar Kapoor D. Mani Ratnam

234. Late Pankaj Udhas was famous in which of the following fields?
A. Singing B. Acting
C. Music D. Literature

235. Who among the following is the director of the film 'Kaho Na Pyar Hai'?
A. Subhash Ghai B. Shekhar Kapoor
C. Ramesh Sippy D. Rakesh Roshan

236. The character played by Jim Carrey in the movie *Man on Moon* is based on:
A. Andy Kaufman B. Edwin Aldrin
C. John Glenn D. Neil Armstrong

237. A popular Hindi film-based on the famous Sanskrit play *Mrichhakatika*, was titled:
A. Meghadoot B. Amrapali
C. Utsav D. Shakuntala

238. Who composed the song 'Zara Yad Karo Kurbani'?
A. Javed Akhtar
B. Pradeep
C. Nusrat Fateh Ali Khan
D. Raghupati Sahay 'Firaq'

239. Who was the producer of the serial 'Mahabharat'?
A. Shyam Benegal B. B.R. Chopra
C. Ramanand Sagar D. Mani Ratnam

240. Which of the following is a folk dance of Rajasthan?
A. Garba B. Dandya
C. Jhumar D. Kathak

241. 'The Colonel' is the nickname of which Indian Test Cricketer?
A. Colonel C.K. Naidu B. Rahul Dravid
C. Mohinder Amarnath D. Dilip Vengsarkar

242. The term 'Grandmaster' is used in which of these games?
A. Judo B. Chess
C. Bridge D. Karate

243. The term "Derby" is related with which of the following?
A. Polo B. Swimming
C. Racing D. Horse Racing

244. With which game is Geet Sethi associated?
A. Basketball B. Chess
C. Snooker D. Tennis

245. Beighton Cup is related with which of the following?
A. Hockey B. Polo
C. Cricket D. Soccer

246. Match List-I with List-II and select the correct answer using the codes given below the Lists :

List-I	*List-II*
(*a*) Basketball	1. Lob
(*b*) Bridge	2. Revoke
(*c*) Golf	3. Pivot
(*d*) Tennis	4. Bunker

Codes :

	(*a*)	(*b*)	(*c*)	(*d*)
A.	2	3	1	4
B.	2	3	4	1
C.	3	2	1	4
D.	3	2	4	1

247. The head office of the International Cricket Council (ICC) is situated in :
A. Zimbabwe B. Australia
C. South Africa D. UAE

248. Match the following :

List-I	*List-II*
(*a*) Deodhar Trophy	1. Volleyball
(*b*) Durand Cup	2. Football
(*c*) Davis Cup	3. Cricket
	4. Tennis

Codes :

	(*a*)	(*b*)	(*c*)
A.	3	2	4
B.	3	1	4
C.	2	3	1
D.	1	2	4

249. Which of the following is called 'Grand Slam'?
A. Winning the highest number of medals in the Olympic games
B. Winning the men's singles title in Wimbledon Championship
C. Winning the Wimbledon Singles title successively for two years
D. Winning all the four championships Australian, French, Wimblendon and US

250. With which game is the term 'butterfly stroke' associated?
A. Swimming B. Cricket
C. Gliding D. Skiing

251. Who is the first Indian to win the 'International Grand Master' title in Chess?
A. Anupama Abhayankar
B. Bhagyashree Sathe Thipsay
C. Vishwanathan Anand
D. D.V. Prasad

252. The XXII Commonwealth Games were held in 2022 in:
A. Kuala Lumpur B. Bangkok
C. Victoria D. Birmingham

253. The term 'Tee' is associated with which of the following sports?
A. Golf B. Table Tennis
C. Polo D. Judo

254. The famous woman Tennis player who was stabbed during a match, is
A. Steffi Graf B. Monica Seles
C. Mary Pierce D. Martina Navratilova

255. The term 'Baseline' is related to which of the following?
A. Golf B. Hockey
C. Badminton D. Polo

256. In which Indian State did the game of Polo originate?
A. Manipur B. Rajasthan
C. Gujarat D. West Bengal

257. World Environment Day is Celebrated on :
A. June 9 B. June 11
C. June 5 D. June 13

258. Rafael Nadal is the well-known player associated with:
A. Hockey B. Cricket
C. Tennis D. Chess

259. Gagan Narang is the well-known player associated with :
A. Shooting B. Golf
C. Table Tennis D. Chess

260. Eden Garden, a famous Cricket stadium, is located in:
A. Kanpur B. Kolkata
C. Jamshedpur D. Pune

261. Maharaja Ranjit Singh Trophy is associated with :
A. Golf B. Hockey
C. Soccer D. Tennis

262. Neeraj Chopra is a distinguished athlete in which of the following games?
A. Swimming B. Weightlifting
C. Javelin Throw D. Archery

263. Cricket was an Olympic event at which of the following Olympics?
A. London, 1908 B. Amsterdam, 1928
C. Paris, 1900 D. Melbourne, 1956

264. WISPA competitions are associated with :
A. Squash B. Yatching
C. Boxing D. Billiards

265. Ryder Cup is the famous trophy of :
A. Golf B. Chess
C. Boxing D. Polo

266. Davis Cup is associated with the sport of :
A. Cricket B. Football
C. Tennis D. Hockey

267. 'Volley', 'Chop' and 'Drive Spine' are the term associated with :
A. Lawn Tennis B. Badminton
C. Table Tennis D. Golf

268. Lal Bahadur Shastri Stadium is located at :
A. Hyderabad B. Chennai
C. Ahmedabad D. Varanasi

269. The first winner of Major Dhyanchand Khel Ratna Award is :
A. Geet Sethi B. Sachin Tendulkar
C. Viswanathan Anand D. Karnam Malleswari

270. 2023 Cricket World Cup was held in :
A. India B. Sri Lanka
C. Bangladesh D. Australia

271. The first team event introduced in 1900 at Paris Olympics was :
A. Hockey B. Football
C. Cricket D. Baseball

272. Which of the following international tennis tournaments is held on grass court?
A. US Open B. French Open
C. Wimbledon D. Australian Open

273. Which cricketer is nicknamed as the pied piper of Punjab?
A. Yuvraj Singh B. Harbhajan Singh
C. Mohinder Amarnath D. Navjot Singh Sidhu

274. 'Merdeka Cup' is associated with ....
A. Golf B. Football
C. Squash D. Hockey

275. The first time athletes marched into the stadium behind their nation's flag in Olympics:
A. at St. Louis 1904 B. at London 1908
C. at Antwerp 1920 D. at Paris 1924

276. The "Dronacharya Award" is associated with:
A. Eminent Surgeons
B. Famous Sports Person
C. Sport Coaches
D. Expert Engineers

277. Which cricketer is nicknamed as 'Jumbo'?
A. Venkatesh Prasad B. Anil Kumble
C. Glenn McGrath D. Shane Warne

278. The first time the Olympic Games were organised by a private company at:
A. Montreal, 1976 B. Los Angeles, 1984
C. Atlanta, 1996 D. Rome, 1960

279. In which Asian Games Cricket was played first?
A. Guangzhou, 2010
B. Doha, 2006
C. Busan, 2002
D. Seoul, 1986

280. The term 'Penalty cick' is used in :
A. Hockey B. Football
C. Baseball D. Golf

281. "Green Revolution" began in India during the year:
A. 1972-73 B. 1977-78
C. 1980-81 D. 1967-68

282. Khmer Rouge is a dictatorial party of :
A. Cambodia B. Indonesia
C. Malaysia D. Thailand

283. Which country is not a member of SAARC?
A. Russia B. Bangladesh
C. Nepal D. Pakistan

284. The headquarters of WTO is located at :
A. Geneva B. Paris
C. The Hague D. Washington

285. The main function of the World Trade Organisation (WTO) is:
A. enforcing of Uruguay Round Agreements
B. facilitating multi-lateral trade relations of member countries and reviewing trade policies
C. administering trade dispute settlement procedures
D. None of the above

286. The Secretary-General of the UNO is appointed by the:
A. General Assembly B. Security Council
C. Trusteeship Council D. World Bank

287. The United Nations officially came into existence in 1945 on :
A. November 24 B. October 14
C. October 24 D. November 14

288. Which one of the following is true of the International Court of Justice?
A. The Judges of the Court are appointed according to the discretion of the Secretary General
B. No two Judges may belong to the same country
C. The Court consists of 20 Judges
D. The statute of the International Court of Justice is not an integral part of the UN Charter

289. Which of the following was not among the six founding countries of the European Community?
A. Belgium B. France
C. Germany D. UK

290. The smallest country in South America is:
A. Ecuador B. Guyana
C. Surinam D. Uruguay

291. In which year "Human Rights Resolution" was adopted by the U.N.?
A. 1945 B. 1946
C. 1947 D. 1948

292. Where is the headquarters of INTERPOL located?
A. Berlin B. California
C. Lyons D. Montreal

293. Parliament of which of the following countries is known as Great People's Khural?
A. Malaysia B. Mongolia
C. Thailand D. Indonesia

294. Numbers of major organs of United Nations are:
A. 3 B. 4
C. 5 D. 6

295. When is the UN Day celebrated?
A. October 24 B. January 24
C. June 24 D. September 24

296. Which one of the following organ of United Nations is known as the 'Policeman of the World'?
A. Security Council
B. International Court of Justice
C. The Secretariat
D. General Assembly

297. The members of the NAFTA include:
A. USA, Canada and Mexico
B. USA, Canada, Mexico and UK
C. USA, UK, Russia and Mexico
D. USA, Canada and Brazil

298. The sits of International Court of Justice is located at:
A. Vienna B. Paris
C. Hague D. New York

299. Which of the following is known as the Constitution of the UN?
A. UN Charter B. UN Assembly
C. UN Security Council D. UN Secretariat

300. The Headquarters of the Amnesty International is located at :
A. New York B. London
C. Geneva D. Addis-Ababa

ANSWERS

1	2	3	4	5	6	7	8	9	10
B	C	D	C	B	C	A	C	C	D
11	**12**	**13**	**14**	**15**	**16**	**17**	**18**	**19**	**20**
C	A	C	A	A	D	A	B	A	D
21	**22**	**23**	**24**	**25**	**26**	**27**	**28**	**29**	**30**
A	C	B	C	D	C	B	D	D	B
31	**32**	**33**	**34**	**35**	**36**	**37**	**38**	**39**	**40**
C	D	C	C	B	C	D	B	C	C
41	**42**	**43**	**44**	**45**	**46**	**47**	**48**	**49**	**50**
A	A	A	B	C	D	C	B	B	D
51	**52**	**53**	**54**	**55**	**56**	**57**	**58**	**59**	**60**
A	C	A	B	B	A	B	C	A	C
61	**62**	**63**	**64**	**65**	**66**	**67**	**68**	**69**	**70**
C	C	B	B	C	C	D	D	D	B
71	**72**	**73**	**74**	**75**	**76**	**77**	**78**	**79**	**80**
B	C	C	C	A	A	A	B	B	A
81	**82**	**83**	**84**	**85**	**86**	**87**	**88**	**89**	**90**
A	B	D	B	C	C	D	C	B	D
91	**92**	**93**	**94**	**95**	**96**	**97**	**98**	**99**	**100**
A	B	A	A	A	B	B	A	A	C
101	**102**	**103**	**104**	**105**	**106**	**107**	**108**	**109**	**110**
C	B	A	D	D	D	A	C	D	C
111	**112**	**113**	**114**	**115**	**116**	**117**	**118**	**119**	**120**
B	B	B	A	D	C	C	D	B	D
121	**122**	**123**	**124**	**125**	**126**	**127**	**128**	**129**	**130**
C	A	A	B	A	D	C	D	B	D
131	**132**	**133**	**134**	**135**	**136**	**137**	**138**	**139**	**140**
B	B	D	A	B	D	B	D	D	C
141	**142**	**143**	**144**	**145**	**146**	**147**	**148**	**149**	**150**
D	C	D	D	D	B	A	D	C	C
151	**152**	**153**	**154**	**155**	**156**	**157**	**158**	**159**	**160**
A	B	A	A	A	D	C	B	D	A
161	**162**	**163**	**164**	**165**	**166**	**167**	**168**	**169**	**170**
B	B	C	B	D	D	C	B	B	B
171	**172**	**173**	**174**	**175**	**176**	**177**	**178**	**179**	**180**
D	C	D	D	C	B	C	A	D	A
181	**182**	**183**	**184**	**185**	**186**	**187**	**188**	**189**	**190**
B	B	C	A	A	A	B	D	D	A
191	**192**	**193**	**194**	**195**	**196**	**197**	**198**	**199**	**200**
B	C	A	A	D	A	B	D	D	A
201	**202**	**203**	**204**	**205**	**206**	**207**	**208**	**209**	**210**
B	B	B	B	A	A	A	A	A	A

211	212	213	214	215	216	217	218	219	220
B	A	A	A	D	C	D	A	B	B
221	222	223	224	225	226	227	228	229	230
D	C	A	D	A	A	D	D	B	B
231	232	233	234	235	236	237	238	239	240
D	B	D	A	D	D	C	B	B	C
241	242	243	244	245	246	247	248	249	250
D	B	D	C	A	D	D	A	D	A
251	252	253	254	255	256	257	258	259	260
C	D	A	B	C	A	C	C	A	B
261	262	263	264	265	266	267	268	269	270
B	C	C	A	A	C	C	A	C	A
271	272	273	274	275	276	277	278	279	280
B	C	A	B	A	C	B	B	A	B
281	282	283	284	285	286	287	288	289	290
D	A	A	A	B	A	C	B	D	C
291	292	293	294	295	296	297	298	299	300
D	C	B	D	A	A	A	C	A	B

❒ ❒ ❒

2603

HARYANA

General Knowledge & Awareness

Multiple Choice Questions

1. During the ancient age, modern Haryana state was known as:
(*a*) Brahmavarta (*b*) Brahmarshi region
(*c*) Uttravedi of Brahma (*d*) All of the above

2. Who of the following rulers of Bharata vamsha (descendants of Bharata, according to Rigveda, who were a group of people who lived in the north-west of India) started his campaign from Haryana for establishing his authority in various other Kingdoms of the time?
(*a*) Sudas (*b*) Arjuna
(*c*) Bharata (*d*) Bhishma

3. The famous war of Mahabharata was fought at which of the following places in Haryana?
(*a*) Panipat (*b*) Kurukshetra
(*c*) Jhajjhar (*d*) Ballabh Garh

4. During Mughals, Janapadas of this state were replaced by
(*a*) Gana Sangha (*b*) Gana System
(*c*) Khaps (*d*) Panchayata

5. The territory of modern Haryana was included in which of the following Mahajanapadas of Buddha period?
(*a*) Kuru and Panchala (*b*) Kosala and Vajji
(*c*) Sursena and Avanti (*d*) Asmaka and Vatsa

6. At which of the following places in the state, capital of the Agreyagana was situated?
(*a*) Rewari (*b*) Sirsa
(*c*) Hansi (*d*) Agroha

7. Mahamud Gaznavi attacked on Thanesar in:
(*a*) 1013 AD (*b*) 1014 AD
(*c*) 1016 AD (*d*) 1017 AD

8. Thanesar (now in Haryana) was the capital of which of the following famous rulers of ancient India?
(*a*) Harsha Vardhan
(*b*) Ashoka
(*c*) Chandragupta Vikramaditya
(*d*) Kanishka

9. During the 12th century A.D. who of the following rulers of Chauhan dynasty defeated Tomars of Haryana?
(*a*) Vigraha Raja VI (*b*) Vigrah Raja II
(*c*) Arno Raja (*d*) Prithvi Raj Chauhan

10. When did Sultan Balban of Ghulam dynasty attacked on Mevas of Haryana with a view to establish his authority on Mevas?
(*a*) 1260 AD (*b*) 1265 AD
(*c*) 1266 AD (*d*) 1267 AD

11. Feroz Tughlaq of Tughlaq dynasty built which of the following cities in Haryana?
(*a*) Tohana (*b*) Hansi
(*c*) Siwani (*d*) Fatehabad

12. Timur made an attack on which of the following cities of Haryana?
(*a*) Sirsa (*b*) Fatehabad
(*c*) Hissar (*d*) All of the above

13. The famous battle of 1526 between Babur and Ibrahim Lodi was fought at which of the following places of Haryana?
(*a*) Panipat (*b*) Kurukshetra
(*c*) Tawaru (*d*) Jind

14. Who was the King of Rewari during the reign of famous Mughal Emperor Akbar?
(*a*) Tularam (*b*) Karna Singh
(*c*) Hemachandra (Hemu) (*d*) Phool Singh

15. The famous second battle of Panipat between Akbar and Hemachandra (Hemu) was fought in:
(*a*) 1550 AD (*b*) 1552 AD
(*c*) 1554 AD (*d*) 1556 AD

16. Which of the following famous battle was fought in the state of Haryana between the Marathas and Ahmadshah Abdali?
(*a*) The third battle of Panipat
(*b*) The second battle of Panipat
(*c*) The first battle of Panipat
(*d*) None of these

17. George Thomas built his capital at which of the following places of the state?
(*a*) Raniya (*b*) Tohana
(*c*) The fort of Hansi (*d*) Behram Pur

18. In 1802 AD George Thomas died at which of the following places in Haryana?
(*a*) Mahendragarh (*b*) Behram Pur
(*c*) Narnaul (*d*) Bawal

19. During 1809-10 AD, entire territories of Haryana was under the control of:
(*a*) Marathas (*b*) Satnamies
(*c*) Mughals (*d*) Britishers

20. Modern Haryana state was built on:
(*a*) 1 November, 1966 (*b*) 5 January, 1967
(*c*) 1 November, 1958 (*d*) 15 August, 1947

21. Evidences of Early-Harappan, Mature Harappan and Late Harappan culture have been found at which of the following places in Haryana?
(*a*) Banawali (*b*) Sosawal
(*c*) Mirzapur (*d*) All of the above

22. The period of Aryans of Kuru Vamsha, centuries before the Mahabharata period was marked with the beginning of which of the following ages?
(*a*) Cultivation Age (*b*) Copper Age
(*c*) Iron Age (*d*) Metal Age

23. The essence of the philosophy of Bhagvad Gita preached by Lord Krishna to Arjuna, a noted Commander of the Mahabharata War in the form of a dialogue between the two was delivered at which of the following places of Haryana?
(*a*) Rewari (*b*) Pehwa
(*c*) Kurukshetra (*d*) Panipat

24. During Youdheya period, Haryana was known as:
(*a*) Youdheya confederacy (*b*) Bahudhanyaka region
(*c*) Matsya region (*d*) Gana region

25. The famous pilgrim Hiuen Tsang in his book Si-Yo-ki, has described the prosperity of which of the following cities of Haryana?
(*a*) Sthaneshwar (Thanesmar)
(*b*) Panipat
(*c*) Rohtak
(*d*) Ambala

26. Which of the following treatise provide valuable information about the advancement of trade, art and culture in Haryana during the reign of Tomar Kings?
(*a*) Tahkik-i-Hind (*b*) Harsh Charita
(*c*) Kadambari (*d*) Yashastilak Champu

27. Who was the ruler of the Tawaroo pargana during the invasion of Babur in 1526-27?
(*a*) Hasan Khan (*b*) Mohan Singh Mandhar
(*c*) Faizal Khan (*d*) Jalal Khan

28. During the period of Babur, the Rajput King Mohan Singh Mandhar had its kingdom in Haryana at:
(*a*) Mandhar Pargana of Kaithal
(*b*) Tawaroo
(*c*) Jind
(*d*) Panipat

29. During 1756-57, Haryana was under the control of:
(*a*) Mughals (*b*) Sikhs
(*c*) Marathas (*d*) Satnamies

30. While returning back to his homeland, Ahmad Shah Abdali put the northern part of Haryana (Ambala, Jind, Kurukshetra and Karnal Districts) under the charge of:
(*a*) Mughals
(*b*) Sikhs
(*c*) Jain Khan, the Governor of Sarhind
(*d*) Gen Khan the Governor of Durrani

31. In the sepoy mutiny that broke out in 1857 at Meerut, majority of soldiers who took part in the revolt hailed from which of the following districts of Haryana?
(*a*) Gurugram (*b*) Rohtak
(*c*) Hissar (*d*) All of these

32. Who of the following great warriors of Haryana was the Naib Kotwal of Meerut at the time of Sepoy mutiny:
(*a*) Abdus Samad Khan (*b*) Vikram Singh
(*c*) Rao Krishna Gopal (*d*) Rameshwar Dayal

33. In the battle (for the freedom of India) fought at the village Naseebpur situated near Narnaul, Britishers destroyed which of the following three powers?
(*a*) Rewari, Jhajjhar and Jodhpur
(*b*) Gurugram, Rewari and Jodhpur
(*c*) Jind, Jagadari and Pehwa
(*d*) Panipat, Jhajjhar and Tawaroo

34. In the first Freedom struggle, who of the following Kings of Ballabhgarh led the revolutionary army in Delhi?
(*a*) Raja Karn Singh (*b*) Raja Nahan Singh
(*c*) Raja Suraj Bhan (*d*) Raja Satyapal

35. Which of the following provinces of Haryana extended valuable cooperation to the British army in the revolt of 1857?
(*a*) Bahadurgarh (*b*) Tawaroo
(*c*) Jhajjhar (*d*) Jind

36. In the second Calcutta session of the Indian National Congress held in the year 1886, Haryana was represented by:
(*a*) Pandit Deen Dayal Sharma
(*b*) Lala Murlidhar
(*c*) Bal Mukund Gupta
(*d*) All of these

37. Lala Lajpat Rai had selected which of the following places situated in Haryana as his political and social work-field?
(*a*) Hissar (*b*) Sonipat
(*c*) Gurugram (*d*) Nooh

38. In the fourth session of the Indian National Congress held in 1888 at Allahabad who of the following national leaders represented Hissar?
(*a*) Lala Sultan Singh (*b*) Baldeo Singh
(*c*) Lala Lajpat Rai (*d*) Baini Singh

39. On 8 April, 1919, Gandhiji was arrested from which of the following places of Haryana?
(*a*) Kaithal (*b*) Palwal
(*c*) Gohana (*d*) Ambala

40. When was a conference held at Rohtak presided by Pt. Rambhaj Dutta in which a decision was taken to implement the Non-cooperation movement launched by Gandhiji?
(*a*) January, 1919 (*b*) November, 1919
(*c*) November, 1920 (*d*) September, 1921

41. In the annual session of Congress held at Nagpur, Haryana was represented by :
(*a*) Sardar Buta Singh (*b*) Lala Ugrasen
(*c*) Babu Shyam Lal (*d*) Pt. Neki Ram Sharma

42. On the appeal of Punjab Pradesh Congress, Independence Day was celebrated in entire Haryana on:
(*a*) 12 January, 1932 (*b*) 10 December, 1932
(*c*) 15 August, 1935 (*d*) 26 January, 1932

43. On which day was the Golden Jubilee of Congress celebrated in Haryana?
(*a*) 18 August, 1930 (*b*) 30 January, 1935
(*c*) 28 December, 1935 (*d*) 10 December, 1936

44. Who of the following was the great hero of Haryana who as a member of the INA hoisted the tricoloured flag for the first time on the land of Manipur?
(*a*) Major Pratap Singh (*b*) Major Suraj Mal
(*c*) Darbara Singh (*d*) Bhajan Lal

45. Chaudhary Chhotu Ram started a vigorous campaigns to popularize the Unionist Party in Haryana. In Haryana state this Party was called as:
(*a*) Zamindara League (*b*) Zamindari System
(*c*) Hindu-Muslim (*d*) None of these

46. Publication of which of the following weekly magazine was started by Chaudhary Chhotu Ram in 1916 from Rohtak?
(*a*) Hindu Gazette (*b*) Sikh Gazette
(*c*) Jat Gazette (*d*) None of the above

47. Chaudhary Chhotu Ram alongwith Shri Fazali Hussain set up the Unionist Party in Punjab in:
(*a*) 1919 (*b*) 1921
(*c*) 1922 (*d*) 1923

48. With a view to keep a control on the political activities in Patiala, Jind and Nabha states, a law was enforced in Samvat 1988 Vikrami. What was that law termed as:
(*a*) Hidayat Samvat (*b*) Hizri Samvat
(*c*) Vikram Samvat (*d*) Saka Samvat

49. In 1938, Jind Prajamandal was set up at Sangrur, the capital of Jind by:
(*a*) Rajendra Kumar Jain (*b*) Sadhu Ram
(*c*) Hansraj Rahbar (*d*) Nand Kishore

50. Gandhji was arrested from Palwal on:
(*a*) 5 January, 1919 (*b*) 8 May, 1920
(*c*) 8 April, 1919 (*d*) 17 April, 1921

51. Pt. Deen Dayal Sharma who made a very important contribution in popularizing Sanatan Dharma in whole of the Northern India, hailed from which of the following places of Haryana?
(*a*) Jhajjhar (*b*) Kaithal
(*c*) Hissar (*d*) Jind

52. In the Lahore Session of the Congress in 1892, Hissar was represented by:
(*a*) Balmukund Gupta (*b*) Lala Murlidhar
(*c*) Lala Lajpat Rai (*d*) Pt. Deen Dayal Sharma

53. When was Lala Lajpat Rai and Sardar Ajit Singh were arrested by the British Government and sent to Mandley Jail?
(*a*) In 1907 (*b*) In 1895
(*c*) In 1902 (*d*) In 1896

54. Mahatma Gandhi accompanied with Muhammad Ali and Shaukat Ali arrived Rohtak on:
(*a*) 10 January, 1919 (*b*) 8 October, 1920
(*c*) 1 October, 1920 (*d*) 18 March, 1920

55. The Divisional Political Conference of Ambala Division which was attended by Mahatma Gandhi alongwith Ali brothers, was held at Bhiwani in:
(*a*) March, 1918 (*b*) June, 1920
(*c*) October, 1919 (*d*) October, 1920

56. Even after India became free in 1947, Haryana remained a part of which of the following Indian Provinces?
(*a*) Delhi (*b*) Punjab
(*c*) Uttra Pradesh (*d*) Rajasthan

57. The state Restructuring Commission set up in 1955 by the Government of India had recommended to include which of the following two places in the state of Haryana?
(*a*) Mahendragarh and Jind (*b*) Patiala and Hissar
(*c*) Panipat and Kaithal (*d*) Rohtak and Gurugram

58. The tourist place called 'Tiliyar' is situated in which of the following districts of Haryana?
(*a*) Jind (*b*) Mahendragarh
(*c*) Rohtak (*d*) Kaithal

59. Who was the first Governor of Haryana?
(*a*) Shri Satyapal (*b*) Shri Dharmvir
(*c*) Shri Devilal (*d*) Shri Bansilal

60. Name of the first Non-Congress Chief Minister of Haryana who assumed this office on 24 March, 1967.
(*a*) Chaudhary Bhajan Lal (*b*) Devi Lal
(*c*) Bansi Lal (*d*) Rao Virendra Singh

61. Which of the following Rivers flow from the adjoining areas of Eastern Haryana and Uttar Pradesh?
(*a*) Ganga (*b*) Saraswati
(*c*) Ghaghghar (*d*) Yamuna

62. The main land of Haryana state stretches from 27° 39° N to 30° 55° N latitudes in the North-West of India. It stretches from .... E to .... E longitudes.
(*a*) 74° 28° E to 77° 36° E (*b*) 65° 33° E to 77° 28° E
(*c*) 50° 28° E to 64° 36° E (*d*) 84° 42° E to 89° 41° E

63. Which of the following states is located to the North of Haryana?
(*a*) Uttar Pradesh (*b*) Punjab
(*e*) Himachal Pradesh (*d*) Rajasthan

64. Which of the following states is located to the west of Haryana?
(*a*) Punjab (*b*) Rajasthan
(*c*) Uttar Pradesh (*d*) Himachal Pradesh

65. What is the area of the state of Haryana?
(*a*) 36,154 Sq. km. (*b*) 44,212 Sq. km.
(*c*) 49,105 Sq. km. (*d*) 51,206 Sq. km.

66. Which of the following state is not larger than Haryana by area?
(*a*) Meghalaya (*b*) Bihar
(*c*) Himachal Pradesh (*d*) Punjab

67. Dabwali is a subdivision of which district?
(*a*) Sirsa (*b*) Hissar
(*c*) Rohtak (*d*) Jhajjar

68. The mainland of Haryana is located at the height of .... from the sea level.
(*a*) 700 to 900 ft. (*b*) 750 to 880 ft.
(*c*) 800 to 1000 ft. (*d*) 900 to 1100 ft.

69. Shivalik range is located in which part of Haryana?
(*a*) North-West (*b*) North-East
(*c*) South-West (*d*) South-East

70. Which of the following rivers originate from Shivalik range to flow through the mainland of Haryana?
(*a*) Ghaghghar (*b*) Markanda
(*c*) Tangri (*d*) All of these

71. Which of the following natural parts of Haryana is the largest?
(*a*) the hilly region of the Shivalik
(*b*) the desert of Haryana
(*c*) the mainland of Haryana
(*d*) the dry plains of Aravali range

72. The famous Bibipur and Najafgarh lakes are located in which natural part of Haryana?
(*a*) The Plain
(*b*) The desert
(*c*) Hilly region of the Shivalik
(*d*) The dry plain of Aravali range

73. Which of the following cities of Haryana is not the part of National Capital Region?
(*a*) Sonipat (*b*) Faridabad
(*c*) Hisar (*d*) Gurugram

74. Which part of Haryana experiences maximum rainfall?
(*a*) South-Western Part (*b*) North-Eastern Part
(*c*) North-Western Part (*d*) South-Eastern Part

75. Which of the following parts of Haryana experiences minimum annual rainfall?
(*a*) North-Eastern Part (*b*) South-Eastern Part
(*c*) North-Western Part (*d*) South-Western Part

76. Which type of soil is found on Morney hills of the state?
(*a*) Sandy Soil (*b*) Brownish Soil
(*c*) Laterite Soil (*d*) Sandy Clayee Soil

77. Generally, which type of soil is found in the plains of Haryana?
(*a*) Fertile Soil of Yellow brownish colour
(*b*) Laterite Soil
(*c*) Sandy Soil
(*d*) Sandy Clayee Soil

78. In which of the following districts of Haryana, red chestnut soil is found?
(*a*) Rohtak (*b*) Sirsa
(*c*) Yamuna Nagar (*d*) Bhivani

79. Which of the following rivers of the state of Haryana joins Markanda river near Mulana?
(*a*) Sahibi (*b*) Tangri
(*c*) Krishnawati (*d*) Dohan

80. Which of the following is the oldest and the most important canal of Haryana?
(*a*) Gurugram Canal (*b*) Bhiwani Canal
(*c*) Bhakra Canal (*d*) Western Yamuna Canal

81. Which of the following canals originates from the Yamuna river near Tazewala situated on the Jagadhari-Pona road?
(*a*) Bhakra Canal
(*b*) Western and Eastern Yamuna Canal
(*c*) Jawahar Lal Nehru Canal
(*d*) None of these

82. Jawahar Lal Nehru canal of Haryana originates from:
(*a*) Bhakra Canal (*b*) Bhiwani Canal
(*c*) Gurugram Canal (*d*) Yamuna Canal

83. Which of the following lakes is located in Haryana?
(*a*) Damdama Lake (*b*) Kotla Lake
(*c*) Khalilpur Lake (*d*) All of these

84. Which of the following lakes is situated in Farrukh Nagar block of the state?
(*a*) Sultanpur lake (*b*) Damdama lake
(*c*) Khalilpur lake (*d*) Kotla lake

85. The famous Badkal lake is situated in which of the following districts of Haryana?
(*a*) Gurugram (*b*) Bhivani
(*c*) Faridabad (*d*) Rohtak

86. Which of the following canals of Haryana originates from Yamuna river at Okhla in Delhi?
(*a*) Bhakra Canal (*b*) Gurugram Canal
(*c*) Eastern Yamuna Canal (*d*) None of these

87. Bhakra Canal provides water for irrigation in which of the following districts of Haryana?
(*a*) Sirsa (*b*) Hissar
(*c*) Rohtak (*d*) All of these

88. Which of the following districts of the state gets water for irrigation from Jawahar Lal Nehru Canal?
(*a*) Sirsa (*b*) Rohtak
(*c*) Mahendragarh (*d*) Jind

89. Bhiwani canal originates from which of the following canals?
(*a*) Bhakra Canal (*b*) Gurugram Canal
(*c*) Western Yamuna Canal (*d*) Eastern Yamuna Canal

90. When was the famous Badkal lake of Haryana built?
(*a*) In 1940 (*b*) In 1950
(*c*) In 1974 (*d*) In 1947

91. The famous tourist place 'Tajewala Headworks' is situated in which of the following districts of Haryana?
(*a*) Rohtak (*b*) Faridabad
(*c*) Gurugram (*d*) Yamuna Nagar

92. Haryana has been divided into:
(*a*) 6 Divisions (*b*) 5 Sub Divisions
(*c*) 4 Divisions (*d*) 8 Divisions

93. How many total sub-divisions exist in Haryana state till January, 2025?
(*a*) 60 Sub-Divisions (*b*) 65 Sub-Divisions
(*c*) 68 Sub-Divisions (*d*) 80 Sub-Divisions

94. How many total Tehsils exist in Haryana till January, 2025?
(*a*) 94 (*b*) 68
(*c*) 70 (*d*) 85

95. How many total sub-Tehsils exist in Haryana till January, 2025?
(*a*) 30 (*b*) 31
(*c*) 49 (*d*) 40

96. How many total Blocks exist in Haryana till January, 2025?
(*a*) 95 (*b*) 143
(*c*) 115 (*d*) 119

97. Total number of populated villages in Haryana is:
(*a*) 4,390 (*b*) 4,950
(*c*) 5,845 (*d*) 6,841

98. According to the Census of 2011, the total population of Haryana is:
(*a*) 2,53,51,462 (*b*) 2,40,55,400
(*c*) 2,25,83,912 (*d*) 2,20,45,657

99. Salarganj Gate is situated near which of the following town of Haryana?
(*a*) Rohtak (*b*) Hissar
(*c*) Panipat (*d*) Ambala

100. In terms of area the largest district of Haryana is:
(*a*) Rohtak (*b*) Sirsa
(*c*) Panipat (*d*) Ambala

101. Which of the following minerals is found in abundance in Mahendragarh district of Haryana?
(*a*) Lime stone (*b*) China clay
(*c*) Copper (*d*) All of these

102. At which of the following places in district Rewari, Slate-stone is found in abundance?
(*a*) Kund (*b*) Baval
(*c*) Kusal (*d*) Khol

103. Consider the following statements:
1. Nada Sahib Gurudwara is situated in Ambala.
2. Nada Sahib Gurudwara is situated on the bank of river Ghaggar.

Which of the above statements is/are correct?
(*a*) 2 only (*b*) Both 1 and 2
(*c*) Neither 1 nor 2 (*d*) 1 only

104. At which of the following places in district Bhiwani Granite stones are found?
(*a*) Village Nigana Kalan (*b*) Delheri
(*c*) Riwasa (*d*) All of these

105. When was Shri Krishna Museum established in Kurukshetra?
(*a*) 1987 (*b*) 1970
(*c*) 1989 (*d*) 1995

106. What is the area of the total forest land in Haryana?
(*a*) 1,428 Sq. km. (*b*) 1,614.26 Sq. km.
(*c*) 1,852 Sq. km. (*d*) 1,812 Sq. km.

107. During which of the following years, a comprehensive afforestation scheme 'Greening of Haryana' was started?
(*a*) 1982 - 83 (*b*) 1983 - 86
(*c*) 1989 - 90 (*d*) 1994 - 95

108. Haryana has announced its new Industrial Policy in ....
(*a*) 1995 (*b*) 2011
(*c*) 2005 (*d*) 2002

109. With the aid of the European Union "Haryana Community Development Scheme" (Haryana Samudayiki) was introduced in Haryana in:
(*a*) 1992 - 93 (*b*) 1994 - 95
(*c*) 1996 - 97 (*d*) 1998 - 99

110. Basai wetland is located in which district of Haryana?
(*a*) Gurugram (*b*) Jhajjar
(*c*) Faridabad (*d*) Kurukshetra

111. As per census 2011, literacy of Haryana is:
(*a*) 80.40% (*b*) 65.72%
(*c*) 75.6% (*d*) 68.85%

112. Which of the following tourist place is situated on Samauli Road Panipat?
(*a*) Jyotisar (*b*) Kala Amb
(*c*) Damdama Lake (*d*) King Fisher

113. Which of the following minerals is found in districts Hissar and Karnal?
(*a*) Pig Iron (*b*) Mica
(*c*) Nitre (*d*) Marble

114. Which of the following minerals is found in Rohtak district?
(*a*) Lime (*b*) Copper
(*c*) Manganese (*d*) Mica

115. Which of the following trees are found in abundance in Jind district of Haryana?
(*a*) Rosewood tree (Sesam) (*b*) Acacia tree (Kikar)
(*c*) Safeda (*d*) All of these

116. In the Agricultural University, Hissar 'research on Paddy' was started in:
(*a*) 1966 (*b*) 1970
(*c*) 1974 (*d*) 1989

117. Where is National Cancer Institute situated?
(*a*) Sampla (*b*) Meham
(*c*) Kalanaur (*d*) Badsa

118. Which of the following districts of Haryana is pre-eminent in the production of mushroom (Khumbhi) in India?
(*a*) Ambala (*b*) Sirsa
(*c*) Sonepat (*d*) Yamuna Nagar

119. Which of the following is a major crop produced in Rohtak district of Haryana?
(*a*) Pearl Millet (*b*) Great Millet
(*c*) Sugar cane (*d*) All of these

120. Sugar Mill is located at which of the following places in Kurukshetra?
(*a*) Pehwa (*b*) Shahabad Markanda
(*c*) Ladawa (*d*) Babain

121. Which of the following districts of Haryana is called "a big bowl of paddy" as it has gained world fame in the production of Basmati rice?
(*a*) Hissar (*b*) Kurukshetra
(*c*) Karnal (*d*) Jind

122. Navagrah temple in Haryana is located at ....
(*a*) Kurukshetra (*b*) Kaithal
(*c*) Gurugram (*d*) Faridabad

123. The total installed capacity of energy available to the state till 2023-24 is ....
(*a*) 8,575 MW (*b*) 8,200 MW
(*c*) 14,026.68 MW (*d*) 9,510 MW

124. What was the quantum of production of horticulture crops in Haryana during 2023-24?
(*a*) 41.20 Lakh M.T. (*b*) 85.63 Lakh M.T.
(*c*) 62.15 Lakh M.T. (*d*) 52.25 Lakh M.T.

125. In which of the following districts of Haryana, with a view to check the soil erosion in Shivalik areas, coordinated water flow Development Project is being implemented?
(*a*) Ambala (*b*) Panchkula
(*c*) Yamuna Nagar (*d*) All of these

126. Indira Gandhi Super Thermal Power Project is situated in which district of Haryana?
(*a*) Sirsa (*b*) Hisar
(*c*) Jind (*d*) Jhajjar

127. In the Ambala district of Haryana, canal irrigation system was made available after completion of which of the following irrigation project?
(*a*) Nangal Lift Irrigation Project
(*b*) Hathni Reservoir Barrage Project
(*c*) Jawahar Lal Nehru Irrigation Project
(*d*) Sewani Lift Irrigation Project

128. Which of the following system of irrigation is used in the sandy plains of Haryana?
(*a*) Canal
(*b*) Well
(*c*) With the help of Tubewell-Fountain irrigation
(*d*) Rain water

129. Water from western Yamuna Canal is used for irrigation in which of the following districts of Haryana?
(*a*) Karnal (*b*) Sonepat
(*c*) Rohtak (*d*) All of these

130. Besides Gurugram, in which of the following districts of Haryana water from Gurgaon canal is used for irrigation?
(*a*) Panipat (*b*) Faridabad
(*c*) Sonepat (*d*) Kaithal

131. Hathni Reservoir Barrage Project is related with which of the following districts of Haryana?
(*a*) Yamuna Nagar (*b*) Gurugram
(*c*) Rohtak (*d*) Faridabad

132. Which of the following irrigation projects was launched in Mahendragarh district of Haryana with a view to bring improvement in the field of agriculture?
(*a*) Loharu Lift Irrigation Project
(*b*) Western Yamuna Nagar Scheme
(*c*) J.L.N. Lift Irrigation Project
(*d*) Hathni Reservoir Barrage Project

133. When water was released for the first time from J.L.N. Lift Irrigation Project launched in Mahendragarh district of Haryana?
(*a*) In 1976 (*b*) In 1980
(*c*) In 1982 (*d*) In 1995

134. Which of the following irrigation projects provided irrigation facilities in Swarup Kalauda, Khurl Kalan, Bhikhewala, Kharadwala, Nehra, Fuliya kalan etc. villages of the state?
(*a*) Jhajjhar Lift Irrigation Project
(*b*) Nakhana Irrigation Project
(*c*) Nangal Lift Irrigation Project
(*d*) Jawahar Lal Nehru Lift Irrigation Project

135. Which of the following irrigation schemes was launched for providing irrigation facility in Ahriwal region of Haryana?
(*a*) Rewari Lift Irrigation Scheme
(*b*) Hathni Reservoir Barrage Irrigation Scheme
(*c*) Mewat Lift Irrigation Scheme
(*d*) Bhakra Canal Irrigation Scheme

136. The largest Animal Farm of Haryana is situated at which of the following places?
(*a*) Rohtak (*b*) Hissar
(*c*) Panch Kula (*d*) Jind

137. Which of the following breeds of the Buffalo of Haryana is famous in entire India?
(*a*) Murra (*b*) Tura
(*c*) Puspa (*d*) Chassa

138. At which of the following places of Haryana cooperative milk plant has been set up?
(*a*) Ambala (*b*) Bhivani
(*c*) Jind (*d*) All of the above

139. In the Thanesar town of district Kurukshetra, the building for Pouttry disease diagnosis Laboratory was built in:
(*a*) 1980 – 81 (*b*) 1984 – 85
(*c*) 1988 – 89 (*d*) 1995 – 96

140. Besides Nilokheri in Haryana, at which of the following places of the state, training in poultry is imparted?
(*a*) Ambala (*b*) Karnal
(*c*) Hissar (*d*) Kaithal

141. Consider the following statements:
1. Rohtak has a Police Commissionerate located there.
2. Sonipat has a Police Commissionerate located there.

Which of the above statements is/are correct?
(*a*) 2 only (*b*) Both 1 and 2
(*c*) Neither 1 nor 2 (*d*) 1 only

142. Intensive Animal Development project in district Bhivani was launched in:
(*a*) 1966 (*b*) 1970
(*c*) 1972 (*d*) 1978

143. At which place in district Mahendragarh a Semen Bank is located and a liquid Nitrogen Plant has been set-up?
(*a*) Ateli (*b*) Narnaul
(*c*) Nangal Chaudhary (*d*) Mahendragarh

144. In district Bhiwani of Haryana, for diagnosing the diseases in animals the District Village Development Body set up the "Animal Disease Diagnosis Laboratory" in:
(*a*) 1978 (*b*) 1980
(*c*) 1984 (*d*) 1990

145. Haryana gets an average rainfall of ....
(*a*) 100 cms. (*b*) 85 cms.
(*c*) 75 cms. (*d*) 45 cms.

146. The ancient town 'Bery' is situated in which of the following districts of Haryana?
(*a*) Jhajjar (*b*) Yamuna Nagar
(*c*) Karnal (*d*) Kurukshetra

147. Where in Haryana, the National Institute of Fashion Technology is located?
(*a*) Panipat (*b*) Ambala
(*c*) Panchkula (*d*) Kurukshetra

148. The products manufactured by the industrial units of district Yamuna Nagar are exported to which of the following countries?
(*a*) Dubai (*b*) Germany
(*c*) South Africa (*d*) All of the above

149. Saraswati Sugar Mill is located in which of the following districts of Haryana?
(*a*) Rohtak (*b*) Panipat
(*c*) Yamuna Nagar (*d*) Faridabad

150. In Yamuna Nagar, Yanuma Gases Limited was set up in:
(*a*) 1973 (*b*) 1975
(*c*) 1980 (*d*) 1981

151. Yamuna Gases Limited operating in Yamuna Nagar attained a leading position in the production of gases in the year:
(*a*) 1969 (*b*) 1973
(*c*) 1972 (*d*) 1975

152. Bharat Starch Chemical Ltd. was established in Yamuna Nagar in:
(*a*) 1929 (*b*) 1932
(*c*) 1938 (*d*) 1948

153. Before 1947, the Timber Market of Yamuna Nagar was known as:
(*a*) Abdullapur Mandi
(*b*) Sadapur Mandi
(*c*) Yamuna Nagar Mandi
(*d*) Yamuna Pur Mandi

154. Charkhi Dadri was carved out from which district?
(*a*) Bhiwani (*b*) Hissar
(*c*) Sirsa (*d*) Rewari

155. "Bhiwani Textile Mill" in Haryana was established in:
(*a*) 1930 (*b*) 1937
(*c*) 1942 (*d*) 1950

156. In Haryana, where the Vulture Conservation Centre is located?
(*a*) Pinjore (*b*) Jind
(*c*) Mahendragarh (*d*) Ambala

157. The Sahibi river does not flow in which of the following district?
(*a*) Rewari (*b*) Jhajjar
(*c*) Gurugram (*d*) Rohtak

158. Consider the following statements in respect of National Security Guards (NSG):
1. Operational Headquarter of NSG is in Manesar.
2. NSG comes under the control of Union Ministry of Home Affairs.

Which of the above statements is/are correct?
(*a*) 2 only (*b*) Both 1 and 2
(*c*) Neither 1 nor 2 (*d*) 1 only

159. Indian Cement Corporation, A Government of India undertaking, took possession of the factory located at Charkhi-Dadri of Haryana on:
(*a*) 5 April, 1980 (*b*) 23 June, 1981
(*c*) 10 June, 1984 (*d*) 23 June, 1988

160. National Beekeeping and Honey Mission (NBHM) Scheme was started in which year in Haryana?
(*a*) 2017 (*b*) 2018
(*c*) 2019 (*d*) 2020

161. Captive Electricity Plant has been set up in which of the following districts of Haryana?
(*a*) Panipat (*b*) Hissar
(*c*) Rohtak (*d*) Karnal

162. At Baholi of district Panipat which of the following factories has been set up?
(*a*) Cloth Factory
(*b*) Agricultural Implements Factory
(*c*) Oil Refinery
(*d*) Slippers Factory

163. 'Ammonia Plant' has been installed in which of the following districts of Haryana?
(*a*) Panipat (*b*) Kaithal
(*c*) Gurugram (*d*) Karnal

164. District Mahanderagarh ranks first in the state of Haryana in the production of:
(*a*) Rice (*b*) Utensils
(*c*) Mustard (*d*) Bicycle

165. According to the 2011 census sex ratio in the state is ....

(*a*) 787 (*b*) 879
(*c*) 987 (*d*) 973

166. Which of the following industries in Rewari district of Haryana is famous all over India?

(*a*) Shoe Sole Industry
(*b*) Brass Utensil Industry
(*c*) Hero Honda Motor Cycle Factory
(*d*) All of these

167. In addition to Bicycle Factory, which of the following other factories are located in Jind district of Haryana?

(*a*) Utensil Factory (*b*) Textile Factory
(*c*) Sugar Factory (*d*) Leather Shoe Factory

168. According to the 2011 census population density in the state is ....

(*a*) 573 (*b*) 752
(*c*) 482 (*d*) 531

169. Total covered area of the Shri Krishna Museum is:

(*a*) 8764 sq.m. (*b*) 8885 sq.m.
(*c*) 8129 sq.m. (*d*) 8649 sq.m.

170. Which of the following articles manufactured in Karnal district are exported to foreign countries also?

(*a*) Liberty Shoes (*b*) Paint
(*c*) Wooden Furnitures (*d*) Steel Furniture

171. Shahabad Cooperative Sugar Mill in district Kurukshetra was established in:

(*a*) 1976 – 77 (*b*) 1984 – 85
(*c*) 1991 – 92 (*d*) 1994 – 95

172. Which of the following factories have been set up in Faridabad District of Haryana?

(*a*) Tractor Factory (*b*) Refrigerator Factory
(*c*) Rubber Tyre Factory (*d*) All of these

173. In which year the strength of Haryana Assembly was raised to 90?

(*a*) 1977 (*b*) 1967
(*c*) 1971 (*d*) 1985

174. At which of the following places in Haryana Maruti Cars are manufactured?

(*a*) Gurugram (*b*) Ambala
(*c*) Faridabad (*d*) Hissar

175. Which among the following is the highly populated district, as per the 2011 census?

(*a*) Rohtak (*b*) Karnal
(*c*) Gurugram (*d*) Faridabad

176. During which of the following years Government of Haryana decided to confer honour on Freedom Fighters?

(*a*) 1980 (*b*) 1981
(*c*) 1985 (*d*) 1997

177. Which of the following districts of Haryana does not share its boundary with any other state of India?

(*a*) Charkhi Dadri (*b*) Palwal
(*c*) Gurugram (*d*) Jind

178. Skylark Tourist Complex is located at ....

(*a*) Faridabad (*b*) Panipat
(*c*) Karnal (*d*) Rohtak

179. Scheme of granting cash amount, amount payable annually and cash in lieu of land to the soldiers awarded with 'Yuddha Sewa Medal' was discontinued in 1988. This scheme was launched again by the Government of Bansi Lal in:

(*a*) April 1995 (*b*) April 1997
(*c*) April 1996 (*d*) April 1998

180. Chaudhary Devi Lal University in Haryana is located at:

(*a*) Hissar (*b*) Karnal
(*c*) Sirsa (*d*) Panipat

181. Who among the following was not the chief minister of Haryana?

(*a*) Babu Parmanand (*b*) B.D. Gupta
(*c*) Devi Lal (*d*) Hukum Singh

182. National Dairy Research Institute is located at ....

(*a*) Karnal (*b*) Hissar
(*c*) Sirsa (*d*) Rohtak

183. Who was the first governor of Haryana?

(*a*) R.S. Narula (*b*) G.D. Tapse
(*c*) Dharamvir (*d*) B.D. Sharma

184. Hostel for the boys of Scheduled Castes who are engaged in unclean occupation is located at:

(*a*) Karnal (*b*) Faridabad
(*c*) Ambala (*d*) All of these

185. Hostel for the boys of exempted castes is located at :

(*a*) Rohtak (*b*) Jind
(*c*) Faridabad (*d*) Gurugram

186. Legal provisions for ban on liquor were enforced in Haryana on:

(*a*) 1 December, 1991 (*b*) 1 June, 1993
(*c*) 1 July, 1996 (*d*) 1 May, 1997

187. Ban on the sale of liquor was lifted by the state government on:

(*a*) 1 May, 1996 (*b*) 1 May, 1997
(*c*) 1 February, 1996 (*d*) 1 April, 1998

188. Which of the following Child Development Projects is related with the State of Haryana?

(*a*) Coordinated Child Development Project
(*b*) Child Health Project
(*c*) Infant Nutrition Programme
(*d*) Helpless Child Development Project

189. Which of the following schemes are being run for the welfare of the girls belonging to poor families?

(*a*) Paraya Dhan Parayee Beti
(*b*) Apni Beti Paraya Dhan
(*c*) Apni Beti Apna Dhan
(*d*) None of these

190. The total length of National Highway in Haryana till November, 2024 is:
(*a*) 1900 kms. (*b*) 1503 kms.
(*c*) 1800 kms. (*d*) 3391 kms.

191. Each and every village of the State of Haryana became electrified on:
(*a*) 10 June, 1966 (*b*) 25 March, 1971
(*c*) 15 April, 1968 (*d*) 29 November, 1970

192. Aruna is the ancient name of which river?
(*a*) Markanda (*b*) Sahibi
(*c*) Ghaggar (*d*) Yamuna

193. Red Soil is found in ....
(*a*) Rohtak (*b*) Sirsa
(*c*) Karnal (*d*) Bihwani

194. With a view to bring improvement in the availability of electricity in Southern Haryana, a new 50 km long single circuit line has been laid from :
(*a*) Gurugram to Badshahpur
(*b*) Badshahpur to Rewari
(*c*) Faridabad to Rewari
(*d*) Jind to Kaithal

195. Which one of the following pairs is not correctly matched?
(*a*) Surajkund Lake – Kurukshetra
(*b*) Tilyaar Lake – Rohtak
(*c*) Damdama Lake – Gurugram
(*d*) Badkhal Lake – Faridabad

196. Sultanpur Lake is located in which district?
(*a*) Bhiwani (*b*) Mahendragarh
(*c*) Gurugram (*d*) Rewari

197. According to the demands made by farmers, which of the following systems for electricity on the basis of the depth of tubewells has been adopted in the entire state?
(*a*) Stove System
(*b*) Electricity Measurement System
(*c*) Test System
(*d*) None of these

198. Thermal Power Station is located at which of the following places in Haryana?
(*a*) Hissar (*b*) Kaithal
(*c*) Jind (*d*) Faridabad

199. At which of the following places, the Power Plant of 432 MW based on Gas has been installed by NTPC in Haryana?
(*a*) Gurugram (*b*) Faridabad
(*c*) Panipat (*d*) Karnal

200. What is the total length of road in Haryana till November, 2024?
(*a*) 33,543 km (*b*) 24,065 km
(*c*) 25,074 km (*d*) 40,760 km

201. The strength of Legislative Assembly of Haryana is ....
(*a*) 102 (*b*) 110
(*c*) 75 (*d*) 90

202. Where is Nahar Wildlife Sanctuary is situated?
(*a*) Ambala (*b*) Sonipat
(*c*) Rewari (*d*) Yamunanagar

203. When the Public Transport in Haryana was brought under the possession of the Government?
(*a*) In 1972 (*b*) In 1976
(*c*) In 1980 (*d*) In 1985

204. 'Rao Tej Singh Pond' is located in:
(*a*) Panipat (*b*) Sonipat
(*c*) Palwal (*d*) Rewari

205. The Magazine of Haryana Sahitya Academy is:
(*a*) Harigandha (*b*) Haryana Samvad
(*c*) Haryana Sandesh (*d*) Panchajanya

206. While travelling on the National Highway from Delhi to Ferozepur, which of the following important town of Haryana comes on the way:
(*a*) Rohtak (*b*) Sirsa
(*c*) Hissar (*d*) All of these

207. Manu Bhaker of Haryana is related with which sports?
(*a*) Badminton (*b*) Boxing
(*c*) Shooting (*d*) Wrestling

208. Which of the following tourist places is situated at Bahadurgarh in Haryana?
(*a*) Dairango Tourist Place (*b*) Gureya
(*c*) Jal Tarang (*d*) Tiliyar

209. In Haryana, in addition to Hissar, Karnal, Bhiwani, Narnaul and Jind, at which of the following airports metalled run-way has been built?
(*a*) Panipat (*b*) Pinjore
(*c*) Faridabad (*d*) Rewari

210. Where is Tilyar lake is situated?
(*a*) Rohtak (*b*) Gurugram
(*c*) Jind (*d*) Faridabad

211. At which of the following places in Haryana, Heavy Vehicle Driving Training Institute is located?
(*a*) Murthal (*b*) Charkhi-Dadri
(*c*) Ambala (*d*) Tawaroo

212. In Shivalik hills near Pinjore-Kalka in Haryana, utensils have been found which pertain to which of the following ages?
(*a*) Stone Age (*b*) Later Vedic Age
(*c*) Harappan Age (*d*) Early Vedic Age

213. In the treatise named "Avanti Sunderi Katha" Vaivast Manu who is known as the father of human beings is said to be the resident of which of the following places?
(*a*) Panipat (*b*) Rohtak
(*c*) Sthaneshwar (*d*) Panchkula

214. Evidences found from the excavations done at Banwali, Siswal, Kunal, Mirzapur, Daulatpur and Bhagawanpura in the state of Haryana revealed links dating back to:

(*a*) Early Harappan Culture
(*b*) Mature Harappan Culture
(*c*) Late Harappan Culture
(*d*) All of the above phases

215. Who of the following started archaeological survey in Haryana for the first time?
(*a*) Sir John (*b*) Alexander Kaningham
(*c*) Lord Munro (*d*) John Marshall

216. Archaeological Survey in Haryana started in:
(*a*) 1862 (*b*) 1892
(*c*) 1900 (*d*) 1905

217. Under the supervision of Dr. Suraj Bhan, excavations at which of the following places of Haryana brought out very valuable historical evidences?
(*a*) Mithathal (*b*) Dadri
(*c*) Ailanabad (*d*) Safidon

218. From which of the following sites of Haryana, evidences have been found for the first time regarding co-existence of the people of Late Harappan culture and Painted Grey Ware (PGW) culture?
(*a*) Narnaul (*b*) Bhagwanpura
(*c*) Sirsa (*d*) Mahendragarh

219. A great mound pertaining to Harappan culture is situated at which of the following places in district Jind of Haryana?
(*a*) Safidon (*b*) Uchana
(*c*) Narwana (*d*) Rakhigarhi

220. Remains of a Stupa have been found at Chaneti which is situated three kilometers east of Jagadhari. Height of this Stupa is 8 m. Its periphery is:
(*a*) 20 m (*b*) 30 m
(*c*) 45 m (*d*) 50 m

221. Consider the following statements:
1. Sonipat and Jhajjar share border with Delhi.
2. Rohtak does not share border with Delhi.

Which of the above statements is/are correct?
(*a*) 2 only (*b*) Both 1 and 2
(*c*) Neither 1 nor 2 (*d*) 1 only

222. A battle axe type Gold Coin which pertains to the age of Samudra Gupta has been found at which of the following places in Haryana?
(*a*) Kosali (*b*) Rohana
(*c*) Mithathal (*d*) Raniya

223. Which of the following areas of Haryana was under the control of Yudheyas during the 3rd century A.D.?
(*a*) Panipat (*b*) Rohtak
(*c*) Hissar (*d*) Ambala

224. The Gold Coin obtained from Jagadhari pertains to which of the following emperors of the ancient India?
(*a*) Kanishka (*b*) Kumar Gupta
(*c*) Pushyamitra Sunga (*d*) Samudragupta

225. From which of the following places in Haryana, copper coin of the age of Harsha Vardhan has been found which contains an account of Pushyabhuti dynasty of Thanesar?
(*a*) Sonepat (*b*) Sirsa
(*c*) Gurugram (*d*) Kaithal

226. At which of the following places located in district Hissar of Haryana excavations was done by Shri H.L. Srivastava of Archaeo-logical Survey of India?
(*a*) Uklana (*b*) Fatehabad
(*c*) Agroha (*d*) Adampur

227. What is the total number of Primary and Pre Primary Schools in Haryana till 2023-24?
(*a*) 9,872 (*b*) 9,399
(*c*) 11,582 (*d*) 8,780

228. What is the total number of Middle Schools in Haryana till 2023-24?
(*a*) 6,215 (*b*) 2,312
(*c*) 5,640 (*d*) 3,850

229. In Haryana 'Brahma Sarovar' is located in:
(*a*) Palwal (*b*) Kurukshetra
(*c*) Panipat (*d*) Sonipat

230. 'Uchana' is located in:
(*a*) Jind (*b*) Karnal
(*c*) Rohtak (*d*) Faridabad

231. The tenure of nagarpalika, municipality or municipal corporation in Haryana is ....
(*a*) 3 years (*b*) 1 year
(*c*) 4 years (*d*) 5 years

232. What is the area of Sirsa district?
(*a*) 4,277 sq.km (*b*) 5,780 sq.km
(*c*) 3,760 sq.km (*d*) 2,765 sq.km

233. What is the total number of literate people in Haryana?
(*a*) 1,66,25,728 (*b*) 1,65,98,988
(*c*) 1,78,10,882 (*d*) 1,32,58,652

234. The historical monument known as the corridor Chhatta of Rai Mukund Das (Birbal Ka Chhatta) is in:
(*a*) Panipat (*b*) Karnal
(*c*) Kaithal (*d*) Narnaul

235. Navodaya Vidyalaya is situated at which of the following places in the state?
(*a*) Titaram (Kurukshetra) (*b*) Odha (Sirsa)
(*c*) Deorala (Bhiwani) (*d*) All of these

236. During which of the following years Government of Haryana introduced 10+2+3 system of Education in Haryana?
(*a*) 1980 - 81 (*b*) 1976 - 77
(*c*) 1988 - 89 (*d*) 1985 - 86

237. M.D. University is located in which of the following towns of Haryana?
(*a*) Rohtak (*b*) Hissar
(*c*) Faridabad (*d*) Rewari

238. Chaudhary Charan Singh Agricultural University is located in which of the following towns of the state?
(*a*) Jind (*b*) Gurugram
(*c*) Hissar (*d*) Kurukshetra

239. In order to promote Punjabi language in Haryana it has been made the .... language of the state.
(*a*) First (*b*) Second
(*c*) Third (*d*) Fourth

240. Chaudhary Devilal University is located in which of the following towns of Haryana?
(*a*) Kurukshetra (*b*) Hissar
(*c*) Rohtak (*d*) Sirsa

241. In order to give promotion to sports in Haryana, the State Government has launched which of the following important schemes?
(*a*) Providing Grant in aid to the Sports Institutions
(*b*) Training Scheme
(*c*) Sports Stadium
(*d*) All of the above

242. In order to impart training to the players through modern and scientific methods, at which of the following places of Haryana a sports hostel has been set up?
(*a*) Gurugram (*b*) Rohtak
(*c*) Faridabad (*d*) Panipat

243. A sports school is situated at Rai in Sonepat district of Haryana. What is the name of this sports school?
(*a*) Jawahar Lal Nehru Sports School
(*b*) Indira Gandhi Sports School
(*c*) Moti Lal Nehru Sports School
(*d*) Rajiv Gandhi Sports School

244. Kamla Nehru School situated in the premises of Moti Lal Nehru Sports School at Rai in Sonepat district was established in
(*a*) 1970 (*b*) 1974
(*c*) 1982 (*d*) 1986

245. Haryana Shehari Vikas Pradhikaran (HSVP), formerly Haryana Urban Development Authority (HUDA) was constituted in ....
(*a*) 1977 (*b*) 1972
(*c*) 1970 (*d*) 1966

246. Who has variously been described as Plato of Jat Tribes?
(*a*) Suraj Mal (*b*) Churaman
(*c*) Raja Ram Bhajja (*d*) None of these

247. Khoria dance is famous in ....
(*a*) Eastern Haryana (*b*) Western Haryana
(*c*) Central Haryana (*d*) Northern Haryana

248. Which player of Haryana won gold medal in Tokyo Olympics 2020?
(*a*) Bajarang Punia (*b*) Neeraj Chopra
(*c*) Ravi Kumar (*d*) Vijendra Singh

249. The Haryana Shawl is known as ....
(*a*) Phulkari (*b*) Ghagra
(*c*) Iungis **(*d*) Bagh**

250. The famous story writer of Hindi Shri Vishvambhar Nath Kaushik was born in Haryana at
(*a*) Ambala Cantt (*b*) Sirsa
(*c*) Panchkula (*d*) Rohtak

251. Famous writer of Haryana Pt. Neki Ram Sharma had brought out which of the following papers from Bhiwani?
(*a*) Samvahak (*b*) Sandesh
(*c*) Nivaran (*d*) Vani

252. Who of the following players of Indian Cricket hails from Haryana?
(*a*) Kapil Dev (*b*) Sunil Gavaskar
(*c*) Ajay Jadeja (*d*) Azharuddin

253. The Cricket Test Match in which Kapil Dev of Haryana took 432nd wicket to make a record of taking maximum number of wickets was held on
(*a*) 10 January, 1992 (*b*) 8 December, 1996
(*c*) 8 February, 1994 (*d*) 12 August, 1997

254. Kapil Dev announced to abandon the international cricket on
(*a*) 6 November, 1993 (*b*) 2 November, 1994
(*c*) 18 November, 1997 (*d*) 15 November, 1998

255. Who of the following players of Haryana is not related with Gymnastic?
(*a*) Sunita Sharma (*b*) Sandhya
(*c*) Nirmala Guliya (*d*) Geeta Jutshi

256. Who of the following first ever poet is considered a native poet of Haryana?
(*a*) Goswami Tulsi Das (*b*) Kabir Das
(*c*) Kavi Chandbardai (*d*) Rahim Das

257. Who of the following Muslim Saints of Haryana had made significant contributions in the development of Hindi literature?
(*a*) Shekh-U-Alishaha Kalander
(*b*) Saint Sadullah
(*c*) Shekh Bahauddin Chishti
(*d*) All of these

258. Who of the following first ever poet is not related with Haryana?
(*a*) Virbhan (*b*) Mahatma Haridas
(*c*) Banarsi Das (*d*) Narottam Das

259. Haryana got the status of a full state on
(*a*) 1 November, 1964 (*b*) 10 December, 1965
(*c*) 1 November, 1966 (*d*) 15 June, 1968

260. The capital city of Haryana is
(*a*) Chandigarh (*b*) Rohtak
(*c*) Karnal (*d*) Yamuna Nagar

261. With a view to administrative convenience, Haryana has been divided into
(*a*) Three Divisions (*b*) Six Divisions
(*c*) Five Divisions (*d*) Four Divisions

262. The number of Districts in Haryana till January, 2026 is:
(*a*) 16 (*b*) 17
(*c*) 18 **(*d*) 23**

263. The tourist place called Oasis is situated at which of the following places in Haryana?
(*a*) Faridabad (*b*) Bhiwani
(*c*) Uchchhana (*d*) Rewari

264. Which of the following famous tourist place of Haryana is located at a distance of about 20 kms from Delhi?
(*a*) Suraj Kund (*b*) Red Robin
(*c*) Paracot (*d*) Damdama Lake

265. In vast rocky areas extended to the west of Faridabad by the Delhi-Mathura National Highway which of the following tourist place is situated?
(*a*) Damdama Lake (*b*) Badkhal Lake
(*c*) King Fisher (*d*) Dabchik

266. Between the hills of Arawali on Delhi-Alwar road which of the following famous tourist place of Haryana is located?
(*a*) Shama (*b*) Blue-ze
(*c*) Sohana (*d*) Dairangon

267. Who had discovered the Sultanpur Bird Sanctuary of Haryana situated on Gurugram Farrukh Nagar road?
(*a*) Peter Jackson (*b*) Thomar Roe
(*c*) Sir John Marshall (*d*) Robin Hood

268. On the Gurugram-Farrukhabad road which of the following tourist places of Haryana is situated?
(*a*) Dab-bich
(*b*) Sultanpur Bird Sanctuary
(*c*) Oasis
(*d*) Red Robin

269. The Turban worn by male in Haryana is called
(*a*) Khandwa (*b*) Paggada
(*c*) Toda (*d*) Pagari

270. The tourist centre called 'Shama' is situated at which of the following towns of Haryana?
(*a*) Faridabad (*b*) Kaithal
(*c*) Gurugram (*d*) Jind

271. In Haryana, the skirt worn by females from waist to ankle which is without any gusset and made of hand-spun coarse cloth knitted by using four blue and four red threads is called
(*a*) Dharna (*b*) Khara
(*c*) Thara (*d*) Kachara

272. Which of the following ornaments used in the state is not worn around neck?
(*a*) Hansla (*b*) Fool
(*c*) Galshree (*d*) Batan

273. Which of the following ornaments is worn on face and head on the ladies of the state?
(*a*) Singar Patti (*b*) Tagga
(*c*) Bessar (*d*) All of these

274. Which of the following ornaments used in the state is not worn on nose?
(*a*) Nath (*b*) Purli
(*c*) Dhede (*d*) Kokka

275. Which of the following ornaments used in the state is not worn on hands?
(*a*) Pauhchi (*b*) Kandulla
(*c*) Pachhelli (*d*) Bankri

276. According to the augury, which of the following is considered a good omen in the state of Haryana?
(*a*) A pitcher full of water
(*b*) To have a view of a deer
(*c*) A sweeper with a broom in hand
(*d*) All of the above

277. According to the augury, which of the following is considered a bad omen in the state of the Haryana?
(*a*) Empty pitcher
(*b*) To have a view of grass
(*c*) To experience an itching sensation in feet
(*d*) Meeting with a water carrier carrying water.

278. Which of the traditional ornaments is worn by males in Haryana?
(*a*) Goph (*b*) Tagari
(*c*) Nada (*d*) Kadi

279. At which of the following places of religious importance, lakhs of people from all over India go for a religious ritual on the occurrence of solar eclipse?
(*a*) Gurugram (*b*) Kurukshetra
(*c*) Jagadhari (*d*) None of these

280. At Islampur in the district Gurugram, which of the following festivals (Mela) is organised on the ninth day of Bhado (the sixth month of the year according to the Hindu calendar)?
(*a*) Guga Naumi (*b*) Nag Pooja
(*c*) Yamuna Snan (*d*) Shiv Mela

281. In the months of Chait and Aashadh (respectively the opening and the fourth month of the year according to the Hindu caldendar) in district Gurugram of Haryana on every Monday and Tuesday which of the following famous festivals (Melas) is organised?
(*a*) Buddho Mata Ka Mela
(*b*) Shivji Ka Mela
(*c*) Shitla Mata Ka Mela
(*d*) Baba Buddha Ka Mela

282. In which of the following districts of Haryana famous festivals of Ramsarai and Bhuteshwar are organised?
(*a*) Faridabad (*b*) Jind
(*c*) Rohtak (*d*) Jhajjhar

283. In the monastery at Asthal Bohar in Rohtak district of Haryana which of the following festivals (Melas) is organised during the months of February and March?
(*a*) Baba Mastnath Ka Mela
(*b*) Kapal Mochan Ka Mela
(*c*) Devi Mela
(*d*) Pathari Mata Ka Mela

284. Which of the following festivals (Melas) is organised on Kartik-Purnima at Bilaspur situated near Jagadhari?
(*a*) Aadi Badri Mela (*b*) Mela Kali Mai
(*c*) Kapal Mochan Mela (*d*) Panchmukhi Mela

285. At Lakhan Majra in Rohtak district "Gurudwara of Manji Sahib" is situated. Here which of the following festivals (Melas) is organised?
(*a*) Festival of Satya Teej
(*b*) Festival of Mohola Halla
(*c*) Bawan Dwadashi
(*d*) Maanu Mela

286. At Pathri in district Sonepat, on every Wednesday in the months of Chait and Aashadh, which of the following festivals (Melas) is organised?
(*a*) Mata Ka Mela (*b*) Shiva Mela
(*c*) Dehati Mela (*d*) Pathri Mata Ka Mela

287. At Kharak Ramji situated in district Jind, which of the following festivals (Melas) is organised on the day of Holi?
(*a*) Mata Ka Mela
(*b*) Nag Devata Ka Mela
(*c*) Baba Bhalu Nath Ka Mela
(*d*) Mela Sachcha Sauda

288. At Dubaldhan Majra in Rohtak district which of the following festivals (Melas) is organised in the months of February-March?
(*a*) Mela Mata (*b*) Mela Devi
(*c*) Mela Shyamji (*d*) Mela Baba Buddha

289. At Khori in the Gurugram district which of the following festivals (Melas) is organised during the months of April-May?
(*a*) Shah Chokha Khori Mela
(*b*) Shiva Ka Mela
(*c*) Nagpooja Ka Mela
(*d*) Baba Mast Nath Ka Mela

290. At which of the following places in district Sonepat, festival (Mela) of Dera Nagn Balaknath is organised during the months of February-March?
(*a*) Bega (Tehsil Sonepat)
(*b*) Mehripur (Tehsil Sonepat)
(*c*) Rabhara (Tehsil Gohana)
(*d*) Chulkana (Tehsil Sonepat)

291. Which of the following festivals (Melas) is oraganised at Khubadu situated in district Sonepat during the months of February-March?
(*a*) Satakumbha Mela (*b*) Mela Baba Shamakshah
(*c*) Mela Sanjhi (*d*) Devi Mela

292. Which amongst the following is the State Tree of Haryana?
(*a*) Sacred Fig (*b*) Mango Tree
(*c*) Sal Tree (*d*) Banyan Tree

293. At which of the following places in Haryana festival (Mela) of Baba Khedewala is organised on the day of Raksha Bandhan?
(*a*) Naurangabad (*b*) Kaharak Kalan
(*c*) Riwasa (*d*) Tosham

294. On which of the following occasions in the state of Haryana auspicious "Piliya" folk song is sung?
(*a*) In the months of July-August
(*b*) On the occasion of the birth of a male child in the family
(*c*) On the occasion of marriage ceremony
(*d*) In the months of February-March

295. On which of the following occasions, in the state of Haryana folk songs are sung?
(*a*) On the occasion of the birth of a male child in the family
(*b*) In the months of July-August
(*c*) On the occasion of a festival
(*d*) On all of the above occasions

296. In the state, males perform which of the following dances in open field at moon-lit night on flute, scooped gourd (Tumbi), etc.?
(*a*) Dhamal Dance (*b*) Manjeera Dance
(*c*) Loor Dance (*d*) Damru Dance

297. Which of the following dance performances is famous in Mewat area of Haryana which is accompanied with beating huge kettle drum, tambourine and cymbals?
(*a*) Ghora Dance (*b*) Dhamal Dance
(*c*) Manjeera Dance (*d*) Chhathi Dance

298. In Bagar area of Haryana which of the following dance performances is famous that is performed during the festival of Holi?
(*a*) Damru Dance (*b*) Manjeera Dance
(*c*) Ghora Dance (*d*) Loor Dance

299. The Ghora folk dance popular in Haryana is generally performed on which of the following occasions?
(*a*) On the occasion of marriage
(*b*) In the month of February-March
(*c*) On the occasion of birth of a male child in the family
(*d*) In the Month of July-August

300. In Haryana, which of the following dances is performed after the worship of Guggapir in the month of August-September?
(*a*) Dhamal Dance (*b*) Chchari Dance
(*c*) Loor Dance (*d*) Damru Dance

301. Which of the following folk dances is performed by women in the state?
(*a*) Teej Dance (*b*) Dhamal Dance
(*c*) Damru Dance (*d*) Khodiya Dance

302. Which dance is performed by males among the following folk dances practised in the state?
(*a*) Chhatthi dance (*b*) Teej dance
(*c*) Damru dance (*d*) Khodia dance

303. Which of the following folk dances is performed by men and women both in the state?
(*a*) Teej Dance (*b*) Loor Dance
(*c*) Khodiya Dance (*d*) Fag Dance

304. Which of the following Gurudwaras is situated near Pratap Gate in Kaithal town of Haryana?
(*a*) Gurudwara Neem Sahib
(*b*) Gurudwara Nauvi Patshahi
(*c*) Ragdhaar Gurudwara
(*d*) Gurudwara Chhathi Patshahi

305. Gurudwara Manji Sahib is situated in which of the following towns of Haryana?
(*a*) Karnal (*b*) Panipat
(*c*) Kaithal (*d*) Ambala

306. Which place in Haryana is called as "Chhoti Kashi" due to presence of "Navagraha Kunds"?
(*a*) Narnaul (*b*) Kaithal
(*c*) Gurugram (*d*) Kurukshetra

307. At a few distance from Kaithal in Haryana the grave of which of the following great men is situated where every year next dayof Dushera a large festival is organised?
(*a*) Baba Kali Kamli Wale
(*b*) Baba Haridas
(*c*) Baba Ladana
(*d*) Baba Ramdas

308. Which of the following famous places of pilgrimage is situated near Thanesar City Station in district Kurukshetra of Haryana?
(*a*) Brahma Sarovar (*b*) Hatakeshwar
(*c*) Dhosi (*d*) Pundarik Sarovar

309. Which of the following places of pilgrimage is situated on the Kurukshetra-Pehwa road near Kurukshetra Railway Station which is considered as the permanent abode of Lord Vishnu?
(*a*) Brahma Sarovar (*b*) Kaleshwar Tirth
(*c*) Sannihit Sarovar (*d*) Markanday Tirth

310. At which place of piligrimage in Kurukshetra district Shri Krishna had preached Arjuna?
(*a*) Brahm Sarovar (*b*) Kamal Nabh Tirth
(*c*) Prachi Tirth (*d*) Jyotishwar Sarovar

311. When did Maharaja Darbhanga build metalled platform around the Akshya Vat located near the Jyotishwar Sarovar situated in district Kurukshetra?
(*a*) In 1924 (*b*) In 1930
(*c*) In 1932 (*d*) In 1949

312. Who had built the Krishna-Arjuna Rath (Chariot) and the temple of Shankaracharya near the Jyotishwar Sarovar situated in district Kurukshetra?
(*a*) Maharaja Darbhanga
(*b*) Shankaracharya of Kam Koti Peeth
(*c*) King of Kashmir
(*d*) Swami Vishuddhananda Maharaj

313. What is the total length of Jyotishwar Sarovar situated in district Kurukshetra?
(*a*) 1000 ft. (*b*) 1500 ft.
(*c*) 2000 ft. (*d*) 2500 ft.

314. Who was the founder of "Baba Kali Kamli Wale Ka Dera" situated in district Kurukshetra?
(*a*) Swami Ram Tirth
(*b*) Shri Swami Vishuddhananda Maharaja
(*c*) Shankaracharya of Kamkoti Peeth
(*d*) Swami Parmananda Maharaj

315. Gaudiya Math (monastery) related with the period of Bhakti movement in India, is situated in which of the following districts of Haryana?
(*a*) Ambala (*b*) Jind
(*c*) Kurukshetra (*d*) Mahendragarh

316. At which of the following places in district Kurukshetra Baba Laxman Giri Maharaj went into eternal trance?
(*a*) Ban Ganga (*b*) Prachi Tirth
(*c*) Gaudiya Math (*d*) Balmiki Aashram

317. Raj Ghat Gurudwara is situated at which of the following places in Haryana?
(*a*) Kurukshetra (*b*) Yamuna Nagar
(*c*) Kaithal (*d*) Bhiwani

318. Which of the following places of pilgrimage is not situated in district Kurukshetra of Haryana?
(*a*) Kalkeshwar Tirth
(*b*) Prachi Tirth
(*c*) Dhosi Tirth
(*d*) Kuber Tirth

319. Which of the following places of pilgrimage is situated at a distance of 1 km. to the North-West of Kurukshetra University in district Kurukshetra of Haryana?
(*a*) Markandya Tirth
(*b*) Narakatari (Anrak Tirth)
(*c*) Prachi Tirth
(*d*) Kuber Tirth

320. Which of the following important places of pilgrimage is situated at a distance of 25 km to the west of Thanesar in Haryana that is given the same importance by the people of Haryana and adjoining areas as is given to Gaya by the people of Eastern region of India?
(*a*) Pehova (*b*) Panchavati
(*c*) Safeedon (*d*) Pandu-Pindara

321. In which district of Haryana the 'National Institute of Animal Genetics' is located?
(*a*) Hisar (*b*) Yamunanagar
(*c*) Karnal (*d*) Rohtak

322. A place of pilgrimage known as "Panchavati" is situated at which of the following districts of Haryana?
(*a*) Ambala (*b*) Jind
(*c*) Kurukshetra (*d*) Palwal

323. Which of the following is an ancient place of pilgrimage located by Jind-Gohana Road near Jind where a fair is organised every year on Somawati Amavasya?
(*a*) Pandu-Pindara
(*b*) Safeedon
(*c*) Hans Daihar
(*d*) None of the above

324. Temple of Sthaneshwar Mahadeva situated at a distance of a few kilometres from Thanesar was built by which of the following kings prior to Harshavardhan?
(*a*) Pushyabhuti (*b*) Adityavardhan
(*c*) Narvardhan (*d*) Prabhakarvardhan

325. Mahmud Ghaznavi during his return course to Ghazni took away with him from Haryana to Ghazni, statue of which of the ancient temple located in Haryana?
(*a*) Dukh Bhanjaneshwar Temple (Kuruk-shetra)
(*b*) Lord Shiva Temple (Narnaul)
(*c*) Sarveshwar Mahadeva Temple (Kuruk-shetra)
(*d*) Sthaneshwar Mahadeva Temple (Thanesar)

326. Sthaneshwar Temple of Haryana was reconstructed by
(*a*) Maratha Sadashiva Rao
(*b*) Chandra Gupta Vikramaditya
(*c*) Harshavardhan
(*d*) Narvardhan

327. Devikoop (Bhadra Kali Temple) is one of the 51 Shakti Peeths (Seats of goddess personifying divine power) of India. This temple is located at which of the following places in the state?
(*a*) Rohtak (*b*) Kurukshetra
(*c*) Panipat (*d*) Thanesar

328. Which of the following temples is situated near Sannihit Sarovar in Kurukshetra?
(*a*) Narayana Temple
(*b*) Laxmi Narayan Temple
(*c*) Dukh Bhanjaneshwar Temple
(*d*) Birla Mandir

329. Which of the following temples of Kurukshetra was built by the perfect Saint of Giri Sect Baba Shiv Giri Maharaj?
(*a*) Sarveshwar Mahadeva Temple
(*b*) Narayana Temple
(*c*) Laxmi Narayan Temple
(*d*) Dukh Bhanajaneshwar Temple

330. Who had built the famous 'Sarveshwar Mahadeva Temple' of Kurukshetra?
(*a*) Baba Shravan Nath (*b*) Baba Shiva Giri
(*c*) Baba Tarak Nath (*d*) Shri Jugal Kishore Birla

331. Birla Temple situated by the Kurukshetra-Pehova road was built by Shri Jugal Kishore Birla in
(*a*) 1950 (*b*) 1955
(*c*) 1965 (*d*) 1978

332. "Gyarah Rudri Shiva Temple" is situated in which of the following towns of Haryana?
(*a*) Jind (*b*) Panipat
(*c*) Hissar (*d*) Kaithal

333. Maratha General Mangal Raghu Nath Ji had built which of the following temples after the third battle of Panipat?
(*a*) Shiva Temple of Devi Pond
(*b*) Hanuman Temple
(*c*) Devi Temple
(*d*) Rudra Temple

334. In Amin village of Kurukshetra district which one of the following ancient temples is situated?
(*a*) Panchvati Temple
(*b*) Shiva Temple
(*c*) Temple of Aditi
(*d*) Temple of Dauji

335. In Vanchari village situated at a distance of 55 km. from Faridabad, which of the following ancient temples is situated?
(*a*) Temple of Dauji
(*b*) Temple of Aditi
(*c*) Panchvati Temple
(*d*) Temple of Chamunda Devi

336. The famous ancient temple of Mata Sheetala Devi is situated at which of the following places in Haryana?
(*a*) Rewari (*b*) Gurugram
(*c*) Narnaul (*d*) Jind

337. Temple of Mata Sheetala Devi situated at Gurugram was built by Maharaja of Bharatpur in
(*a*) 1620 (*b*) 1645
(*c*) 1648 (*d*) 1650

338. The ancient Shiva temple where the grave of Baba Thandipuri is also located, is situated at which of the following places?
(*a*) Pundrik Tirth (*b*) Gurugram
(*c*) Hissar (*d*) Rohtak

339. Which of the following ancient temples is situated at village Beri of district Jhajjar in Haryana?
(*a*) Old Shiva-Parvati Temple
(*b*) Temple of Mata Sheetala Devi
(*c*) Lal Rudhmal Temple
(*d*) Temple of Dauji

340. The height of the Shivalaya located in Rudhmal temple at village Beri in district Jhajjar of Haryana is
(*a*) 116 ft. (*b*) 122 ft.
(*c*) 132 ft. (*d*) 140 ft.

341. The Shivalaya located in Rudhmal temple at village Beri in district Jhajjar of Haryana was built in
(*a*) 1842 (*b*) 1850
(*c*) 1892 (*d*) 1899

342. The Shivalaya located in Rudhmal temple at village Beri in district Jhajjar was resurrected for the first time in
(*a*) 1943 (*b*) 1945
(*c*) 1950 (*d*) 1953

343. The temple of Chamunda Devi situated at Narnaul was built and resurrected by
(*a*) Raja Parikshit (*b*) Raja Dilip
(*c*) Raja Noorkaran (*d*) Pandavas

344. Chisti sect was established in Haryana by
(*a*) Boo Alishah Kalandar
(*b*) Shekh Farid (Farid-ud-din-Shakarganj)
(*c*) Altaf Hussain
(*d*) Ibrahim Abidullah

345. The eminent saint of Chisti sect Boo Alishah Kalandar made which of the following places the centre of his meditation?
(*a*) Panipat (*b*) Rohtak
(*c*) Sonepat (*d*) Gurugram

346. Dargah of Sufi Saint Altaf Hussain Hali is situated at which of the following places in Haryana?
(*a*) Jhajjhar (*b*) Rewari
(*c*) Panipat (*d*) Rohtak

347. Regarding which of the following Dargahs (tombs of saints which are pilgrimage spots and places of worship) situated at Panipat is believed that bowing heads by believers accomplishes their attending in celebration of Urs of Khwaza of Ajmer?
(*a*) Dargah of Khwaza Shamshuddin Makhdoom Zalaluddin
(*b*) Dargah of Shekh Usman Jindapeer
(*c*) Dargah of Gauss Alishah
(*d*) Dargah of Boo Alishah Kalandar

348. Dargah of which of the following famous saints is situated at village Dharsun which is at a distance of about 10 kms from Narnaul?
(*a*) Hazarat Shah Kalmuddin Hamzapeer Hussain
(*b*) Meer Shah (Baba Shah Khan)
(*c*) Sheikh Nijamuddin
(*d*) Sheikh Junaid

349. At Fatehabad in the courtyard of the tomb of which of the following Sufi saints inscription of Mughal emperor Humayun is engraved on a stone?
(*a*) Mir Taki Khan
(*b*) Mir Junaidi
(*c*) Sheikh Nizamuddin
(*d*) Mir Shah (Baba Shah Khan)

350. Which of the following tombs situated in Haryana has been declared a monument of National importance under the Archaeological Site and Remnant Act, 1958?
(*a*) Sheikh Chehli
(*b*) Boo Alishah Kalandar
(*c*) Sheikh Farid (Farid-ud-din-Shakarganj)
(*d*) Peer Jamal

351. Tomb of Baba Shah Kamal is situated at which of the following places in Haryana?
(*a*) Gohan (*b*) Fatehabad
(*c*) Kaithal (*d*) Rohtak

352. At which one of the following places in the state, tombs of four Sufi-saints (Kutub Sheikh Jamaluddin Ahmad, Kutub Maulana, Basohddin Sufi Qutubuddin Mannawar, Qutub Nuruddin) are located?
(*a*) Karnal (*b*) Hissar
(*c*) Palwal (*d*) Hansi

353. The tomb of who of the following Sufi-saints is situated between Shahabad and Ambala where watch is offered after a desire is fulfilled?
(*a*) Peer Nagauji (*b*) Hamja Peer
(*c*) Peer Naugaja (*d*) Ibrahim Abidullah

354. Which of the following mosques in Rohtak which was previously a temple was turned into a mosque during the reign of Aurangzeb?
(*a*) Qazi Ki Masjid (*b*) Dini Masjid
(*c*) Lal Masjid (*d*) None of these

355. The Lal Masjid situated in Rohtak was built by famous trader Haji Aashiq Ali in
(*a*) 1930 (*b*) 1931
(*c*) 1935 (*d*) 1939

356. Mosque at Sarai Alawardi village in district Gurugram was built during the reign of
(*a*) Babur (*b*) Jahangir
(*c*) Shahjahan (*d*) Alauddin Khilji

357. Which of the following ancient historical Mosques is situated at village Dujana, situated at a distance of 22 km by Jhajjhar road from Rohtak?
(*a*) Lal Masjid (*b*) Qaji Ki Masjid
(*c*) Karim Ji Ki Masjid (*d*) Jama Masjid

358. The famous historic Lal Masjid at Rewari was built during the reign of which of the following Mughal Emperors?
(*a*) Babur (*b*) Humayun
(*c*) Akbar (*d*) Jahangir

359. In addition to Narnaul, Panipat and Ambala, Sufi-saints made which of the following towns of Haryana as a centre of Sufi-sect?
(*a*) Kaithal (*b*) Thanesar
(*c*) Karnal (*d*) Sonepat

360. The majority of Sufi-saints who lived in Haryana for propagating sufi cult belonged to which of the following sects?
(*a*) Chisti (*b*) Nakshbandi
(*c*) Kadari (*d*) All of the above

361. Tomb of famous Sufi-saint Sheikh Chehli which is called as the Tajmahal of Haryana is situated at
(*a*) Hissar (*b*) Fatehabad
(*c*) Thanesar (*d*) Panipat

362. Tomb of which of the following saints is situated at Kalyana village of Charkhi Dadri district where fair is organised on every Wednesday?
(*a*) Peer Mubarak Shah
(*b*) Sheikh Usman Jindapeer
(*c*) Sheikh Nizamuddin
(*d*) Muhammad Afzal

363. Tomb of Meeran Sahib is situated in which of the following towns of Haryana?
(*a*) Ambala (*b*) Panipat
(*c*) Karnal (*d*) Kaithal

364. Where did Lord Krishna delivered his inspirational messages to Arjuna which have been described in "Gita" as a dialogue between the two?
(*a*) Panipat (*b*) Kurukshetra
(*c*) Hodal (*d*) Thanesar

365. Which of the following towns of Haryana was the capital of Shrikantha Janapada during ancient times?
(*a*) Thanesar (*b*) Chandigarh
(*c*) Rohtak (*d*) Gurugram

366. The detailed description of which of the following ancient cities of Haryana is given in the account presented by Chinese pilgrim Huen Tsang?
(*a*) Rohtak (*b*) Ambala
(*c*) Thaneshwar (*d*) Bhiwani

367. Thaneshwar City of this state was at the pinnacle of its glory during
(*a*) Vardhan period (*b*) Gupta period
(*c*) Sunga period (*d*) Maurya period

368. The famous battle between the armies of Babur and Ibrahim Lodi in 1526 was fought at which of the following places in Haryana?
(*a*) Jhajjhar (*b*) Kurukshetra
(*c*) Rohtak (*d*) Panipat

369. Panipat town was given the status of District on
(*a*) 1 January, 1988 (*b*) 1 November, 1989
(*c*) 1 December, 1990 (*d*) 17 June, 1980

370. Rewari district was formed on
(*a*) 10 June, 1977 (*b*) 5 February, 1979
(*c*) 1 November, 1989 (*d*) 17 June, 1980

371. Hissar is the birth place of which of the following famous kings?
(*a*) Shershah Suri (*b*) Akbar
(*c*) Muhammad Tughlaq (*d*) Feroz Tughlaq

372. In which of the following towns has the largest cattle farm of Haryana?
(*a*) Narnaul (*b*) Hissar
(*c*) Panipat (*d*) Karnal

373. In 1354, who of the following famous ruler of the medieval India built the town of Hissar as a fort?
(*a*) Muhammad Tughlaq (*b*) Balban
(*c*) Feroz Tughlaq (*d*) Alauddin Khilji

374. During ancient times, Mahendragarh town of this state was known as
(*a*) Janauva (*b*) Karnpur
(*c*) Mahipgarh (*d*) Kanaud

375. Name the last king of Ballabhgarh who died as a martyr during freedom struggle of 1857.
(*a*) Nahar Singh (*b*) Vijay Singh
(*c*) Pratap Singh (*d*) Mahar Singh

376. Ballabhgarh town is included in which of the following districts of Haryana?
(*a*) Rohtak (*b*) Faridabad
(*c*) Gurugram (*d*) Karnal

377. Narwana Tehsil is situated in which of the following Districts of the state?
(*a*) Sirsa (*b*) Bhiwani
(*c*) Jind (*d*) Fatehabad

378. Grave of the famous Sultana Raziya of Ghulam dynasty is located in which of the following districts of the state?
(*a*) Kaithal (*b*) Gurugram
(*c*) Ambala (*d*) Faridabad

379. Which of the following towns of Haryana is termed as 'a big bowl of paddy' and 'Paris of Haryana'?
(*a*) Rohtak (*b*) Sonepat
(*c*) Faridabad (*d*) Karnal

380. In 1607, Faridabad town was built by
(*a*) Feroz Shah (*b*) Mubarakshah
(*c*) Baba Farid (*d*) Mansub Ali

381. During the Mahabharata period Sirsa was known as
(*a*) Shishira (*b*) Shairishkam
(*c*) Saurish (*d*) Sirisa

382. During ancient times, Gohana town of the state was known as
(*a*) Gawabh Bhawana (*b*) Gadhana
(*c*) Gapat Zamana (*d*) None of these

383. During ancient times, Bahadurgarh town of the state was known as
(*a*) Bahawalgarh (*b*) Shafirabad
(*c*) Sharfabad (*d*) Balramgarh

384. Britishers confiscated Bahadurgarh from Scindia King and handed it as a Jaghir to the brother of Nawab of Jhajjhar in
(*a*) 1800 AD (*b*) 1801 AD
(*c*) 1805 AD (*d*) 1803 AD

385. Which of the following towns of the state was built by a Rajput named Amba in the 14th century?
(*a*) Jhajjhar (*b*) Rohtak
(*c*) Ambala (*d*) Bhiwani

386. Abdur Rahman Khan who sacrificed his life during freedom struggle, hailed from which of the following towns of Haryana?
(*a*) Kurukshetra (*b*) Jhajjhar
(*c*) Farrukh Nagar (*d*) Rewari

387. Farrukh Nagar was built by which of the following Biloch rulers?
(*a*) Dalel Khan (Faujdar Khan)
(*b*) Shaffuddin Khan
(*c*) Badar Khan
(*d*) Jamaluddin Khan

388. Biloch ruler Dalel Khan (Faujdar Khan) built the town of Farrukh Nagar in the name of which of the following Emperors?
(*a*) Fakhruddin Ahmad (*b*) Farukh Ali
(*c*) Ferozshah Tughlaq (*d*) Farrukh Siyar

389. Great epic Mahabharata was composed by Maharshi Ved Vyas in which of the following towns of Haryana?
(*a*) Panipat (*b*) Rewari
(*c*) Kurukshetra (*d*) Hissar

390. Rise of Vardhan dynasty took place in which of the following towns of Haryana?
(*a*) Thanesar (Sthaneshwar)
(*b*) Rohtak
(*c*) Panipat
(*d*) Kurukshetra

391. In 1556, the famous battle between the forces of Akbar and Hemchandra (Hemu) of Rewari was fought at which of the following places in Haryana?
(*a*) Rewari (*b*) Jind
(*c*) Kurukshetra (*d*) Panipat

392. In 1761 the third battle of Panipat was fought between the forces of
(*a*) Babur and Ibrahim Lodi
(*b*) Akbar and Hemchandra (Hemu)
(*c*) Afghans and Marathas
(*d*) Britishers and Sikhs

393. The town of Panipat was under which of the following districts of Haryana till 31 October, 1989?
(*a*) Rewari (*b*) Ambala
(*c*) Karnal (*d*) Hissar

394. Which of the following districts of the state was included under Gurugram and Mahendragarh districts before 1989?
(*a*) Mahendragarh (*b*) Faridabad
(*c*) Jind (*d*) Rewari

395. Jind was given the status of district in
(*a*) 1966 (*b*) 1972
(*c*) 1968 (*d*) 1975

396. Which of the following districts of Haryana has its headquarters at Narnaul?
(*a*) Hissar (*b*) Faridabad
(*c*) Mahendragarh (*d*) Karnal

397. Who amongst the following did not play for Haryana in Ranji Trophy?
(*a*) Kapil Dev (*b*) Rajinder Goel
(*c*) Sarkar Talwar (*d*) Maninder Singh

398. When Hansi came into existence as the 23rd districts of Haryana?
(*a*) 2024 (*b*) 2023
(*c*) 2025 (*d*) 2022

399. During Mahabharat period, which of the following places was given by Raja Yudhishthir to his Guru Dronacharya as a gift?
(*a*) Gurugram village (*b*) Kaithal
(*c*) Hodal (*d*) Sirsa

400. Who was the Collector of Gurugram during the freedom struggle of 1857?
(*a*) Henry (*b*) Sir Helley
(*c*) John Marshall (*d*) Shri Ford

401. In 1858, which of the following districts of Haryana was included in Punjab?
(*a*) Faridabad (*b*) Gurugram
(*c*) Hissar (*d*) Mahendragarh

402. When Faridabad came into existence as the 12th district of Haryana?
(*a*) 15 August, 1970 (*b*) 02 August, 1979
(*c*) 26 January, 1979 (*d*) 8 March, 1982

403. Bahadurgarh town is included in which of the following districts of Haryana?
(*a*) Jhajjar (*b*) Karnal
(*c*) Yamun Nagar (*d*) Faridabad

404. The historical town Gohana is included in which of the following districts of Haryana?
(*a*) Panipat (*b*) Sirsa
(*c*) Sonepat (*d*) Rewari

405. In which year 'Sirsa' became a district?
(*a*) 1980 (*b*) 1975
(*c*) 1990 (*d*) 1995

406. Hodal Sub-division is located in which district of Haryana?
(*a*) Rohtak (*b*) Sonepat
(*c*) Palwal (*d*) Panipat

407. Tosham town of district Bhiwani was given the status of Sub-Division on
(*a*) 27 April, 1993 (*b*) 10 June, 1995
(*c*) 5 March, 1997 (*d*) 27 April, 1998

408. Which of the following famous temples is situated at historical town "Sadhaura"of district Yamuna Nagar?
(*a*) Manokamna Temple (*b*) Gagarwala Temple
(*c*) Toranwala Temple (*d*) All of these

409. In which of the following historical towns of Yamuna Nagar district, the Gurudwara of Buddhushah is situated which had helped Guru Govind Singh in the battle of Bhagani?
(*a*) Sadhaura (*b*) Radaur
(*c*) Bilaspur (*d*) Chhachhrauli

410. In ancient times Bahadurgarh town of Haryana was called as
(*a*) Charkhabad (*b*) Hasinpur
(*c*) Sharfabad (*d*) Betawabad

411. The historical town of Maham is situated in which of the following districts of the state?
(*a*) Bhiwani (*b*) Rohtak
(*c*) Yamuna Nagar (*d*) Jhajjhar

412. Maham town situated in district Rohtak was rebuilt by a person called Peshora of Kayastha (Baniya) Community in
(*a*) 1266 (*b*) 1295
(*c*) 1298 (*d*) 1299

413. Ailanabad town situated in district Sirsa was earlier known as
(*a*) Ailisabad (*b*) Chavipur
(*c*) Kalisabad (*d*) Khariyal

414. What was the earlier name of the historical town 'Raniyan' situated in district Sirsa?
(*a*) Rajabpur (*b*) Sajupur
(*c*) Rajipur (*d*) Ratipur

415. Which of the following towns situated in district Ambala was built by the King of Sirmour (Himachal Pradesh) Raja Laxmi Narayan?
(*a*) Barara (*b*) Mulana
(*c*) Narayangarh (*d*) Raipur Rani

416. By excavations done in which of the following historical towns of Sonepat district, earthen utensils belonging to Mahabharata period have been found?
(*a*) Rai (*b*) Kheri Gujjar
(*c*) Gankaur (*d*) Gohana

417. Mythological village Aadi Badri is situated in which of the following districts of Haryana?
(*a*) Yamuna Nagar (*b*) Bhiwani
(*c*) Sirsa (*d*) Rewari

418. Which of the following historical villages situated in district Yamuna Nagar is associated with King Santanu of the Mahabharata period?
(*a*) Chhachhrauli (*b*) Aadi Badri
(*c*) Basantar (*d*) None of these

419. At which of the following places Mazaar of Altaf Hussain Hali is located?
(*a*) Sonepat (*b*) Gurugram
(*c*) Panipat (*d*) Jind

420. Which of the following places was made a powerful centre of Afghan chiefs by Ahmadshah Abdali before the third battle of Panipat?
(*a*) Gharauda (*b*) Nilpe Khedi
(*c*) Asangh (*d*) Kunjpura

ANSWERS

1	**2**	**3**	**4**	**5**	**6**	**7**	**8**	**9**	**10**
(*d*)	(*a*)	(*b*)	(*c*)	(*a*)	(*d*)	(*b*)	(*a*)	(*c*)	(*b*)
11	**12**	**13**	**14**	**15**	**16**	**17**	**18**	**19**	**20**
(*d*)	(*d*)	(*a*)	(*c*)	(*d*)	(*a*)	(*c*)	(*b*)	(*d*)	(*a*)
21	**22**	**23**	**24**	**25**	**26**	**27**	**28**	**29**	**30**
(*d*)	(*a*)	(*c*)	(*b*)	(*a*)	(*d*)	(*d*)	(*a*)	(*c*)	(*c*)
31	**32**	**33**	**34**	**35**	**36**	**37**	**38**	**39**	**40**
(*d*)	(*c*)	(*a*)	(*b*)	(*d*)	(*d*)	(*a*)	(*c*)	(*b*)	(*c*)
41	**42**	**43**	**44**	**45**	**46**	**47**	**48**	**49**	**50**
(*d*)	(*a*)	(*c*)	(*b*)	(*a*)	(*c*)	(*d*)	(*a*)	(*c*)	(*c*)
51	**52**	**53**	**54**	**55**	**56**	**57**	**58**	**59**	**60**
(*a*)	(*c*)	(*a*)	(*b*)	(*d*)	(*b*)	(*a*)	(*c*)	(*b*)	(*d*)
61	**62**	**63**	**64**	**65**	**66**	**67**	**68**	**69**	**70**
(*d*)	(*a*)	(*c*)	(*a*)	(*b*)	(*a*)	(*a*)	(*a*)	(*b*)	(*d*)
71	**72**	**73**	**74**	**75**	**76**	**77**	**78**	**79**	**80**
(*c*)	(*a*)	(*c*)	(*b*)	(*d*)	(*c*)	(*a*)	(*c*)	(*b*)	(*d*)
81	**82**	**83**	**84**	**85**	**86**	**87**	**88**	**89**	**90**
(*b*)	(*a*)	(*d*)	(*a*)	(*c*)	(*b*)	(*d*)	(*c*)	(*a*)	(*d*)
91	**92**	**93**	**94**	**95**	**96**	**97**	**98**	**99**	**100**
(*d*)	(*a*)	(*d*)	(*a*)	(*c*)	(*b*)	(*d*)	(*a*)	(*c*)	(*b*)
101	**102**	**103**	**104**	**105**	**106**	**107**	**108**	**109**	**110**
(*d*)	(*a*)	(*a*)	(*d*)	(*a*)	(*b*)	(*c*)	(*b*)	(*d*)	(*a*)
111	**112**	**113**	**114**	**115**	**116**	**117**	**118**	**119**	**120**
(*c*)	(*b*)	(*c*)	(*a*)	(*d*)	(*b*)	(*d*)	(*c*)	(*a*)	(*b*)
121	**122**	**123**	**124**	**125**	**126**	**127**	**128**	**129**	**130**
(*c*)	(*b*)	(*c*)	(*b*)	(*d*)	(*d*)	(*a*)	(*c*)	(*d*)	(*b*)
131	**132**	**133**	**134**	**135**	**136**	**137**	**138**	**139**	**140**
(*a*)	(*c*)	(*a*)	(*b*)	(*a*)	(*b*)	(*a*)	(*d*)	(*c*)	(*b*)
141	**142**	**143**	**144**	**145**	**146**	**147**	**148**	**149**	**150**
(*a*)	(*c*)	(*b*)	(*a*)	(*d*)	(*a*)	(*c*)	(*d*)	(*c*)	(*a*)
151	**152**	**153**	**154**	**155**	**156**	**157**	**158**	**159**	**160**
(*d*)	(*c*)	(*a*)	(*a*)	(*b*)	(*a*)	(*d*)	(*b*)	(*b*)	(*d*)
161	**162**	**163**	**164**	**165**	**166**	**167**	**168**	**169**	**170**
(*a*)	(*c*)	(*a*)	(*c*)	(*b*)	(*d*)	(*c*)	(*a*)	(*b*)	(*a*)

171 (*b*)	172 (*d*)	173 (*a*)	174 (*a*)	175 (*d*)	176 (*b*)	177 (*a*)	178 (*b*)	179 (*b*)	180 (*c*)
181 (*a*)	182 (*a*)	183 (*c*)	184 (*d*)	185 (*b*)	186 (*c*)	187 (*d*)	188 (*a*)	189 (*c*)	190 (*d*)
191 (*d*)	192 (*a*)	193 (*b*)	194 (*b*)	195 (*a*)	196 (*c*)	197 (*a*)	198 (*d*)	199 (*b*)	200 (*a*)
201 (*d*)	202 (*c*)	203 (*a*)	204 (*d*)	205 (*a*)	206 (*d*)	207 (*c*)	208 (*b*)	209 (*b*)	210 (*a*)
211 (*a*)	212 (*a*)	213 (*c*)	214 (*d*)	215 (*b*)	216 (*a*)	217 (*a*)	218 (*b*)	219 (*d*)	220 (*a*)
221 (*b*)	222 (*c*)	223 (*b*)	224 (*d*)	225 (*a*)	226 (*c*)	227 (*a*)	228 (*d*)	229 (*b*)	230 (*a*)
231 (*d*)	232 (*a*)	233 (*b*)	234 (*a*)	235 (*d*)	236 (*d*)	237 (*a*)	238 (*c*)	239 (*b*)	240 (*d*)
241 (*d*)	242 (*a*)	243 (*c*)	244 (*b*)	245 (*a*)	246 (*a*)	247 (*c*)	248 (*b*)	249 (*a*)	250 (*a*)
251 (*b*)	252 (*a*)	253 (*c*)	254 (*b*)	255 (*d*)	256 (*c*)	257 (*d*)	258 (*d*)	259 (*c*)	260 (*a*)
261 (*b*)	262 (*d*)	263 (*c*)	264 (*a*)	265 (*b*)	266 (*c*)	267 (*a*)	268 (*b*)	269 (*a*)	270 (*c*)
271 (*b*)	272 (*b*)	273 (*d*)	274 (*c*)	275 (*d*)	276 (*d*)	277 (*a*)	278 (*a*)	279 (*b*)	280 (*a*)
281 (*c*)	282 (*b*)	283 (*a*)	284 (*c*)	285 (*b*)	286 (*d*)	287 (*c*)	288 (*c*)	289 (*a*)	290 (*c*)
291 (*b*)	292 (*a*)	293 (*a*)	294 (*b*)	295 (*d*)	296 (*a*)	297 (*c*)	298 (*d*)	299 (*a*)	300 (*b*)
301 (*a*)	302 (*c*)	303 (*d*)	304 (*a*)	305 (*c*)	306 (*b*)	307 (*c*)	308 (*a*)	309 (*c*)	310 (*d*)
311 (*a*)	312 (*b*)	313 (*a*)	314 (*b*)	315 (*c*)	316 (*d*)	317 (*a*)	318 (*c*)	319 (*b*)	320 (*a*)
321 (*c*)	322 (*d*)	323 (*a*)	324 (*a*)	325 (*d*)	326 (*a*)	327 (*b*)	328 (*d*)	329 (*c*)	330 (*a*)
331 (*b*)	332 (*d*)	333 (*a*)	334 (*c*)	335 (*a*)	336 (*b*)	337 (*d*)	338 (*a*)	339 (*c*)	340 (*a*)
341 (*c*)	342 (*d*)	343 (*c*)	344 (*b*)	345 (*a*)	346 (*c*)	347 (*d*)	348 (*a*)	349 (*d*)	350 (*a*)
351 (*c*)	352 (*d*)	353 (*c*)	354 (*b*)	355 (*d*)	356 (*d*)	357 (*b*)	358 (*c*)	359 (*b*)	360 (*d*)
361 (*c*)	362 (*a*)	363 (*c*)	364 (*b*)	365 (*a*)	366 (*c*)	367 (*a*)	368 (*d*)	369 (*b*)	370 (*c*)
371 (*a*)	372 (*b*)	373 (*c*)	374 (*d*)	375 (*a*)	376 (*b*)	377 (*c*)	378 (*a*)	379 (*d*)	380 (*c*)
381 (*b*)	382 (*a*)	383 (*c*)	384 (*d*)	385 (*c*)	386 (*b*)	387 (*a*)	388 (*d*)	389 (*c*)	390 (*a*)
391 (*d*)	392 (*c*)	393 (*c*)	394 (*d*)	395 (*a*)	396 (*c*)	397 (*d*)	398 (*c*)	399 (*a*)	400 (*d*)
401 (*b*)	402 (*b*)	403 (*a*)	404 (*c*)	405 (*b*)	406 (*c*)	407 (*a*)	408 (*d*)	409 (*a*)	410 (*c*)
411 (*b*)	412 (*a*)	413 (*d*)	414 (*a*)	415 (*c*)	416 (*b*)	417 (*a*)	418 (*c*)	419 (*c*)	420 (*d*)

❑❑❑

CURRENT AFFAIRS

1. 25th Shanghai Cooperation Organisation (SCO) summit 2025 was held in:
A. Wuhan B. Shanghai
C. Tianjin D. Beijing

2. In which state Indiramma Atmiya Bharosa Scheme was launched in 2025?
A. Andhra Pradesh B. Telangana
C. Karnataka D. Tamil Nadu

3. Integrated Sohra Tourism Circuit is being developed in which state:
A. Mizoram B. Arunachal Pradesh
C. Meghalaya D. Tripura

4. Who inaugurated the Handloom conclave Manthan?
A. Narendra Modi B. Giriraj Singh
C. Piyush Goyal D. Smriti Irani

5. How many children were awarded the Pradhan Mantri Rashtriya Bal Puraskar 2025 by President Droupadi Murmu?
A. 15 B. 20
C. 18 D. 17

6. Which city hosted the AI Action Summit 2025?
A. New York B. Paris
C. Geneva D. Tokyo

7. How many individuals were honoured with the Padma Vibhushan Award in 2026?
A. 4 B. 8
C. 5 D. 6

8. Jitendra Pal Singh has been appointed as India's new Ambassador to which country?
A. United States of America
B. Israel
C. France
D. Germany

9. On which date the USA launched a military strike on Venezuela and captured president Nicolas Maduro and his wife Cilia Flores?
A. Jan 1, 2026 B. Jan 3, 2026
C. Jan 8, 2026 D. Jan 12, 2026

10. In January 2026, which State/UT government signed a MoU with the RBI to strengthen financial governance?
A. Bihar Government
B. Sikkim Government
C. Assam Government
D. Delhi Government

11. Who has been elected as the President of Belarus?
A. Michel Martin
B. Francois Barua
C. Alexander Lukashenko
D. NOT

12. Which organization has launched the enhanced Certificate of Origin (eCoO) 2.0 system?
A. Reserve Bank of India (RBI)
B. Export Promotion Council (EPC)
C. Directorate General of Foreign Trade (DGFT)
D. Federation of Indian Export Organisations (FIEO)

13. Which is the first Indian organisation received the Ramon Magsaysay Award 2025?
A. Pratham Education Foundation
B. The Foundation to Educate Girls Globally
C. The Akshaya Patra Foundation
D. Help Age India

14. In which of the following states the World's largest data centre will be built?
A. Gujarat B. Odisha
C. Maharashtra D. Uttar Pradesh

15. Who among the following has been appointed as the Director of the Liquid Propulsion Systems Centre of ISRO?
A. M. Mohan B. S. Somnath
C. V. Narayanan D. K. Sivan

16. Madhav Gadgil died in Pune on 7th January, 2026 was related to which field?
A. Sports B. Music
C. Ecology D. Social Service

17. Who among the following has won the Men's singles title in the recently held Australian Open 2025?
A. Jannik Sinner B. Alexander Zverev
C. Novac Djokovic D. Carlos Alcaraz

18. How many people have been announced to be given the Padma Award by the government of India in 2026?
A. 121 B. 131
C. 140 D. 155

19. Which bank becomes the first Indian bank to implement Clari5's NCRP Integration Solution?
A. Punjab National Bank B. Bank of Baroda
C. Bank of India D. Canara Bank

20. Polavaram Multipurpose Project, which was seen in the news, is located in which state?
A. Kerala B. Karnataka
C. Andhra Pradesh D. Maharashtra

21. Rani Durgavati Tiger Reserve is located in which state?
A. Odisha B. Madhya Pradesh
C. Rajasthan D. Gujarat

22. Pangsau Pass, which was seen in the news, lies between which two countries?
A. India and Bhutan B. China and Nepal
C. India and Myanmar D. India and Bangladesh

23. India hosted the Second BIMSTEC Expert Group Meeting on Cyber Security Cooperation in which city?
A. Hyderabad B. Chennai
C. New Delhi D. Bengaluru

24. Who was appointed as the brand ambassador of FICCI FRAMES?
A. Sachin Tendulkar B. Akshay Kumar
C. Virat Kohli D. Ayushmann Khurrana

25. Which country hosted the Chess World Cup 2025?
A. India B. Germany
C. USA D. Norway

26. Which Ministry of the Government of India is responsible for the Kalagram for Mahakumbh 2025?
A. Ministry of Culture, Government of India
B. Ministry of Tourism, Government of India
C. Indian Council for Cultural Relations
D. Ministry of External Affairs, Government of India

27. The 14th edition of the India - Thailand joint military Exercise MAITREE-XIV was organised at:
A. Fort Vachiraprakan, Thailand
B. Umroi, Meghalaya
C. Mhow, Madhya Pradesh
D. Jodhpur, Rajasthan

28. Which day is observed as the International Day of Education every year?
A. 24 January B. 25 January
C. 26 January D. 27 January

29. Which Indian Navy ship conducted the hydrographic survey of Mauritius recently?
A. INS Viraat B. INS Sarvekshak
C. INS Kalvari D. INS Saryu

30. The United States jointly develops National Advanced Surface-to-Air Missile Systems (NASAMS) with which country?
A. France B. Norway
C. Greece D. Australia

31. What is "Australopithecus" that was recently seen in the news?
A. A genus of extinct Primates
B. A prehistoric species of Fish
C. Traditional irrigation technique
D. Newly discovered species of Frog

32. With which of the following, the First EAN Rupay Credit Card is seamlessly integrated?
A. BHIM B. Rupay Card
C. UPI D. None of these

33. IDFC First Bank has partnered with whom to launch the First EA₹N Credit Card?
A. VISA Card B. Rupay Card
C. Master Card D. None of these

34. What is SANJAY, recently seen in the news?
A. Battlefield Surveillance System
B. Light Weight Battle Tank
C. Drone
D. None of these

35. The Dhanauri wetland, recently which is seen in the news, is .located in?
A. Maharashtra B. Uttarakhand
C. Uttar Pradesh D. Bihar

36. Which state is at the top of the Fiscal Health Index Report 2025, recently released by NITI Aayog?
A. Karnataka B. Tamil Nadu
C. Kerala D. Odisha

37. Typhoon Missile System was developed by which country?
A. Russia B. France
C. United States D. Japan

38. Who inaugurated the All India Campaign 'Our Constitution, Our Respect'?
A. J.P. Nadda B. PM Narendra Modi
C. Mr. Rajnath Singh D. Om Birla

39. Which player won the ICC Men's T20I Cricketer of the Year Award?
A. Kuldeep Yadav B. Rishabh Pant
C. Suryakumar Yadav D. None of these

40. Recently, Russian President Putin signed a new comprehensive strategic partnership agreement with which country after bilateral talks?
A. Brazil B. Ukraine
C. Iran D. None of these

41. Karpoori Thakur will be honoured with Bharat Ratna (posthumously), he was the former Chief Minister of which state?
A. Karnataka B. Jharkhand
C. Uttar Pradesh D. Bihar

42. Mount Ibu, which was seen in the news, is located in which country?
A. Indonesia B. America
C. Latvia D. Egypt

43. Which German company, along with its Indian partner, cleared field trials for submarines for the Indian Navy?
A. ThyssenKrupp B. BAE Systems
C. Siemens D. Rheinmetall

44. In which state the army launched two new Bailey bridges on the Shyok River?
A. Jammu and Kashmir
B. Arunachal Pradesh
C. Ladakh
D. Mizoram

45. What is the name of India's first indigenous micro-missile system designed to counter swarm drones?
A. Bhargavastra B. Agni
C. Vayu D. Saryu

46. Which day is observed as Kokborok Day in Tripura?
A. 18 January B. 19 January
C. 20 January D. 21 January

47. Who among the following Won Booker Prize 2025?
A. Andrew Miller
B. David Szalay
C. Katie Kitamura
D. Susan Chai

48. M JANMAN scheme, which was seen in the news, is associated with which category of people?
A. MSME Owners
B. Farmers
C. Particularly Vulnerable Tribal Groups
D. Non-Resident Indians

49. Recently, which country has pulled out of the Paris Climate Agreement?
A. France B. Germany
C. America D. None of these

50. Which three states were granted full statehood on January 21, 1972?
A. Nagaland, Manipur and Tripura
B. Tripura, Manipur and Meghalaya
C. Assam, Manipur and Mizoram
D. Sikkim, Meghalaya and Tripura

51. Who is the author of the recently launched book 'The World after Gaza'?
A. Arundhati Roy B. Pankaj Mishra
C. Chetan Bhagat D. Shashi Jharool

52. Which country recently became a partner state of the BRICS group?
A. Nigeria B. Saudi Arabia
C. Iran D. Argentina

53. When was the recently discussed Beti Bachao Beti Padhao (BBBP) Scheme launched?
A. 2014 B. 2015
C. 2016 D. 2017

54. In the Vijay Hazare Trophy 2024-25 final, which team defeated Vidarbha to win the title?
A. Tamil Nadu B. Karnataka
C. Maharashtra D. Uttar Pradesh

55. Which organization has launched the quantum processor 'Willow'?
A. Amazon B. Meta
C. Google D. Microsoft

56. When does the National Disaster Response Force (NDRF) celebrate its foundation day every year?
A. 18th January B. 20th January
C. 19th January D. 21st January

57. In which state is Kokborak Day celebrated?
A. Tripura B. Ladakh
C. Arunachal Pradesh D. Rajasthan

58. Donald Trump is which number president of the United States?
A. 46th B. 47th
C. 45th D. 44th

59. Who recently won the India Open 2025 men's singles title?
A. Kidambi Srikanth B. H.S. Prannoy
C. Viktor Axelsen D. Anthony Ginting

60. Which heritage site from India has been recently included in the World Monuments Watch List 2025?
A. Kaziranga National Park
B. Taj Mahal
C. Ajanta – Ellora Caves
D. Historic Building along the Musi River

61. Abdal-Kuri Island, which was seen in the news, is located in which ocean?
A. Pacific Ocean B. Indian Ocean
C. Atlantic Ocean D. Arctic Ocean

62. Which organisation released the Global Risks Report 2025?
A. International Monetary Fund
B. United Nations Development Programme
C. World Economic Forum
D. United Nations Environment Programme

63. The Nord Stream pipeline is constructed under which sea?
A. Red Sea B. Arabian Sea
C. Black Sea D. Baltic Sea

64. The Trajan 155 mm towed artillery gun system was developed by India and which country?
A. Russia B. Australia
C. Japan D. France

65. Which Indian Naval Ship (INS) participated in the fourth edition of the multinational exercise LA PEROUSE?
A. INS Surat B. INS Kolkata
C. INS Mumbai D. INS Vikrant

66. Project Veer Gatha 4.0 is a joint initiative of which ministries?
A. Ministry of Home Affairs and Ministry of Youth Affairs
B. Ministry of Defence and Ministry of Education
C. Ministry of Culture and Ministry of Defence
D. Ministry of Education and Ministry of Sports

67. Which ministry has launched the National River Traffic and Navigation System (NRT & NS)?
A. Ministry of Road Transport and Highways
B. Ministry of Ports, Shipping & Waterways
C. Ministry of Jal Shakti
D. Ministry of Defence

68. Cyber-Security Grand Challenge (CSGC 2.0) has been launched by whom?
A. Ministry of Defence and the Indian Army
B. Ministry of Science and Technology and ISRO
C. Ministry of Home Affairs and NITI Aayog
D. Ministry of Technology and Data Security Council of India

69. Who has been sworn in as the new Chief Justice of the Supreme Court?
A. Justice Ashok Ganguly
B. Justice Surya Kant
C. Justice Vinod Kumar
D. Justice Deepak Mishra

70. The falcated duck was recently spotted at which protected area in Haryana?
A. Nahar Wildlife Sanctuary
B. Bhindawas Wildlife Sanctuary
C. Sultanpur National Park
D. Kalesar National Park

71. Which institution developed the Central Suspect Registry?
A. Reserve Bank of India (RBI)
B. Indian Cyber Crime Coordination Centre (I4C)
C. Central Bureau of Investigation (CBI)
D. National Investigation Agency (NIA)

72. With which country has India signed a deal for the export of BrahMos supersonic cruise missiles?
A. Indonesia B. Bangladesh
C. Ukraine D. India

73. Which state government has launched the SHE COHORT 3.0 initiative to empower women-led startups?
A. Odisha B. Haryana
C. Punjab D. Gujarat

74. Which of the following is the best description of 'Nag Mk 2 Missile'?
A. It is a land variant of short-range submarine-launched Ballistic Missile (SLBM).
B. It is the third-generation Anti-Tank Fire-and-Forget Guided Missile.
C. It is India's first indigenously produced medium-range Surface to Air missile.
D. None of the above

75. What is the main objective of Exercise Devil Strike conducted by the Indian Army?
A. Testing new technologies
B. Expanding international military alliances
C. Enhancing combat preparedness and operational capabilities
D. Conducting humanitarian assistance missions

76. Which player of the Indian women's cricket team was appointed as DSP in UP Police?
A. Harmanpreet Kaur B. Smriti Mandhana
C. Deepti Sharma D. Richa Ghosh

77. Which State has inaugurated the International Saraswati Mahotsav?
A. Andhra Pradesh B. Haryana
C. Karnataka D. Uttar Pradesh

78. Recently, which scheme was launched by the government to provide loan guarantees for MSMEs?
A. Mutual Credit Guarantee Scheme for MSMEs (MCGS-MSMEs)
B. Credit-Linked Capital Subsidy Scheme
C. Stand-Up India Scheme
D. Pradhan Mantri Mudra Yojana

79. Who was named ICC Women's Cricketer of the Year 2024?
A. Smriti Mandhana B. Ellyse Perry
C. Amelia Kerr D. Alyssa Healy

80. In which of the following cities did the Inland Waterways Authority of India (IWAI) establish a new regional office?
A. Haridwar B. Varanasi
C. Kashi D. Ujjain

81. Which of the following is NOT a member of the Selection Committee for appointing the CEC and ECs?
A. The Prime Minister
B. The Chief Justice of India
C. The Leader of the Opposition in the Lok Sabha
D. A Cabinet Minister nominated by the Prime Minister

82. What is the limit of non-taxable income as per the new regime 2025?
A. 10 lakhs B. 12 lakhs
C. 11 lakhs D. 13 lakhs

83. When Indian Coast Guard Raising Day is celebrated every year?
A. 1st Feb B. 31st Jan
C. 30th Jan D. 2nd Feb

84. Which of the following has been added as the newest member of ASEAN?
A. East Timor B. Western New Guinea
C. Bangladesh D. South Korea

85. Which country recently became the first in Africa to be acknowledged by the WHO for interrupting the transmission of Onchocerca volvulus?
A. Kenya B. Egypt
C. Nigeria D. Niger

86. Who was the pilot of the Axiom-4 mission to the International Space Station (ISS)?
A. Stawosz Uznanski-Wisniewski
B. Peggy Whitson
C. Group Captain Shubhanshu Shukla
D. Tibor Kapu

87. Which state recently approved a pilot study for regulated cannabis cultivation?
A. Himachal Pradesh B. Uttar Pradesh
C. Andhra Pradesh D. Haryana

88. Which board was established to promote Makhana cultivation in Bihar as part of the budget initiatives?
A. Fisheries and Aquaculture Board
B. Bihar Crop Improvement Board
C. Makhana Board
D. Agricultural Development Board

89. Greg Bell, who recently passed away, was a famous long jumper from which country?
A. Australia B. Germany
C. USA D. Canada

90. Point Nemo, which was seen in the news, is located in which ocean?
A. Atlantic Ocean B. Indian Ocean
C. Arctic Ocean D. Pacific Ocean

91. Which institution recently extracted silicon carbide from simulated moon soil?
A. IIT Bombay B. IIT Kanpur
C. IIT Delhi D. IIT Madras

92. Which city is the host of the first Raisina Middle East Conference?
A. Riyadh B. Abu Dhabi
C. Cairo D. Beirut

93. Ramappa Temple is located in which state?
A. Telangana B. Gujarat
C. Tamil Nadu D. Maharashtra

94. What is the name of the indigenous dog breed recently recognized by ICAR-NBAGR from the Himalayas?
A. Damchi B. Gaddi
C. Bakharwal D. Bangara

95. Who has taken oath as the New Governor of Bihar?
A. Sanjay Malhotra B. Sushil Kumar
C. Junaid Ahmad D. Arif Mohammad

96. India has recently rolled out Digital pilot licenses (Electronic Personnel License - EPL). What position does India hold globally in implementing this initiative?
A. 1st B. 2nd
C. 3rd D. 4th

97. Which state has Recently Launched the N proud (New Programme for Removal of Unused) initiative?
A. Tamil Nadu B. Maharashtra
C. Karnataka D. Kerala

98. Recently launched NAKSHA campaign is associated with which Ministry?
A. Ministry of Housing and Urban Affairs
B. Ministry of Rural Development and Agriculture Farmer's welfare
C. Ministry of Environment, forest and climate change
D. Ministry of Home Affairs

99. India and Qatar have set a target to double their bilateral trade to show much by 2030.
A. $20 Billion B. $35 Billion
C. $28 Billion D. $40 Billion

100. Recently, which organization developed the 10-tonne vertical planetary Mixer, the world's largest for solid propellants?
A. DRDO B. HAL
C. IISC D. ISRO

101. What is unique about the NISAR satellite, launched on 30 July 2025?
A. It is India's first satellite
B. It is the first to carry humans
C. It uses dual-frequency radar (L-band & S-band)
D. It is designed for lunar missions

102. Gen Z protests on mass scale erupted in which country?
A. Bangladesh B. Pakistan
C. Nepal D. Sri Lanka

103. When is International Tiger Day celebrated every year?
A. 28 July B. 15 August
C. 29 July D. 30 June

104. What is the full form of NISAR, the satellite launched by ISRO on July 30, 2025?
A. National Indian Satellite for Agricultural Research
B. NASA-ISRO Synthetic Aperture Radar
C. New Indian Satellite for Aerial Reconnaissance
D. None of the above

105. Which country's Prime Minister mediated and announced the ceasefire to resolve the Thailand-Cambodia border clashes in July 2025?
A. Thailand B. Cambodia
C. Vietnam D. Malaysia

106. Who won the FIDE Women's World Cup 2025?
A. Koneru Humpy B. Harika Dronavalli
C. Divya Deshmukh D. Tania Sachdev

107. Central Reserve Police Force (CRPF) Raising Day is observed on 27 July every year, What was the original name of the Central Reserve Police Force (CRPF) established in 1939?
A. British Reserve Police
B. Crown Representative's Police
C. Indian Territorial Force
D. Royal Indian Constabulary

108. Which historical site is at the center of the territorial dispute between Thailand and Cambodia that led to clashes in July 2025?
A. Angkor Wat B. Preah Vihear Temple
C. Golden Pagoda D. Phnom Penh Palace

109. What is the name of the joint military exercise between India and Singapore held in July–August 2025?
A. SIMBEX B. Garuda Shakti
C. Bold Kurukshetra D. Mitra Shakti

110. Where was the first hydrogen-powered train coach tested in July 2025?
A. Bhopal Rail Coach Factory
B. RCF Kapurthala
C. Integral Coach Factory, Chennai
D. Lucknow Workshop

111. Whose record did Narendra Modi surpass to become the second-longest-serving PM in consecutive terms in July 2025?
A. Atal Bihari Vajpayee
B. Jawaharlal Nehru
C. Indira Gandhi
D. Lal Bahadur Shastri

112. Kargil Vijay Diwas is observed on which date every year?
A. 15 August B. 3 December
C. 26 July D. 26 June

113. Which military operation was launched by India during the Kargil War?
A. Operation Blue Star B. Operation Meghdoot
C. Operation Vijay D. Operation Shakti

114. When was the National Cooperative Policy 2025 launched by Amit Shah, Union Minister of Home and Cooperation?
A. 15 August 2025 B. 24 July 2025
C. 1 January 2025 D. 30 June 2025

115. Under which constitutional amendment were cooperative societies recognized as a fundamental right?
A. 74th Amendment B. 86th Amendment
C. 97th Amendment D. 102nd Amendment

116. Which two leaders signed the India–UK Free Trade Agreement (FTA) in July 2025?
A. Narendra Modi and Rishi Sunak
B. Amit Shah and Keir Starmer
C. Narendra Modi and Keir Starmer
D. Rishi Sunak and Nirmala Sitharaman

117. India has achieved how much percentage ethanol blending in petrol in 2025, five years ahead of its original 2030 target?
A. 15%　　B. 20%
C. 18%　　D. 10%

118. Which two countries is PM Narendra Modi visited from July 23 to 26, 2025?
A. UK and Sri Lanka
B. UK and Maldives
C. France and Maldives
D. UAE and UK

119. What is the primary objective of the Indian Government's "World's Largest Grain Storage Plan in the Cooperative Sector"?
A. To increase grain exports
B. To promote organic farming
C. To centralize food procurement
D. To improve rural grain storage infrastructure and strengthen PACS

120. Who resigned as the Vice President of India in July 2025?
A. M. Venkaiah Naidu　　B. Jagdeep Dhankhar
C. Ram Nath Kovind　　D. Om Birla

121. When did FIDE Chess World Cup 2025 held in India?
A. August 10 – September 5
B. September 15 – October 12
C. October 30 – November 27
D. November 10 – December 5

122. How many gold medals did India win at the 66th International Mathematical Olympiad (IMO) 2025 held in Sunshine Coast, Australia in July 2025?
A. Two　　B. Three
C. Four　　D. One

123. When is International Moon Day observed?
A. July 16　　B. July 20
C. August 5　　D. June 21

124. Purple Fest 2025, organised on 10-11th September, 2025 in New Delhi is related to:
A. Deserted women　　B. Transgenders
C. LGBTQIA+　　D. Divangjan

125. Which organization was designated as a Foreign Terrorist Organization (FTO) by the United States in July 2025 for its involvement in the deadly April 22 Pahalgam attack?
A. Jaish-e-Mohammed
B. The Resistance Front (TRF)
C. Hizbul Mujahideen
D. Indian Mujahideen

126. What is the name of the annual maritime bilateral exercise between India and Singapore, conducted in July 2025?
A. MILAN　　B. SIMBEX
C. VARUNA　　D. INDRA

127. Where did the 56th International Film Festival of India (IFFI) held in November 2025?
A. Mumbai　　B. New Delhi
C. Goa　　D. Hyderabad

128. Which city was declared India's cleanest city for the 8th consecutive year in the Swachh Survekshan 2024–25?
A. Ahmedabad　　B. Surat
C. Indore　　D. Navi Mumbai

129. What is the range of the Agni-I missile, which is capable of carrying both nuclear and conventional warheads?
A. 150 – 300 km　　B. 350 – 500 km
C. 700 – 900 km　　D. 1,000 – 1,500 km

130. What is the name of the government scheme launched in July 2025 to improve agriculture in low-productivity districts?
A. Pradhan Mantri Krishi Samriddhi Yojana
B. Dhan-Vikas Gramin Krishi Yojana
C. Prime Minister Dhan-Dhaanya Krishi Yojana
D. Kisan Utthan Abhiyan

131. What age group of children is required to complete the Mandatory Biometric Update (MBU) as per UIDAI guidelines?
A. Below 5 years
B. 5 to 7 years
C. 7 years and above
D. 10 years and above

132. Which government agency is responsible for issuing, updating, and managing Aadhaar in India?
A. National Informatics Centre (NIC)
B. Ministry of Home Affairs (MHA)
C. Unique Identification Authority of India (UIDAI)
D. Central Bureau of Investigation (CBI)

133. Ancy Sojan secured third place in the Lignano Meeting – World Athletics Continental Tour Bronze in July 2025 in which event?
A. 100m Sprint　　B. High Jump
C. Long Jump　　D. Triple Jump

134. What is the name of the mission that carried Shubhanshu Shukla to the International Space Station (ISS) in July 2025?
A. Chandrayaan-3
B. Gaganyaan-1
C. Axiom-4 (Akash Ganga)
D. Mission Prithvi

135. When is the 10th Anniversary of the Skill India Mission observed?
A. 12 July 2025　　B. 15 July 2025
C. 1 August 2025　　D. 5 June 2025

136. Which football club won the first-ever FIFA Club World Cup in 2025?
A. Paris Saint-Germain
B. Bayern Munich
C. Manchester City
D. Chelsea

137. Who has been appointed as the new Governor of Haryana in July 2025?
A. Prof. Ashim Kumar Ghosh
B. B. D. Mishra
C. Pusapati Ashok Gajapathi Raju
D. Kavinder Gupta

138. Who has been appointed as the new Governor of Goa in July 2025?
A. Prof. Ashim Kumar Ghosh
B. B. D. Mishra
C. Pusapati Ashok Gajapathi Raju
D. Kavinder Gupta

139. What is the name of India's second-longest cable-stayed bridge inaugurated in July 2025?
A. Bandra-Worli Sea Link
B. Sharavathi Bridge
C. Sigandur Bridge
D. Kalasavalli Bridge

140. What is India's longest cable-stayed bridge overall?
A. Pamban Bridge
B. Bandra-Worli Sea Link
C. Sigandur Bridge
D. Bogibeel Bridge

141. Under which Article of the Indian Constitution does the President nominate members to the Rajya Sabha?
A. Article 78 B. Article 370
C. Article 80(1)(a) D. Article 356

142. Who won the Wimbledon 2025 Men's Singles title?
A. Novak Djokovic B. Carlos Alcaraz
C. Jannik Sinner D. Daniil Medvedev

143. Who won the Wimbledon 2025 Women's Singles title?
A. Aryna Sabalenka B. Amanda Anisimova
C. Iga Swiatek D. Elena Rybakina

144. Which Indian heritage site was inscribed as the 44th UNESCO World Heritage Site in July 2025?
A. Hill Forts of Rajasthan
B. Maratha Military Landscapes of India
C. Ajanta Caves
D. Chola Temples

145. What is the primary objective of Operation SHIVA 2025, launched by the Indian Army in July 2025?
A. Border surveillance in Ladakh
B. Rescue operations in flood-hit areas
C. Ensuring safe conduct of the Shri Amarnath Yatra
D. Conducting joint military drills with foreign forces

146. According to the Aircraft Accident Investigation Bureau (AAIB) report, what caused the crash of the Air India flight AI 171?
A. Bird strike
B. Weather turbulence
C. Fuel supply to engines was cut off
D. Engine fire

147. Who recently (in July 2025) became the fastest Indian sprinter in the 100 meters?
A. Gurindervir Singh B. Neeraj Chopra
C. Animesh Kujur D. Amlan Borgohain

148. What is the name of the revolution that helped India's fish production double in 11 years (2013–14) to (2024–25)?
A. Green Revolution B. White Revolution
C. Blue Revolution D. Yellow Revolution

149. What is the name of the Indian Navy's first indigenously designed and built Diving Support Vessel (DSV)?
A. Samarth B. Nistar
C. Varun D. Rakshak

150. Dr. Syama Prasad Mookerjee was the founder of which political party?
A. Indian National Congress
B. Bharatiya Jana Sangh
C. Hindu Mahasabha
D. Swatantra Party

151. Who was appointed as the new CEO of the International Cricket Council (ICC) in July 2025?
A. Jay Shah
B. Manu Sawhney
C. Sanjog Gupta
D. Anurag Thakur

152. In July 2025, Prime Minister Narendra Modi was conferred which civilian honour by Brazil?
A. Order of the Star of Africa
B. Grand Collar of the National Order of the Southern Cross
C. Order of the Condor of the Andes
D. Order of Rio Branco

153. Who scored 430 runs across both innings and was named Player of the Match in the second Test of the Anderson-Tendulkar Trophy at Edgbaston, Birmingham?
A. Virat Kohli B. Shubman Gill
C. Rohit Sharma D. Rishabh Pant

154. Indonesia was formally inducted as a full member of BRICS during which summit?
A. 16th BRICS Summit, South Africa
B. 17th BRICS Summit, Brazil
C. 18th BRICS Summit, India
D. 15th BRICS Summit, China

155. Who will chair the BRICS Summit in 2026?
A. Brazil B. China
C. India D. Russia

156. Which of the following is not accepted as valid proof of citizenship during Special Intensive Revision (SIR) of electoral rolls in Bihar?
A. Passport B. Birth Certificate
C. School Certificate D. Aadhaar Card

157. Where was the 17th BRICS Summit held in 2025?
A. New Delhi, India
B. Beijing, China
C. Rio de Janeiro, Brazil
D. Cape Town, South Africa

158. Who among the following Indian boxers won gold medals at the World Boxing Cup 2025 held in Astana in July 2025?
A. Meenakshi, Sanju, Jaismine
B. Sakshi, Jaismine, Nupur
C. Jaismine, Pooja Rani, Hitesh Gulia
D. Nupur, Narender, Abhinash Jamwal

159. India recently qualified for the AFC Women's Asian Cup 2026 after how many years?

A. 18 years B. 20 years
C. 22 years D. 25 years

160. India ranks _______ in terms of income equality globally, based on the Gini Index of World Bank.

A. First B. Fourth
C. Tenth D. Fifteenth

161. Who won the Rapid section of the Grand Chess Tour 2025 in Zagreb?

A. Magnus Carlsen
B. Jan-Krzyszt of Duda
C. Gukesh Dommaraju
D. Praggnanandhaa Rameshbabu

162. Where has India set up its first Equine Disease-Free Compartment (EDFC) in July 2025?

A. Pune B. Bikaner
C. Meerut Cantonment D. Chennai

163. What is the name of the award PM Modi received from Trinidad and Tobago in July 2025?

A. Order of the Caribbean
B. National Hero Award
C. Order of the Republic of Trinidad and Tobago
D. West Indies Medal of Honour

164. Where did the first Khelo India Water Sports Festival held in August 2025?

A. Goa B. Chilika Lake
C. Dal Lake, Srinagar D. Naini Lake

165. What is the name of the sweeping legislation passed by the US House on July 3, 2025?

A. The Liberty Act
B. Build Back Better Bill
C. One Big Beautiful Bill
D. Freedom Finance Act

166. Which honour was conferred upon PM Modi during his visit to Ghana in July 2025?

A. Order of Africa
B. Commander of the Golden Star
C. Officer of the Order of the Star of Ghana
D. Star of Africa

167. Who is the current and 14th Dalai Lama?

A. Lobsang Sangay B. Tenzin Gyatso
C. Gyalwa Rinpoche D. Penpa Tsering

168. Who won the gold medal in U-15 Girls' Singles at the 29th Asian Youth Table Tennis Championships 2025?

A. Liu Ziling
B. Zhu Qihi
C. Divyanshi Bhowmick
D. P. B. Abhinand

169. What is the total outlay of the Employment-Linked Incentive (ELI) Scheme approved by the Union Cabinet on 1 July 2025?

A. ₹ 50,000 crore B. ₹ 1 lakh crore
C. ₹ 2 lakh crore D. ₹ 75,000 crore

170. What is the name of the new Indian Railways app launched on 1 July 2025?

A. RailConnect B. RailOne
C. RailMate D. UTSonMobile

171. What is the name of the advanced stealth frigate that was commissioned on 1 July 2025 at Yantar Shipyard, Kaliningrad, Russia?

A. INS Vikrant B. INS Talwar
C. INS Tamal D. INS Shivalik

172. Who became the first Indian to win a BWF World Tour title in 2025?

A. Lakshya Sen B. Kidambi Srikanth
C. Ayush Shetty D. Prannoy H.S.

173. Who has been appointed as the Secretary of RAW from July 1, 2025?

A. Ravi Sinha B. Rakesh Asthana
C. Parag Jain D. Samant Goel

174. Which two hydroelectric projects are at the center of the Indus Waters Treaty dispute?

A. Baglihar and Uri
B. Kishenganga and Ratle
C. Sardar Sarovar and Tehri
D. Dulhasti and Salal

175. Where was the NATO Summit 2025 held?

A. Brussels, Belgium B. The Hague, Netherlands
C. Berlin, Germany D. Paris, France

176. Samvidhaan Hatya Diwas is observed annually in remembrance of the Emergency, which was declared in India on which date?

A. 15 August 1975 B. 26 January 1975
C. 25 June 1975 D. 25 July 1975

177. Which major Government scheme for urban infrastructure development completed 10 years on 25 June 2025?

A. Smart Cities Mission
B. AMRUT (Atal Mission for Rejuvenation and Urban Transformation)
C. PM Awas Yojana - Urban
D. Swachh Bharat Mission - Urban

178. What is the name of the evacuation mission launched by India from Iran amid the conflict in June 2025?

A. Operation Vande Bharat
B. Operation Samudra Setu
C. Operation Sindhu
D. Operation Suraksha

179. Neeraj Chopra won the men's javelin throw at which Diamond League event in June 2025?

A. Doha Diamond League
B. Zurich Diamond League
C. Paris Diamond League
D. Rome Diamond League

180. Where did Prime Minister Narendra Modi lead the International Yoga Day 2025 celebrations?

A. Rishikesh B. Varanasi
C. Visakhapatnam D. New Delhi

181. Which university topped the QS World University Rankings 2026?
A. Stanford University
B. University of Oxford
C. Massachusetts Institute of Technology (MIT)
D. Harvard University

182. Which Indian institute ranked highest among Indian University in the QS World University Rankings 2026?
A. IIT Kanpur B. IIT Madras
C. IIT Bombay D. IIT Delhi

183. What is the theme for the 11th International Day of Yoga (IDY) 2025?
A. Yoga for Global Peace
B. Yoga for Wellness and Harmony
C. Yoga for One Earth, One Health
D. Yoga for Climate and Community

184. Which judge is facing possible impeachment over allegations of misconduct related to half-burnt cash found at his residence in March 2025?
A. Justice G.S. Sandhawalia
B. Justice Anu Sivaraman
C. Justice Yashwant Varma
D. Justice Sheel Nagu

185. What is the name of India's first Anti-Submarine Warfare Shallow Water Craft (ASW-SWC)?
A. INS Vikrant B. INS Kalvari
C. INS Arnala D. INS Vagir

186. Where was the G7 Summit 2025 held from 16 to 17 June 2025?
A. Paris B. Kananaskis
C. Berlin D. Tokyo

187. What is the name of the Indo-French joint military exercise held in June 2025?
A. Varuna B. Shakti
C. Indra D. Surya Kiran

188. Which is the number of the national Census to be conducted in 2026–2027?
A. 14th B. 15th
C. 16th D. 17th

189. A major armed conflict broke out between which two countries in June 2025?
A. Russia and Ukraine
B. Iran and Israel
C. China and Taiwan
D. North Korea and South Korea

190. Which team won the ICC World Test Championship Final 2025?
A. Australia B. England
C. India D. South Africa

191. What type of aircraft was involved in the Air India London Flight Crash on June, 12 2025?
A. Airbus A320
B. Boeing 777
C. Boeing 737 Max
D. Boeing 787-8 Dreamliner

192. What is the name of the new postal service launched by the Department of Posts in June 2025 for affordable delivery of books?
A. Book Post B. Gyan Setu
C. Gyan Post D. Shiksha Mail

193. What is the name of Israel's military operation targeting Iran's nuclear and military sites in June 2025?
A. Desert Thunder B. Iron Shield
C. Rising Lion D. Storm Falcon

194. What are the two main routes for the Shri Amarnath Ji Yatra?
A. Jammu and Leh
B. Pahalgam and Baltal
C. Gulmarg and Sonmarg
D. Kargil and Pulwama

195. In terms of social protection beneficiaries, what is India's global rank, as per ILO's ILOSTAT data released in June 2025?
A. First B. Second
C. Third D. Fourth

196. Which Indian cricketer was included in the ICC Hall of Fame in June 2025?
A. Virat Kohli B. Rahul Dravid
C. MS Dhoni D. Sachin Tendulkar

197. Who won the Women's Singles title at French Open 2025?
A. Aryna Sabalenka B. Serena Williams
C. Coco Gauff D. Iga Swiatek

198. What is the revised policy repo rate after the June 2025 MPC meeting?
A. 5.0% B. 5.25%
C. 5.5% D. 6.0%

199. Which of the following bridges is the world's highest railway arch bridge inaugurated by PM Modi in June 2025?
A. Howrah Bridge B. Anji Khad Bridge
C. Pamban Bridge D. Chenab Bridge

200. Which of the following is India's first cable-stayed rail bridge?
A. Chenab Bridge B. Pamban Bridge
C. Anji Khad Bridge D. Godavari Arch Bridge

201. The PM Modi-led NDA government completed how many years at the Centre in June 2025?
A. 10 years B. 11 years
C. 12 years D. 9 years

202. When will the reference date for the Population Census 2027 be, for most parts of India?
A. January 1, 2027 B. March 1, 2027
C. April 1, 2027 D. February 28, 2027

203. What significant new feature is included in Census 2027?
A. Online data collection
B. Biometric verification
C. Caste enumeration
D. Use of Aadhaar-linked data only

204. What is the main theme of World Environment Day 2025, observed on June 5?
A. Climate Action
B. Clean Energy
C. Ending Plastic Pollution
D. Reforestation

205. Who won the Indian Premier League (IPL) 2025 title?
A. Punjab Kings
B. Chennai Super Kings
C. Royal Challengers Bengaluru
D. Gujarat Titans

206. Who won the 2025 presidential runoff election in Poland?
A. Rafal Trzaskowski B. Andrzej Duda
C. Karol Nawrocki D. Helga Schmid

207. Who was crowned Miss World 2025?
A. Hasset (Ethiopia)
B. Krystyna Pyszková
C. Opal Suchata Chuangsri
D. Nandini Gupta

208. What is the name of the joint military exercise between India and Mongolia?
A. Desert Eagle
B. Nomadic Elephant
C. Mountain Tiger
D. Steppe Warrior

209. What is the purpose of next-generation defence technologies trials conducted by the Indian Army in June 2025?
A. Training cadets for disaster response
B. Enhancing public awareness
C. Evaluating advanced systems under near-combat conditions
D. Demonstrating systems to foreign allies

210. What award is conferred to recognize exceptional nursing professionals for outstanding contributions to India's healthcare system?
A. Padma Shri Award
B. Bharat Ratna Award
C. National Florence Nightingale Award
D. National Health Excellence Award

211. What historic first took place during the 148th Passing Out Parade of NDA in May 2025?
A. First foreign cadet graduated
B. First women cadets were commissioned into the Indian Armed Forces
C. President attended the ceremony for the first time
D. First drone display at NDA parade

212. Who won two gold medals at the Asian Athletics Championships 2025 for India?
A. Avinash Sable B. Gulveer Singh
C. Tejas Bhat D. Animesh Kujur

213. Which Indian state became the second to cross the nationally prescribed 95% benchmark for full literacy?
A. Kerala B. Goa
C. Tamil Nadu D. Himachal Pradesh

214. Which event did Avinash Sable win gold in 26th Asian Athletics Championships in Gumi, South Korea, on 29 May 2025?
A. 1500 m
B. 10,000 m
C. 3000 m steeplechase
D. 5000 m

215. AdFalciVax is being used in India against:
A. Malaria B. Filaria
C. Influenza D. Diphtheria

216. Chandrapuram Ponnusami Radhakrishnan took oath as the ……….. Vice President of India.
A. 14th B. 15th
C. 16th D. 17th

217. Which ministry released the industrial production data?
A. Ministry of Finance
B. Ministry of Commerce and Industry
C. Ministry of Statistics and Programme Implementation
D. Ministry of Labour and Employment

218. Who won the gold medal in the Men's 10,000-metre race at the Asian Athletics Championships 2025?
A. Servin Sebasthiyan B. Wang Zhaozhao
C. Gulveer Singh D. Amit

219. Which of the following received the Padma Vibhushan posthumously in 2025 for his contribution in Folk Music?
A. Bibek Debroy B. Sharda Sinha
C. Colleen Gantzer D. Ajay Bhatt

220. Kunjiparamba caves were in the news recently. They are in which state?
A. Kerala B. Odisha
C. Madhya Pradesh D. Tamil Nadu

221. According to World Economic Forum's 'The Future of Jobs Report 2025' unemployment rate in India is:
A. 2% B. 3%
C. 4% D. 5%

222. Who set a new world record in the F42 javelin category in May 2025?
A. Sumit Antil
B. Roberto Floriani Edenilson
C. Mahendra Gurjar
D. Neeraj Chopra

223. Where did Prime Minister Narendra Modi inaugurate the new Locomotive Manufacturing Plant in May 2025?
A. Vadodara, Gujarat B. Surat, Gujarat
C. Dahod, Gujarat D. Rajkot, Gujarat

224. Who won the Palme d'Or at the 78th Cannes Film Festival?
A. Hayakawa Chie B. Suzuki Yui
C. Jafar Panahi D. Asghar Farhadi

225. Which country did India surpass to become the world's fourth-largest economy?
A. Germany B. China
C. Japan D. United Kingdom

226. Who is the current CEO of NITI Aayog (as of December 2025)?
A. Amitabh Kant
B. Parameswaran Iyer
C. B.V.R. Subrahmanyam
D. Rajiv Kumar

227. Who is the current Prime Minister of Singapore as of December 2025?
A. Lee Hsien Loong B. K. Shanmugam
C. Lawrence Wong D. Vivian Balakrishnan

228. Which forces are included in the cadre review order issued by the Supreme Court in May 2025?
A. ITBP and Indian Army
B. BSF, CISF, and Indian Navy
C. ITBP, BSF, CRPF, CISF, and SSB
D. Police and Coast Guard

229. Who among the following has been appointed as an Executive Director of International Monetary Fund?
A. Dr. Raghuram Rajan
B. Dr. Urjit Patel
C. Arvind Subramanian
D. Dr. Rajiv Kumar

230. What is the name of the islands that the UK returned to Mauritius in an agreement in May 2025?
A. Maldives B. Lakshadweep
C. Chagos Islands D. Seychelles

231. Where did the Rising North East Investors Summit 2025 held in May 2025?
A. Mumbai B. Guwahati
C. New Delhi D. Kolkata

232. Which state became the first in India to achieve full functional literacy in May 2025?
A. Kerala B. Tamil Nadu
C. Mizoram D. Himachal Pradesh

233. What is the name of the national literacy program that helped Mizoram achieve full literacy?
A. Sarva Shiksha Abhiyan
B. Digital India Literacy Mission
C. ULLAS – Nav Bharat Saaksharta Karyakram
D. Shiksha Setu Abhiyan

234. What is the primary purpose of the Golden Dome shield, announced by US President in May 2025?
A. To launch satellites for GPS
B. To detect and intercept long-range missile threats
C. To replace the U.S. Navy defense systems
D. To prevent cyber attacks

235. How many Asiatic lions were recorded in Gujarat's 16th lion census in 2025?
A. 721 B. 817
C. 891 D. 956

236. How many public EV charging stations are planned to be established under the PM E-Drive scheme?
A. 50,000 B. 60,000
C. 72,000 D. 75,000

237. What was the theme of the 78th World Health Assembly addressed by PM Modi on May 20, 2025?
A. Health for All
B. One Earth, One Health
C. Universal Health Coverage
D. One World for Health

238. Which core industry carries the highest individual weight in the Index of Eight Core Industries?
A. Coal
B. Steel
C. Electricity
D. Petroleum Refinery Products

239. Indian Navy inducted an Ancient Stitched Ship in May 2025. This recreation of a 5th-century CE ship was inspired by which of the following?
A. Ancient Sanskrit manuscripts
B. A painting from the Ajanta Caves
C. Shipwrecks found along the western coast of India
D. Ancient texts from the Vedic period

240. Which country is known for its traditional tea ceremony called 'Chanoyu'?
A. India B. China
C. Japan D. Sri Lanka

241. Where was the first edition of the Khelo India Beach Games (KIBG) held in May 2025?
A. Marina Beach, Chennai
B. Baga Beach, Goa
C. Ghoghla Beach, Diu
D. Juhu Beach, Mumbai

242. What caused the failure of ISRO's PSLV-C61 mission to place the EOS-09 satellite in orbit on May 18, 2025?
A. An issue with the rocket's first stage
B. Launch pad malfunction
C. An anomaly in the rocket's third stage
D. None of these

243. Who won the South Asian Football Federation (SAFF) Under-19 Football Championship 2025?
A. Nepal B. Bangladesh
C. India D. Sri Lanka

244. India has signed Bilateral Investment Agreement (BIA) with which country?
A. UK B. Italy
C. Israel D. Germany

245. What milestone did Neeraj Chopra achieve at 2025 Doha Diamond League?
A. First Diamond League win
B. First throw over 85 meters
C. First time crossing the 90-meter mark
D. First time beating Julian Weber

246. Who won the Superbet Chess Classic 2025 held in Bucharest, Romania in May 2025?
A. Alireza Firouzja
B. Maxime Vachier-Lagrave
C. D Gukesh
D. R Praggnanandhaa

247. Jagadguru Rambhadracharya was awarded the 58th Jnanpith Award for his contribution to the literature of which language?
A. Hindi B. Urdu
C. Sanskrit D. Tamil

248. According to United Nations' mid-year World Economic Situation and Prospects (WESP) report, which economy is expected to grow faster than China, the US, and the EU in 2025?
A. United States B. European Union
C. India D. Japan

249. Which state emerged as the overall champion in the Khelo India Youth Games 2025?
A. Haryana B. Rajasthan
C. Uttar Pradesh D. Maharashtra

250. Why did the government revoke the security clearance of Celebi Airport Services India Pvt. Ltd., a Turkish ground handling firm, in May 2025?
A. The Turkish support to Pakistan during Operation Sindoor
B. Poor financial performance of the company in India
C. Celebi's failure to comply with aviation safety standards
D. Allegations of employee exploitation and labour violations

251. Which scheme was launched by the Haryana Government in July 2025 to encourage help to road accident victims?
A. Jeevan Raksha Scheme
B. Raha-Veer Scheme
C. Safe Roads Scheme
D. Accident Insurance Scheme

252. What incentive amount is given under the Raha-Veer Scheme?
A. ₹ 10,000 B. ₹ 15,000
C. ₹ 25,000 D. ₹ 50,000

253. Under which law helpers are given legal protection in the Raha-Veer Scheme?
A. BNS
B. BNSS
C. Motor Vehicles Act
D. Evidence Act

254. In July 2025, approval was given for a kinnow juice processing plant in which district of Haryana?
A. Hisar B. Sirsa
C. Fatehabad D. Karnal

255. The kinnow processing plant will be set up under which model?
A. Government model
B. Cooperative model
C. PPP (Public-Private Partnership)
D. FDI

256. In July 2025, the EWS income limit in Haryana was increased to:
A. ₹ 6 lakh B. ₹ 7 lakh
C. ₹ 8 lakh D. ₹ 10 lakh

257. The increase in EWS income limit mainly benefits:
A. Private sector jobs
B. Government recruitment & admissions
C. Traders
D. Farmers

258. Which city was announced to get a new medical college in July 2025?
A. Palwal B. Charkhi Dadri
C. Jind D. Mahendragarh

259. Which portal was launched in July 2025 to support education policy implementation in Haryana?
A. Shiksha Sathi B. NEEV
C. Gyan Deep D. Shiksha Setu

260. The NEEV portal is related to which department?
A. IT B. Finance
C. Education D. Planning

261. In July 2025, electricity tariff of ₹ 2 per unit was announced for which industries?
A. Large industries
B. Medium industries
C. Micro & Small industries
D. IT companies

262. The main objective of this electricity subsidy is to:
A. Increase revenue B. Promote MSMEs
C. Reduce exports D. Privatise power sector

263. In July 2025, farmers held a mahapanchayat in Jind against which issue?
A. MSP B. Crop insurance
C. Smart meters D. Land acquisition

264. The farmers' protest was linked to amendments in which law?
A. Labour laws
B. Agriculture laws
C. Electricity Amendment Bill
D. Environment laws

265. In July 2025, Haryana decided to establish which type of colleges in all districts?
A. Engineering colleges
B. Model Sanskriti colleges
C. Medical colleges
D. IT colleges

266. In August 2025, Haryana announced a State Research Fund of how much amount?
A. ₹ 10 crore B. ₹ 20 crore
C. ₹ 50 crore D. ₹ 100 crore

267. State Research Fund is mainly aimed at promoting:
A. Sports B. Higher education
C. Tourism D. Industry

268. By August 2025, how many beneficiaries had crossed under the Chirayu Haryana Scheme?
A. 15 lakh B. 20 lakh
C. 25 lakh D. 30 lakh

269. Chirayu Haryana Scheme is related to:
A. Insurance B. Health
C. Education D. Pension

270. Approximately how many Chirayu cards were issued in Haryana by August 2025?
A. 80 lakh B. 1 crore
C. 1.3 crore D. 2 crore

271. In August 2025, the Chief Minister admitted shortage of a civil hospital in which city?
A. Faridabad B. Gurugram
C. Sonipat D. Rohtak

272. About how many MSMEs benefited from electricity subsidy by August 2025?
A. 2 lakh B. 4 lakh
C. 6–7 lakh D. 10 lakh

273. Which sector was identified as a major source of employment generation in August 2025?
A. IT B. Agriculture
C. MSME D. Tourism

274. Digital tracking was introduced in August 2025 under which scheme?
A. Ration B. Chirayu
C. Pension D. Scholarship

275. Which district was announced as a food-processing hub in August 2025?
A. Karnal B. Sirsa
C. Jhajjar D. Nuh

276. What was the total size of Haryana Budget 2025–26 announced in September 2025?
A. ₹1.5 lakh crore B. ₹1.8 lakh crore
C. ₹2.05 lakh crore D. ₹2.5 lakh crore

277. Which sector received the highest priority in the Haryana Budget 2025–26?
A. Tourism B. Education
C. Infrastructure D. Defence

278. Work was accelerated on which expressway project in September 2025?
A. KMP Expressway
B. Panipat–Dabwali Expressway
C. Ambala–Yamunanagar
D. Faridabad–Noida

279. The main objective of Panipat–Dabwali Expressway is to boost:
A. Tourism
B. Defence
C. Logistics and trade
D. Irrigation

280. The Haryana Orbital Rail Corridor aims to:
A. Increase freight movement
B. Reduce load on Delhi rail network
C. Expand metro
D. Promote tourism

281. The rail corridor is being developed along which expressway?
A. NH-44
B. Eastern Peripheral Expressway
C. Western Peripheral Expressway
D. KMP

282. Which district got a Startup Support Centre in September 2025?
A. Karnal B. Hisar
C. Jind D. Sirsa

283. The main objective of the startup policy is:
A. Foreign investment
B. Local employment
C. Tax collection
D. Privatisation

284. In September 2025, women SHGs were linked with which scheme?
A. Aajeevika B. Lakhpati Didi
C. Mudra D. Svanidhi

285. The aim of this initiative is to promote:
A. Credit access
B. Women entrepreneurship
C. Education
D. Pension

286. In October 2025, a new industrial cluster was announced in which district?
A. Rewari B. Jind
C. Sirsa D. Kaithal

287. The new industrial cluster mainly focuses on which sector?
A. IT B. Auto & manufacturing
C. Textile D. Mining

288. DBT mechanism was strengthened in October 2025 for which scheme?
A. Old-age pension B. Scholarship
C. Ration D. Insurance

289. The main objective of DBT is to ensure:
A. Tax collection B. Transparency
C. Privatisation D. Control

290. Skill training was expanded in October 2025 mainly in which sector?
A. IT B. Health
C. Industry D. Agriculture

291. Which road safety campaign was intensified in October 2025?
A. Safe India B. Raha-Veer
C. Jeevan Raksha D. Road Mitra

292. The objective of road safety campaign was to:
A. Issue challans B. Reduce road accidents
C. Increase tax D. Promote insurance

293. A new bus terminal was approved in October 2025 in which district?
A. Nuh B. Palwal
C. Jhajjar D. Fatehabad

294. This project mainly benefits which sector?
A. Agriculture B. Tourism
C. Transport D. Education

295. Which mission gained momentum in October 2025?
A. Har Ghar Jal B. Har Ghar Solar
C. Swachh Bharat D. AMRUT

296. Which district recorded the highest solar installations in November 2025?
A. Ambala B. Hisar
C. Rohtak D. Sonipat

297. The main benefit of the solar mission is:
A. Job reduction
B. Reduction in carbon footprint
C. Revenue loss
D. Industrial shutdown

298. In November 2025, Haryana athletes won international medals mainly in which sport?
A. Cricket B. Wrestling
C. Hockey D. Tennis

299. Haryana is nationally famous for which sport?
A. Badminton B. Wrestling
C. Football D. Swimming

300. Under which policy were cash rewards given to sportspersons in November 2025?
A. Khelo India
B. Haryana Sports Policy
C. Fit India
D. Arjuna Scheme

301. In November 2025, new assistance was announced for which group?
A. Farmers B. Senior citizens
C. Students D. Traders

302. This assistance was provided in the form of:
A. Loan B. Pension enhancement
C. Insurance D. Scholarship

303. Which city saw a new women safety initiative in November 2025?
A. Gurugram B. Panipat
C. Karnal D. Kaithal

304. This initiative was related to:
A. CCTV B. Helpline
C. Fast-track courts D. Police recruitment

305. E-governance was expanded in November 2025 mainly in which department?
A. Education B. Revenue
C. Health D. Agriculture

306. The sharp rise in gold prices in December 2025 was mainly due to:
A. Tax increase
B. Global economic uncertainty
C. Local production
D. Export surge

307. By December 2025, the price of 24-carat gold in Haryana reached around:
A. ₹ 1.2 lakh B. ₹ 1.3 lakh
C. ₹ 1.4 lakh D. ₹ 1.5 lakh

308. Which sector was most affected by rising gold prices?
A. Agriculture B. Jewellery
C. Transport D. Education

309. Which scheme was reviewed by the Haryana Government in December 2025?
A. Raha-Veer B. Ujjwala
C. Mudra D. Svanidhi

310. The purpose of the review was to:
A. Cut budget B. Improve effectiveness
C. Discontinue scheme D. Privatise

311. A new IT park was announced in December 2025 in which city?
A. Gurugram B. Rohtak
C. Jind D. Sirsa

312. The main objective of this IT park is:
A. Tourism promotion
B. Employment generation
C. Tax collection
D. Education

313. Which service was integrated with a digital platform in December 2025?
A. Ration B. Pension
C. Scholarship D. Insurance

314. The main benefit of this integration is:
A. Delay B. Transparency
C. Extra cost D. Control

315. In December 2025, Haryana increased investment mainly in which sector?
A. Defence B. Infrastructure
C. Mining D. Fisheries

316. Which scheme was expanded by the Haryana Government in January 2026?
A. Chirayu B. Ujjwala
C. Mudra D. Central Ayushman

317. The objective of Chirayu scheme expansion was to:
A. Privatise healthcare
B. Cover more families under health insurance
C. Reduce budget
D. End scheme

318. In January 2026, which city recorded the highest gold trade in Haryana?
A. Hisar B. Panipat
C. Sirsa D. Kaithal

319. A new policy was announced in January 2026 for which sector?
A. Startups B. Mining
C. Fisheries D. Tourism

320. The main aim of startups policy is to promote:
- A. Tax increase
- B. Innovation and employment
- C. Privatisation
- D. Regulation

321. Which district was announced as a logistics hub in January 2026?
- A. Sonipat
- B. Rohtak
- C. Jind
- D. Fatehabad

322. The logistics hub will mainly benefit which sector?
- A. Education
- B. Trade
- C. Health
- D. Tourism

323. Road safety awareness campaign in January 2026 was run under which scheme?
- A. Jeevan Raksha
- B. Raha-Veer
- C. Safe India
- D. Transport Mitra

324. The main objective of this campaign was to:
- A. Issue challans
- B. Reduce road accident deaths
- C. Increase tax
- D. Promote insurance

325. In January 2026, Haryana identified which sector as its "growth engine"?
- A. Agriculture
- B. MSME
- C. Tourism
- D. Defence

ANSWERS

1	**2**	**3**	**4**	**5**	**6**	**7**	**8**	**9**	**10**
C	B	C	B	B	B	C	B	B	D
11	**12**	**13**	**14**	**15**	**16**	**17**	**18**	**19**	**20**
C	C	B	A	A	C	A	B	A	C
21	**22**	**23**	**24**	**25**	**26**	**27**	**28**	**29**	**30**
B	C	C	D	A	A	B	A	B	B
31	**32**	**33**	**34**	**35**	**36**	**37**	**38**	**39**	**40**
A	C	B	A	C	D	C	A	C	C
41	**42**	**43**	**44**	**45**	**46**	**47**	**48**	**49**	**50**
D	A	A	C	B	B	B	D	C	B
51	**52**	**53**	**54**	**55**	**56**	**57**	**58**	**59**	**60**
B	A	B	B	C	C	A	B	C	B
61	**62**	**63**	**64**	**65**	**66**	**67**	**68**	**69**	**70**
B	C	D	D	C	B	B	D	B	C
71	**72**	**73**	**74**	**75**	**76**	**77**	**78**	**79**	**80**
B	A	C	B	C	C	B	A	C	B
81	**82**	**83**	**84**	**85**	**86**	**87**	**88**	**89**	**90**
B	B	A	A	D	C	A	C	C	D
91	**92**	**93**	**94**	**95**	**96**	**97**	**98**	**99**	**100**
D	B	A	B	D	B	D	B	C	D
101	**102**	**103**	**104**	**105**	**106**	**107**	**108**	**109**	**110**
C	C	C	B	D	C	B	B	C	C
111	**112**	**113**	**114**	**115**	**116**	**117**	**118**	**119**	**120**
C	C	C	B	C	C	B	B	D	B
121	**122**	**123**	**124**	**125**	**126**	**127**	**128**	**129**	**130**
C	B	B	D	B	B	C	C	C	C
131	**132**	**133**	**134**	**135**	**136**	**137**	**138**	**139**	**140**
C	C	C	C	B	D	A	C	C	B
141	**142**	**143**	**144**	**145**	**146**	**147**	**148**	**149**	**150**
C	C	C	B	C	C	C	C	B	B
151	**152**	**153**	**154**	**155**	**156**	**157**	**158**	**159**	**160**
C	B	B	B	C	D	C	B	C	B

161	162	163	164	165	166	167	168	169	170
C	C	C	C	C	C	B	C	B	B
171	**172**	**173**	**174**	**175**	**176**	**177**	**178**	**179**	**180**
C	C	C	B	B	C	B	C	C	C
181	**182**	**183**	**184**	**185**	**186**	**187**	**188**	**189**	**190**
C	D	C	C	C	B	B	C	B	D
191	**192**	**193**	**194**	**195**	**196**	**197**	**198**	**199**	**200**
D	C	C	B	B	C	C	C	D	C
201	**202**	**203**	**204**	**205**	**206**	**207**	**208**	**209**	**210**
B	B	C	C	C	C	C	B	C	C
211	**212**	**213**	**214**	**215**	**216**	**217**	**218**	**219**	**220**
B	B	B	C	A	B	C	C	B	A
221	**222**	**223**	**224**	**225**	**226**	**227**	**228**	**229**	**230**
A	C	C	C	C	C	C	C	B	C
231	**232**	**233**	**234**	**235**	**236**	**237**	**238**	**239**	**240**
C	C	C	B	C	C	D	D	B	C
241	**242**	**243**	**244**	**245**	**246**	**247**	**248**	**249**	**250**
C	C	C	C	C	D	C	C	D	A
251	**252**	**253**	**254**	**255**	**256**	**257**	**258**	**259**	**260**
B	C	C	B	C	C	B	B	B	C
261	**262**	**263**	**264**	**265**	**266**	**267**	**268**	**269**	**270**
C	B	C	C	B	B	B	C	B	C
271	**272**	**273**	**274**	**275**	**276**	**277**	**278**	**279**	**280**
B	C	C	B	B	C	C	B	C	B
281	**282**	**283**	**284**	**285**	**286**	**287**	**288**	**289**	**290**
B	B	B	B	B	A	B	A	B	C
291	**292**	**293**	**294**	**295**	**296**	**297**	**298**	**299**	**300**
B	B	B	C	B	B	B	B	B	B
301	**302**	**303**	**304**	**305**	**306**	**307**	**308**	**309**	**310**
B	B	A	B	B	B	C	B	A	B
311	**312**	**313**	**314**	**315**	**316**	**317**	**318**	**319**	**320**
A	B	A	B	B	A	B	B	A	B
321	**322**	**323**	**324**	**325**					
A	B	B	B	B					

●●●